[redacted]

[redacted]

[redacted]

THE GREEN LANTERN

ARCHIVES ▼ VOLUME 1

BROOME ▼ KANE ▼ GIELLA

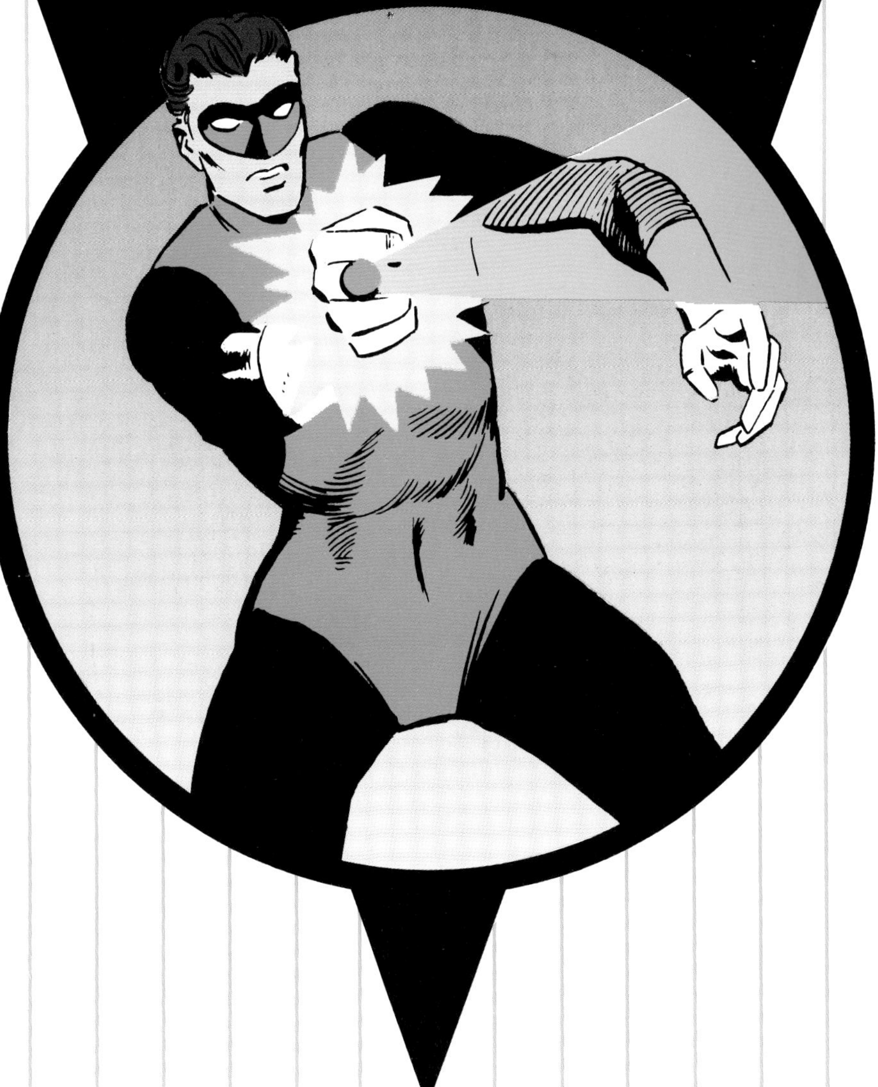

ARCHIVE DC EDITIONS

DC COMICS

JENETTE KAHN
PRESIDENT & EDITOR-IN-CHIEF

PAUL LEVITZ
EXECUTIVE VICE PRESIDENT
& PUBLISHER

MIKE CARLIN
EXECUTIVE EDITOR

BOB KAHAN
EDITOR
COLLECTED EDITION

GEORG BREWER
DESIGN DIRECTOR

ROBBIN BROSTERMAN
ART DIRECTOR

RICHARD BRUNING
VP-CREATIVE DIRECTOR

PATRICK CALDON
VP-FINANCE & OPERATIONS

DOROTHY CROUCH
VP-LICENSED PUBLISHING

TERRI CUNNINGHAM
VP-MANAGING EDITOR

JOEL EHRLICH
SENIOR VP-ADVERTISING &
PROMOTIONS

ALISON GILL
EXEC. DIRECTOR-
MANUFACTURING

LILLIAN LASERSON
VP & GENERAL COUNSEL

JIM LEE
EDITORIAL DIRECTOR-
WILDSTORM

JOHN NEE
VP & GENERAL MANAGER-
WILDSTORM

BOB WAYNE
VP-DIRECT SALES

GREEN LANTERN ARCHIVES
VOLUME ONE

ISBN 1-56389-087-9

PUBLISHED BY DC COMICS
COPYRIGHT ©1993 DC COMICS
ALL RIGHTS RESERVED

ORIGINALLY PUBLISHED IN SINGLE MAGAZINE
FORM IN SHOWCASE 22-24 AND GREEN
LANTERN 1-5. COPYRIGHT © 1959, 1960, 1961
DC COMICS. ALL RIGHTS RESERVED.

GREEN LANTERN AND ALL RELATED
CHARACTERS, THE DISTINCTIVE LIKENESSES
THEREOF, AND ALL RELATED INDICIA ARE
TRADEMARKS OF DC COMICS. THE STORIES,
CHARACTERS, AND INCIDENTS FEATURED IN
THIS PUBLICATION ARE ENTIRELY FICTIONAL.

DC COMICS
1700 BROADWAY
NEW YORK, NY 10019

A DIVISION OF WARNER BROS. -
A TIME WARNER ENTERTAINMENT COMPANY.
PRINTED IN HONG KONG.
THIRD PRINTING.

THE DC ARCHIVE EDITIONS

COVER ILLUSTRATION BY GIL KANE
AND JOE GIELLA.
COVER COLOR BY RICK TAYLOR.

SERIES DESIGN BY ALEX JAY/STUDIO J.

PUBLICATION DESIGN BY BRIAN PEARCE.

BLACK-AND-WHITE RECONSTRUCTION
BY RICK KEENE.

COLOR RECONSTRUCTION
BY ANTHONY TOLLIN.

TABLE OF CONTENTS

STORIES BY JOHN BROOME
ART BY GIL KANE AND JOE GIELLA
EXCEPT WHERE NOTED

TABLE OF CONTENTS

FOREWORD

Working for DC in the 1940s, '50s and '60s was fun, like going to a musical college run by the Marx Brothers and overseen by an awesome father figure. As long as we did our best we were given the only security of its kind in the business. Nowhere else could people work for a comics publishing company for twenty-five years or better. (I, myself, have been with DC for most of fifty years.)

We were all social and convivial. Many of us became lifelong friends and associates; but while the situation in the workplace was nearly ideal, the possibilities for real creativity were far from ideal.

By the beginning of the 1950s a smothering conformism had extinguished the exhilarating reforms of the 1940s . . . and settled down most heavily on comics. The attacks by these watchdog forces culminated in the figure of Fredric Wertham and his vicious indictments. He was aided and abetted by a Senate investigating committee headed by Estes Kefauver.

Comics publishers tried to avoid the tarring of Wertham's dripping brush by appointing a watchdog committee of their own called the Comics Code. It was headed by a distinguished jurist and its job was to scrutinize and sanitize every comics page published under their emblem. It was like being forced to wear an unyielding corset under your coat. But, it did the trick. Comics survived . . . barely. All violence was eliminated from the pages of comics and the equivalent of "true confessions" magazines — romance comics — dominated sales for a stifling decade. However, we all learned that nothing lasts forever, including official attitudes about what constitutes free expression. After all, '50s conformism was to give way to the liberating '60s looming just over the horizon. DC decided to run a new version of The Flash in SHOWCASE. The sales were excellent and were sustained for three additional issues.

The super-hero was back in business.

THE FLASH became a regular title and, at Julie Schwartz's suggestion, DC management decided that Green Lantern would be the next character to be resuscitated.

In those days DC had a half dozen editors under the immediate supervision of Whitney Ellsworth. Each editor was assigned six or seven monthly titles which were then handed out to his own stable of writers and artists.

Julie was chosen as the editor for the new GREEN LANTERN and he picked writer John Broome and myself to do it.

I went to work on the look of the character while the script was being written. Julie had given me some rough indications of what he wanted

and, coupled with some ideas I'd had, the drawing began to develop. I submitted them to Julie, taking care to color the one I favored. That was the one he chose.

That began a ten-year involvement with the character that was written by John Broome and Gardner Fox. Julie oversaw all of the plots and scripts.

There was still a lingering cloud of repression that was yet to be dissipated. Characters could run, fly, jump, ride horses but they could not hurt each other badly.

Plots were generally puzzles with an unexpected resolution that left the artist with about one or two panels of concluding action in which to punch the villain out. How to extend the physical action and not raise Julie's blood pressure became my job for the immediate future.

Ultimately, the '60s took hold and comics, like everything else, became reflections of their time.

They became freer, more expressive, and more involving because they were a more accurate barometer of current tastes.

It was during the run of GREEN LANTERN and THE ATOM that I first began to apply myself seriously to the idea of craft. The strips became a basis for self-development and the beginning of a mature professional identity.

Despite having drawn (and occasionally written) almost every mainstream title at one time or another for every major company and having done newspaper strips, animation films, paperback books, about 2,000 comics covers (I also did the first original comic book graphic novel, HIS NAME IS SAVAGE) GREEN LANTERN still remains the strip I'm most associated with.

These strips were done so long ago I feel as though I did them working with charcoal on cave walls.

It is all different all over again.

Comics have changed with the times as all things must. The range of possibilities — subject matter . . . interpretation — has greatly expanded. They are printed differently. They are sold differently. They are created under different circumstances.

I have always felt that comics would have an influential place amongst mainstream forms. It has found it.

This is just the beginning. Enjoy the ride.

Gil Kane – *Los Angeles 1993*

(A biography of Gil Kane appears on page 223.)

FOREWORD

I'm writing this because a better writer had to decline. John Broome — who wrote the bulk and the best of Green Lantern's adventures in the 1960s — was too busy with his post-comics life in Japan to join his old collaborator Gil Kane for a double-barrelled blast of memories. It's a pity. But at least you have me to tell you what Mr. Broome never would: just what a master of comic book writing John Broome really was.

What you will read here is not the birth of Green Lantern but his re-incarnation. When invented in 1940 by Mart Nodell, Bill Finger, and Sheldon Mayer, GL was a mystical figure, with a magic lantern echoing Aladdin's, a mysterious weakness to wood, a chanted oath. In the mid-'40s he took a spin toward the science-fictional, as a former SF literary agent named Julius Schwartz became his editor and brought in some of his former clients as writers: Henry Kuttner, Alfred Bester, John Broome. Yet the series remained as colorful, bizarre and amusing as the costume Mart had designed for his hero: Green Lantern's was a world of goofy cab-driver sidekicks, wonder dogs, and villains as strange as the Sportsmaster.

Super-heroes faded in the postwar years, and GL lost his comic book in 1949. A decade later, when the heroes were coming tentatively back into vogue, Julie Schwartz conceived a souped-up post-Sputnik version of the ring-wielder: sleek costume, outer-space origin, jet-pilot secret identity, Gil Kane art, and John

Broome stories. Broome by then was nearing the peak of his craft, telling his little stories with perfect economy, delicacy, and grace.

Grace is a faculty badly undervalued in our information-driven culture. The worth of a work is too often judged by its novelty or intellectual content, not by the beauty of its form. Yet a perfectly danced tango has far more art in it than an *avant-garde* performance piece laden with concept but lacking in rhythm.

Broome's stories are tangos. Or maybe something less passionate than that. The humor of a jitterbug, cuteness of a polka, lightness of a waltz. They're formula stories, and their conflicts are easy, but they're danced with perfect rhythm, lightness and charm. Like any good dance, they're built on deadly-perfect precision that comes across as sheer fun.

It's a strange world these stories create. Drawing-room parties at suburban estates, old barns in the countryside, dates at amusement parks, convertible sports cars, snappily-dressed singles at a nightclub, manly test pilots, and headstrong dames. And dinosaurs. Radiation monsters. Giant robots. Cosmic wiseguys guarding the universe. Fifties domesticity and Hollywood-tinted sophistication meld with the rawest of kid-culture grotesqueries. I can see Rock Hudson and Jane Wyman wheeling in an overcolored Ross Hunter farmscape to find a Roger Corman Crab Monster smashing through the hedge.

In the last story in this collection, Broome brought to an odd synthesis the pop-culture dream-stuff of the end of the Ike Age: sleazy playboy Hector Hammond finds a meteor that evolves organisms, uses it to turn four captive scientists into super-brains, becomes the ascotted idol of martini society, moves in on Green Lantern's girl, steals his power ring, and turns his Eskimo sidekick into a chimpanzee. Pseudoscience, strapless gowns, apes, and a power-ring duel . . . what else could you ask for?

Broome and Kane and Schwartz had a gift for charm more than anything, a lightness of touch and a wry but never condescending self-awareness that let fresh air into stuffy formulas. Even the predictable boy-girl mix-up of these early issues — Carol Ferris wants Green Lantern but fends off alter ego Hal Jordan — is played out with a wit and sexual sophistication that brings it to life. In the issues that followed those in this volume, when Carol found herself transformed into the dominating and marriage-minded villainess Star Sapphire, that mix-up would become perversely delightful.

Green Lantern himself is a minimal character, like all comic-book heroes of those days, but with intimations of an uncommon depth. There's something in his masculinity, his emotional urgency, his playboy life, his fearlessness with foes and awkwardness with Carol, that has tempted other comic-book writers for twenty-two years to find the core of his personality. I'm not sure any of us have quite succeeded. Somehow, in Broome's hands, GL was mysterious but complete.

Carol Ferris was the best-realized of all those headstrong professional women who populated the comics of Julie Schwartz. She's far from a feminist paragon: daddy's girl, fickle, hung up on her big, strong superhero. But she's no scheming, insecure goofball Lois Lane, either. Read any scene with Carol and you can tell that Schwartz and Broome knew and liked women.

Even the figure of the smiling, boyish, non-white sidekick takes on an uncommon humanity in these sto-ries. His name, "Pieface," is the only cheap Eskimo gag in the whole series. Pie is "a wizard with jet engines" and unlike most side-boys he's given a real name — Thomas Kalmaku — and a genuine ethnic context. He shows a deep loyalty to "my people" and fights back against an injustice. A short time after this volume leaves off he gets a wife, in a sense becoming more of an adult than his confidant-hero.

The villains in these stories are gimmicks. But they're clever gimmicks, and Broome could give even them a mysterious dignity. The oversized microbe thanking GL for shrinking him; the Venusian cavemen celebrating by their fires; the refugee from Qward begging GL for aid . . . these are strangely powerful moments in the context of these superheroic jitterbugs. Then there are those bits of atmosphere that Broome and Kane made so simple but so vivid: the frozen ghost town in the Arctic, the council of the Guardians, the desert where Abin Sur dies. It's in such details that these little stories transcend their formula and become remarkable. Reviewing them now, for the purpose of this foreword, I find they become more enchanting with every visit.

As this volume ends, Green Lantern's best was still to come: the introduction of the wonderful Green Lantern Corps, beginning with Tomar Re, one of Kane's most winning character designs; the delightfully wicked renegade GL named Sinestro, and Broome's most amusing work with the antimatter universe of Qward; the Jordan family, Star Sapphire, and GL's amnesiac other-life in the 58th Century. In the mid-1960s would come the Hal-Carol breakup, and GL's colorful ramblings around the American West, and Gil Kane's emergence as a master of action-art. I hope this Archives series runs long enough to revive those joys.

Since 1970, and the last of the John Broome stories, Green Lantern has been on an emotional and conceptual rollercoaster. He's flitted through political relevance and personal collapse and replacement by other Green Lanterns and, most recently, the slow rebuilding of his smashed-up mythos. A number of writers have struggled to find the best way to handle this magical and difficult concept. Denny O'Neil. Marv Wolfman. Len Wein. Steve Englehart. Me. We've all had our moments, but none quite like these. For me, these stories of the late 1950s and early 1960s are the purest instant in the life of one of comics' most enduring characters. In writing Green Lantern's current adventures, my happiest moments come when I can transcend my content, tap into that rhythm, and for a few pages dance a dance like John Broome.

— GERARD JONES

(Gerard Jones has written GREEN LANTERN, GREEN LANTERN: MOSAIC, JUSTICE LEAGUE EUROPE (in which Green Lantern has appeared), and portions of GREEN LANTERN CORPS QUARTERLY.)

"In brightest day...
In blackest night...
No evil shall
escape my sight!
Let those
who worship
evil's might
Beware my power—

GREEN
LANTERN'S
LIGHT!"

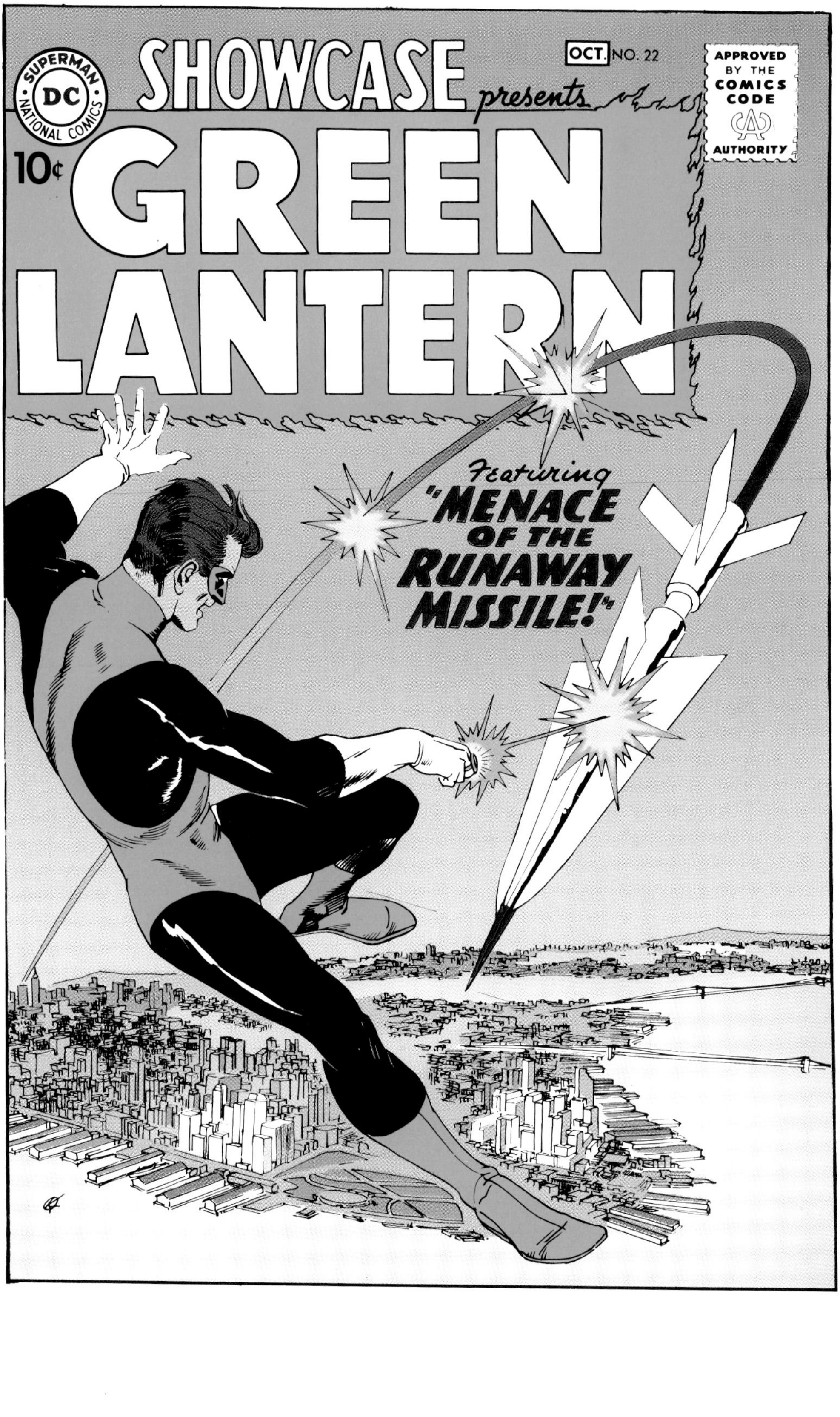
SUPERMAN DC NATIONAL COMICS
10¢
SHOWCASE presents
OCT. NO. 22
APPROVED BY THE COMICS CODE AUTHORITY
GREEN LANTERN
Featuring "MENACE OF THE RUNAWAY MISSILE!"

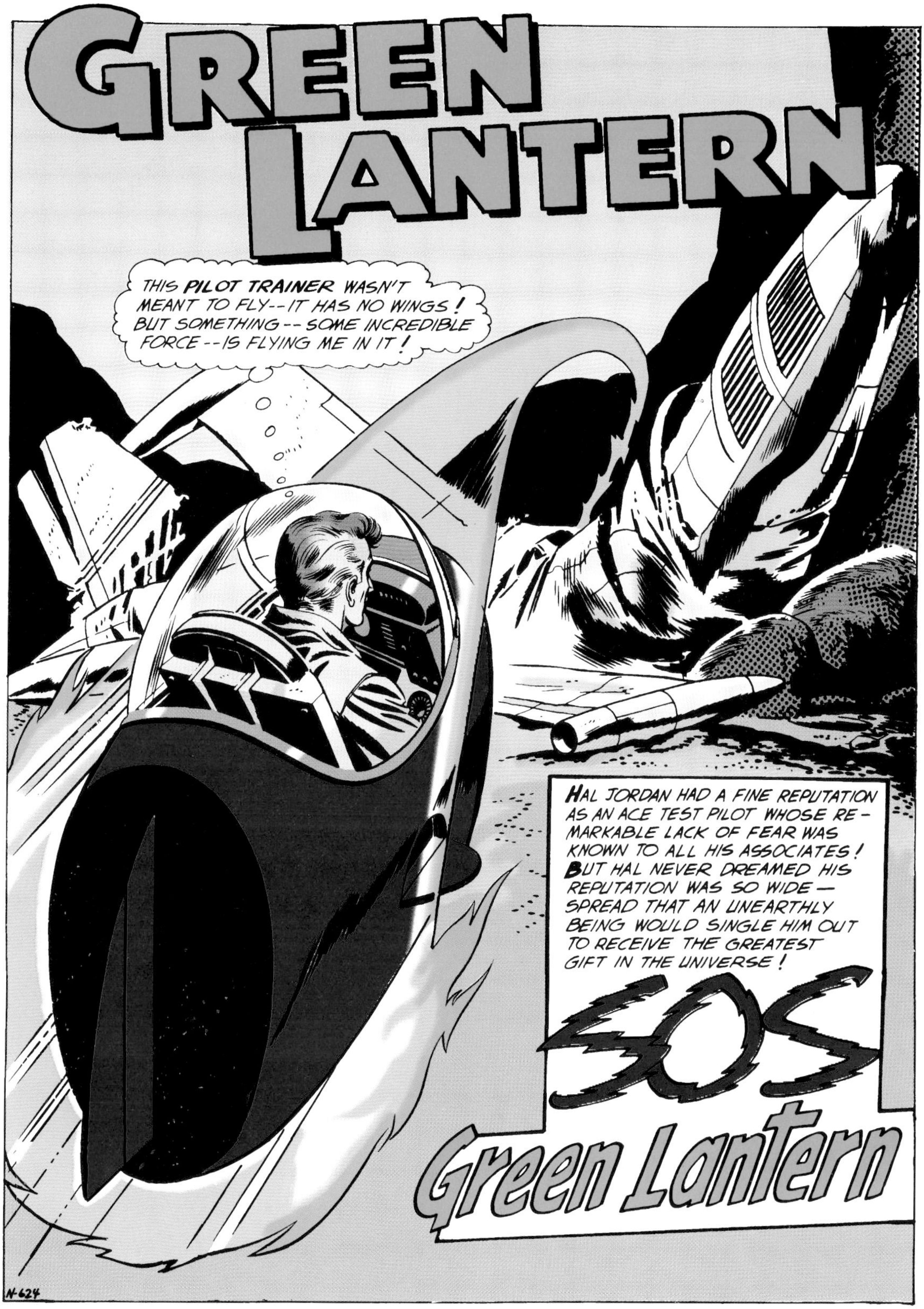
GREEN LANTERN
THIS PILOT TRAINER WASN'T MEANT TO FLY--IT HAS NO WINGS! BUT SOMETHING--SOME INCREDIBLE FORCE--IS FLYING ME IN IT!
HAL JORDAN HAD A FINE REPUTATION AS AN ACE TEST PILOT WHOSE RE-MARKABLE LACK OF FEAR WAS KNOWN TO ALL HIS ASSOCIATES! BUT HAL NEVER DREAMED HIS REPUTATION WAS SO WIDE-SPREAD THAT AN UNEARTHLY BEING WOULD SINGLE HIM OUT TO RECEIVE THE GREATEST GIFT IN THE UNIVERSE!
SOS Green Lantern
N-624

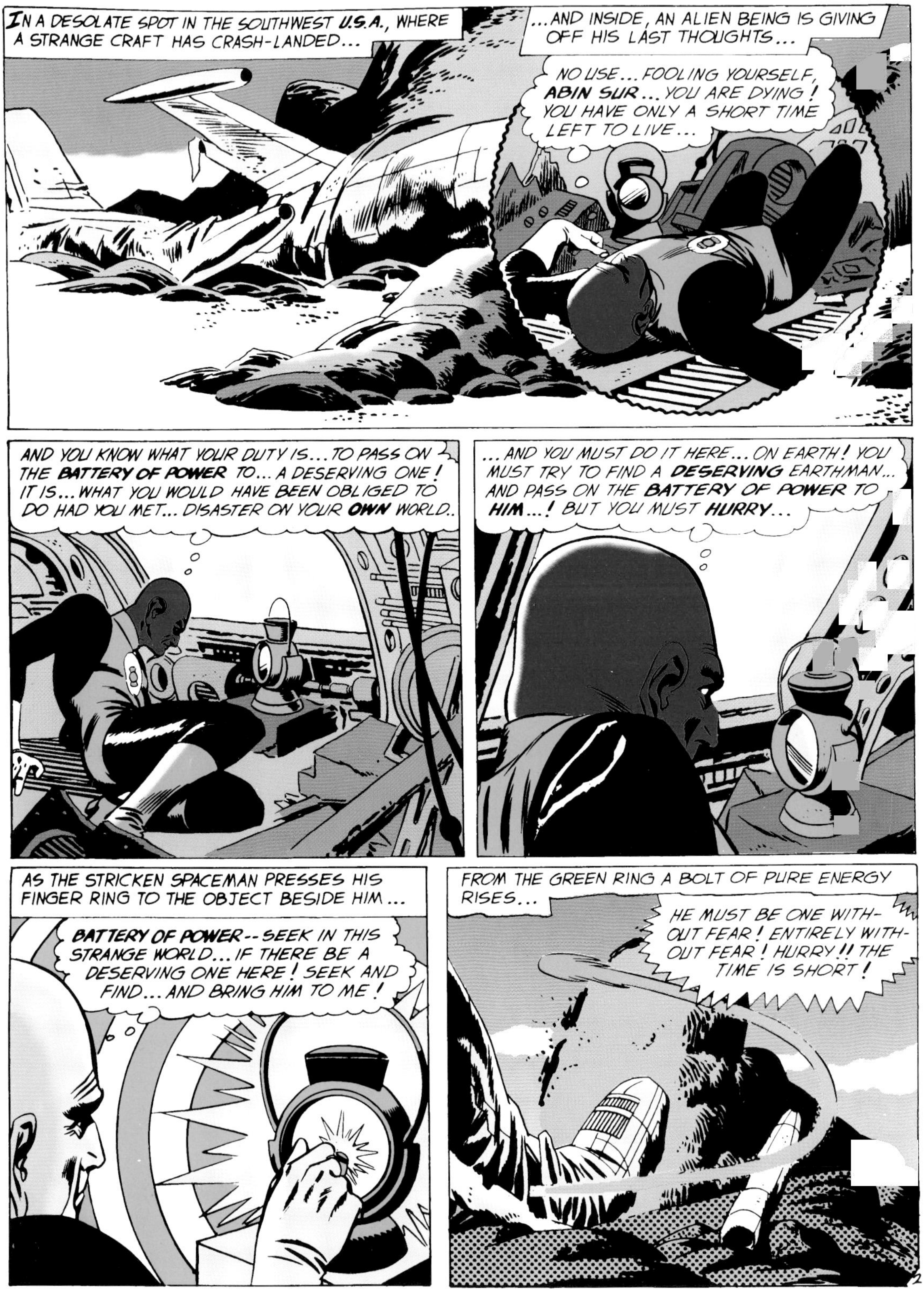
IN A DESOLATE SPOT IN THE SOUTHWEST U.S.A., WHERE A STRANGE CRAFT HAS CRASH-LANDED...
...AND INSIDE, AN ALIEN BEING IS GIVING OFF HIS LAST THOUGHTS...
NO USE... FOOLING YOURSELF, ABIN SUR... YOU ARE DYING! YOU HAVE ONLY A SHORT TIME LEFT TO LIVE...
AND YOU KNOW WHAT YOUR DUTY IS... TO PASS ON THE BATTERY OF POWER TO... A DESERVING ONE! IT IS... WHAT YOU WOULD HAVE BEEN OBLIGED TO DO HAD YOU MET... DISASTER ON YOUR OWN WORLD..
...AND YOU MUST DO IT HERE... ON EARTH! YOU MUST TRY TO FIND A DESERVING EARTHMAN... AND PASS ON THE BATTERY OF POWER TO HIM...! BUT YOU MUST HURRY...
AS THE STRICKEN SPACEMAN PRESSES HIS FINGER RING TO THE OBJECT BESIDE HIM...
BATTERY OF POWER -- SEEK IN THIS STRANGE WORLD... IF THERE BE A DESERVING ONE HERE! SEEK AND FIND... AND BRING HIM TO ME!
FROM THE GREEN RING A BOLT OF PURE ENERGY RISES...
HE MUST BE ONE WITHOUT FEAR! ENTIRELY WITHOUT FEAR! HURRY!! THE TIME IS SHORT!
2

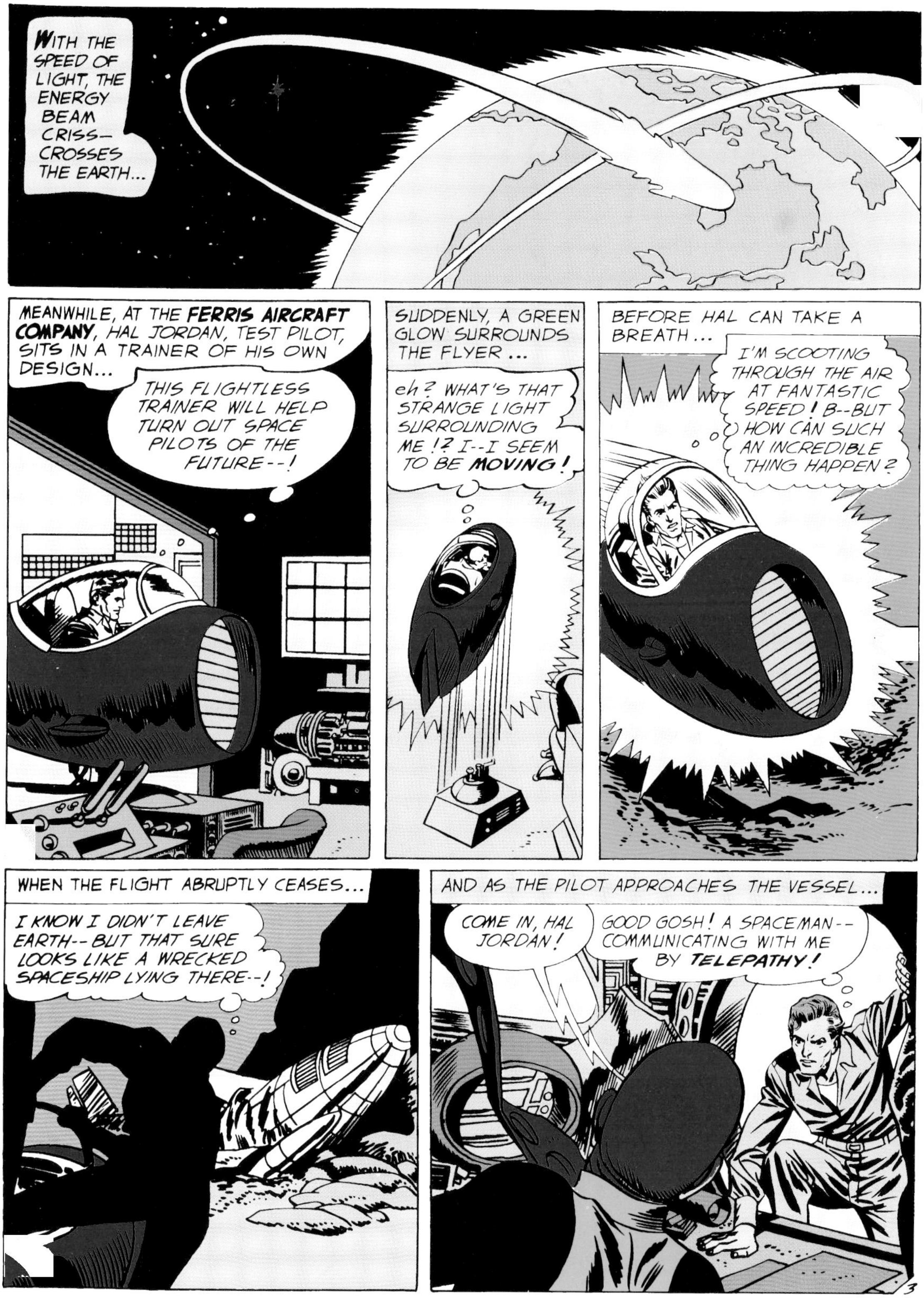
WITH THE SPEED OF LIGHT, THE ENERGY BEAM CRISS-CROSSES THE EARTH...
MEANWHILE, AT THE FERRIS AIRCRAFT COMPANY, HAL JORDAN, TEST PILOT, SITS IN A TRAINER OF HIS OWN DESIGN...
THIS FLIGHTLESS TRAINER WILL HELP TURN OUT SPACE PILOTS OF THE FUTURE--!
SUDDENLY, A GREEN GLOW SURROUNDS THE FLYER...
eh? WHAT'S THAT STRANGE LIGHT SURROUNDING ME!? I--I SEEM TO BE MOVING!
BEFORE HAL CAN TAKE A BREATH...
I'M SCOOTING THROUGH THE AIR AT FANTASTIC SPEED! B--BUT HOW CAN SUCH AN INCREDIBLE THING HAPPEN?
WHEN THE FLIGHT ABRUPTLY CEASES...
I KNOW I DIDN'T LEAVE EARTH--BUT THAT SURE LOOKS LIKE A WRECKED SPACESHIP LYING THERE--!
AND AS THE PILOT APPROACHES THE VESSEL...
COME IN, HAL JORDAN!
GOOD GOSH! A SPACEMAN--COMMUNICATING WITH ME BY TELEPATHY!
3

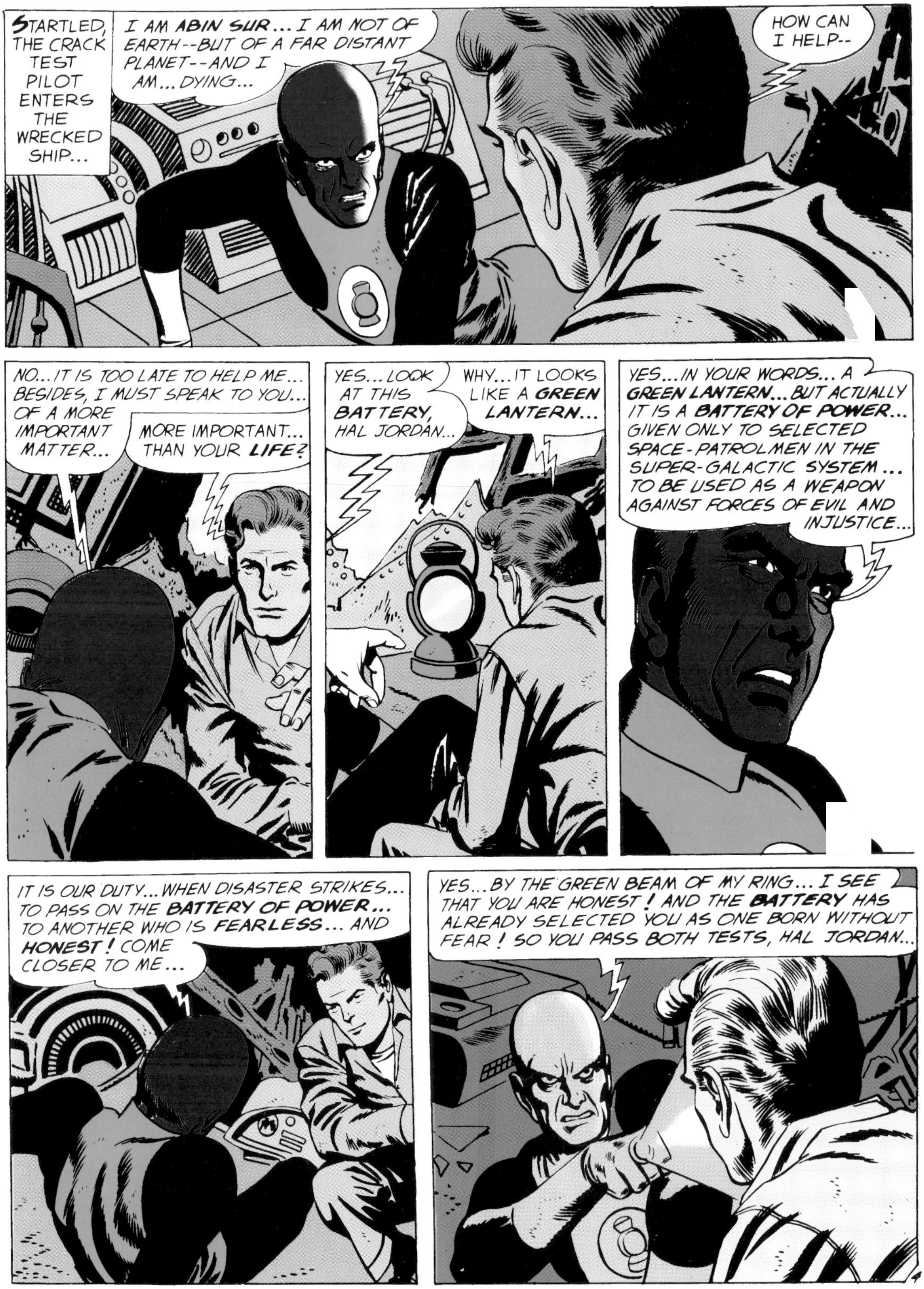
STARTLED, THE CRACK TEST PILOT ENTERS THE WRECKED SHIP...
I AM ABIN SUR... I AM NOT OF EARTH--BUT OF A FAR DISTANT PLANET--AND I AM... DYING...
HOW CAN I HELP--
NO... IT IS TOO LATE TO HELP ME... BESIDES, I MUST SPEAK TO YOU... OF A MORE IMPORTANT MATTER...
MORE IMPORTANT... THAN YOUR LIFE?
YES... LOOK AT THIS BATTERY, HAL JORDAN...
WHY... IT LOOKS LIKE A GREEN LANTERN...
YES... IN YOUR WORDS... A GREEN LANTERN... BUT ACTUALLY IT IS A BATTERY OF POWER... GIVEN ONLY TO SELECTED SPACE-PATROLMEN IN THE SUPER-GALACTIC SYSTEM... TO BE USED AS A WEAPON AGAINST FORCES OF EVIL AND INJUSTICE...
IT IS OUR DUTY... WHEN DISASTER STRIKES... TO PASS ON THE BATTERY OF POWER... TO ANOTHER WHO IS FEARLESS... AND HONEST! COME CLOSER TO ME...
YES... BY THE GREEN BEAM OF MY RING... I SEE THAT YOU ARE HONEST! AND THE BATTERY HAS ALREADY SELECTED YOU AS ONE BORN WITHOUT FEAR! SO YOU PASS BOTH TESTS, HAL JORDAN...
4

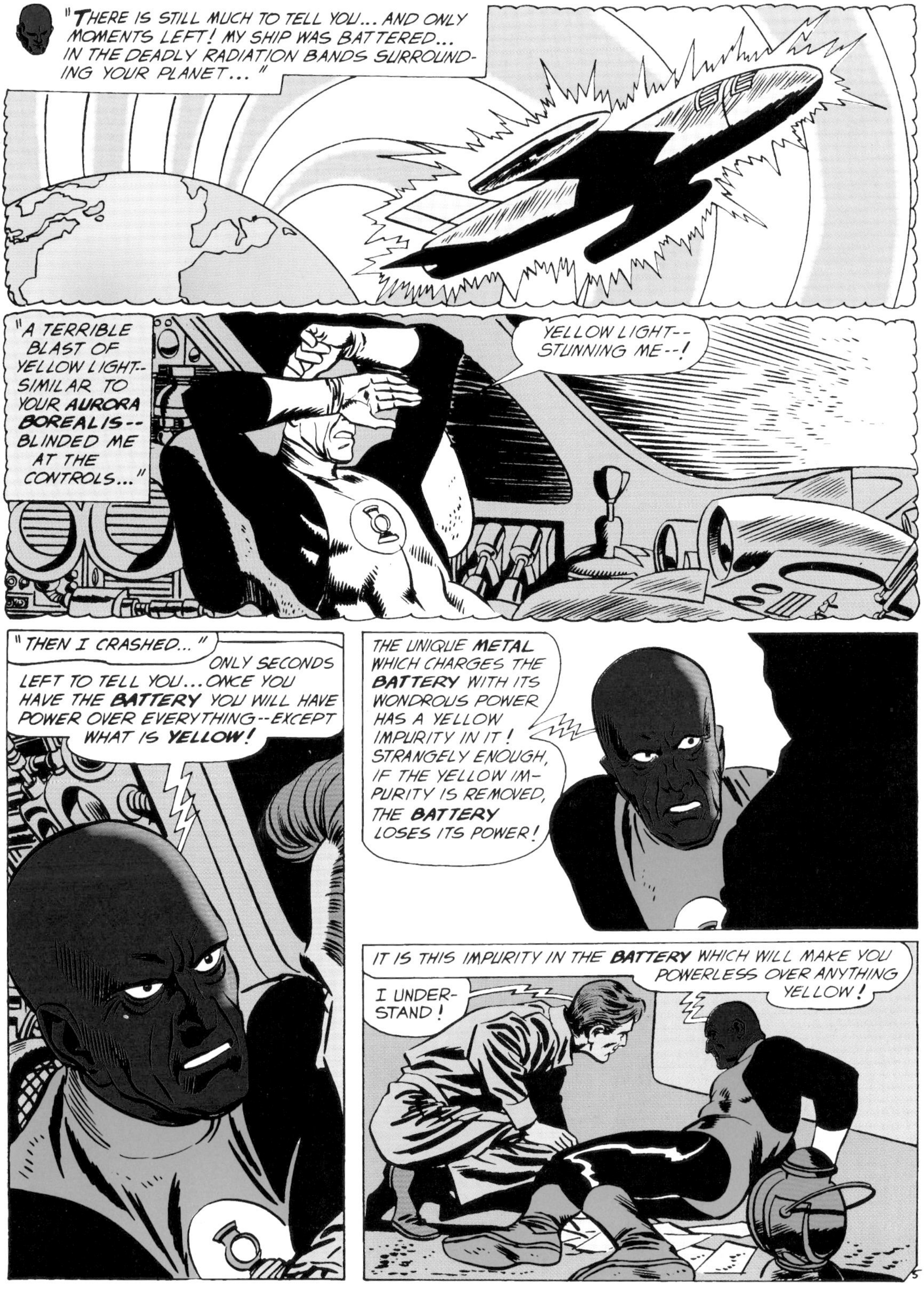
"THERE IS STILL MUCH TO TELL YOU... AND ONLY MOMENTS LEFT! MY SHIP WAS BATTERED... IN THE DEADLY RADIATION BANDS SURROUNDING YOUR PLANET..."
"A TERRIBLE BLAST OF YELLOW LIGHT-- SIMILAR TO YOUR AURORA BOREALIS-- BLINDED ME AT THE CONTROLS..."
YELLOW LIGHT-- STUNNING ME--!
"THEN I CRASHED..."
ONLY SECONDS LEFT TO TELL YOU... ONCE YOU HAVE THE BATTERY YOU WILL HAVE POWER OVER EVERYTHING--EXCEPT WHAT IS YELLOW!
THE UNIQUE METAL WHICH CHARGES THE BATTERY WITH ITS WONDROUS POWER HAS A YELLOW IMPURITY IN IT! STRANGELY ENOUGH, IF THE YELLOW IMPURITY IS REMOVED, THE BATTERY LOSES ITS POWER!
IT IS THIS IMPURITY IN THE BATTERY WHICH WILL MAKE YOU POWERLESS OVER ANYTHING YELLOW!
I UNDERSTAND!
5

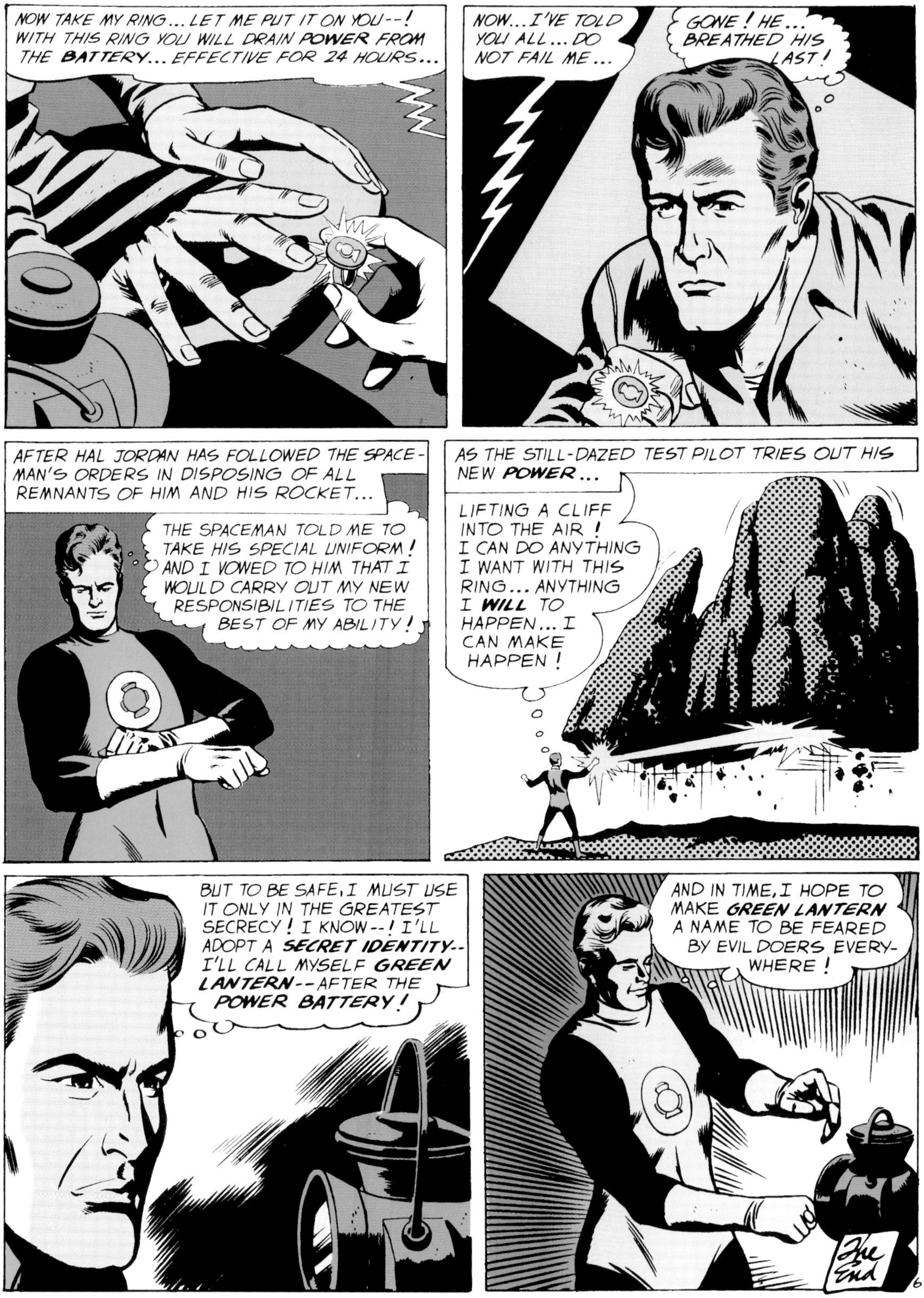
NOW TAKE MY RING... LET ME PUT IT ON YOU--! WITH THIS RING YOU WILL DRAIN POWER FROM THE BATTERY... EFFECTIVE FOR 24 HOURS...
NOW... I'VE TOLD YOU ALL... DO NOT FAIL ME...
GONE! HE... BREATHED HIS LAST!
AFTER HAL JORDAN HAS FOLLOWED THE SPACE-MAN'S ORDERS IN DISPOSING OF ALL REMNANTS OF HIM AND HIS ROCKET...
THE SPACEMAN TOLD ME TO TAKE HIS SPECIAL UNIFORM! AND I VOWED TO HIM THAT I WOULD CARRY OUT MY NEW RESPONSIBILITIES TO THE BEST OF MY ABILITY!
AS THE STILL-DAZED TEST PILOT TRIES OUT HIS NEW POWER...
LIFTING A CLIFF INTO THE AIR! I CAN DO ANYTHING I WANT WITH THIS RING... ANYTHING I WILL TO HAPPEN... I CAN MAKE HAPPEN!
BUT TO BE SAFE, I MUST USE IT ONLY IN THE GREATEST SECRECY! I KNOW--! I'LL ADOPT A SECRET IDENTITY--I'LL CALL MYSELF GREEN LANTERN--AFTER THE POWER BATTERY!
AND IN TIME, I HOPE TO MAKE GREEN LANTERN A NAME TO BE FEARED BY EVIL DOERS EVERY-WHERE!
The End

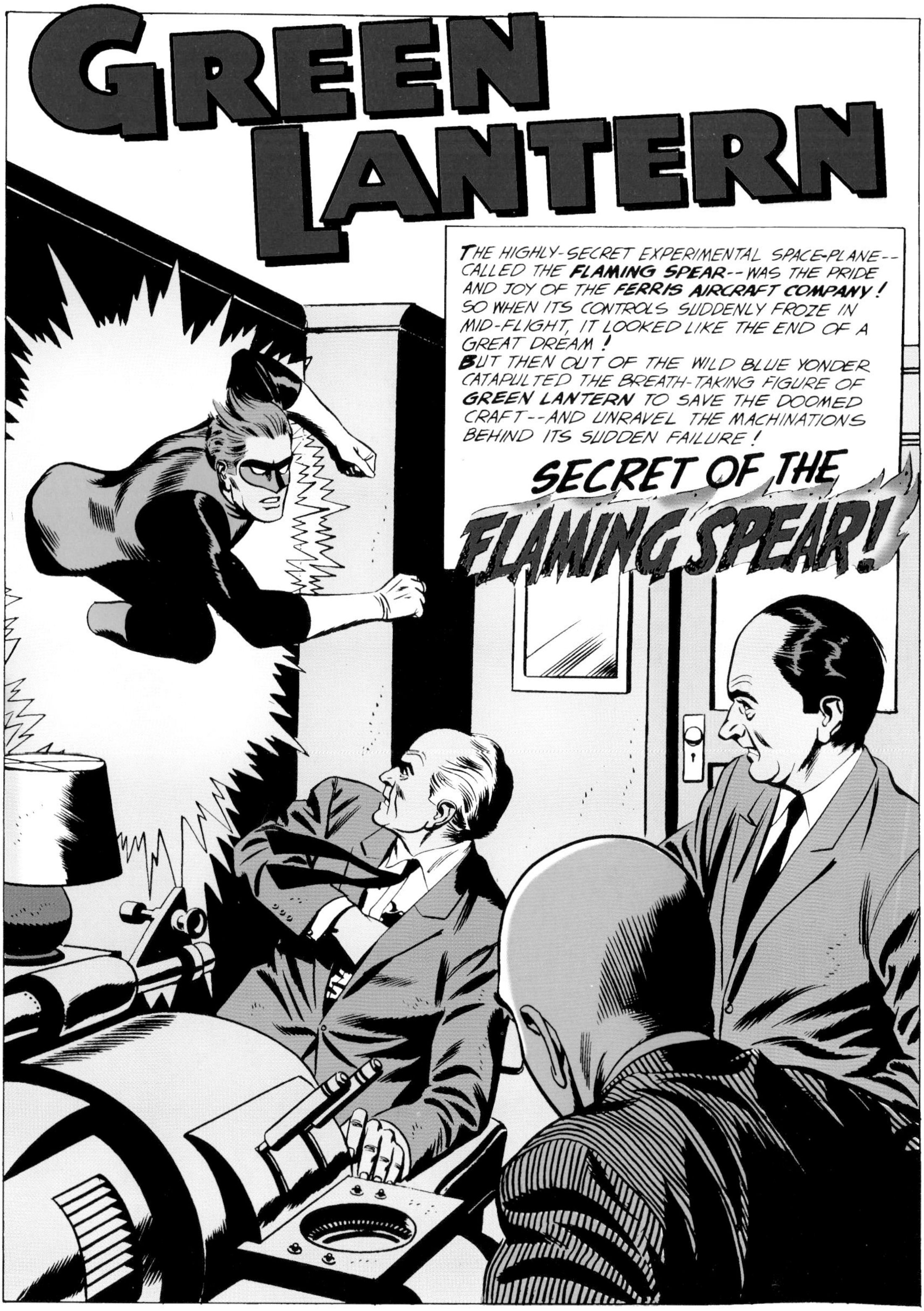
GREEN LANTERN
THE HIGHLY-SECRET EXPERIMENTAL SPACE-PLANE--CALLED THE FLAMING SPEAR--WAS THE PRIDE AND JOY OF THE FERRIS AIRCRAFT COMPANY! SO WHEN ITS CONTROLS SUDDENLY FROZE IN MID-FLIGHT, IT LOOKED LIKE THE END OF A GREAT DREAM!
BUT THEN OUT OF THE WILD BLUE YONDER CATAPULTED THE BREATH-TAKING FIGURE OF GREEN LANTERN TO SAVE THE DOOMED CRAFT--AND UNRAVEL THE MACHINATIONS BEHIND ITS SUDDEN FAILURE!
SECRET OF THE FLAMING SPEAR!

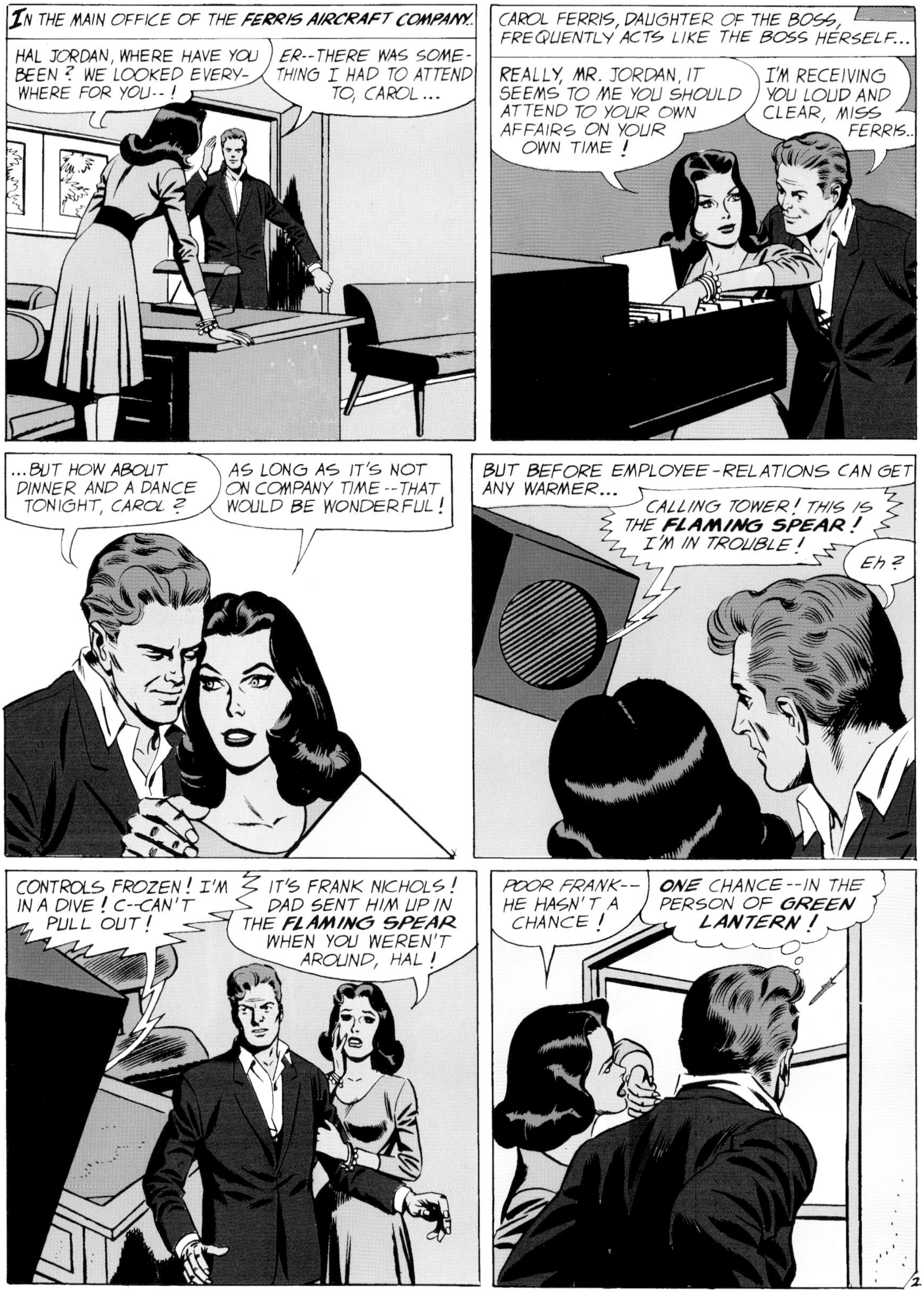
IN THE MAIN OFFICE OF THE FERRIS AIRCRAFT COMPANY.
HAL JORDAN, WHERE HAVE YOU BEEN? WE LOOKED EVERYWHERE FOR YOU--!
ER--THERE WAS SOMETHING I HAD TO ATTEND TO, CAROL...
CAROL FERRIS, DAUGHTER OF THE BOSS, FREQUENTLY ACTS LIKE THE BOSS HERSELF...
REALLY, MR. JORDAN, IT SEEMS TO ME YOU SHOULD ATTEND TO YOUR OWN AFFAIRS ON YOUR OWN TIME!
I'M RECEIVING YOU LOUD AND CLEAR, MISS FERRIS..
...BUT HOW ABOUT DINNER AND A DANCE TONIGHT, CAROL?
AS LONG AS IT'S NOT ON COMPANY TIME--THAT WOULD BE WONDERFUL!
BUT BEFORE EMPLOYEE-RELATIONS CAN GET ANY WARMER...
CALLING TOWER! THIS IS THE FLAMING SPEAR! I'M IN TROUBLE!
Eh?
CONTROLS FROZEN! I'M IN A DIVE! C--CAN'T PULL OUT!
IT'S FRANK NICHOLS! DAD SENT HIM UP IN THE FLAMING SPEAR WHEN YOU WEREN'T AROUND, HAL!
POOR FRANK--HE HASN'T A CHANCE!
ONE CHANCE--IN THE PERSON OF GREEN LANTERN!
2

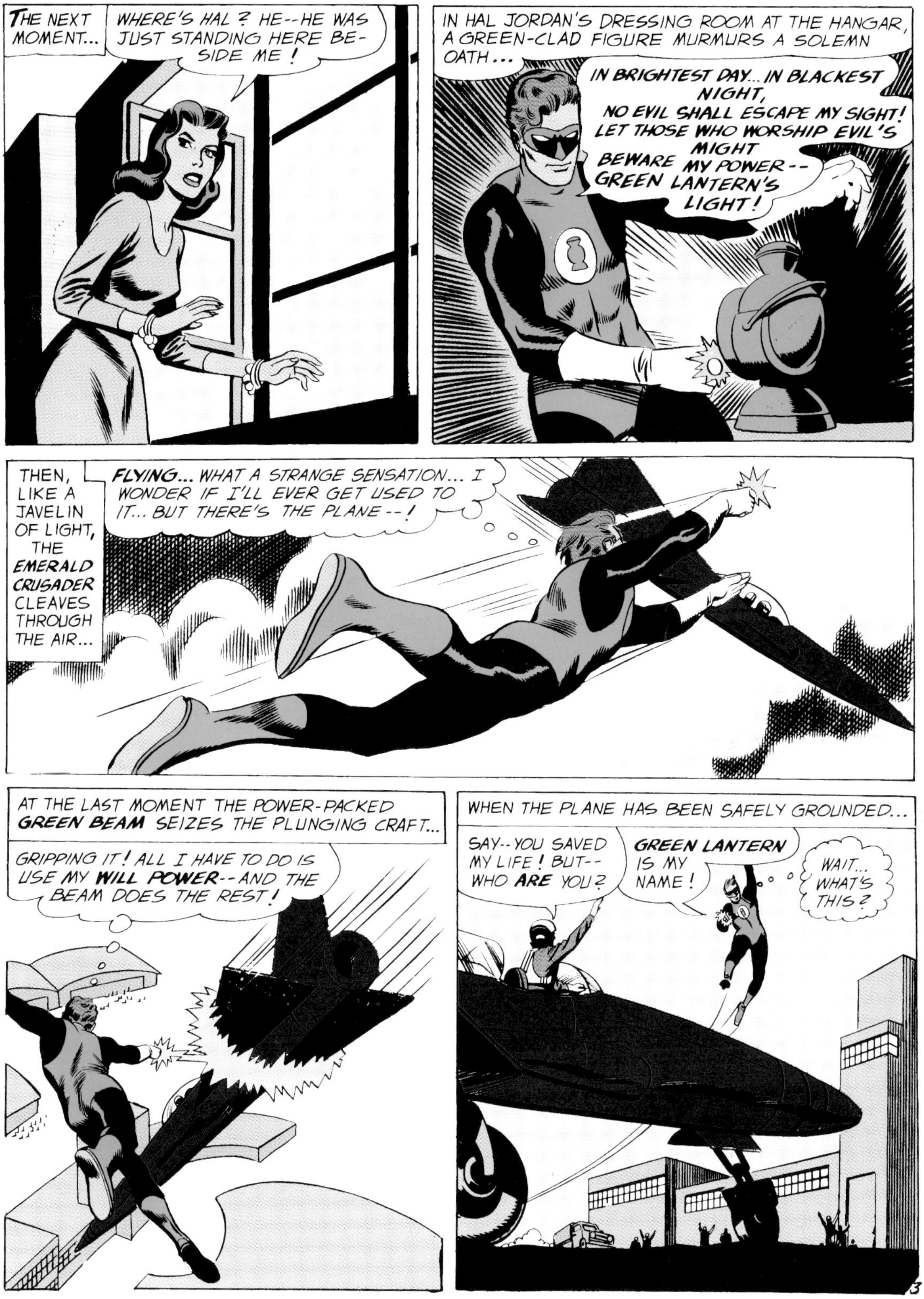
THE NEXT MOMENT...
WHERE'S HAL? HE--HE WAS JUST STANDING HERE BESIDE ME!
IN HAL JORDAN'S DRESSING ROOM AT THE HANGAR, A GREEN-CLAD FIGURE MURMURS A SOLEMN OATH...
IN BRIGHTEST DAY... IN BLACKEST NIGHT, NO EVIL SHALL ESCAPE MY SIGHT! LET THOSE WHO WORSHIP EVIL'S MIGHT BEWARE MY POWER--GREEN LANTERN'S LIGHT!
THEN, LIKE A JAVELIN OF LIGHT, THE EMERALD CRUSADER CLEAVES THROUGH THE AIR...
FLYING... WHAT A STRANGE SENSATION... I WONDER IF I'LL EVER GET USED TO IT... BUT THERE'S THE PLANE--!
AT THE LAST MOMENT THE POWER-PACKED GREEN BEAM SEIZES THE PLUNGING CRAFT...
GRIPPING IT! ALL I HAVE TO DO IS USE MY WILL POWER--AND THE BEAM DOES THE REST!
WHEN THE PLANE HAS BEEN SAFELY GROUNDED...
SAY--YOU SAVED MY LIFE! BUT--WHO ARE YOU?
GREEN LANTERN IS MY NAME!
WAIT... WHAT'S THIS?
3

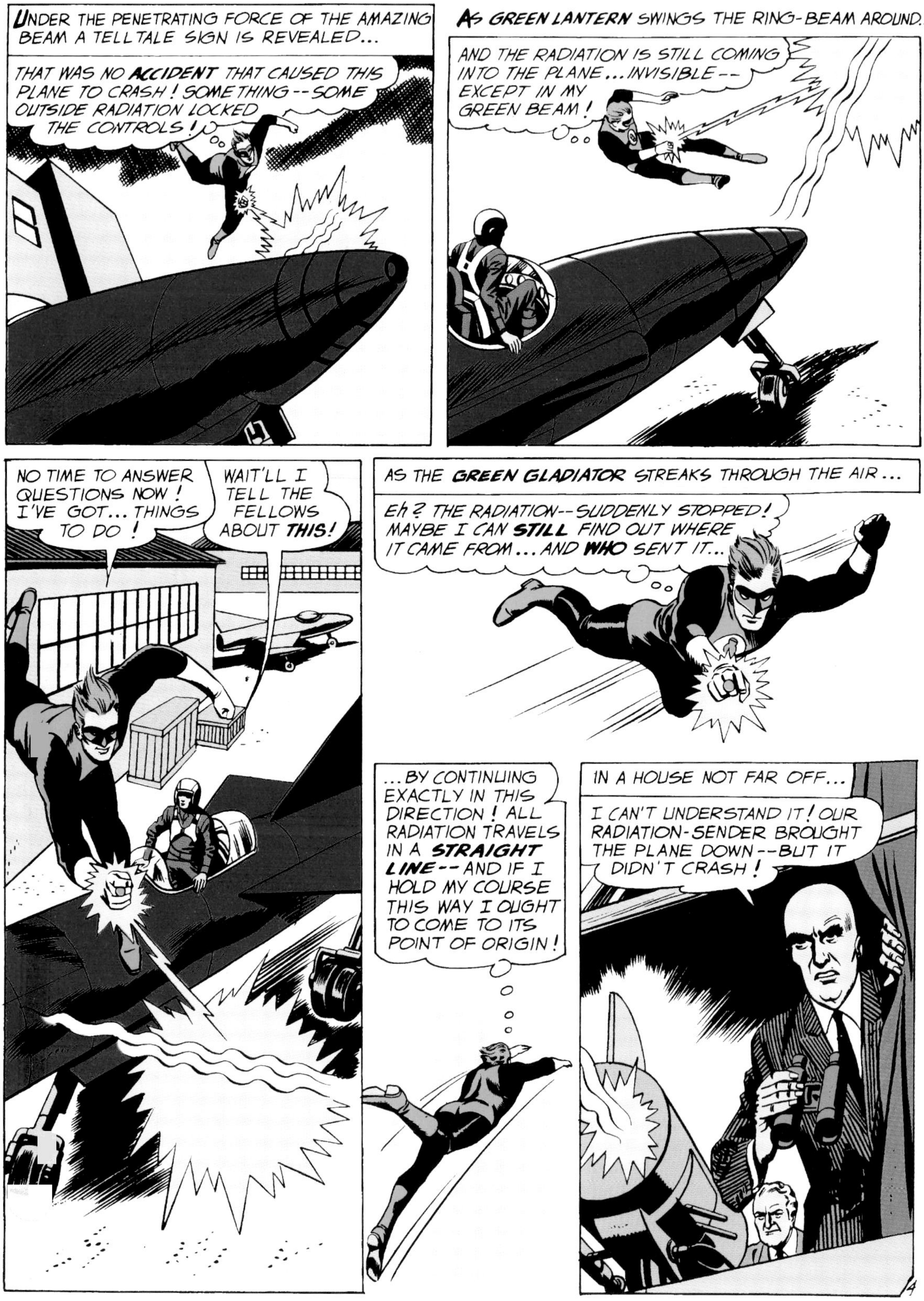
UNDER THE PENETRATING FORCE OF THE AMAZING BEAM A TELLTALE SIGN IS REVEALED...
THAT WAS NO ACCIDENT THAT CAUSED THIS PLANE TO CRASH! SOMETHING--SOME OUTSIDE RADIATION LOCKED THE CONTROLS!
AS GREEN LANTERN SWINGS THE RING-BEAM AROUND..
AND THE RADIATION IS STILL COMING INTO THE PLANE...INVISIBLE--EXCEPT IN MY GREEN BEAM!
NO TIME TO ANSWER QUESTIONS NOW! I'VE GOT... THINGS TO DO!
WAIT'LL I TELL THE FELLOWS ABOUT THIS!
AS THE GREEN GLADIATOR STREAKS THROUGH THE AIR...
Eh? THE RADIATION--SUDDENLY STOPPED! MAYBE I CAN STILL FIND OUT WHERE IT CAME FROM...AND WHO SENT IT...
...BY CONTINUING EXACTLY IN THIS DIRECTION! ALL RADIATION TRAVELS IN A STRAIGHT LINE--AND IF I HOLD MY COURSE THIS WAY I OUGHT TO COME TO ITS POINT OF ORIGIN!
IN A HOUSE NOT FAR OFF...
I CAN'T UNDERSTAND IT! OUR RADIATION-SENDER BROUGHT THE PLANE DOWN--BUT IT DIDN'T CRASH!
4

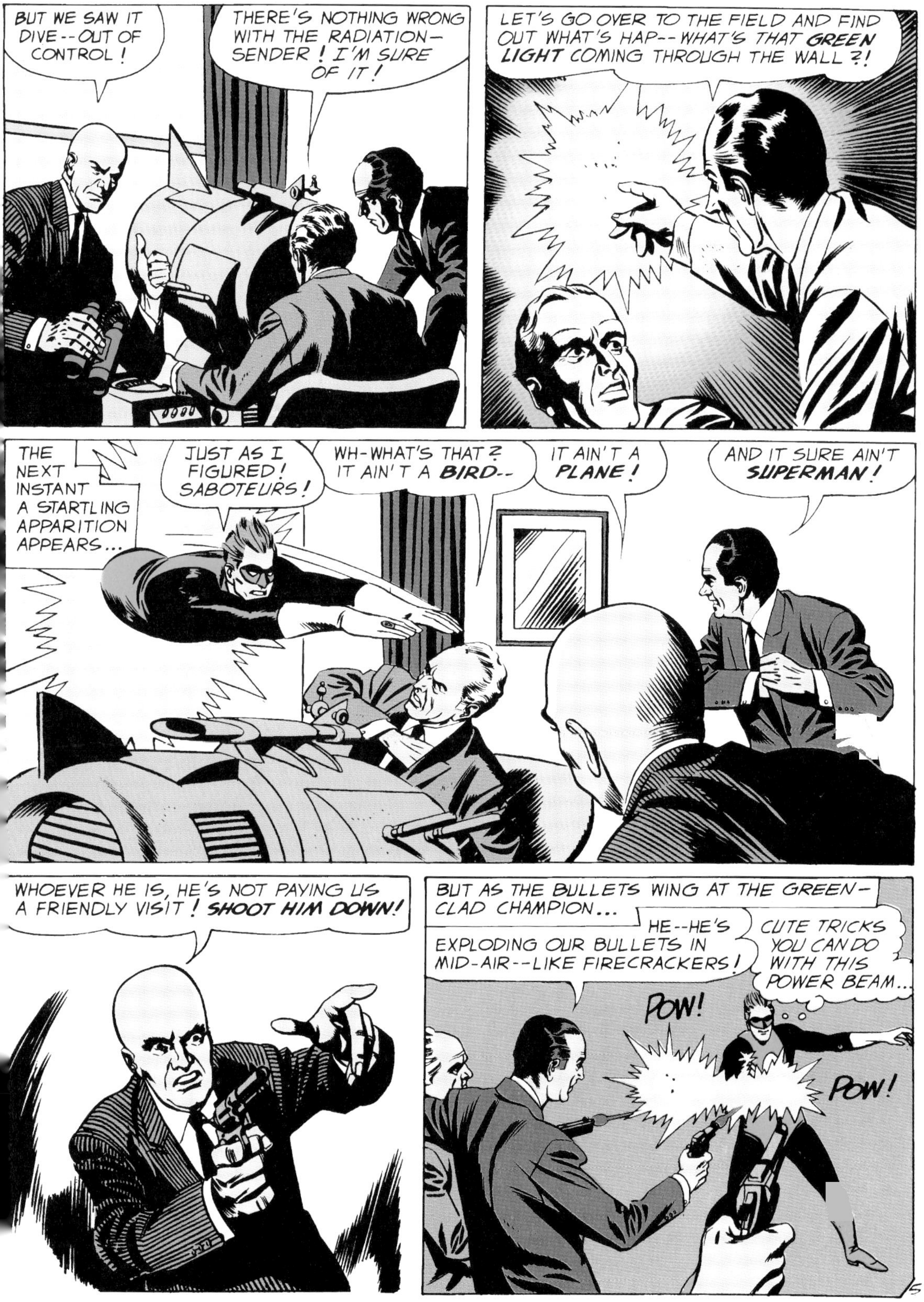
BUT WE SAW IT DIVE--OUT OF CONTROL!
THERE'S NOTHING WRONG WITH THE RADIATION-SENDER! I'M SURE OF IT!
LET'S GO OVER TO THE FIELD AND FIND OUT WHAT'S HAP--WHAT'S THAT GREEN LIGHT COMING THROUGH THE WALL?!
THE NEXT INSTANT A STARTLING APPARITION APPEARS...
JUST AS I FIGURED! SABOTEURS!
WH-WHAT'S THAT? IT AIN'T A BIRD--
IT AIN'T A PLANE!
AND IT SURE AIN'T SUPERMAN!
WHOEVER HE IS, HE'S NOT PAYING US A FRIENDLY VISIT! SHOOT HIM DOWN!
BUT AS THE BULLETS WING AT THE GREEN-CLAD CHAMPION...
HE--HE'S EXPLODING OUR BULLETS IN MID-AIR--LIKE FIRECRACKERS!
CUTE TRICKS YOU CAN DO WITH THIS POWER BEAM...
POW!
POW!
5

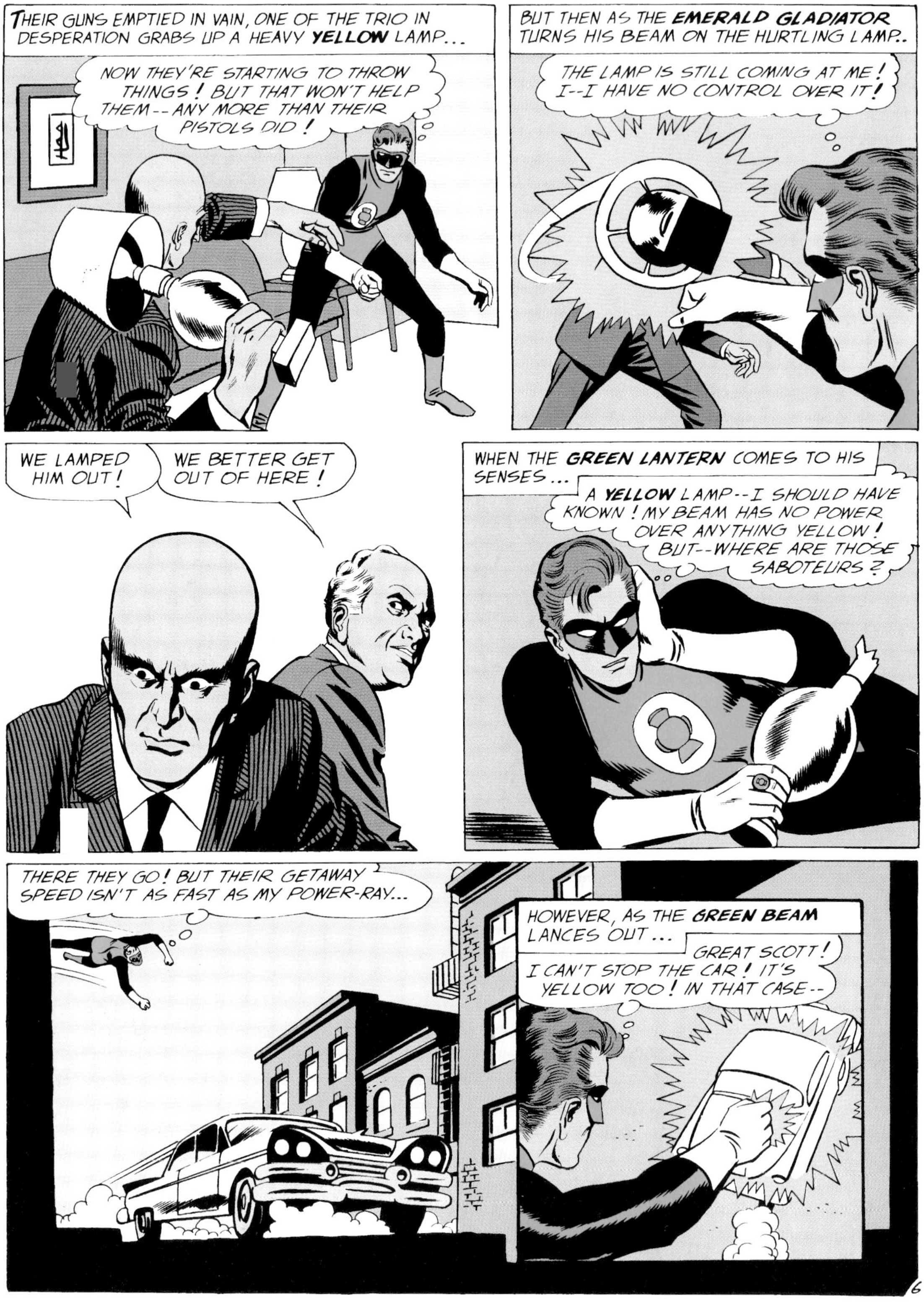
THEIR GUNS EMPTIED IN VAIN, ONE OF THE TRIO IN DESPERATION GRABS UP A HEAVY YELLOW LAMP...
NOW THEY'RE STARTING TO THROW THINGS! BUT THAT WON'T HELP THEM--ANY MORE THAN THEIR PISTOLS DID!
BUT THEN AS THE EMERALD GLADIATOR TURNS HIS BEAM ON THE HURTLING LAMP..
THE LAMP IS STILL COMING AT ME! I--I HAVE NO CONTROL OVER IT!
WE LAMPED HIM OUT!
WE BETTER GET OUT OF HERE!
WHEN THE GREEN LANTERN COMES TO HIS SENSES...
A YELLOW LAMP--I SHOULD HAVE KNOWN! MY BEAM HAS NO POWER OVER ANYTHING YELLOW! BUT--WHERE ARE THOSE SABOTEURS?
THERE THEY GO! BUT THEIR GETAWAY SPEED ISN'T AS FAST AS MY POWER-RAY...
HOWEVER, AS THE GREEN BEAM LANCES OUT...
GREAT SCOTT! I CAN'T STOP THE CAR! IT'S YELLOW TOO! IN THAT CASE--
6

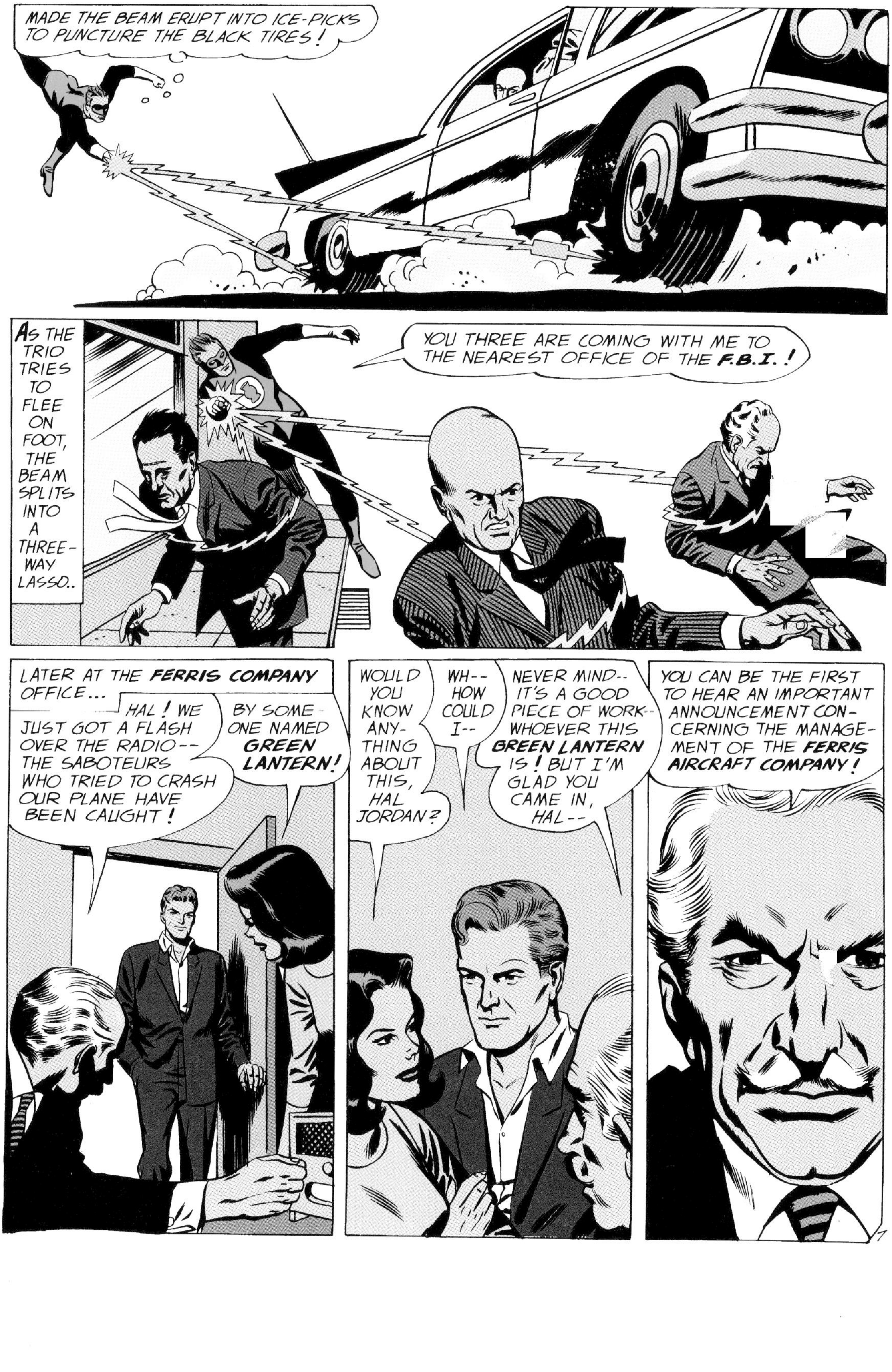
MADE THE BEAM ERUPT INTO ICE-PICKS TO PUNCTURE THE BLACK TIRES!
AS THE TRIO TRIES TO FLEE ON FOOT, THE BEAM SPLITS INTO A THREE-WAY LASSO..
YOU THREE ARE COMING WITH ME TO THE NEAREST OFFICE OF THE F.B.I.!
LATER AT THE FERRIS COMPANY OFFICE...
HAL! WE JUST GOT A FLASH OVER THE RADIO--THE SABOTEURS WHO TRIED TO CRASH OUR PLANE HAVE BEEN CAUGHT!
BY SOME-ONE NAMED GREEN LANTERN!
WOULD YOU KNOW ANY-THING ABOUT THIS, HAL JORDAN?
WH--HOW COULD I--
NEVER MIND--IT'S A GOOD PIECE OF WORK--WHOEVER THIS GREEN LANTERN IS! BUT I'M GLAD YOU CAME IN, HAL--
YOU CAN BE THE FIRST TO HEAR AN IMPORTANT ANNOUNCEMENT CON-CERNING THE MANAGE-MENT OF THE FERRIS AIRCRAFT COMPANY!
7

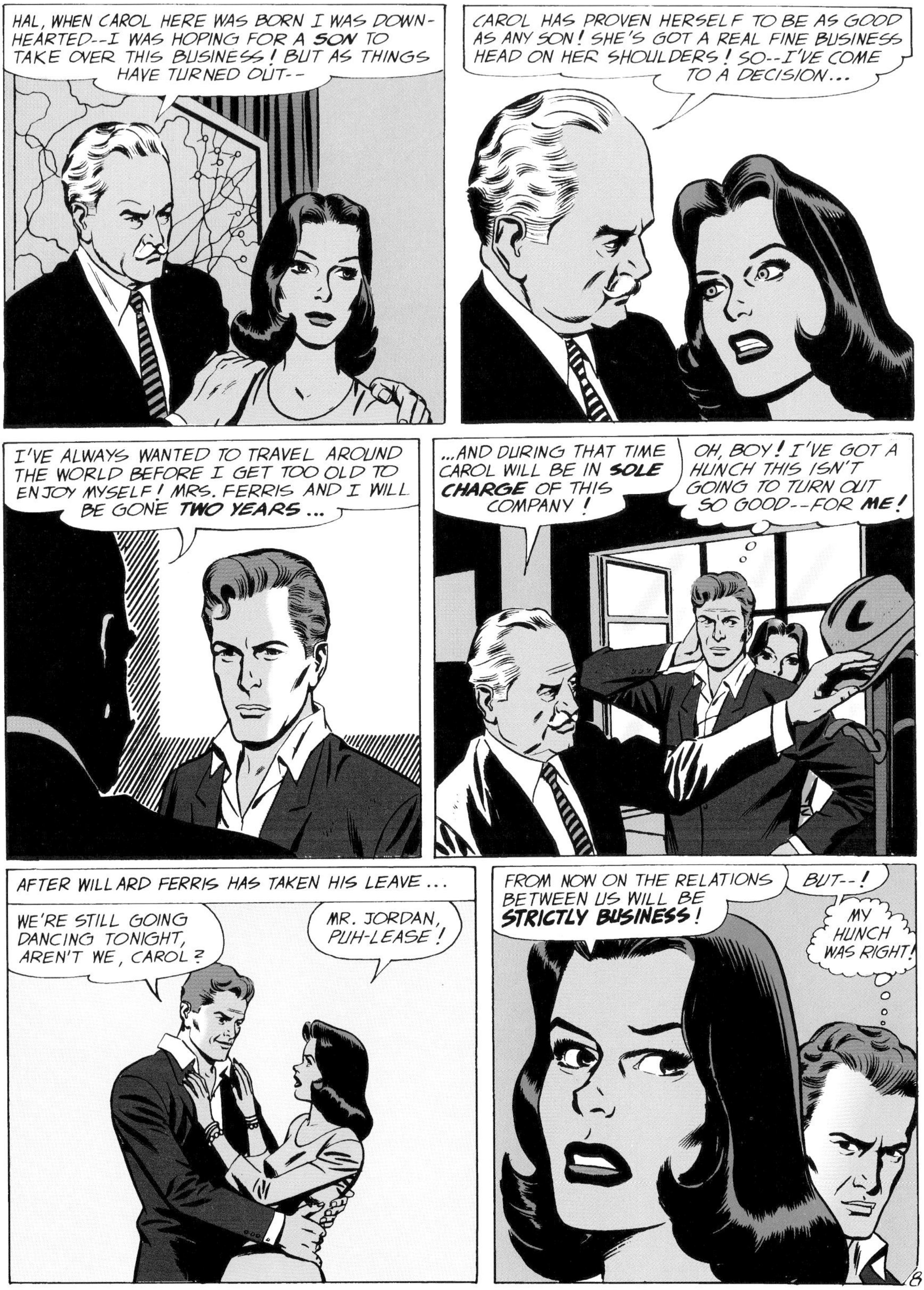
HAL, WHEN CAROL HERE WAS BORN I WAS DOWN-HEARTED--I WAS HOPING FOR A SON TO TAKE OVER THIS BUSINESS! BUT AS THINGS HAVE TURNED OUT--
CAROL HAS PROVEN HERSELF TO BE AS GOOD AS ANY SON! SHE'S GOT A REAL FINE BUSINESS HEAD ON HER SHOULDERS! SO--I'VE COME TO A DECISION...
I'VE ALWAYS WANTED TO TRAVEL AROUND THE WORLD BEFORE I GET TOO OLD TO ENJOY MYSELF! MRS. FERRIS AND I WILL BE GONE TWO YEARS...
...AND DURING THAT TIME CAROL WILL BE IN SOLE CHARGE OF THIS COMPANY!
OH, BOY! I'VE GOT A HUNCH THIS ISN'T GOING TO TURN OUT SO GOOD--FOR ME!
AFTER WILLARD FERRIS HAS TAKEN HIS LEAVE...
WE'RE STILL GOING DANCING TONIGHT, AREN'T WE, CAROL?
MR. JORDAN, PUH-LEASE!
FROM NOW ON THE RELATIONS BETWEEN US WILL BE STRICTLY BUSINESS!
BUT--!
MY HUNCH WAS RIGHT!
8

NO HARM IN MIXING BUSINESS WITH PLEASURE--

YOU HEARD WHAT DAD SAID! I'VE GOT TO SATISFY HIS FAITH IN ME--

AND THAT MEANS THAT DURING THE NEXT TWO YEARS I'LL HAVE ABSOLUTELY NO TIME FOR ROMANCE! I'M YOUR BOSS, MR. JORDAN-- AND THAT'S **ORDERS**!

Whew!

TWO YEARS!?

LATER, A CRESTFALLEN PILOT MOONS OVER HIS FATE...

(sigh) MY **POWER RING** CAN DO ANYTHING FOR ME EXCEPT GET ME THE ONE THING IN THE WORLD I WANT MOST--**CAROL**!

The End

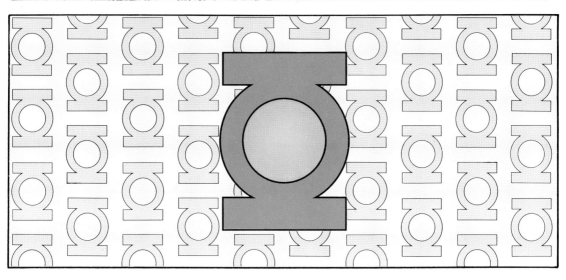

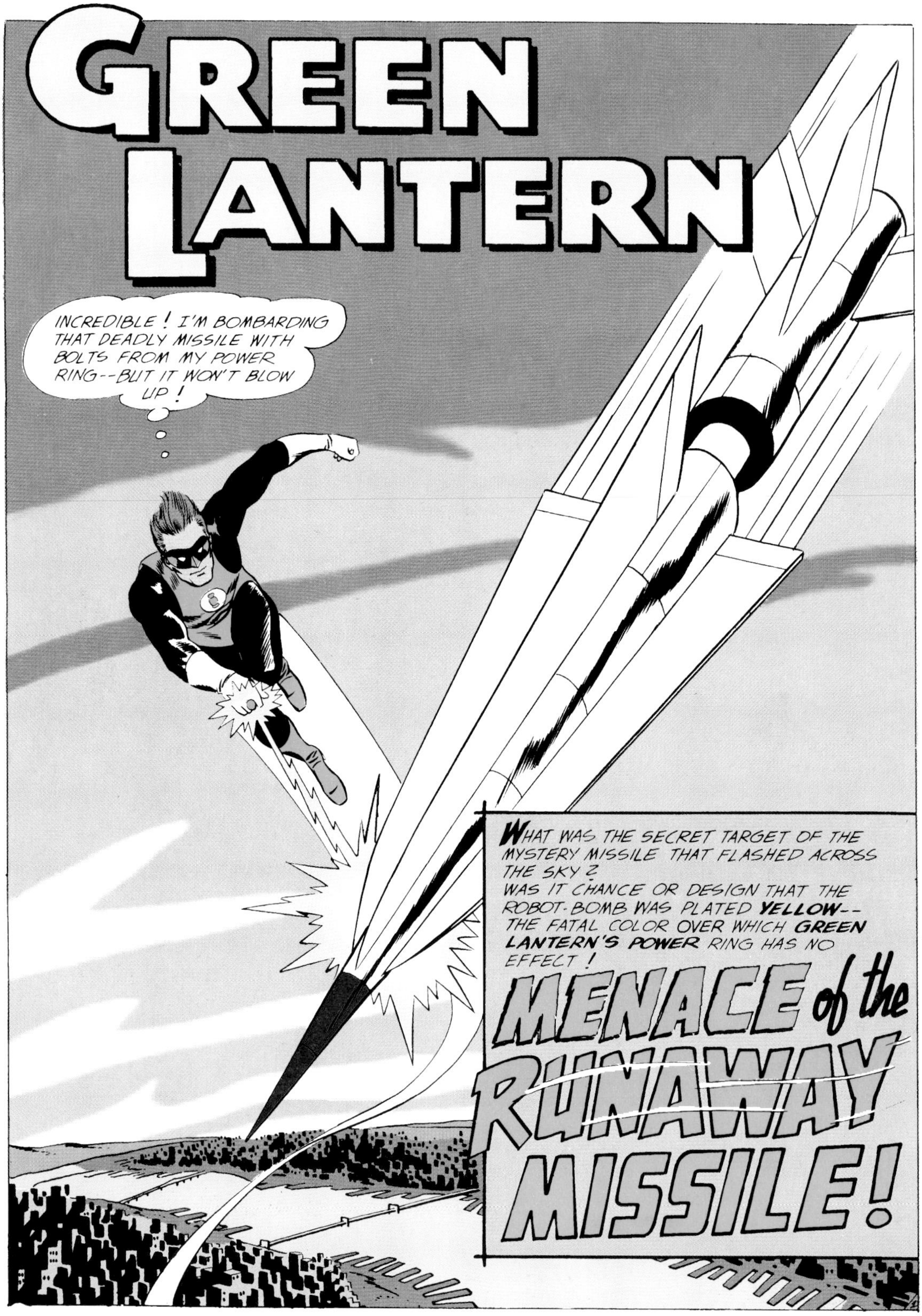
GREEN LANTERN
INCREDIBLE! I'M BOMBARDING THAT DEADLY MISSILE WITH BOLTS FROM MY POWER RING--BUT IT WON'T BLOW UP!
WHAT WAS THE SECRET TARGET OF THE MYSTERY MISSILE THAT FLASHED ACROSS THE SKY? WAS IT CHANCE OR DESIGN THAT THE ROBOT-BOMB WAS PLATED YELLOW-- THE FATAL COLOR OVER WHICH GREEN LANTERN'S POWER RING HAS NO EFFECT!
MENACE of the RUNAWAY MISSILE!

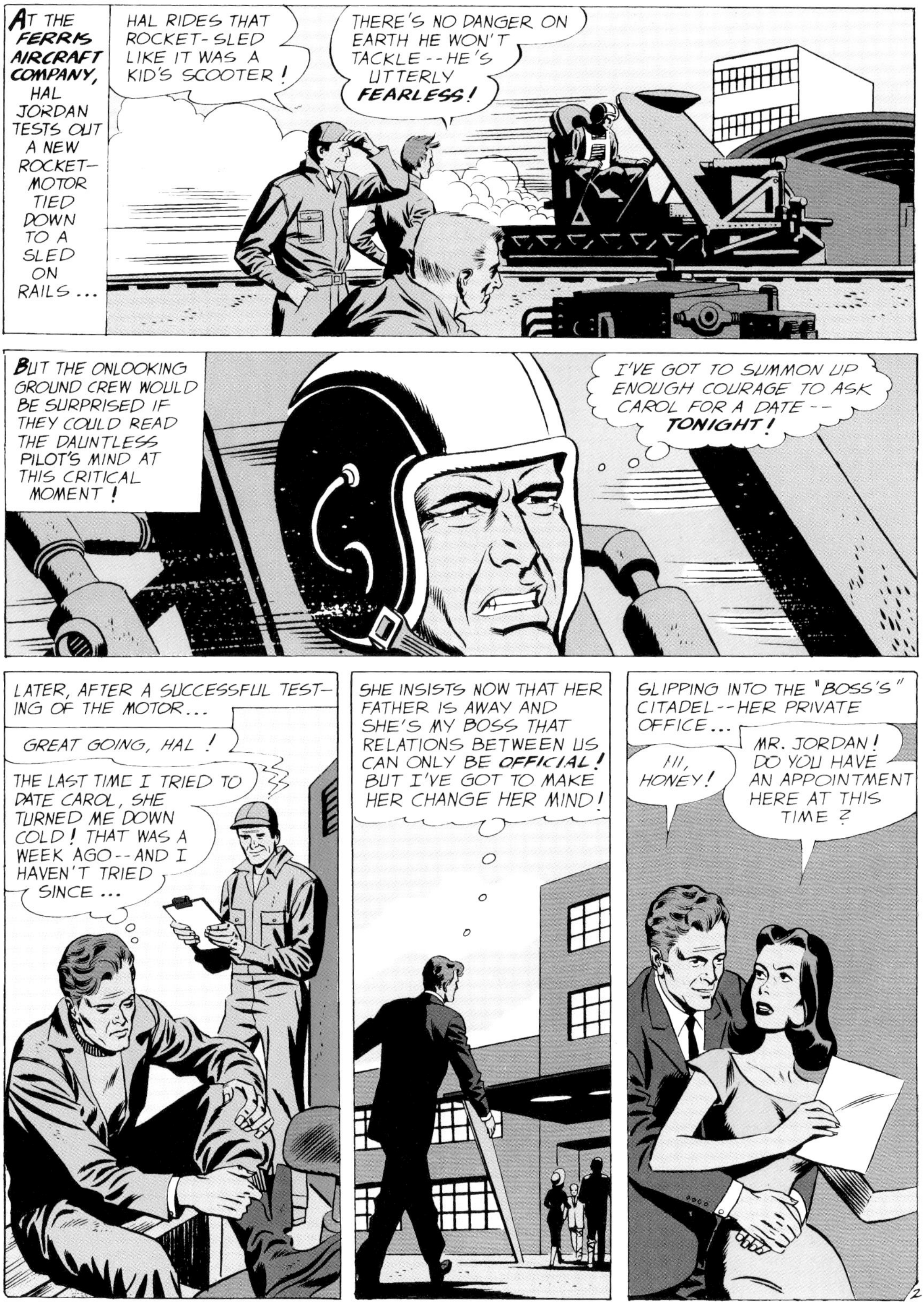
AT THE FERRIS AIRCRAFT COMPANY, HAL JORDAN TESTS OUT A NEW ROCKET-MOTOR TIED DOWN TO A SLED ON RAILS...
HAL RIDES THAT ROCKET-SLED LIKE IT WAS A KID'S SCOOTER!
THERE'S NO DANGER ON EARTH HE WON'T TACKLE--HE'S UTTERLY FEARLESS!
BUT THE ONLOOKING GROUND CREW WOULD BE SURPRISED IF THEY COULD READ THE DAUNTLESS PILOT'S MIND AT THIS CRITICAL MOMENT!
I'VE GOT TO SUMMON UP ENOUGH COURAGE TO ASK CAROL FOR A DATE--TONIGHT!
LATER, AFTER A SUCCESSFUL TESTING OF THE MOTOR...
GREAT GOING, HAL!
THE LAST TIME I TRIED TO DATE CAROL, SHE TURNED ME DOWN COLD! THAT WAS A WEEK AGO--AND I HAVEN'T TRIED SINCE...
SHE INSISTS NOW THAT HER FATHER IS AWAY AND SHE'S MY BOSS THAT RELATIONS BETWEEN US CAN ONLY BE OFFICIAL! BUT I'VE GOT TO MAKE HER CHANGE HER MIND!
SLIPPING INTO THE "BOSS'S" CITADEL--HER PRIVATE OFFICE...
HI, HONEY!
MR. JORDAN! DO YOU HAVE AN APPOINTMENT HERE AT THIS TIME?
2

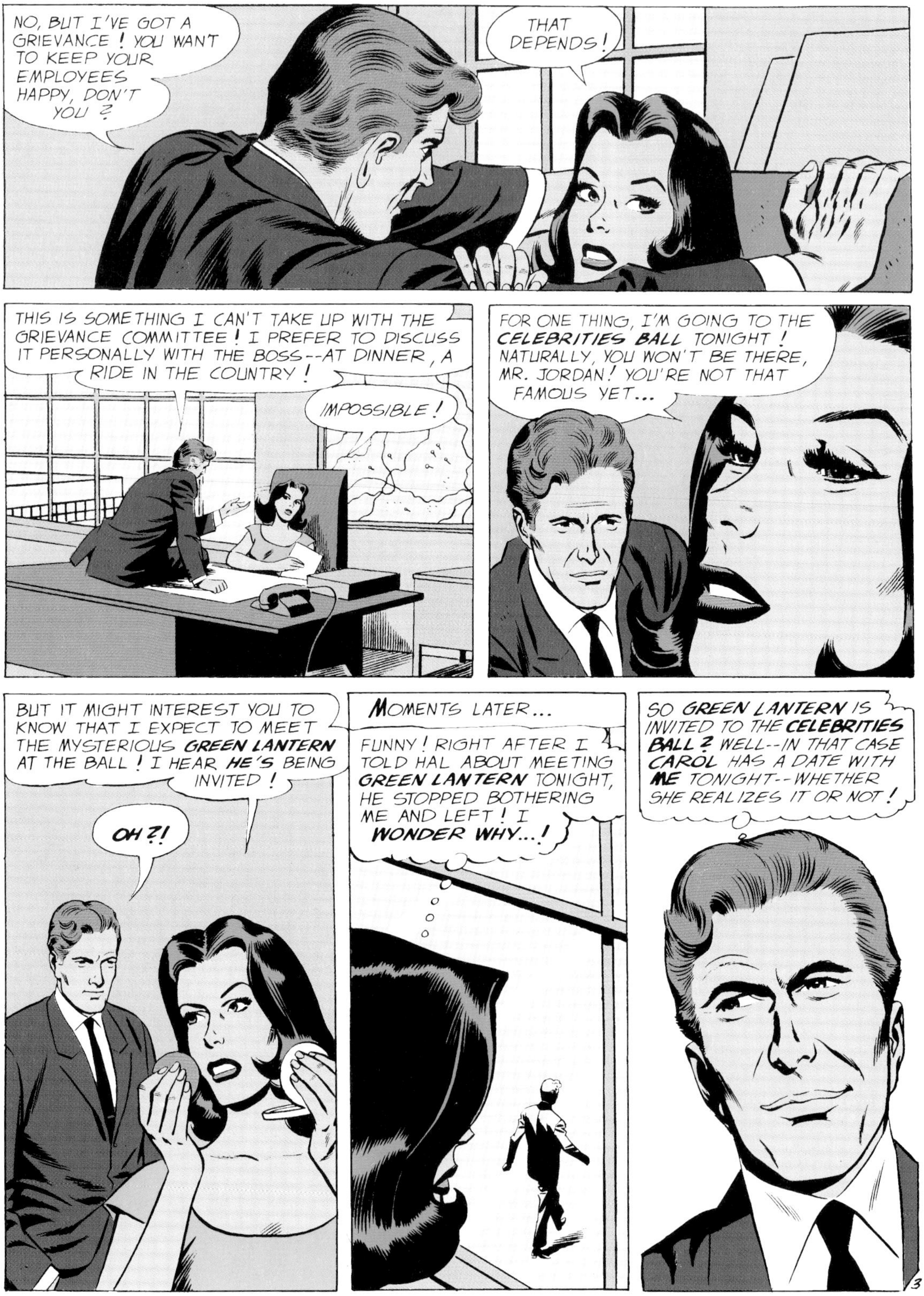
NO, BUT I'VE GOT A GRIEVANCE! YOU WANT TO KEEP YOUR EMPLOYEES HAPPY, DON'T YOU?
THAT DEPENDS!
THIS IS SOMETHING I CAN'T TAKE UP WITH THE GRIEVANCE COMMITTEE! I PREFER TO DISCUSS IT PERSONALLY WITH THE BOSS--AT DINNER, A RIDE IN THE COUNTRY!
IMPOSSIBLE!
FOR ONE THING, I'M GOING TO THE CELEBRITIES BALL TONIGHT! NATURALLY, YOU WON'T BE THERE, MR. JORDAN! YOU'RE NOT THAT FAMOUS YET...
BUT IT MIGHT INTEREST YOU TO KNOW THAT I EXPECT TO MEET THE MYSTERIOUS GREEN LANTERN AT THE BALL! I HEAR HE'S BEING INVITED!
OH?!
MOMENTS LATER...
FUNNY! RIGHT AFTER I TOLD HAL ABOUT MEETING GREEN LANTERN TONIGHT, HE STOPPED BOTHERING ME AND LEFT! I WONDER WHY...!
SO GREEN LANTERN IS INVITED TO THE CELEBRITIES BALL? WELL--IN THAT CASE CAROL HAS A DATE WITH ME TONIGHT--WHETHER SHE REALIZES IT OR NOT!
3

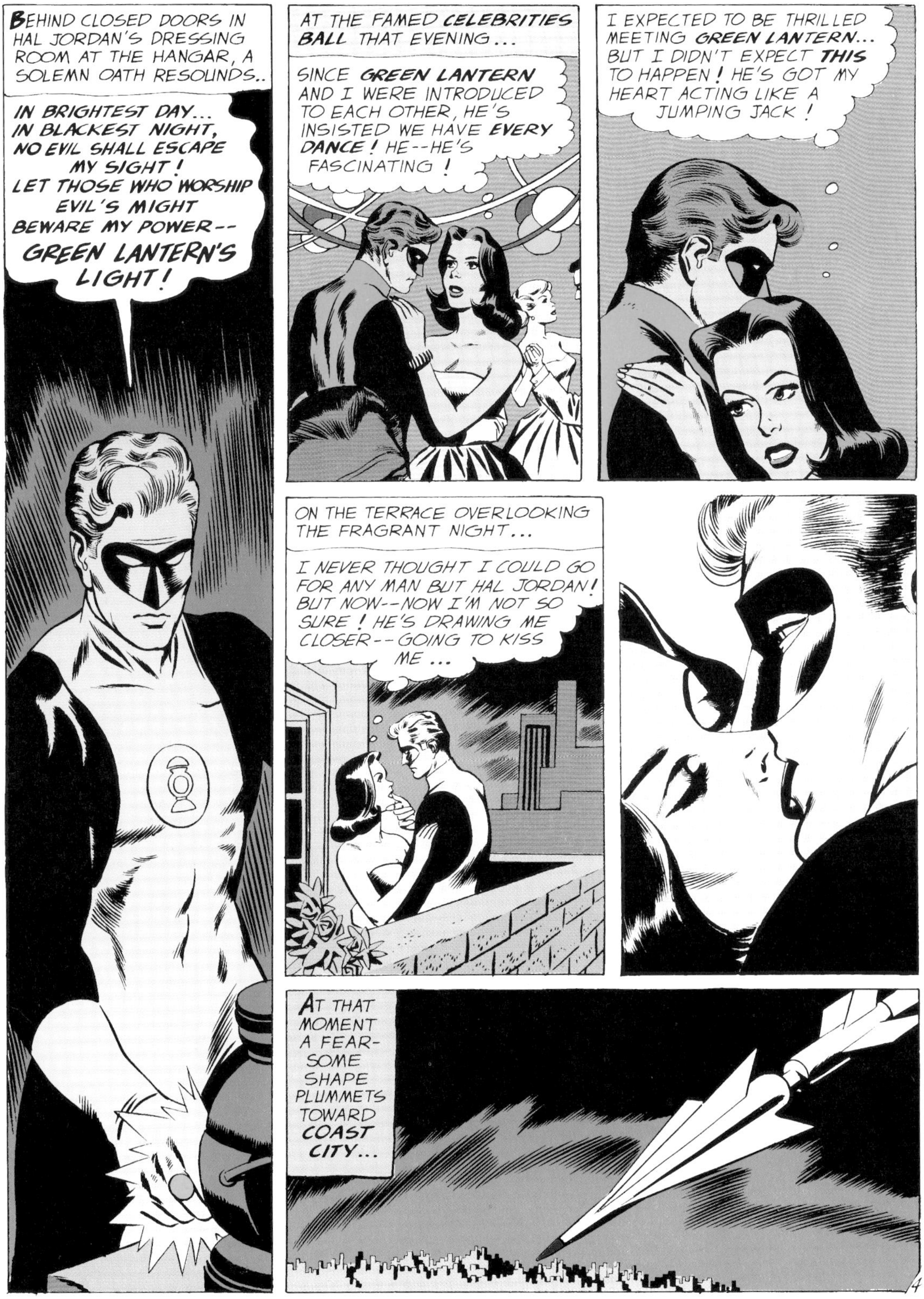
BEHIND CLOSED DOORS IN HAL JORDAN'S DRESSING ROOM AT THE HANGAR, A SOLEMN OATH RESOUNDS..
IN BRIGHTEST DAY... IN BLACKEST NIGHT, NO EVIL SHALL ESCAPE MY SIGHT! LET THOSE WHO WORSHIP EVIL'S MIGHT BEWARE MY POWER-- GREEN LANTERN'S LIGHT!
AT THE FAMED CELEBRITIES BALL THAT EVENING...
SINCE GREEN LANTERN AND I WERE INTRODUCED TO EACH OTHER, HE'S INSISTED WE HAVE EVERY DANCE! HE--HE'S FASCINATING!
I EXPECTED TO BE THRILLED MEETING GREEN LANTERN... BUT I DIDN'T EXPECT THIS TO HAPPEN! HE'S GOT MY HEART ACTING LIKE A JUMPING JACK!
ON THE TERRACE OVERLOOKING THE FRAGRANT NIGHT...
I NEVER THOUGHT I COULD GO FOR ANY MAN BUT HAL JORDAN! BUT NOW--NOW I'M NOT SO SURE! HE'S DRAWING ME CLOSER--GOING TO KISS ME...
AT THAT MOMENT A FEAR-SOME SHAPE PLUMMETS TOWARD COAST CITY...
4

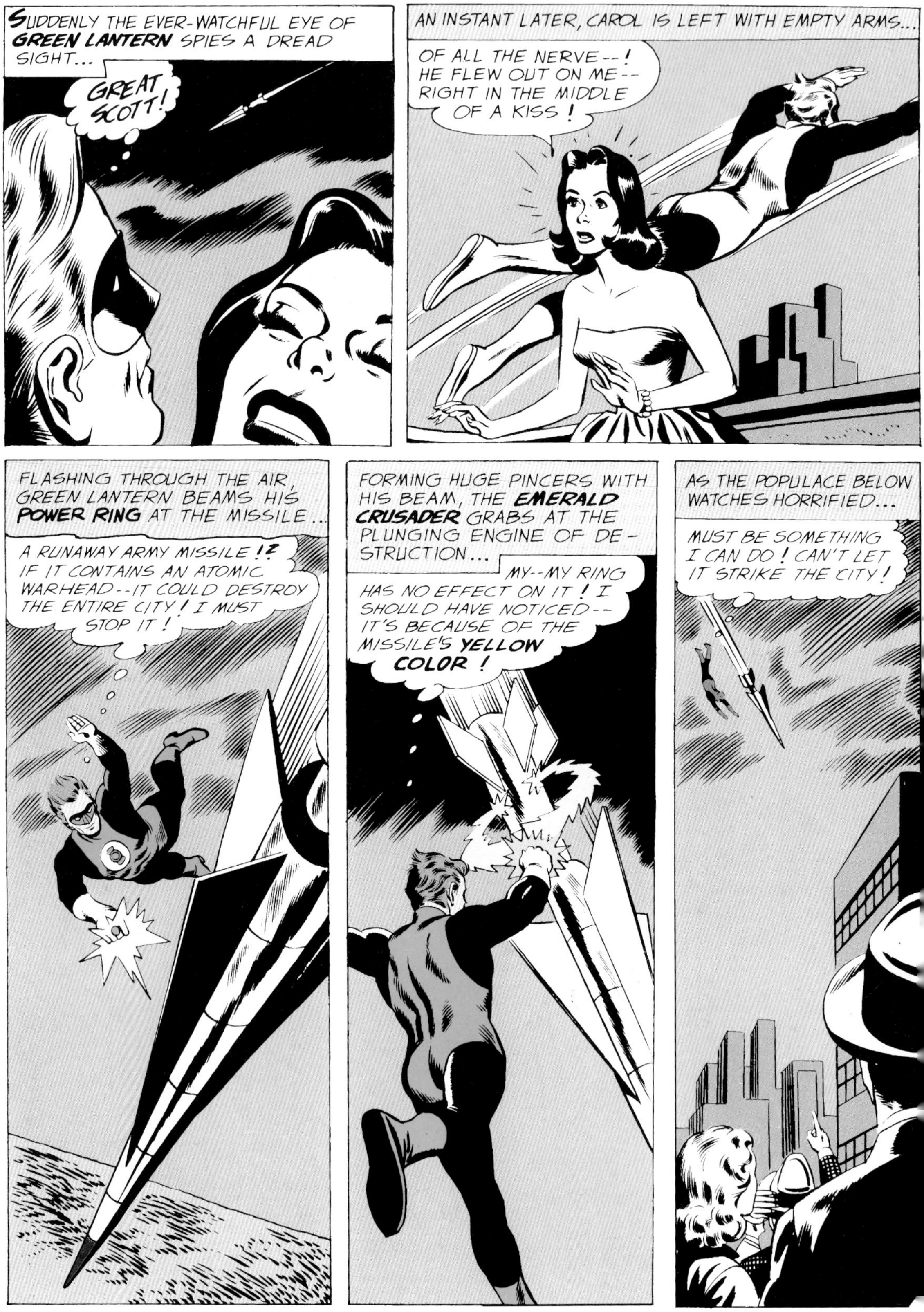
SUDDENLY THE EVER-WATCHFUL EYE OF GREEN LANTERN SPIES A DREAD SIGHT...
GREAT SCOTT!
AN INSTANT LATER, CAROL IS LEFT WITH EMPTY ARMS...
OF ALL THE NERVE--! HE FLEW OUT ON ME--RIGHT IN THE MIDDLE OF A KISS!
FLASHING THROUGH THE AIR, GREEN LANTERN BEAMS HIS POWER RING AT THE MISSILE...
A RUNAWAY ARMY MISSILE!? IF IT CONTAINS AN ATOMIC WARHEAD--IT COULD DESTROY THE ENTIRE CITY! I MUST STOP IT!
FORMING HUGE PINCERS WITH HIS BEAM, THE EMERALD CRUSADER GRABS AT THE PLUNGING ENGINE OF DE-STRUCTION...
MY--MY RING HAS NO EFFECT ON IT! I SHOULD HAVE NOTICED--IT'S BECAUSE OF THE MISSILE'S YELLOW COLOR!
AS THE POPULACE BELOW WATCHES HORRIFIED...
MUST BE SOMETHING I CAN DO! CAN'T LET IT STRIKE THE CITY!

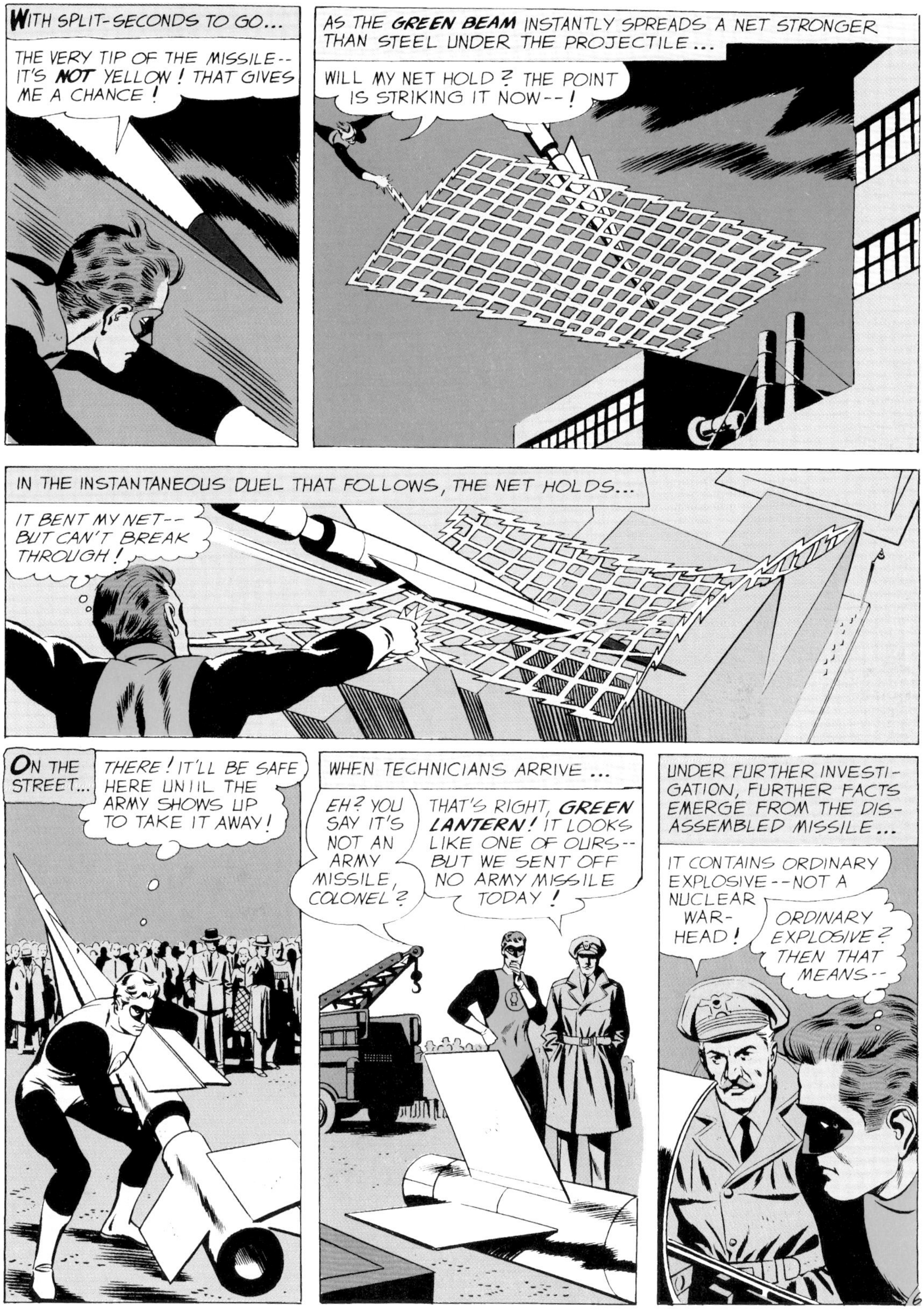
WITH SPLIT-SECONDS TO GO...
THE VERY TIP OF THE MISSILE-- IT'S NOT YELLOW! THAT GIVES ME A CHANCE!
AS THE GREEN BEAM INSTANTLY SPREADS A NET STRONGER THAN STEEL UNDER THE PROJECTILE...
WILL MY NET HOLD? THE POINT IS STRIKING IT NOW--!
IN THE INSTANTANEOUS DUEL THAT FOLLOWS, THE NET HOLDS...
IT BENT MY NET-- BUT CAN'T BREAK THROUGH!
ON THE STREET...
THERE! IT'LL BE SAFE HERE UNTIL THE ARMY SHOWS UP TO TAKE IT AWAY!
WHEN TECHNICIANS ARRIVE...
EH? YOU SAY IT'S NOT AN ARMY MISSILE, COLONEL?
THAT'S RIGHT, GREEN LANTERN! IT LOOKS LIKE ONE OF OURS-- BUT WE SENT OFF NO ARMY MISSILE TODAY!
UNDER FURTHER INVESTIGATION, FURTHER FACTS EMERGE FROM THE DISASSEMBLED MISSILE...
IT CONTAINS ORDINARY EXPLOSIVE--NOT A NUCLEAR WAR-HEAD!
ORDINARY EXPLOSIVE? THEN THAT MEANS--
6

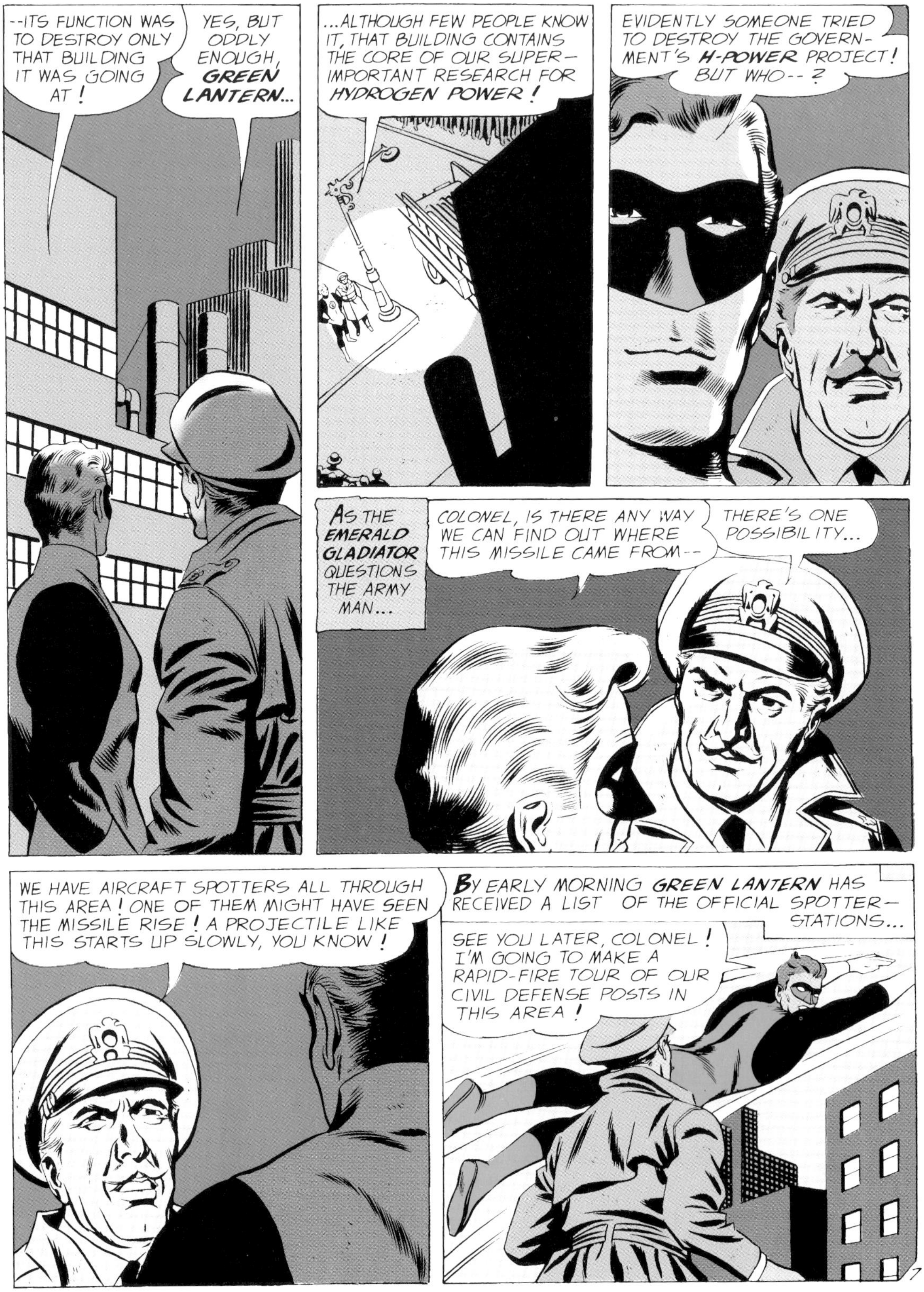
--ITS FUNCTION WAS TO DESTROY ONLY THAT BUILDING IT WAS GOING AT!
YES, BUT ODDLY ENOUGH, GREEN LANTERN...
...ALTHOUGH FEW PEOPLE KNOW IT, THAT BUILDING CONTAINS THE CORE OF OUR SUPER-IMPORTANT RESEARCH FOR HYDROGEN POWER!
EVIDENTLY SOMEONE TRIED TO DESTROY THE GOVERNMENT'S H-POWER PROJECT! BUT WHO--?
AS THE EMERALD GLADIATOR QUESTIONS THE ARMY MAN...
COLONEL, IS THERE ANY WAY WE CAN FIND OUT WHERE THIS MISSILE CAME FROM--
THERE'S ONE POSSIBILITY...
WE HAVE AIRCRAFT SPOTTERS ALL THROUGH THIS AREA! ONE OF THEM MIGHT HAVE SEEN THE MISSILE RISE! A PROJECTILE LIKE THIS STARTS UP SLOWLY, YOU KNOW!
BY EARLY MORNING GREEN LANTERN HAS RECEIVED A LIST OF THE OFFICIAL SPOTTER-STATIONS...
SEE YOU LATER, COLONEL! I'M GOING TO MAKE A RAPID-FIRE TOUR OF OUR CIVIL DEFENSE POSTS IN THIS AREA!
7

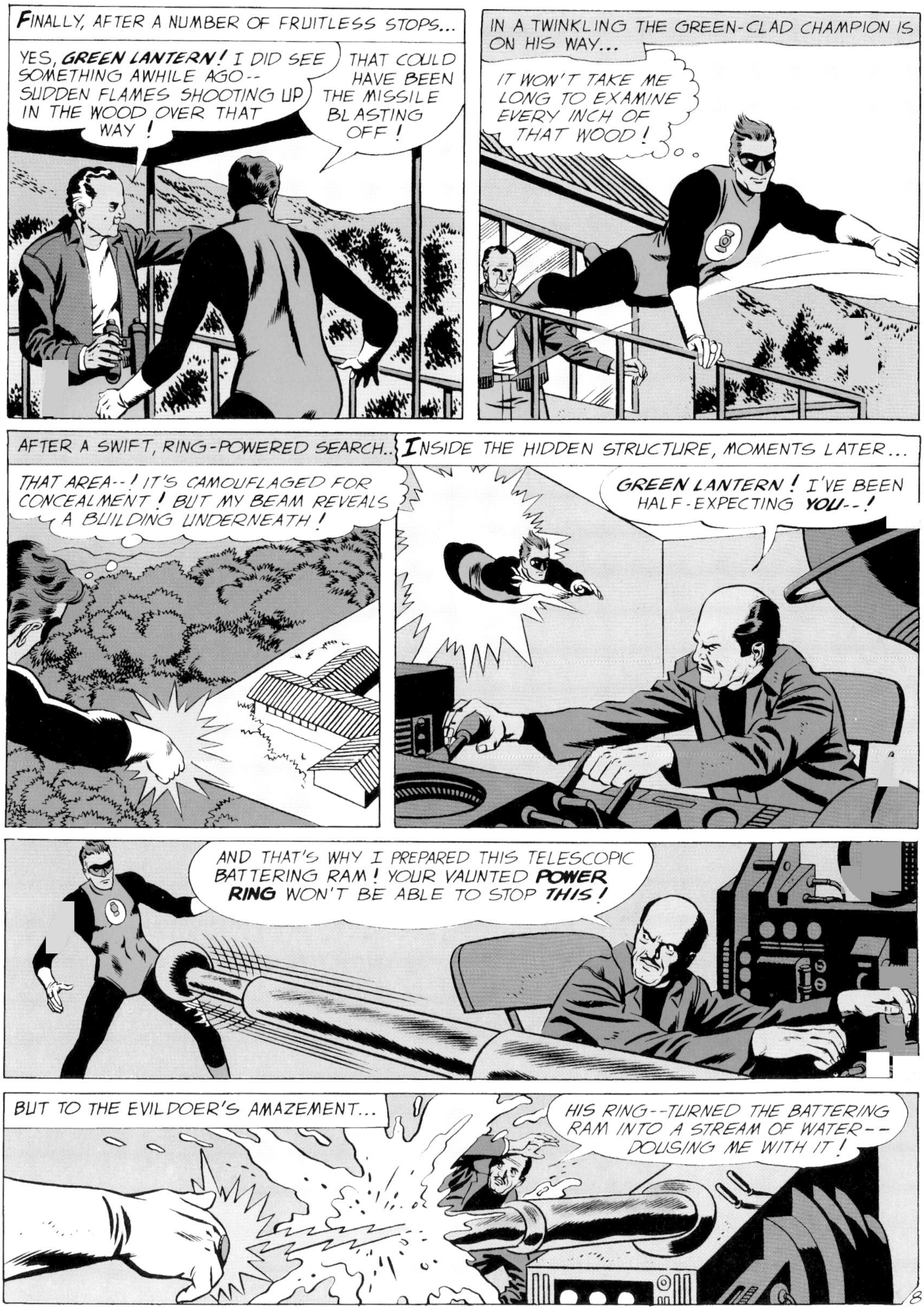
FINALLY, AFTER A NUMBER OF FRUITLESS STOPS...
YES, GREEN LANTERN! I DID SEE SOMETHING AWHILE AGO-- SUDDEN FLAMES SHOOTING UP IN THE WOOD OVER THAT WAY!
THAT COULD HAVE BEEN THE MISSILE BLASTING OFF!
IN A TWINKLING THE GREEN-CLAD CHAMPION IS ON HIS WAY...
IT WON'T TAKE ME LONG TO EXAMINE EVERY INCH OF THAT WOOD!
AFTER A SWIFT, RING-POWERED SEARCH..
THAT AREA--! IT'S CAMOUFLAGED FOR CONCEALMENT! BUT MY BEAM REVEALS A BUILDING UNDERNEATH!
INSIDE THE HIDDEN STRUCTURE, MOMENTS LATER...
GREEN LANTERN! I'VE BEEN HALF-EXPECTING YOU--!
AND THAT'S WHY I PREPARED THIS TELESCOPIC BATTERING RAM! YOUR VAUNTED POWER RING WON'T BE ABLE TO STOP THIS!
BUT TO THE EVILDOER'S AMAZEMENT...
HIS RING--TURNED THE BATTERING RAM INTO A STREAM OF WATER-- DOUSING ME WITH IT!
8

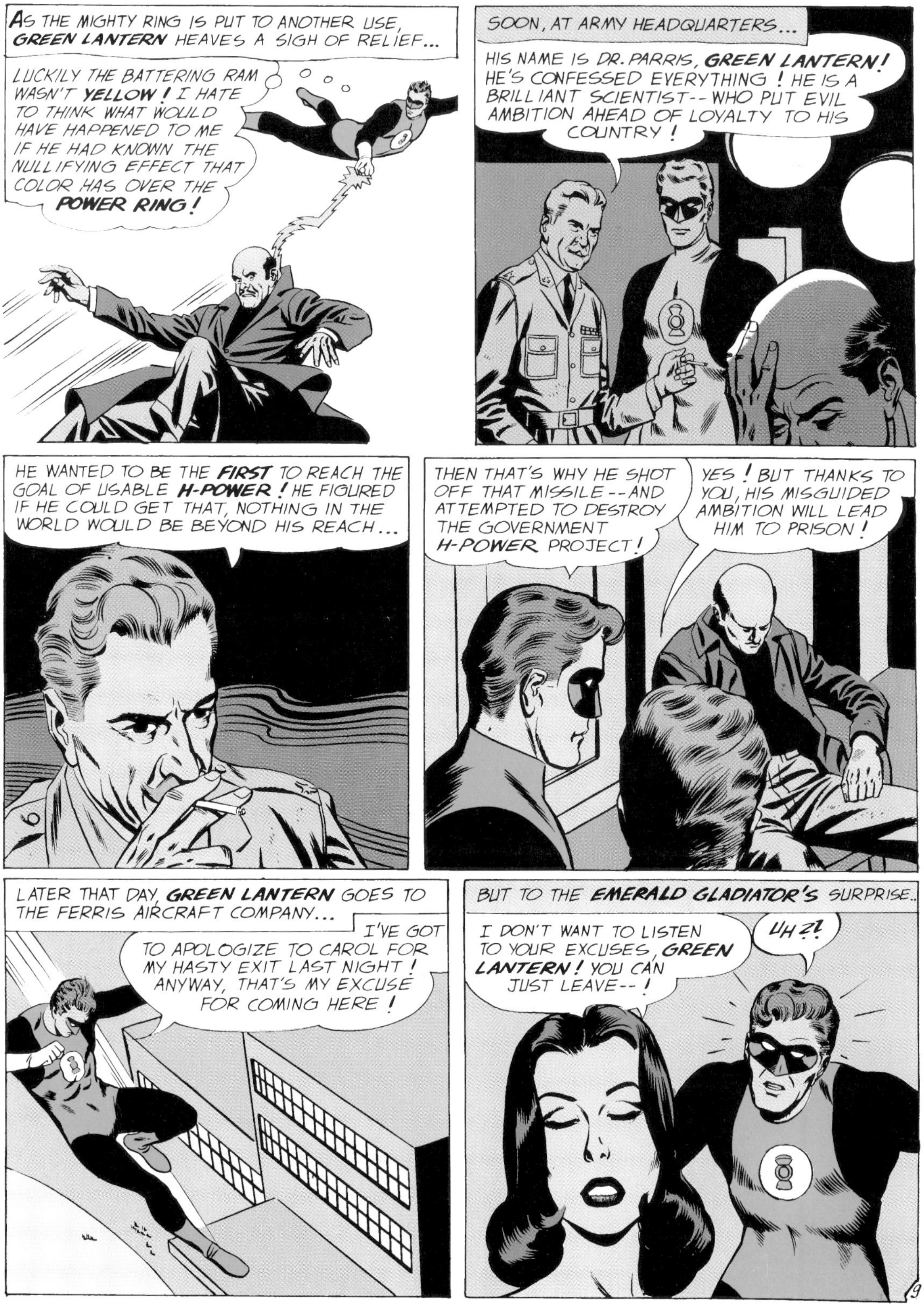
AS THE MIGHTY RING IS PUT TO ANOTHER USE, GREEN LANTERN HEAVES A SIGH OF RELIEF...
LUCKILY THE BATTERING RAM WASN'T YELLOW! I HATE TO THINK WHAT WOULD HAVE HAPPENED TO ME IF HE HAD KNOWN THE NULLIFYING EFFECT THAT COLOR HAS OVER THE POWER RING!
SOON, AT ARMY HEADQUARTERS...
HIS NAME IS DR. PARRIS, GREEN LANTERN! HE'S CONFESSED EVERYTHING! HE IS A BRILLIANT SCIENTIST--WHO PUT EVIL AMBITION AHEAD OF LOYALTY TO HIS COUNTRY!
HE WANTED TO BE THE FIRST TO REACH THE GOAL OF USABLE H-POWER! HE FIGURED IF HE COULD GET THAT, NOTHING IN THE WORLD WOULD BE BEYOND HIS REACH...
THEN THAT'S WHY HE SHOT OFF THAT MISSILE--AND ATTEMPTED TO DESTROY THE GOVERNMENT H-POWER PROJECT!
YES! BUT THANKS TO YOU, HIS MISGUIDED AMBITION WILL LEAD HIM TO PRISON!
LATER THAT DAY, GREEN LANTERN GOES TO THE FERRIS AIRCRAFT COMPANY...
I'VE GOT TO APOLOGIZE TO CAROL FOR MY HASTY EXIT LAST NIGHT! ANYWAY, THAT'S MY EXCUSE FOR COMING HERE!
BUT TO THE EMERALD GLADIATOR'S SURPRISE..
I DON'T WANT TO LISTEN TO YOUR EXCUSES, GREEN LANTERN! YOU CAN JUST LEAVE--!
UH?!
9

BUT, CAROL-- MISS FERRIS-- WHAT HAVE I DONE?
WHAT HAVE YOU DONE? YOU-- YOU HEEL! LAST NIGHT YOU KISSED ME--
YOU'RE NOT OBJECTING TO THAT? THE WAY YOU KISSED ME, I COULD TELL--
IT'S THE WAY YOU KISSED ME THAT I'M REFERRING TO...
IF YOU HAD LOST YOURSELF IN THAT KISS...THE WAY I DID...YOUR EYES WOULD HAVE NATURALLY CLOSED...
BUT CAROL--BE REASONABLE! IF MY EYES HAD BEEN CLOSED, I WOULDN'T HAVE SEEN THAT MISSILE AND...
GOOD DAY, MR. GREEN LANTERN! I AM BUSY!
CAROL FERRIS PRIVATE
SLAM!
WHEW! NOW I'M IN A DOUBLE DOGHOUSE AS FAR AS CAROL IS CONCERNED! BOTH AS HAL JORDAN--AND AS GREEN LANTERN! HOW COULD THINGS GET WORSE?
IN THE NEXT ISSUE OF SHOWCASE, MORE THRILLING ADVENTURES WITH GREEN LANTERN!
The End
10

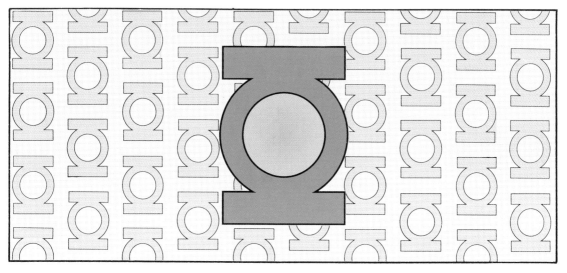

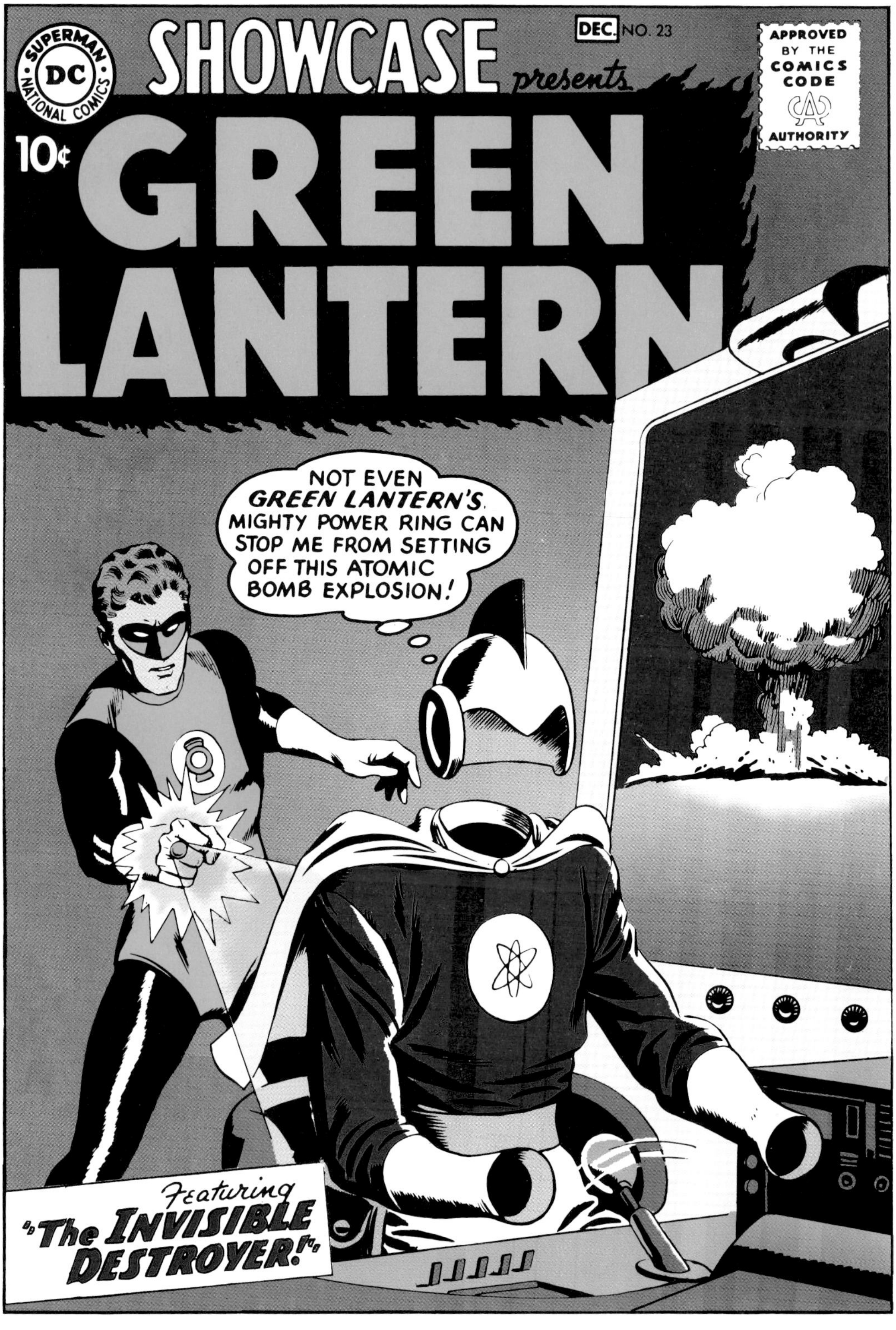
SUPERMAN DC NATIONAL COMICS
SHOWCASE presents
DEC. NO. 23
APPROVED BY THE COMICS CODE AUTHORITY
10¢
GREEN LANTERN
NOT EVEN GREEN LANTERN'S MIGHTY POWER RING CAN STOP ME FROM SETTING OFF THIS ATOMIC BOMB EXPLOSION!
Featuring "The INVISIBLE DESTROYER!"

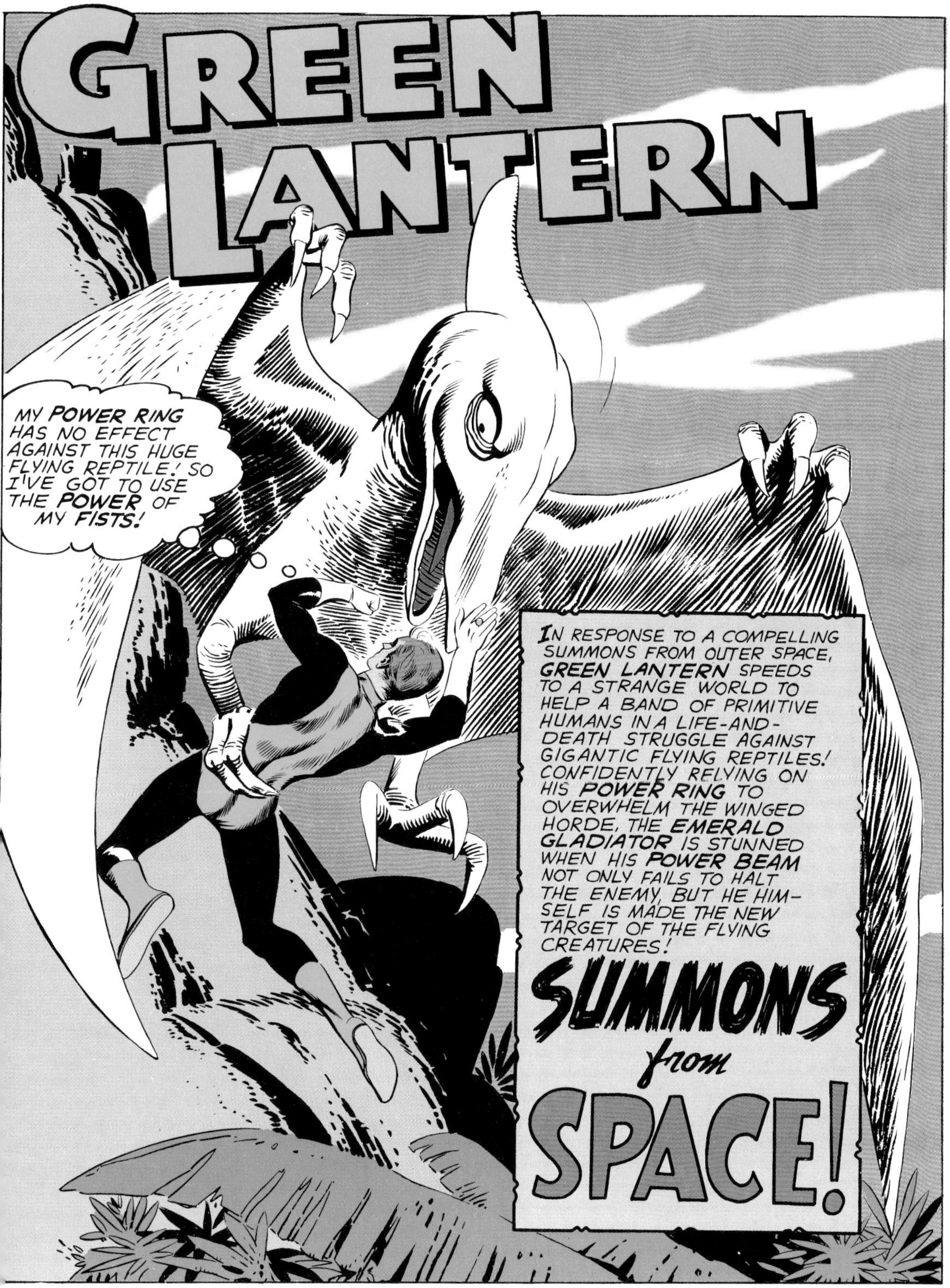
GREEN LANTERN
MY POWER RING HAS NO EFFECT AGAINST THIS HUGE FLYING REPTILE! SO I'VE GOT TO USE THE POWER OF MY FISTS!
IN RESPONSE TO A COMPELLING SUMMONS FROM OUTER SPACE, GREEN LANTERN SPEEDS TO A STRANGE WORLD TO HELP A BAND OF PRIMITIVE HUMANS IN A LIFE-AND-DEATH STRUGGLE AGAINST GIGANTIC FLYING REPTILES! CONFIDENTLY RELYING ON HIS POWER RING TO OVERWHELM THE WINGED HORDE, THE EMERALD GLADIATOR IS STUNNED WHEN HIS POWER BEAM NOT ONLY FAILS TO HALT THE ENEMY, BUT HE HIMSELF IS MADE THE NEW TARGET OF THE FLYING CREATURES!
SUMMONS from SPACE!

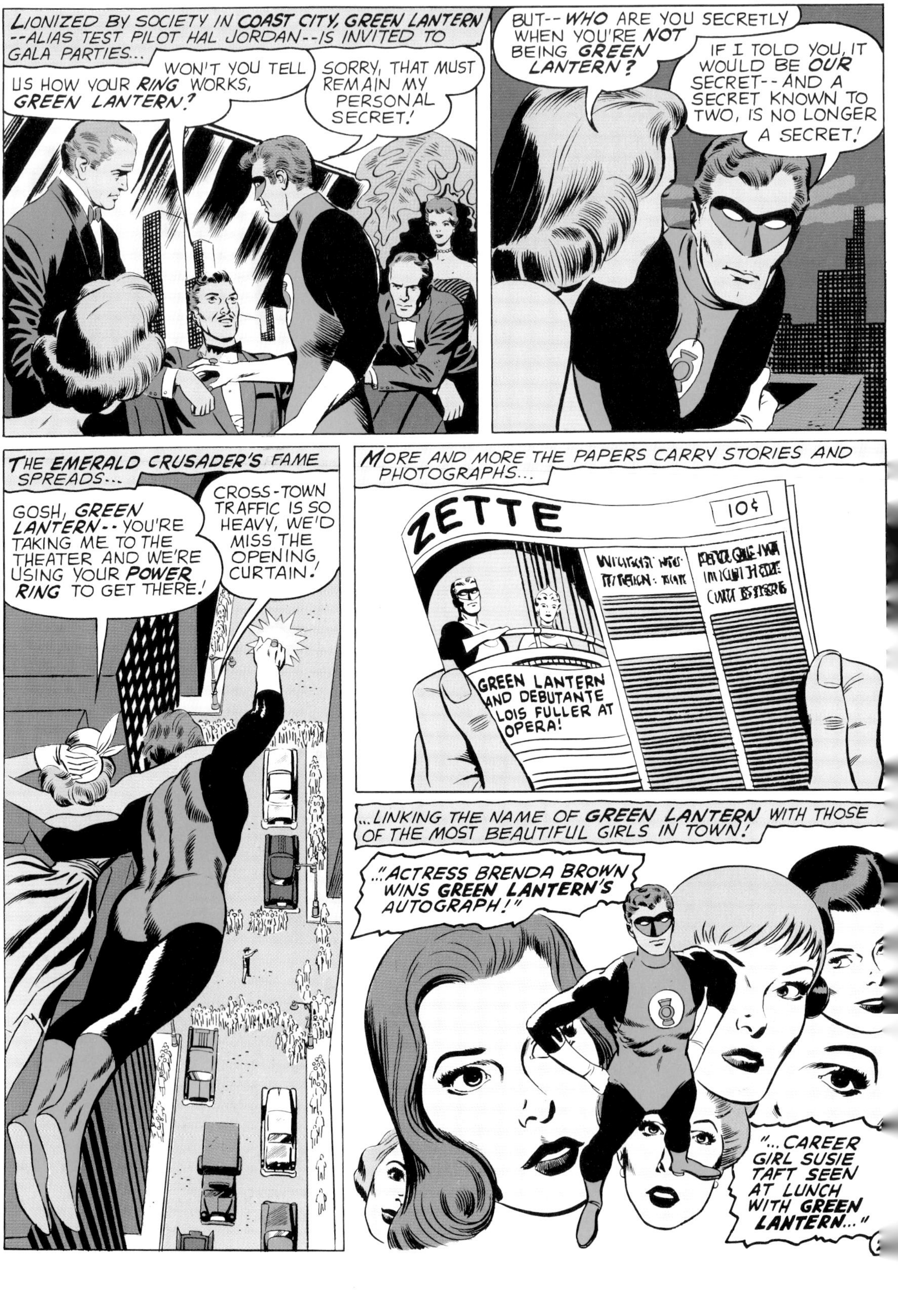
LIONIZED BY SOCIETY IN COAST CITY, GREEN LANTERN --ALIAS TEST PILOT HAL JORDAN--IS INVITED TO GALA PARTIES...
WON'T YOU TELL US HOW YOUR RING WORKS, GREEN LANTERN?
SORRY, THAT MUST REMAIN MY PERSONAL SECRET!
BUT--WHO ARE YOU SECRETLY WHEN YOU'RE NOT BEING GREEN LANTERN?
IF I TOLD YOU, IT WOULD BE OUR SECRET--AND A SECRET KNOWN TO TWO, IS NO LONGER A SECRET!
THE EMERALD CRUSADER'S FAME SPREADS...
GOSH, GREEN LANTERN--YOU'RE TAKING ME TO THE THEATER AND WE'RE USING YOUR POWER RING TO GET THERE!
CROSS-TOWN TRAFFIC IS SO HEAVY, WE'D MISS THE OPENING CURTAIN!
MORE AND MORE THE PAPERS CARRY STORIES AND PHOTOGRAPHS...
ZETTE
10¢
GREEN LANTERN AND DEBUTANTE LOIS FULLER AT OPERA!
...LINKING THE NAME OF GREEN LANTERN WITH THOSE OF THE MOST BEAUTIFUL GIRLS IN TOWN!
..."ACTRESS BRENDA BROWN WINS GREEN LANTERN'S AUTOGRAPH!"
"...CAREER GIRL SUSIE TAFT SEEN AT LUNCH WITH GREEN LANTERN..."

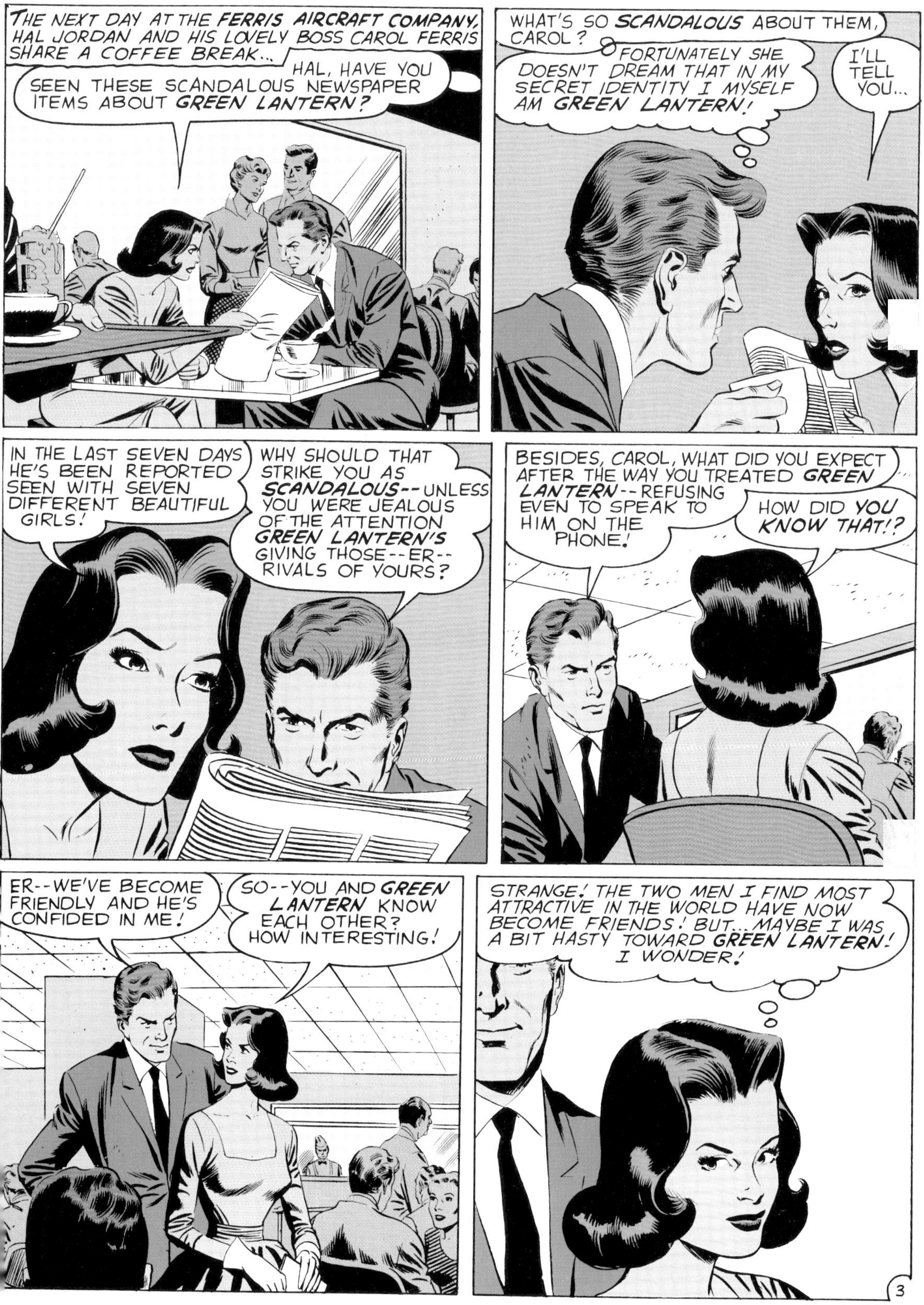
THE NEXT DAY AT THE FERRIS AIRCRAFT COMPANY, HAL JORDAN AND HIS LOVELY BOSS CAROL FERRIS SHARE A COFFEE BREAK...
HAL, HAVE YOU SEEN THESE SCANDALOUS NEWSPAPER ITEMS ABOUT GREEN LANTERN?
WHAT'S SO SCANDALOUS ABOUT THEM, CAROL?
FORTUNATELY SHE DOESN'T DREAM THAT IN MY SECRET IDENTITY I MYSELF AM GREEN LANTERN!
I'LL TELL YOU...
IN THE LAST SEVEN DAYS HE'S BEEN REPORTED SEEN WITH SEVEN DIFFERENT BEAUTIFUL GIRLS!
WHY SHOULD THAT STRIKE YOU AS SCANDALOUS--UNLESS YOU WERE JEALOUS OF THE ATTENTION GREEN LANTERN'S GIVING THOSE--ER--RIVALS OF YOURS?
BESIDES, CAROL, WHAT DID YOU EXPECT AFTER THE WAY YOU TREATED GREEN LANTERN--REFUSING EVEN TO SPEAK TO HIM ON THE PHONE!
HOW DID YOU KNOW THAT!?
ER--WE'VE BECOME FRIENDLY AND HE'S CONFIDED IN ME!
SO--YOU AND GREEN LANTERN KNOW EACH OTHER? HOW INTERESTING!
STRANGE! THE TWO MEN I FIND MOST ATTRACTIVE IN THE WORLD HAVE NOW BECOME FRIENDS! BUT... MAYBE I WAS A BIT HASTY TOWARD GREEN LANTERN! I WONDER!
3

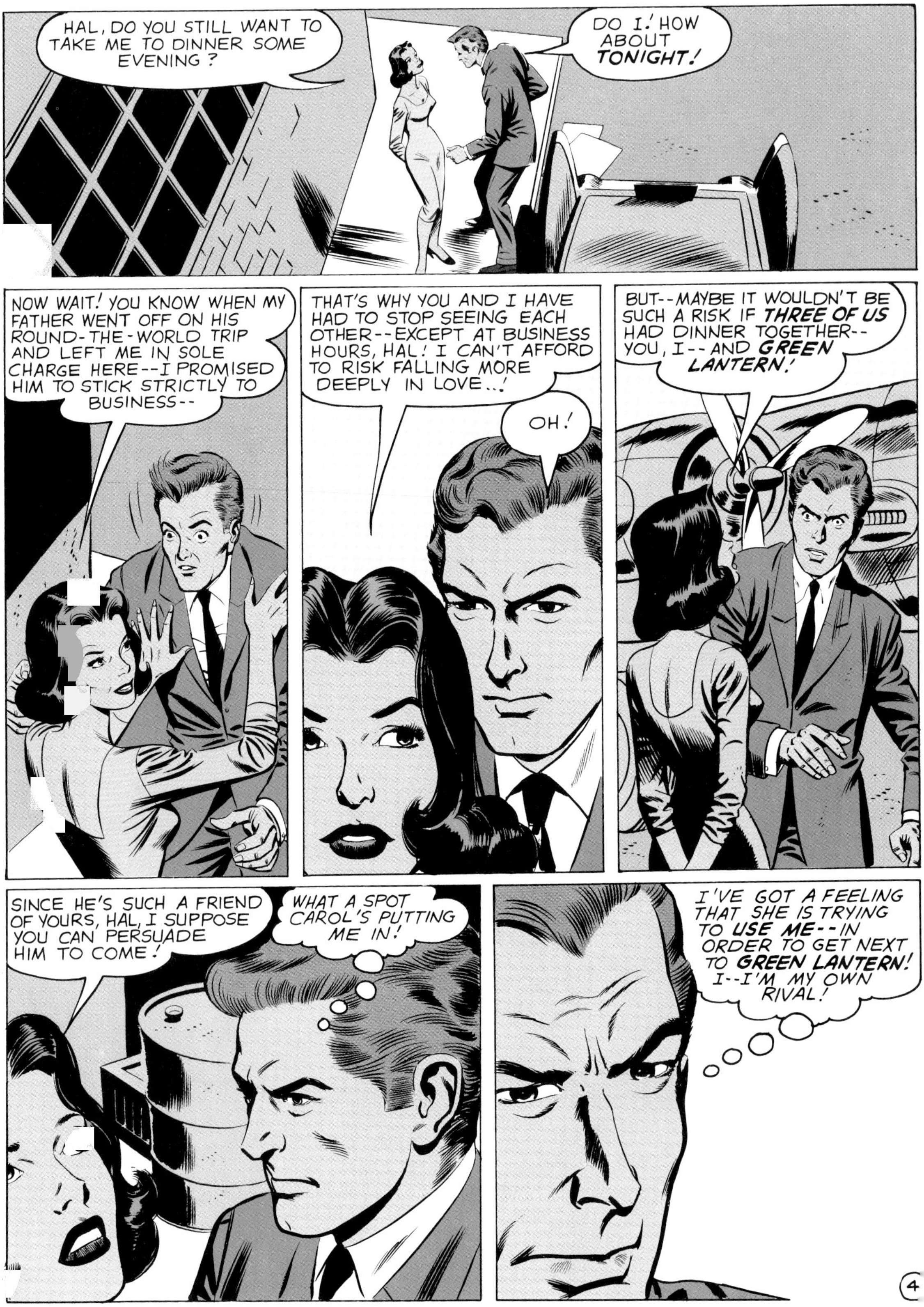
HAL, DO YOU STILL WANT TO TAKE ME TO DINNER SOME EVENING?
DO I.! HOW ABOUT TONIGHT!
NOW WAIT! YOU KNOW WHEN MY FATHER WENT OFF ON HIS ROUND-THE-WORLD TRIP AND LEFT ME IN SOLE CHARGE HERE--I PROMISED HIM TO STICK STRICTLY TO BUSINESS--
THAT'S WHY YOU AND I HAVE HAD TO STOP SEEING EACH OTHER--EXCEPT AT BUSINESS HOURS, HAL! I CAN'T AFFORD TO RISK FALLING MORE DEEPLY IN LOVE..!
OH!
BUT--MAYBE IT WOULDN'T BE SUCH A RISK IF THREE OF US HAD DINNER TOGETHER--YOU, I--AND GREEN LANTERN!
SINCE HE'S SUCH A FRIEND OF YOURS, HAL, I SUPPOSE YOU CAN PERSUADE HIM TO COME!
WHAT A SPOT CAROL'S PUTTING ME IN!
I'VE GOT A FEELING THAT SHE IS TRYING TO USE ME--IN ORDER TO GET NEXT TO GREEN LANTERN! I--I'M MY OWN RIVAL!
4

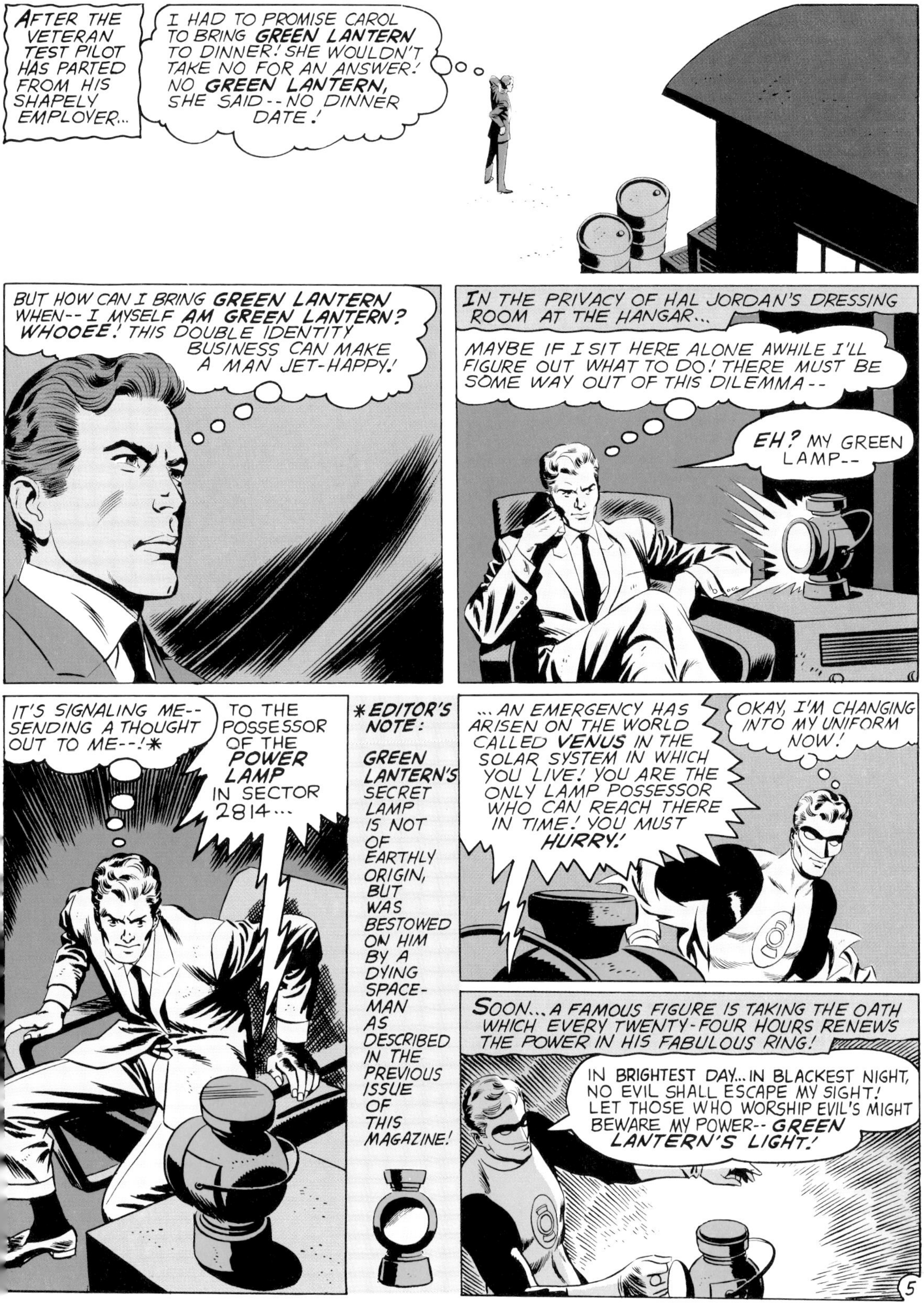
AFTER THE VETERAN TEST PILOT HAS PARTED FROM HIS SHAPELY EMPLOYER...
I HAD TO PROMISE CAROL TO BRING GREEN LANTERN TO DINNER! SHE WOULDN'T TAKE NO FOR AN ANSWER! NO GREEN LANTERN, SHE SAID--NO DINNER DATE!
BUT HOW CAN I BRING GREEN LANTERN WHEN-- I MYSELF AM GREEN LANTERN? WHOOEE! THIS DOUBLE IDENTITY BUSINESS CAN MAKE A MAN JET-HAPPY!
IN THE PRIVACY OF HAL JORDAN'S DRESSING ROOM AT THE HANGAR...
MAYBE IF I SIT HERE ALONE AWHILE I'LL FIGURE OUT WHAT TO DO! THERE MUST BE SOME WAY OUT OF THIS DILEMMA--
EH? MY GREEN LAMP--
IT'S SIGNALING ME-- SENDING A THOUGHT OUT TO ME--!*
TO THE POSSESSOR OF THE POWER LAMP IN SECTOR 2814...
*EDITOR'S NOTE: GREEN LANTERN'S SECRET LAMP IS NOT OF EARTHLY ORIGIN, BUT WAS BESTOWED ON HIM BY A DYING SPACE-MAN AS DESCRIBED IN THE PREVIOUS ISSUE OF THIS MAGAZINE!
...AN EMERGENCY HAS ARISEN ON THE WORLD CALLED VENUS IN THE SOLAR SYSTEM IN WHICH YOU LIVE! YOU ARE THE ONLY LAMP POSSESSOR WHO CAN REACH THERE IN TIME! YOU MUST HURRY!
OKAY, I'M CHANGING INTO MY UNIFORM NOW!
SOON...A FAMOUS FIGURE IS TAKING THE OATH WHICH EVERY TWENTY-FOUR HOURS RENEWS THE POWER IN HIS FABULOUS RING!
IN BRIGHTEST DAY...IN BLACKEST NIGHT, NO EVIL SHALL ESCAPE MY SIGHT! LET THOSE WHO WORSHIP EVIL'S MIGHT BEWARE MY POWER-- GREEN LANTERN'S LIGHT!
5

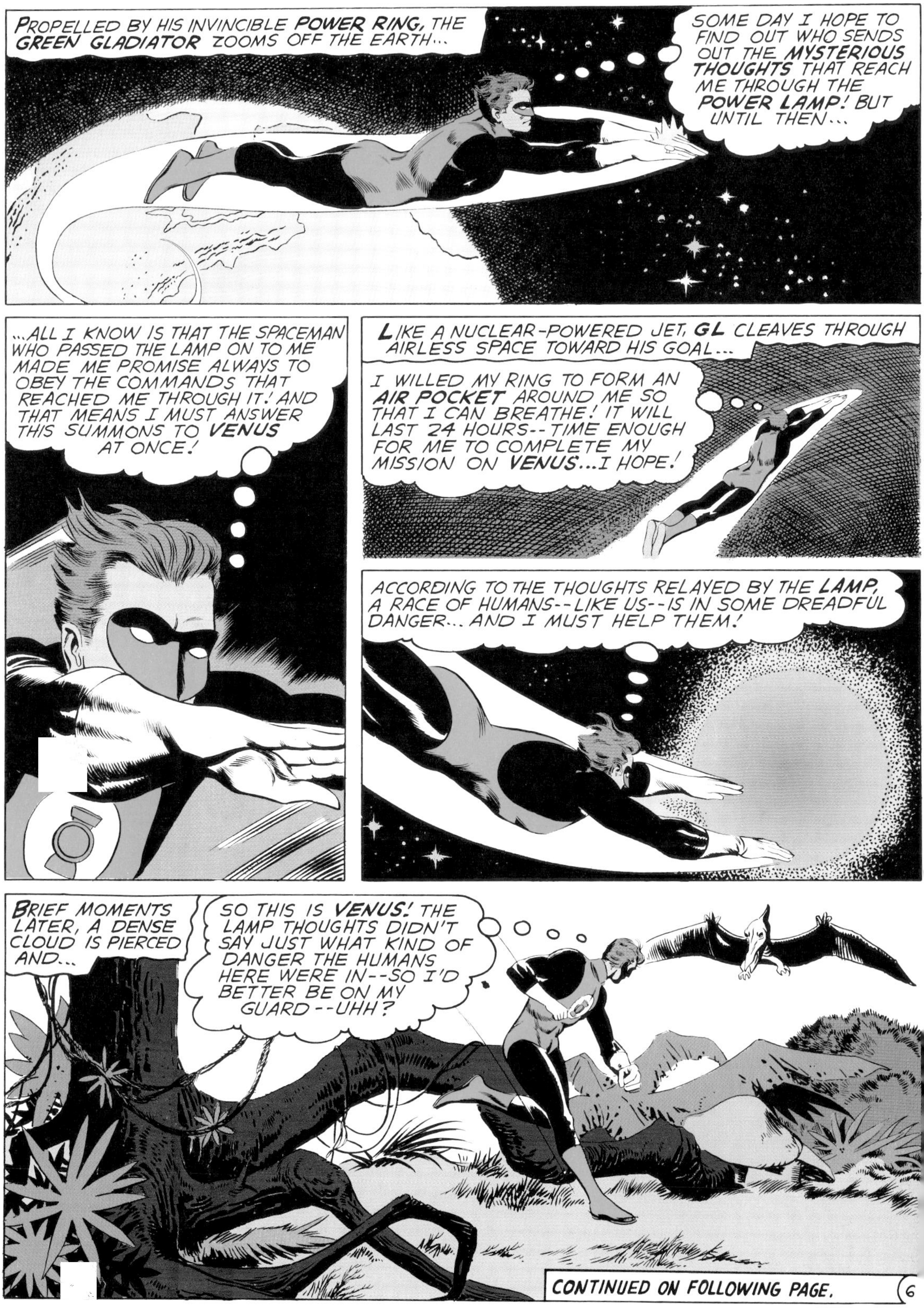
PROPELLED BY HIS INVINCIBLE POWER RING, THE GREEN GLADIATOR ZOOMS OFF THE EARTH...
SOME DAY I HOPE TO FIND OUT WHO SENDS OUT THE MYSTERIOUS THOUGHTS THAT REACH ME THROUGH THE POWER LAMP! BUT UNTIL THEN...
...ALL I KNOW IS THAT THE SPACEMAN WHO PASSED THE LAMP ON TO ME MADE ME PROMISE ALWAYS TO OBEY THE COMMANDS THAT REACHED ME THROUGH IT! AND THAT MEANS I MUST ANSWER THIS SUMMONS TO VENUS AT ONCE!
LIKE A NUCLEAR-POWERED JET, GL CLEAVES THROUGH AIRLESS SPACE TOWARD HIS GOAL...
I WILLED MY RING TO FORM AN AIR POCKET AROUND ME SO THAT I CAN BREATHE! IT WILL LAST 24 HOURS--TIME ENOUGH FOR ME TO COMPLETE MY MISSION ON VENUS...I HOPE!
ACCORDING TO THE THOUGHTS RELAYED BY THE LAMP, A RACE OF HUMANS--LIKE US--IS IN SOME DREADFUL DANGER... AND I MUST HELP THEM!
BRIEF MOMENTS LATER, A DENSE CLOUD IS PIERCED AND...
SO THIS IS VENUS! THE LAMP THOUGHTS DIDN'T SAY JUST WHAT KIND OF DANGER THE HUMANS HERE WERE IN--SO I'D BETTER BE ON MY GUARD--UHH?
CONTINUED ON FOLLOWING PAGE.
6

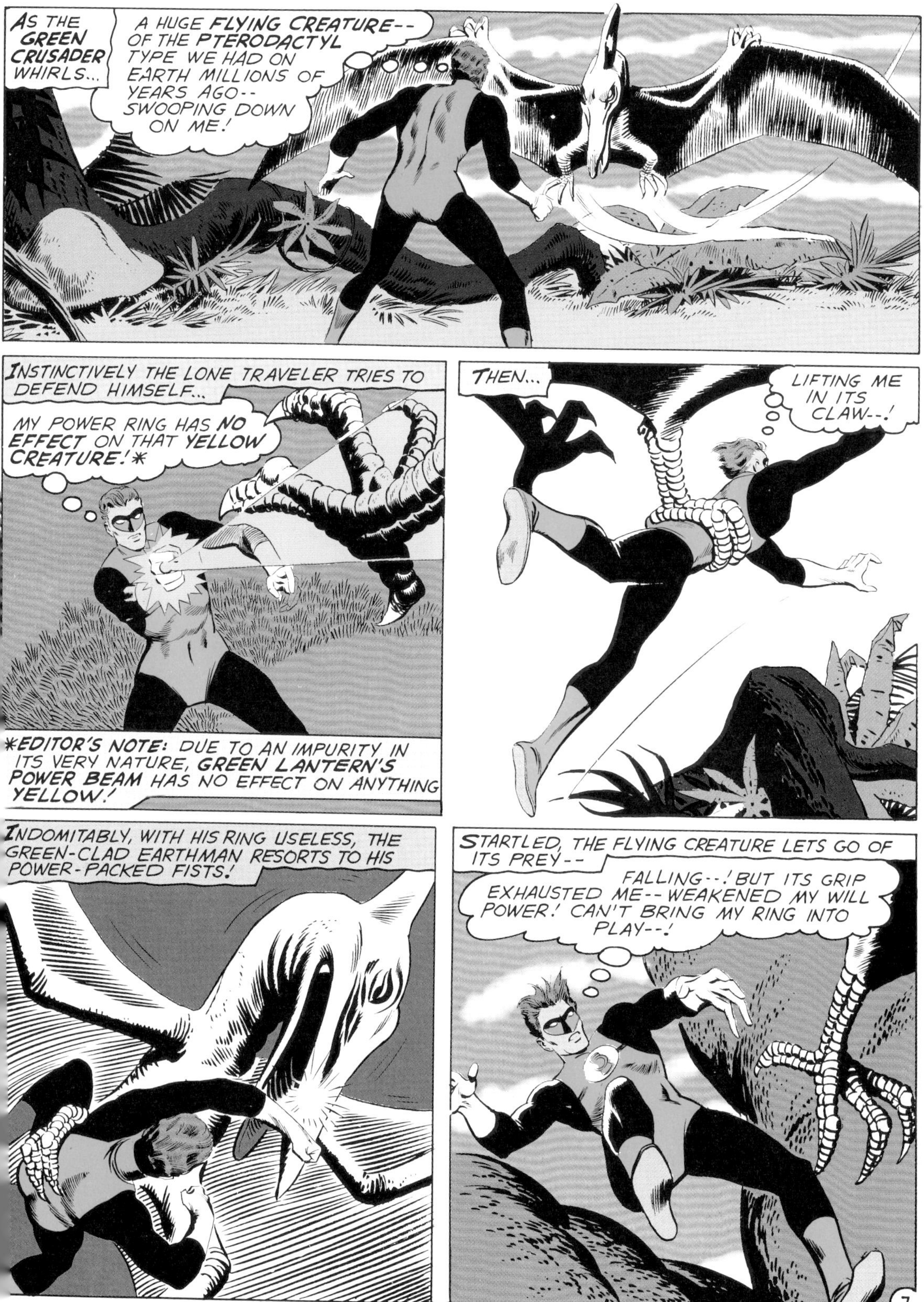
AS THE GREEN CRUSADER WHIRLS...
A HUGE FLYING CREATURE-- OF THE PTERODACTYL TYPE WE HAD ON EARTH MILLIONS OF YEARS AGO-- SWOOPING DOWN ON ME!
INSTINCTIVELY THE LONE TRAVELER TRIES TO DEFEND HIMSELF...
MY POWER RING HAS NO EFFECT ON THAT YELLOW CREATURE!*
*EDITOR'S NOTE: DUE TO AN IMPURITY IN ITS VERY NATURE, GREEN LANTERN'S POWER BEAM HAS NO EFFECT ON ANYTHING YELLOW!
THEN...
LIFTING ME IN ITS CLAW--!
INDOMITABLY, WITH HIS RING USELESS, THE GREEN-CLAD EARTHMAN RESORTS TO HIS POWER-PACKED FISTS!
STARTLED, THE FLYING CREATURE LETS GO OF ITS PREY--
FALLING--! BUT ITS GRIP EXHAUSTED ME--WEAKENED MY WILL POWER! CAN'T BRING MY RING INTO PLAY--!
7

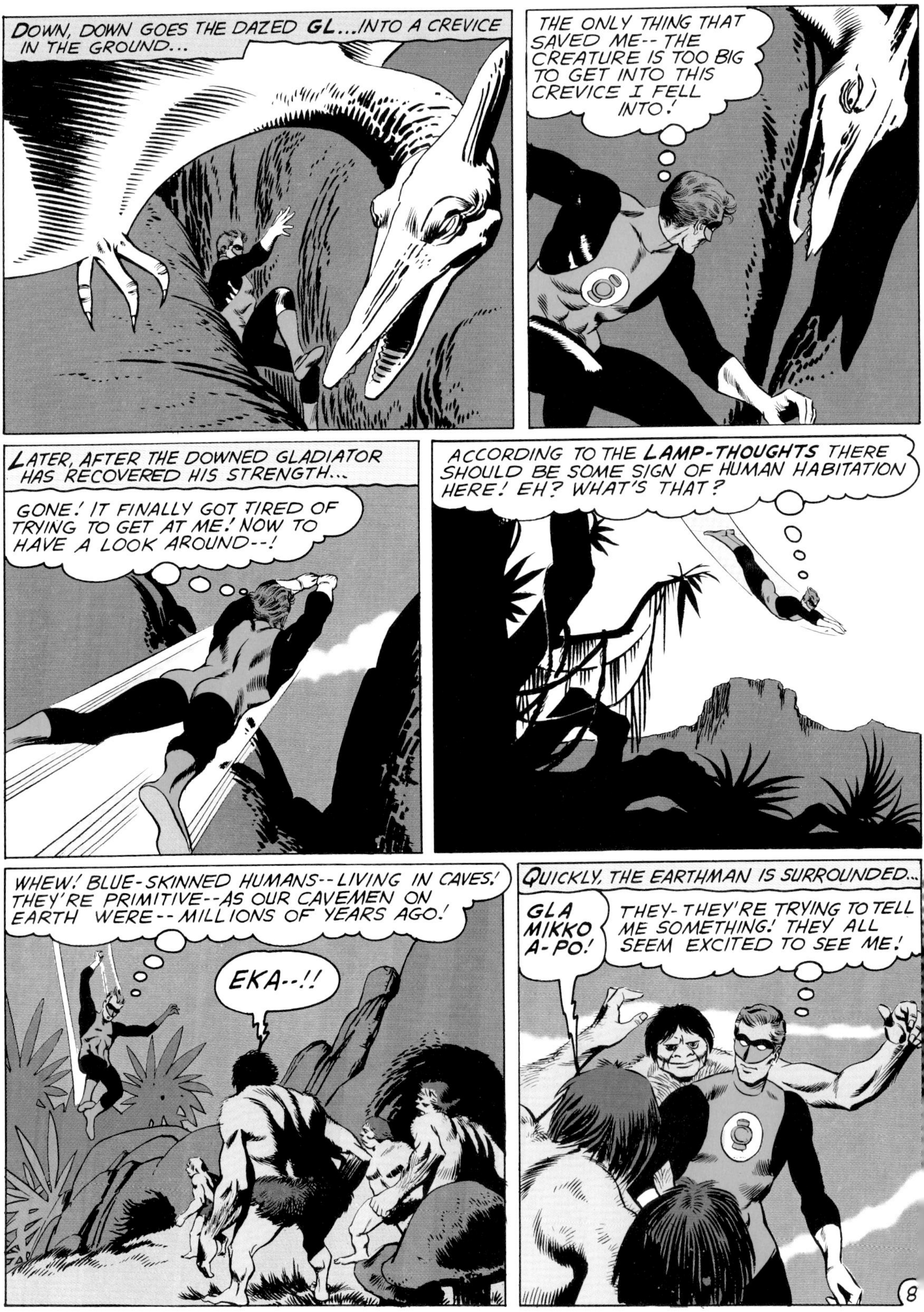
DOWN, DOWN GOES THE DAZED GL...INTO A CREVICE IN THE GROUND...
THE ONLY THING THAT SAVED ME-- THE CREATURE IS TOO BIG TO GET INTO THIS CREVICE I FELL INTO!
LATER, AFTER THE DOWNED GLADIATOR HAS RECOVERED HIS STRENGTH...
GONE! IT FINALLY GOT TIRED OF TRYING TO GET AT ME! NOW TO HAVE A LOOK AROUND--!
ACCORDING TO THE LAMP-THOUGHTS THERE SHOULD BE SOME SIGN OF HUMAN HABITATION HERE! EH? WHAT'S THAT?
WHEW! BLUE-SKINNED HUMANS--LIVING IN CAVES! THEY'RE PRIMITIVE--AS OUR CAVEMEN ON EARTH WERE--MILLIONS OF YEARS AGO!
EKA--!!
QUICKLY, THE EARTHMAN IS SURROUNDED...
GLA MIKKO A-PO!
THEY-THEY'RE TRYING TO TELL ME SOMETHING! THEY ALL SEEM EXCITED TO SEE ME!
8

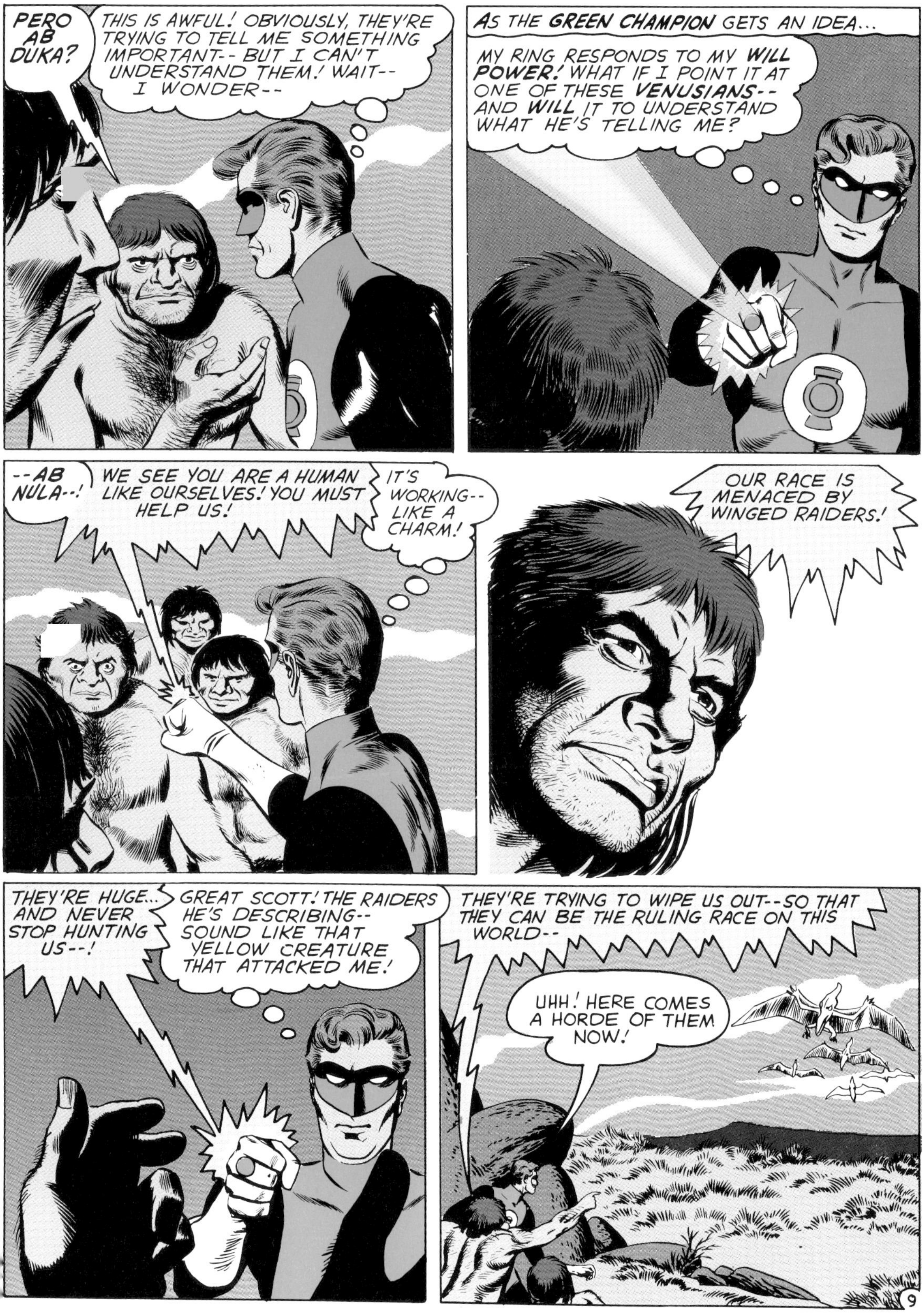
PERO AB DUKA?
THIS IS AWFUL! OBVIOUSLY, THEY'RE TRYING TO TELL ME SOMETHING IMPORTANT-- BUT I CAN'T UNDERSTAND THEM! WAIT-- I WONDER--
AS THE GREEN CHAMPION GETS AN IDEA...
MY RING RESPONDS TO MY WILL POWER! WHAT IF I POINT IT AT ONE OF THESE VENUSIANS-- AND WILL IT TO UNDERSTAND WHAT HE'S TELLING ME?
--AB NULA--!
WE SEE YOU ARE A HUMAN LIKE OURSELVES! YOU MUST HELP US!
IT'S WORKING-- LIKE A CHARM!
OUR RACE IS MENACED BY WINGED RAIDERS!
THEY'RE HUGE... AND NEVER STOP HUNTING US--!
GREAT SCOTT! THE RAIDERS HE'S DESCRIBING-- SOUND LIKE THAT YELLOW CREATURE THAT ATTACKED ME!
THEY'RE TRYING TO WIPE US OUT--SO THAT THEY CAN BE THE RULING RACE ON THIS WORLD--
UHH! HERE COMES A HORDE OF THEM NOW!
9

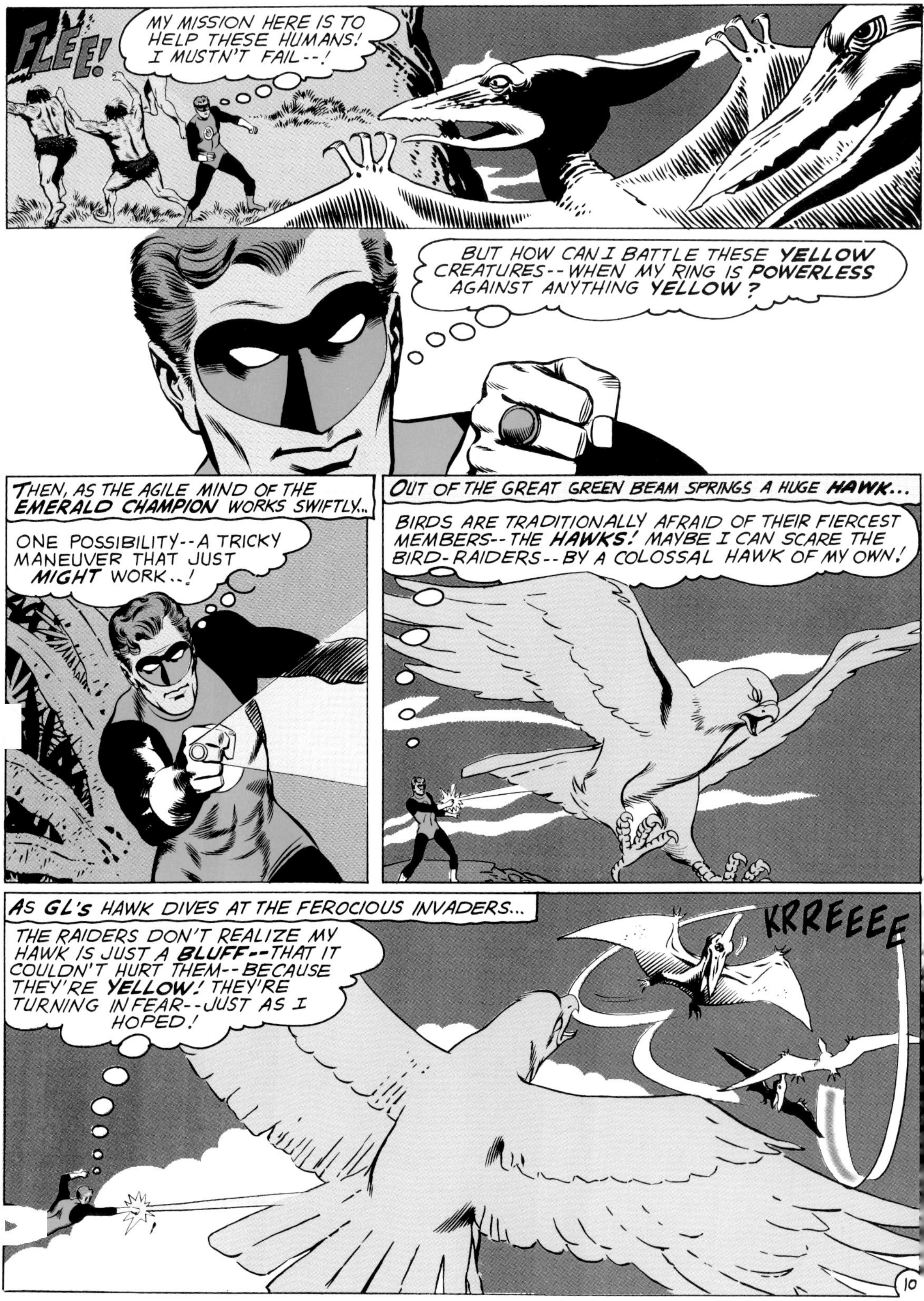
FLEE!
MY MISSION HERE IS TO HELP THESE HUMANS! I MUSTN'T FAIL--!
BUT HOW CAN I BATTLE THESE YELLOW CREATURES--WHEN MY RING IS POWERLESS AGAINST ANYTHING YELLOW?
THEN, AS THE AGILE MIND OF THE EMERALD CHAMPION WORKS SWIFTLY...
ONE POSSIBILITY--A TRICKY MANEUVER THAT JUST MIGHT WORK..!
OUT OF THE GREAT GREEN BEAM SPRINGS A HUGE HAWK...
BIRDS ARE TRADITIONALLY AFRAID OF THEIR FIERCEST MEMBERS--THE HAWKS! MAYBE I CAN SCARE THE BIRD-RAIDERS--BY A COLOSSAL HAWK OF MY OWN!
AS GL's HAWK DIVES AT THE FEROCIOUS INVADERS...
THE RAIDERS DON'T REALIZE MY HAWK IS JUST A BLUFF--THAT IT COULDN'T HURT THEM--BECAUSE THEY'RE YELLOW! THEY'RE TURNING IN FEAR--JUST AS I HOPED!
KRREEEEE
10

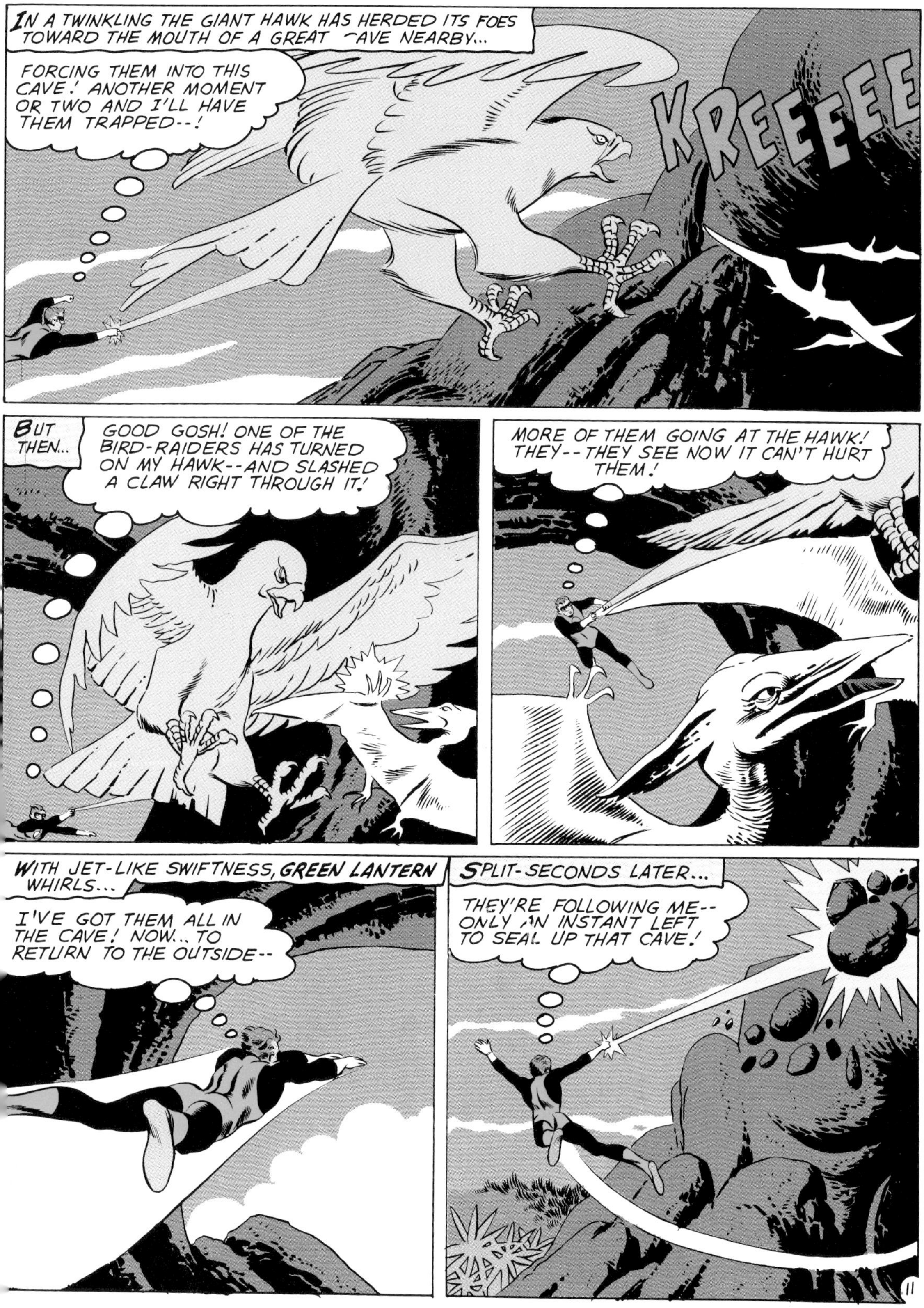
IN A TWINKLING THE GIANT HAWK HAS HERDED ITS FOES TOWARD THE MOUTH OF A GREAT CAVE NEARBY...
FORCING THEM INTO THIS CAVE! ANOTHER MOMENT OR TWO AND I'LL HAVE THEM TRAPPED--!
KREEEEE
BUT THEN...
GOOD GOSH! ONE OF THE BIRD-RAIDERS HAS TURNED ON MY HAWK--AND SLASHED A CLAW RIGHT THROUGH IT!
MORE OF THEM GOING AT THE HAWK! THEY--THEY SEE NOW IT CAN'T HURT THEM!
WITH JET-LIKE SWIFTNESS, GREEN LANTERN WHIRLS...
I'VE GOT THEM ALL IN THE CAVE! NOW... TO RETURN TO THE OUTSIDE--
SPLIT-SECONDS LATER...
THEY'RE FOLLOWING ME--ONLY AN INSTANT LEFT TO SEAL UP THAT CAVE!
11

AS THE GREAT GREEN BEAM CAUSES A HUGE LANDSLIDE BLOCKING THE CAVE MOUTH UP FOREVER...

YOU HAVE TRAPPED OUR ENEMIES THE BIRD-RAIDERS!

THANKS TO OUR FELLOW-HUMAN, WE ARE SAVED!

LATER... THE *VENUSIAN* HUMANS ARE PREPARING A GREAT VICTORY FEAST-- TO WHICH I'M INVITED! THEY'RE JUST ABOUT AT THE CAVEMAN LEVEL NOW...

MAKING THEIR FIRES OUT IN THE OPEN... AND KEEPING THE FIRES LIT AND GUARDING THEM EVERY DAY! BUT THEY WON'T ALWAYS BE LIKE THIS-- ONE DAY THERE'LL BE A GREAT CIVILIZATION HERE!

AFTERWARD, AS THE *EMERALD GLADIATOR* STARTS HOMEWARD...

I SEE NOW WHY I WAS SENT HERE.... TO PREVENT THIS BAND OF HUMANS FROM BEING WIPED OUT! HUMANS EVERYWHERE ARE IMPORTANT FOR ALL OTHER HUMANS!

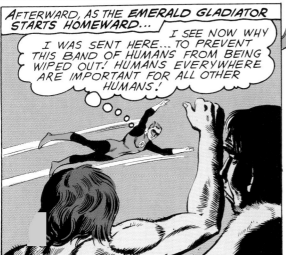

HMM! BUT TO COME DOWN TO PERSONAL MATTERS--I'D BETTER HURRY! I HAVEN'T FORGOTTEN THAT I HAVE A VERY IMPORTANT DATE TONIGHT BACK HOME!

12

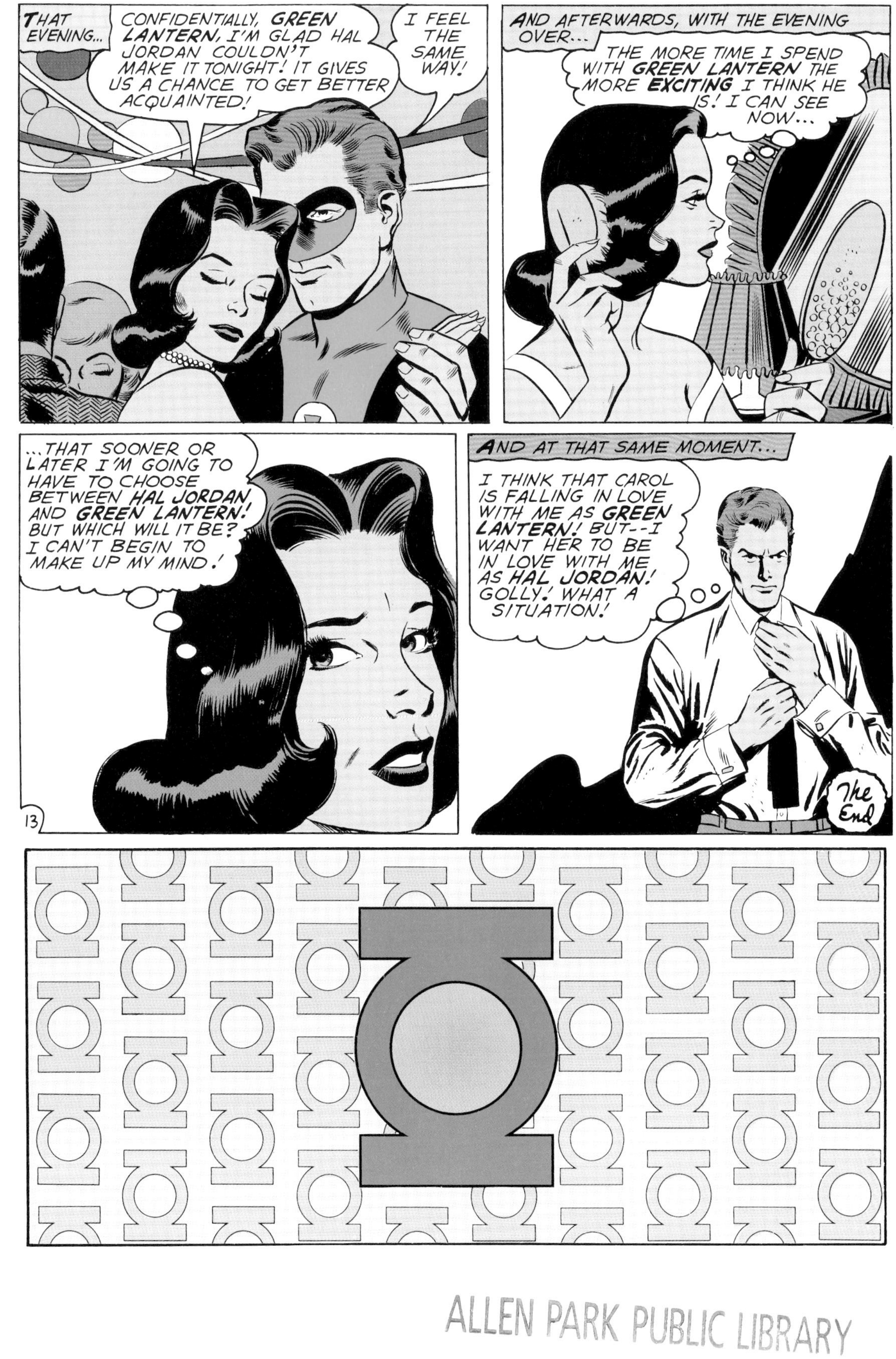
THAT EVENING...
CONFIDENTIALLY, GREEN LANTERN, I'M GLAD HAL JORDAN COULDN'T MAKE IT TONIGHT! IT GIVES US A CHANCE TO GET BETTER ACQUAINTED!
I FEEL THE SAME WAY!
AND AFTERWARDS, WITH THE EVENING OVER...
THE MORE TIME I SPEND WITH GREEN LANTERN THE MORE EXCITING I THINK HE IS! I CAN SEE NOW...
...THAT SOONER OR LATER I'M GOING TO HAVE TO CHOOSE BETWEEN HAL JORDAN AND GREEN LANTERN! BUT WHICH WILL IT BE? I CAN'T BEGIN TO MAKE UP MY MIND!
13
AND AT THAT SAME MOMENT...
I THINK THAT CAROL IS FALLING IN LOVE WITH ME AS GREEN LANTERN! BUT--I WANT HER TO BE IN LOVE WITH ME AS HAL JORDAN! GOLLY! WHAT A SITUATION!
The End

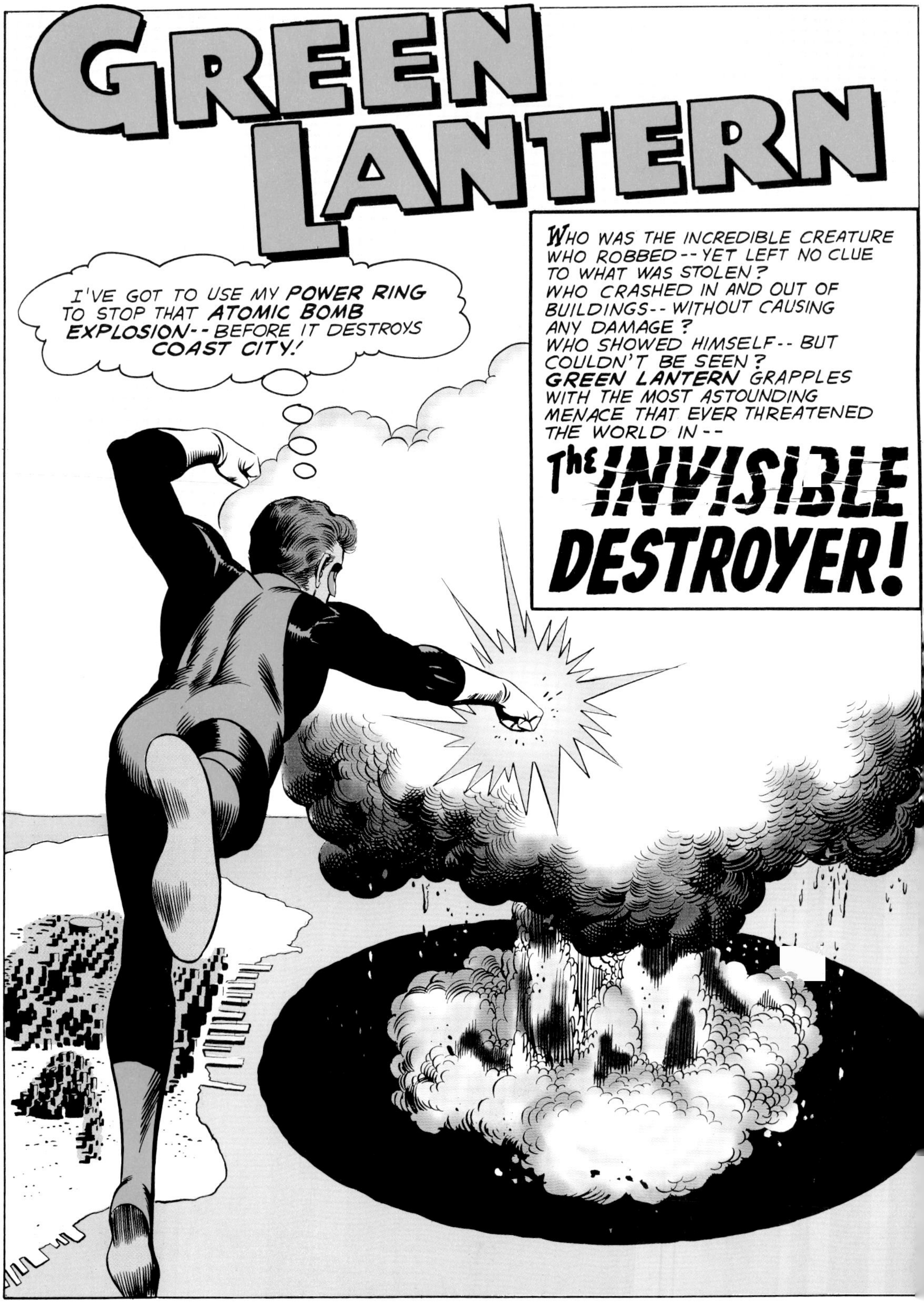
GREEN LANTERN
WHO WAS THE INCREDIBLE CREATURE WHO ROBBED--YET LEFT NO CLUE TO WHAT WAS STOLEN? WHO CRASHED IN AND OUT OF BUILDINGS--WITHOUT CAUSING ANY DAMAGE? WHO SHOWED HIMSELF--BUT COULDN'T BE SEEN? GREEN LANTERN GRAPPLES WITH THE MOST ASTOUNDING MENACE THAT EVER THREATENED THE WORLD IN--
The INVISIBLE DESTROYER!
I'VE GOT TO USE MY POWER RING TO STOP THAT ATOMIC BOMB EXPLOSION--BEFORE IT DESTROYS COAST CITY!

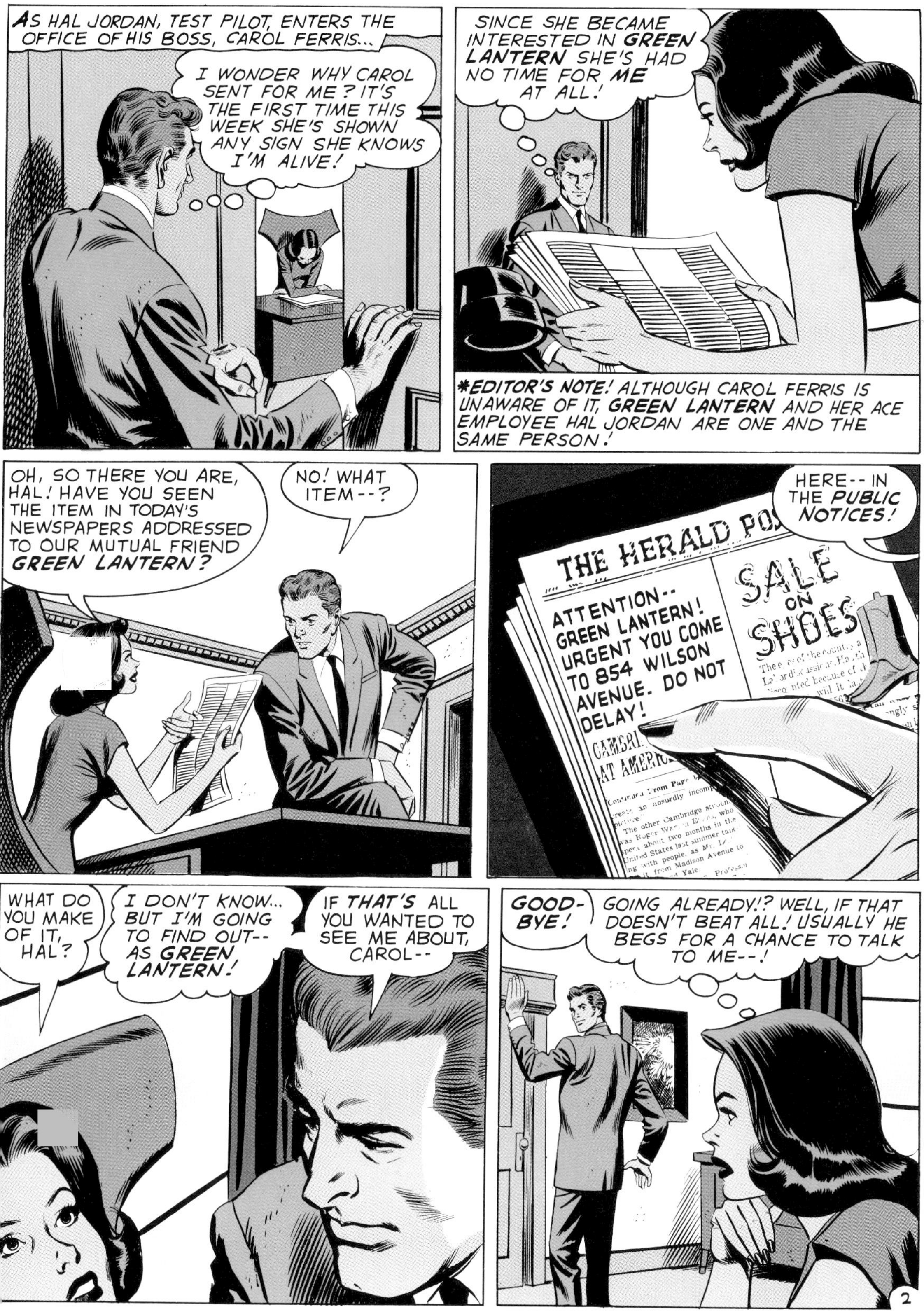
AS HAL JORDAN, TEST PILOT, ENTERS THE OFFICE OF HIS BOSS, CAROL FERRIS...
I WONDER WHY CAROL SENT FOR ME? IT'S THE FIRST TIME THIS WEEK SHE'S SHOWN ANY SIGN SHE KNOWS I'M ALIVE!
SINCE SHE BECAME INTERESTED IN GREEN LANTERN SHE'S HAD NO TIME FOR ME AT ALL!
*EDITOR'S NOTE! ALTHOUGH CAROL FERRIS IS UNAWARE OF IT, GREEN LANTERN AND HER ACE EMPLOYEE HAL JORDAN ARE ONE AND THE SAME PERSON!
OH, SO THERE YOU ARE, HAL! HAVE YOU SEEN THE ITEM IN TODAY'S NEWSPAPERS ADDRESSED TO OUR MUTUAL FRIEND GREEN LANTERN?
NO! WHAT ITEM--?
HERE--IN THE PUBLIC NOTICES!
THE HERALD PO
ATTENTION-- GREEN LANTERN! URGENT YOU COME TO 854 WILSON AVENUE. DO NOT DELAY!
SALE ON SHOES
WHAT DO YOU MAKE OF IT, HAL?
I DON'T KNOW... BUT I'M GOING TO FIND OUT-- AS GREEN LANTERN!
IF THAT'S ALL YOU WANTED TO SEE ME ABOUT, CAROL--
GOOD-BYE!
GOING ALREADY!? WELL, IF THAT DOESN'T BEAT ALL! USUALLY HE BEGS FOR A CHANCE TO TALK TO ME--!
2

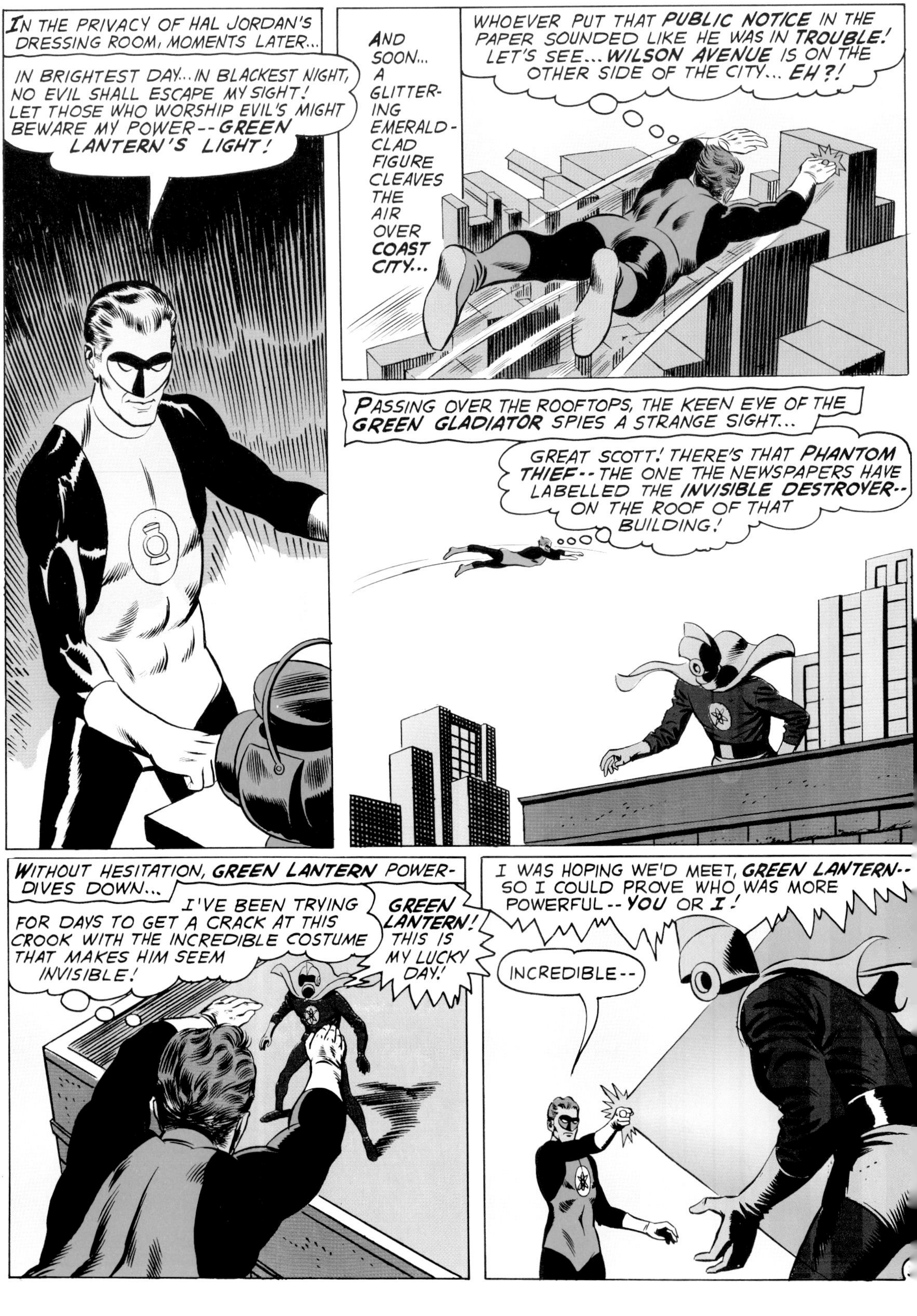
IN THE PRIVACY OF HAL JORDAN'S DRESSING ROOM, MOMENTS LATER...
IN BRIGHTEST DAY...IN BLACKEST NIGHT, NO EVIL SHALL ESCAPE MY SIGHT! LET THOSE WHO WORSHIP EVIL'S MIGHT BEWARE MY POWER--GREEN LANTERN'S LIGHT!
AND SOON... A GLITTERING EMERALD-CLAD FIGURE CLEAVES THE AIR OVER COAST CITY...
WHOEVER PUT THAT PUBLIC NOTICE IN THE PAPER SOUNDED LIKE HE WAS IN TROUBLE! LET'S SEE...WILSON AVENUE IS ON THE OTHER SIDE OF THE CITY... EH?!
PASSING OVER THE ROOFTOPS, THE KEEN EYE OF THE GREEN GLADIATOR SPIES A STRANGE SIGHT...
GREAT SCOTT! THERE'S THAT PHANTOM THIEF--THE ONE THE NEWSPAPERS HAVE LABELLED THE INVISIBLE DESTROYER--ON THE ROOF OF THAT BUILDING!
WITHOUT HESITATION, GREEN LANTERN POWER-DIVES DOWN...
I'VE BEEN TRYING FOR DAYS TO GET A CRACK AT THIS CROOK WITH THE INCREDIBLE COSTUME THAT MAKES HIM SEEM INVISIBLE!
GREEN LANTERN! THIS IS MY LUCKY DAY!
I WAS HOPING WE'D MEET, GREEN LANTERN--SO I COULD PROVE WHO WAS MORE POWERFUL--YOU OR I!
INCREDIBLE--

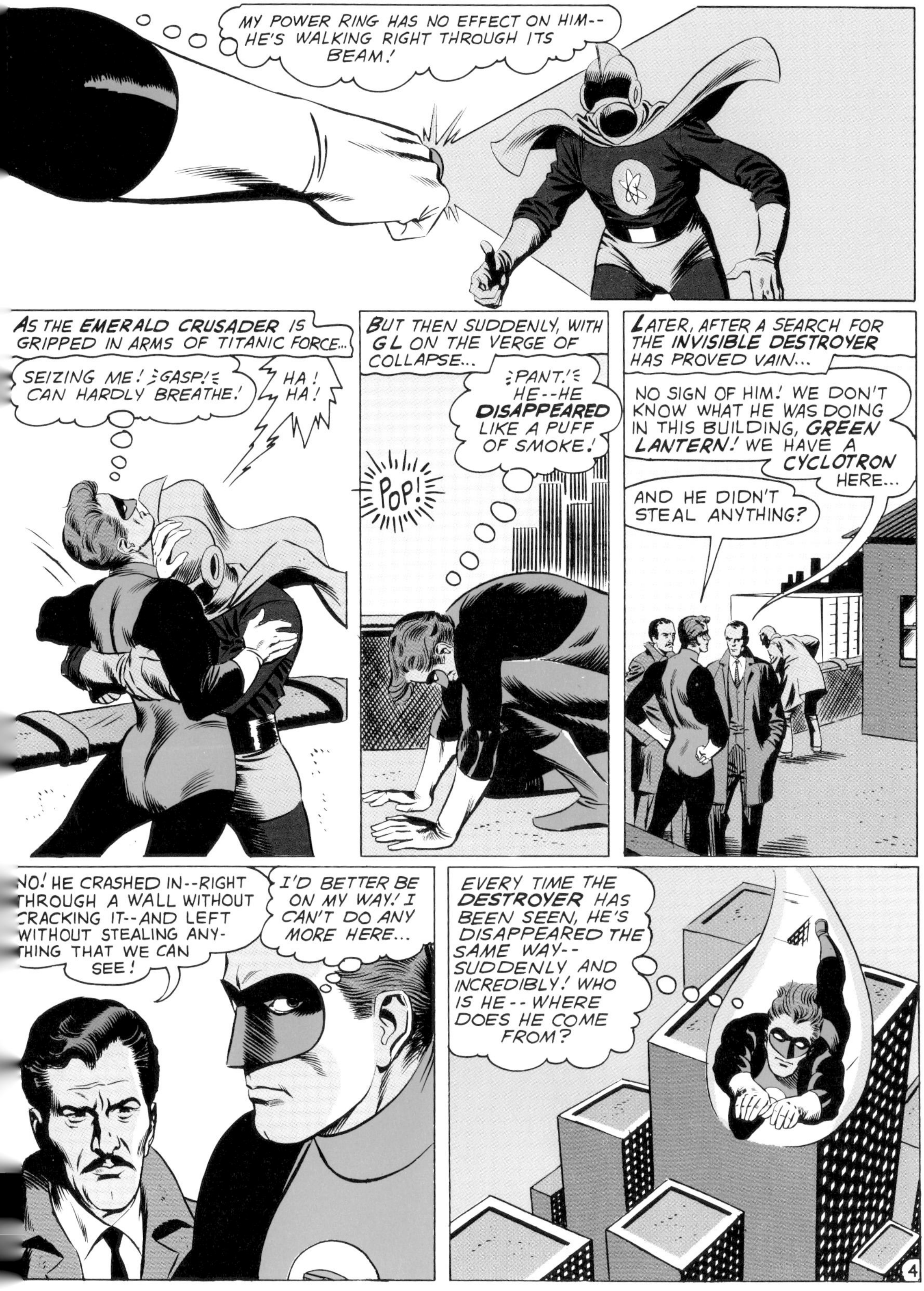
MY POWER RING HAS NO EFFECT ON HIM-- HE'S WALKING RIGHT THROUGH ITS BEAM!
AS THE EMERALD CRUSADER IS GRIPPED IN ARMS OF TITANIC FORCE...
SEIZING ME! GASP! CAN HARDLY BREATHE!
HA! HA!
BUT THEN SUDDENLY, WITH GL ON THE VERGE OF COLLAPSE...
PANT! HE--HE DISAPPEARED LIKE A PUFF OF SMOKE!
POP!
LATER, AFTER A SEARCH FOR THE INVISIBLE DESTROYER HAS PROVED VAIN...
NO SIGN OF HIM! WE DON'T KNOW WHAT HE WAS DOING IN THIS BUILDING, GREEN LANTERN! WE HAVE A CYCLOTRON HERE...
AND HE DIDN'T STEAL ANYTHING?
NO! HE CRASHED IN--RIGHT THROUGH A WALL WITHOUT CRACKING IT--AND LEFT WITHOUT STEALING ANYTHING THAT WE CAN SEE!
I'D BETTER BE ON MY WAY! I CAN'T DO ANY MORE HERE...
EVERY TIME THE DESTROYER HAS BEEN SEEN, HE'S DISAPPEARED THE SAME WAY-- SUDDENLY AND INCREDIBLY! WHO IS HE--WHERE DOES HE COME FROM?
4

SOON... HERE IT IS...854 WILSON... BUT WAIT--! I'VE BEEN TO THIS HOUSE-- AS *HAL JORDAN!* DR. PHILLIPS, THE FAMOUS AND BRILLIANT SCIENTIST, LIVES HERE!

AS GREEN LANTERN ENTERS THE IMPOSING RESIDENCE...

HE WON'T RECOGNIZE ME AS HAL JORDAN, OF COURSE...

GREEN LANTERN! I'M HAPPY YOU COULD COME!

854 WILSON

WITHOUT DELAY THE EMINENT SCIENTIST UNBURDENS HIMSELF TO THE GREEN-CLAD CHAMPION...

WHAT I HAVE TO TELL YOU WILL SOUND FANTASTIC-- UNBELIEVABLE! YOU'VE HEARD OF THE *INVISIBLE DESTROYER?*

NOT ONLY HEARD OF HIM-- BUT HAD AN ALMOST DISASTROUS ENCOUNTER WITH HIM! ON THE WAY HERE, I SAW--

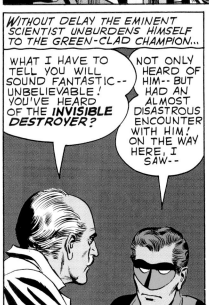

NERVOUSLY THE PHYSICIST INTERRUPTS...

LISTEN! I HAVE A HABIT OF DOODLING WHILE I WORK-- YOU KNOW, MAKING DRAWINGS ON A PIECE OF PAPER-- HARDLY REALIZING WHAT I'M DOING! LOOK AT THESE, PLEASE--

IT'S THE *INVISIBLE DESTROYER!* YOU MUST HAVE SEEN HIS PICTURE IN THE PAPERS--! SOMEONE SNAPPED HIM--

I MADE THESE DRAWINGS OVER A PERIOD OF THREE DAYS, *GREEN LANTERN...*

...*BEFORE* I SAW HIS PICTURE IN THE PAPERS!

I TOLD YOU WHAT I HAD TO SAY WOULD SOUND FANTASTIC, *GREEN LANTERN!* BUT, WAIT-- HERE'S THE REAL *SHOCKER!*

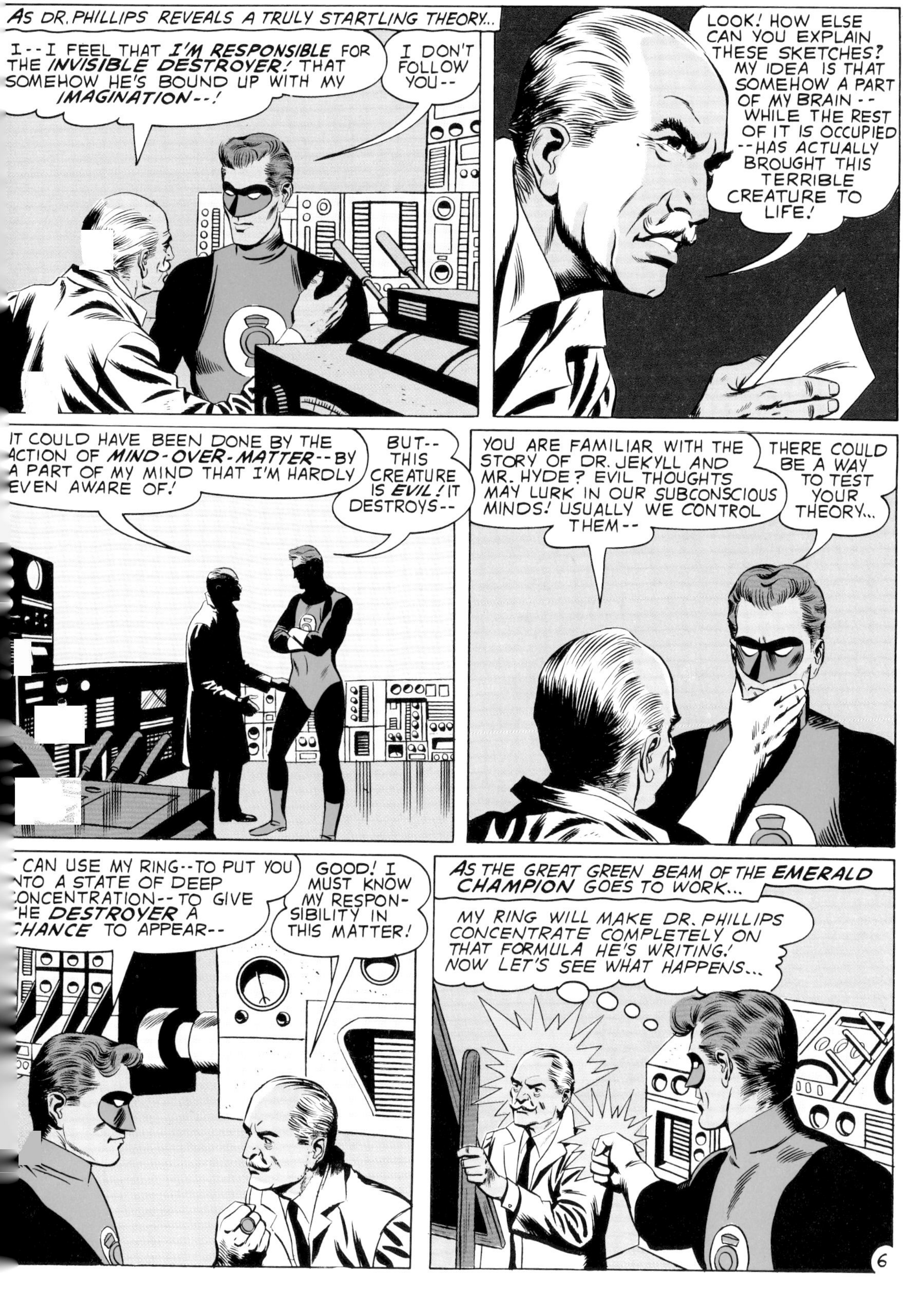
AS DR. PHILLIPS REVEALS A TRULY STARTLING THEORY...
I--I FEEL THAT I'M RESPONSIBLE FOR THE INVISIBLE DESTROYER! THAT SOMEHOW HE'S BOUND UP WITH MY IMAGINATION--!
I DON'T FOLLOW YOU--
LOOK! HOW ELSE CAN YOU EXPLAIN THESE SKETCHES? MY IDEA IS THAT SOMEHOW A PART OF MY BRAIN--WHILE THE REST OF IT IS OCCUPIED--HAS ACTUALLY BROUGHT THIS TERRIBLE CREATURE TO LIFE!
IT COULD HAVE BEEN DONE BY THE ACTION OF MIND-OVER-MATTER--BY A PART OF MY MIND THAT I'M HARDLY EVEN AWARE OF!
BUT--THIS CREATURE IS EVIL! IT DESTROYS--
YOU ARE FAMILIAR WITH THE STORY OF DR. JEKYLL AND MR. HYDE? EVIL THOUGHTS MAY LURK IN OUR SUBCONSCIOUS MINDS! USUALLY WE CONTROL THEM--
THERE COULD BE A WAY TO TEST YOUR THEORY...
CAN USE MY RING--TO PUT YOU NTO A STATE OF DEEP CONCENTRATION--TO GIVE HE DESTROYER A CHANCE TO APPEAR--
GOOD! I MUST KNOW MY RESPONSIBILITY IN THIS MATTER!
AS THE GREAT GREEN BEAM OF THE EMERALD CHAMPION GOES TO WORK...
MY RING WILL MAKE DR. PHILLIPS CONCENTRATE COMPLETELY ON THAT FORMULA HE'S WRITING! NOW LET'S SEE WHAT HAPPENS...
6

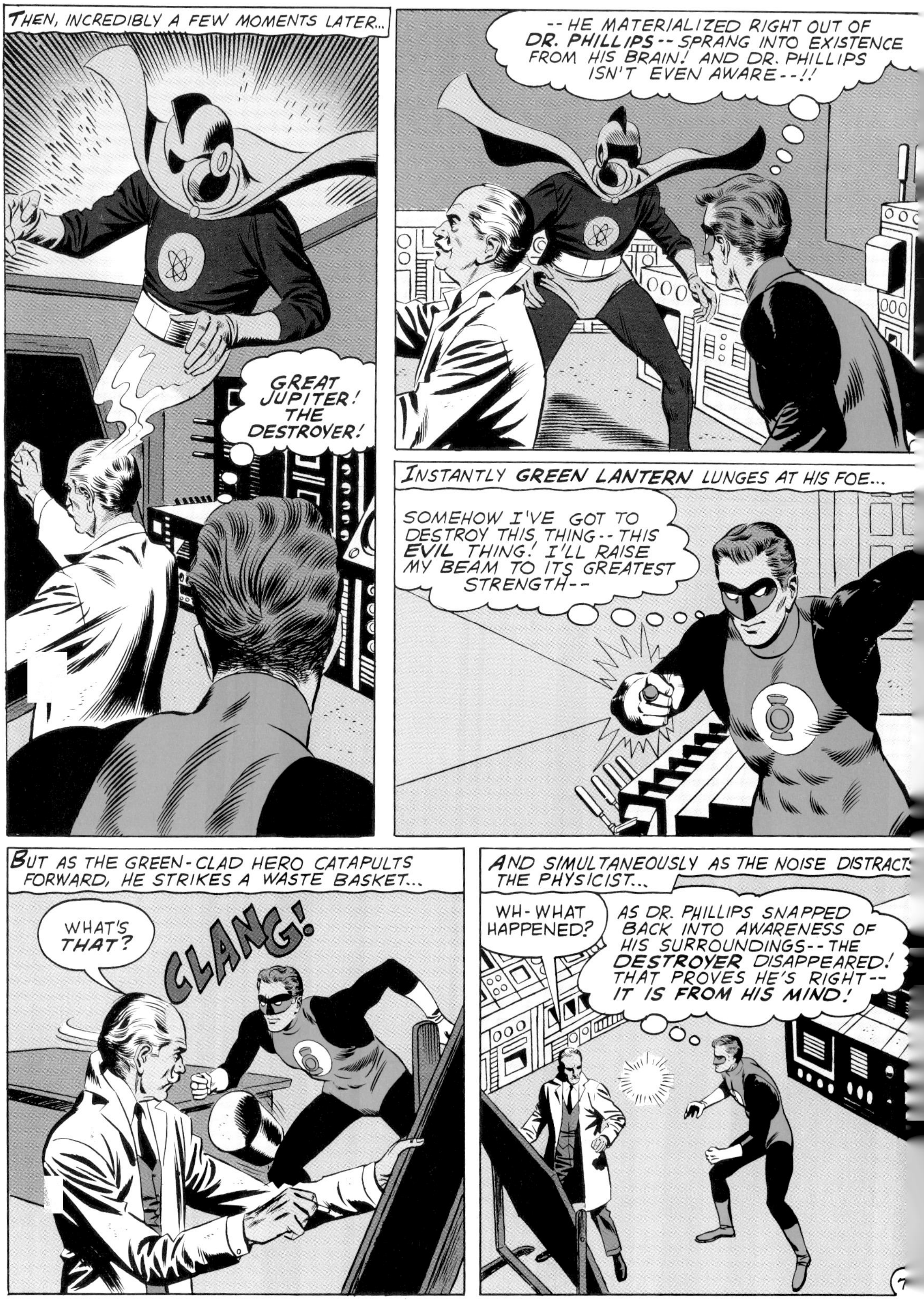
THEN, INCREDIBLY A FEW MOMENTS LATER...
GREAT JUPITER! THE DESTROYER!
-- HE MATERIALIZED RIGHT OUT OF DR. PHILLIPS -- SPRANG INTO EXISTENCE FROM HIS BRAIN! AND DR. PHILLIPS ISN'T EVEN AWARE--!!
INSTANTLY GREEN LANTERN LUNGES AT HIS FOE...
SOMEHOW I'VE GOT TO DESTROY THIS THING -- THIS EVIL THING! I'LL RAISE MY BEAM TO ITS GREATEST STRENGTH--
BUT AS THE GREEN-CLAD HERO CATAPULTS FORWARD, HE STRIKES A WASTE BASKET...
WHAT'S THAT?
CLANG!
AND SIMULTANEOUSLY AS THE NOISE DISTRACTS THE PHYSICIST...
WH-WHAT HAPPENED?
AS DR. PHILLIPS SNAPPED BACK INTO AWARENESS OF HIS SURROUNDINGS -- THE DESTROYER DISAPPEARED! THAT PROVES HE'S RIGHT -- IT IS FROM HIS MIND!
7

As GL and the scientist confer over the dreadful development...

SO THE *DESTROYER IS PART OF ME!* I'M RESPONSIBLE FOR HIM--!

NO--NOT CONSCIOUSLY! THE GOOD PART OF YOUR MIND REFUSES TO ACKNOWLEDGE THE *DESTROYER'S* EXISTENCE! THAT'S WHY IT BLANKS OUT THE *DESTROYER'S* FACE-- SO IT APPEARS *INVISIBLE!*

OUR PROBLEM IS TO DESTROY THE *DESTROYER*-- WITHOUT HARMING YOU! WAIT--! SUPPOSE I USE MY RING TO PROBE INTO YOUR BRAIN! MAYBE I CAN *FORCE* THE CREATURE TO REVEAL ITS PLANS-- WHAT IT'S UP TO!

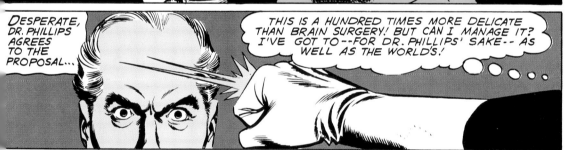

Desperate, Dr. Phillips agrees to the proposal...

THIS IS A HUNDRED TIMES MORE DELICATE THAN BRAIN SURGERY! BUT CAN I MANAGE IT? I'VE GOT TO--FOR DR. PHILLIPS' SAKE-- AS WELL AS THE WORLD'S!

Then, after numerous vain efforts, suddenly...

GOT IT! WHEN MY RING TOUCHED A CERTAIN *TINY SPOT* IT SPRANG INTO VIEW!

SO...YOU WANT TO KNOW MY PLANS, *GREEN LANTERN?* WELL, I DON'T MIND TELLING YOU, BECAUSE YOU WON'T BE ABLE TO STOP THEM!

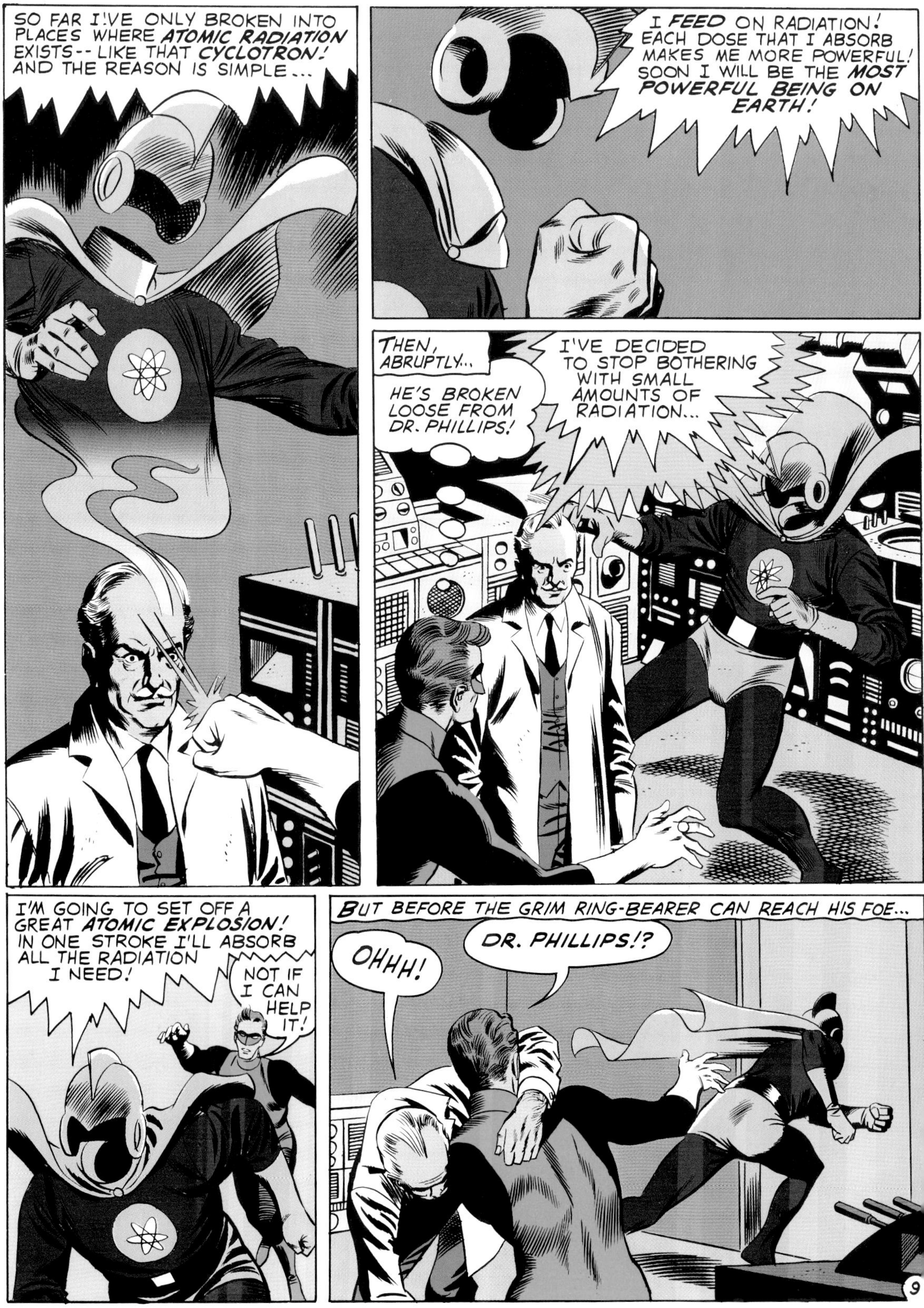
SO FAR I'VE ONLY BROKEN INTO PLACES WHERE ATOMIC RADIATION EXISTS-- LIKE THAT CYCLOTRON! AND THE REASON IS SIMPLE...
I FEED ON RADIATION! EACH DOSE THAT I ABSORB MAKES ME MORE POWERFUL! SOON I WILL BE THE MOST POWERFUL BEING ON EARTH!
THEN, ABRUPTLY...
HE'S BROKEN LOOSE FROM DR. PHILLIPS!
I'VE DECIDED TO STOP BOTHERING WITH SMALL AMOUNTS OF RADIATION...
I'M GOING TO SET OFF A GREAT ATOMIC EXPLOSION! IN ONE STROKE I'LL ABSORB ALL THE RADIATION I NEED!
NOT IF I CAN HELP IT!
BUT BEFORE THE GRIM RING-BEARER CAN REACH HIS FOE...
OHHH!
DR. PHILLIPS!?
9

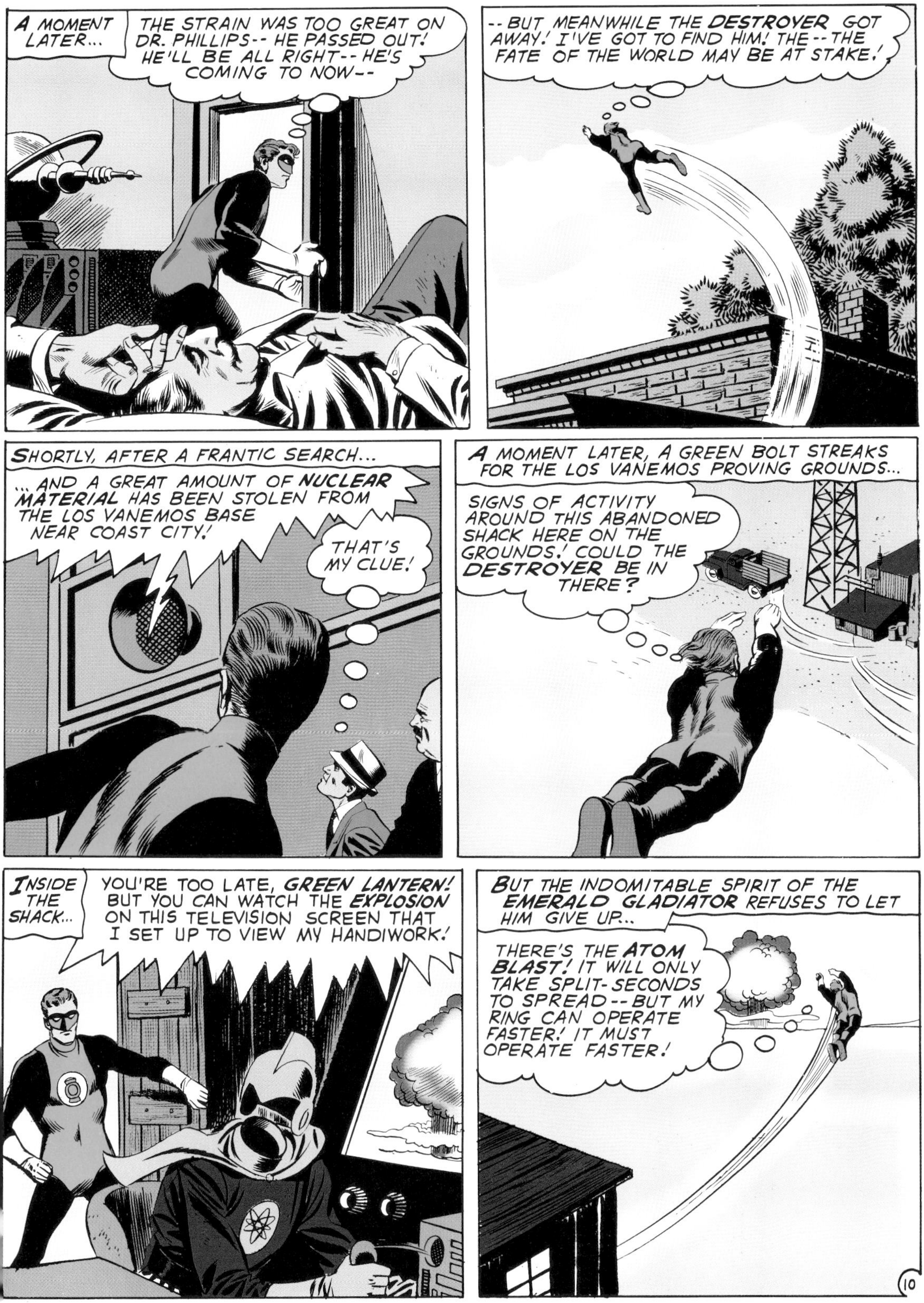
A MOMENT LATER...
THE STRAIN WAS TOO GREAT ON DR. PHILLIPS-- HE PASSED OUT! HE'LL BE ALL RIGHT-- HE'S COMING TO NOW--
-- BUT MEANWHILE THE DESTROYER GOT AWAY! I'VE GOT TO FIND HIM! THE--THE FATE OF THE WORLD MAY BE AT STAKE!
SHORTLY, AFTER A FRANTIC SEARCH...
...AND A GREAT AMOUNT OF NUCLEAR MATERIAL HAS BEEN STOLEN FROM THE LOS VANEMOS BASE NEAR COAST CITY!
THAT'S MY CLUE!
A MOMENT LATER, A GREEN BOLT STREAKS FOR THE LOS VANEMOS PROVING GROUNDS...
SIGNS OF ACTIVITY AROUND THIS ABANDONED SHACK HERE ON THE GROUNDS! COULD THE DESTROYER BE IN THERE?
INSIDE THE SHACK...
YOU'RE TOO LATE, GREEN LANTERN! BUT YOU CAN WATCH THE EXPLOSION ON THIS TELEVISION SCREEN THAT I SET UP TO VIEW MY HANDIWORK!
BUT THE INDOMITABLE SPIRIT OF THE EMERALD GLADIATOR REFUSES TO LET HIM GIVE UP...
THERE'S THE ATOM BLAST! IT WILL ONLY TAKE SPLIT-SECONDS TO SPREAD--BUT MY RING CAN OPERATE FASTER! IT MUST OPERATE FASTER!
10

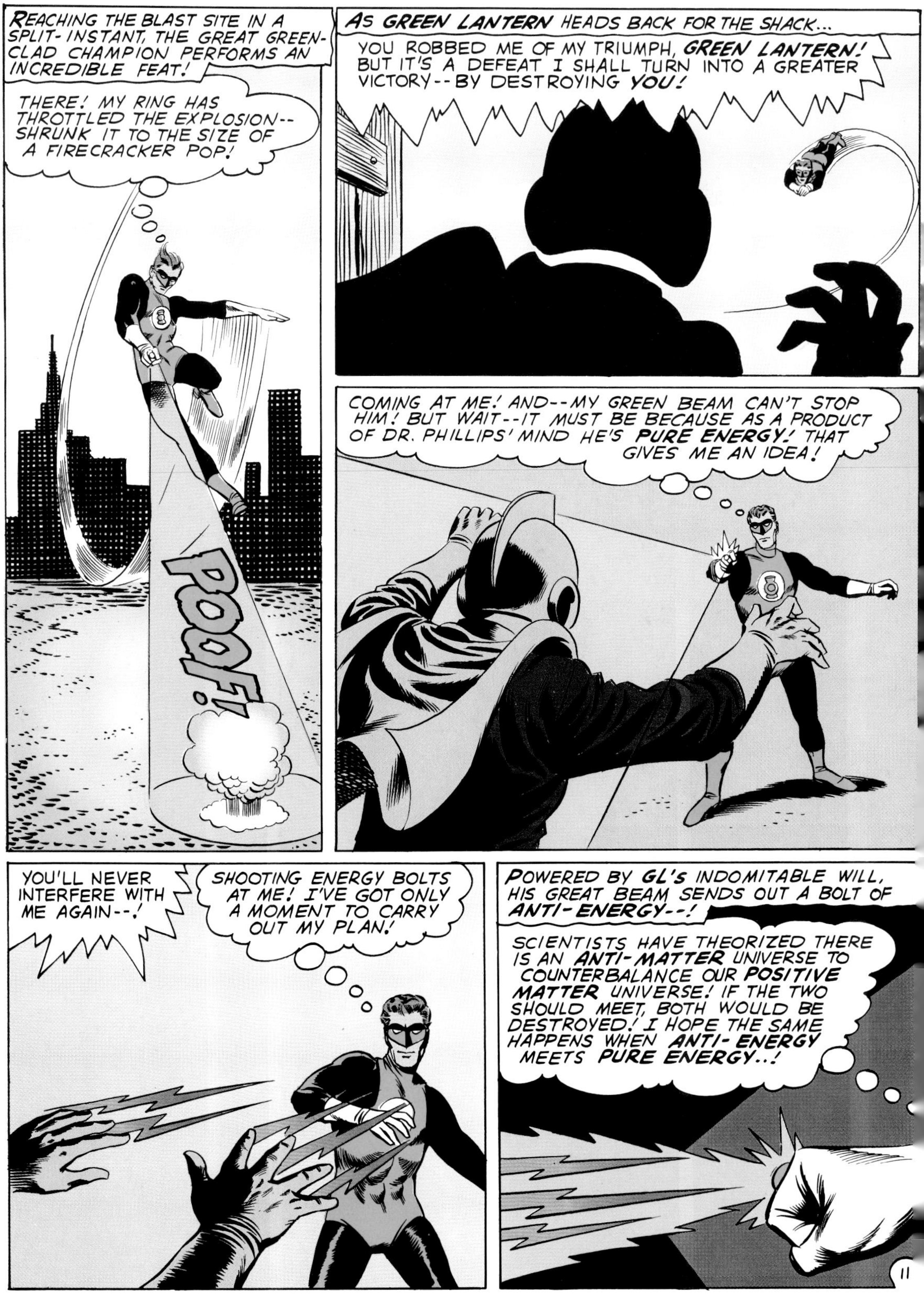
REACHING THE BLAST SITE IN A SPLIT-INSTANT, THE GREAT GREEN-CLAD CHAMPION PERFORMS AN INCREDIBLE FEAT!
THERE! MY RING HAS THROTTLED THE EXPLOSION--SHRUNK IT TO THE SIZE OF A FIRECRACKER POP!
POOF!
AS GREEN LANTERN HEADS BACK FOR THE SHACK...
YOU ROBBED ME OF MY TRIUMPH, GREEN LANTERN! BUT IT'S A DEFEAT I SHALL TURN INTO A GREATER VICTORY--BY DESTROYING YOU!
COMING AT ME! AND--MY GREEN BEAM CAN'T STOP HIM! BUT WAIT--IT MUST BE BECAUSE AS A PRODUCT OF DR. PHILLIPS' MIND HE'S PURE ENERGY! THAT GIVES ME AN IDEA!
YOU'LL NEVER INTERFERE WITH ME AGAIN--!
SHOOTING ENERGY BOLTS AT ME! I'VE GOT ONLY A MOMENT TO CARRY OUT MY PLAN!
POWERED BY GL'S INDOMITABLE WILL, HIS GREAT BEAM SENDS OUT A BOLT OF ANTI-ENERGY--!
SCIENTISTS HAVE THEORIZED THERE IS AN ANTI-MATTER UNIVERSE TO COUNTERBALANCE OUR POSITIVE MATTER UNIVERSE! IF THE TWO SHOULD MEET, BOTH WOULD BE DESTROYED! I HOPE THE SAME HAPPENS WHEN ANTI-ENERGY MEETS PURE ENERGY..!
11

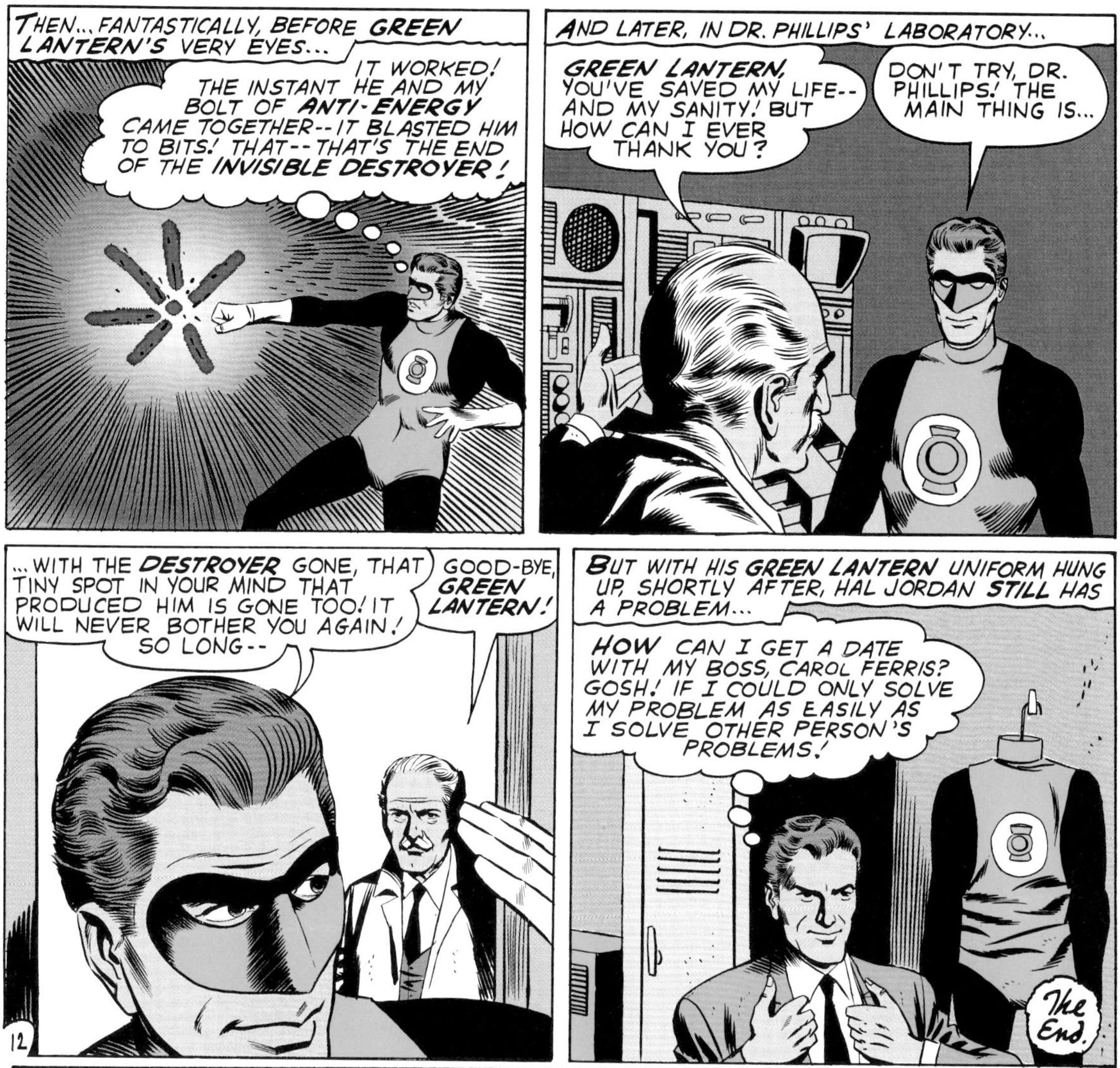
THEN... FANTASTICALLY, BEFORE GREEN LANTERN'S VERY EYES...
IT WORKED! THE INSTANT HE AND MY BOLT OF ANTI-ENERGY CAME TOGETHER--IT BLASTED HIM TO BITS! THAT--THAT'S THE END OF THE INVISIBLE DESTROYER!
AND LATER, IN DR. PHILLIPS' LABORATORY...
GREEN LANTERN, YOU'VE SAVED MY LIFE--AND MY SANITY! BUT HOW CAN I EVER THANK YOU?
DON'T TRY, DR. PHILLIPS! THE MAIN THING IS...
...WITH THE DESTROYER GONE, THAT TINY SPOT IN YOUR MIND THAT PRODUCED HIM IS GONE TOO! IT WILL NEVER BOTHER YOU AGAIN! SO LONG--
GOOD-BYE, GREEN LANTERN!
12
BUT WITH HIS GREEN LANTERN UNIFORM HUNG UP, SHORTLY AFTER, HAL JORDAN STILL HAS A PROBLEM...
HOW CAN I GET A DATE WITH MY BOSS, CAROL FERRIS? GOSH! IF I COULD ONLY SOLVE MY PROBLEM AS EASILY AS I SOLVE OTHER PERSON'S PROBLEMS!
The End.

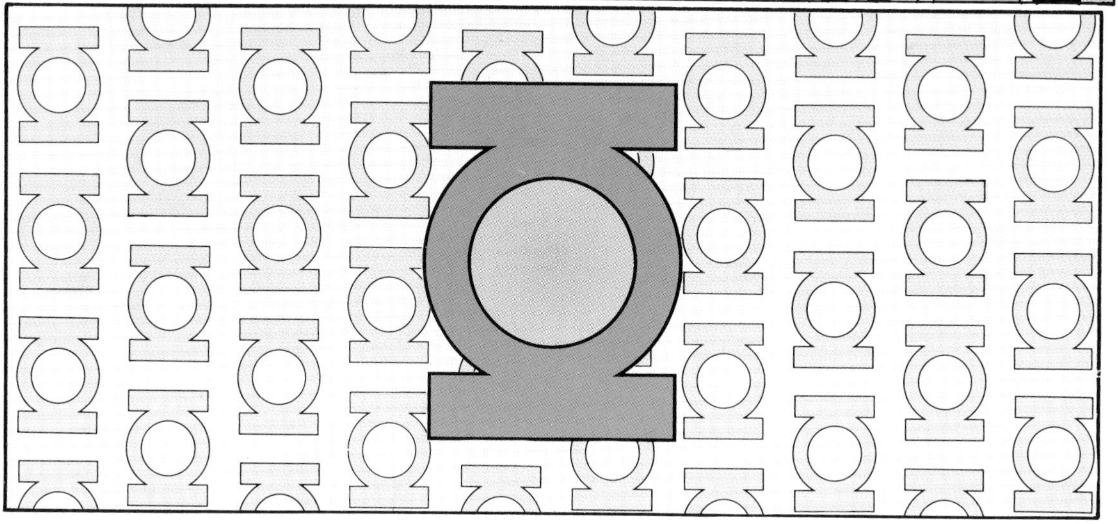

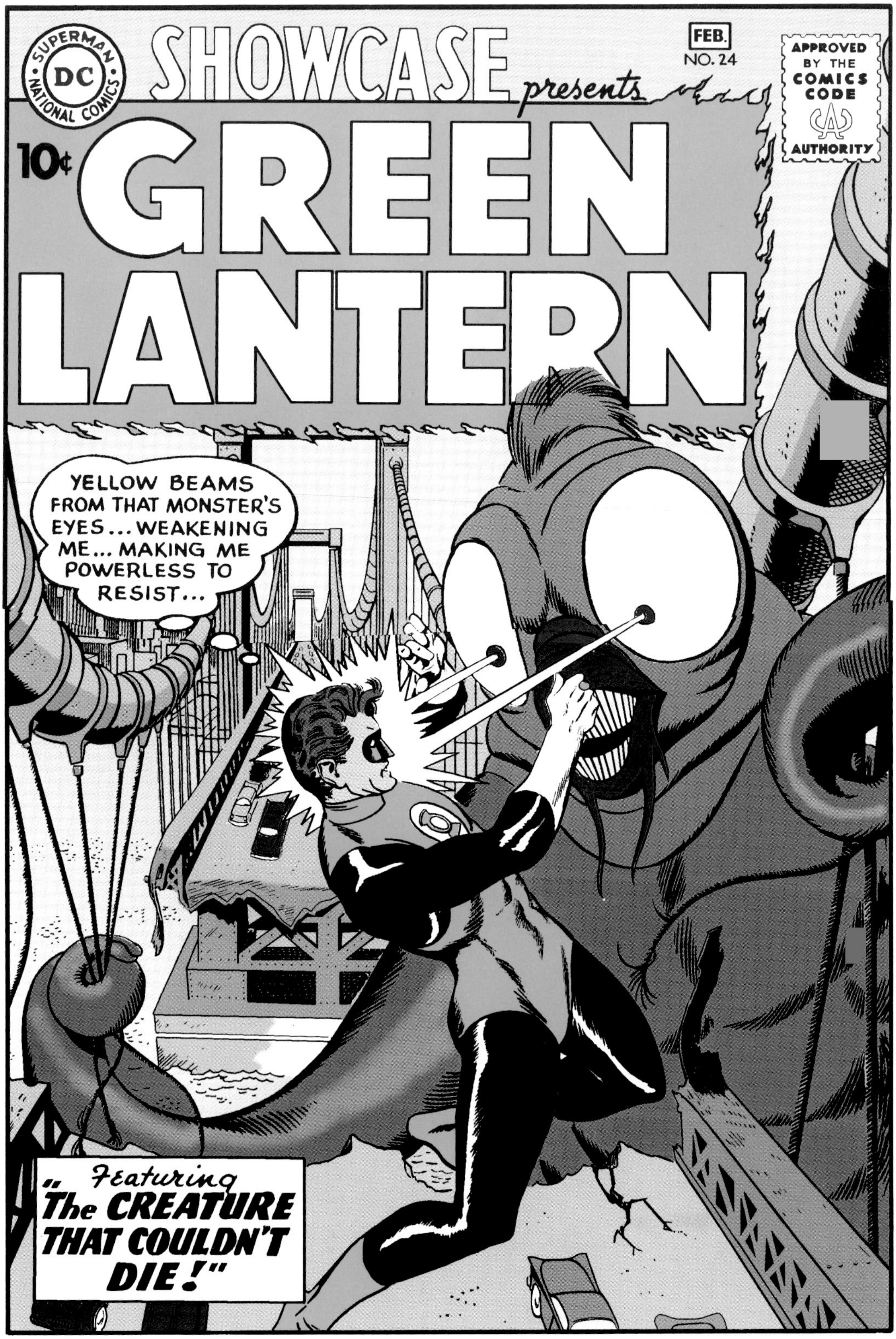
SUPERMAN DC NATIONAL COMICS
SHOWCASE presents
FEB. NO. 24
APPROVED BY THE COMICS CODE AUTHORITY
10¢
GREEN LANTERN
YELLOW BEAMS FROM THAT MONSTER'S EYES... WEAKENING ME... MAKING ME POWERLESS TO RESIST...
Featuring "The CREATURE THAT COULDN'T DIE!"

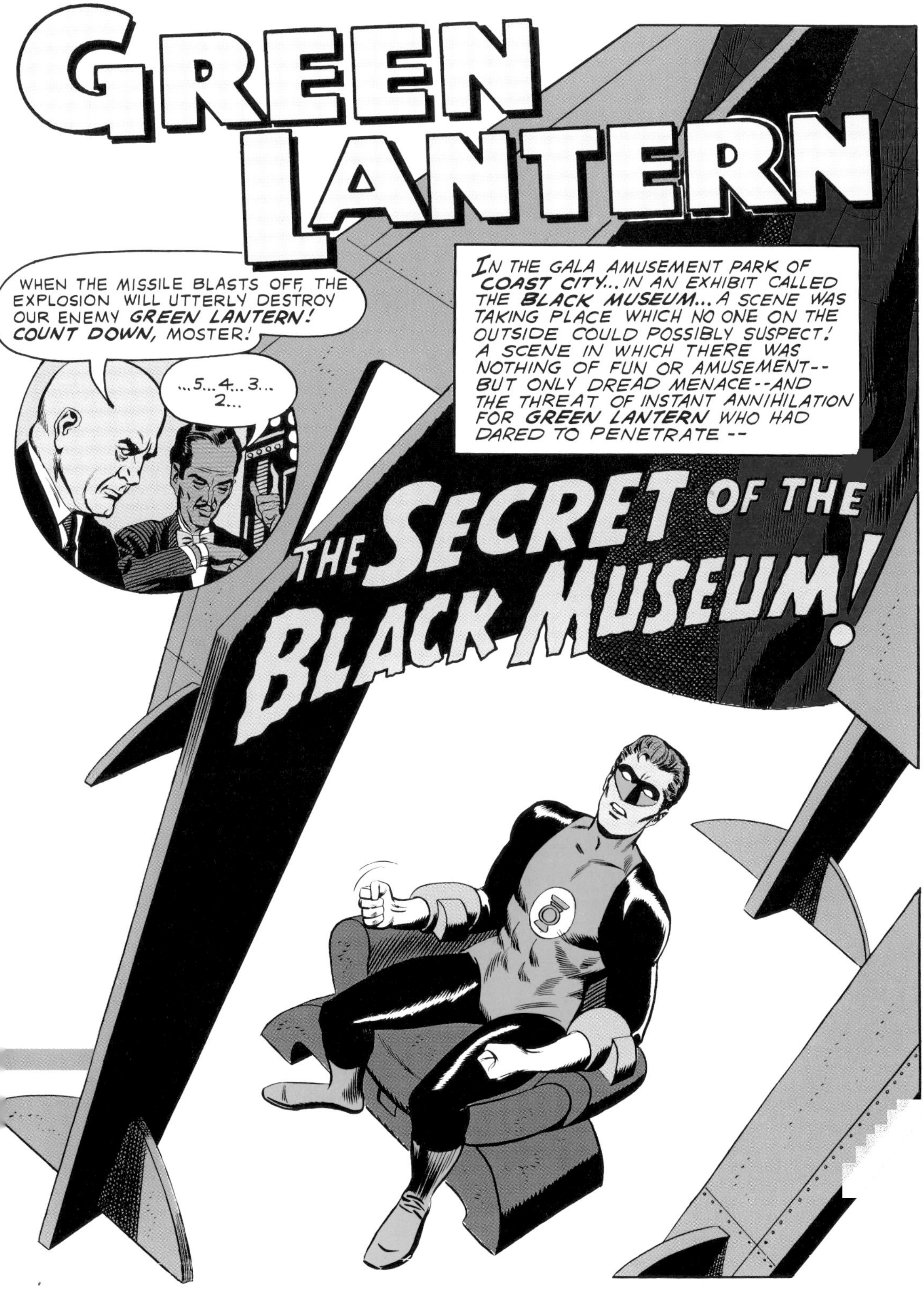
GREEN LANTERN
WHEN THE MISSILE BLASTS OFF, THE EXPLOSION WILL UTTERLY DESTROY OUR ENEMY GREEN LANTERN! COUNT DOWN, MOSTER!
...5...4...3... 2...
IN THE GALA AMUSEMENT PARK OF COAST CITY...IN AN EXHIBIT CALLED THE BLACK MUSEUM...A SCENE WAS TAKING PLACE WHICH NO ONE ON THE OUTSIDE COULD POSSIBLY SUSPECT! A SCENE IN WHICH THERE WAS NOTHING OF FUN OR AMUSEMENT--BUT ONLY DREAD MENACE--AND THE THREAT OF INSTANT ANNIHILATION FOR GREEN LANTERN WHO HAD DARED TO PENETRATE --
THE SECRET OF THE BLACK MUSEUM!

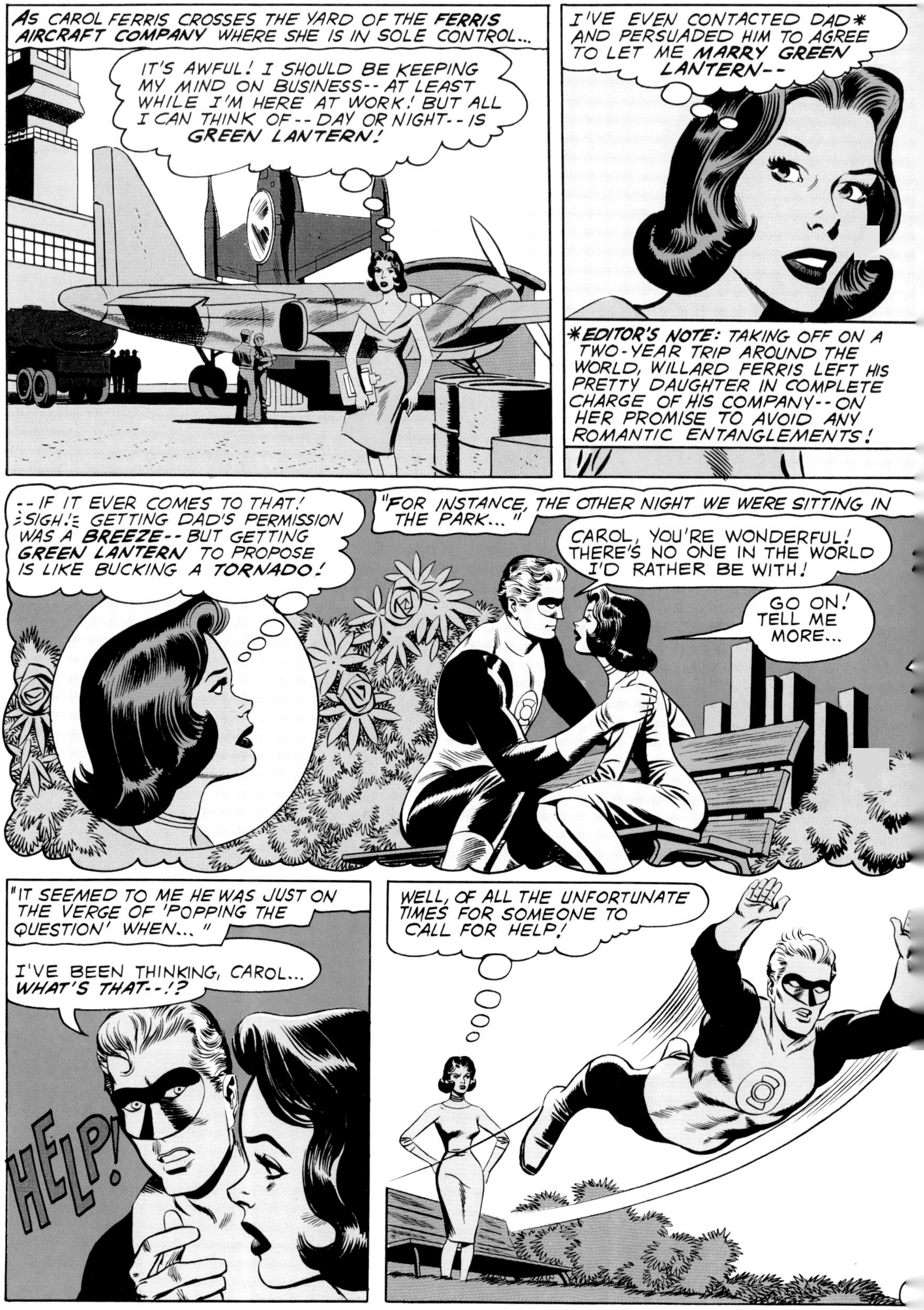
AS CAROL FERRIS CROSSES THE YARD OF THE FERRIS AIRCRAFT COMPANY WHERE SHE IS IN SOLE CONTROL...
IT'S AWFUL! I SHOULD BE KEEPING MY MIND ON BUSINESS-- AT LEAST WHILE I'M HERE AT WORK! BUT ALL I CAN THINK OF-- DAY OR NIGHT-- IS GREEN LANTERN!
I'VE EVEN CONTACTED DAD* AND PERSUADED HIM TO AGREE TO LET ME MARRY GREEN LANTERN--
*EDITOR'S NOTE: TAKING OFF ON A TWO-YEAR TRIP AROUND THE WORLD, WILLARD FERRIS LEFT HIS PRETTY DAUGHTER IN COMPLETE CHARGE OF HIS COMPANY-- ON HER PROMISE TO AVOID ANY ROMANTIC ENTANGLEMENTS!
--IF IT EVER COMES TO THAT! SIGH! GETTING DAD'S PERMISSION WAS A BREEZE-- BUT GETTING GREEN LANTERN TO PROPOSE IS LIKE BUCKING A TORNADO!
"FOR INSTANCE, THE OTHER NIGHT WE WERE SITTING IN THE PARK..."
CAROL, YOU'RE WONDERFUL! THERE'S NO ONE IN THE WORLD I'D RATHER BE WITH!
GO ON! TELL ME MORE...
"IT SEEMED TO ME HE WAS JUST ON THE VERGE OF 'POPPING THE QUESTION' WHEN..."
I'VE BEEN THINKING, CAROL... WHAT'S THAT--!?
HELP!
WELL, OF ALL THE UNFORTUNATE TIMES FOR SOMEONE TO CALL FOR HELP!

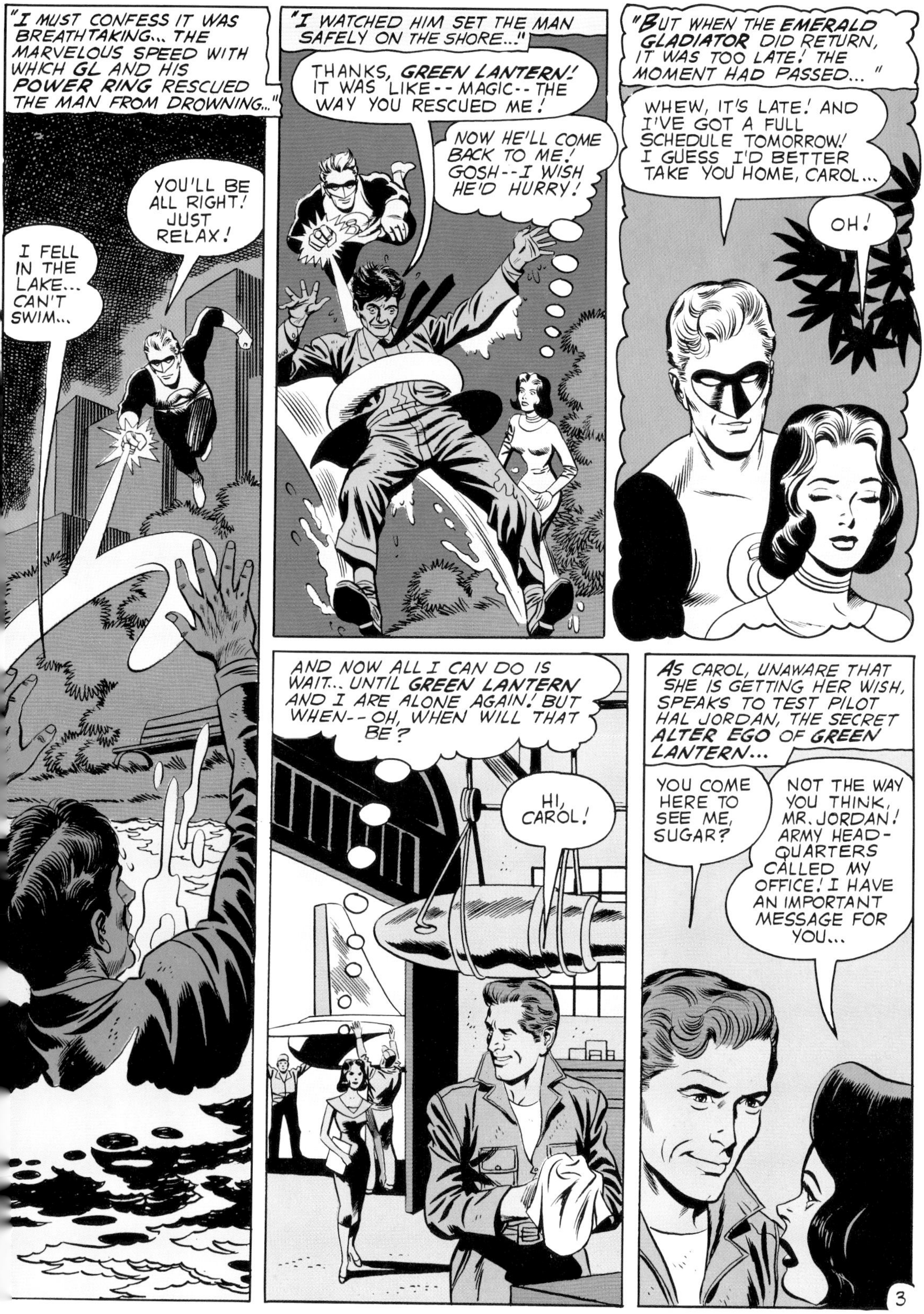
"I MUST CONFESS IT WAS BREATHTAKING... THE MARVELOUS SPEED WITH WHICH GL AND HIS POWER RING RESCUED THE MAN FROM DROWNING..."
YOU'LL BE ALL RIGHT! JUST RELAX!
I FELL IN THE LAKE... CAN'T SWIM...
"I WATCHED HIM SET THE MAN SAFELY ON THE SHORE..."
THANKS, GREEN LANTERN! IT WAS LIKE--MAGIC--THE WAY YOU RESCUED ME!
NOW HE'LL COME BACK TO ME! GOSH--I WISH HE'D HURRY!
"BUT WHEN THE EMERALD GLADIATOR DID RETURN, IT WAS TOO LATE! THE MOMENT HAD PASSED..."
WHEW, IT'S LATE! AND I'VE GOT A FULL SCHEDULE TOMORROW! I GUESS I'D BETTER TAKE YOU HOME, CAROL...
OH!
AND NOW ALL I CAN DO IS WAIT... UNTIL GREEN LANTERN AND I ARE ALONE AGAIN! BUT WHEN--OH, WHEN WILL THAT BE?
HI, CAROL!
AS CAROL, UNAWARE THAT SHE IS GETTING HER WISH, SPEAKS TO TEST PILOT HAL JORDAN, THE SECRET ALTER EGO OF GREEN LANTERN...
YOU COME HERE TO SEE ME, SUGAR?
NOT THE WAY YOU THINK, MR. JORDAN! ARMY HEAD-QUARTERS CALLED MY OFFICE! I HAVE AN IMPORTANT MESSAGE FOR YOU...

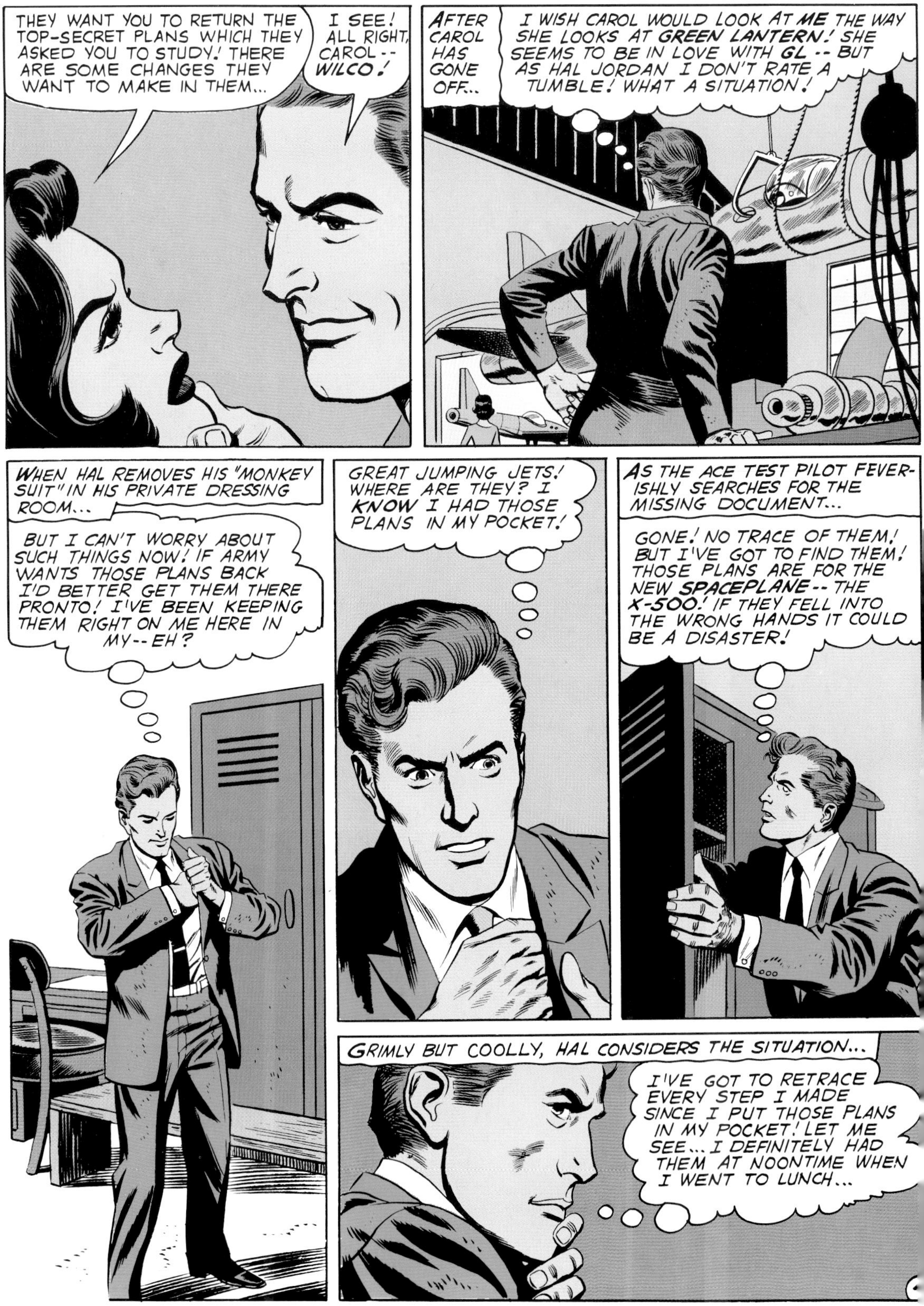
THEY WANT YOU TO RETURN THE TOP-SECRET PLANS WHICH THEY ASKED YOU TO STUDY! THERE ARE SOME CHANGES THEY WANT TO MAKE IN THEM...
I SEE! ALL RIGHT, CAROL -- WILCO!
AFTER CAROL HAS GONE OFF...
I WISH CAROL WOULD LOOK AT ME THE WAY SHE LOOKS AT GREEN LANTERN! SHE SEEMS TO BE IN LOVE WITH GL -- BUT AS HAL JORDAN I DON'T RATE A TUMBLE! WHAT A SITUATION!
WHEN HAL REMOVES HIS "MONKEY SUIT" IN HIS PRIVATE DRESSING ROOM...
BUT I CAN'T WORRY ABOUT SUCH THINGS NOW! IF ARMY WANTS THOSE PLANS BACK I'D BETTER GET THEM THERE PRONTO! I'VE BEEN KEEPING THEM RIGHT ON ME HERE IN MY--EH?
GREAT JUMPING JETS! WHERE ARE THEY? I KNOW I HAD THOSE PLANS IN MY POCKET!
AS THE ACE TEST PILOT FEVERISHLY SEARCHES FOR THE MISSING DOCUMENT...
GONE! NO TRACE OF THEM! BUT I'VE GOT TO FIND THEM! THOSE PLANS ARE FOR THE NEW SPACEPLANE -- THE X-500! IF THEY FELL INTO THE WRONG HANDS IT COULD BE A DISASTER!
GRIMLY BUT COOLLY, HAL CONSIDERS THE SITUATION...
I'VE GOT TO RETRACE EVERY STEP I MADE SINCE I PUT THOSE PLANS IN MY POCKET! LET ME SEE... I DEFINITELY HAD THEM AT NOONTIME WHEN I WENT TO LUNCH...

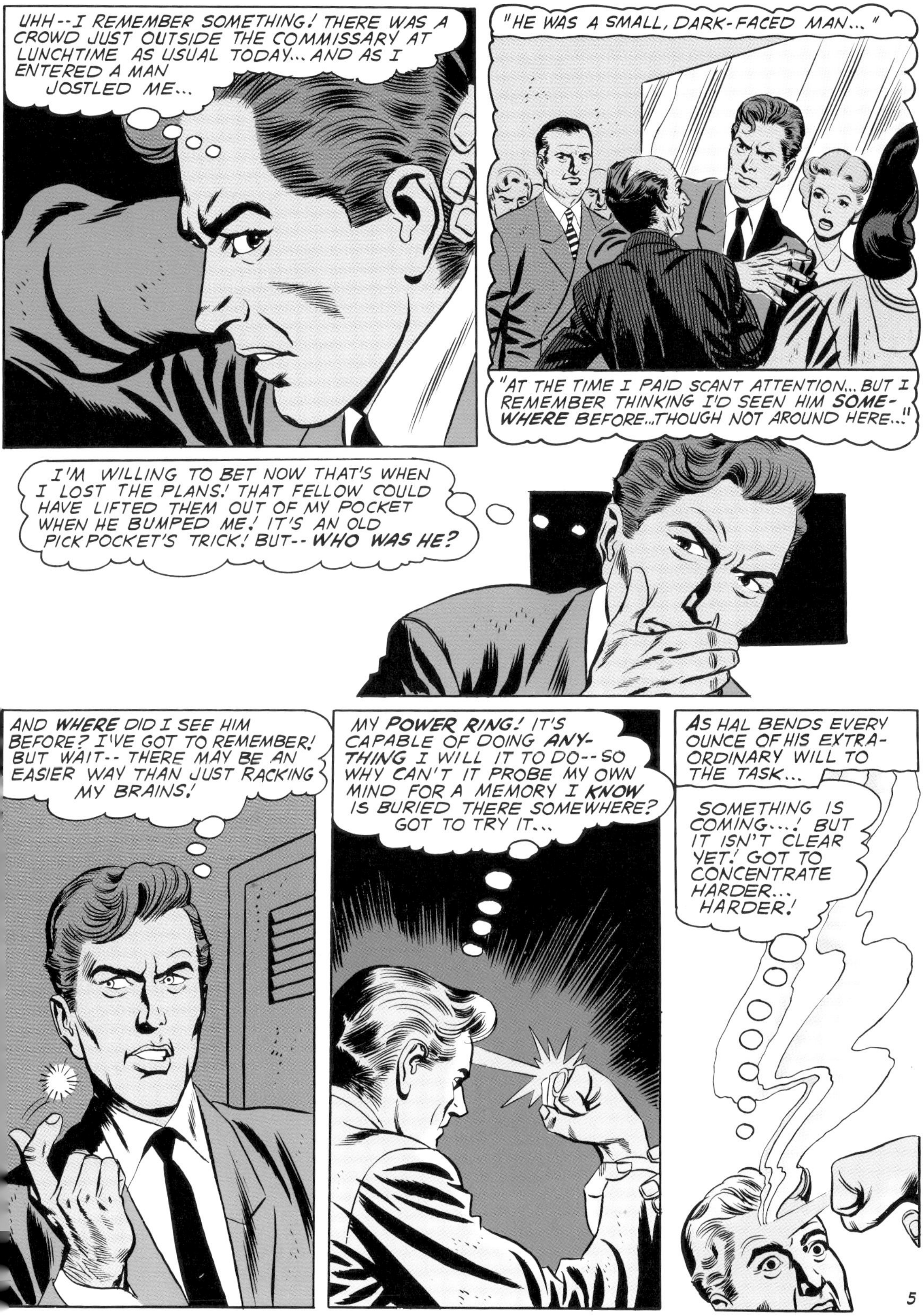
UHH--I REMEMBER SOMETHING! THERE WAS A CROWD JUST OUTSIDE THE COMMISSARY AT LUNCHTIME AS USUAL TODAY... AND AS I ENTERED A MAN JOSTLED ME...
"HE WAS A SMALL, DARK-FACED MAN..."
"AT THE TIME I PAID SCANT ATTENTION... BUT I REMEMBER THINKING I'D SEEN HIM SOME-WHERE BEFORE...THOUGH NOT AROUND HERE...!"
I'M WILLING TO BET NOW THAT'S WHEN I LOST THE PLANS! THAT FELLOW COULD HAVE LIFTED THEM OUT OF MY POCKET WHEN HE BUMPED ME! IT'S AN OLD PICKPOCKET'S TRICK! BUT-- WHO WAS HE?
AND WHERE DID I SEE HIM BEFORE? I'VE GOT TO REMEMBER! BUT WAIT-- THERE MAY BE AN EASIER WAY THAN JUST RACKING MY BRAINS!
MY POWER RING! IT'S CAPABLE OF DOING ANY-THING I WILL IT TO DO--SO WHY CAN'T IT PROBE MY OWN MIND FOR A MEMORY I KNOW IS BURIED THERE SOMEWHERE? GOT TO TRY IT...
AS HAL BENDS EVERY OUNCE OF HIS EXTRA-ORDINARY WILL TO THE TASK...
SOMETHING IS COMING...! BUT IT ISN'T CLEAR YET! GOT TO CONCENTRATE HARDER... HARDER!

THEN SUDDENLY...

GOT HIM! I REMEMBER WHERE I SAW THAT MAN **NOW**-- AT THE *AMUSEMENT PARK!*

IT WAS LAST WEEK-- WHEN I SPENT A FEW HOURS THERE DURING MY DAY OFF! GOLLY! THAT MAY NOT BE MUCH OF A CLUE BUT--

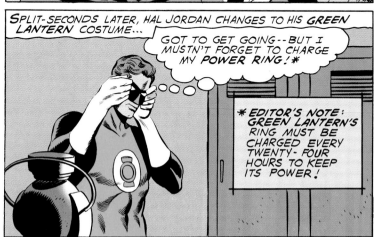

SPLIT-SECONDS LATER, HAL JORDAN CHANGES TO HIS *GREEN LANTERN* COSTUME...

GOT TO GET GOING--BUT I MUSTN'T FORGET TO CHARGE MY *POWER RING!* *

*EDITOR'S NOTE: GREEN LANTERN'S RING MUST BE CHARGED EVERY TWENTY-FOUR HOURS TO KEEP ITS POWER!

IN THE PRIVACY OF HAL JORDAN'S DRESSING ROOM A SOLEMN SCENE TAKES PLACE UNWITNESSED BY ANY INTRUDING EYE...

IN BRIGHTEST DAY... IN BLACKEST NIGHT, NO EVIL SHALL ESCAPE MY SIGHT! LET THOSE WHO WORSHIP EVIL'S MIGHT BEWARE MY POWER-- *GREEN LANTERN'S LIGHT!*

ACROSS THE CITY, MOMENTS AFTER, STREAKS THE AWESOME FIGURE OF THE FAMED *GREEN GLADIATOR*...

MY ONLY HOPE IS THAT THE MAN IS AN *EMPLOYEE* AT THE PARK--OR THAT HE COMES THERE REGULARLY!

ROCKET

CONTINUED ON FOLLOWING PAGE

6

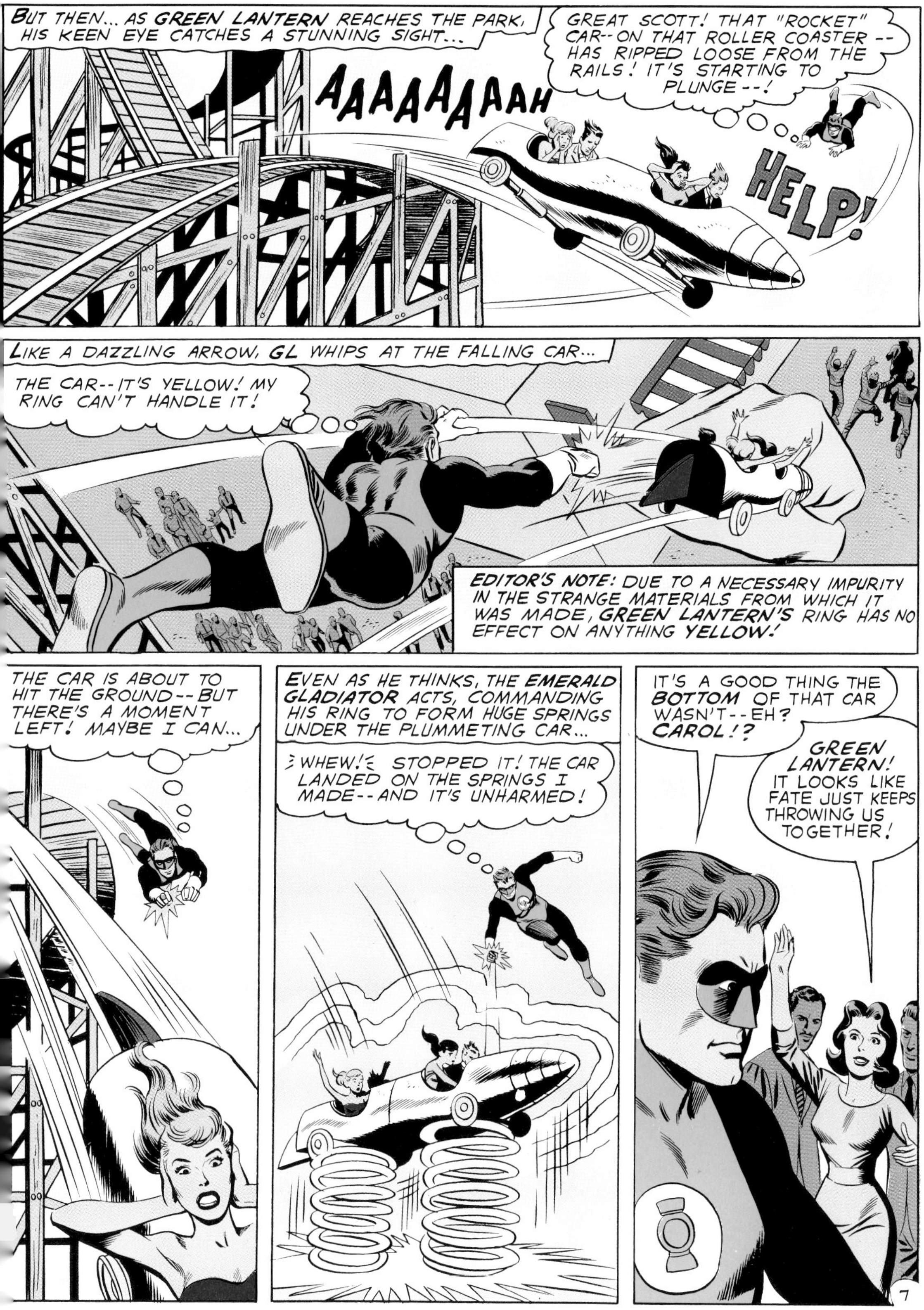
BUT THEN... AS GREEN LANTERN REACHES THE PARK, HIS KEEN EYE CATCHES A STUNNING SIGHT...
GREAT SCOTT! THAT "ROCKET" CAR--ON THAT ROLLER COASTER--HAS RIPPED LOOSE FROM THE RAILS! IT'S STARTING TO PLUNGE--!
AAAAAAAAAH
HELP!
LIKE A DAZZLING ARROW, GL WHIPS AT THE FALLING CAR...
THE CAR--IT'S YELLOW! MY RING CAN'T HANDLE IT!
EDITOR'S NOTE: DUE TO A NECESSARY IMPURITY IN THE STRANGE MATERIALS FROM WHICH IT WAS MADE, GREEN LANTERN'S RING HAS NO EFFECT ON ANYTHING YELLOW!
THE CAR IS ABOUT TO HIT THE GROUND--BUT THERE'S A MOMENT LEFT! MAYBE I CAN...
EVEN AS HE THINKS, THE EMERALD GLADIATOR ACTS, COMMANDING HIS RING TO FORM HUGE SPRINGS UNDER THE PLUMMETING CAR...
WHEW! STOPPED IT! THE CAR LANDED ON THE SPRINGS I MADE--AND IT'S UNHARMED!
IT'S A GOOD THING THE BOTTOM OF THAT CAR WASN'T--EH? CAROL!?
GREEN LANTERN! IT LOOKS LIKE FATE JUST KEEPS THROWING US TOGETHER!
7

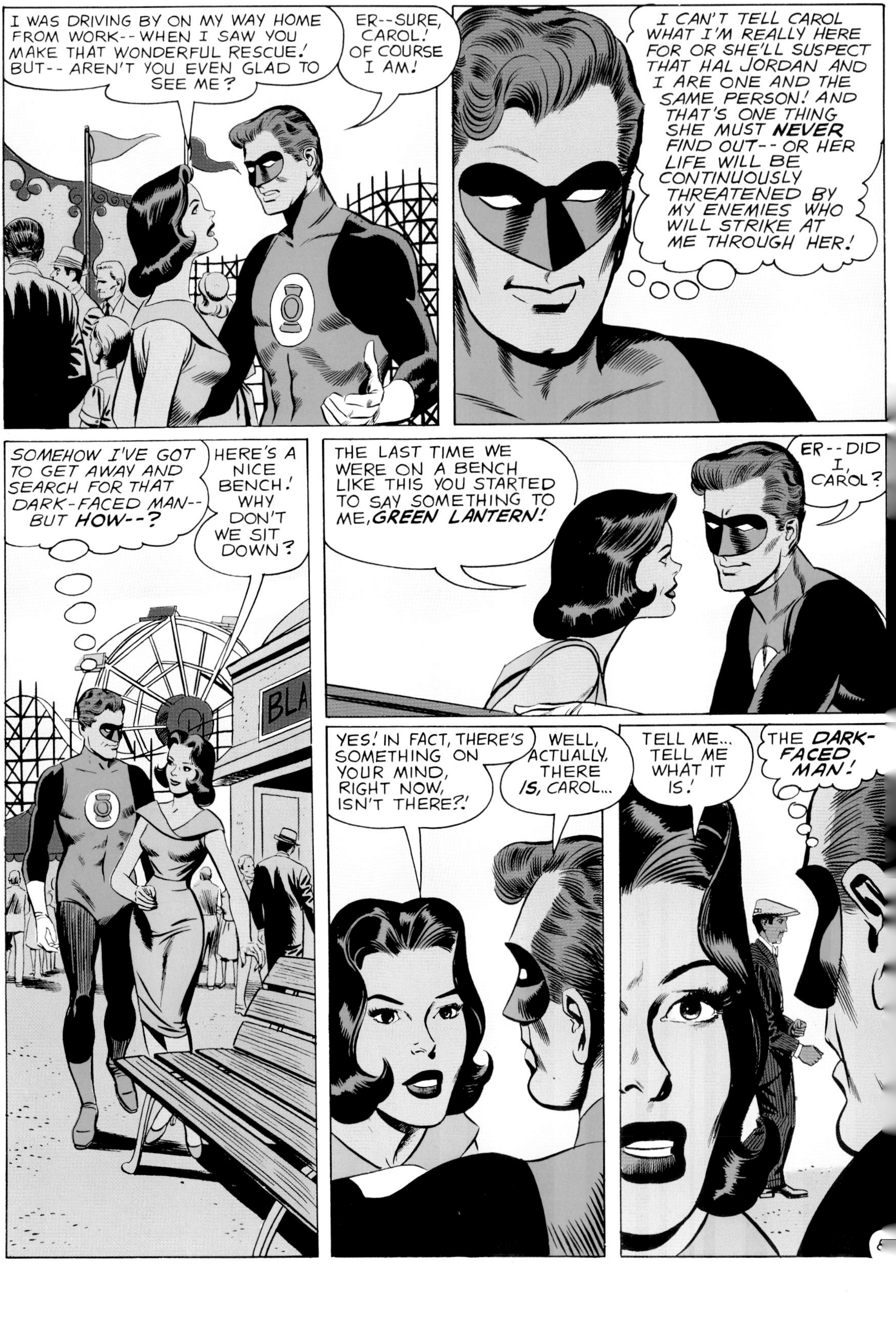

I WAS DRIVING BY ON MY WAY HOME FROM WORK--WHEN I SAW YOU MAKE THAT WONDERFUL RESCUE! BUT--AREN'T YOU EVEN GLAD TO SEE ME?
ER--SURE, CAROL! OF COURSE I AM!
I CAN'T TELL CAROL WHAT I'M REALLY HERE FOR OR SHE'LL SUSPECT THAT HAL JORDAN AND I ARE ONE AND THE SAME PERSON! AND THAT'S ONE THING SHE MUST **NEVER** FIND OUT--OR HER LIFE WILL BE CONTINUOUSLY THREATENED BY MY ENEMIES WHO WILL STRIKE AT ME THROUGH HER!
SOMEHOW I'VE GOT TO GET AWAY AND SEARCH FOR THAT DARK-FACED MAN--BUT **HOW--?**
HERE'S A NICE BENCH! WHY DON'T WE SIT DOWN?
BLA
THE LAST TIME WE WERE ON A BENCH LIKE THIS YOU STARTED TO SAY SOMETHING TO ME, **GREEN LANTERN!**
ER--DID I, CAROL?
YES! IN FACT, THERE'S SOMETHING ON YOUR MIND, RIGHT NOW, ISN'T THERE?!
WELL, ACTUALLY, THERE *IS*, CAROL...
TELL ME... TELL ME WHAT IT IS!
THE ***DARK-FACED MAN!***

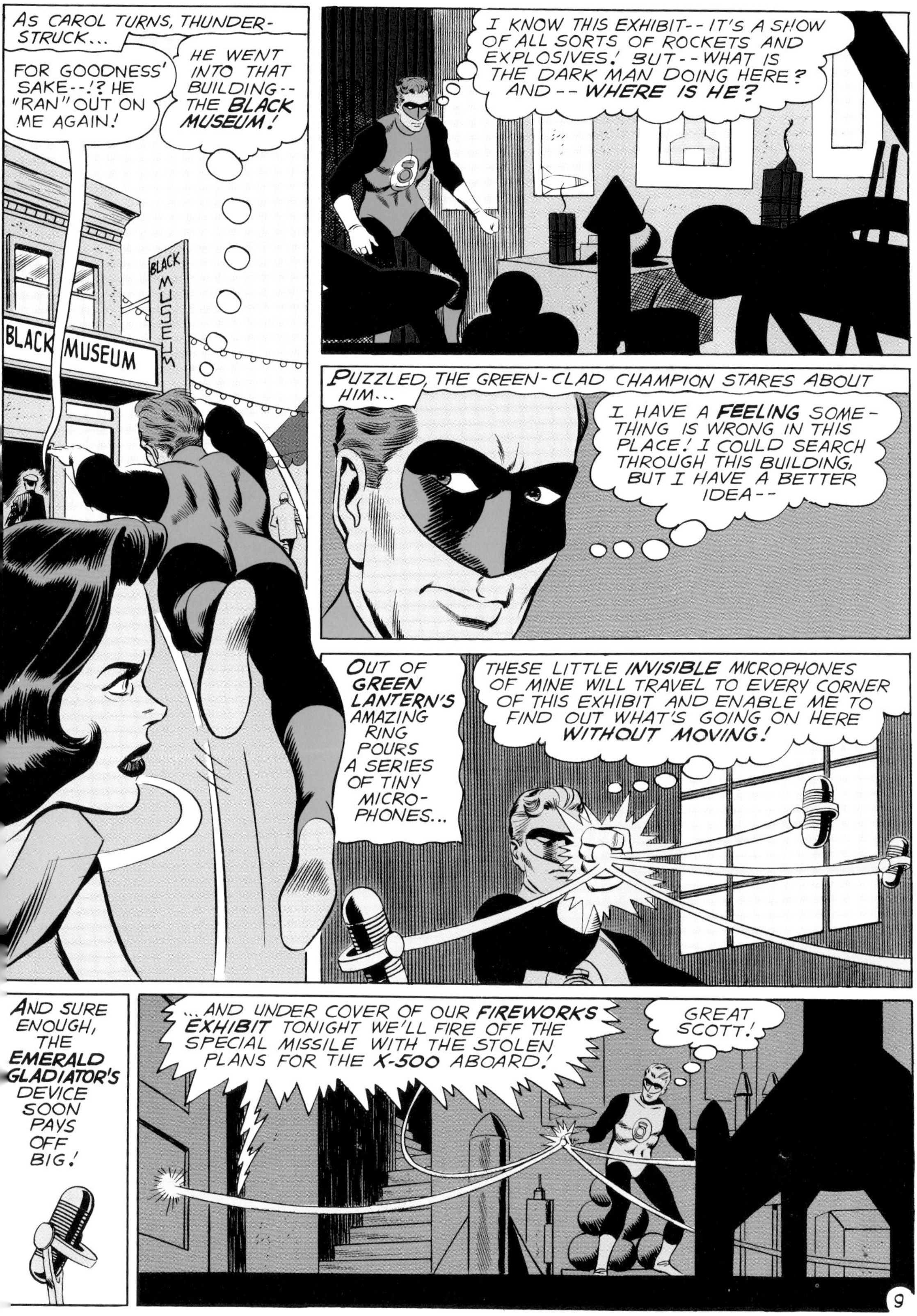
AS CAROL TURNS, THUNDER-STRUCK...
FOR GOODNESS' SAKE--!? HE "RAN" OUT ON ME AGAIN!
HE WENT INTO THAT BUILDING-- THE BLACK MUSEUM!
BLACK MUSEUM
BLACK MUSEUM
I KNOW THIS EXHIBIT-- IT'S A SHOW OF ALL SORTS OF ROCKETS AND EXPLOSIVES! BUT--WHAT IS THE DARK MAN DOING HERE? AND--WHERE IS HE?
PUZZLED, THE GREEN-CLAD CHAMPION STARES ABOUT HIM...
I HAVE A FEELING SOMETHING IS WRONG IN THIS PLACE! I COULD SEARCH THROUGH THIS BUILDING, BUT I HAVE A BETTER IDEA--
OUT OF GREEN LANTERN'S AMAZING RING POURS A SERIES OF TINY MICRO-PHONES...
THESE LITTLE INVISIBLE MICROPHONES OF MINE WILL TRAVEL TO EVERY CORNER OF THIS EXHIBIT AND ENABLE ME TO FIND OUT WHAT'S GOING ON HERE WITHOUT MOVING!
AND SURE ENOUGH, THE EMERALD GLADIATOR'S DEVICE SOON PAYS OFF BIG!
...AND UNDER COVER OF OUR FIREWORKS EXHIBIT TONIGHT WE'LL FIRE OFF THE SPECIAL MISSILE WITH THE STOLEN PLANS FOR THE X-500 ABOARD!
GREAT SCOTT!
9

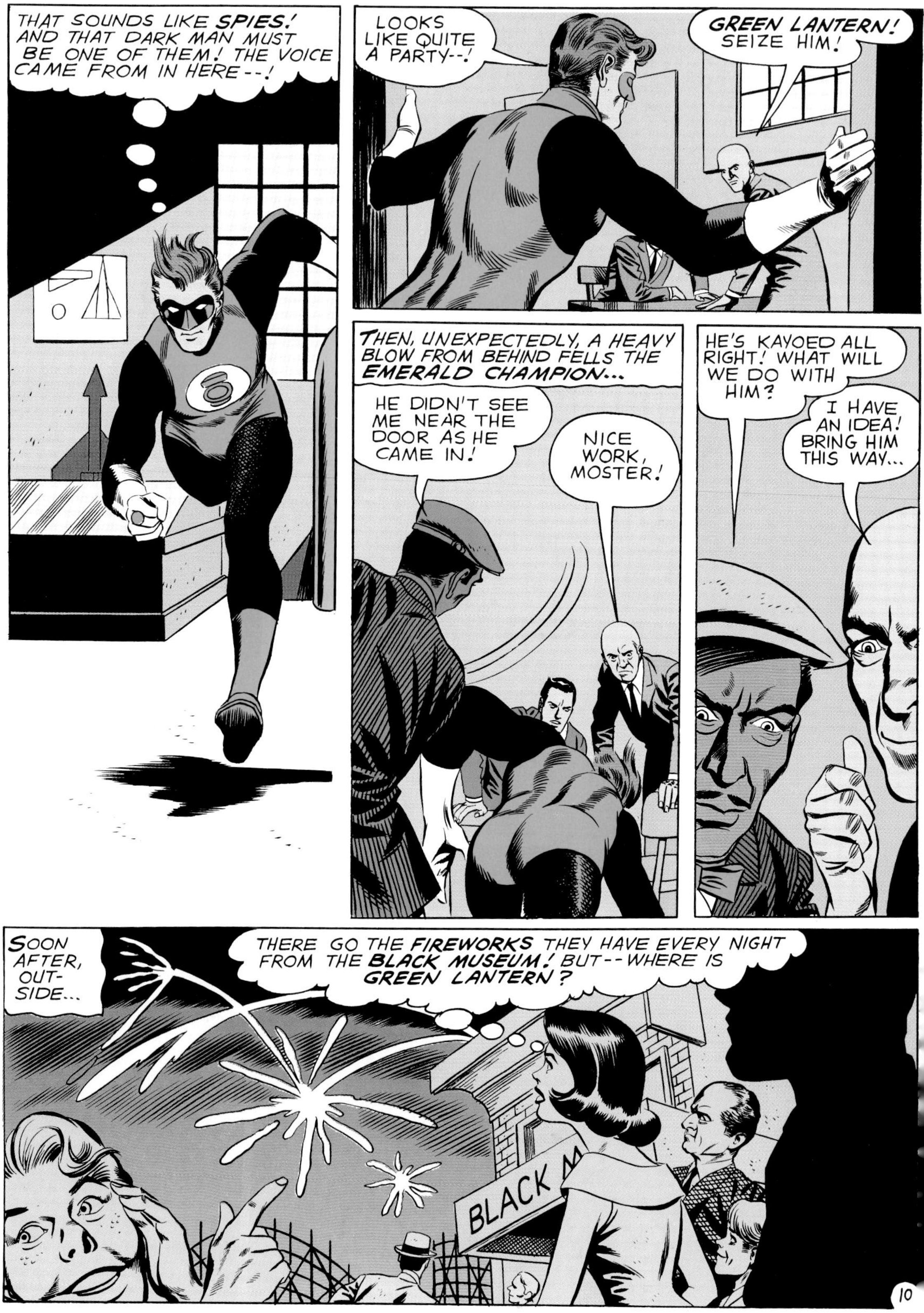
THAT SOUNDS LIKE SPIES! AND THAT DARK MAN MUST BE ONE OF THEM! THE VOICE CAME FROM IN HERE--!
LOOKS LIKE QUITE A PARTY--!
GREEN LANTERN! SEIZE HIM!
THEN, UNEXPECTEDLY, A HEAVY BLOW FROM BEHIND FELLS THE EMERALD CHAMPION...
HE DIDN'T SEE ME NEAR THE DOOR AS HE CAME IN!
NICE WORK, MOSTER!
HE'S KAYOED ALL RIGHT! WHAT WILL WE DO WITH HIM?
I HAVE AN IDEA! BRING HIM THIS WAY...
SOON AFTER, OUT-SIDE...
THERE GO THE FIREWORKS THEY HAVE EVERY NIGHT FROM THE BLACK MUSEUM! BUT--WHERE IS GREEN LANTERN?
BLACK M
10

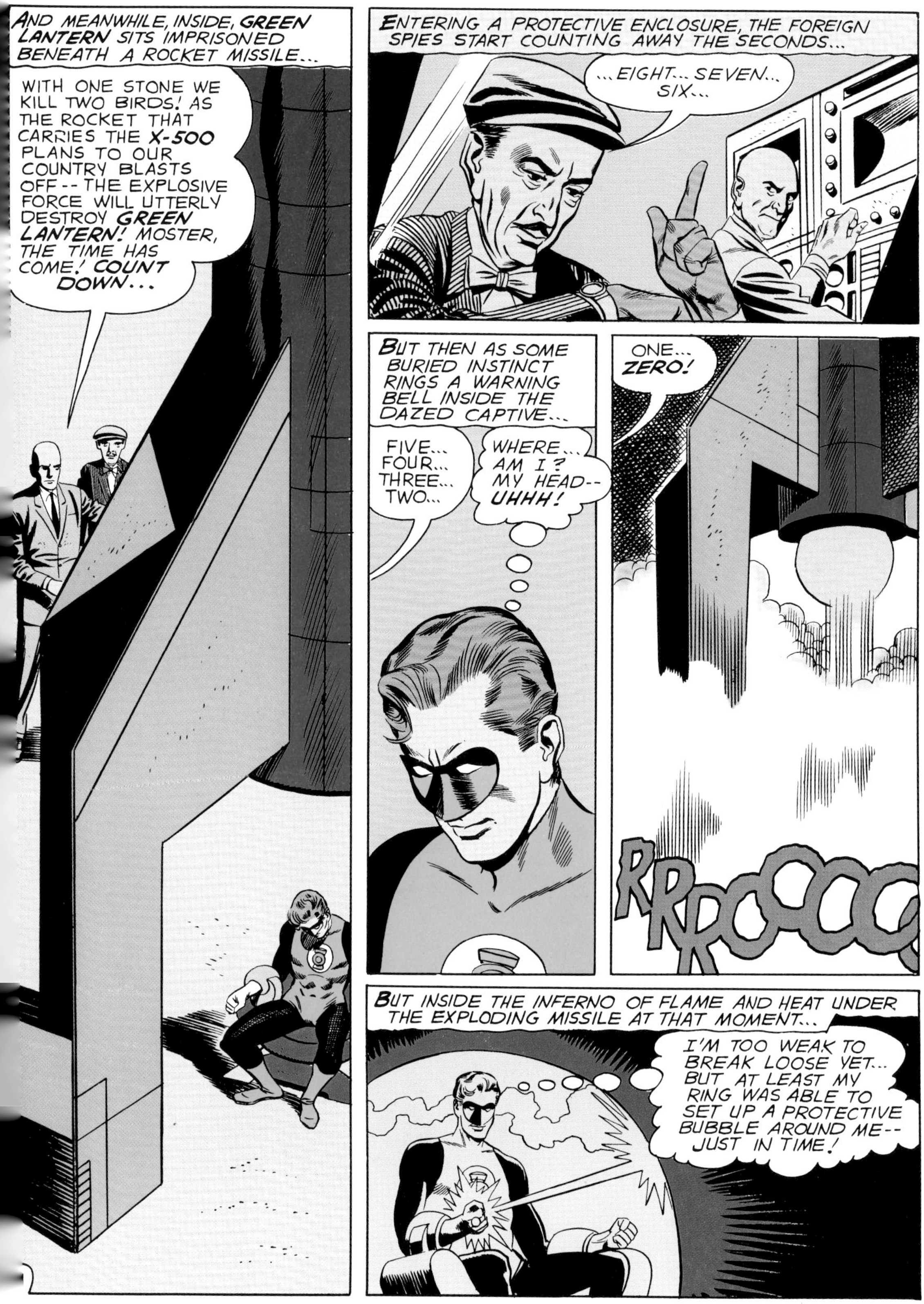
AND MEANWHILE, INSIDE, GREEN LANTERN SITS IMPRISONED BENEATH A ROCKET MISSILE...
WITH ONE STONE WE KILL TWO BIRDS! AS THE ROCKET THAT CARRIES THE X-500 PLANS TO OUR COUNTRY BLASTS OFF -- THE EXPLOSIVE FORCE WILL UTTERLY DESTROY GREEN LANTERN! MOSTER, THE TIME HAS COME! COUNT DOWN...
ENTERING A PROTECTIVE ENCLOSURE, THE FOREIGN SPIES START COUNTING AWAY THE SECONDS...
...EIGHT... SEVEN... SIX...
BUT THEN AS SOME BURIED INSTINCT RINGS A WARNING BELL INSIDE THE DAZED CAPTIVE...
FIVE... FOUR... THREE... TWO...
WHERE... AM I? MY HEAD-- UHHH!
ONE... ZERO!
RRROOOOO
BUT INSIDE THE INFERNO OF FLAME AND HEAT UNDER THE EXPLODING MISSILE AT THAT MOMENT...
I'M TOO WEAK TO BREAK LOOSE YET... BUT AT LEAST MY RING WAS ABLE TO SET UP A PROTECTIVE BUBBLE AROUND ME-- JUST IN TIME!

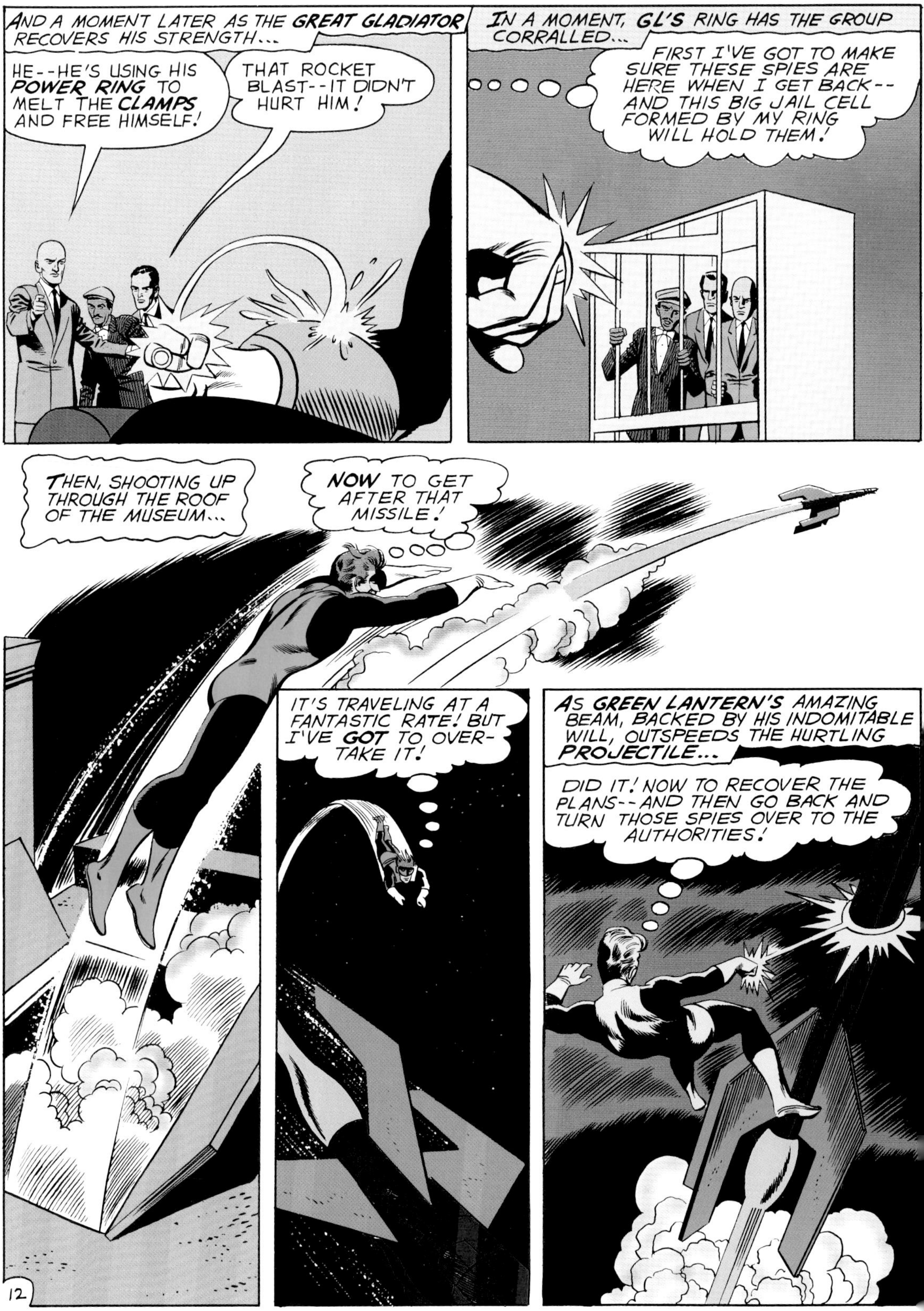
AND A MOMENT LATER AS THE GREAT GLADIATOR RECOVERS HIS STRENGTH...
HE--HE'S USING HIS POWER RING TO MELT THE CLAMPS AND FREE HIMSELF!
THAT ROCKET BLAST--IT DIDN'T HURT HIM!
IN A MOMENT, GL'S RING HAS THE GROUP CORRALLED...
FIRST I'VE GOT TO MAKE SURE THESE SPIES ARE HERE WHEN I GET BACK--AND THIS BIG JAIL CELL FORMED BY MY RING WILL HOLD THEM!
THEN, SHOOTING UP THROUGH THE ROOF OF THE MUSEUM...
NOW TO GET AFTER THAT MISSILE!
IT'S TRAVELING AT A FANTASTIC RATE! BUT I'VE GOT TO OVER-TAKE IT!
AS GREEN LANTERN'S AMAZING BEAM, BACKED BY HIS INDOMITABLE WILL, OUTSPEEDS THE HURTLING PROJECTILE...
DID IT! NOW TO RECOVER THE PLANS--AND THEN GO BACK AND TURN THOSE SPIES OVER TO THE AUTHORITIES!
12

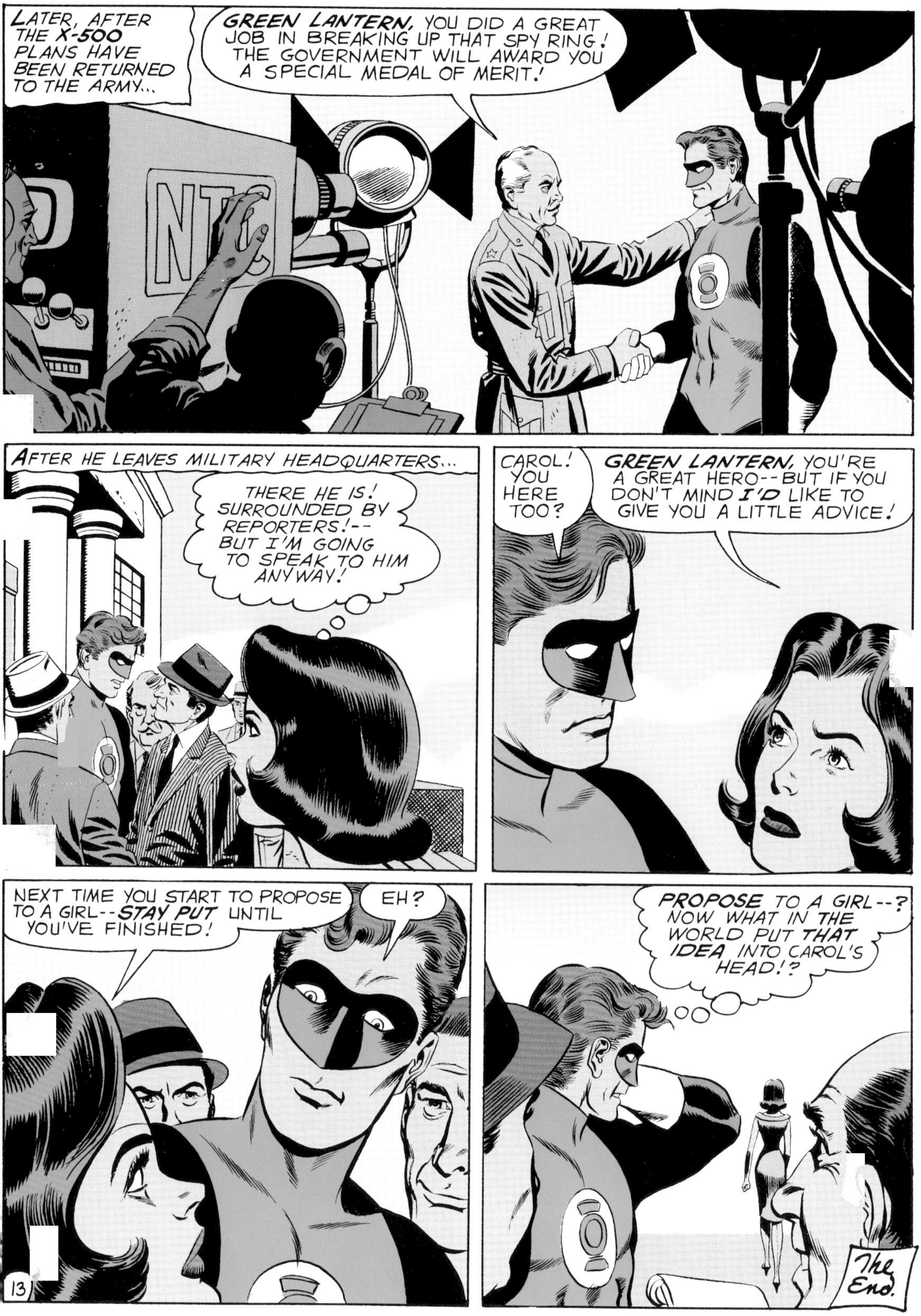
LATER, AFTER THE X-500 PLANS HAVE BEEN RETURNED TO THE ARMY...
GREEN LANTERN, YOU DID A GREAT JOB IN BREAKING UP THAT SPY RING! THE GOVERNMENT WILL AWARD YOU A SPECIAL MEDAL OF MERIT!
NTC
AFTER HE LEAVES MILITARY HEADQUARTERS...
THERE HE IS! SURROUNDED BY REPORTERS!-- BUT I'M GOING TO SPEAK TO HIM ANYWAY!
CAROL! YOU HERE TOO?
GREEN LANTERN, YOU'RE A GREAT HERO-- BUT IF YOU DON'T MIND I'D LIKE TO GIVE YOU A LITTLE ADVICE!
NEXT TIME YOU START TO PROPOSE TO A GIRL--STAY PUT UNTIL YOU'VE FINISHED!
EH?
PROPOSE TO A GIRL--? NOW WHAT IN THE WORLD PUT THAT IDEA INTO CAROL'S HEAD!?
The End.
13

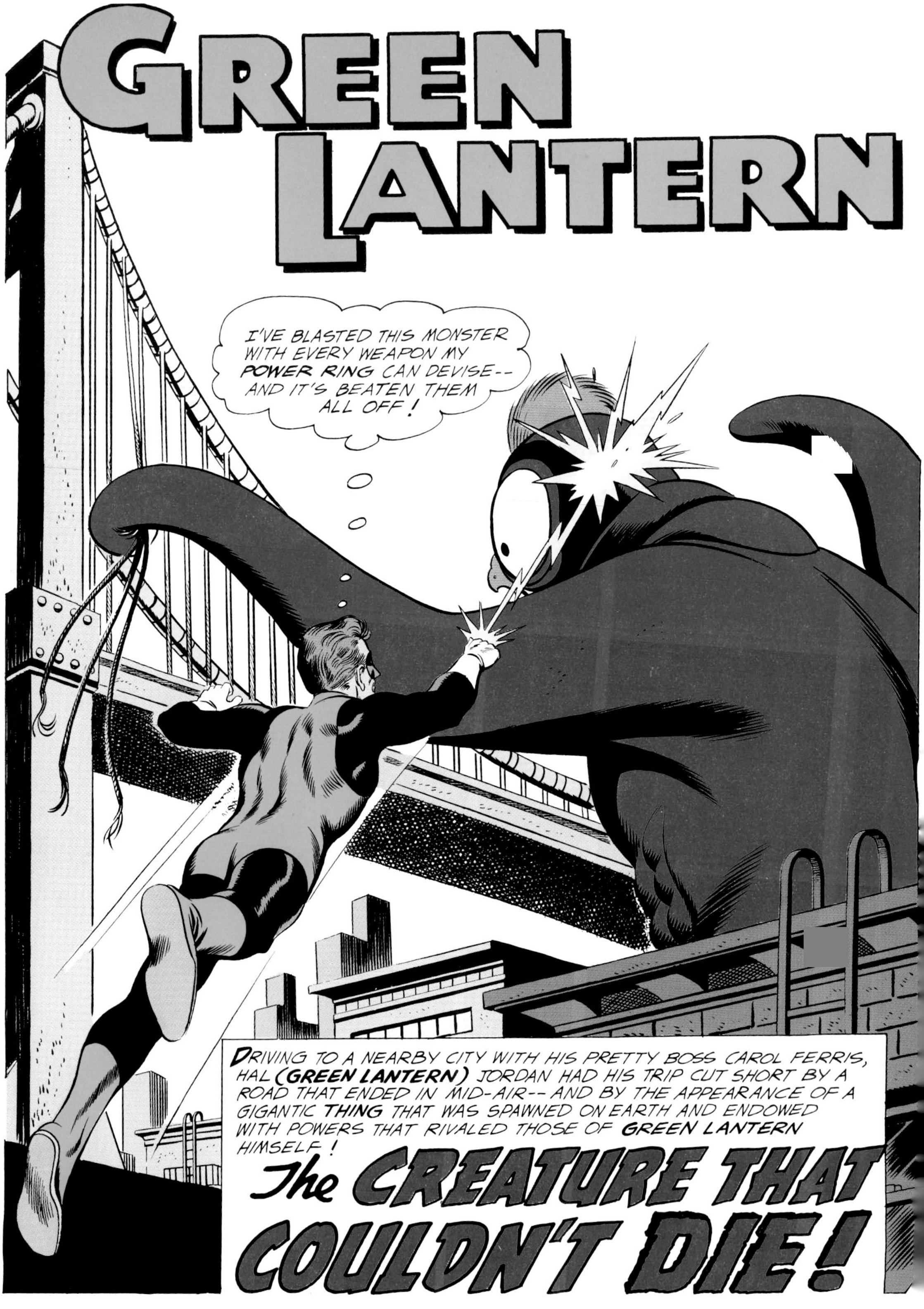
GREEN LANTERN
I'VE BLASTED THIS MONSTER WITH EVERY WEAPON MY POWER RING CAN DEVISE-- AND IT'S BEATEN THEM ALL OFF!
DRIVING TO A NEARBY CITY WITH HIS PRETTY BOSS CAROL FERRIS, HAL (GREEN LANTERN) JORDAN HAD HIS TRIP CUT SHORT BY A ROAD THAT ENDED IN MID-AIR-- AND BY THE APPEARANCE OF A GIGANTIC THING THAT WAS SPAWNED ON EARTH AND ENDOWED WITH POWERS THAT RIVALED THOSE OF GREEN LANTERN HIMSELF!
The CREATURE THAT COULDN'T DIE!

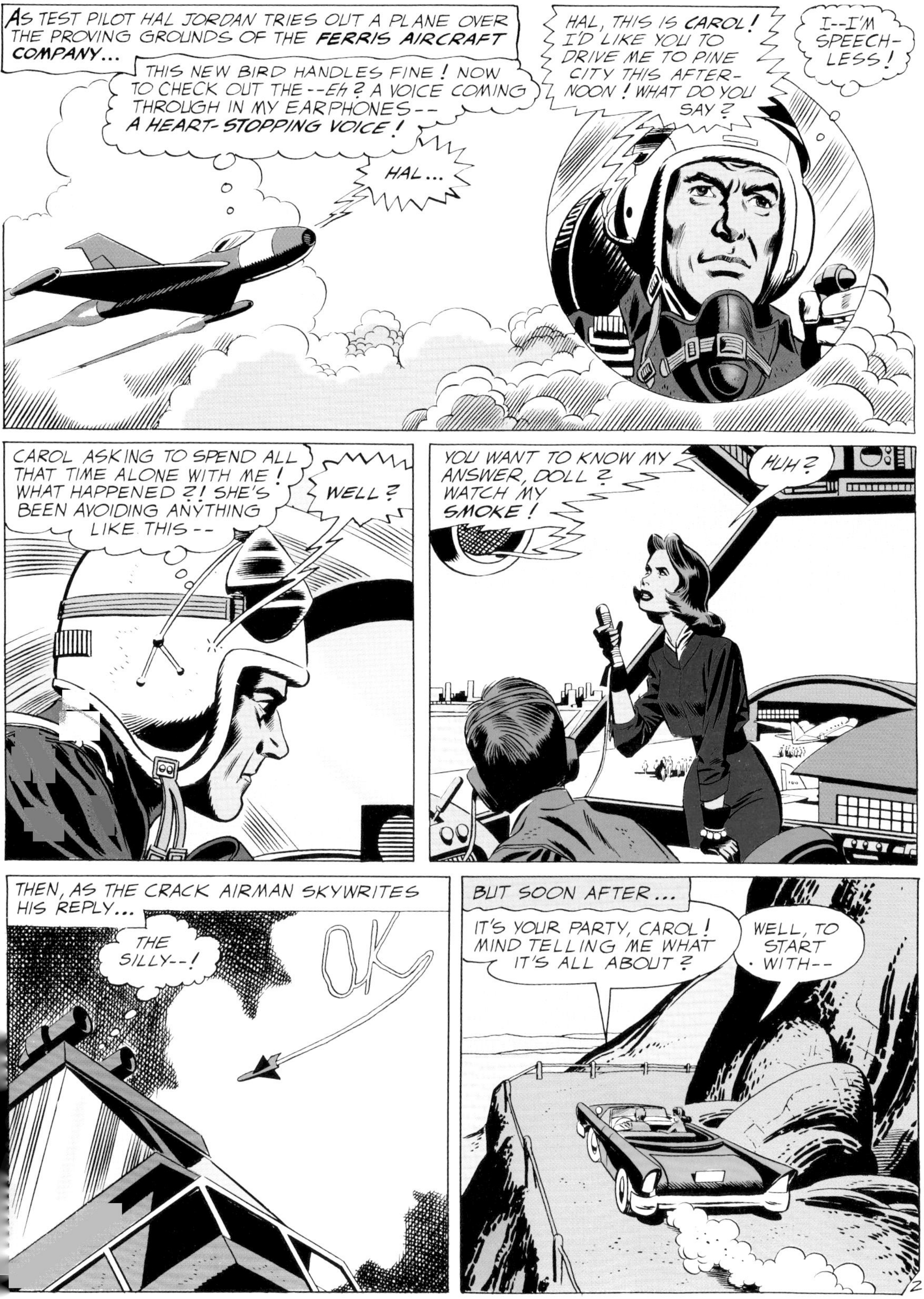
AS TEST PILOT HAL JORDAN TRIES OUT A PLANE OVER THE PROVING GROUNDS OF THE FERRIS AIRCRAFT COMPANY...
THIS NEW BIRD HANDLES FINE! NOW TO CHECK OUT THE--Eh? A VOICE COMING THROUGH IN MY EARPHONES-- A HEART-STOPPING VOICE!
HAL...
HAL, THIS IS CAROL! I'D LIKE YOU TO DRIVE ME TO PINE CITY THIS AFTERNOON! WHAT DO YOU SAY?
I--I'M SPEECHLESS!
CAROL ASKING TO SPEND ALL THAT TIME ALONE WITH ME! WHAT HAPPENED?! SHE'S BEEN AVOIDING ANYTHING LIKE THIS--
WELL?
YOU WANT TO KNOW MY ANSWER, DOLL? WATCH MY SMOKE!
HUH?
THEN, AS THE CRACK AIRMAN SKYWRITES HIS REPLY...
THE SILLY--!
OK
BUT SOON AFTER...
IT'S YOUR PARTY, CAROL! MIND TELLING ME WHAT IT'S ALL ABOUT?
WELL, TO START WITH--
2

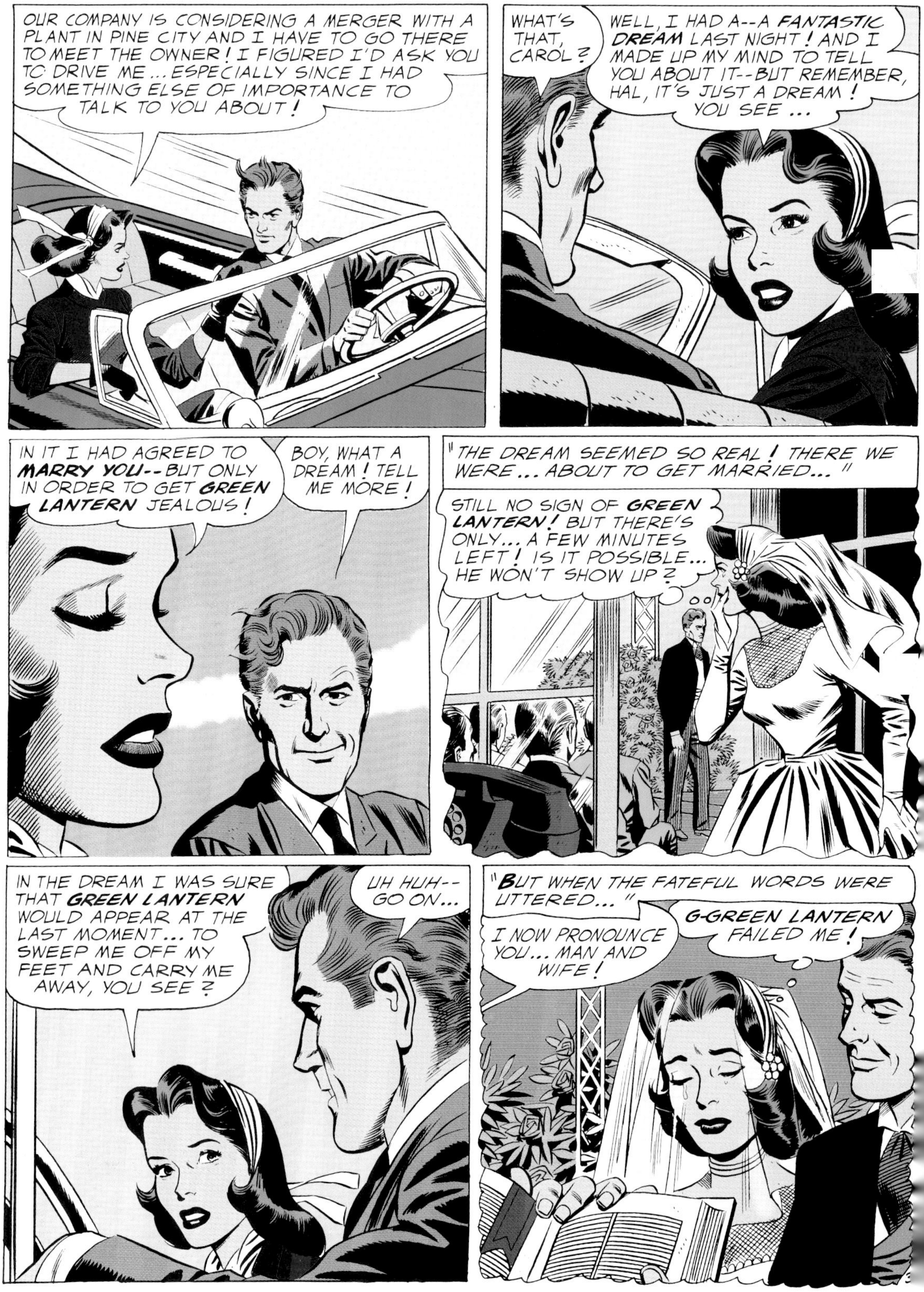
OUR COMPANY IS CONSIDERING A MERGER WITH A PLANT IN PINE CITY AND I HAVE TO GO THERE TO MEET THE OWNER! I FIGURED I'D ASK YOU TO DRIVE ME... ESPECIALLY SINCE I HAD SOMETHING ELSE OF IMPORTANCE TO TALK TO YOU ABOUT!
WHAT'S THAT, CAROL?
WELL, I HAD A--A FANTASTIC DREAM LAST NIGHT! AND I MADE UP MY MIND TO TELL YOU ABOUT IT--BUT REMEMBER, HAL, IT'S JUST A DREAM! YOU SEE...
IN IT I HAD AGREED TO MARRY YOU--BUT ONLY IN ORDER TO GET GREEN LANTERN JEALOUS!
BOY, WHAT A DREAM! TELL ME MORE!
"THE DREAM SEEMED SO REAL! THERE WE WERE... ABOUT TO GET MARRIED..."
STILL NO SIGN OF GREEN LANTERN! BUT THERE'S ONLY... A FEW MINUTES LEFT! IS IT POSSIBLE... HE WON'T SHOW UP?
IN THE DREAM I WAS SURE THAT GREEN LANTERN WOULD APPEAR AT THE LAST MOMENT... TO SWEEP ME OFF MY FEET AND CARRY ME AWAY, YOU SEE?
UH HUH--GO ON...
"BUT WHEN THE FATEFUL WORDS WERE UTTERED..."
I NOW PRONOUNCE YOU... MAN AND WIFE!
G-GREEN LANTERN FAILED ME!

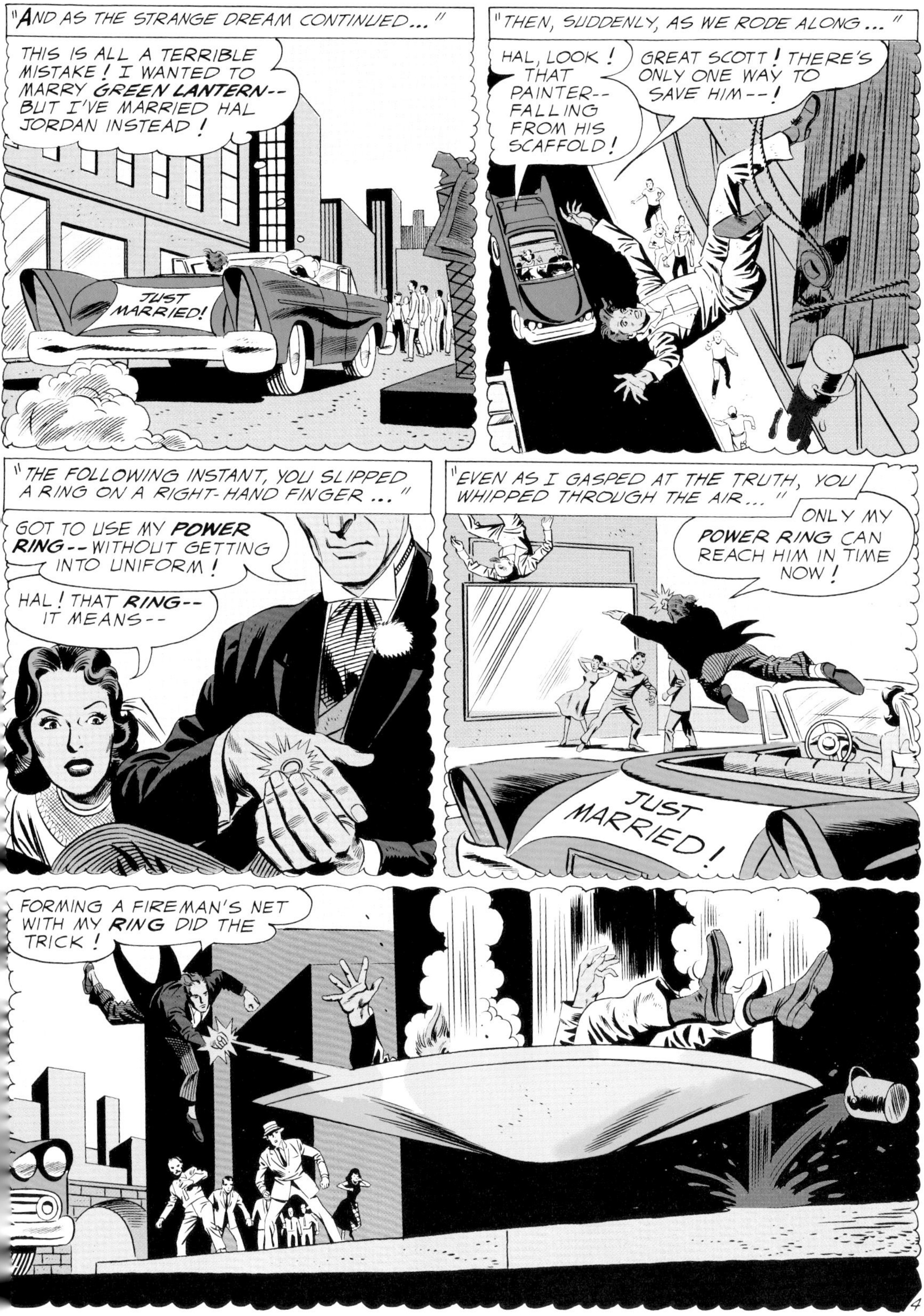
"AND AS THE STRANGE DREAM CONTINUED..."
THIS IS ALL A TERRIBLE MISTAKE! I WANTED TO MARRY GREEN LANTERN-- BUT I'VE MARRIED HAL JORDAN INSTEAD!
JUST MARRIED!
"THEN, SUDDENLY, AS WE RODE ALONG..."
HAL, LOOK! THAT PAINTER-- FALLING FROM HIS SCAFFOLD!
GREAT SCOTT! THERE'S ONLY ONE WAY TO SAVE HIM--!
"THE FOLLOWING INSTANT, YOU SLIPPED A RING ON A RIGHT-HAND FINGER..."
GOT TO USE MY POWER RING--WITHOUT GETTING INTO UNIFORM!
HAL! THAT RING-- IT MEANS--
"EVEN AS I GASPED AT THE TRUTH, YOU WHIPPED THROUGH THE AIR..."
ONLY MY POWER RING CAN REACH HIM IN TIME NOW!
JUST MARRIED!
FORMING A FIREMAN'S NET WITH MY RING DID THE TRICK!
4

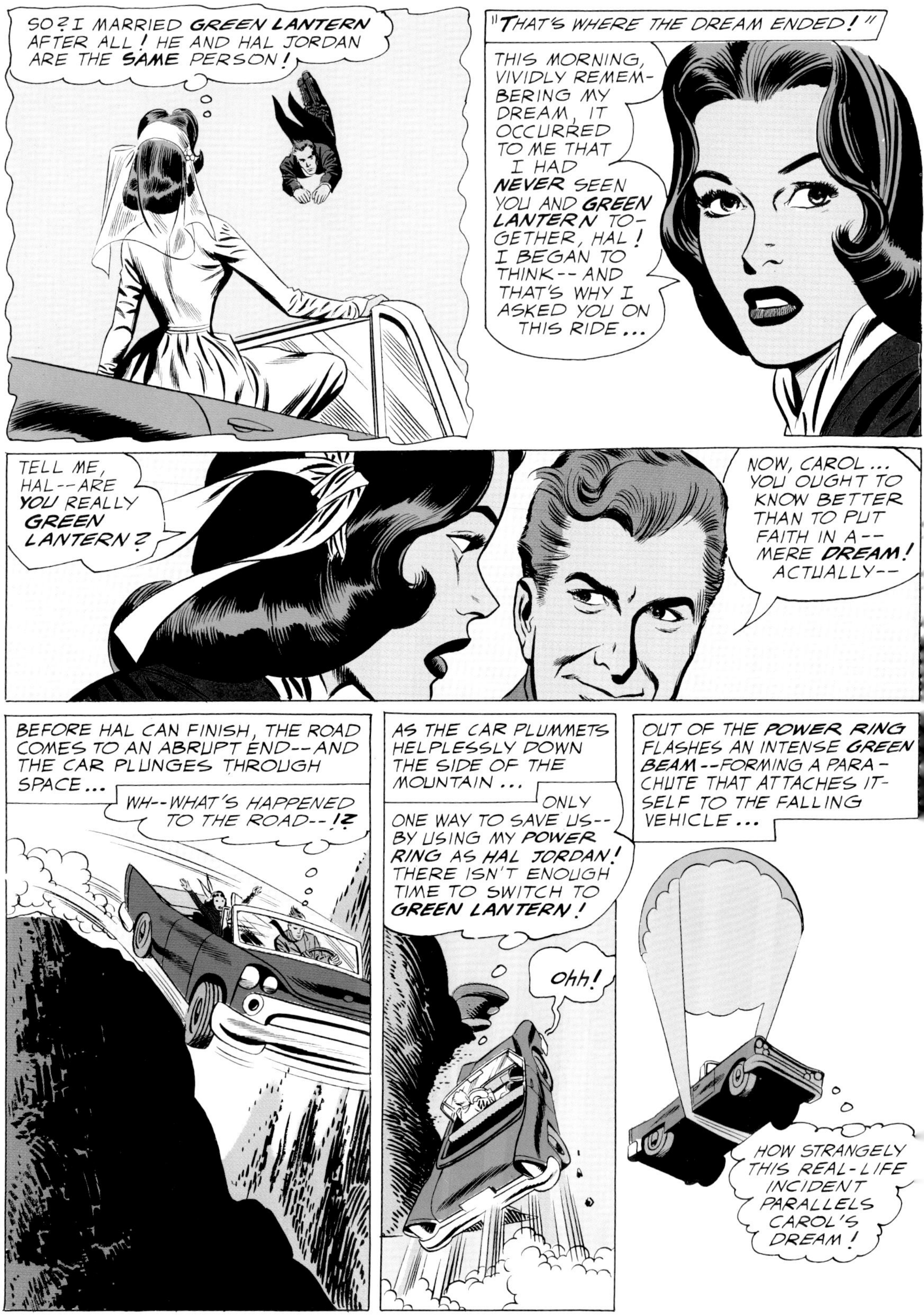
SO?I MARRIED GREEN LANTERN AFTER ALL! HE AND HAL JORDAN ARE THE SAME PERSON!
"THAT'S WHERE THE DREAM ENDED!"
THIS MORNING, VIVIDLY REMEMBERING MY DREAM, IT OCCURRED TO ME THAT I HAD NEVER SEEN YOU AND GREEN LANTERN TOGETHER, HAL! I BEGAN TO THINK--AND THAT'S WHY I ASKED YOU ON THIS RIDE...
TELL ME, HAL--ARE YOU REALLY GREEN LANTERN?
NOW, CAROL... YOU OUGHT TO KNOW BETTER THAN TO PUT FAITH IN A--MERE DREAM! ACTUALLY--
BEFORE HAL CAN FINISH, THE ROAD COMES TO AN ABRUPT END--AND THE CAR PLUNGES THROUGH SPACE...
WH--WHAT'S HAPPENED TO THE ROAD--!?
AS THE CAR PLUMMETS HELPLESSLY DOWN THE SIDE OF THE MOUNTAIN...
ONLY ONE WAY TO SAVE US--BY USING MY POWER RING AS HAL JORDAN! THERE ISN'T ENOUGH TIME TO SWITCH TO GREEN LANTERN!
Ohh!
OUT OF THE POWER RING FLASHES AN INTENSE GREEN BEAM--FORMING A PARACHUTE THAT ATTACHES ITSELF TO THE FALLING VEHICLE...
HOW STRANGELY THIS REAL-LIFE INCIDENT PARALLELS CAROL'S DREAM!

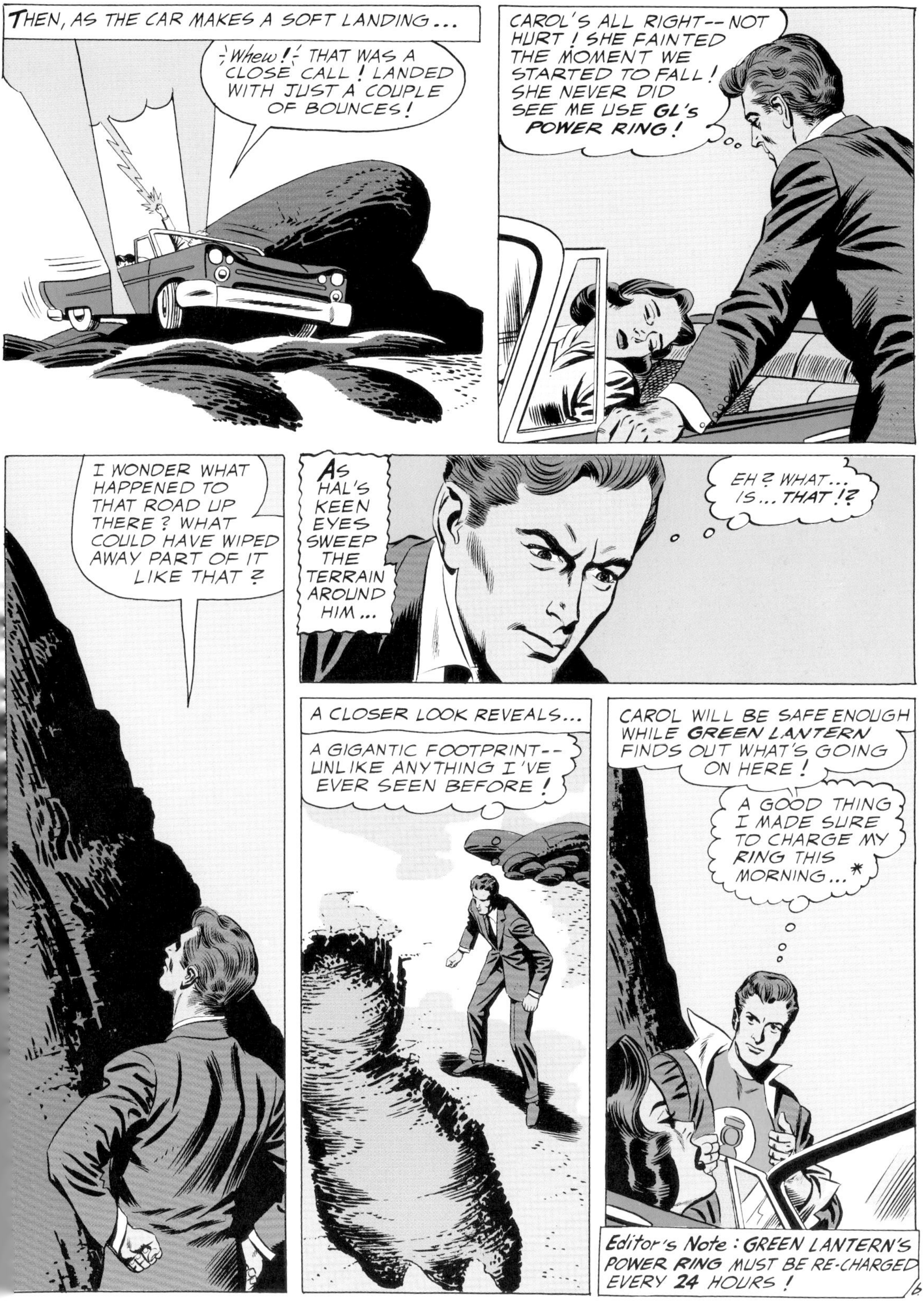
THEN, AS THE CAR MAKES A SOFT LANDING...
Whew! THAT WAS A CLOSE CALL! LANDED WITH JUST A COUPLE OF BOUNCES!
CAROL'S ALL RIGHT-- NOT HURT! SHE FAINTED THE MOMENT WE STARTED TO FALL! SHE NEVER DID SEE ME USE GL's POWER RING!
I WONDER WHAT HAPPENED TO THAT ROAD UP THERE? WHAT COULD HAVE WIPED AWAY PART OF IT LIKE THAT?
AS HAL'S KEEN EYES SWEEP THE TERRAIN AROUND HIM...
EH? WHAT... IS... THAT!?
A CLOSER LOOK REVEALS...
A GIGANTIC FOOTPRINT-- UNLIKE ANYTHING I'VE EVER SEEN BEFORE!
CAROL WILL BE SAFE ENOUGH WHILE GREEN LANTERN FINDS OUT WHAT'S GOING ON HERE!
A GOOD THING I MADE SURE TO CHARGE MY RING THIS MORNING...*
Editor's Note: GREEN LANTERN'S POWER RING MUST BE RE-CHARGED EVERY 24 HOURS!
6

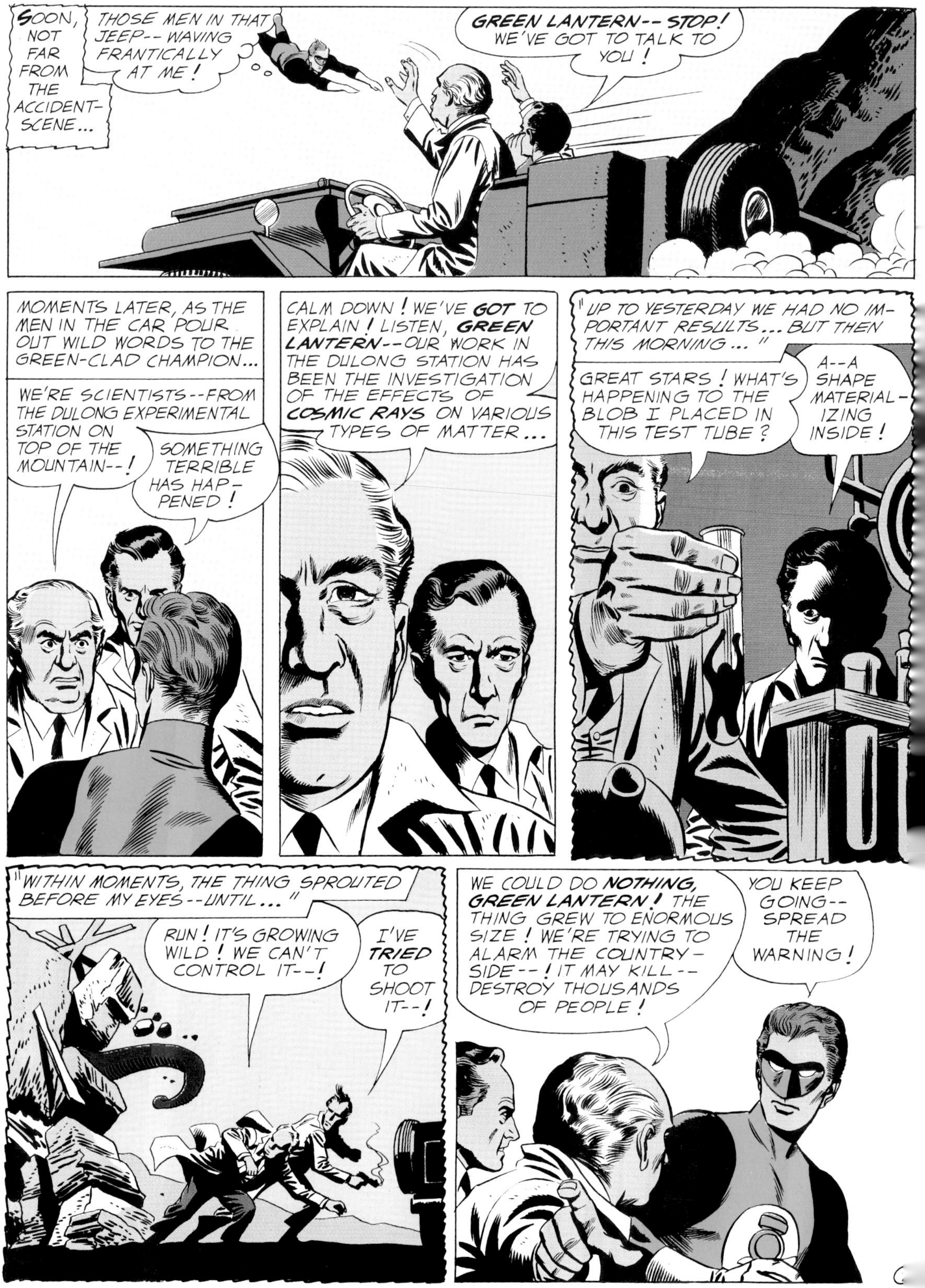
SOON, NOT FAR FROM THE ACCIDENT-SCENE...
THOSE MEN IN THAT JEEP-- WAVING FRANTICALLY AT ME!
GREEN LANTERN-- STOP! WE'VE GOT TO TALK TO YOU!
MOMENTS LATER, AS THE MEN IN THE CAR POUR OUT WILD WORDS TO THE GREEN-CLAD CHAMPION...
WE'RE SCIENTISTS--FROM THE DULONG EXPERIMENTAL STATION ON TOP OF THE MOUNTAIN--!
SOMETHING TERRIBLE HAS HAPPENED!
CALM DOWN! WE'VE GOT TO EXPLAIN! LISTEN, GREEN LANTERN--OUR WORK IN THE DULONG STATION HAS BEEN THE INVESTIGATION OF THE EFFECTS OF COSMIC RAYS ON VARIOUS TYPES OF MATTER...
"UP TO YESTERDAY WE HAD NO IMPORTANT RESULTS... BUT THEN THIS MORNING..."
GREAT STARS! WHAT'S HAPPENING TO THE BLOB I PLACED IN THIS TEST TUBE?
A--A SHAPE MATERIALIZING INSIDE!
"WITHIN MOMENTS, THE THING SPROUTED BEFORE MY EYES--UNTIL..."
RUN! IT'S GROWING WILD! WE CAN'T CONTROL IT--!
I'VE TRIED TO SHOOT IT--!
WE COULD DO NOTHING, GREEN LANTERN! THE THING GREW TO ENORMOUS SIZE! WE'RE TRYING TO ALARM THE COUNTRYSIDE--! IT MAY KILL--DESTROY THOUSANDS OF PEOPLE!
YOU KEEP GOING--SPREAD THE WARNING!

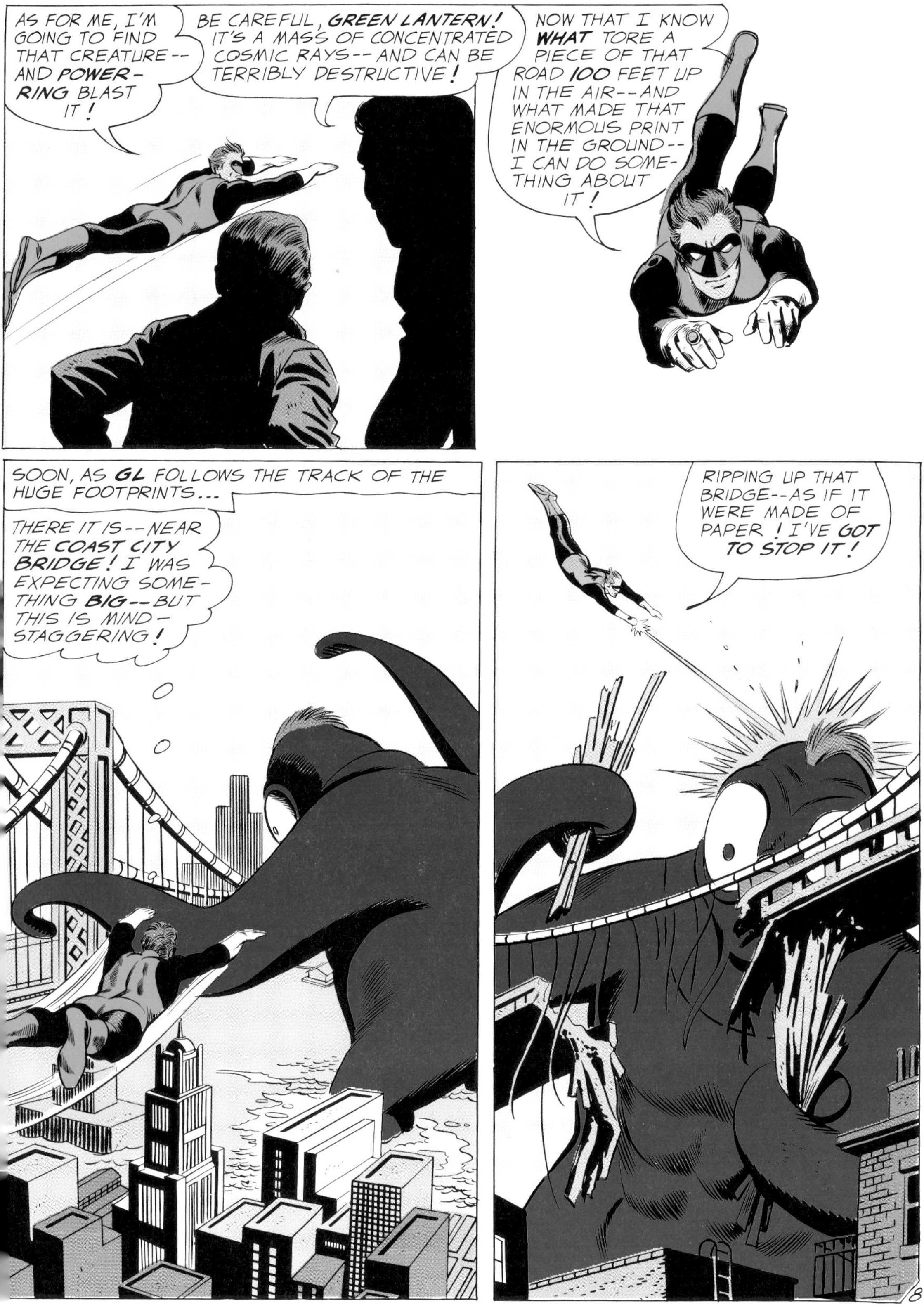
AS FOR ME, I'M GOING TO FIND THAT CREATURE-- AND POWER-RING BLAST IT!
BE CAREFUL, GREEN LANTERN! IT'S A MASS OF CONCENTRATED COSMIC RAYS-- AND CAN BE TERRIBLY DESTRUCTIVE!
NOW THAT I KNOW WHAT TORE A PIECE OF THAT ROAD 100 FEET UP IN THE AIR--AND WHAT MADE THAT ENORMOUS PRINT IN THE GROUND-- I CAN DO SOMETHING ABOUT IT!
SOON, AS GL FOLLOWS THE TRACK OF THE HUGE FOOTPRINTS...
THERE IT IS--NEAR THE COAST CITY BRIDGE! I WAS EXPECTING SOMETHING BIG--BUT THIS IS MIND-STAGGERING!
RIPPING UP THAT BRIDGE--AS IF IT WERE MADE OF PAPER! I'VE GOT TO STOP IT!
8

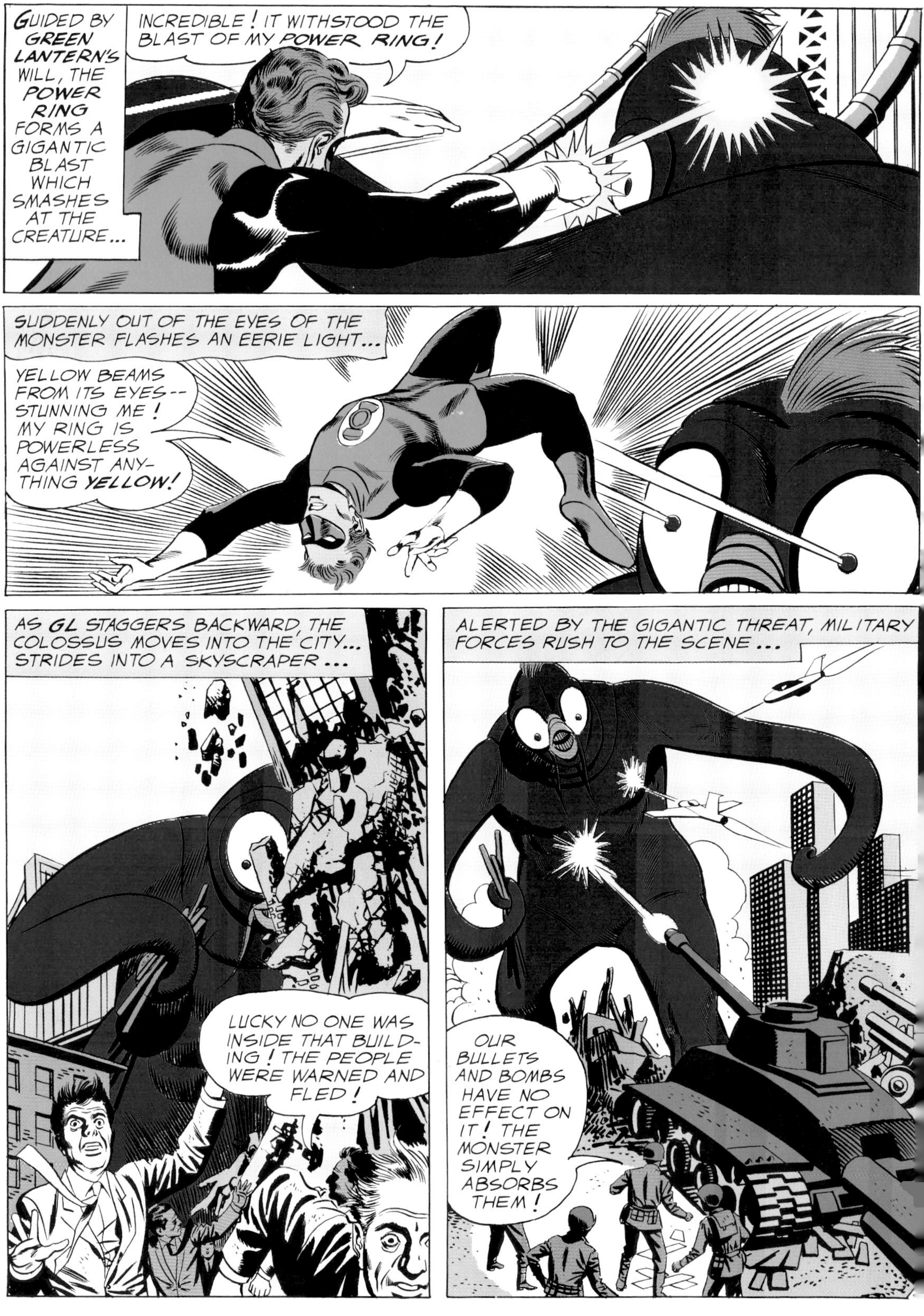
GUIDED BY GREEN LANTERN'S WILL, THE POWER RING FORMS A GIGANTIC BLAST WHICH SMASHES AT THE CREATURE...
INCREDIBLE! IT WITHSTOOD THE BLAST OF MY POWER RING!
SUDDENLY OUT OF THE EYES OF THE MONSTER FLASHES AN EERIE LIGHT...
YELLOW BEAMS FROM ITS EYES--STUNNING ME! MY RING IS POWERLESS AGAINST ANYTHING YELLOW!
AS GL STAGGERS BACKWARD, THE COLOSSUS MOVES INTO THE CITY... STRIDES INTO A SKYSCRAPER...
LUCKY NO ONE WAS INSIDE THAT BUILDING! THE PEOPLE WERE WARNED AND FLED!
ALERTED BY THE GIGANTIC THREAT, MILITARY FORCES RUSH TO THE SCENE...
OUR BULLETS AND BOMBS HAVE NO EFFECT ON IT! THE MONSTER SIMPLY ABSORBS THEM!

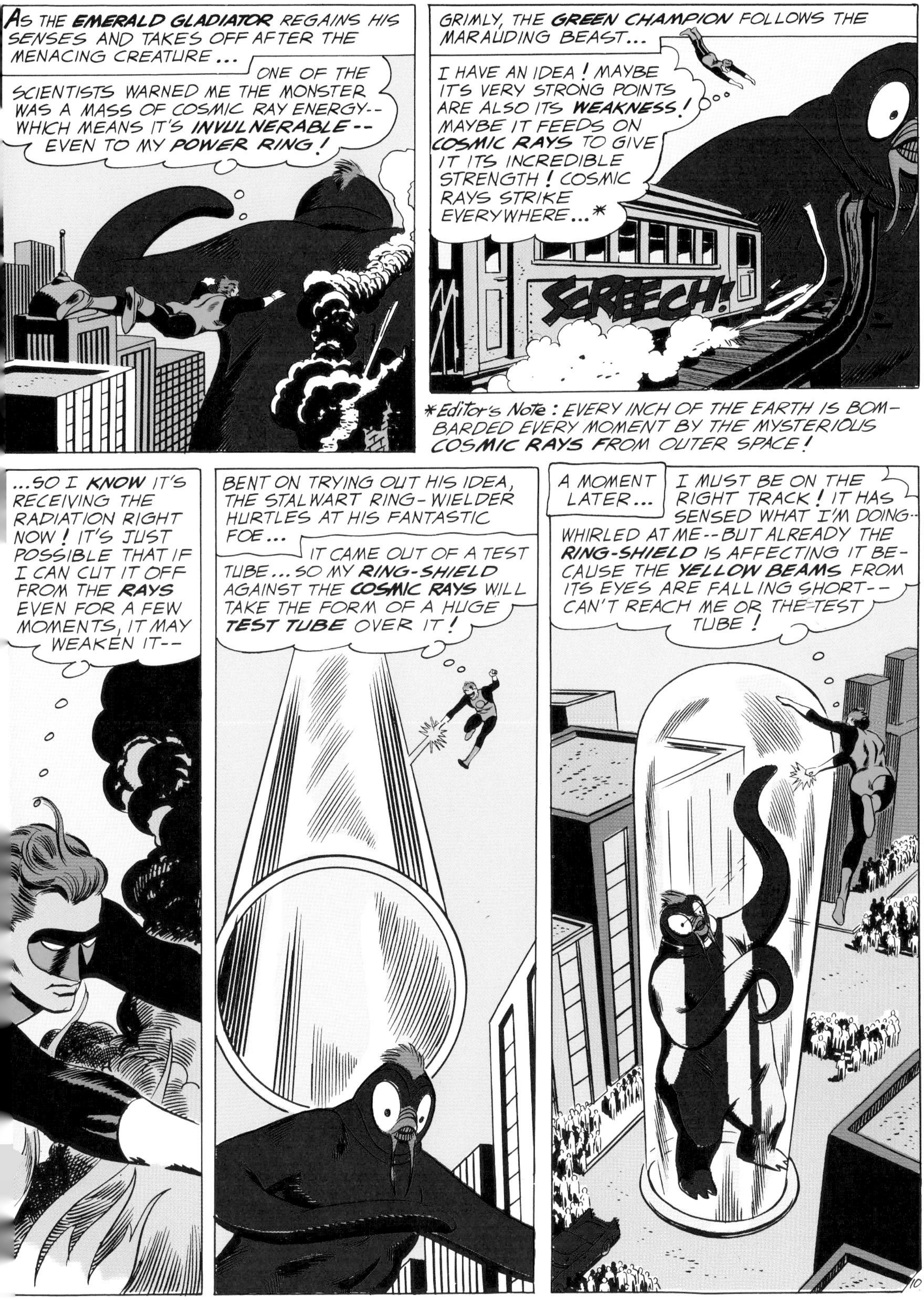
AS THE EMERALD GLADIATOR REGAINS HIS SENSES AND TAKES OFF AFTER THE MENACING CREATURE...
ONE OF THE SCIENTISTS WARNED ME THE MONSTER WAS A MASS OF COSMIC RAY ENERGY-- WHICH MEANS IT'S INVULNERABLE -- EVEN TO MY POWER RING!
GRIMLY, THE GREEN CHAMPION FOLLOWS THE MARAUDING BEAST...
I HAVE AN IDEA! MAYBE ITS VERY STRONG POINTS ARE ALSO ITS WEAKNESS! MAYBE IT FEEDS ON COSMIC RAYS TO GIVE IT ITS INCREDIBLE STRENGTH! COSMIC RAYS STRIKE EVERYWHERE...*
SCREECH!
*Editor's Note: EVERY INCH OF THE EARTH IS BOMBARDED EVERY MOMENT BY THE MYSTERIOUS COSMIC RAYS FROM OUTER SPACE!
...SO I KNOW IT'S RECEIVING THE RADIATION RIGHT NOW! IT'S JUST POSSIBLE THAT IF I CAN CUT IT OFF FROM THE RAYS EVEN FOR A FEW MOMENTS, IT MAY WEAKEN IT--
BENT ON TRYING OUT HIS IDEA, THE STALWART RING-WIELDER HURTLES AT HIS FANTASTIC FOE...
IT CAME OUT OF A TEST TUBE...SO MY RING-SHIELD AGAINST THE COSMIC RAYS WILL TAKE THE FORM OF A HUGE TEST TUBE OVER IT!
A MOMENT LATER...
I MUST BE ON THE RIGHT TRACK! IT HAS SENSED WHAT I'M DOING-- WHIRLED AT ME--BUT ALREADY THE RING-SHIELD IS AFFECTING IT BECAUSE THE YELLOW BEAMS FROM ITS EYES ARE FALLING SHORT-- CAN'T REACH ME OR THE TEST TUBE!
10

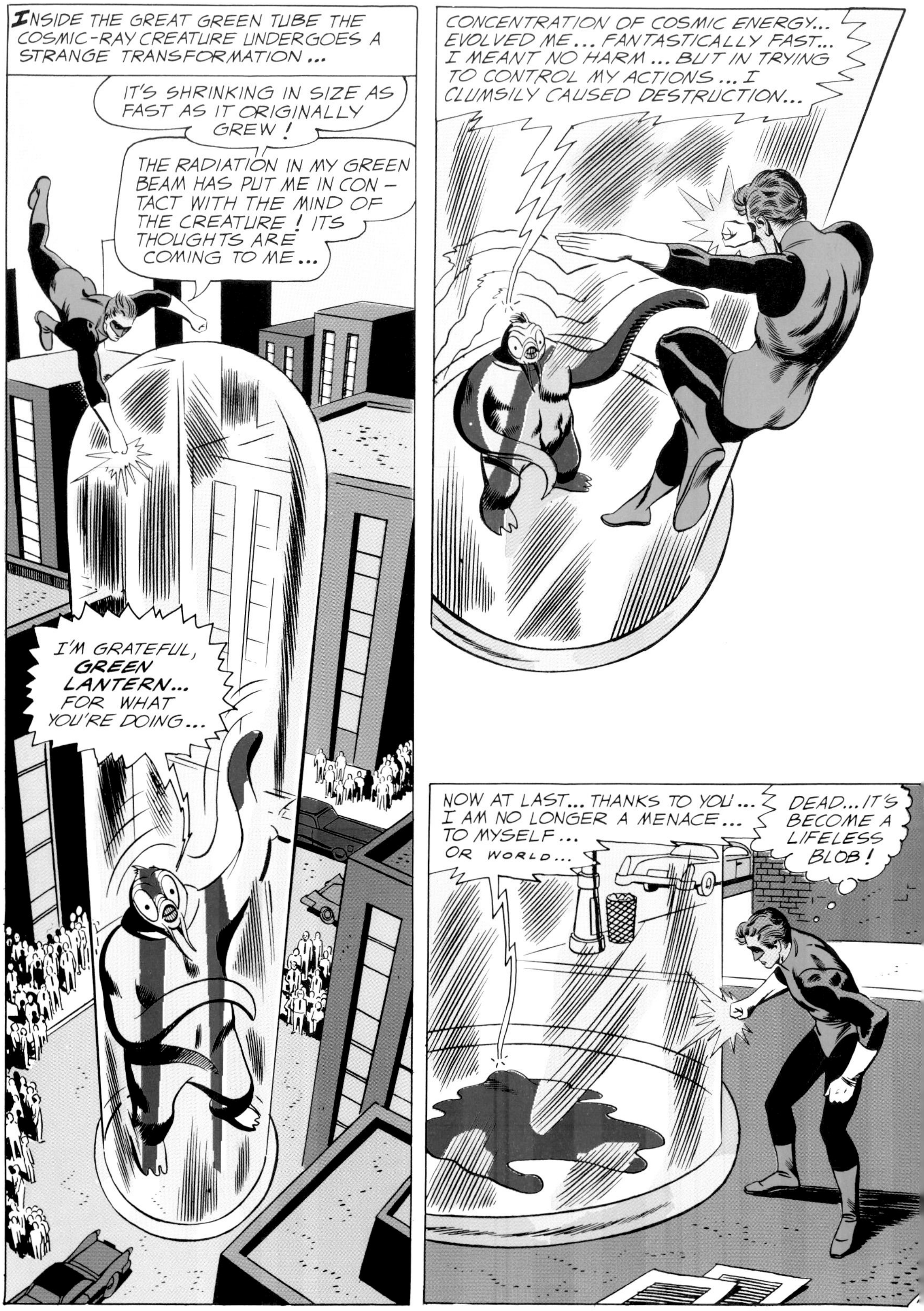
INSIDE THE GREAT GREEN TUBE THE COSMIC-RAY CREATURE UNDERGOES A STRANGE TRANSFORMATION ...
IT'S SHRINKING IN SIZE AS FAST AS IT ORIGINALLY GREW!
THE RADIATION IN MY GREEN BEAM HAS PUT ME IN CON-TACT WITH THE MIND OF THE CREATURE! ITS THOUGHTS ARE COMING TO ME ...
I'M GRATEFUL, GREEN LANTERN... FOR WHAT YOU'RE DOING...
CONCENTRATION OF COSMIC ENERGY... EVOLVED ME... FANTASTICALLY FAST... I MEANT NO HARM ... BUT IN TRYING TO CONTROL MY ACTIONS ... I CLUMSILY CAUSED DESTRUCTION...
NOW AT LAST... THANKS TO YOU ... I AM NO LONGER A MENACE ... TO MYSELF ... OR WORLD...
DEAD... IT'S BECOME A LIFELESS BLOB!

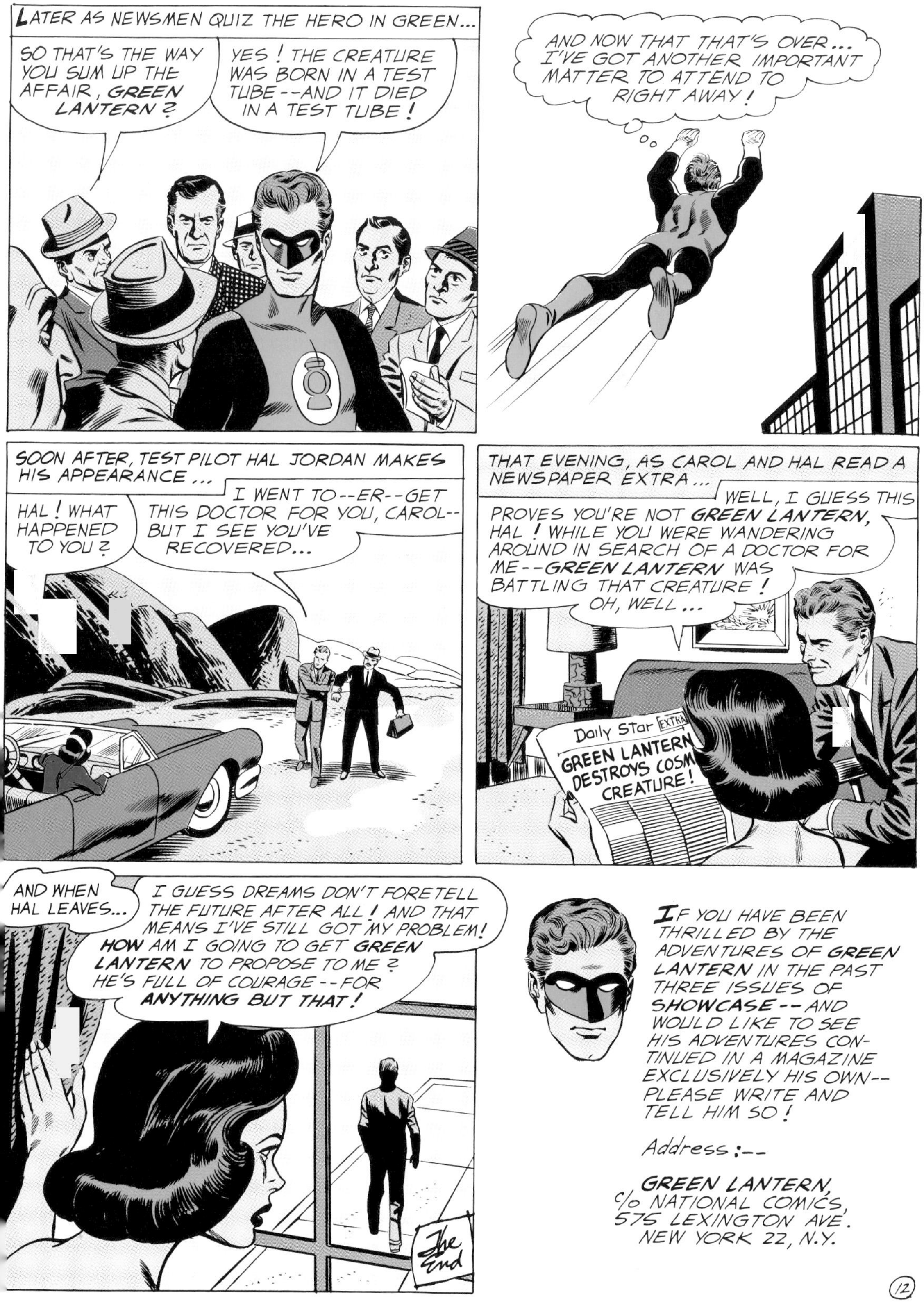
LATER AS NEWSMEN QUIZ THE HERO IN GREEN...
SO THAT'S THE WAY YOU SUM UP THE AFFAIR, GREEN LANTERN?
YES! THE CREATURE WAS BORN IN A TEST TUBE--AND IT DIED IN A TEST TUBE!
AND NOW THAT THAT'S OVER... I'VE GOT ANOTHER IMPORTANT MATTER TO ATTEND TO RIGHT AWAY!
SOON AFTER, TEST PILOT HAL JORDAN MAKES HIS APPEARANCE...
HAL! WHAT HAPPENED TO YOU?
I WENT TO--ER--GET THIS DOCTOR FOR YOU, CAROL--BUT I SEE YOU'VE RECOVERED...
THAT EVENING, AS CAROL AND HAL READ A NEWSPAPER EXTRA...
WELL, I GUESS THIS PROVES YOU'RE NOT GREEN LANTERN, HAL! WHILE YOU WERE WANDERING AROUND IN SEARCH OF A DOCTOR FOR ME--GREEN LANTERN WAS BATTLING THAT CREATURE! OH, WELL...
Daily Star EXTRA
GREEN LANTERN DESTROYS COSM CREATURE!
AND WHEN HAL LEAVES...
I GUESS DREAMS DON'T FORETELL THE FUTURE AFTER ALL! AND THAT MEANS I'VE STILL GOT MY PROBLEM! HOW AM I GOING TO GET GREEN LANTERN TO PROPOSE TO ME? HE'S FULL OF COURAGE--FOR ANYTHING BUT THAT!
The End
IF YOU HAVE BEEN THRILLED BY THE ADVENTURES OF GREEN LANTERN IN THE PAST THREE ISSUES OF SHOWCASE--AND WOULD LIKE TO SEE HIS ADVENTURES CONTINUED IN A MAGAZINE EXCLUSIVELY HIS OWN--PLEASE WRITE AND TELL HIM SO!
Address:--
GREEN LANTERN, c/o NATIONAL COMICS, 575 LEXINGTON AVE. NEW YORK 22, N.Y.
12

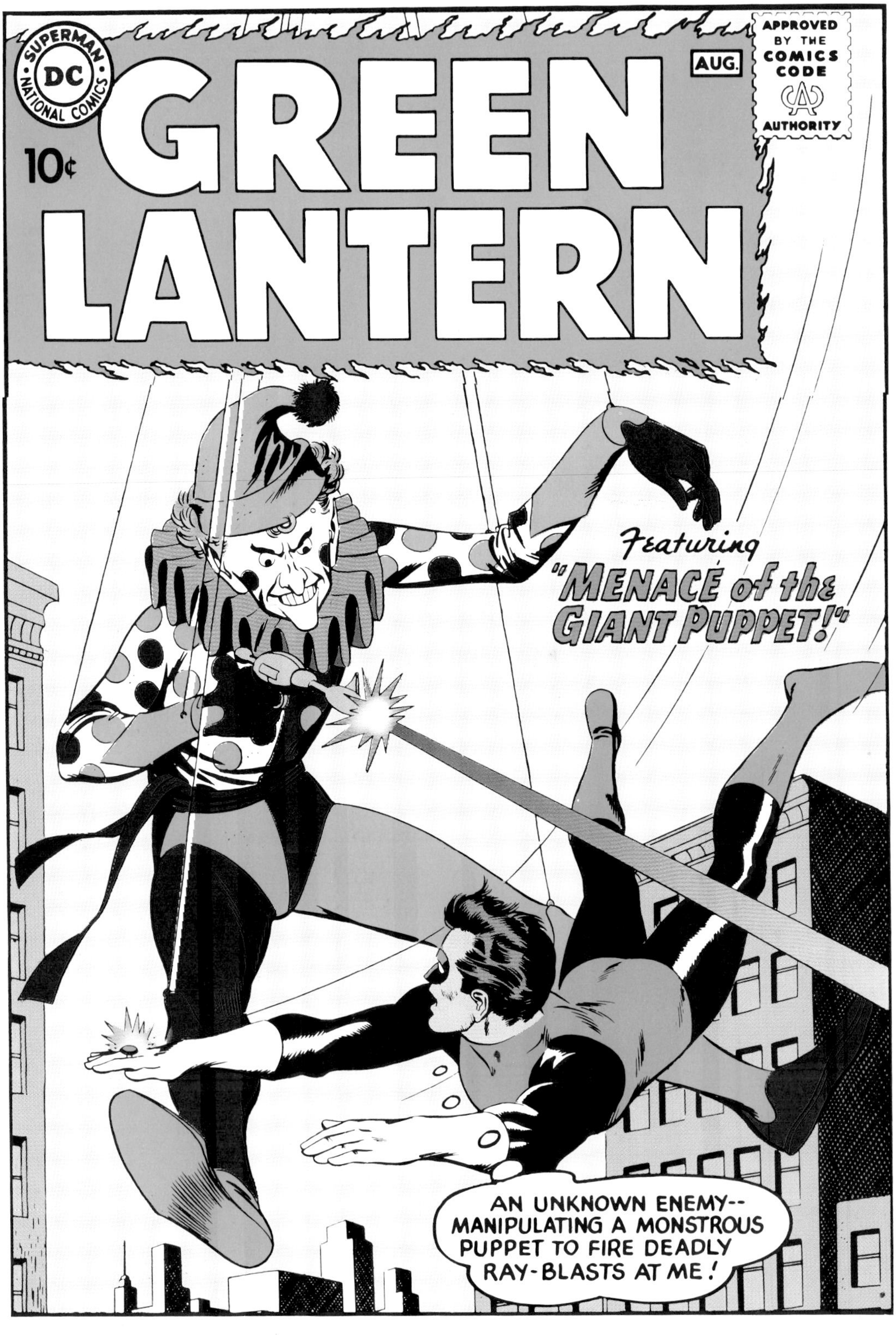
SUPERMAN DC NATIONAL COMICS
10¢
GREEN LANTERN
AUG.
APPROVED BY THE COMICS CODE AUTHORITY
Featuring
"MENACE of the GIANT PUPPET!"
AN UNKNOWN ENEMY-- MANIPULATING A MONSTROUS PUPPET TO FIRE DEADLY RAY-BLASTS AT ME!

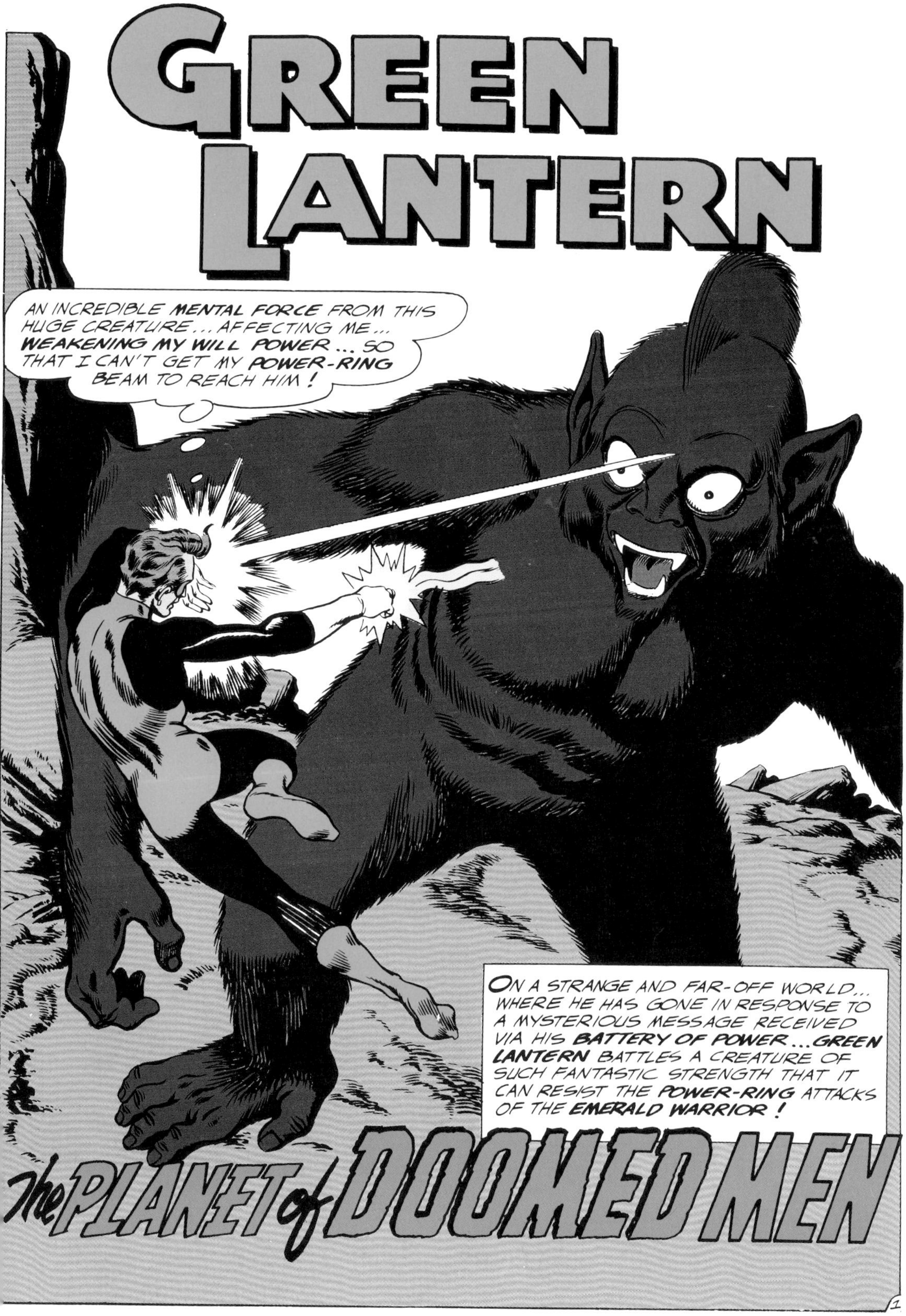
GREEN LANTERN
AN INCREDIBLE MENTAL FORCE FROM THIS HUGE CREATURE... AFFECTING ME... WEAKENING MY WILL POWER... SO THAT I CAN'T GET MY POWER-RING BEAM TO REACH HIM!
ON A STRANGE AND FAR-OFF WORLD... WHERE HE HAS GONE IN RESPONSE TO A MYSTERIOUS MESSAGE RECEIVED VIA HIS BATTERY OF POWER... GREEN LANTERN BATTLES A CREATURE OF SUCH FANTASTIC STRENGTH THAT IT CAN RESIST THE POWER-RING ATTACKS OF THE EMERALD WARRIOR!
The PLANET of DOOMED MEN
1

AS ACE TEST PILOT *HAL JORDAN* PUTS A NEW EXPERIMENTAL SPACE-PLANE THROUGH ITS PACES...

HANDLES FINE... EASY AS RIDING A KIDDIE-CAR! EXCEPT THAT THIS BABY CAN **GO**...!

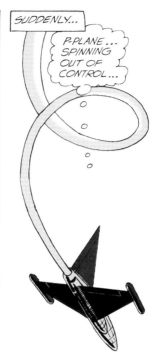

SUDDENLY...

P-PLANE... SPINNING OUT OF CONTROL...

WITH PRACTICED SKILL, AND LIGHTNING REFLEXES, THE CRACK AIRMAN BRINGS HIS CRAFT OUT OF ITS DIVE...

; *Whew!* ; NOTHING WENT WRONG WITH THE PLANE -- **I** WAS AT FAULT! SUDDENLY I WENT LIMP -- AS IF EVERY BIT OF ENERGY HAD BEEN DRAINED OUT OF ME --

I'M ALL RIGHT NOW! BUT WHAT IN THE WORLD HAPPENED TO ME IN THAT BRIEF MOMENT?

AT THE SAME TIME ON THE FAR-DISTANT PLANET OF **OA**, IN THE CENTRAL GALAXY OF THE UNIVERSE, A GROUP SIMPLY KNOWN AS THE **GUARDIANS** IS MEETING IN SOLEMN COUNCIL...

THE **ENERGY-DUPLICATE** OF THE POSSESSOR OF A **POWER BATTERY** IN SECTOR 2814 WILL ARRIVE IN A MOMENT...

WE MUST FIND OUT IF THIS NEW POSSESSOR IS WORTHY OF HIS GREAT TRUST!

YES! AND ALSO WHETHER HE IS CAPABLE OF DEALING WITH THE TERRIBLE EMERGENCY WHICH HAS ARISEN IN HIS SECTOR...

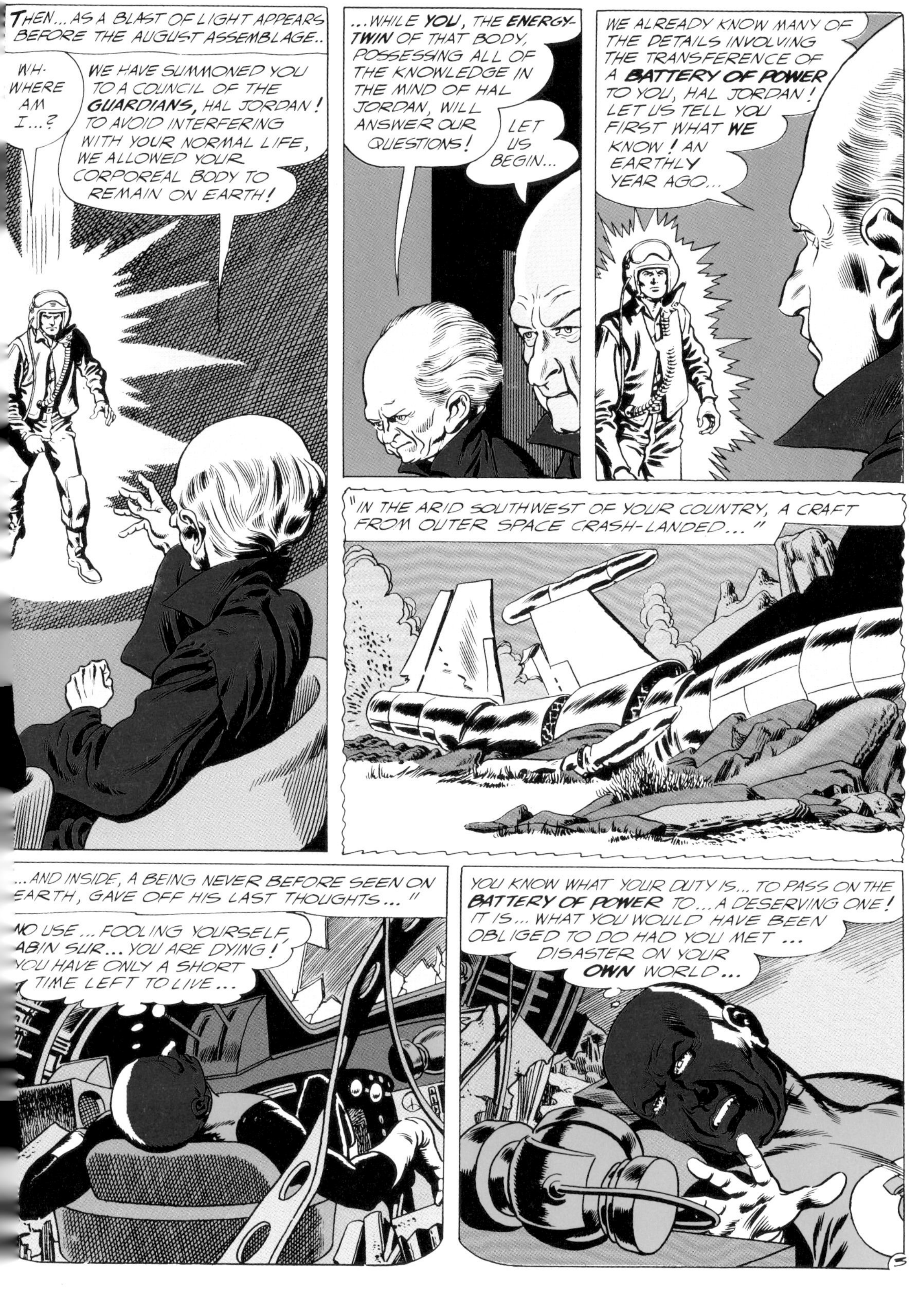
THEN... AS A BLAST OF LIGHT APPEARS BEFORE THE AUGUST ASSEMBLAGE..
WH-WHERE AM I...?
WE HAVE SUMMONED YOU TO A COUNCIL OF THE GUARDIANS, HAL JORDAN! TO AVOID INTERFERING WITH YOUR NORMAL LIFE, WE ALLOWED YOUR CORPOREAL BODY TO REMAIN ON EARTH!
...WHILE YOU, THE ENERGY-TWIN OF THAT BODY, POSSESSING ALL OF THE KNOWLEDGE IN THE MIND OF HAL JORDAN, WILL ANSWER OUR QUESTIONS!
LET US BEGIN...
WE ALREADY KNOW MANY OF THE DETAILS INVOLVING THE TRANSFERENCE OF A BATTERY OF POWER TO YOU, HAL JORDAN! LET US TELL YOU FIRST WHAT WE KNOW! AN EARTHLY YEAR AGO...
"IN THE ARID SOUTHWEST OF YOUR COUNTRY, A CRAFT FROM OUTER SPACE CRASH-LANDED..."
...AND INSIDE, A BEING NEVER BEFORE SEEN ON EARTH, GAVE OFF HIS LAST THOUGHTS..."
NO USE... FOOLING YOURSELF, ABIN SUR... YOU ARE DYING! YOU HAVE ONLY A SHORT TIME LEFT TO LIVE...
YOU KNOW WHAT YOUR DUTY IS... TO PASS ON THE BATTERY OF POWER TO... A DESERVING ONE! IT IS... WHAT YOU WOULD HAVE BEEN OBLIGED TO DO HAD YOU MET ... DISASTER ON YOUR OWN WORLD...
5

...AND YOU MUST DO IT HERE...ON EARTH! YOU MUST FIND A **DESERVING** EARTHMAN... AND PASS ON THE **BATTERY OF POWER** TO **HIM**...! BUT YOU MUST **HURRY**...

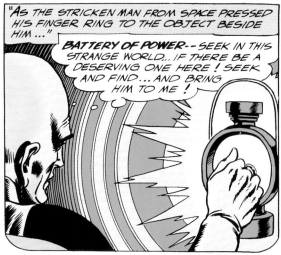

"AS THE STRICKEN MAN FROM SPACE PRESSED HIS FINGER RING TO THE OBJECT BESIDE HIM..."

BATTERY OF POWER-- SEEK IN THIS STRANGE WORLD...IF THERE BE A DESERVING ONE HERE! SEEK AND FIND...AND BRING HIM TO ME!

"FROM THE **GREEN RING** A BOLT OF PURE ENERGY EXPLODED..."

HE MUST BE ONE WITHOUT FEAR! ENTIRELY WITHOUT FEAR! HURRY! THE TIME IS SHORT!

"WITH THE SPEED OF LIGHT, THE ENERGY-BEAM CRISS-CROSSED THE SURFACE OF YOUR PLANET..."

BUT IT WAS AT THAT POINT THAT AN ION-STORM UPSET COMMUNICATIONS BETWEEN OUR PLANET AND YOURS! AS A RESULT, WHEN WE COULD RE-CEIVE INFORMATION FROM YOUR WORLD AGAIN, WE FOUND THAT AN INDIVIDUAL NAMED **GREEN LANTERN** HAD COME INTO POSSESSION OF **ABIN SUR'S POWER BATTERY**!

GREEN LANTERN... AND I...ARE ONE AND THE SAME PERSON...

YES! SO WE GATHERED FROM OUR SURVEY AFTER THE STORM...

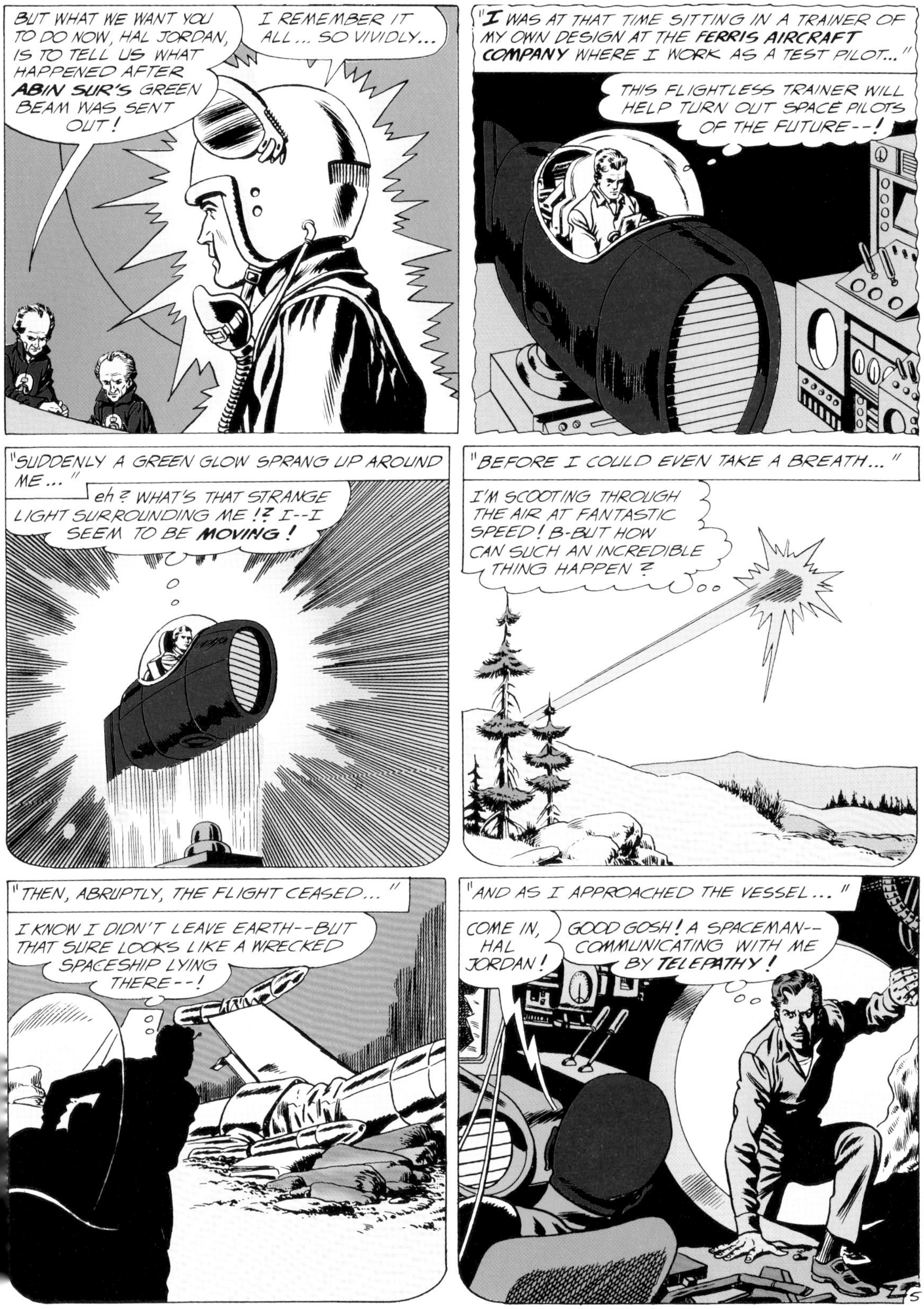
BUT WHAT WE WANT YOU TO DO NOW, HAL JORDAN, IS TO TELL US WHAT HAPPENED AFTER ABIN SUR'S GREEN BEAM WAS SENT OUT!
I REMEMBER IT ALL... SO VIVIDLY...
"I WAS AT THAT TIME SITTING IN A TRAINER OF MY OWN DESIGN AT THE FERRIS AIRCRAFT COMPANY WHERE I WORK AS A TEST PILOT..."
THIS FLIGHTLESS TRAINER WILL HELP TURN OUT SPACE PILOTS OF THE FUTURE--!
"SUDDENLY A GREEN GLOW SPRANG UP AROUND ME..."
eh? WHAT'S THAT STRANGE LIGHT SURROUNDING ME!? I--I SEEM TO BE MOVING!
"BEFORE I COULD EVEN TAKE A BREATH..."
I'M SCOOTING THROUGH THE AIR AT FANTASTIC SPEED! B-BUT HOW CAN SUCH AN INCREDIBLE THING HAPPEN?
"THEN, ABRUPTLY, THE FLIGHT CEASED..."
I KNOW I DIDN'T LEAVE EARTH--BUT THAT SURE LOOKS LIKE A WRECKED SPACESHIP LYING THERE--!
"AND AS I APPROACHED THE VESSEL..."
COME IN, HAL JORDAN!
GOOD GOSH! A SPACEMAN-- COMMUNICATING WITH ME BY TELEPATHY!
5

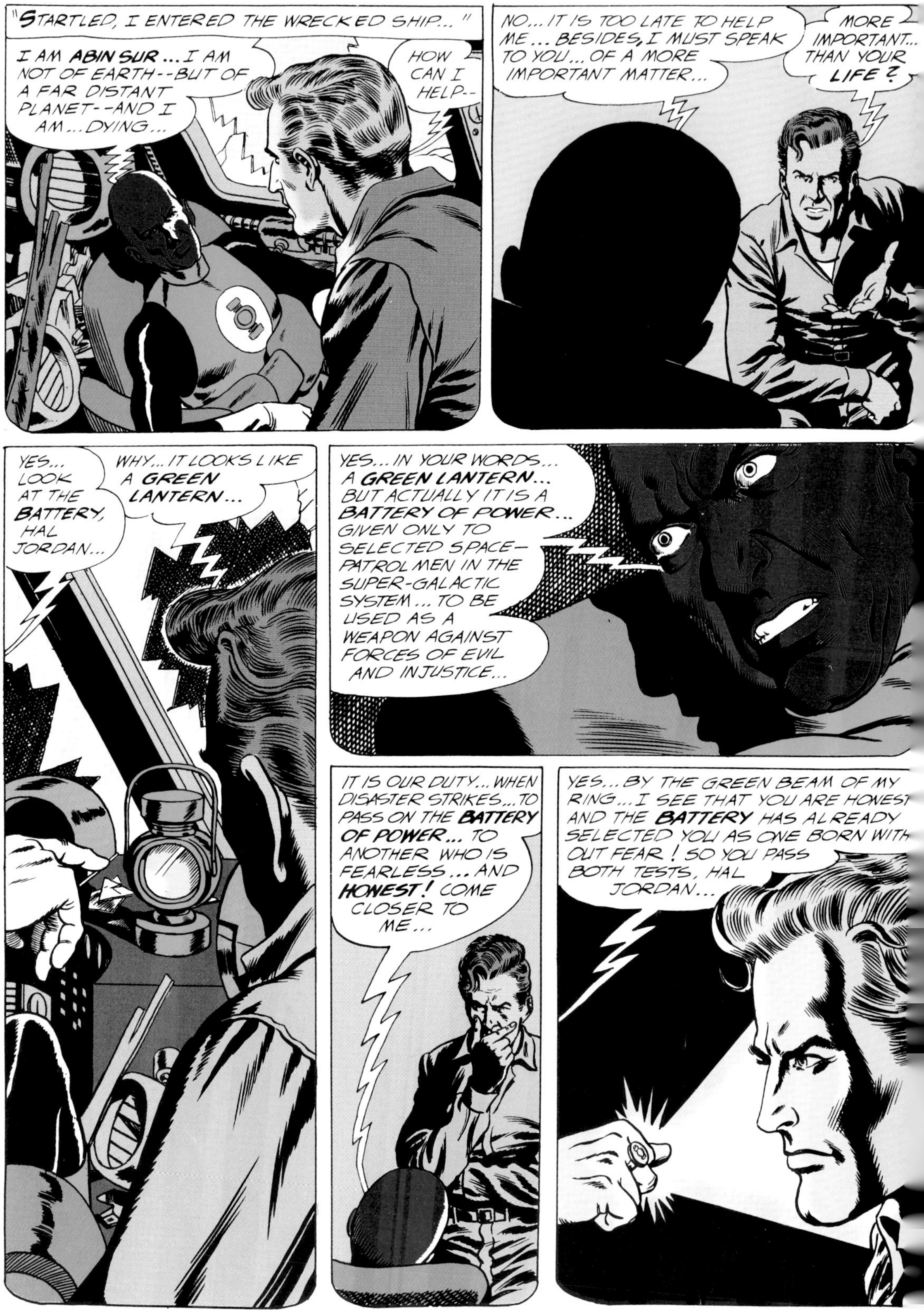
"STARTLED, I ENTERED THE WRECKED SHIP..."
I AM ABIN SUR... I AM NOT OF EARTH--BUT OF A FAR DISTANT PLANET--AND I AM... DYING...
HOW CAN I HELP--
NO... IT IS TOO LATE TO HELP ME... BESIDES, I MUST SPEAK TO YOU... OF A MORE IMPORTANT MATTER...
MORE IMPORTANT... THAN YOUR LIFE?
YES... LOOK AT THE BATTERY, HAL JORDAN...
WHY... IT LOOKS LIKE A GREEN LANTERN...
YES... IN YOUR WORDS... A GREEN LANTERN... BUT ACTUALLY IT IS A BATTERY OF POWER... GIVEN ONLY TO SELECTED SPACE-PATROLMEN IN THE SUPER-GALACTIC SYSTEM... TO BE USED AS A WEAPON AGAINST FORCES OF EVIL AND INJUSTICE...
IT IS OUR DUTY... WHEN DISASTER STRIKES... TO PASS ON THE BATTERY OF POWER... TO ANOTHER WHO IS FEARLESS... AND HONEST! COME CLOSER TO ME...
YES... BY THE GREEN BEAM OF MY RING... I SEE THAT YOU ARE HONEST AND THE BATTERY HAS ALREADY SELECTED YOU AS ONE BORN WITHOUT FEAR! SO YOU PASS BOTH TESTS, HAL JORDAN...

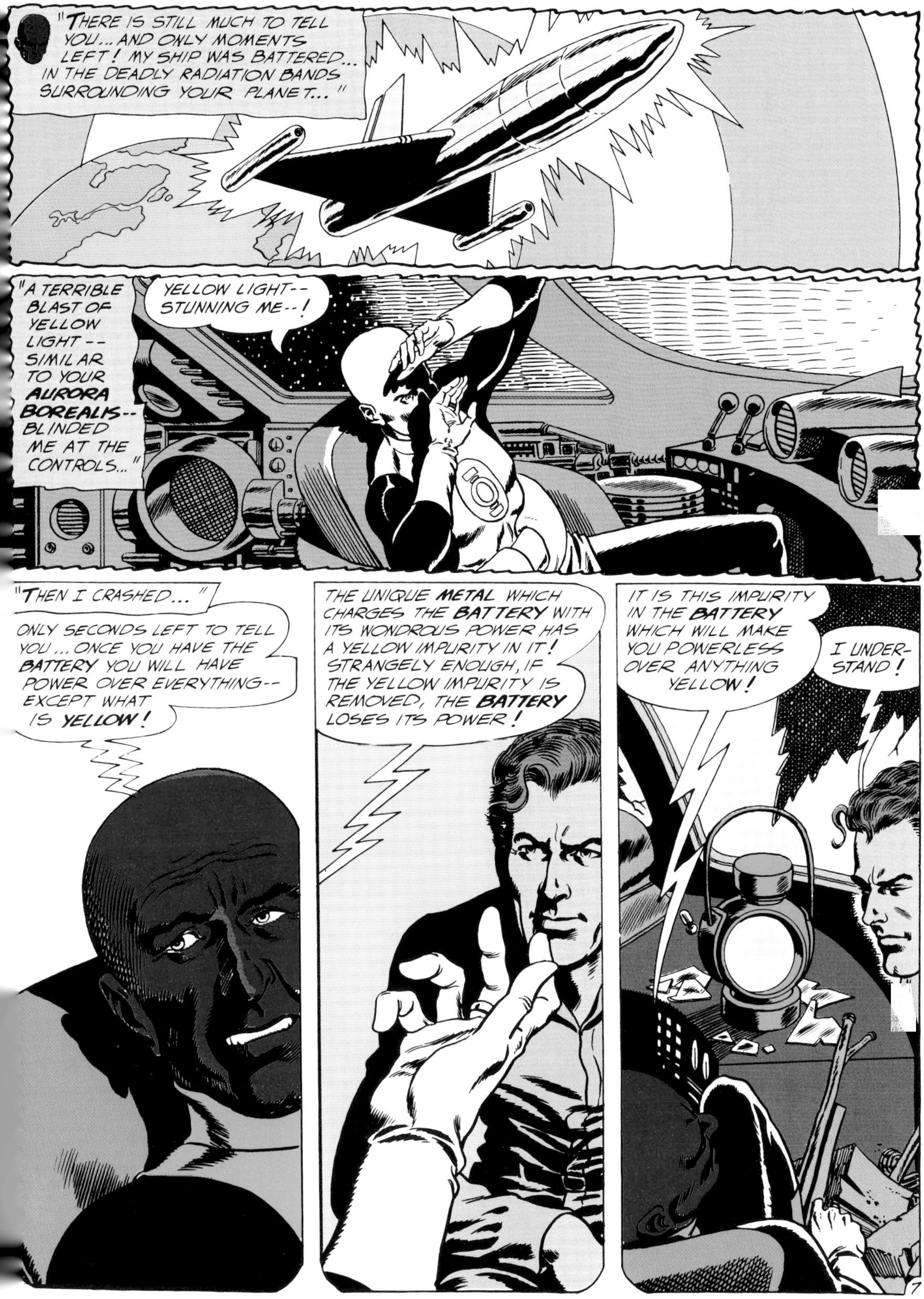
"THERE IS STILL MUCH TO TELL YOU... AND ONLY MOMENTS LEFT! MY SHIP WAS BATTERED... IN THE DEADLY RADIATION BANDS SURROUNDING YOUR PLANET..."
"A TERRIBLE BLAST OF YELLOW LIGHT -- SIMILAR TO YOUR AURORA BOREALIS -- BLINDED ME AT THE CONTROLS..."
YELLOW LIGHT -- STUNNING ME -- !
"THEN I CRASHED..."
ONLY SECONDS LEFT TO TELL YOU... ONCE YOU HAVE THE BATTERY YOU WILL HAVE POWER OVER EVERYTHING -- EXCEPT WHAT IS YELLOW!
THE UNIQUE METAL WHICH CHARGES THE BATTERY WITH ITS WONDROUS POWER HAS A YELLOW IMPURITY IN IT! STRANGELY ENOUGH, IF THE YELLOW IMPURITY IS REMOVED, THE BATTERY LOSES ITS POWER!
IT IS THIS IMPURITY IN THE BATTERY WHICH WILL MAKE YOU POWERLESS OVER ANYTHING YELLOW!
I UNDERSTAND!
7

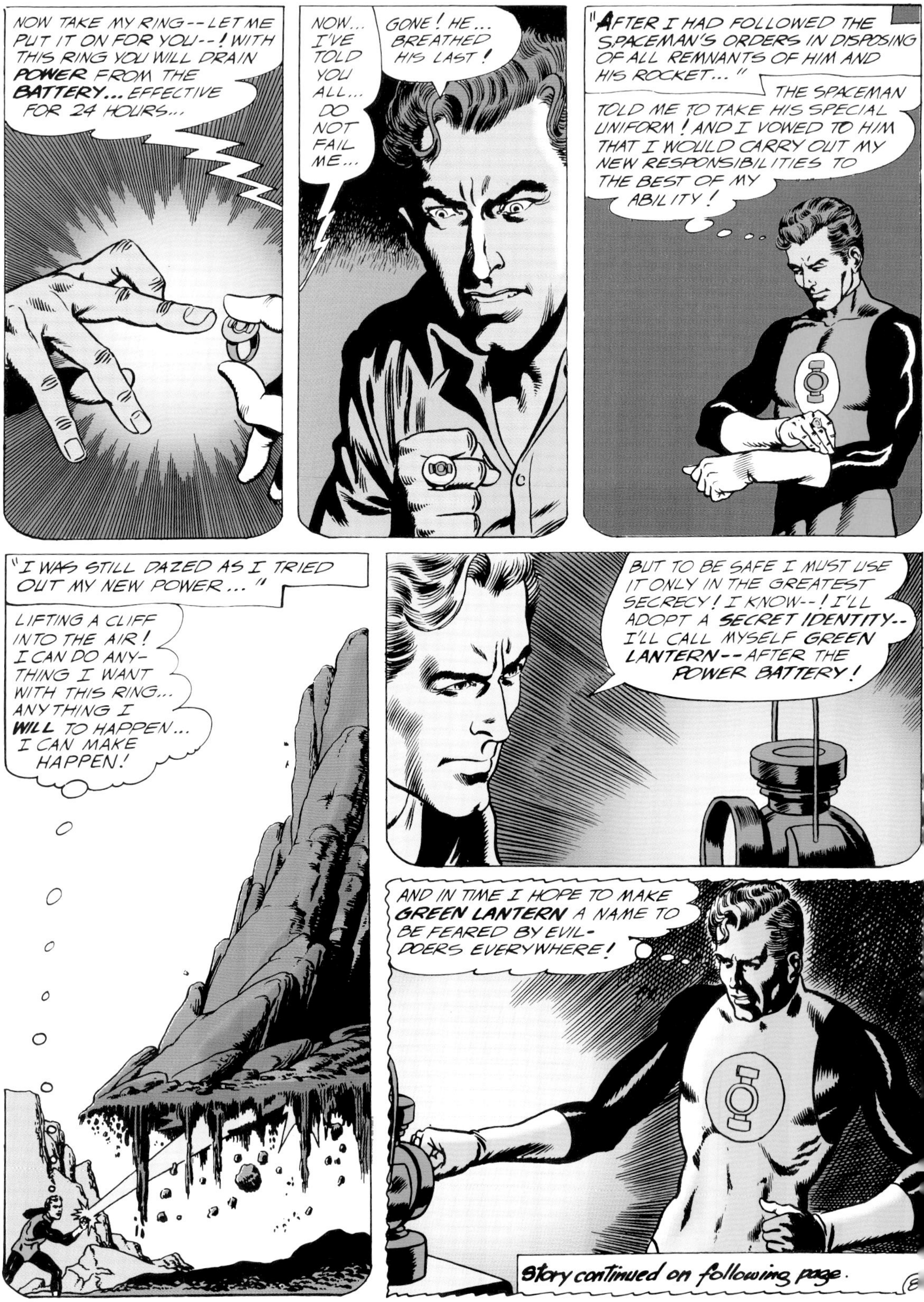
NOW TAKE MY RING--LET ME PUT IT ON FOR YOU--! WITH THIS RING YOU WILL DRAIN **POWER** FROM THE **BATTERY...** EFFECTIVE FOR 24 HOURS...
NOW... I'VE TOLD YOU ALL... DO NOT FAIL ME...
GONE! HE... BREATHED HIS LAST!
"AFTER I HAD FOLLOWED THE SPACEMAN'S ORDERS IN DISPOSING OF ALL REMNANTS OF HIM AND HIS ROCKET..."
THE SPACEMAN TOLD ME TO TAKE HIS SPECIAL UNIFORM! AND I VOWED TO HIM THAT I WOULD CARRY OUT MY NEW RESPONSIBILITIES TO THE BEST OF MY ABILITY!
"I WAS STILL DAZED AS I TRIED OUT MY NEW POWER..."
LIFTING A CLIFF INTO THE AIR! I CAN DO ANYTHING I WANT WITH THIS RING... ANYTHING I **WILL** TO HAPPEN... I CAN MAKE HAPPEN!
BUT TO BE SAFE I MUST USE IT ONLY IN THE GREATEST SECRECY! I KNOW--! I'LL ADOPT A **SECRET IDENTITY**-- I'LL CALL MYSELF **GREEN LANTERN**--AFTER THE **POWER BATTERY!**
AND IN TIME I HOPE TO MAKE **GREEN LANTERN** A NAME TO BE FEARED BY EVIL-DOERS EVERYWHERE!
Story continued on following page.

As the **ENERGY-TWIN** of the real Hal Jordan finishes his account, the **GUARDIANS** come to a unanimous decision...

HAL JORDAN, WE DEEM YOU WORTHY OF BEING A POSSESSOR OF A **BATTERY OF POWER!**

YOU WILL NOW RETURN TO YOUR WORLD TO REJOIN THE CORPOREAL BODY OF YOUR REAL SELF!

AND THIS INTERVIEW WILL BE ERASED FROM YOUR MIND... UNTIL IT IS PROPER FOR YOU TO LEARN ABOUT US...

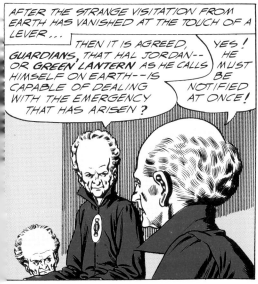

AFTER THE STRANGE VISITATION FROM EARTH HAS VANISHED AT THE TOUCH OF A LEVER...

THEN IT IS AGREED, **GUARDIANS,** THAT HAL JORDAN-- OR **GREEN LANTERN** AS HE CALLS HIMSELF ON EARTH--IS CAPABLE OF DEALING WITH THE EMERGENCY THAT HAS ARISEN?

YES! HE MUST BE NOTIFIED AT ONCE!

BACK ON EARTH AT THIS MOMENT...

FUNNY ABOUT THAT SENSATION I HAD--BUT EVIDENTLY IT DIDN'T DO ANY HARM! I FEEL OKAY!

...BUT I'D FEEL EVEN BETTER IF I COULD GET A DATE WITH CAROL * TONIGHT!

***Editor's Note:** MISS CAROL FERRIS, IN THE ABSENCE OF HER FATHER, IS IN SOLE CHARGE OF THE **FERRIS AIRCRAFT COMPANY** WHERE HAL IS EMPLOYED AS TEST PILOT.

IN HIS PRIVATE DRESSING ROOM AT THE HANGAR, AS HAL TAKES OFF HIS FLYING TOGS...

THE TROUBLE IS, EVER SINCE CAROL MET MY ALTER EGO **GREEN LANTERN,** SHE DOESN'T SEEM TO FIND ANY TIME FOR ME! WHAT A SITUATION I'M UP AGAINST...

I'M MY OWN RIVAL FOR CAROL'S AFFECTIONS! BUT I'LL NEVER TELL HER--OR ANYONE ELSE--THAT I'M **GREEN LANTERN!** I WANT TO WIN CAROL AS MYSELF-- AS **HAL JORDAN!**

EH?

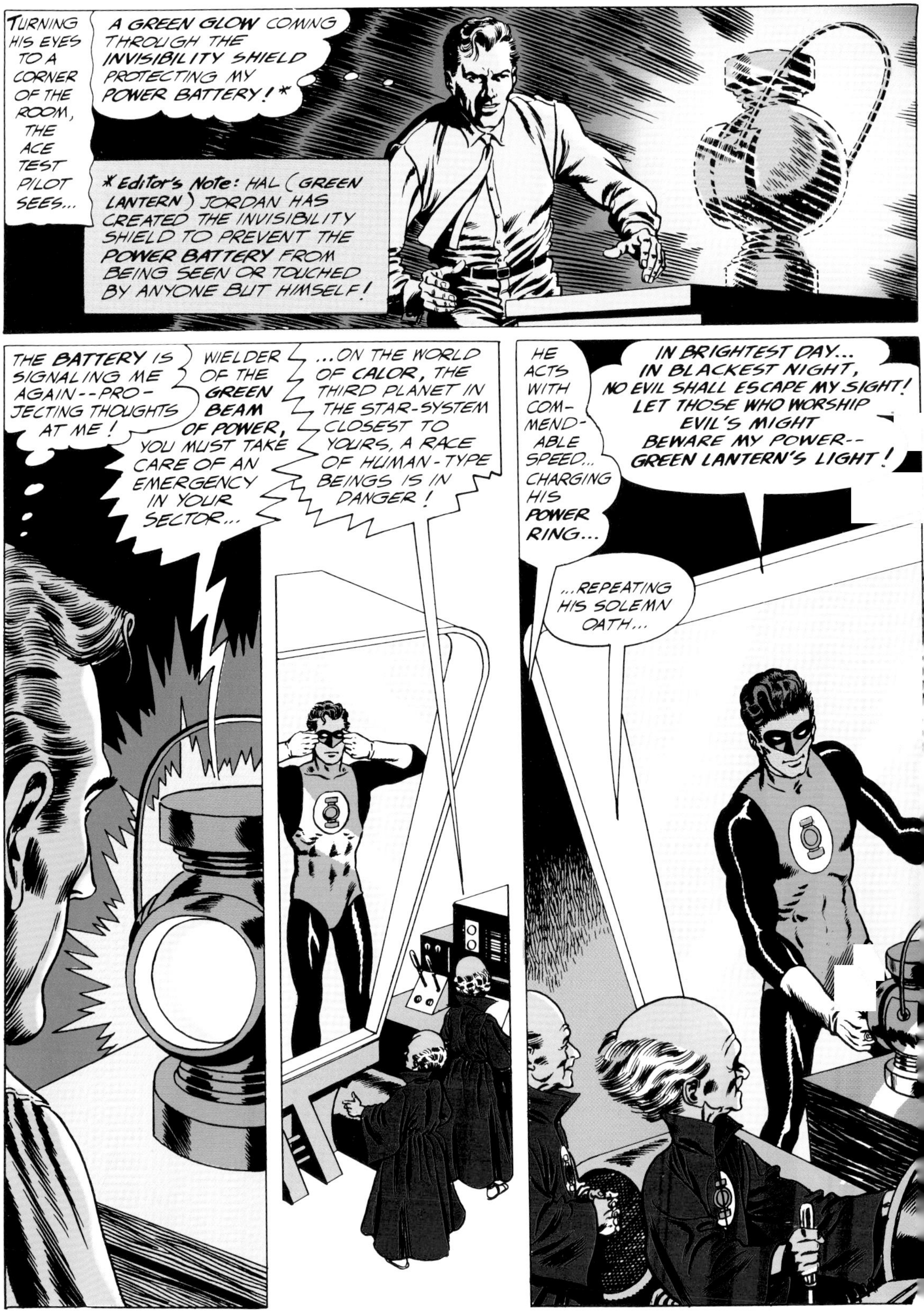
TURNING HIS EYES TO A CORNER OF THE ROOM, THE ACE TEST PILOT SEES...
A GREEN GLOW COMING THROUGH THE INVISIBILITY SHIELD PROTECTING MY POWER BATTERY! *
* Editor's Note: HAL (GREEN LANTERN) JORDAN HAS CREATED THE INVISIBILITY SHIELD TO PREVENT THE POWER BATTERY FROM BEING SEEN OR TOUCHED BY ANYONE BUT HIMSELF!
THE BATTERY IS SIGNALING ME AGAIN--PROJECTING THOUGHTS AT ME!
WIELDER OF THE GREEN BEAM OF POWER, YOU MUST TAKE CARE OF AN EMERGENCY IN YOUR SECTOR...
...ON THE WORLD OF CALOR, THE THIRD PLANET IN THE STAR-SYSTEM CLOSEST TO YOURS, A RACE OF HUMAN-TYPE BEINGS IS IN DANGER!
HE ACTS WITH COMMENDABLE SPEED... CHARGING HIS POWER RING...
...REPEATING HIS SOLEMN OATH...
IN BRIGHTEST DAY... IN BLACKEST NIGHT, NO EVIL SHALL ESCAPE MY SIGHT! LET THOSE WHO WORSHIP EVIL'S MIGHT BEWARE MY POWER-- GREEN LANTERN'S LIGHT!

AND SOON A FORMIDABLE FIGURE CLEAVES THE DARKNESS OF OUTER SPACE AROUND EARTH...

MY *RING*, OBEYING MY WILL POWER, HAS FORMED AN INVULNERABLE POCKET OF AIR AROUND ME... TO ENABLE ME TO BREATHE UNTIL I GET TO THAT STAR-SYSTEM THE *LANTERN* VOICE TOLD ABOUT!

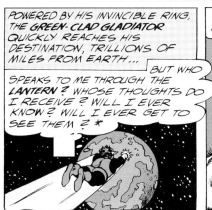

POWERED BY HIS INVINCIBLE RING, THE *GREEN-CLAD GLADIATOR* QUICKLY REACHES HIS DESTINATION, TRILLIONS OF MILES FROM EARTH...

BUT WHO SPEAKS TO ME THROUGH THE *LANTERN*? WHOSE THOUGHTS DO I RECEIVE? WILL I EVER KNOW? WILL I EVER GET TO SEE THEM? *

Editor's Note: GL IS UNAWARE THAT IN THE PERSON OF HIS *ENERGY-DUPLICATE* HE HAS ALREADY SEEN THE INCREDIBLE *GUARDIANS*!

ON THE PLANET...

KE-GRA-UM-NU--

WE HAVE BEEN ASKING THE SPIRIT KA-MA TO SEND US HELP--!

AS THE EMERALD CRUSADER APPROACHES...

GU-BARO! GU-NARU--

I CAN'T UNDERSTAND THEM--BUT MY RING WILL FIX THAT--!

UNDER GL'S AMAZING *POWER RING*, BACKED BY HIS INDOMITABLE WILL, THE WORDS OF THE NATIVES COME CLEAR...

WE EXPECTED YOU! WE KNEW THAT YOU WOULD COME!

WHAT?! HOW COULD THAT BE?

AFTER THE *RING-WIELDER* HAS BEEN MADE TO UNDERSTAND...

SO THAT'S IT! THEY BELIEVE THAT THIS STRANGE TREE HAS THE POWER TO GRANT THEM FAVORS--AND THEY WERE BEGGING IT FOR HELP! THEY THINK *THAT'S* HOW I CAME HERE!

11

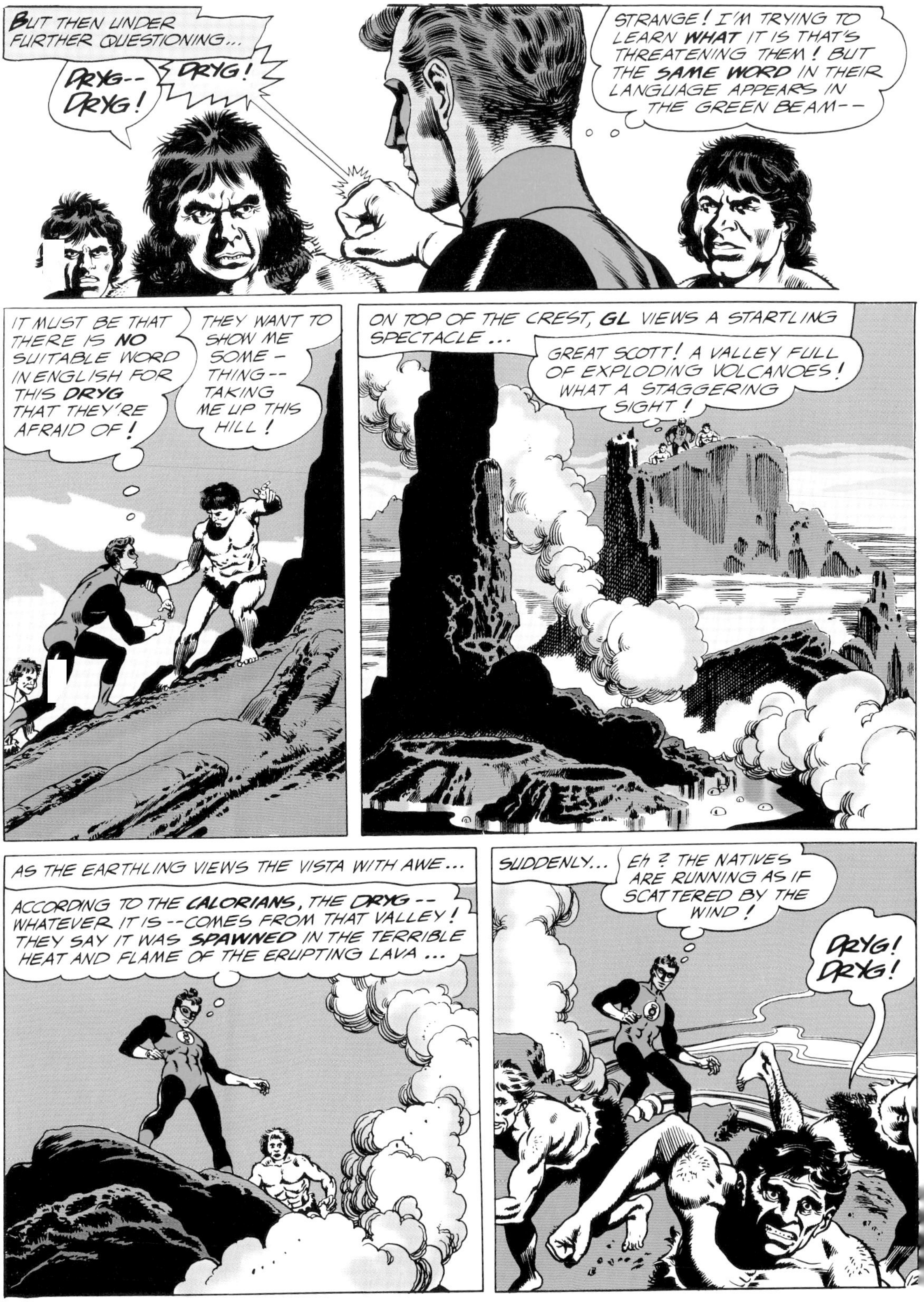
BUT THEN UNDER FURTHER QUESTIONING...
DRYG-- DRYG!
DRYG!
STRANGE! I'M TRYING TO LEARN WHAT IT IS THAT'S THREATENING THEM! BUT THE SAME WORD IN THEIR LANGUAGE APPEARS IN THE GREEN BEAM--
IT MUST BE THAT THERE IS NO SUITABLE WORD IN ENGLISH FOR THIS DRYG THAT THEY'RE AFRAID OF!
THEY WANT TO SHOW ME SOME-THING-- TAKING ME UP THIS HILL!
ON TOP OF THE CREST, GL VIEWS A STARTLING SPECTACLE...
GREAT SCOTT! A VALLEY FULL OF EXPLODING VOLCANOES! WHAT A STAGGERING SIGHT!
AS THE EARTHLING VIEWS THE VISTA WITH AWE...
ACCORDING TO THE CALORIANS, THE DRYG -- WHATEVER IT IS --COMES FROM THAT VALLEY! THEY SAY IT WAS SPAWNED IN THE TERRIBLE HEAT AND FLAME OF THE ERUPTING LAVA...
SUDDENLY...
Eh? THE NATIVES ARE RUNNING AS IF SCATTERED BY THE WIND!
DRYG! DRYG!

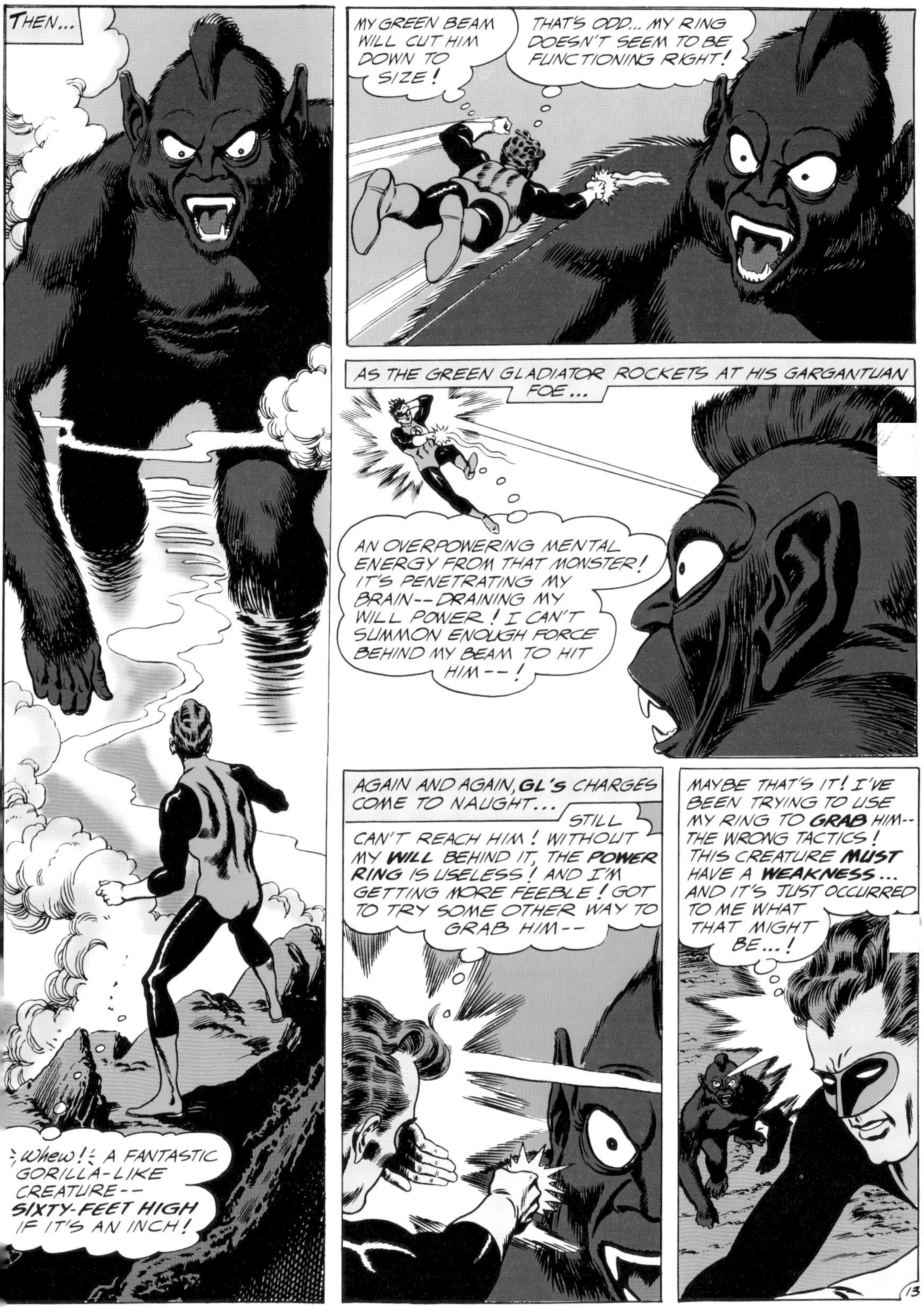
THEN...
WHEW! A FANTASTIC GORILLA-LIKE CREATURE--SIXTY-FEET HIGH IF IT'S AN INCH!
MY GREEN BEAM WILL CUT HIM DOWN TO SIZE!
THAT'S ODD... MY RING DOESN'T SEEM TO BE FUNCTIONING RIGHT!
AS THE GREEN GLADIATOR ROCKETS AT HIS GARGANTUAN FOE...
AN OVERPOWERING MENTAL ENERGY FROM THAT MONSTER! IT'S PENETRATING MY BRAIN--DRAINING MY WILL POWER! I CAN'T SUMMON ENOUGH FORCE BEHIND MY BEAM TO HIT HIM--!
AGAIN AND AGAIN, GL'S CHARGES COME TO NAUGHT...
STILL CAN'T REACH HIM! WITHOUT MY WILL BEHIND IT, THE POWER RING IS USELESS! AND I'M GETTING MORE FEEBLE! GOT TO TRY SOME OTHER WAY TO GRAB HIM--
MAYBE THAT'S IT! I'VE BEEN TRYING TO USE MY RING TO GRAB HIM--THE WRONG TACTICS! THIS CREATURE MUST HAVE A WEAKNESS... AND IT'S JUST OCCURRED TO ME WHAT THAT MIGHT BE...!
13

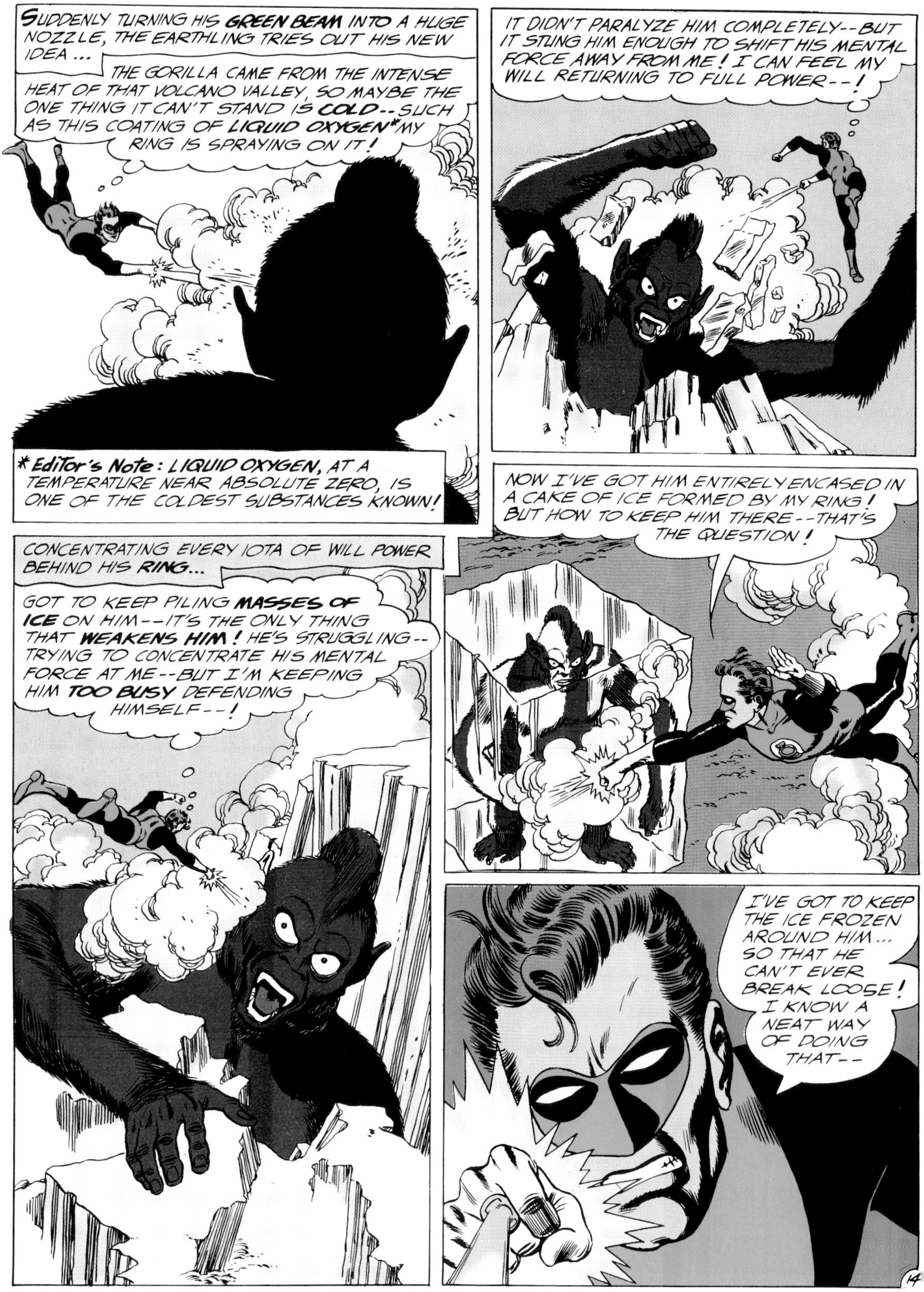
SUDDENLY TURNING HIS GREEN BEAM INTO A HUGE NOZZLE, THE EARTHLING TRIES OUT HIS NEW IDEA ...
THE GORILLA CAME FROM THE INTENSE HEAT OF THAT VOLCANO VALLEY, SO MAYBE THE ONE THING IT CAN'T STAND IS COLD--SUCH AS THIS COATING OF LIQUID OXYGEN* MY RING IS SPRAYING ON IT!
*Editor's Note: LIQUID OXYGEN, AT A TEMPERATURE NEAR ABSOLUTE ZERO, IS ONE OF THE COLDEST SUBSTANCES KNOWN!
IT DIDN'T PARALYZE HIM COMPLETELY--BUT IT STUNG HIM ENOUGH TO SHIFT HIS MENTAL FORCE AWAY FROM ME! I CAN FEEL MY WILL RETURNING TO FULL POWER--!
CONCENTRATING EVERY IOTA OF WILL POWER BEHIND HIS RING...
GOT TO KEEP PILING MASSES OF ICE ON HIM--IT'S THE ONLY THING THAT WEAKENS HIM! HE'S STRUGGLING--TRYING TO CONCENTRATE HIS MENTAL FORCE AT ME--BUT I'M KEEPING HIM TOO BUSY DEFENDING HIMSELF--!
NOW I'VE GOT HIM ENTIRELY ENCASED IN A CAKE OF ICE FORMED BY MY RING! BUT HOW TO KEEP HIM THERE--THAT'S THE QUESTION!
I'VE GOT TO KEEP THE ICE FROZEN AROUND HIM... SO THAT HE CAN'T EVER BREAK LOOSE! I KNOW A NEAT WAY OF DOING THAT--
14

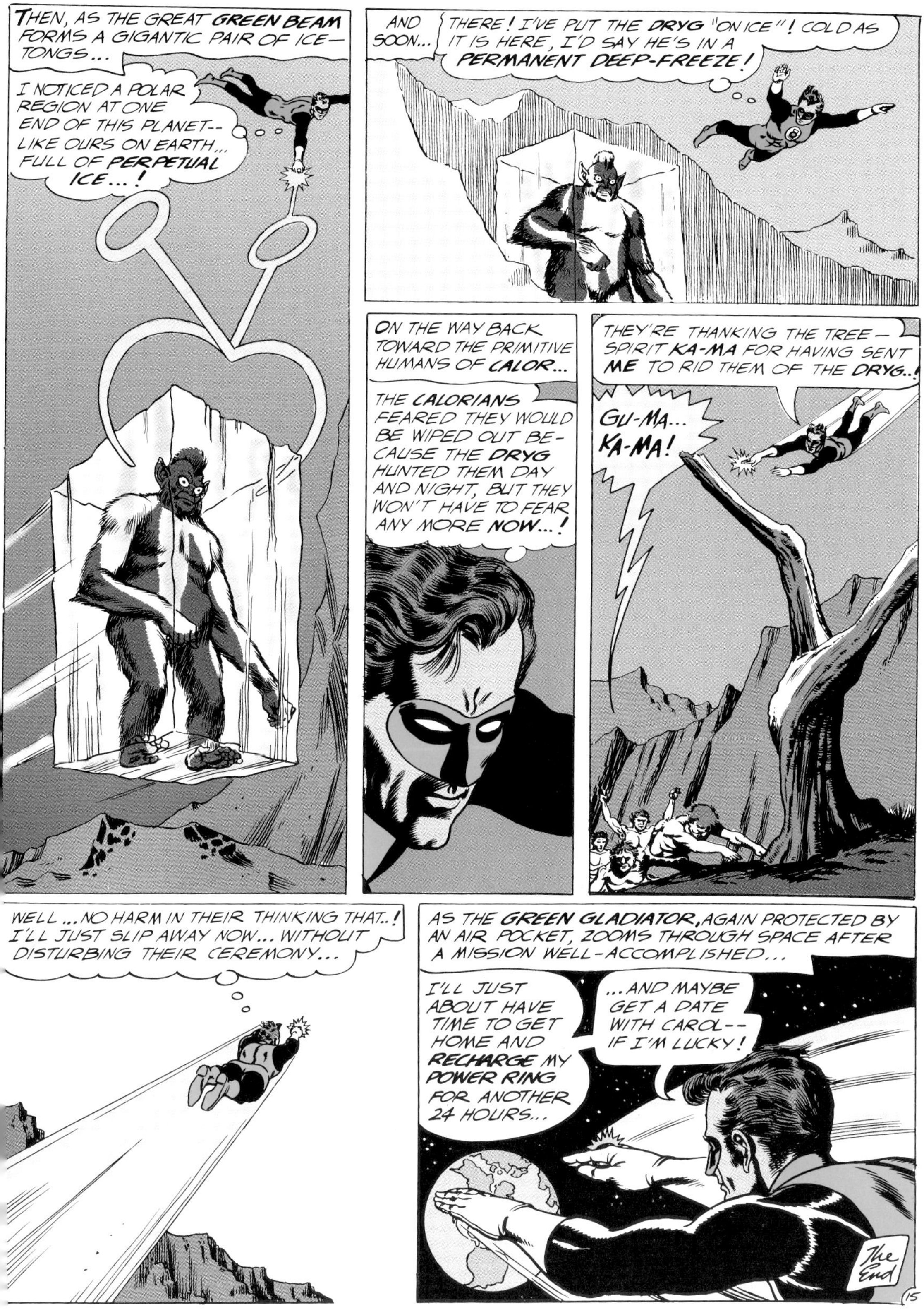
THEN, AS THE GREAT GREEN BEAM FORMS A GIGANTIC PAIR OF ICE-TONGS...
I NOTICED A POLAR REGION AT ONE END OF THIS PLANET-- LIKE OURS ON EARTH... FULL OF PERPETUAL ICE...!
AND SOON...
THERE! I'VE PUT THE DRYG "ON ICE"! COLD AS IT IS HERE, I'D SAY HE'S IN A PERMANENT DEEP-FREEZE!
ON THE WAY BACK TOWARD THE PRIMITIVE HUMANS OF CALOR...
THE CALORIANS FEARED THEY WOULD BE WIPED OUT BECAUSE THE DRYG HUNTED THEM DAY AND NIGHT, BUT THEY WON'T HAVE TO FEAR ANY MORE NOW...!
THEY'RE THANKING THE TREE-SPIRIT KA-MA FOR HAVING SENT ME TO RID THEM OF THE DRYG..!
GU-MA... KA-MA!
WELL ... NO HARM IN THEIR THINKING THAT..! I'LL JUST SLIP AWAY NOW... WITHOUT DISTURBING THEIR CEREMONY...
AS THE GREEN GLADIATOR, AGAIN PROTECTED BY AN AIR POCKET, ZOOMS THROUGH SPACE AFTER A MISSION WELL-ACCOMPLISHED...
I'LL JUST ABOUT HAVE TIME TO GET HOME AND RECHARGE MY POWER RING FOR ANOTHER 24 HOURS...
...AND MAYBE GET A DATE WITH CAROL-- IF I'M LUCKY!
The End
15

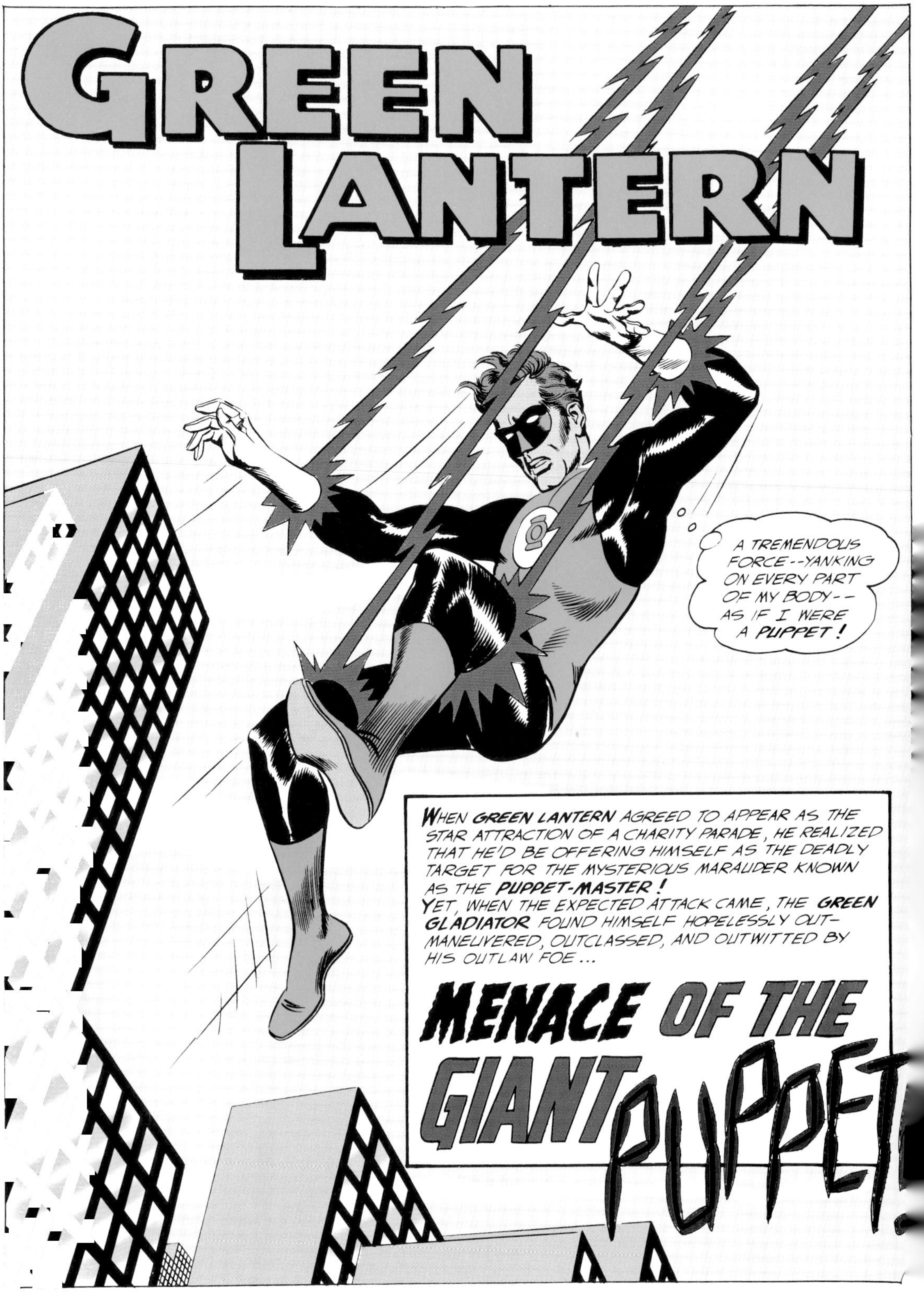
GREEN LANTERN
A TREMENDOUS FORCE--YANKING ON EVERY PART OF MY BODY--AS IF I WERE A PUPPET!
WHEN GREEN LANTERN AGREED TO APPEAR AS THE STAR ATTRACTION OF A CHARITY PARADE, HE REALIZED THAT HE'D BE OFFERING HIMSELF AS THE DEADLY TARGET FOR THE MYSTERIOUS MARAUDER KNOWN AS THE PUPPET-MASTER! YET, WHEN THE EXPECTED ATTACK CAME, THE GREEN GLADIATOR FOUND HIMSELF HOPELESSLY OUT-MANEUVERED, OUTCLASSED, AND OUTWITTED BY HIS OUTLAW FOE ...
MENACE OF THE GIANT PUPPET!

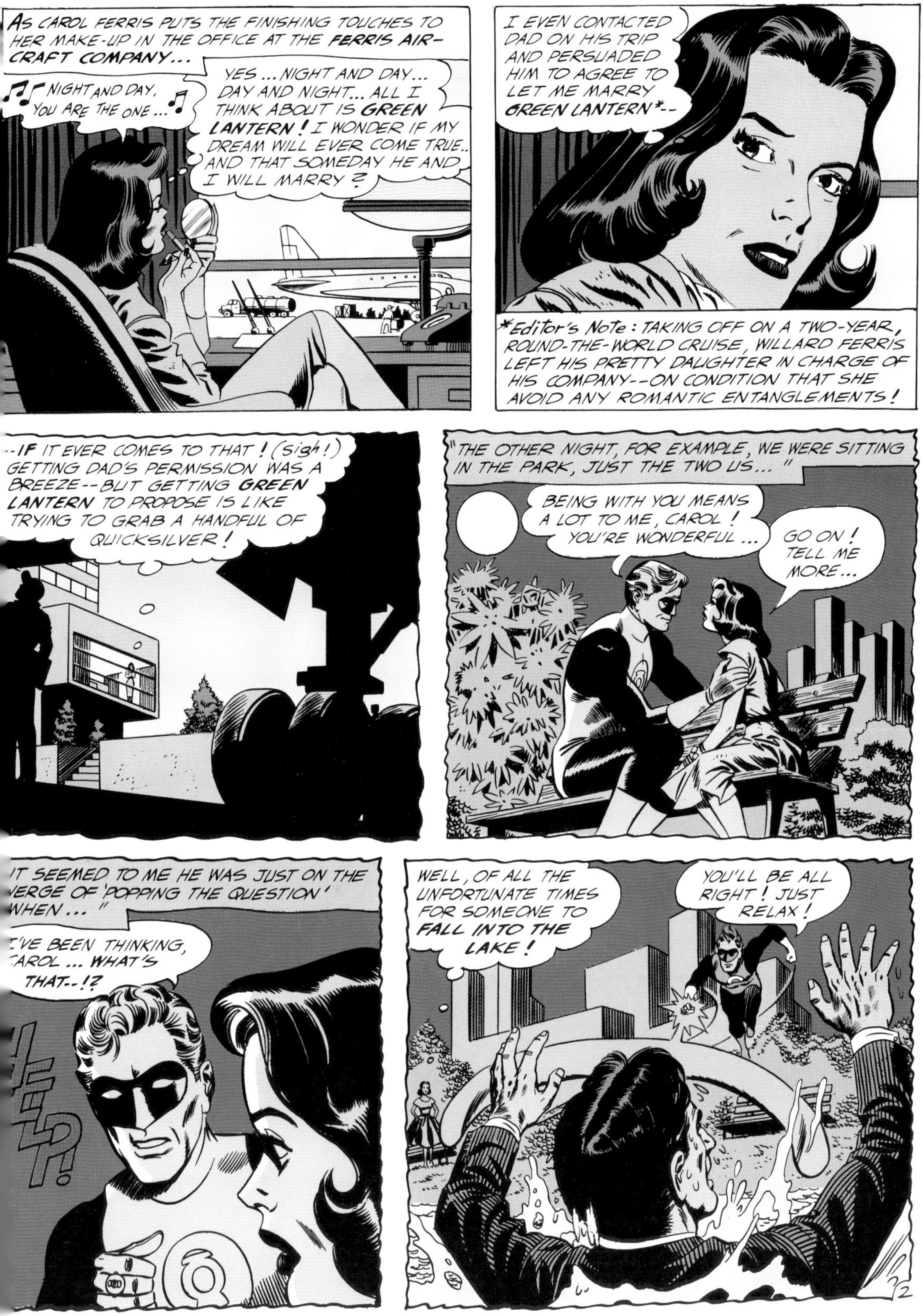
AS CAROL FERRIS PUTS THE FINISHING TOUCHES TO HER MAKE-UP IN THE OFFICE AT THE FERRIS AIR-CRAFT COMPANY...
NIGHT AND DAY, YOU ARE THE ONE...
YES... NIGHT AND DAY... DAY AND NIGHT... ALL I THINK ABOUT IS GREEN LANTERN! I WONDER IF MY DREAM WILL EVER COME TRUE.. AND THAT SOMEDAY HE AND I WILL MARRY?
I EVEN CONTACTED DAD ON HIS TRIP AND PERSUADED HIM TO AGREE TO LET ME MARRY GREEN LANTERN*--
*Editor's Note: TAKING OFF ON A TWO-YEAR, ROUND-THE-WORLD CRUISE, WILLARD FERRIS LEFT HIS PRETTY DAUGHTER IN CHARGE OF HIS COMPANY--ON CONDITION THAT SHE AVOID ANY ROMANTIC ENTANGLEMENTS!
--IF IT EVER COMES TO THAT! (sigh!) GETTING DAD'S PERMISSION WAS A BREEZE--BUT GETTING GREEN LANTERN TO PROPOSE IS LIKE TRYING TO GRAB A HANDFUL OF QUICKSILVER!
"THE OTHER NIGHT, FOR EXAMPLE, WE WERE SITTING IN THE PARK, JUST THE TWO US..."
BEING WITH YOU MEANS A LOT TO ME, CAROL! YOU'RE WONDERFUL...
GO ON! TELL ME MORE...
IT SEEMED TO ME HE WAS JUST ON THE VERGE OF 'POPPING THE QUESTION' WHEN..."
I'VE BEEN THINKING, CAROL... WHAT'S THAT--!?
HELP!
WELL, OF ALL THE UNFORTUNATE TIMES FOR SOMEONE TO FALL INTO THE LAKE!
YOU'LL BE ALL RIGHT! JUST RELAX!
2

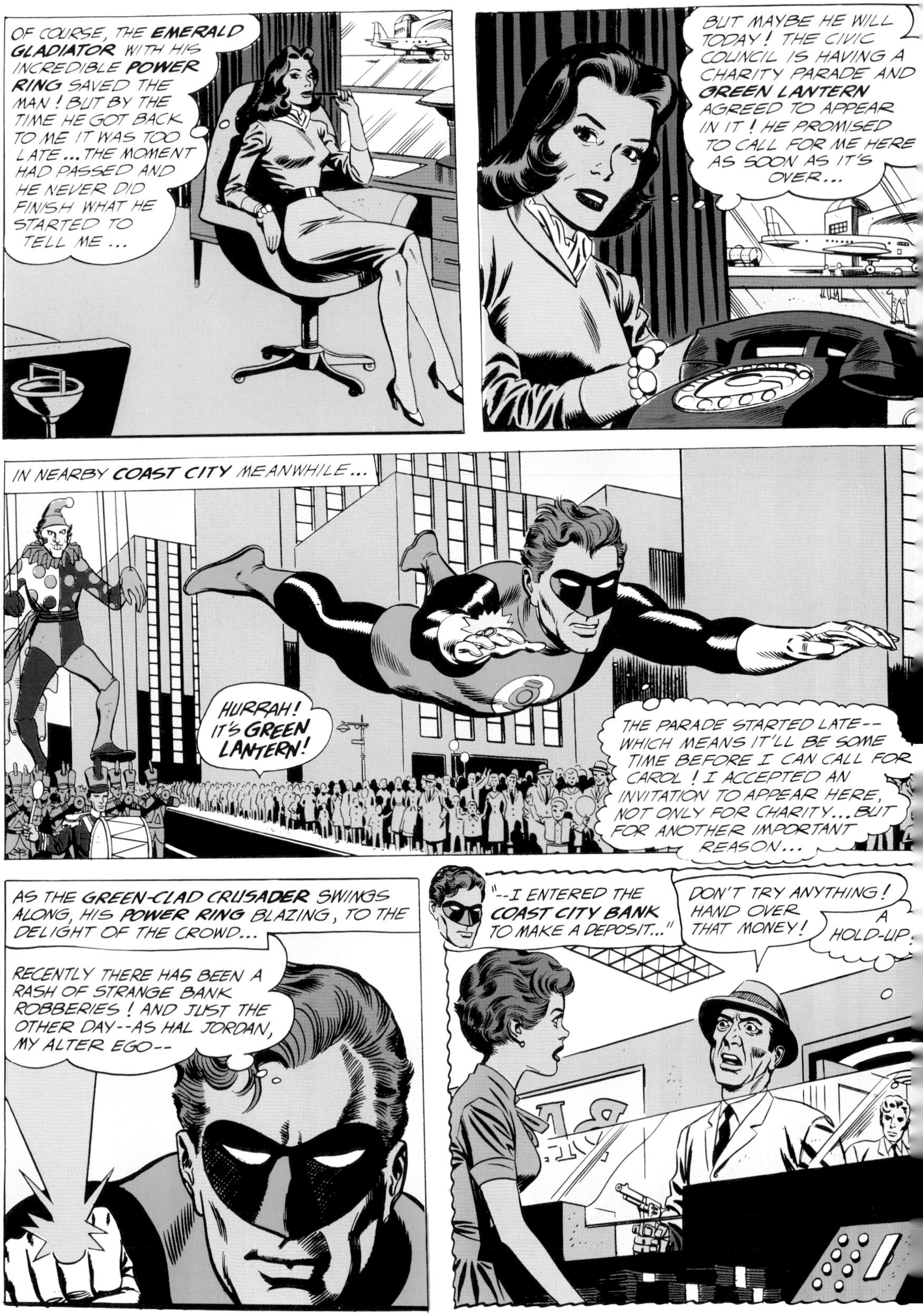
OF COURSE, THE EMERALD GLADIATOR WITH HIS INCREDIBLE POWER RING SAVED THE MAN! BUT BY THE TIME HE GOT BACK TO ME IT WAS TOO LATE...THE MOMENT HAD PASSED AND HE NEVER DID FINISH WHAT HE STARTED TO TELL ME...
BUT MAYBE HE WILL TODAY! THE CIVIC COUNCIL IS HAVING A CHARITY PARADE AND GREEN LANTERN AGREED TO APPEAR IN IT! HE PROMISED TO CALL FOR ME HERE AS SOON AS IT'S OVER...
IN NEARBY COAST CITY MEANWHILE...
HURRAH! IT'S GREEN LANTERN!
THE PARADE STARTED LATE--WHICH MEANS IT'LL BE SOME TIME BEFORE I CAN CALL FOR CAROL! I ACCEPTED AN INVITATION TO APPEAR HERE, NOT ONLY FOR CHARITY...BUT FOR ANOTHER IMPORTANT REASON...
AS THE GREEN-CLAD CRUSADER SWINGS ALONG, HIS POWER RING BLAZING, TO THE DELIGHT OF THE CROWD...
RECENTLY THERE HAS BEEN A RASH OF STRANGE BANK ROBBERIES! AND JUST THE OTHER DAY--AS HAL JORDAN, MY ALTER EGO--
"--I ENTERED THE COAST CITY BANK TO MAKE A DEPOSIT..."
DON'T TRY ANYTHING! HAND OVER THAT MONEY!
A HOLD-UP!

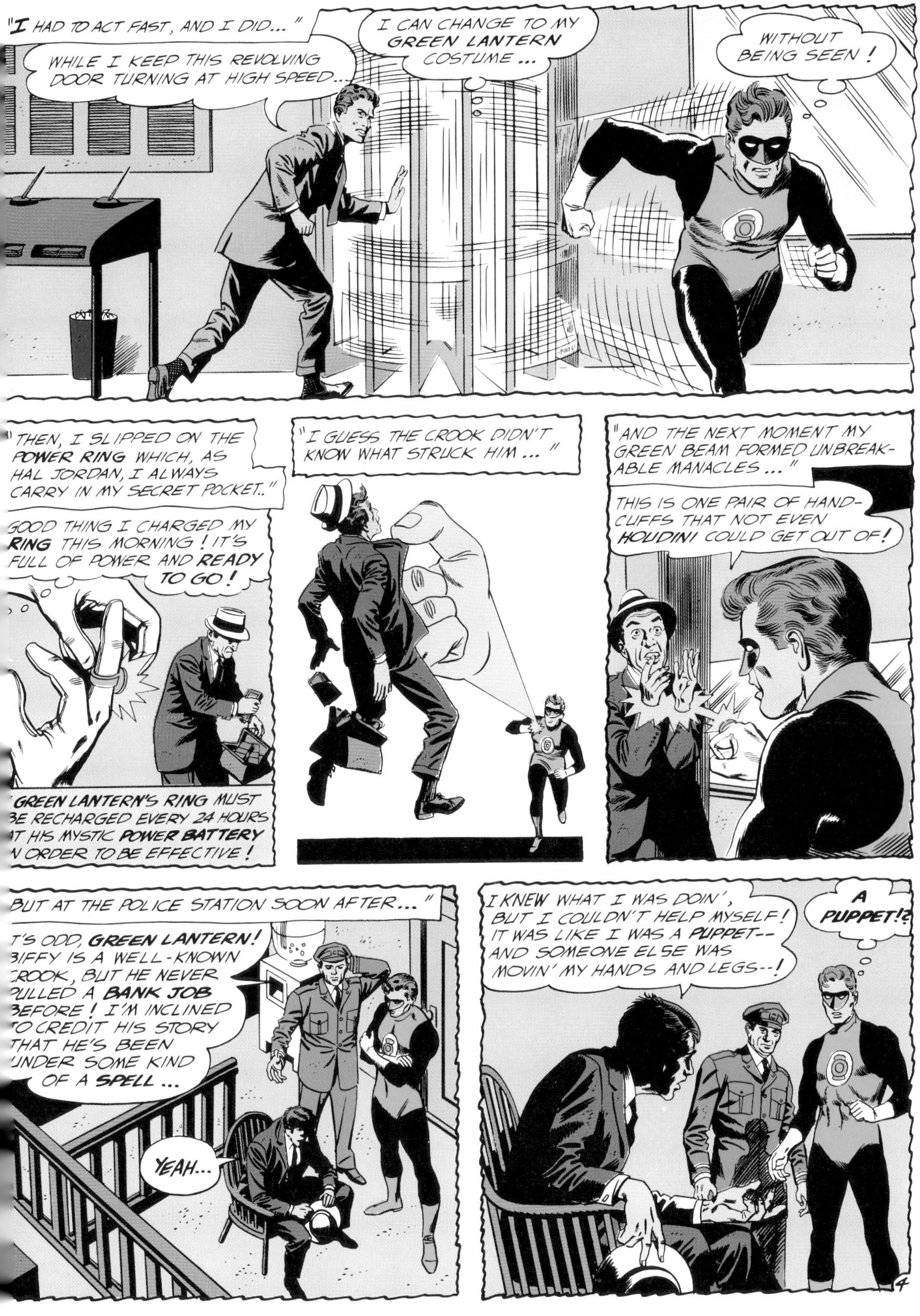
"I HAD TO ACT FAST, AND I DID..."
WHILE I KEEP THIS REVOLVING DOOR TURNING AT HIGH SPEED...
I CAN CHANGE TO MY GREEN LANTERN COSTUME ...
WITHOUT BEING SEEN !
"THEN, I SLIPPED ON THE POWER RING WHICH, AS HAL JORDAN, I ALWAYS CARRY IN MY SECRET POCKET.."
GOOD THING I CHARGED MY RING THIS MORNING ! IT'S FULL OF POWER AND READY TO GO !
GREEN LANTERN'S RING MUST BE RECHARGED EVERY 24 HOURS AT HIS MYSTIC POWER BATTERY IN ORDER TO BE EFFECTIVE !
"I GUESS THE CROOK DIDN'T KNOW WHAT STRUCK HIM ..."
"AND THE NEXT MOMENT MY GREEN BEAM FORMED UNBREAKABLE MANACLES ..."
THIS IS ONE PAIR OF HANDCUFFS THAT NOT EVEN HOUDINI COULD GET OUT OF!
"BUT AT THE POLICE STATION SOON AFTER..."
IT'S ODD, GREEN LANTERN! BIFFY IS A WELL-KNOWN CROOK, BUT HE NEVER PULLED A BANK JOB BEFORE ! I'M INCLINED TO CREDIT HIS STORY THAT HE'S BEEN UNDER SOME KIND OF A SPELL ...
YEAH...
I KNEW WHAT I WAS DOIN', BUT I COULDN'T HELP MYSELF! IT WAS LIKE I WAS A PUPPET-- AND SOMEONE ELSE WAS MOVIN' MY HANDS AND LEGS--!
A PUPPET!?
4

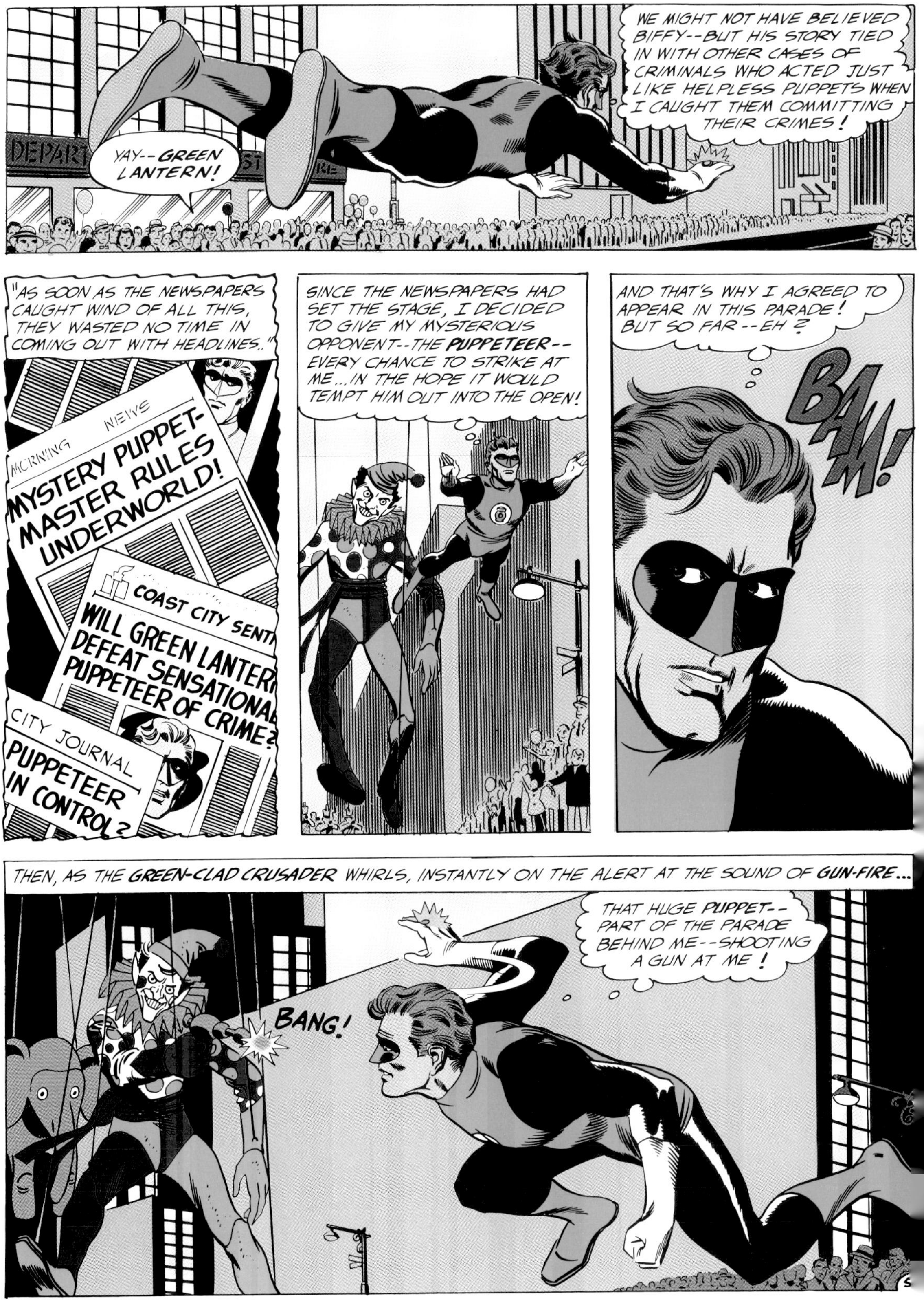
WE MIGHT NOT HAVE BELIEVED BIFFY--BUT HIS STORY TIED IN WITH OTHER CASES OF CRIMINALS WHO ACTED JUST LIKE HELPLESS PUPPETS WHEN I CAUGHT THEM COMMITTING THEIR CRIMES!
YAY--GREEN LANTERN!
DEPART
"AS SOON AS THE NEWSPAPERS CAUGHT WIND OF ALL THIS, THEY WASTED NO TIME IN COMING OUT WITH HEADLINES.."
MORNING NEWS
MYSTERY PUPPET-MASTER RULES UNDERWORLD!
COAST CITY SENT
WILL GREEN LANTER DEFEAT SENSATIONAL PUPPETEER OF CRIME?
CITY JOURNAL
PUPPETEER IN CONTROL?
SINCE THE NEWSPAPERS HAD SET THE STAGE, I DECIDED TO GIVE MY MYSTERIOUS OPPONENT--THE PUPPETEER--EVERY CHANCE TO STRIKE AT ME...IN THE HOPE IT WOULD TEMPT HIM OUT INTO THE OPEN!
AND THAT'S WHY I AGREED TO APPEAR IN THIS PARADE! BUT SO FAR--EH?
BAM!
THEN, AS THE GREEN-CLAD CRUSADER WHIRLS, INSTANTLY ON THE ALERT AT THE SOUND OF GUN-FIRE...
THAT HUGE PUPPET--PART OF THE PARADE BEHIND ME--SHOOTING A GUN AT ME!
BANG!

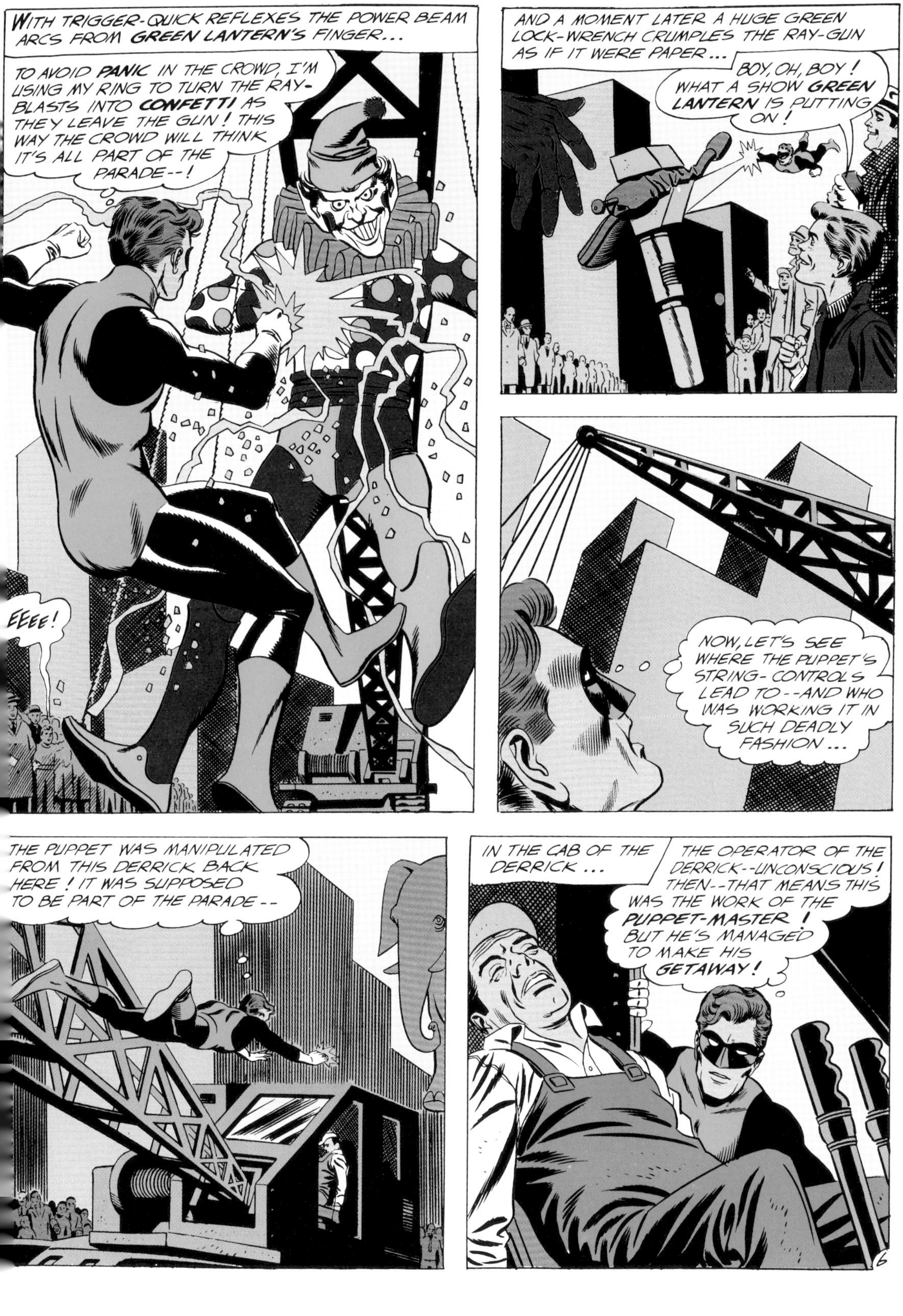
WITH TRIGGER-QUICK REFLEXES THE POWER BEAM ARCS FROM GREEN LANTERN'S FINGER...
TO AVOID PANIC IN THE CROWD, I'M USING MY RING TO TURN THE RAY-BLASTS INTO CONFETTI AS THEY LEAVE THE GUN! THIS WAY THE CROWD WILL THINK IT'S ALL PART OF THE PARADE--!
EEEE!
AND A MOMENT LATER A HUGE GREEN LOCK-WRENCH CRUMPLES THE RAY-GUN AS IF IT WERE PAPER...
BOY, OH, BOY! WHAT A SHOW GREEN LANTERN IS PUTTING ON!
NOW, LET'S SEE WHERE THE PUPPET'S STRING-CONTROLS LEAD TO--AND WHO WAS WORKING IT IN SUCH DEADLY FASHION...
THE PUPPET WAS MANIPULATED FROM THIS DERRICK BACK HERE! IT WAS SUPPOSED TO BE PART OF THE PARADE--
IN THE CAB OF THE DERRICK...
THE OPERATOR OF THE DERRICK--UNCONSCIOUS! THEN--THAT MEANS THIS WAS THE WORK OF THE PUPPET-MASTER! BUT HE'S MANAGED TO MAKE HIS GETAWAY!
6

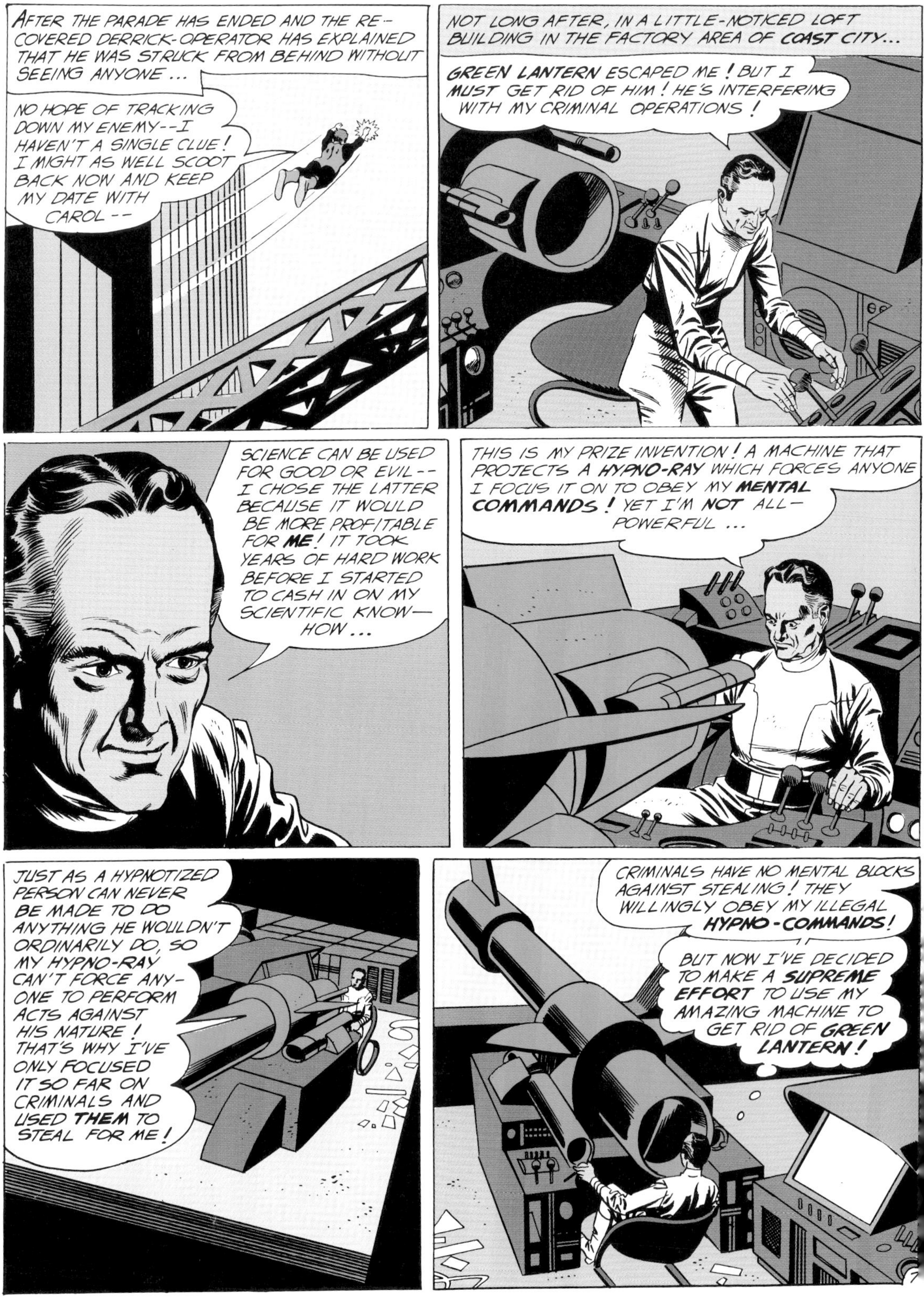
AFTER THE PARADE HAS ENDED AND THE RE-COVERED DERRICK-OPERATOR HAS EXPLAINED THAT HE WAS STRUCK FROM BEHIND WITHOUT SEEING ANYONE ...
NO HOPE OF TRACKING DOWN MY ENEMY--I HAVEN'T A SINGLE CLUE! I MIGHT AS WELL SCOOT BACK NOW AND KEEP MY DATE WITH CAROL--
NOT LONG AFTER, IN A LITTLE-NOTICED LOFT BUILDING IN THE FACTORY AREA OF COAST CITY...
GREEN LANTERN ESCAPED ME! BUT I MUST GET RID OF HIM! HE'S INTERFERING WITH MY CRIMINAL OPERATIONS!
SCIENCE CAN BE USED FOR GOOD OR EVIL-- I CHOSE THE LATTER BECAUSE IT WOULD BE MORE PROFITABLE FOR ME! IT TOOK YEARS OF HARD WORK BEFORE I STARTED TO CASH IN ON MY SCIENTIFIC KNOW-HOW...
THIS IS MY PRIZE INVENTION! A MACHINE THAT PROJECTS A HYPNO-RAY WHICH FORCES ANYONE I FOCUS IT ON TO OBEY MY MENTAL COMMANDS! YET I'M NOT ALL-POWERFUL ...
JUST AS A HYPNOTIZED PERSON CAN NEVER BE MADE TO DO ANYTHING HE WOULDN'T ORDINARILY DO, SO MY HYPNO-RAY CAN'T FORCE ANY-ONE TO PERFORM ACTS AGAINST HIS NATURE! THAT'S WHY I'VE ONLY FOCUSED IT SO FAR ON CRIMINALS AND USED THEM TO STEAL FOR ME!
CRIMINALS HAVE NO MENTAL BLOCKS AGAINST STEALING! THEY WILLINGLY OBEY MY ILLEGAL HYPNO-COMMANDS!
BUT NOW I'VE DECIDED TO MAKE A SUPREME EFFORT TO USE MY AMAZING MACHINE TO GET RID OF GREEN LANTERN!
7

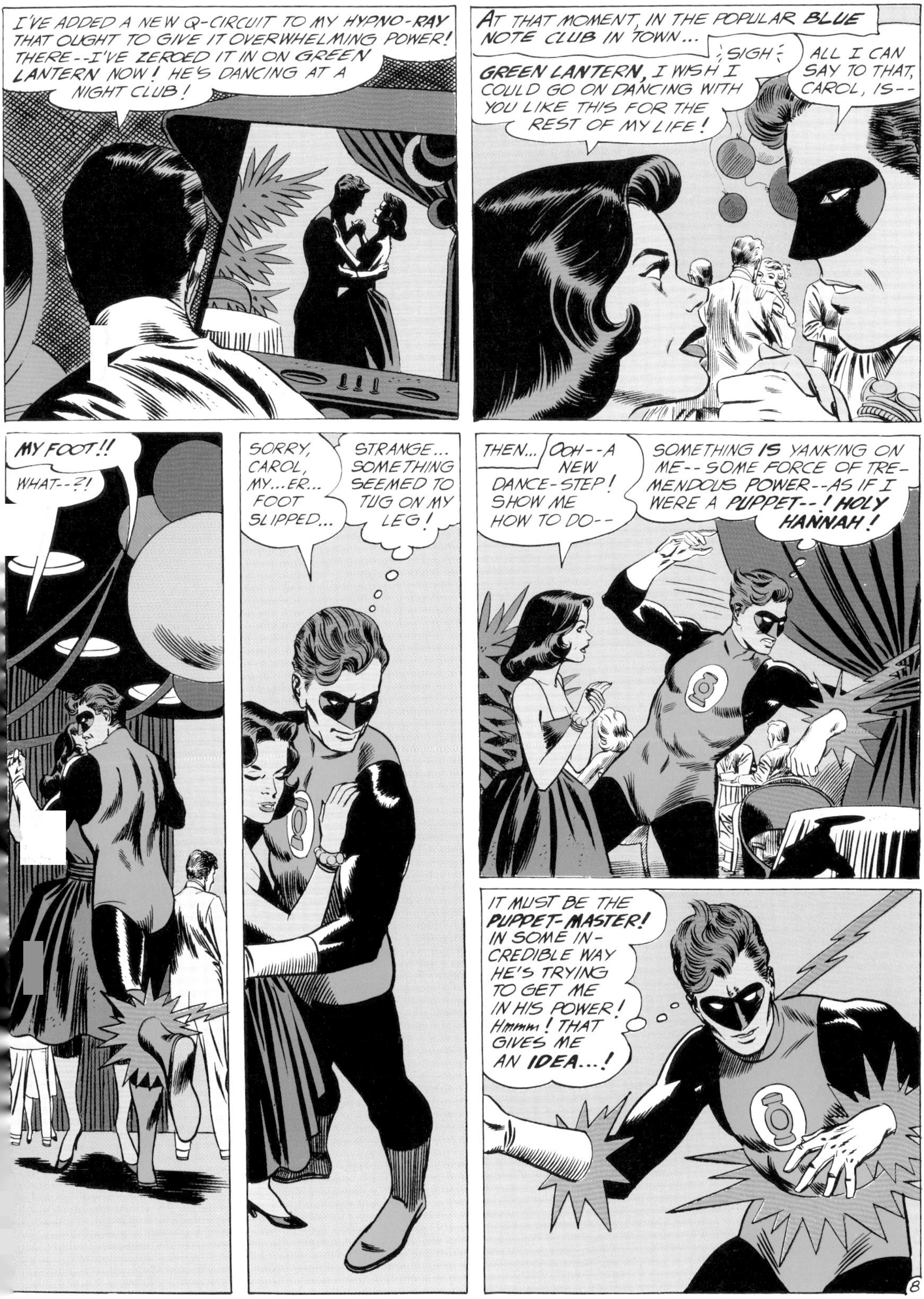
I'VE ADDED A NEW Q-CIRCUIT TO MY HYPNO-RAY THAT OUGHT TO GIVE IT OVERWHELMING POWER! THERE--I'VE ZEROED IT IN ON GREEN LANTERN NOW! HE'S DANCING AT A NIGHT CLUB!
AT THAT MOMENT, IN THE POPULAR BLUE NOTE CLUB IN TOWN...
:SIGH: GREEN LANTERN, I WISH I COULD GO ON DANCING WITH YOU LIKE THIS FOR THE REST OF MY LIFE!
ALL I CAN SAY TO THAT, CAROL, IS--
MY FOOT!!
WHAT--?!
SORRY, CAROL, MY...ER... FOOT SLIPPED...
STRANGE... SOMETHING SEEMED TO TUG ON MY LEG!
THEN...
OOH--A NEW DANCE-STEP! SHOW ME HOW TO DO--
SOMETHING IS YANKING ON ME--SOME FORCE OF TREMENDOUS POWER--AS IF I WERE A PUPPET--! HOLY HANNAH!
IT MUST BE THE PUPPET-MASTER! IN SOME INCREDIBLE WAY HE'S TRYING TO GET ME IN HIS POWER! Hmmm! THAT GIVES ME AN IDEA...!
8

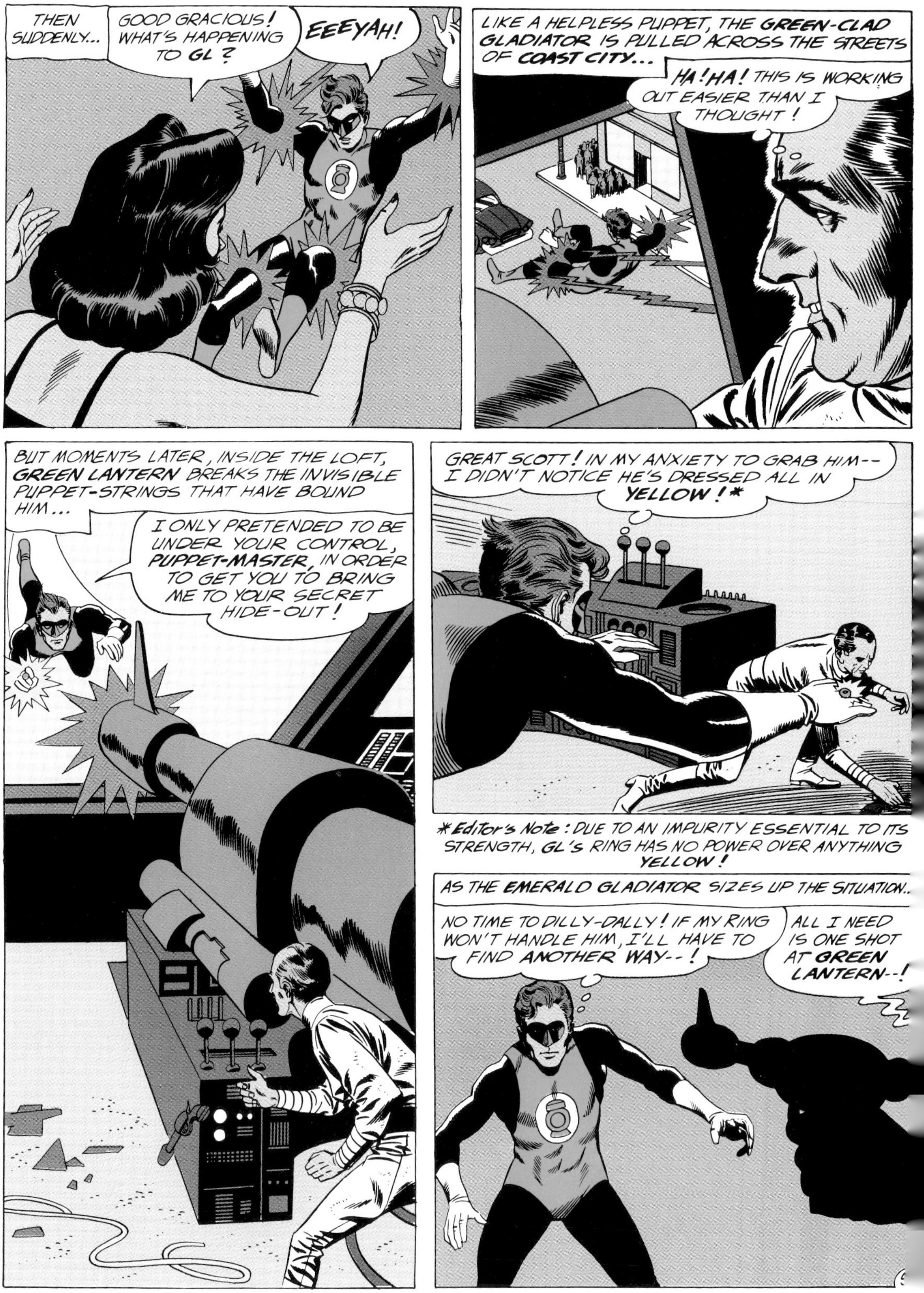
THEN SUDDENLY...
GOOD GRACIOUS! WHAT'S HAPPENING TO GL?
EEEYAH!
LIKE A HELPLESS PUPPET, THE GREEN-CLAD GLADIATOR IS PULLED ACROSS THE STREETS OF COAST CITY...
HA! HA! THIS IS WORKING OUT EASIER THAN I THOUGHT!
BUT MOMENTS LATER, INSIDE THE LOFT, GREEN LANTERN BREAKS THE INVISIBLE PUPPET-STRINGS THAT HAVE BOUND HIM...
I ONLY PRETENDED TO BE UNDER YOUR CONTROL, PUPPET-MASTER, IN ORDER TO GET YOU TO BRING ME TO YOUR SECRET HIDE-OUT!
GREAT SCOTT! IN MY ANXIETY TO GRAB HIM-- I DIDN'T NOTICE HE'S DRESSED ALL IN YELLOW! *
* Editor's Note: DUE TO AN IMPURITY ESSENTIAL TO ITS STRENGTH, GL'S RING HAS NO POWER OVER ANYTHING YELLOW!
AS THE EMERALD GLADIATOR SIZES UP THE SITUATION...
NO TIME TO DILLY-DALLY! IF MY RING WON'T HANDLE HIM, I'LL HAVE TO FIND ANOTHER WAY--!
ALL I NEED IS ONE SHOT AT GREEN LANTERN--!

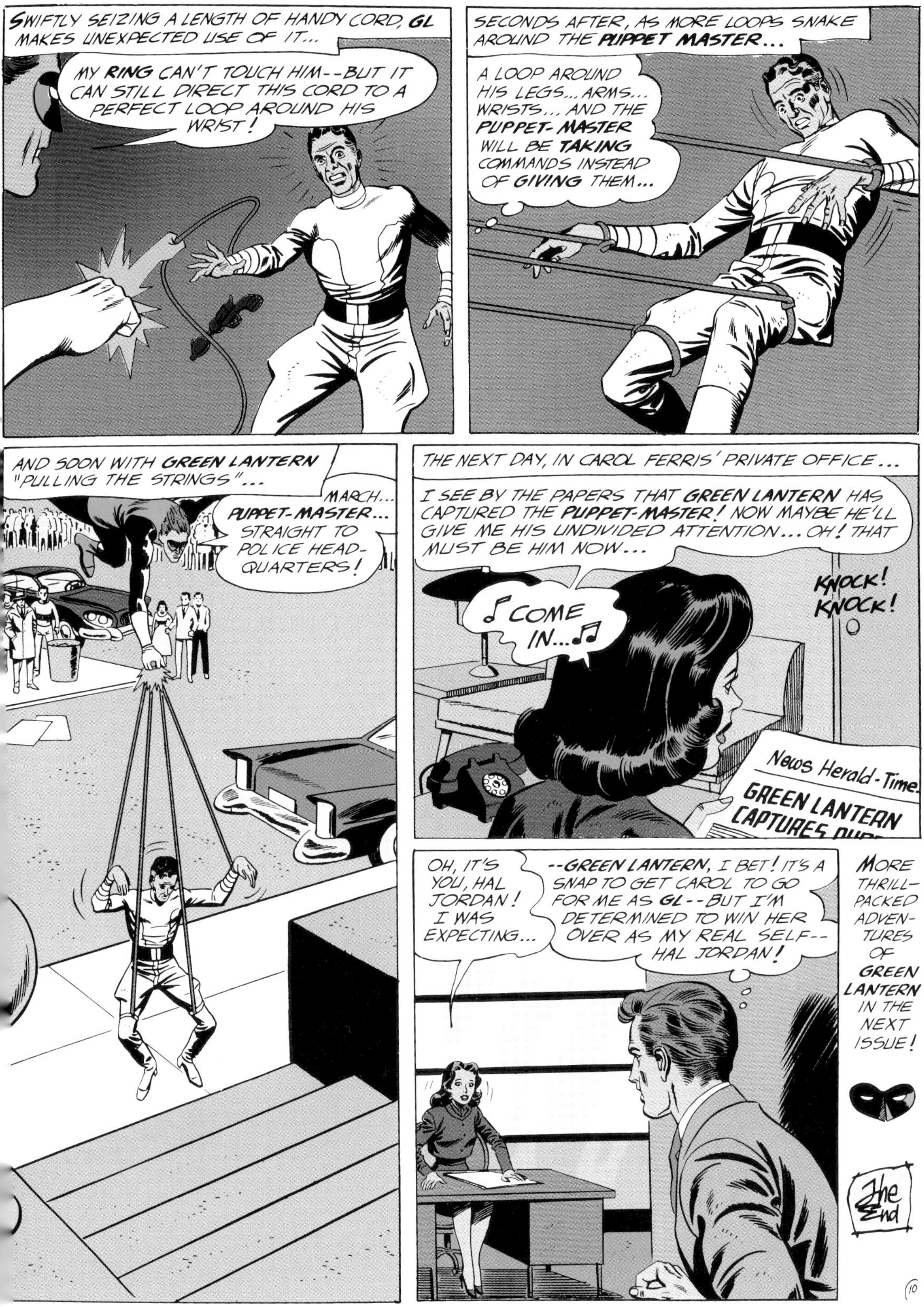
SWIFTLY SEIZING A LENGTH OF HANDY CORD, GL MAKES UNEXPECTED USE OF IT...
MY RING CAN'T TOUCH HIM--BUT IT CAN STILL DIRECT THIS CORD TO A PERFECT LOOP AROUND HIS WRIST!
SECONDS AFTER, AS MORE LOOPS SNAKE AROUND THE PUPPET MASTER...
A LOOP AROUND HIS LEGS... ARMS... WRISTS... AND THE PUPPET-MASTER WILL BE TAKING COMMANDS INSTEAD OF GIVING THEM...
AND SOON WITH GREEN LANTERN "PULLING THE STRINGS"...
MARCH... PUPPET-MASTER... STRAIGHT TO POLICE HEAD-QUARTERS!
THE NEXT DAY, IN CAROL FERRIS' PRIVATE OFFICE...
I SEE BY THE PAPERS THAT GREEN LANTERN HAS CAPTURED THE PUPPET-MASTER! NOW MAYBE HE'LL GIVE ME HIS UNDIVIDED ATTENTION... OH! THAT MUST BE HIM NOW...
KNOCK! KNOCK!
COME IN...
News Herald-Time
GREEN LANTERN CAPTURES
OH, IT'S YOU, HAL JORDAN! I WAS EXPECTING...
--GREEN LANTERN, I BET! IT'S A SNAP TO GET CAROL TO GO FOR ME AS GL--BUT I'M DETERMINED TO WIN HER OVER AS MY REAL SELF--HAL JORDAN!
MORE THRILL-PACKED ADVEN-TURES OF GREEN LANTERN IN THE NEXT ISSUE!
The End
10

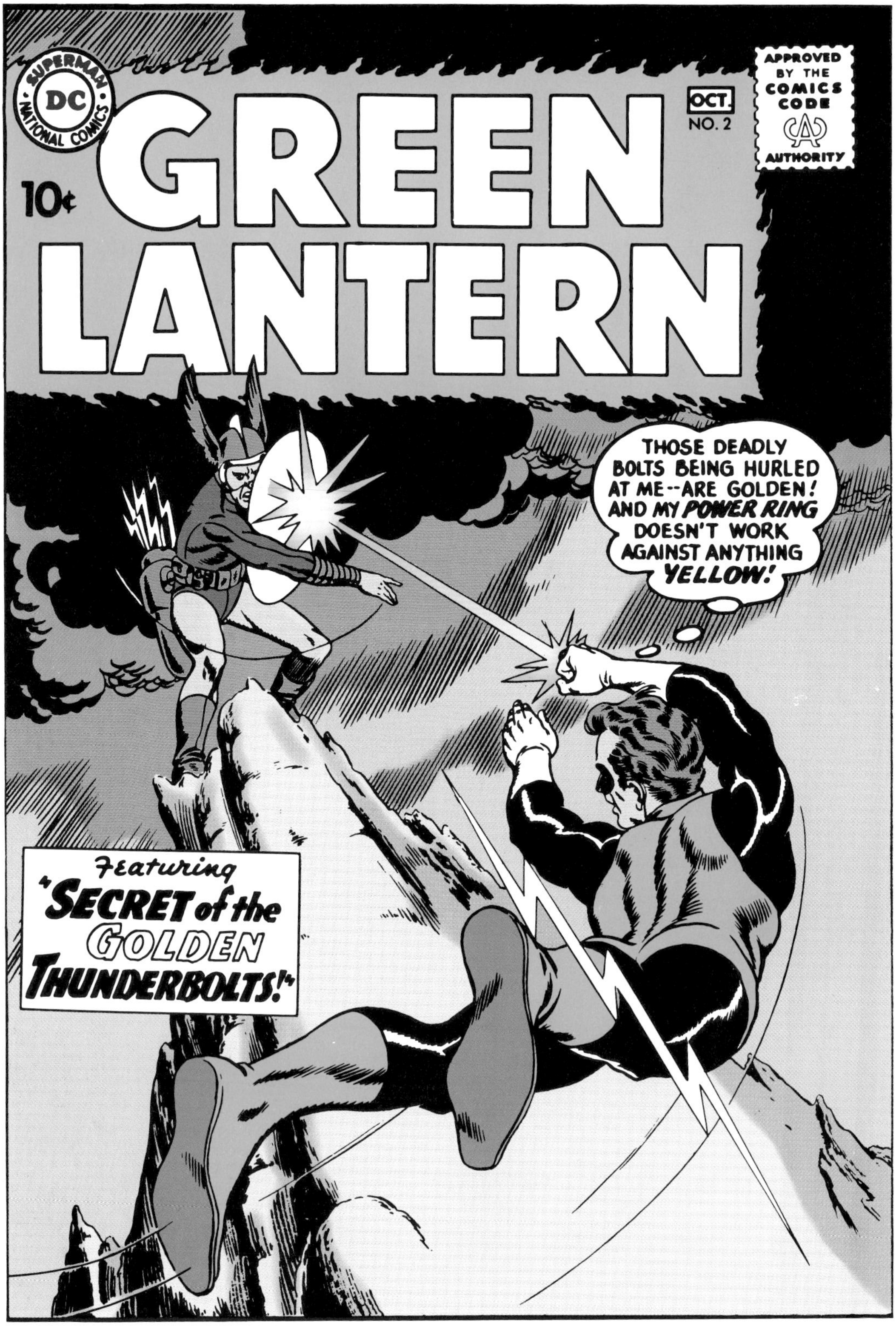
SUPERMAN DC NATIONAL COMICS
10¢
GREEN LANTERN
OCT. NO. 2
APPROVED BY THE COMICS CODE AUTHORITY
THOSE DEADLY BOLTS BEING HURLED AT ME--ARE GOLDEN! AND MY POWER RING DOESN'T WORK AGAINST ANYTHING YELLOW!
Featuring "SECRET of the GOLDEN THUNDERBOLTS!"

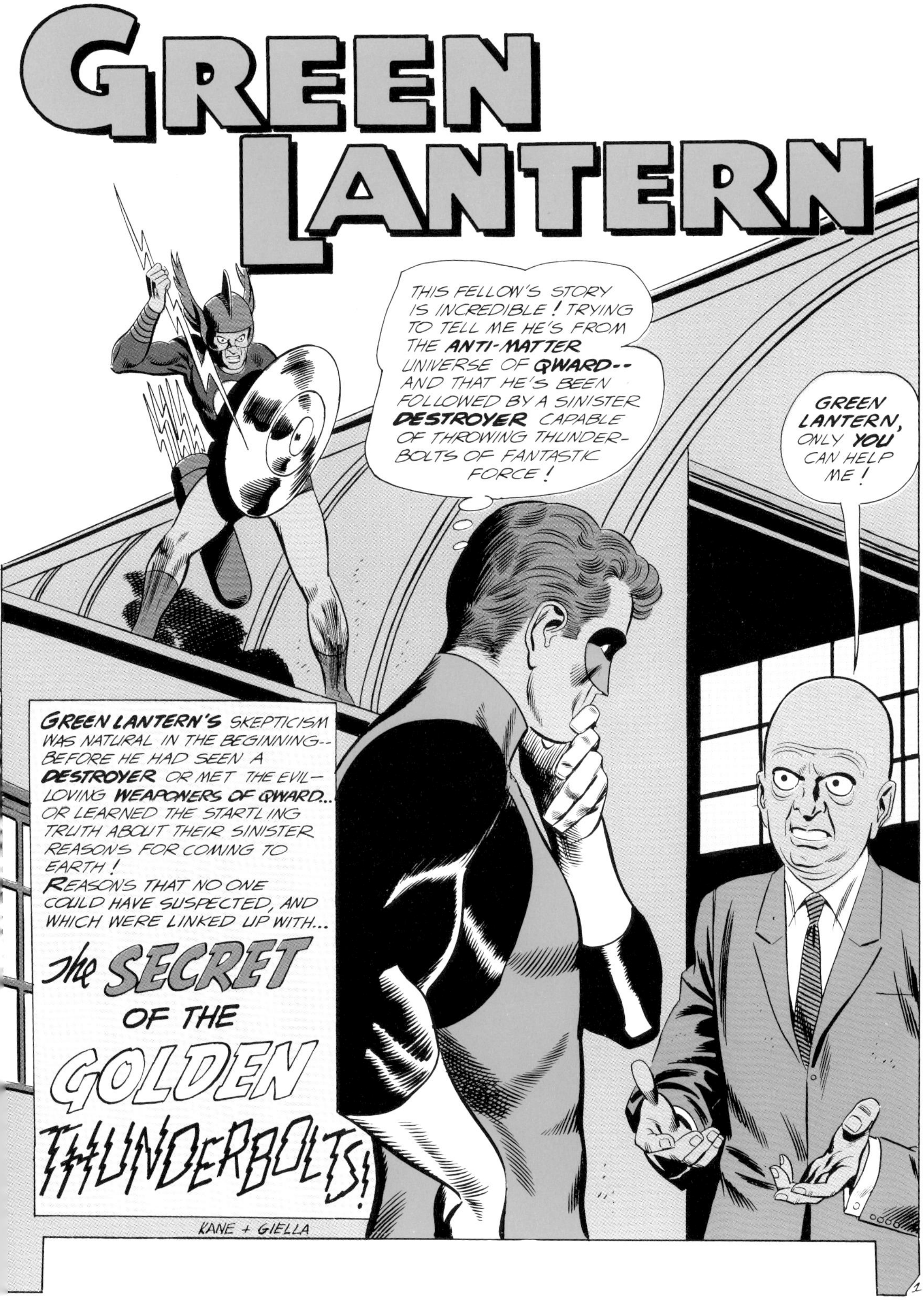
GREEN LANTERN
THIS FELLOW'S STORY IS INCREDIBLE! TRYING TO TELL ME HE'S FROM THE ANTI-MATTER UNIVERSE OF QWARD-- AND THAT HE'S BEEN FOLLOWED BY A SINISTER DESTROYER CAPABLE OF THROWING THUNDER-BOLTS OF FANTASTIC FORCE!
GREEN LANTERN, ONLY YOU CAN HELP ME!
GREEN LANTERN'S SKEPTICISM WAS NATURAL IN THE BEGINNING-- BEFORE HE HAD SEEN A DESTROYER OR MET THE EVIL-LOVING WEAPONERS OF QWARD... OR LEARNED THE STARTLING TRUTH ABOUT THEIR SINISTER REASONS FOR COMING TO EARTH! REASONS THAT NO ONE COULD HAVE SUSPECTED, AND WHICH WERE LINKED UP WITH...
The SECRET OF THE GOLDEN THUNDERBOLTS!
KANE + GIELLA
1

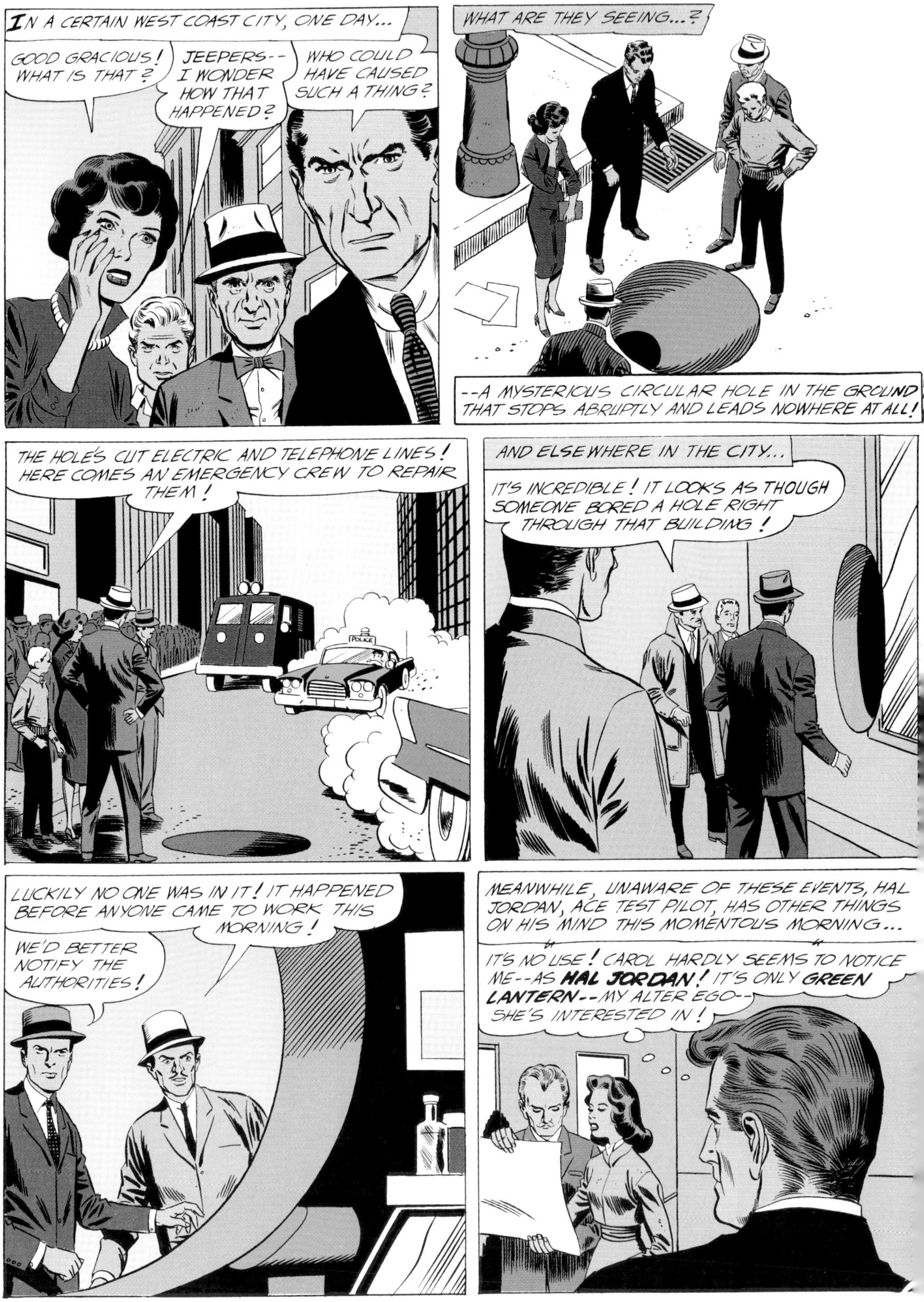
IN A CERTAIN WEST COAST CITY, ONE DAY...
GOOD GRACIOUS! WHAT IS THAT?
JEEPERS-- I WONDER HOW THAT HAPPENED?
WHO COULD HAVE CAUSED SUCH A THING?
WHAT ARE THEY SEEING...?
--A MYSTERIOUS CIRCULAR HOLE IN THE GROUND THAT STOPS ABRUPTLY AND LEADS NOWHERE AT ALL!
THE HOLE'S CUT ELECTRIC AND TELEPHONE LINES! HERE COMES AN EMERGENCY CREW TO REPAIR THEM!
POLICE
AND ELSEWHERE IN THE CITY...
IT'S INCREDIBLE! IT LOOKS AS THOUGH SOMEONE BORED A HOLE RIGHT THROUGH THAT BUILDING!
LUCKILY NO ONE WAS IN IT! IT HAPPENED BEFORE ANYONE CAME TO WORK THIS MORNING!
WE'D BETTER NOTIFY THE AUTHORITIES!
MEANWHILE, UNAWARE OF THESE EVENTS, HAL JORDAN, ACE TEST PILOT, HAS OTHER THINGS ON HIS MIND THIS MOMENTOUS MORNING...
IT'S NO USE! CAROL HARDLY SEEMS TO NOTICE ME--AS HAL JORDAN! IT'S ONLY GREEN LANTERN--MY ALTER EGO--SHE'S INTERESTED IN!

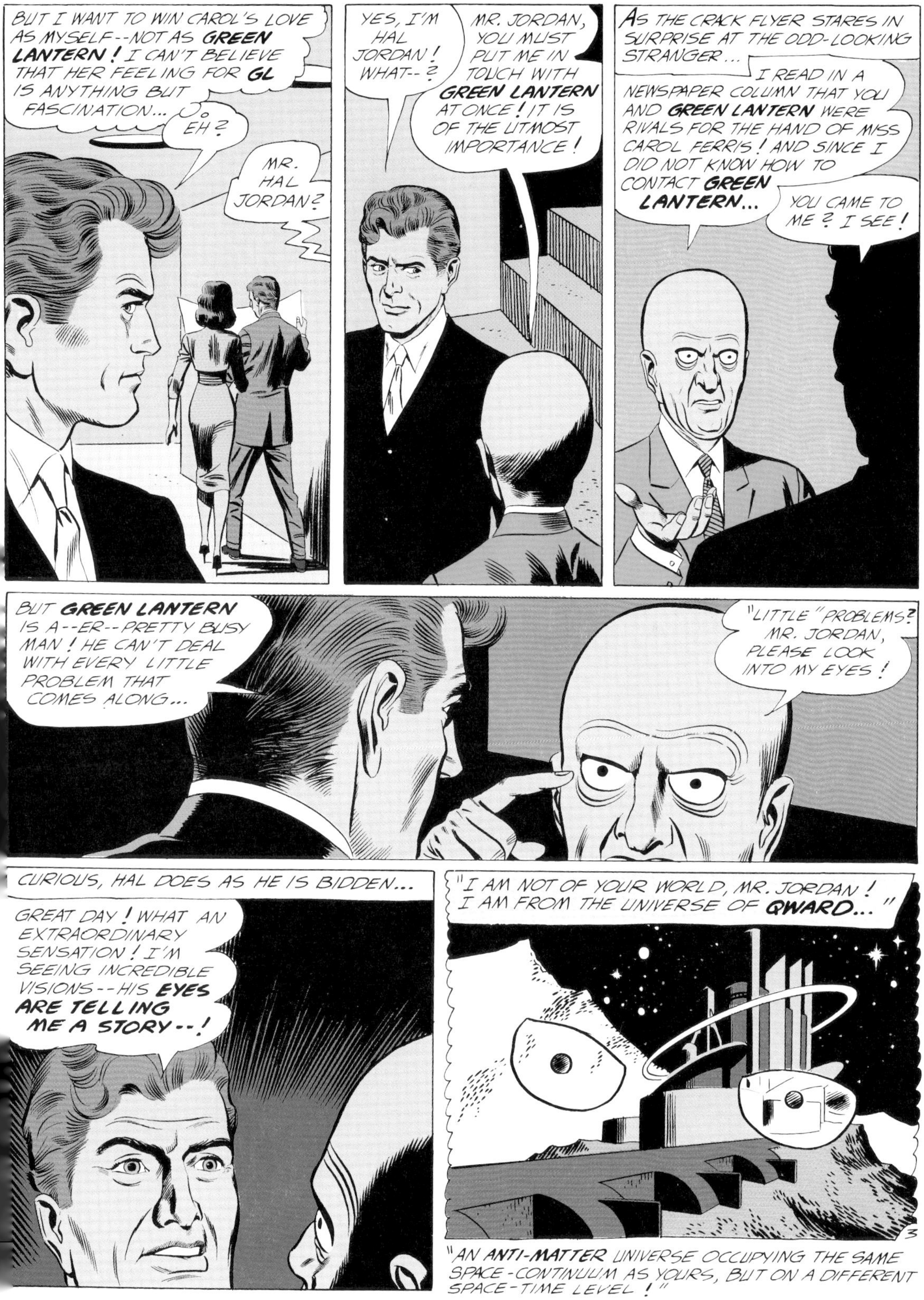
BUT I WANT TO WIN CAROL'S LOVE AS MYSELF--NOT AS GREEN LANTERN! I CAN'T BELIEVE THAT HER FEELING FOR GL IS ANYTHING BUT FASCINATION...
EH?
MR. HAL JORDAN?
YES, I'M HAL JORDAN! WHAT--?
MR. JORDAN, YOU MUST PUT ME IN TOUCH WITH GREEN LANTERN AT ONCE! IT IS OF THE UTMOST IMPORTANCE!
AS THE CRACK FLYER STARES IN SURPRISE AT THE ODD-LOOKING STRANGER...
I READ IN A NEWSPAPER COLUMN THAT YOU AND GREEN LANTERN WERE RIVALS FOR THE HAND OF MISS CAROL FERRIS! AND SINCE I DID NOT KNOW HOW TO CONTACT GREEN LANTERN...
YOU CAME TO ME? I SEE!
BUT GREEN LANTERN IS A--ER--PRETTY BUSY MAN! HE CAN'T DEAL WITH EVERY LITTLE PROBLEM THAT COMES ALONG...
"LITTLE" PROBLEMS? MR. JORDAN, PLEASE LOOK INTO MY EYES!
CURIOUS, HAL DOES AS HE IS BIDDEN...
GREAT DAY! WHAT AN EXTRAORDINARY SENSATION! I'M SEEING INCREDIBLE VISIONS--HIS EYES ARE TELLING ME A STORY--!
"I AM NOT OF YOUR WORLD, MR. JORDAN! I AM FROM THE UNIVERSE OF QWARD..."
3
"AN ANTI-MATTER UNIVERSE OCCUPYING THE SAME SPACE-CONTINUUM AS YOURS, BUT ON A DIFFERENT SPACE-TIME LEVEL!"

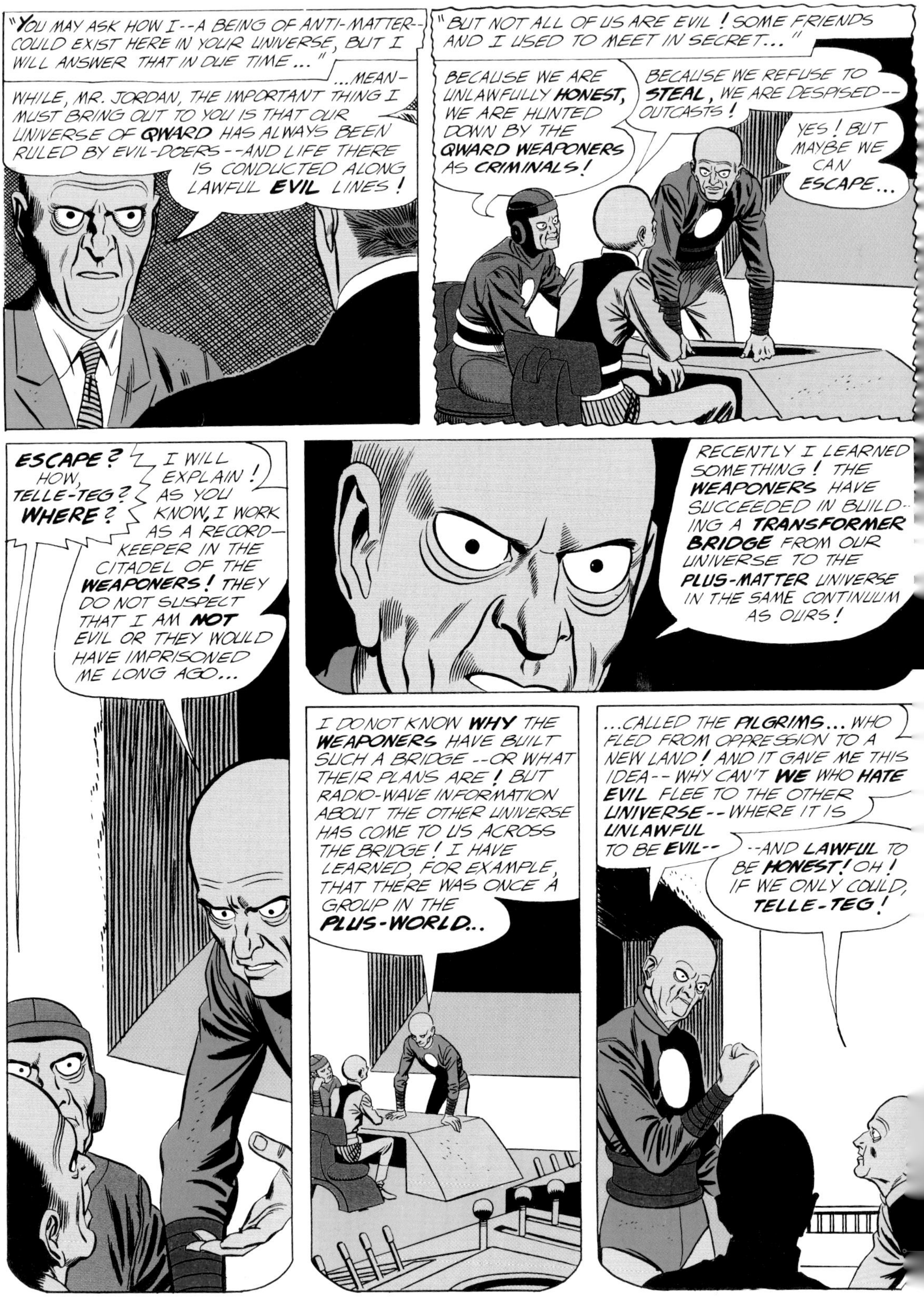
"YOU MAY ASK HOW I--A BEING OF ANTI-MATTER--COULD EXIST HERE IN YOUR UNIVERSE, BUT I WILL ANSWER THAT IN DUE TIME..."
...MEANWHILE, MR. JORDAN, THE IMPORTANT THING I MUST BRING OUT TO YOU IS THAT OUR UNIVERSE OF QWARD HAS ALWAYS BEEN RULED BY EVIL-DOERS--AND LIFE THERE IS CONDUCTED ALONG LAWFUL EVIL LINES!
"BUT NOT ALL OF US ARE EVIL! SOME FRIENDS AND I USED TO MEET IN SECRET..."
BECAUSE WE ARE UNLAWFULLY HONEST, WE ARE HUNTED DOWN BY THE QWARD WEAPONERS AS CRIMINALS!
BECAUSE WE REFUSE TO STEAL, WE ARE DESPISED--OUTCASTS!
YES! BUT MAYBE WE CAN ESCAPE...
ESCAPE? HOW, TELLE-TEG? WHERE?
I WILL EXPLAIN! AS YOU KNOW, I WORK AS A RECORD-KEEPER IN THE CITADEL OF THE WEAPONERS! THEY DO NOT SUSPECT THAT I AM NOT EVIL OR THEY WOULD HAVE IMPRISONED ME LONG AGO...
RECENTLY I LEARNED SOMETHING! THE WEAPONERS HAVE SUCCEEDED IN BUILDING A TRANSFORMER BRIDGE FROM OUR UNIVERSE TO THE PLUS-MATTER UNIVERSE IN THE SAME CONTINUUM AS OURS!
I DO NOT KNOW WHY THE WEAPONERS HAVE BUILT SUCH A BRIDGE--OR WHAT THEIR PLANS ARE! BUT RADIO-WAVE INFORMATION ABOUT THE OTHER UNIVERSE HAS COME TO US ACROSS THE BRIDGE! I HAVE LEARNED, FOR EXAMPLE, THAT THERE WAS ONCE A GROUP IN THE PLUS-WORLD...
...CALLED THE PILGRIMS... WHO FLED FROM OPPRESSION TO A NEW LAND! AND IT GAVE ME THIS IDEA--WHY CAN'T WE WHO HATE EVIL FLEE TO THE OTHER UNIVERSE--WHERE IT IS UNLAWFUL TO BE EVIL--
--AND LAWFUL TO BE HONEST! OH! IF WE ONLY COULD, TELLE-TEG!

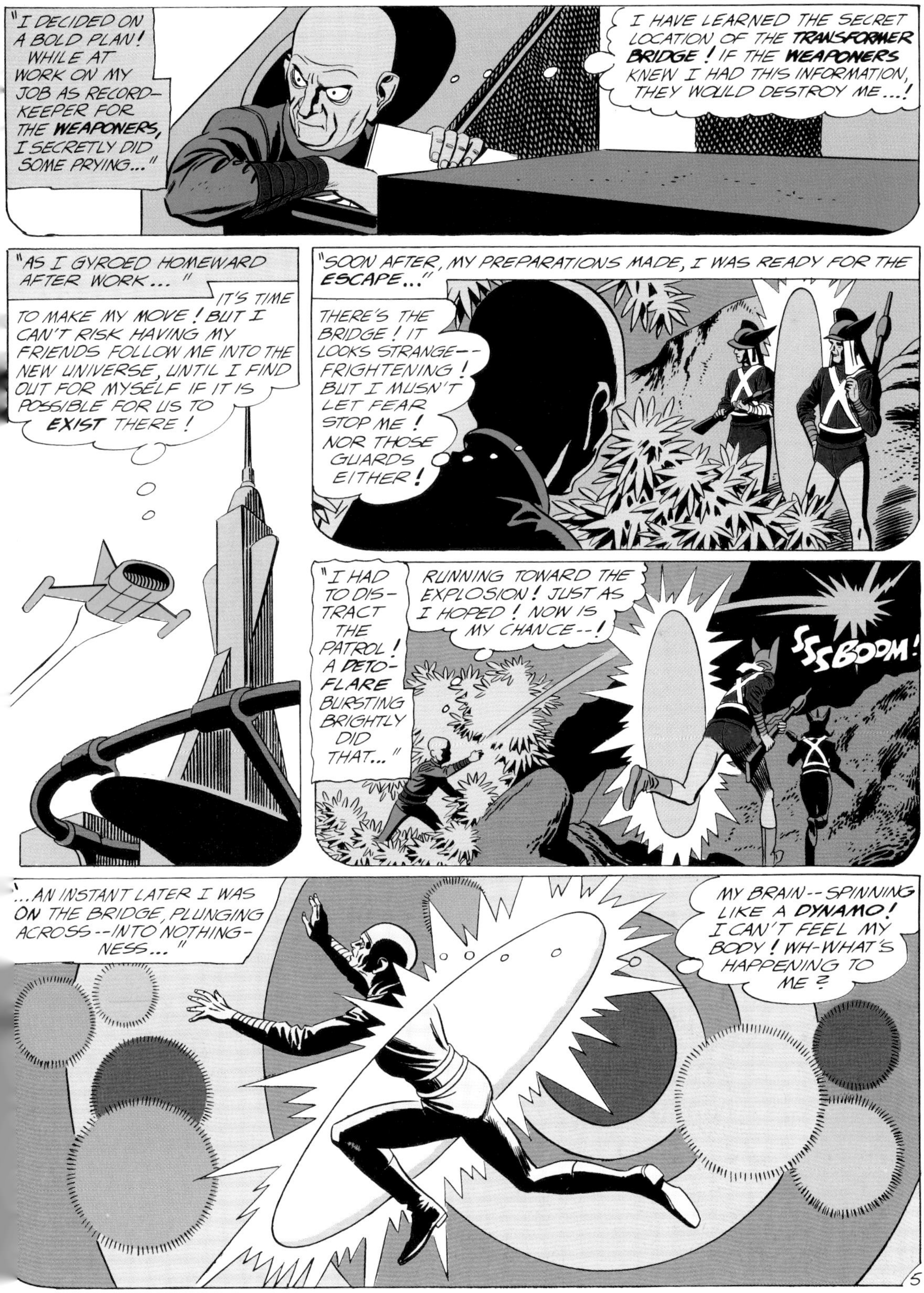
"I DECIDED ON A BOLD PLAN! WHILE AT WORK ON MY JOB AS RECORD-KEEPER FOR THE WEAPONERS, I SECRETLY DID SOME PRYING..."
I HAVE LEARNED THE SECRET LOCATION OF THE TRANSFORMER BRIDGE! IF THE WEAPONERS KNEW I HAD THIS INFORMATION, THEY WOULD DESTROY ME...!
"AS I GYROED HOMEWARD AFTER WORK..."
IT'S TIME TO MAKE MY MOVE! BUT I CAN'T RISK HAVING MY FRIENDS FOLLOW ME INTO THE NEW UNIVERSE, UNTIL I FIND OUT FOR MYSELF IF IT IS POSSIBLE FOR US TO EXIST THERE!
"SOON AFTER, MY PREPARATIONS MADE, I WAS READY FOR THE ESCAPE..."
THERE'S THE BRIDGE! IT LOOKS STRANGE--FRIGHTENING! BUT I MUSN'T LET FEAR STOP ME! NOR THOSE GUARDS EITHER!
"I HAD TO DISTRACT THE PATROL! A DETO-FLARE BURSTING BRIGHTLY DID THAT..."
RUNNING TOWARD THE EXPLOSION! JUST AS I HOPED! NOW IS MY CHANCE--!
SSSBOOM!
"...AN INSTANT LATER I WAS ON THE BRIDGE, PLUNGING ACROSS--INTO NOTHINGNESS..."
MY BRAIN--SPINNING LIKE A DYNAMO! I CAN'T FEEL MY BODY! WH-WHAT'S HAPPENING TO ME?
5

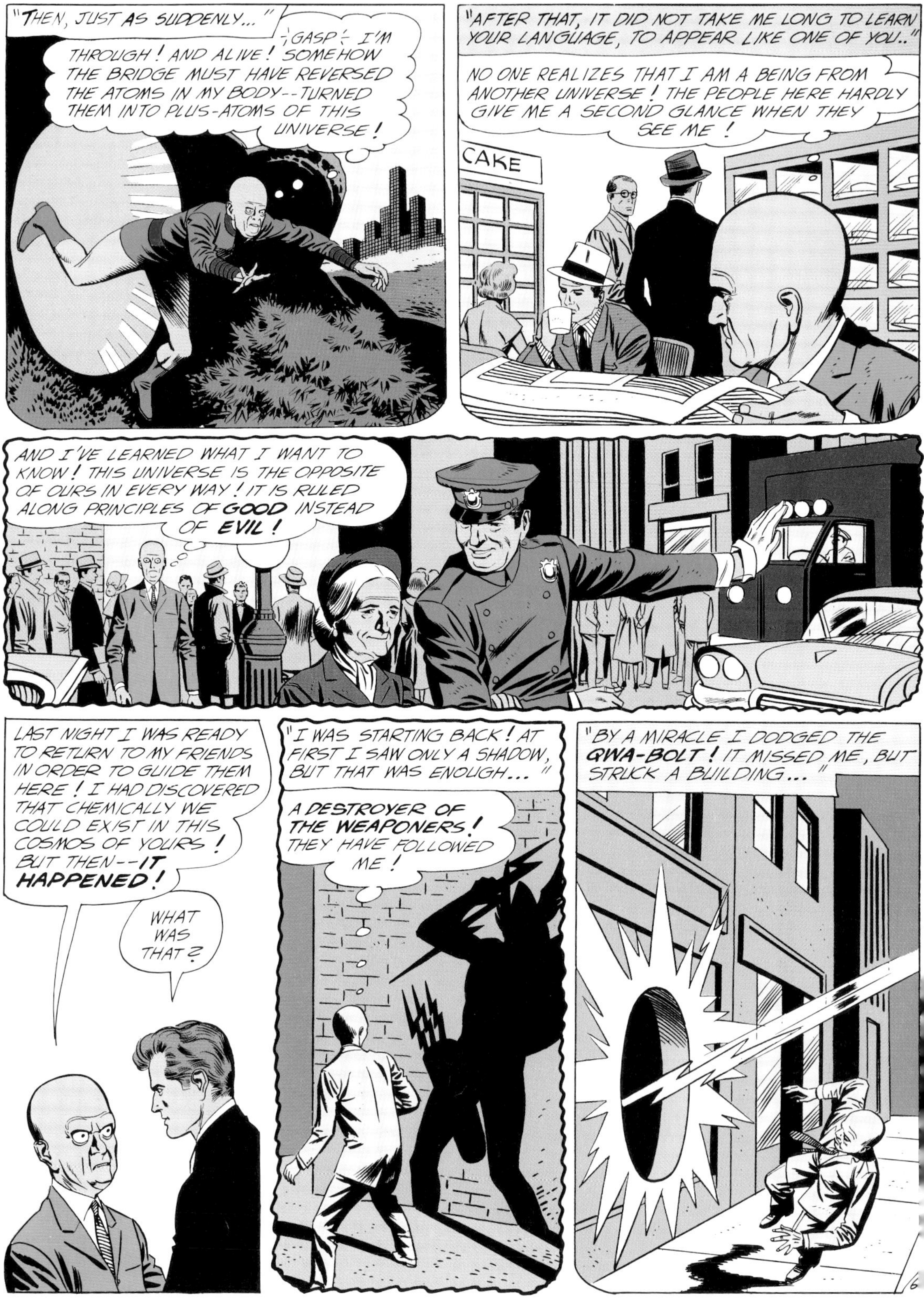
"THEN, JUST AS SUDDENLY..."
GASP -- I'M THROUGH! AND ALIVE! SOMEHOW THE BRIDGE MUST HAVE REVERSED THE ATOMS IN MY BODY--TURNED THEM INTO PLUS-ATOMS OF THIS UNIVERSE!
"AFTER THAT, IT DID NOT TAKE ME LONG TO LEARN YOUR LANGUAGE, TO APPEAR LIKE ONE OF YOU.."
NO ONE REALIZES THAT I AM A BEING FROM ANOTHER UNIVERSE! THE PEOPLE HERE HARDLY GIVE ME A SECOND GLANCE WHEN THEY SEE ME!
CAKE
AND I'VE LEARNED WHAT I WANT TO KNOW! THIS UNIVERSE IS THE OPPOSITE OF OURS IN EVERY WAY! IT IS RULED ALONG PRINCIPLES OF GOOD INSTEAD OF EVIL!
LAST NIGHT I WAS READY TO RETURN TO MY FRIENDS IN ORDER TO GUIDE THEM HERE! I HAD DISCOVERED THAT CHEMICALLY WE COULD EXIST IN THIS COSMOS OF YOURS! BUT THEN--IT HAPPENED!
WHAT WAS THAT?
"I WAS STARTING BACK! AT FIRST I SAW ONLY A SHADOW, BUT THAT WAS ENOUGH..."
A DESTROYER OF THE WEAPONERS! THEY HAVE FOLLOWED ME!
"BY A MIRACLE I DODGED THE QWA-BOLT! IT MISSED ME, BUT STRUCK A BUILDING..."
6

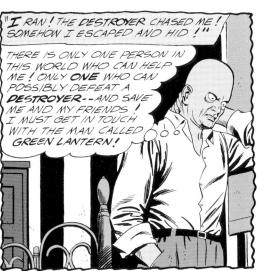

"I RAN! THE DESTROYER CHASED ME! SOMEHOW I ESCAPED AND HID!"

THERE IS ONLY ONE PERSON IN THIS WORLD WHO CAN HELP ME! ONLY **ONE** WHO CAN POSSIBLY DEFEAT A **DESTROYER**--AND SAVE ME AND MY FRIENDS! I MUST GET IN TOUCH WITH THE MAN CALLED GREEN LANTERN!

AND THAT'S WHY I HAVE COME TO YOU, MR. JORDAN!

AN INCREDIBLE TALE, AND YET IT HAS THE RING OF TRUTH! BUT THERE'S ONE WAY I CAN FIND OUT FOR CERTAIN...

WAIT HERE A MOMENT, MR. TELLE-TEG! THERE'S--ER--JUST A POSSIBILITY THAT I MIGHT BE ABLE TO CONTACT GREEN LANTERN FOR YOU...

PLEASE, MR. JORDAN-- HURRY!

BEHIND THE LOCKED DOORS OF HIS DRESSING ROOM AT THE AIRFIELD HANGAR...

I'LL TAKE TELLE-TEG BACK TO THAT BRIDGE OF HIS! IF IT REALLY EXISTS, I'LL KNOW HE ISN'T JUST SOME CRACKPOT WHO HAD A BAD DREAM!

AT HIS MYSTIC LAMP, THE **GREEN GLADIATOR** RECHARGES HIS RING FOR ANOTHER TWENTY-FOUR HOURS OF POWER...

IN BRIGHTEST DAY, IN BLACKEST NIGHT, NO EVIL SHALL ESCAPE MY SIGHT! LET THOSE WHO WORSHIP EVIL'S MIGHT BEWARE MY POWER-- GREEN LANTERN'S LIGHT!

THEN...

GREEN LANTERN! LOOK OUT!

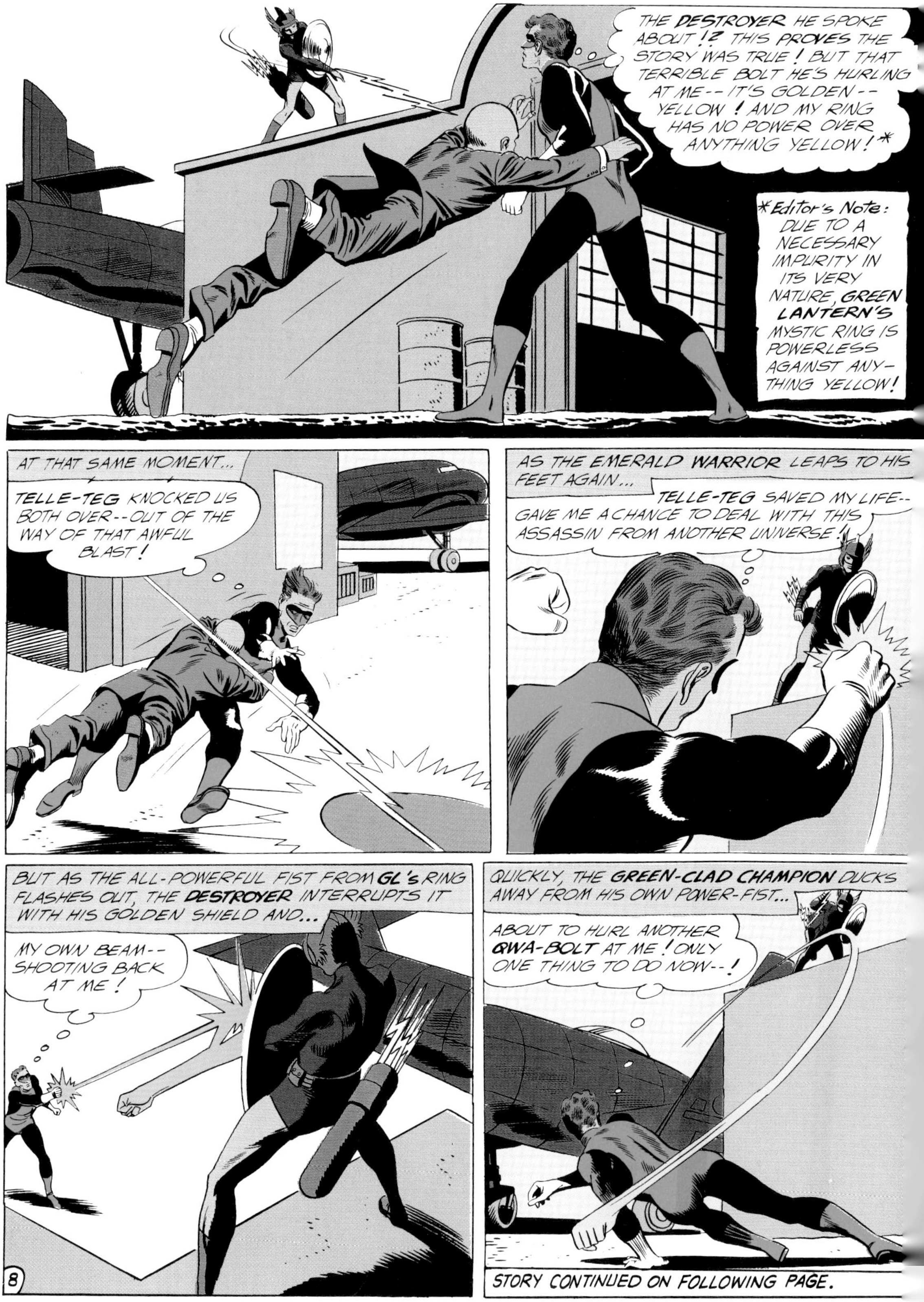
THE DESTROYER HE SPOKE ABOUT !? THIS PROVES THE STORY WAS TRUE ! BUT THAT TERRIBLE BOLT HE'S HURLING AT ME-- IT'S GOLDEN--YELLOW ! AND MY RING HAS NO POWER OVER ANYTHING YELLOW !*
*Editor's Note: DUE TO A NECESSARY IMPURITY IN ITS VERY NATURE, GREEN LANTERN'S MYSTIC RING IS POWERLESS AGAINST ANYTHING YELLOW!
AT THAT SAME MOMENT...
TELLE-TEG KNOCKED US BOTH OVER--OUT OF THE WAY OF THAT AWFUL BLAST!
AS THE EMERALD WARRIOR LEAPS TO HIS FEET AGAIN...
TELLE-TEG SAVED MY LIFE--GAVE ME A CHANCE TO DEAL WITH THIS ASSASSIN FROM ANOTHER UNIVERSE!
BUT AS THE ALL-POWERFUL FIST FROM GL's RING FLASHES OUT, THE DESTROYER INTERRUPTS IT WITH HIS GOLDEN SHIELD AND...
MY OWN BEAM--SHOOTING BACK AT ME!
8
QUICKLY, THE GREEN-CLAD CHAMPION DUCKS AWAY FROM HIS OWN POWER-FIST...
ABOUT TO HURL ANOTHER QWA-BOLT AT ME! ONLY ONE THING TO DO NOW--!
STORY CONTINUED ON FOLLOWING PAGE.

USING THE FULL POWERS OF HIS MAGIC BEAM, **GL** RENDERS HIMSELF **INVISIBLE**...

WHERE--

HE CAN'T SEE ME--DOESN'T KNOW WHERE TO THROW THAT BOLT! I'VE GOT TO USE THIS OPPORTUNITY TO THROW MY BEAM PAST HIS SHIELD--!

BEFORE HIS UNCANNY FOE CAN MAKE ANOTHER MOVE, **GREEN LANTERN** CASTS A **POWER-LASSO** OVER HIM...

SNARED HIM-- EH?

UHH!

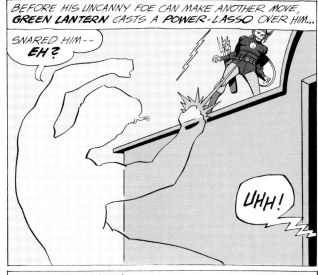

AS THE CRUSADER'S EYES WHIRL MOMENTARILY TO A STRICKEN FIGURE BESIDE HIM...

TELLE-TEG! HE'S HURT--!!

GROAN!

AN INSTANT LATER, WHEN THE **RING-WIELDER** TURNS HIS ATTENTION BACK TOWARD HIS FOE...

GETTING AWAY! DURING THE DISTRACTING MOMENT THAT I TURNED ASIDE, HE MANAGED TO BREAK LOOSE FROM MY GREEN BEAM! BUT I CAN'T CHASE HIM-- MUST SEE TO **TELLE-TEG**!

BUT THEN...

DEAD... IT'S ALL OVER FOR HIM! THAT BLAST HE SAVED ME FROM--HE MUST HAVE BEEN NICKED BY THE EDGE OF IT--ENOUGH TO FINISH HIM! HE SACRIFICED HIS LIFE... TO SAVE MINE!

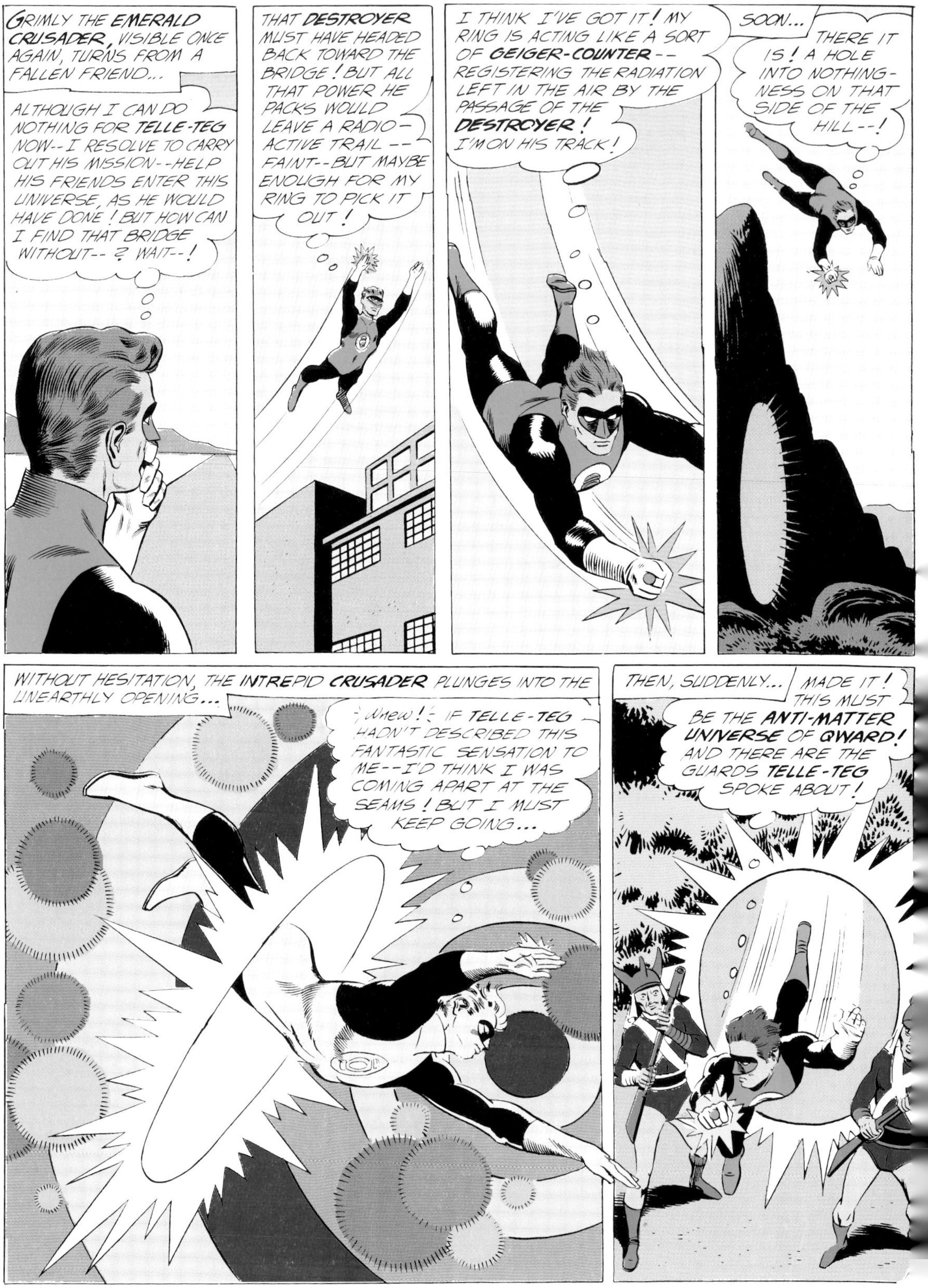
GRIMLY THE EMERALD CRUSADER, VISIBLE ONCE AGAIN, TURNS FROM A FALLEN FRIEND...
ALTHOUGH I CAN DO NOTHING FOR TELLE-TEG NOW--I RESOLVE TO CARRY OUT HIS MISSION--HELP HIS FRIENDS ENTER THIS UNIVERSE, AS HE WOULD HAVE DONE! BUT HOW CAN I FIND THAT BRIDGE WITHOUT--? WAIT--!
THAT DESTROYER MUST HAVE HEADED BACK TOWARD THE BRIDGE! BUT ALL THAT POWER HE PACKS WOULD LEAVE A RADIO-ACTIVE TRAIL--FAINT--BUT MAYBE ENOUGH FOR MY RING TO PICK IT OUT!
I THINK I'VE GOT IT! MY RING IS ACTING LIKE A SORT OF GEIGER-COUNTER--REGISTERING THE RADIATION LEFT IN THE AIR BY THE PASSAGE OF THE DESTROYER! I'M ON HIS TRACK!
SOON...
THERE IT IS! A HOLE INTO NOTHINGNESS ON THAT SIDE OF THE HILL--!
WITHOUT HESITATION, THE INTREPID CRUSADER PLUNGES INTO THE UNEARTHLY OPENING...
WHEW! IF TELLE-TEG HADN'T DESCRIBED THIS FANTASTIC SENSATION TO ME--I'D THINK I WAS COMING APART AT THE SEAMS! BUT I MUST KEEP GOING...
THEN, SUDDENLY...
MADE IT! THIS MUST BE THE ANTI-MATTER UNIVERSE OF QWARD! AND THERE ARE THE GUARDS TELLE-TEG SPOKE ABOUT!

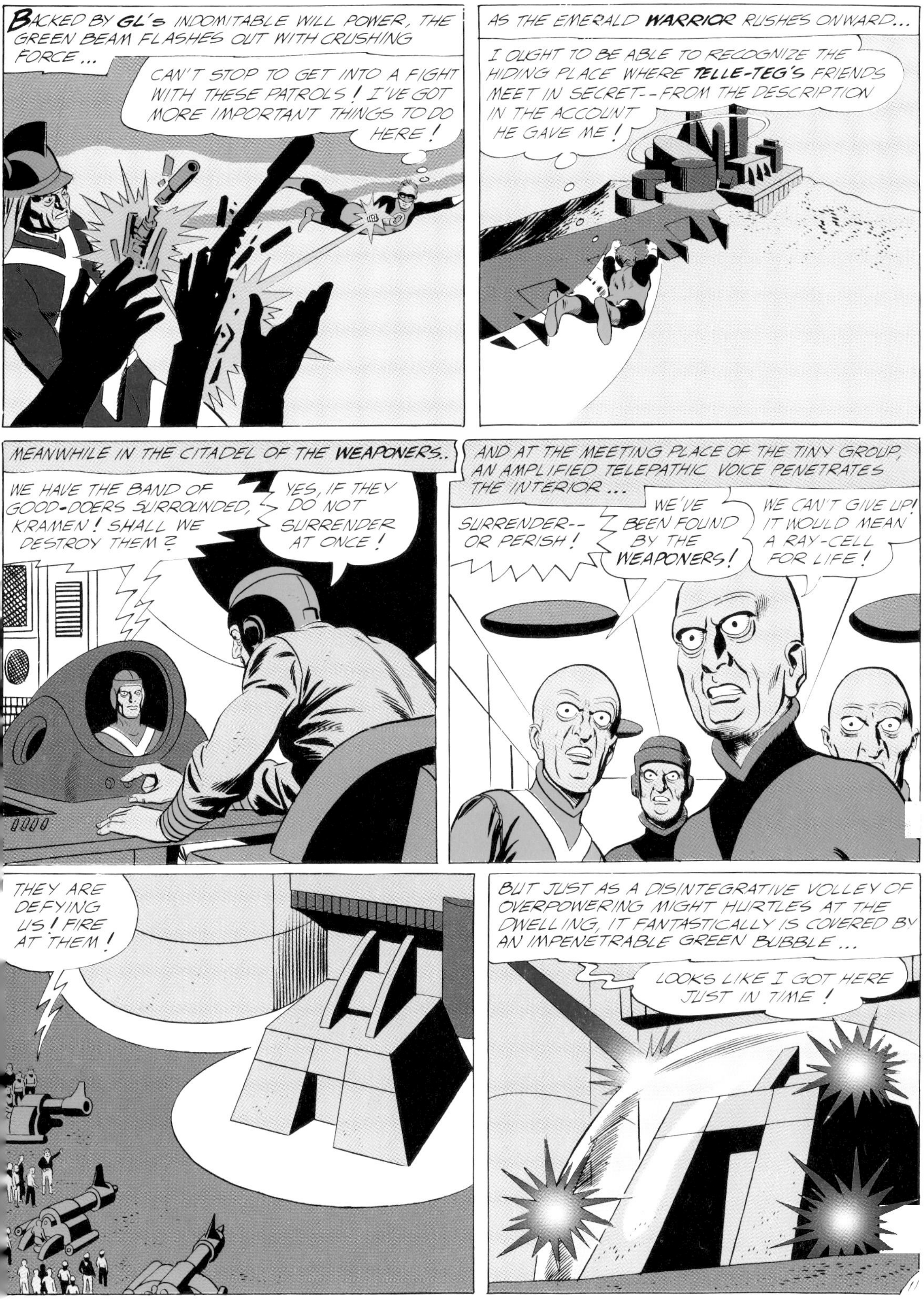
BACKED BY GL'S INDOMITABLE WILL POWER, THE GREEN BEAM FLASHES OUT WITH CRUSHING FORCE ...
CAN'T STOP TO GET INTO A FIGHT WITH THESE PATROLS! I'VE GOT MORE IMPORTANT THINGS TO DO HERE!
AS THE EMERALD WARRIOR RUSHES ONWARD...
I OUGHT TO BE ABLE TO RECOGNIZE THE HIDING PLACE WHERE TELLE-TEG'S FRIENDS MEET IN SECRET--FROM THE DESCRIPTION IN THE ACCOUNT HE GAVE ME!
MEANWHILE IN THE CITADEL OF THE WEAPONERS..
WE HAVE THE BAND OF GOOD-DOERS SURROUNDED, KRAMEN! SHALL WE DESTROY THEM?
YES, IF THEY DO NOT SURRENDER AT ONCE!
AND AT THE MEETING PLACE OF THE TINY GROUP, AN AMPLIFIED TELEPATHIC VOICE PENETRATES THE INTERIOR ...
SURRENDER-- OR PERISH!
WE'VE BEEN FOUND BY THE WEAPONERS!
WE CAN'T GIVE UP! IT WOULD MEAN A RAY-CELL FOR LIFE!
THEY ARE DEFYING US! FIRE AT THEM!
BUT JUST AS A DISINTEGRATIVE VOLLEY OF OVERPOWERING MIGHT HURTLES AT THE DWELLING, IT FANTASTICALLY IS COVERED BY AN IMPENETRABLE GREEN BUBBLE ...
LOOKS LIKE I GOT HERE JUST IN TIME!
11

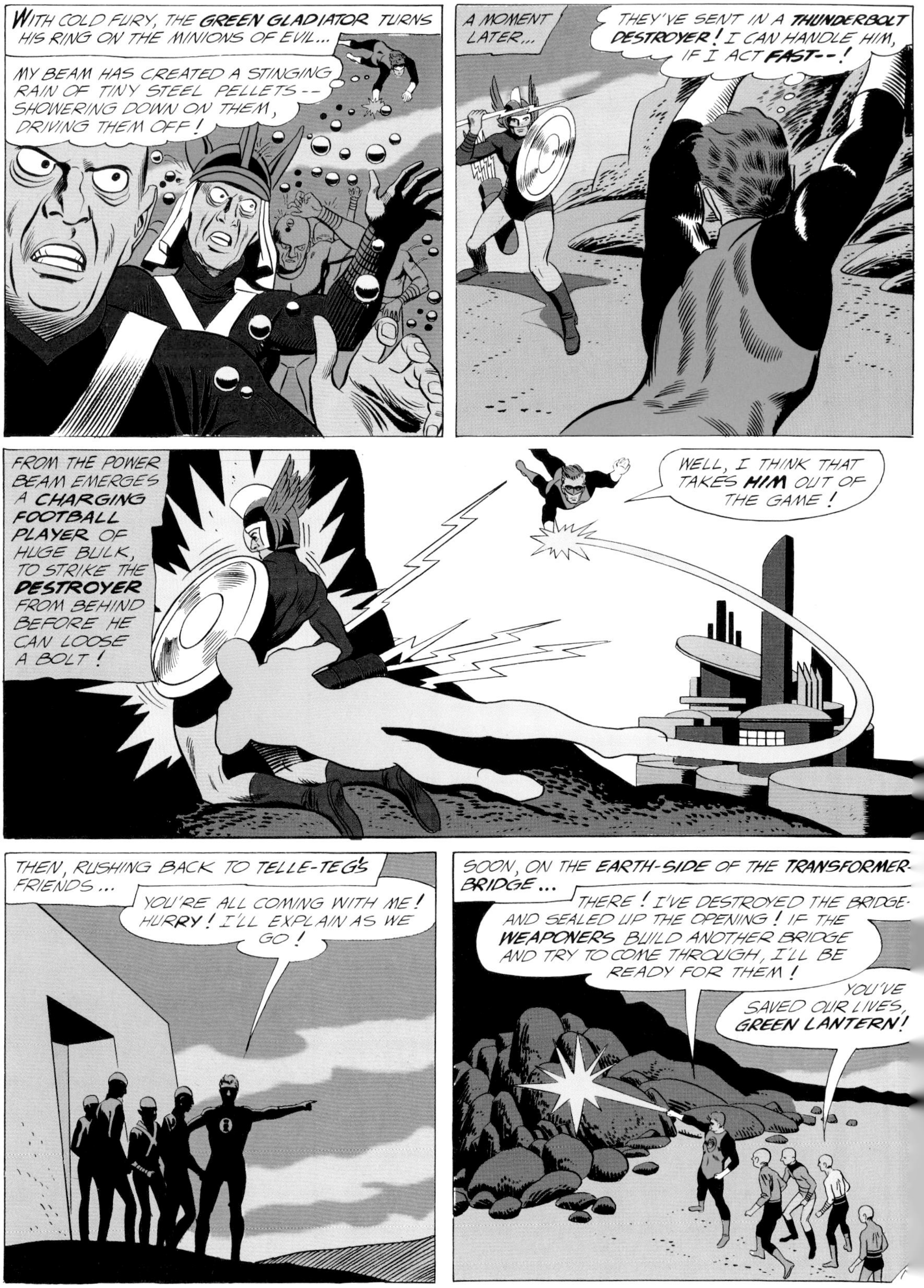
WITH COLD FURY, THE GREEN GLADIATOR TURNS HIS RING ON THE MINIONS OF EVIL...
MY BEAM HAS CREATED A STINGING RAIN OF TINY STEEL PELLETS -- SHOWERING DOWN ON THEM, DRIVING THEM OFF!
A MOMENT LATER...
THEY'VE SENT IN A THUNDERBOLT DESTROYER! I CAN HANDLE HIM, IF I ACT FAST--!
FROM THE POWER BEAM EMERGES A CHARGING FOOTBALL PLAYER OF HUGE BULK, TO STRIKE THE DESTROYER FROM BEHIND BEFORE HE CAN LOOSE A BOLT!
WELL, I THINK THAT TAKES HIM OUT OF THE GAME!
THEN, RUSHING BACK TO TELLE-TEG'S FRIENDS...
YOU'RE ALL COMING WITH ME! HURRY! I'LL EXPLAIN AS WE GO!
SOON, ON THE EARTH-SIDE OF THE TRANSFORMER-BRIDGE...
THERE! I'VE DESTROYED THE BRIDGE-AND SEALED UP THE OPENING! IF THE WEAPONERS BUILD ANOTHER BRIDGE AND TRY TO COME THROUGH, I'LL BE READY FOR THEM!
YOU'VE SAVED OUR LIVES, GREEN LANTERN!

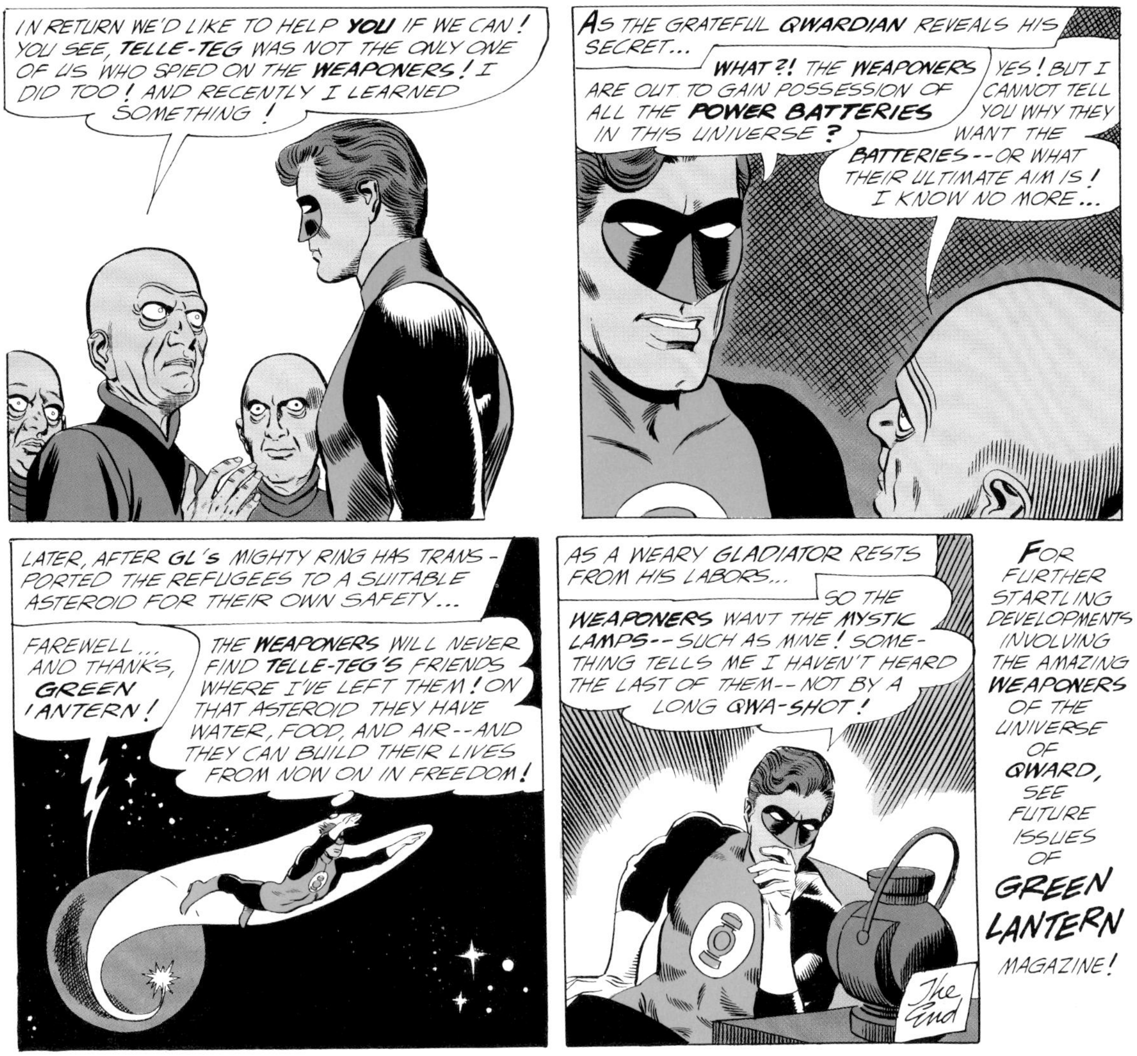

IN RETURN WE'D LIKE TO HELP **YOU** IF WE CAN! YOU SEE, **TELLE-TEG** WAS NOT THE ONLY ONE OF US WHO SPIED ON THE **WEAPONERS**! I DID TOO! AND RECENTLY I LEARNED SOMETHING!

AS THE GRATEFUL **QWARDIAN** REVEALS HIS SECRET...

WHAT?! THE **WEAPONERS** ARE OUT TO GAIN POSSESSION OF ALL THE **POWER BATTERIES** IN THIS UNIVERSE?

YES! BUT I CANNOT TELL YOU WHY THEY WANT THE **BATTERIES**--OR WHAT THEIR ULTIMATE AIM IS! I KNOW NO MORE...

LATER, AFTER **GL'S** MIGHTY RING HAS TRANSPORTED THE REFUGEES TO A SUITABLE ASTEROID FOR THEIR OWN SAFETY...

FAREWELL... AND THANKS, **GREEN LANTERN**!

THE **WEAPONERS** WILL NEVER FIND **TELLE-TEG'S** FRIENDS WHERE I'VE LEFT THEM! ON THAT ASTEROID THEY HAVE WATER, FOOD, AND AIR--AND THEY CAN BUILD THEIR LIVES FROM NOW ON IN FREEDOM!

AS A WEARY GLADIATOR RESTS FROM HIS LABORS...

SO THE **WEAPONERS** WANT THE **MYSTIC LAMPS**--SUCH AS MINE! SOMETHING TELLS ME I HAVEN'T HEARD THE LAST OF THEM-- NOT BY A LONG QWA-SHOT!

FOR FURTHER STARTLING DEVELOPMENTS INVOLVING THE AMAZING **WEAPONERS** OF THE UNIVERSE OF **QWARD**, SEE FUTURE ISSUES OF **GREEN LANTERN** MAGAZINE!

The End

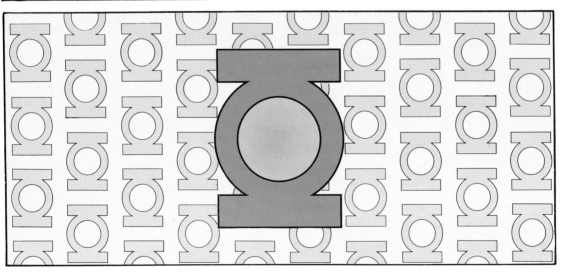

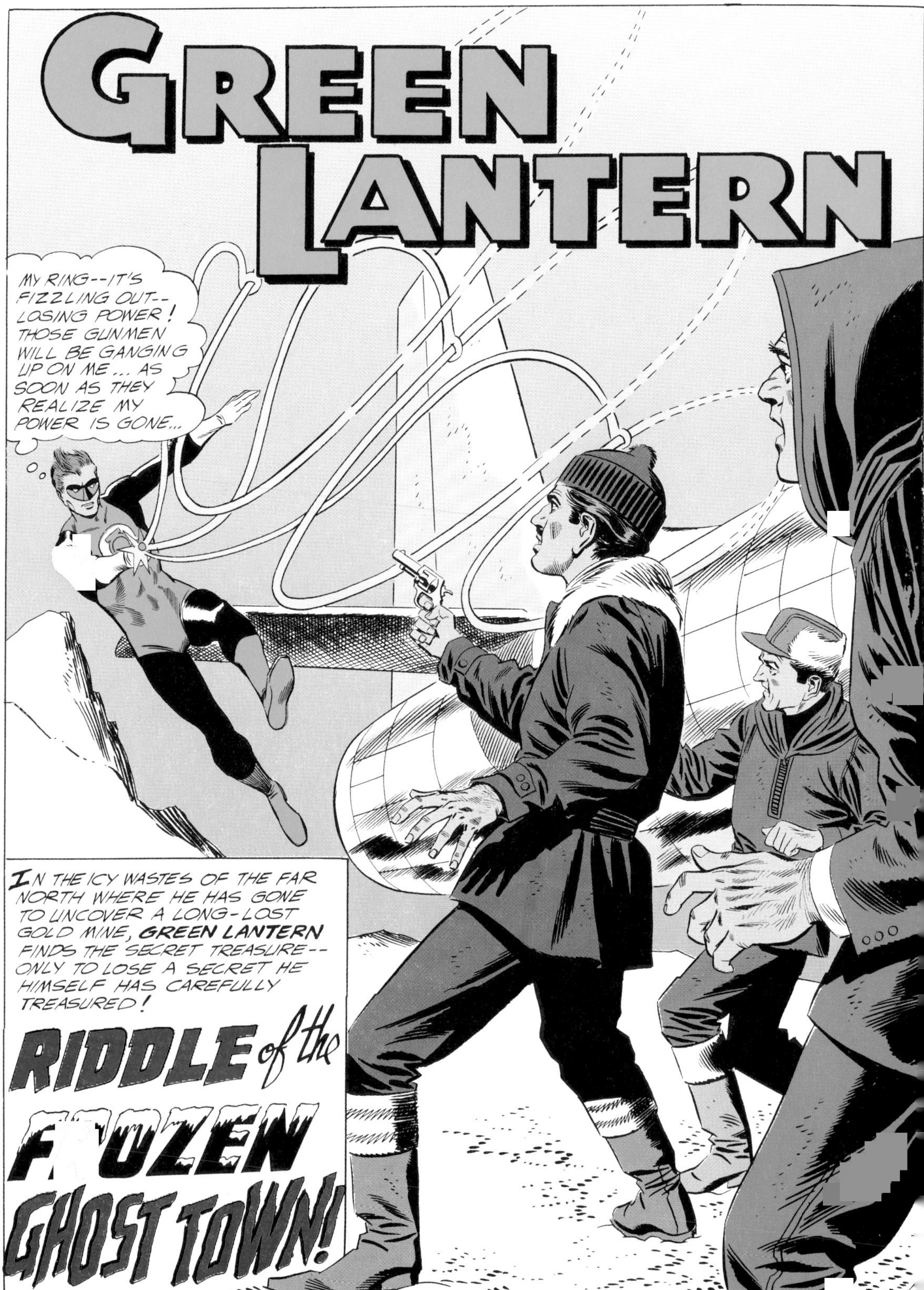
GREEN LANTERN
MY RING--IT'S FIZZLING OUT--LOSING POWER! THOSE GUNMEN WILL BE GANGING UP ON ME... AS SOON AS THEY REALIZE MY POWER IS GONE...
IN THE ICY WASTES OF THE FAR NORTH WHERE HE HAS GONE TO UNCOVER A LONG-LOST GOLD MINE, GREEN LANTERN FINDS THE SECRET TREASURE--ONLY TO LOSE A SECRET HE HIMSELF HAS CAREFULLY TREASURED!
RIDDLE of the FROZEN GHOST TOWN!

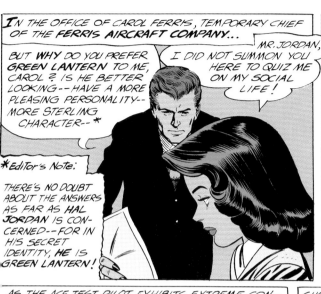

IN THE OFFICE OF CAROL FERRIS, TEMPORARY CHIEF OF THE FERRIS AIRCRAFT COMPANY...

BUT **WHY** DO YOU PREFER **GREEN LANTERN** TO ME, CAROL? IS HE BETTER LOOKING-- HAVE A MORE PLEASING PERSONALITY-- MORE STERLING CHARACTER-- *

I DID NOT SUMMON YOU HERE TO QUIZ ME ON MY SOCIAL LIFE!

Editor's Note:

THERE'S NO DOUBT ABOUT THE ANSWERS AS FAR AS **HAL JORDAN** IS CONCERNED-- FOR IN HIS SECRET IDENTITY, **HE** IS GREEN LANTERN!

NOW-- DOWN TO **BUSINESS**! WE'VE JUST RECEIVED NOTICE-- **THOMAS KALMAKU**, YOUR MECHANIC, IS LEAVING AT THE END OF THE WEEK! WE'LL HAVE TO HIRE SOMEONE ELSE!

PIEFACE-- QUITTING?!

AS THE ACE TEST PILOT EXHIBITS EXTREME CONCERN AT THE NEWS...

LET HIM GO, CAROL! THAT ESKIMO IS A WIZARD WITH JET ENGINES AND I COULDN'T DO WITHOUT HIM! GIVE HIM A RAISE! HE'S GOT TO STAY!

WE CAN'T! HE SAID IT WASN'T MONEY! BUT IF YOU WANT TO TALK TO HIM, HAL, GO AHEAD...

SHORTLY... I WONDER WHAT'S GOT INTO **PIEFACE**? LAST TIME I SAW HIM, HE DIDN'T ACT LIKE THERE WAS ANYTHING WRONG! BUT I REALIZE NOW HOW LITTLE I KNOW ABOUT HIM-- ONLY THAT HE SERVED WITH OUR ARMED FORCES IN ALASKA...

...WHERE HE GOT TO BE AN EXPERT ON SERVICING JETS! AND THAT AFTERWARDS HE CAME DOWN HERE TO THE STATES AND GOT A JOB WITH THE **FERRIS COMPANY** -- AS MY MECHANIC! HE AND I ALWAYS WORKED TOGETHER PERFECTLY --

EH?

GREAT DAY! THERE'S **PIEFACE** NOW-- IN A TUSSLE WITH TWO BIG LUGS! NO TIME TO CHANGE TO MY **GREEN LANTERN** COSTUME!

2

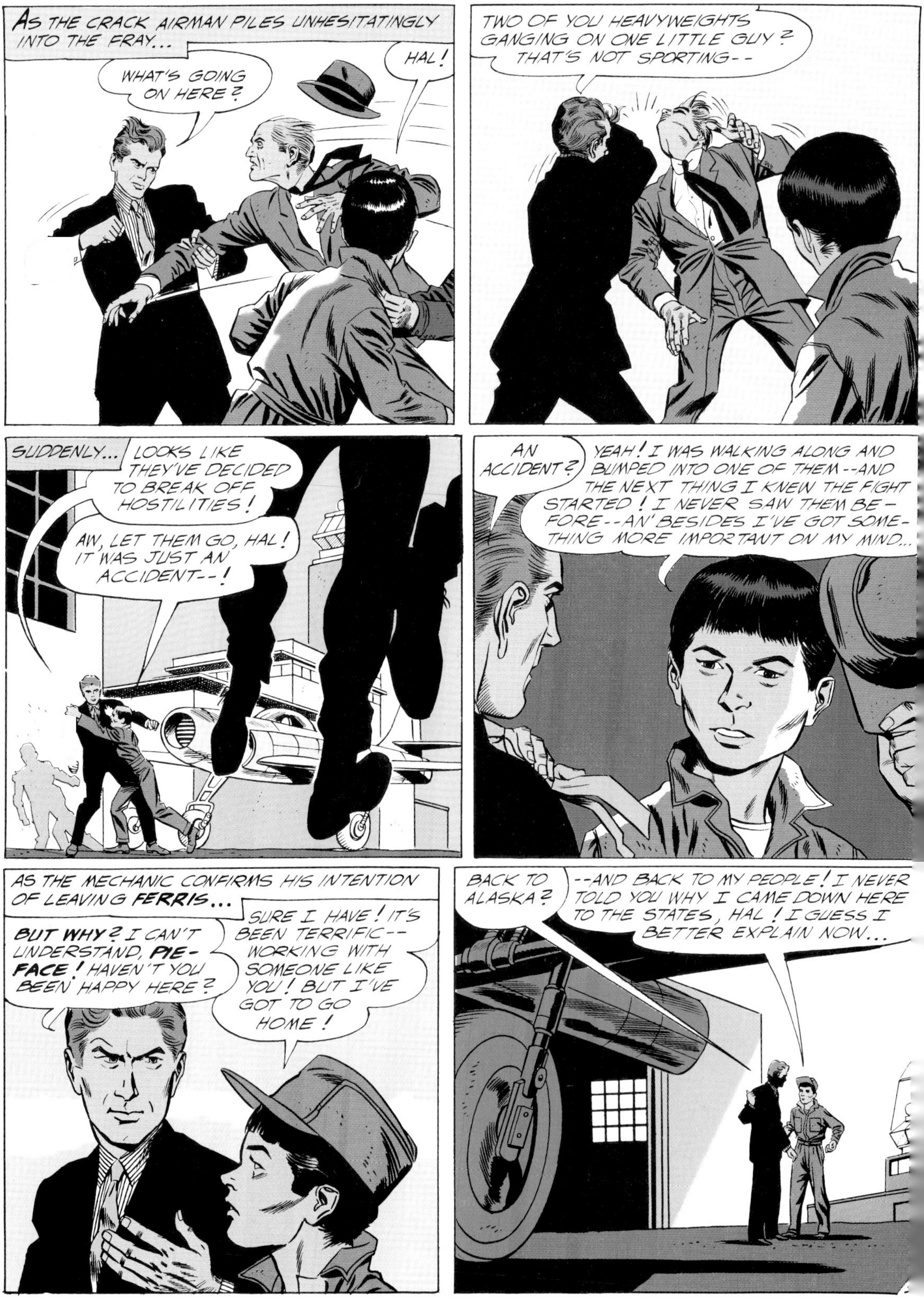
AS THE CRACK AIRMAN PILES UNHESITATINGLY INTO THE FRAY...
WHAT'S GOING ON HERE?
HAL!
TWO OF YOU HEAVYWEIGHTS GANGING ON ONE LITTLE GUY? THAT'S NOT SPORTING--
SUDDENLY...
LOOKS LIKE THEY'VE DECIDED TO BREAK OFF HOSTILITIES!
AW, LET THEM GO, HAL! IT WAS JUST AN ACCIDENT--!
AN ACCIDENT?
YEAH! I WAS WALKING ALONG AND BUMPED INTO ONE OF THEM--AND THE NEXT THING I KNEW THE FIGHT STARTED! I NEVER SAW THEM BE-FORE--AN' BESIDES I'VE GOT SOME-THING MORE IMPORTANT ON MY MIND...
AS THE MECHANIC CONFIRMS HIS INTENTION OF LEAVING FERRIS...
BUT WHY? I CAN'T UNDERSTAND, PIE-FACE! HAVEN'T YOU BEEN HAPPY HERE?
SURE I HAVE! IT'S BEEN TERRIFIC--WORKING WITH SOMEONE LIKE YOU! BUT I'VE GOT TO GO HOME!
BACK TO ALASKA?
--AND BACK TO MY PEOPLE! I NEVER TOLD YOU WHY I CAME DOWN HERE TO THE STATES, HAL! I GUESS I BETTER EXPLAIN NOW...

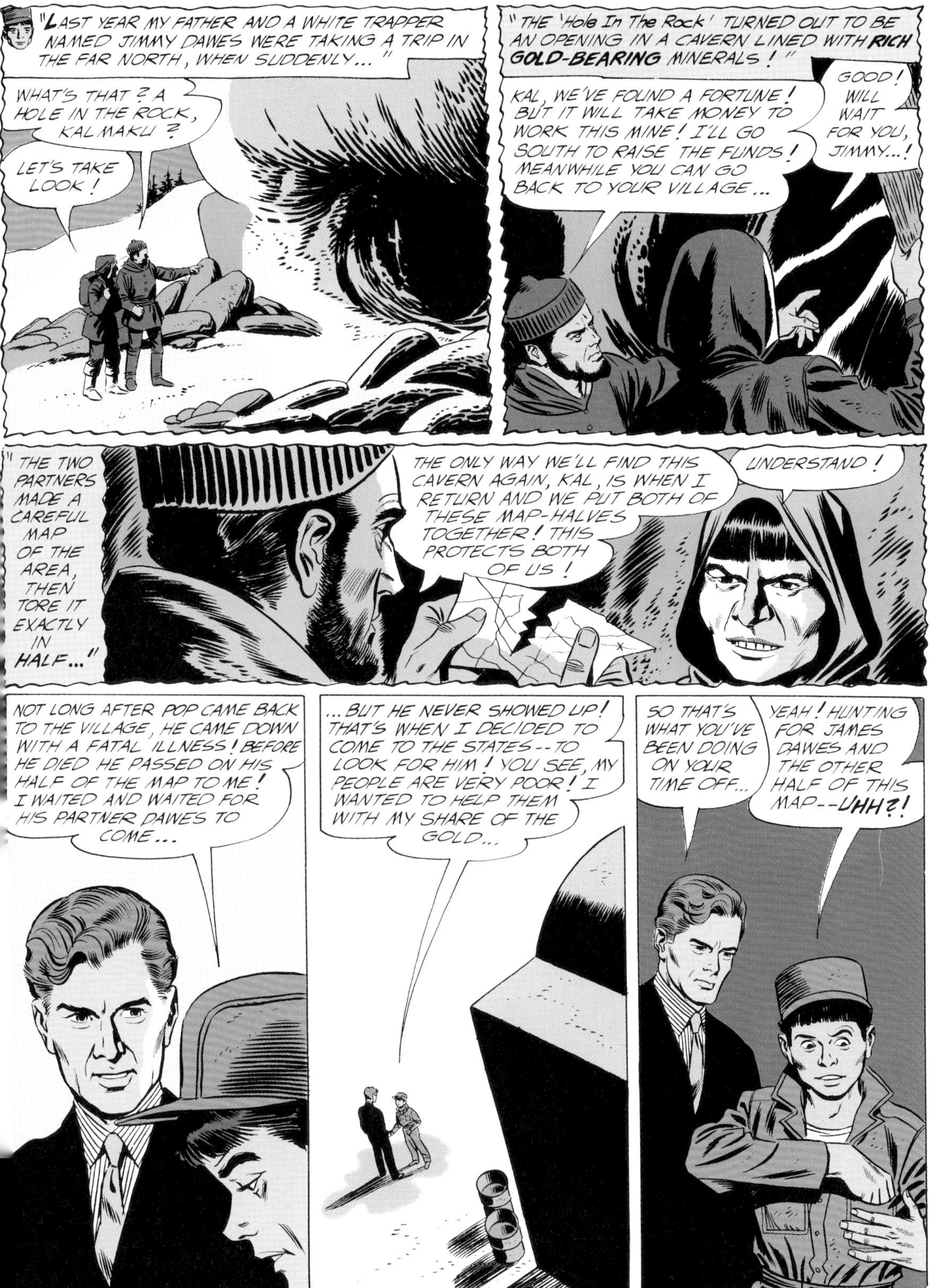
"LAST YEAR MY FATHER AND A WHITE TRAPPER NAMED JIMMY DAWES WERE TAKING A TRIP IN THE FAR NORTH, WHEN SUDDENLY..."
WHAT'S THAT? A HOLE IN THE ROCK, KALMAKU?
LET'S TAKE LOOK!
"THE 'Hole In The Rock' TURNED OUT TO BE AN OPENING IN A CAVERN LINED WITH RICH GOLD-BEARING MINERALS!"
KAL, WE'VE FOUND A FORTUNE! BUT IT WILL TAKE MONEY TO WORK THIS MINE! I'LL GO SOUTH TO RAISE THE FUNDS! MEANWHILE YOU CAN GO BACK TO YOUR VILLAGE...
GOOD! WILL WAIT FOR YOU, JIMMY...!
"THE TWO PARTNERS MADE A CAREFUL MAP OF THE AREA, THEN TORE IT EXACTLY IN HALF..."
THE ONLY WAY WE'LL FIND THIS CAVERN AGAIN, KAL, IS WHEN I RETURN AND WE PUT BOTH OF THESE MAP-HALVES TOGETHER! THIS PROTECTS BOTH OF US!
UNDERSTAND!
NOT LONG AFTER POP CAME BACK TO THE VILLAGE, HE CAME DOWN WITH A FATAL ILLNESS! BEFORE HE DIED HE PASSED ON HIS HALF OF THE MAP TO ME! I WAITED AND WAITED FOR HIS PARTNER DAWES TO COME...
...BUT HE NEVER SHOWED UP! THAT'S WHEN I DECIDED TO COME TO THE STATES--TO LOOK FOR HIM! YOU SEE, MY PEOPLE ARE VERY POOR! I WANTED TO HELP THEM WITH MY SHARE OF THE GOLD...
SO THAT'S WHAT YOU'VE BEEN DOING ON YOUR TIME OFF...
YEAH! HUNTING FOR JAMES DAWES AND THE OTHER HALF OF THIS MAP--UHH?!
4

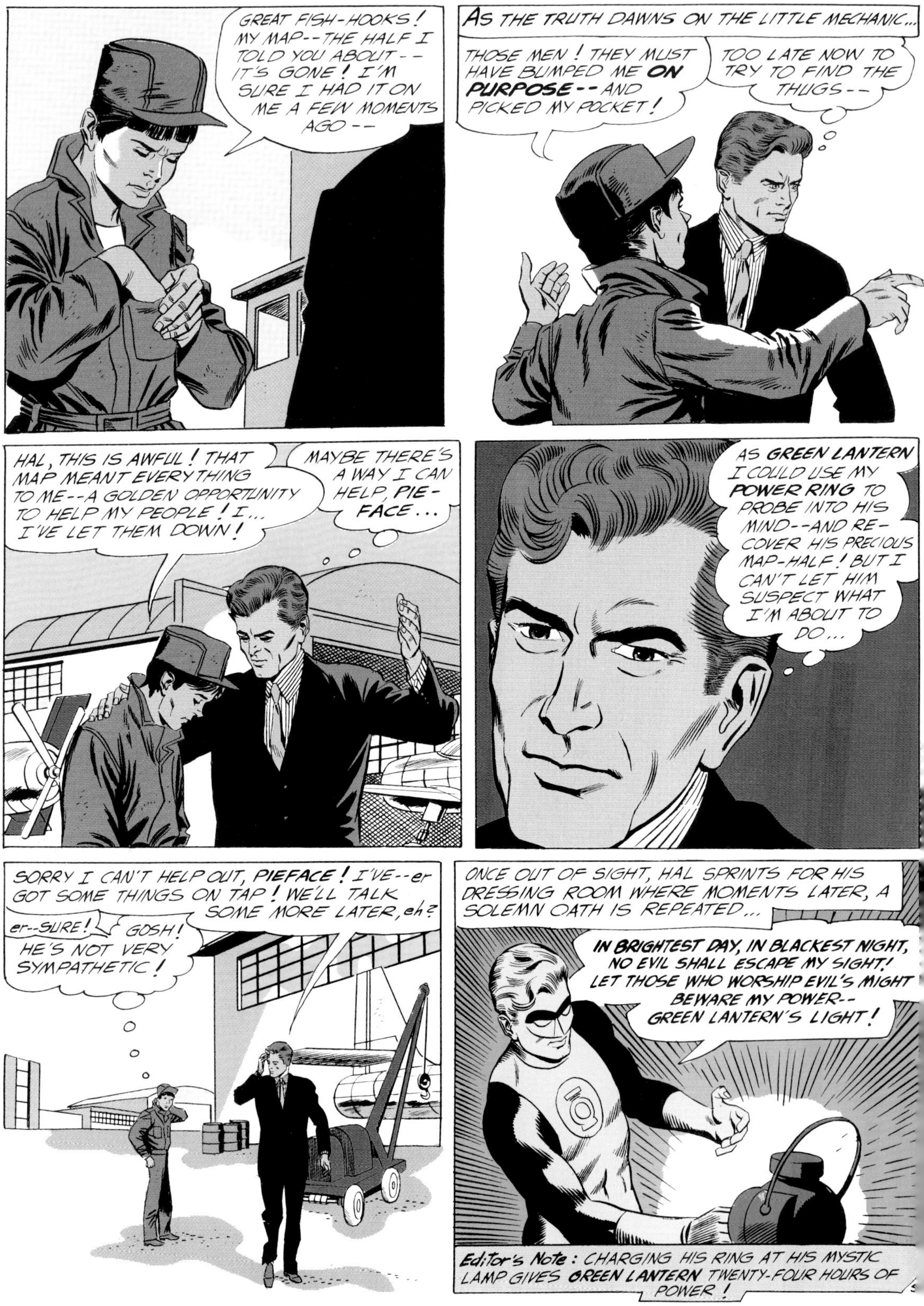
GREAT FISH-HOOKS! MY MAP--THE HALF I TOLD YOU ABOUT--IT'S GONE! I'M SURE I HAD IT ON ME A FEW MOMENTS AGO--
AS THE TRUTH DAWNS ON THE LITTLE MECHANIC...
THOSE MEN! THEY MUST HAVE BUMPED ME ON PURPOSE--AND PICKED MY POCKET!
TOO LATE NOW TO TRY TO FIND THE THUGS--
HAL, THIS IS AWFUL! THAT MAP MEANT EVERYTHING TO ME--A GOLDEN OPPORTUNITY TO HELP MY PEOPLE! I... I'VE LET THEM DOWN!
MAYBE THERE'S A WAY I CAN HELP, PIE-FACE...
AS GREEN LANTERN I COULD USE MY POWER RING TO PROBE INTO HIS MIND--AND RE-COVER HIS PRECIOUS MAP-HALF! BUT I CAN'T LET HIM SUSPECT WHAT I'M ABOUT TO DO...
SORRY I CAN'T HELP OUT, PIEFACE! I'VE--er GOT SOME THINGS ON TAP! WE'LL TALK SOME MORE LATER, eh?
er--SURE!
GOSH! HE'S NOT VERY SYMPATHETIC!
ONCE OUT OF SIGHT, HAL SPRINTS FOR HIS DRESSING ROOM WHERE MOMENTS LATER, A SOLEMN OATH IS REPEATED...
IN BRIGHTEST DAY, IN BLACKEST NIGHT, NO EVIL SHALL ESCAPE MY SIGHT! LET THOSE WHO WORSHIP EVIL'S MIGHT BEWARE MY POWER--GREEN LANTERN'S LIGHT!
Editor's Note: CHARGING HIS RING AT HIS MYSTIC LAMP GIVES GREEN LANTERN TWENTY-FOUR HOURS OF POWER!

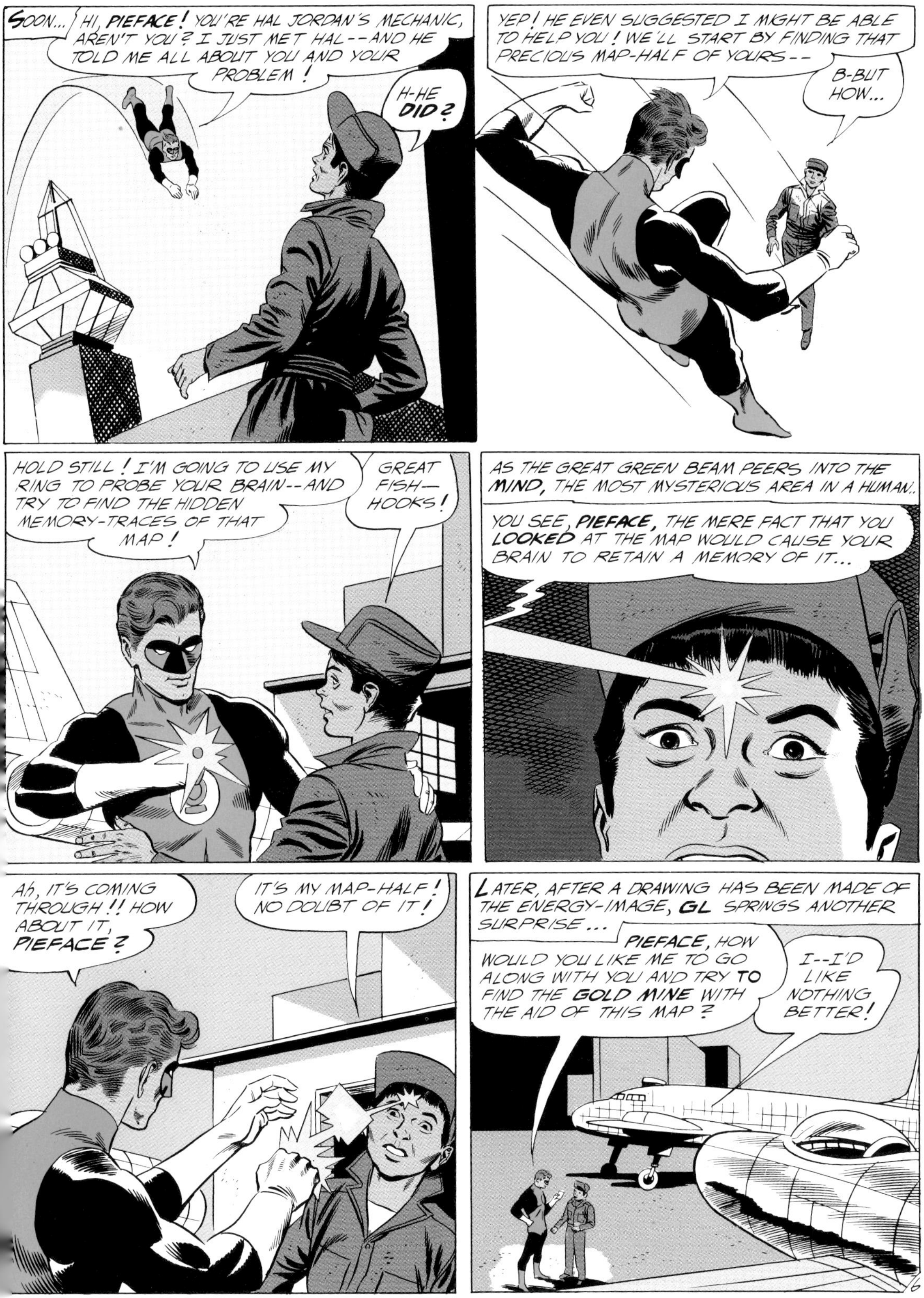
SOON...
HI, PIEFACE! YOU'RE HAL JORDAN'S MECHANIC, AREN'T YOU? I JUST MET HAL--AND HE TOLD ME ALL ABOUT YOU AND YOUR PROBLEM!
H-HE DID?
YEP! HE EVEN SUGGESTED I MIGHT BE ABLE TO HELP YOU! WE'LL START BY FINDING THAT PRECIOUS MAP-HALF OF YOURS--
B-BUT HOW...
HOLD STILL! I'M GOING TO USE MY RING TO PROBE YOUR BRAIN--AND TRY TO FIND THE HIDDEN MEMORY-TRACES OF THAT MAP!
GREAT FISH-HOOKS!
AS THE GREAT GREEN BEAM PEERS INTO THE MIND, THE MOST MYSTERIOUS AREA IN A HUMAN..
YOU SEE, PIEFACE, THE MERE FACT THAT YOU LOOKED AT THE MAP WOULD CAUSE YOUR BRAIN TO RETAIN A MEMORY OF IT...
Ah, IT'S COMING THROUGH!! HOW ABOUT IT, PIEFACE?
IT'S MY MAP-HALF! NO DOUBT OF IT!
LATER, AFTER A DRAWING HAS BEEN MADE OF THE ENERGY-IMAGE, GL SPRINGS ANOTHER SURPRISE...
PIEFACE, HOW WOULD YOU LIKE ME TO GO ALONG WITH YOU AND TRY TO FIND THE GOLD MINE WITH THE AID OF THIS MAP?
I--I'D LIKE NOTHING BETTER!
6

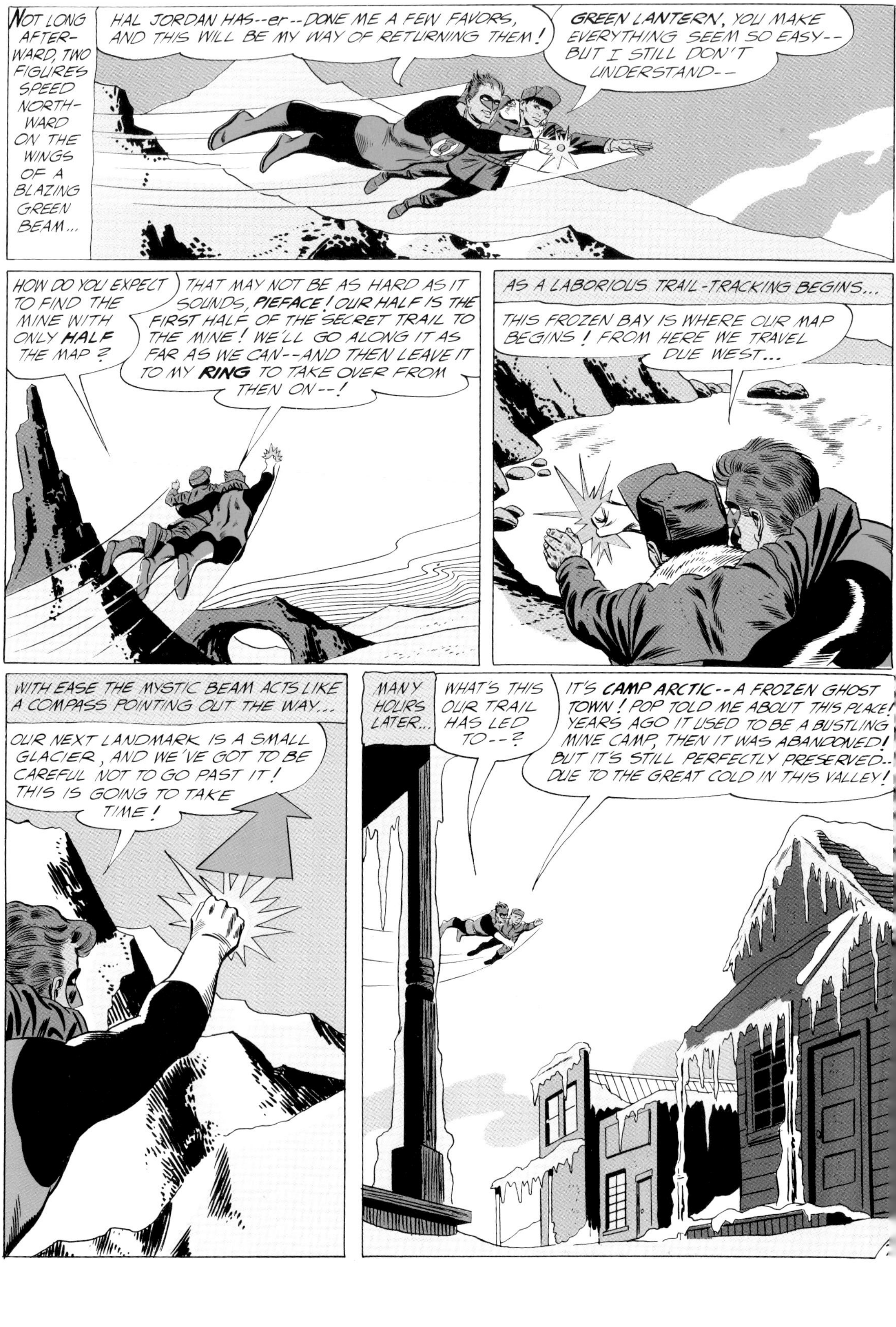
NOT LONG AFTERWARD, TWO FIGURES SPEED NORTHWARD ON THE WINGS OF A BLAZING GREEN BEAM...
HAL JORDAN HAS--er--DONE ME A FEW FAVORS, AND THIS WILL BE MY WAY OF RETURNING THEM!
GREEN LANTERN, YOU MAKE EVERYTHING SEEM SO EASY--BUT I STILL DON'T UNDERSTAND--
HOW DO YOU EXPECT TO FIND THE MINE WITH ONLY HALF THE MAP?
THAT MAY NOT BE AS HARD AS IT SOUNDS, PIEFACE! OUR HALF IS THE FIRST HALF OF THE SECRET TRAIL TO THE MINE! WE'LL GO ALONG IT AS FAR AS WE CAN--AND THEN LEAVE IT TO MY RING TO TAKE OVER FROM THEN ON--!
AS A LABORIOUS TRAIL-TRACKING BEGINS...
THIS FROZEN BAY IS WHERE OUR MAP BEGINS! FROM HERE WE TRAVEL DUE WEST...
WITH EASE THE MYSTIC BEAM ACTS LIKE A COMPASS POINTING OUT THE WAY...
OUR NEXT LANDMARK IS A SMALL GLACIER, AND WE'VE GOT TO BE CAREFUL NOT TO GO PAST IT! THIS IS GOING TO TAKE TIME!
MANY HOURS LATER...
WHAT'S THIS OUR TRAIL HAS LED TO--?
IT'S CAMP ARCTIC--A FROZEN GHOST TOWN! POP TOLD ME ABOUT THIS PLACE! YEARS AGO IT USED TO BE A BUSTLING MINE CAMP, THEN IT WAS ABANDONED! BUT IT'S STILL PERFECTLY PRESERVED--DUE TO THE GREAT COLD IN THIS VALLEY!

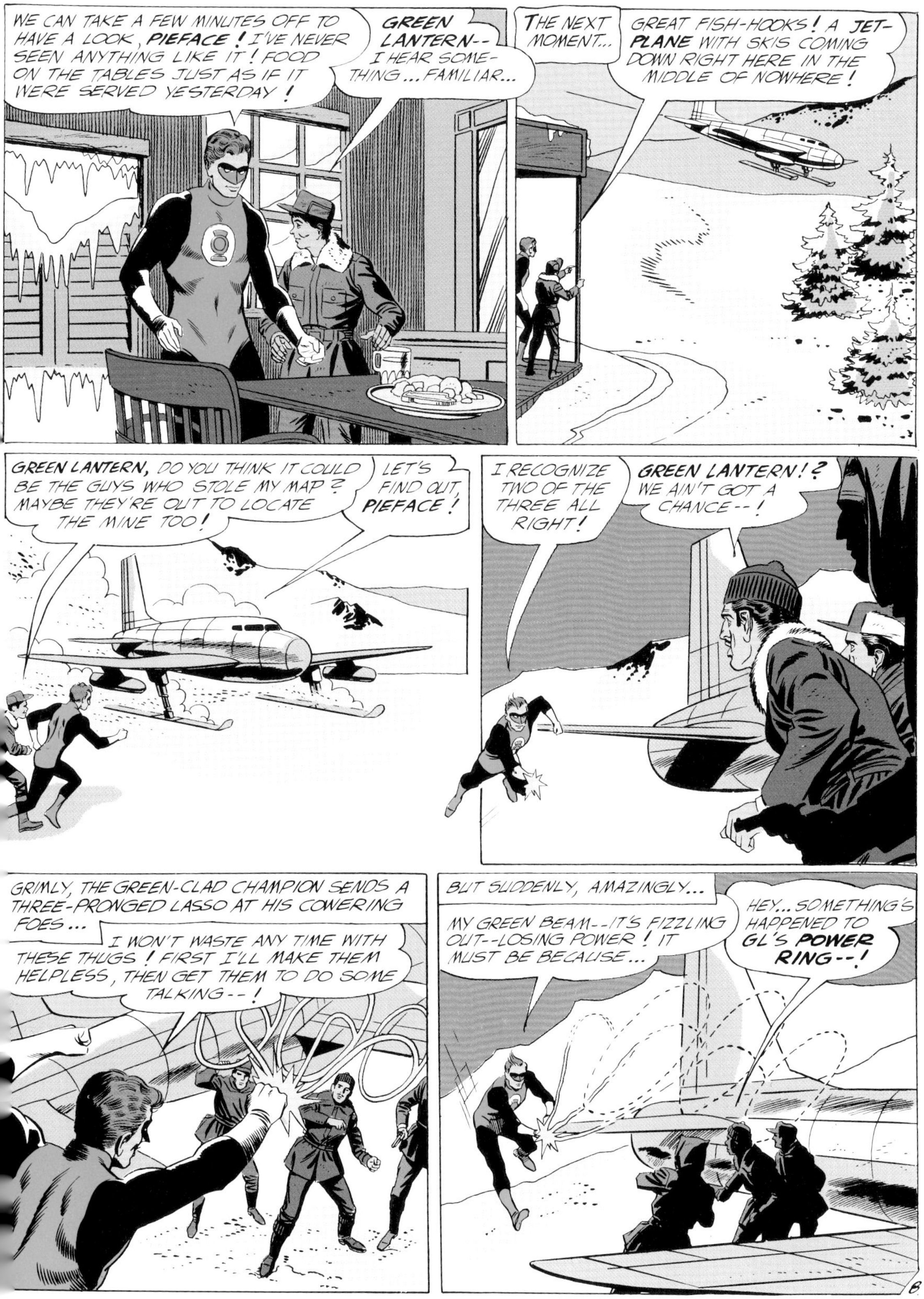
WE CAN TAKE A FEW MINUTES OFF TO HAVE A LOOK, PIEFACE! I'VE NEVER SEEN ANYTHING LIKE IT! FOOD ON THE TABLES JUST AS IF IT WERE SERVED YESTERDAY!
GREEN LANTERN-- I HEAR SOMETHING... FAMILIAR...
THE NEXT MOMENT...
GREAT FISH-HOOKS! A JET-PLANE WITH SKIS COMING DOWN RIGHT HERE IN THE MIDDLE OF NOWHERE!
GREEN LANTERN, DO YOU THINK IT COULD BE THE GUYS WHO STOLE MY MAP? MAYBE THEY'RE OUT TO LOCATE THE MINE TOO!
LET'S FIND OUT, PIEFACE!
I RECOGNIZE TWO OF THE THREE ALL RIGHT!
GREEN LANTERN!? WE AIN'T GOT A CHANCE--!
GRIMLY, THE GREEN-CLAD CHAMPION SENDS A THREE-PRONGED LASSO AT HIS COWERING FOES...
I WON'T WASTE ANY TIME WITH THESE THUGS! FIRST I'LL MAKE THEM HELPLESS, THEN GET THEM TO DO SOME TALKING--!
BUT SUDDENLY, AMAZINGLY...
MY GREEN BEAM--IT'S FIZZLING OUT--LOSING POWER! IT MUST BE BECAUSE...
HEY... SOMETHING'S HAPPENED TO GL'S POWER RING--!
8

AS THE TRUTH DAWNS ON THE EMERALD WARRIOR...

THE TWENTY-FOUR HOURS ARE ALMOST UP-- MY RING NEEDS **RECHARGING**--!

PILE INTO HIM--WHILE WE STILL GOT A CHANCE!

GREAT FISH-HOOKS!

UNDER THE COMBINED ATTACK, THE **GREEN GLADIATOR** GOES DOWN, AND OUT...

HOLD IT, SHRIMP--!

YOU MUGS DON'T SCARE ME--

THAT'LL HOLD HIM!

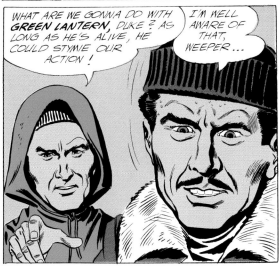

WHAT ARE WE GONNA DO WITH **GREEN LANTERN**, DUKE? AS LONG AS HE'S ALIVE, HE COULD STYMIE OUR ACTION!

I'M WELL AWARE OF THAT, WEEPER...

...THAT'S WHY I'M GOING TO PLAY A GAME OF **FREEZE-OUT** WITH HIM! WEEPER, THERE'S A WATER SPRAY CAN IN OUR PLANE! BRING IT TO ME...

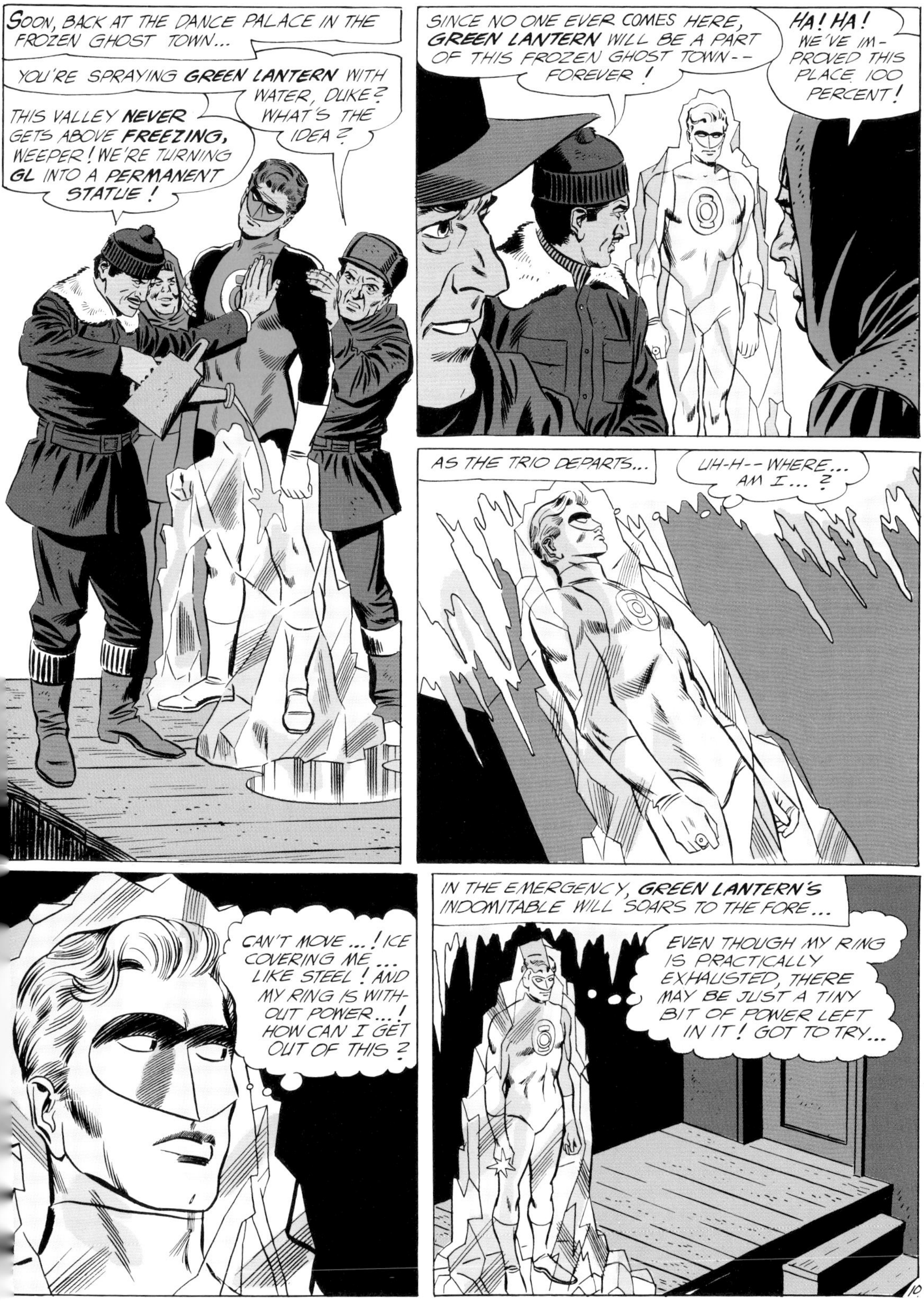
SOON, BACK AT THE DANCE PALACE IN THE FROZEN GHOST TOWN...
YOU'RE SPRAYING GREEN LANTERN WITH WATER, DUKE? WHAT'S THE IDEA?
THIS VALLEY NEVER GETS ABOVE FREEZING, WEEPER! WE'RE TURNING GL INTO A PERMANENT STATUE!
SINCE NO ONE EVER COMES HERE, GREEN LANTERN WILL BE A PART OF THIS FROZEN GHOST TOWN--FOREVER!
HA! HA! WE'VE IMPROVED THIS PLACE 100 PERCENT!
AS THE TRIO DEPARTS...
UH-H--WHERE... AM I...?
CAN'T MOVE...! ICE COVERING ME... LIKE STEEL! AND MY RING IS WITHOUT POWER...! HOW CAN I GET OUT OF THIS?
IN THE EMERGENCY, GREEN LANTERN'S INDOMITABLE WILL SOARS TO THE FORE...
EVEN THOUGH MY RING IS PRACTICALLY EXHAUSTED, THERE MAY BE JUST A TINY BIT OF POWER LEFT IN IT! GOT TO TRY...
10

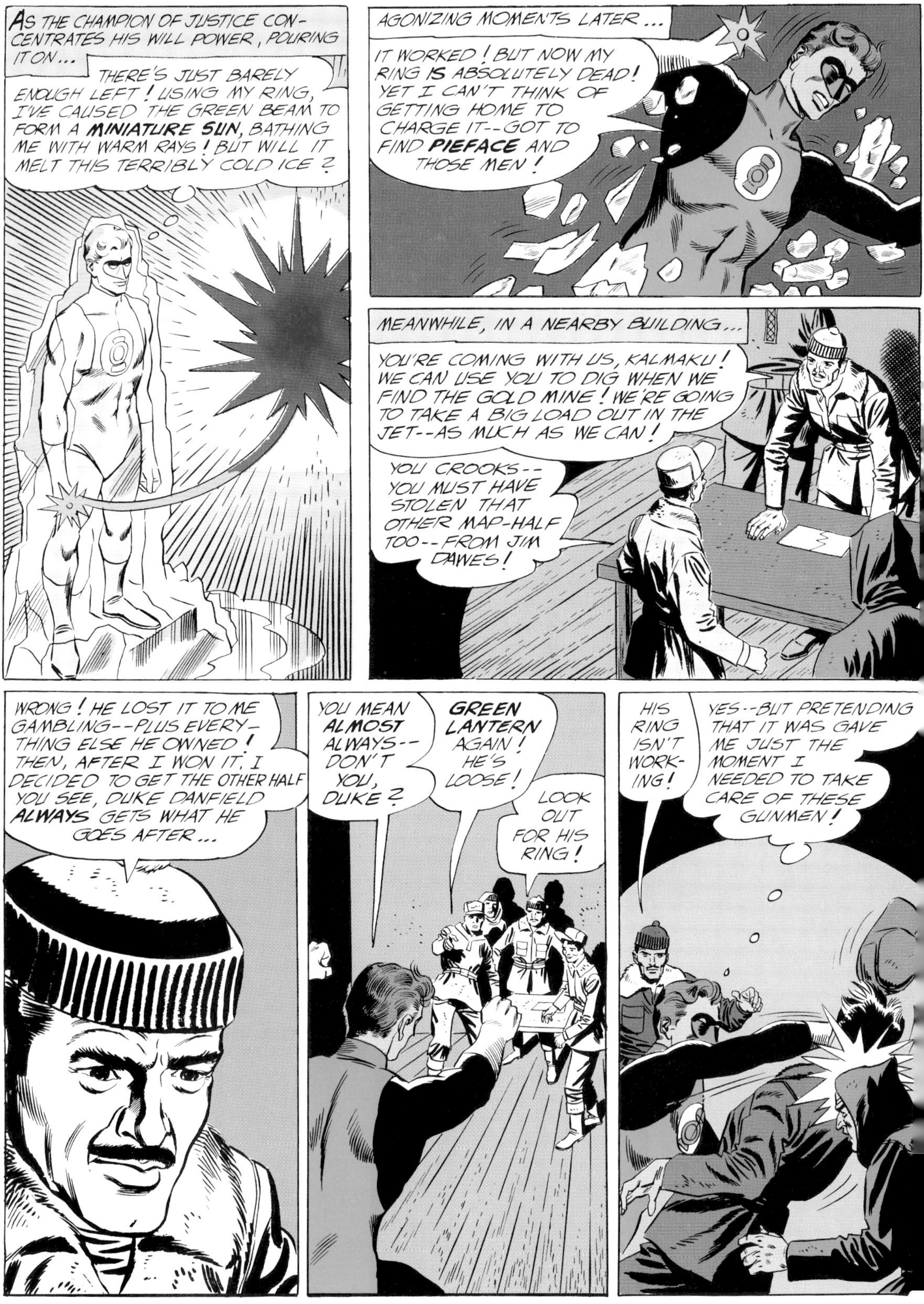
AS THE CHAMPION OF JUSTICE CONCENTRATES HIS WILL POWER, POURING IT ON...
THERE'S JUST BARELY ENOUGH LEFT! USING MY RING, I'VE CAUSED THE GREEN BEAM TO FORM A MINIATURE SUN, BATHING ME WITH WARM RAYS! BUT WILL IT MELT THIS TERRIBLY COLD ICE?
AGONIZING MOMENTS LATER...
IT WORKED! BUT NOW MY RING IS ABSOLUTELY DEAD! YET I CAN'T THINK OF GETTING HOME TO CHARGE IT--GOT TO FIND PIEFACE AND THOSE MEN!
MEANWHILE, IN A NEARBY BUILDING...
YOU'RE COMING WITH US, KALMAKU! WE CAN USE YOU TO DIG WHEN WE FIND THE GOLD MINE! WE'RE GOING TO TAKE A BIG LOAD OUT IN THE JET--AS MUCH AS WE CAN!
YOU CROOKS--YOU MUST HAVE STOLEN THAT OTHER MAP-HALF TOO--FROM JIM DAWES!
WRONG! HE LOST IT TO ME GAMBLING--PLUS EVERYTHING ELSE HE OWNED! THEN, AFTER I WON IT, I DECIDED TO GET THE OTHER HALF. YOU SEE, DUKE DANFIELD ALWAYS GETS WHAT HE GOES AFTER...
YOU MEAN ALMOST ALWAYS--DON'T YOU, DUKE?
GREEN LANTERN AGAIN! HE'S LOOSE!
LOOK OUT FOR HIS RING!
HIS RING ISN'T WORKING!
YES--BUT PRETENDING THAT IT WAS GAVE ME JUST THE MOMENT I NEEDED TO TAKE CARE OF THESE GUNMEN!

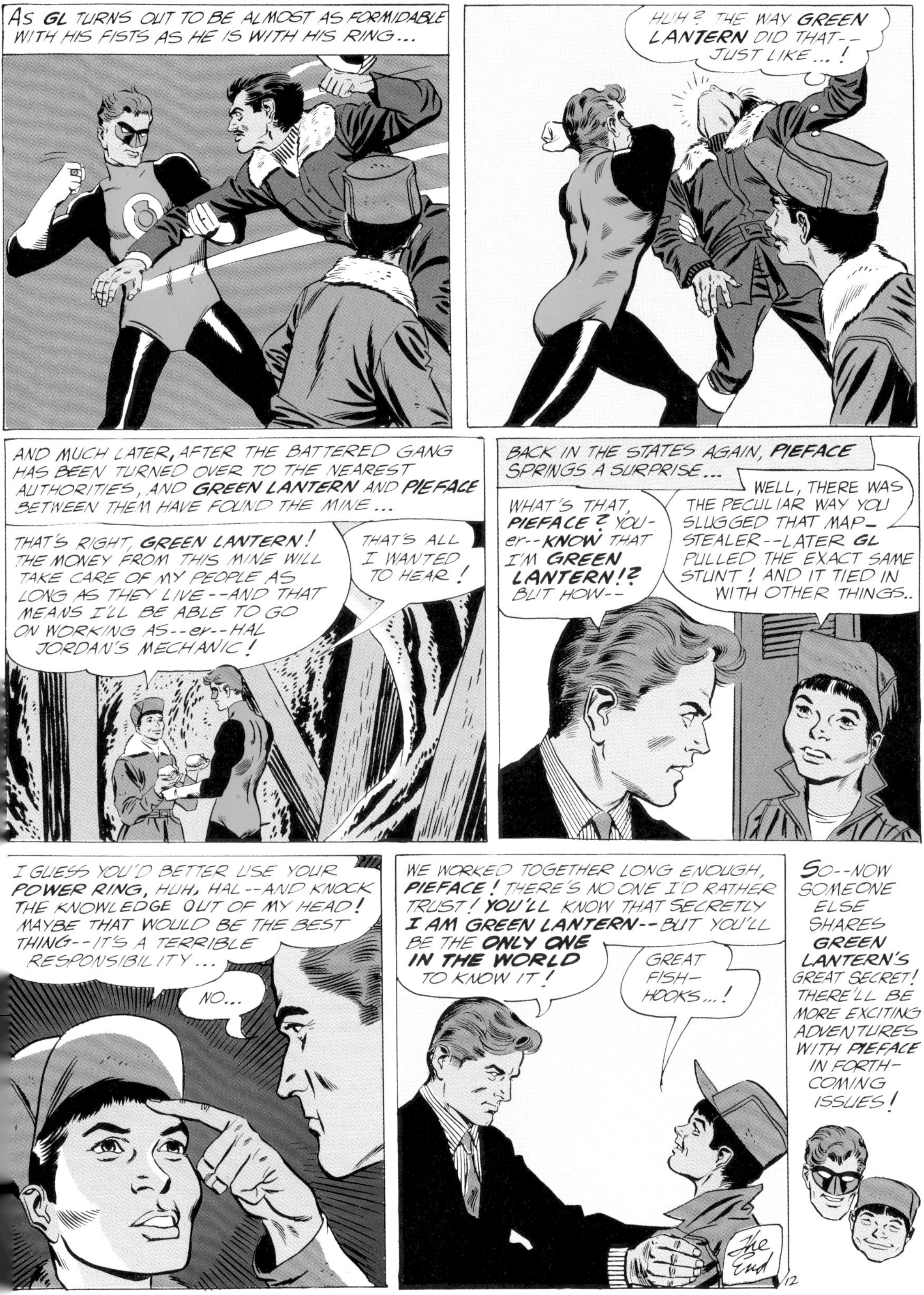
AS GL TURNS OUT TO BE ALMOST AS FORMIDABLE WITH HIS FISTS AS HE IS WITH HIS RING...
HUH? THE WAY GREEN LANTERN DID THAT-- JUST LIKE...!
AND MUCH LATER, AFTER THE BATTERED GANG HAS BEEN TURNED OVER TO THE NEAREST AUTHORITIES, AND GREEN LANTERN AND PIEFACE BETWEEN THEM HAVE FOUND THE MINE...
THAT'S RIGHT, GREEN LANTERN! THE MONEY FROM THIS MINE WILL TAKE CARE OF MY PEOPLE AS LONG AS THEY LIVE--AND THAT MEANS I'LL BE ABLE TO GO ON WORKING AS--er--HAL JORDAN'S MECHANIC!
THAT'S ALL I WANTED TO HEAR!
BACK IN THE STATES AGAIN, PIEFACE SPRINGS A SURPRISE...
WHAT'S THAT, PIEFACE? YOU--er--KNOW THAT I'M GREEN LANTERN!? BUT HOW--
WELL, THERE WAS THE PECULIAR WAY YOU SLUGGED THAT MAP-STEALER--LATER GL PULLED THE EXACT SAME STUNT! AND IT TIED IN WITH OTHER THINGS..
I GUESS YOU'D BETTER USE YOUR POWER RING, HUH, HAL--AND KNOCK THE KNOWLEDGE OUT OF MY HEAD! MAYBE THAT WOULD BE THE BEST THING--IT'S A TERRIBLE RESPONSIBILITY...
NO...
WE WORKED TOGETHER LONG ENOUGH, PIEFACE! THERE'S NO ONE I'D RATHER TRUST! YOU'LL KNOW THAT SECRETLY I AM GREEN LANTERN--BUT YOU'LL BE THE ONLY ONE IN THE WORLD TO KNOW IT!
GREAT FISH-HOOKS...!
The End
12
SO--NOW SOMEONE ELSE SHARES GREEN LANTERN'S GREAT SECRET! THERE'LL BE MORE EXCITING ADVENTURES WITH PIEFACE IN FORTH-COMING ISSUES!

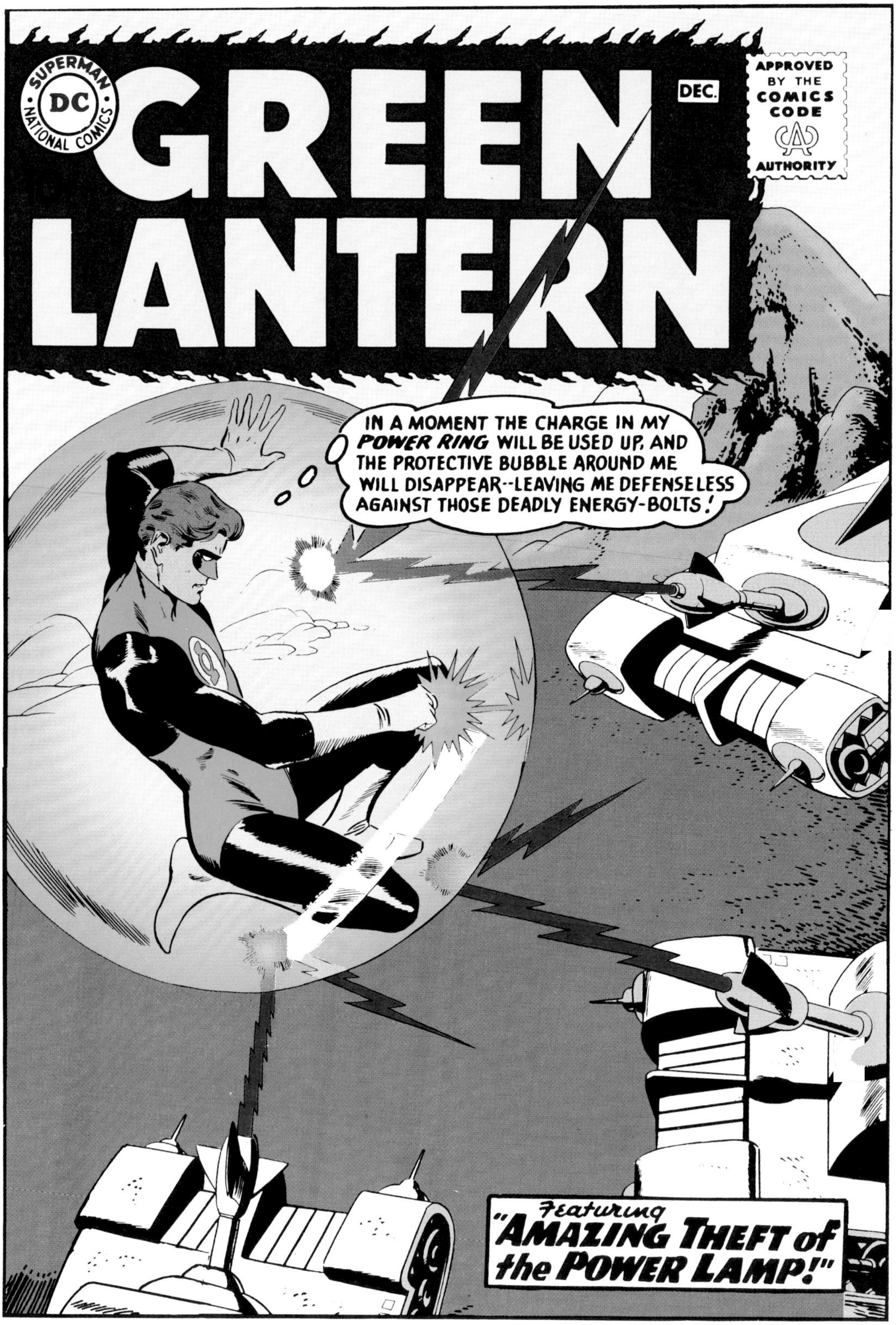
SUPERMAN
DC
NATIONAL COMICS
GREEN LANTERN
DEC.
APPROVED BY THE COMICS CODE AUTHORITY
IN A MOMENT THE CHARGE IN MY POWER RING WILL BE USED UP, AND THE PROTECTIVE BUBBLE AROUND ME WILL DISAPPEAR--LEAVING ME DEFENSELESS AGAINST THOSE DEADLY ENERGY-BOLTS!
Featuring "AMAZING THEFT of the POWER LAMP!"

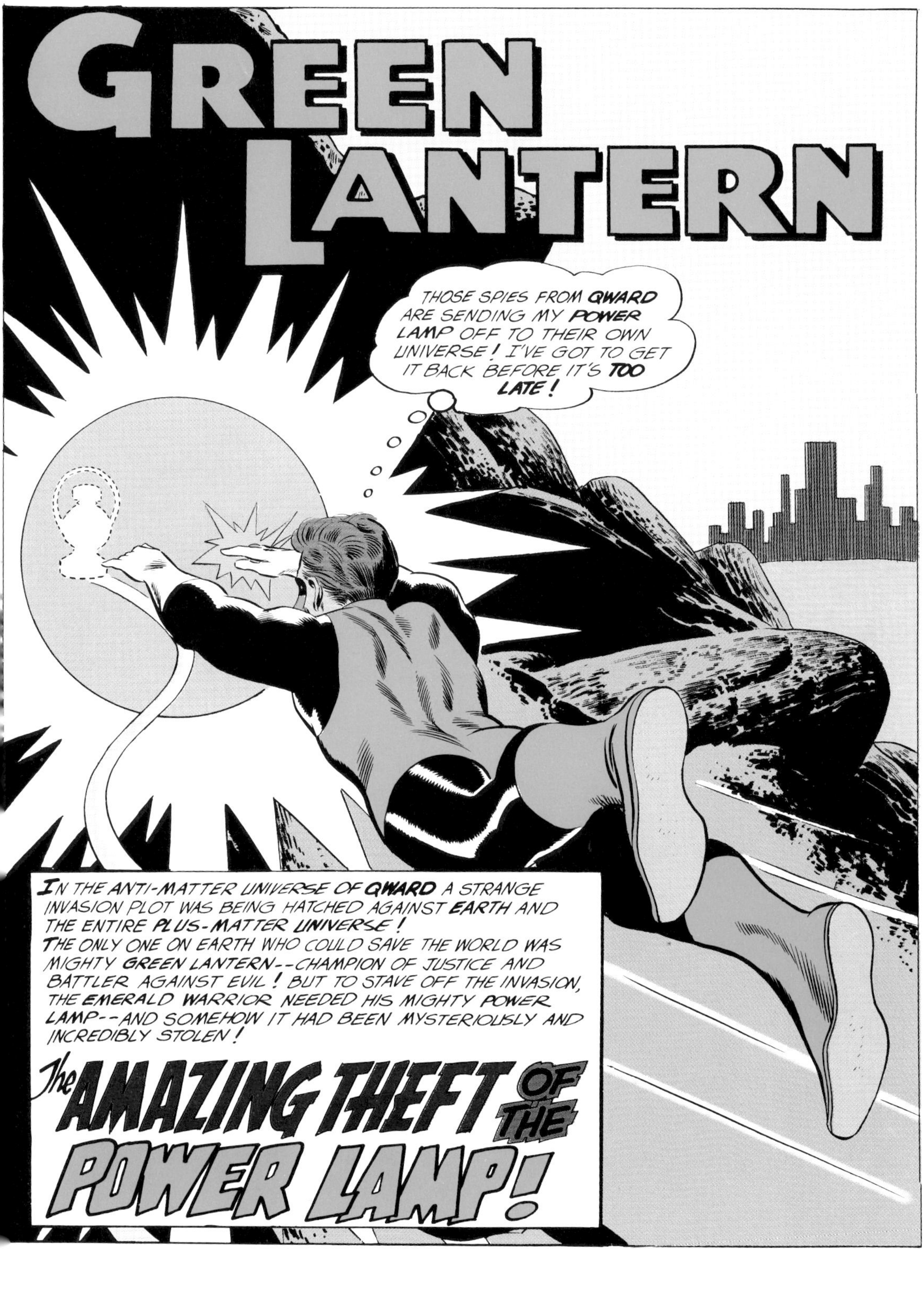
GREEN LANTERN
THOSE SPIES FROM QWARD ARE SENDING MY POWER LAMP OFF TO THEIR OWN UNIVERSE! I'VE GOT TO GET IT BACK BEFORE IT'S TOO LATE!
IN THE ANTI-MATTER UNIVERSE OF QWARD A STRANGE INVASION PLOT WAS BEING HATCHED AGAINST EARTH AND THE ENTIRE PLUS-MATTER UNIVERSE! THE ONLY ONE ON EARTH WHO COULD SAVE THE WORLD WAS MIGHTY GREEN LANTERN--CHAMPION OF JUSTICE AND BATTLER AGAINST EVIL! BUT TO STAVE OFF THE INVASION, THE EMERALD WARRIOR NEEDED HIS MIGHTY POWER LAMP--AND SOMEHOW IT HAD BEEN MYSTERIOUSLY AND INCREDIBLY STOLEN!
The AMAZING THEFT OF THE POWER LAMP!

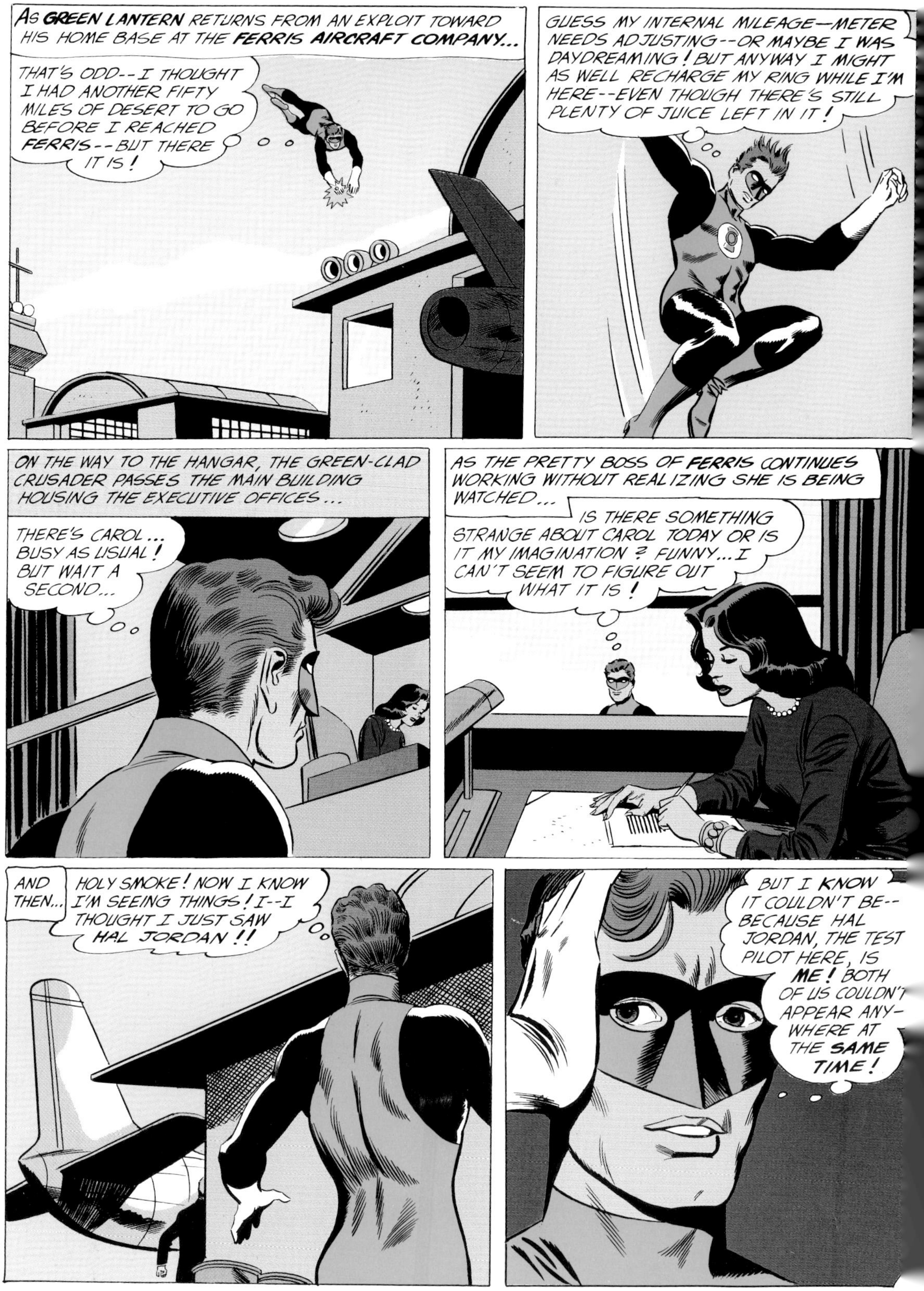
AS GREEN LANTERN RETURNS FROM AN EXPLOIT TOWARD HIS HOME BASE AT THE FERRIS AIRCRAFT COMPANY...
THAT'S ODD--I THOUGHT I HAD ANOTHER FIFTY MILES OF DESERT TO GO BEFORE I REACHED FERRIS--BUT THERE IT IS!
GUESS MY INTERNAL MILEAGE--METER NEEDS ADJUSTING--OR MAYBE I WAS DAYDREAMING! BUT ANYWAY I MIGHT AS WELL RECHARGE MY RING WHILE I'M HERE--EVEN THOUGH THERE'S STILL PLENTY OF JUICE LEFT IN IT!
ON THE WAY TO THE HANGAR, THE GREEN-CLAD CRUSADER PASSES THE MAIN BUILDING HOUSING THE EXECUTIVE OFFICES...
THERE'S CAROL... BUSY AS USUAL! BUT WAIT A SECOND...
AS THE PRETTY BOSS OF FERRIS CONTINUES WORKING WITHOUT REALIZING SHE IS BEING WATCHED...
IS THERE SOMETHING STRANGE ABOUT CAROL TODAY OR IS IT MY IMAGINATION? FUNNY...I CAN'T SEEM TO FIGURE OUT WHAT IT IS!
AND THEN...
HOLY SMOKE! NOW I KNOW I'M SEEING THINGS! I--I THOUGHT I JUST SAW HAL JORDAN!!
BUT I KNOW IT COULDN'T BE--BECAUSE HAL JORDAN, THE TEST PILOT HERE, IS ME! BOTH OF US COULDN'T APPEAR ANY-WHERE AT THE SAME TIME!

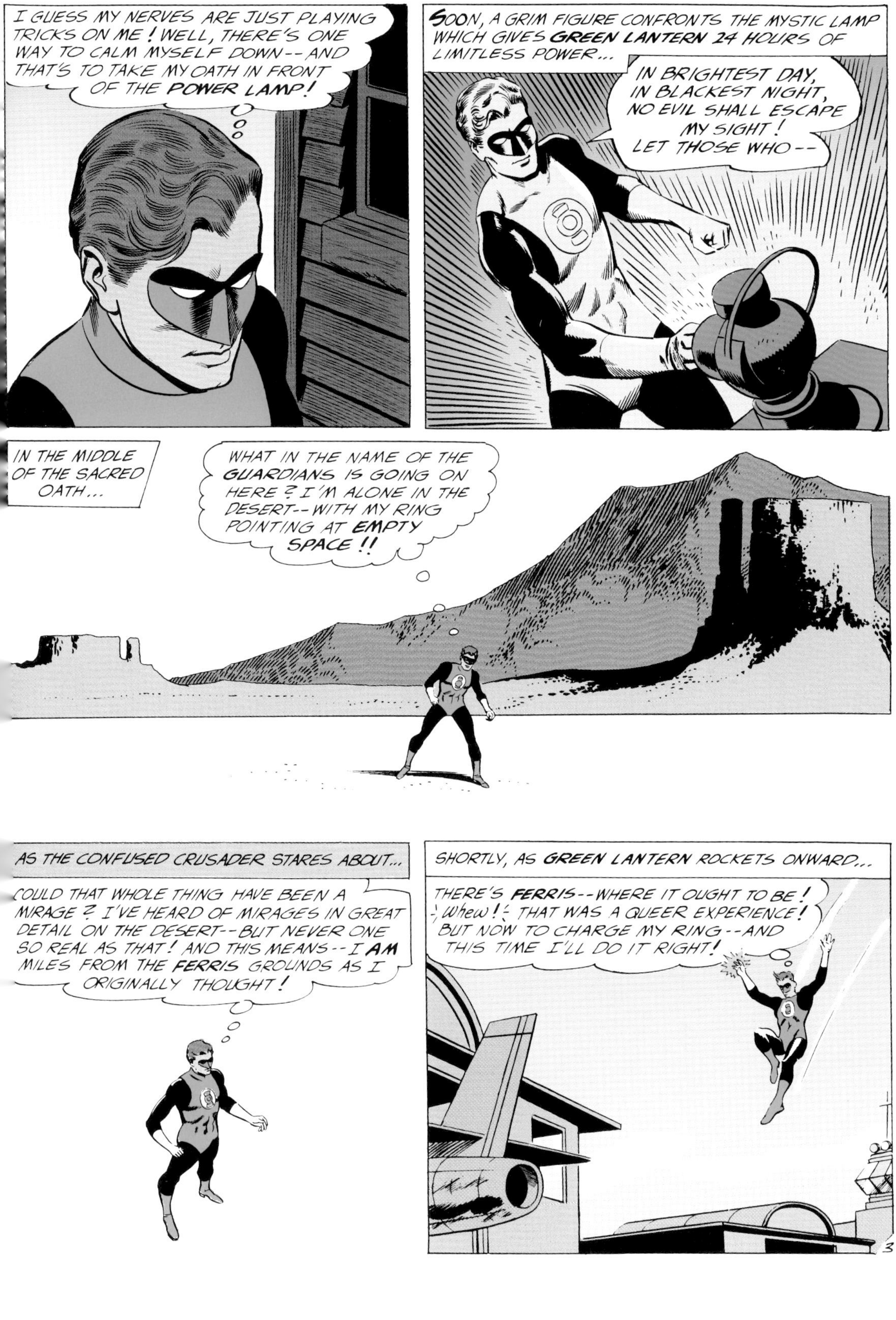
I GUESS MY NERVES ARE JUST PLAYING TRICKS ON ME! WELL, THERE'S ONE WAY TO CALM MYSELF DOWN--AND THAT'S TO TAKE MY OATH IN FRONT OF THE POWER LAMP!
SOON, A GRIM FIGURE CONFRONTS THE MYSTIC LAMP WHICH GIVES GREEN LANTERN 24 HOURS OF LIMITLESS POWER...
IN BRIGHTEST DAY, IN BLACKEST NIGHT, NO EVIL SHALL ESCAPE MY SIGHT! LET THOSE WHO--
IN THE MIDDLE OF THE SACRED OATH...
WHAT IN THE NAME OF THE GUARDIANS IS GOING ON HERE? I'M ALONE IN THE DESERT--WITH MY RING POINTING AT EMPTY SPACE!!
AS THE CONFUSED CRUSADER STARES ABOUT...
COULD THAT WHOLE THING HAVE BEEN A MIRAGE? I'VE HEARD OF MIRAGES IN GREAT DETAIL ON THE DESERT--BUT NEVER ONE SO REAL AS THAT! AND THIS MEANS--I AM MILES FROM THE FERRIS GROUNDS AS I ORIGINALLY THOUGHT!
SHORTLY, AS GREEN LANTERN ROCKETS ONWARD...
THERE'S FERRIS--WHERE IT OUGHT TO BE! -Whew!- THAT WAS A QUEER EXPERIENCE! BUT NOW TO CHARGE MY RING--AND THIS TIME I'LL DO IT RIGHT!
3

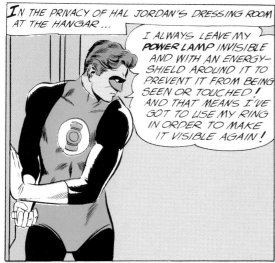

IN THE PRIVACY OF HAL JORDAN'S DRESSING ROOM AT THE HANGAR...

I ALWAYS LEAVE MY *POWER LAMP* INVISIBLE AND WITH AN ENERGY-SHIELD AROUND IT TO PREVENT IT FROM BEING SEEN OR TOUCHED! AND THAT MEANS I'VE GOT TO USE MY RING IN ORDER TO MAKE IT VISIBLE AGAIN!

BUT AS THE GREEN BEAM FLARES INTO THE FAMILIAR CORNER...

GREAT JUPITER!! MY LAMP--IT'S GONE!!!

AT THAT MOMENT ON THE ROOF OF A BOARDING HOUSE IN NEARBY *COAST CITY*...

I PROMISED MRS. HENDRICKS, MY LANDLADY, THAT I'D TRY TO FIX HER *TV* AERIAL TODAY!

SUDDENLY, AS *PIEFACE*--HAL JORDAN'S ESKIMO MECHANIC--GRIPS THE METAL PRONGS...

GREAT FISH-HOOKS! I'M GETTING SOME KIND OF RECEPTION--LIKE THOUGHTS FROM THE AERIAL!

BELOW, BEHIND CAREFULLY LOCKED DOORS...

CALLING *UNIVERSE OF QWARD**... HEADQUARTERS OF THE WEAPONERS! CALLING...

WE ARE RECEIVING YOU, DRIK! MAKE YOUR REPORT...

*Editor's Note: AS EXPLAINED IN THE LAST ISSUE, *QWARD* IS AN ANTI-MATTER UNIVERSE, ON A DIFFERENT SPACE-TIME LEVEL FROM OUR *PLUS-MATTER UNIVERSE!*

WE HAVE A GREAT SUCCESS TO REPORT--BUT ALSO A PROBLEM! LET US RELATE WHAT HAS HAPPENED...

4

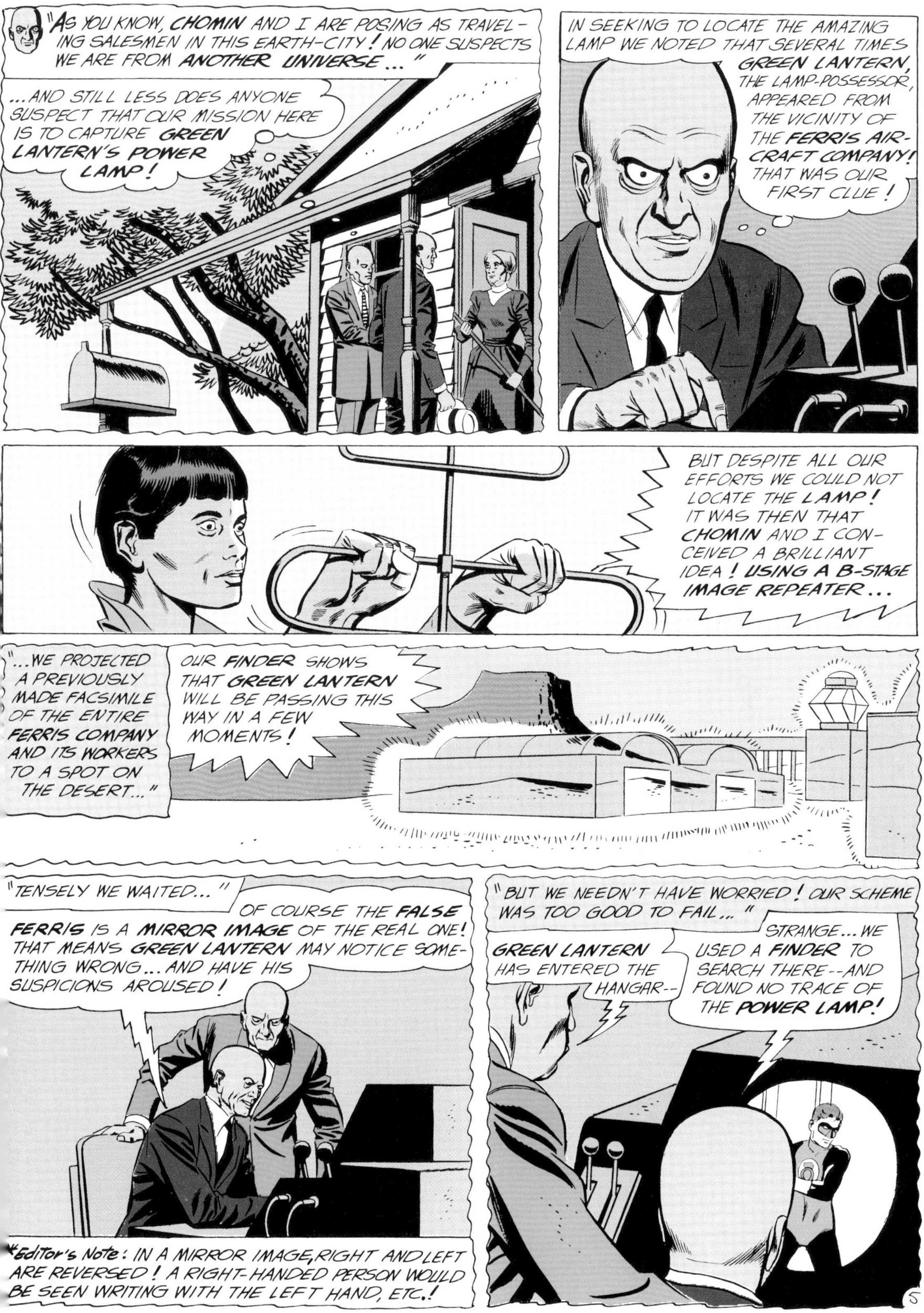
"AS YOU KNOW, CHOMIN AND I ARE POSING AS TRAVEL-ING SALESMEN IN THIS EARTH-CITY! NO ONE SUSPECTS WE ARE FROM ANOTHER UNIVERSE..."
...AND STILL LESS DOES ANYONE SUSPECT THAT OUR MISSION HERE IS TO CAPTURE GREEN LANTERN'S POWER LAMP!
IN SEEKING TO LOCATE THE AMAZING LAMP WE NOTED THAT SEVERAL TIMES
GREEN LANTERN, THE LAMP-POSSESSOR, APPEARED FROM THE VICINITY OF THE FERRIS AIR-CRAFT COMPANY! THAT WAS OUR FIRST CLUE!
BUT DESPITE ALL OUR EFFORTS WE COULD NOT LOCATE THE LAMP! IT WAS THEN THAT CHOMIN AND I CON-CEIVED A BRILLIANT IDEA! USING A B-STAGE IMAGE REPEATER...
"...WE PROJECTED A PREVIOUSLY MADE FACSIMILE OF THE ENTIRE FERRIS COMPANY AND ITS WORKERS TO A SPOT ON THE DESERT..."
OUR FINDER SHOWS THAT GREEN LANTERN WILL BE PASSING THIS WAY IN A FEW MOMENTS!
"TENSELY WE WAITED..."
OF COURSE THE FALSE FERRIS IS A MIRROR IMAGE OF THE REAL ONE! THAT MEANS GREEN LANTERN MAY NOTICE SOME-THING WRONG... AND HAVE HIS SUSPICIONS AROUSED!
*Editor's Note: IN A MIRROR IMAGE, RIGHT AND LEFT ARE REVERSED! A RIGHT-HANDED PERSON WOULD BE SEEN WRITING WITH THE LEFT HAND, ETC.!
"BUT WE NEEDN'T HAVE WORRIED! OUR SCHEME WAS TOO GOOD TO FAIL..."
GREEN LANTERN HAS ENTERED THE HANGAR--
STRANGE... WE USED A FINDER TO SEARCH THERE--AND FOUND NO TRACE OF THE POWER LAMP!
5

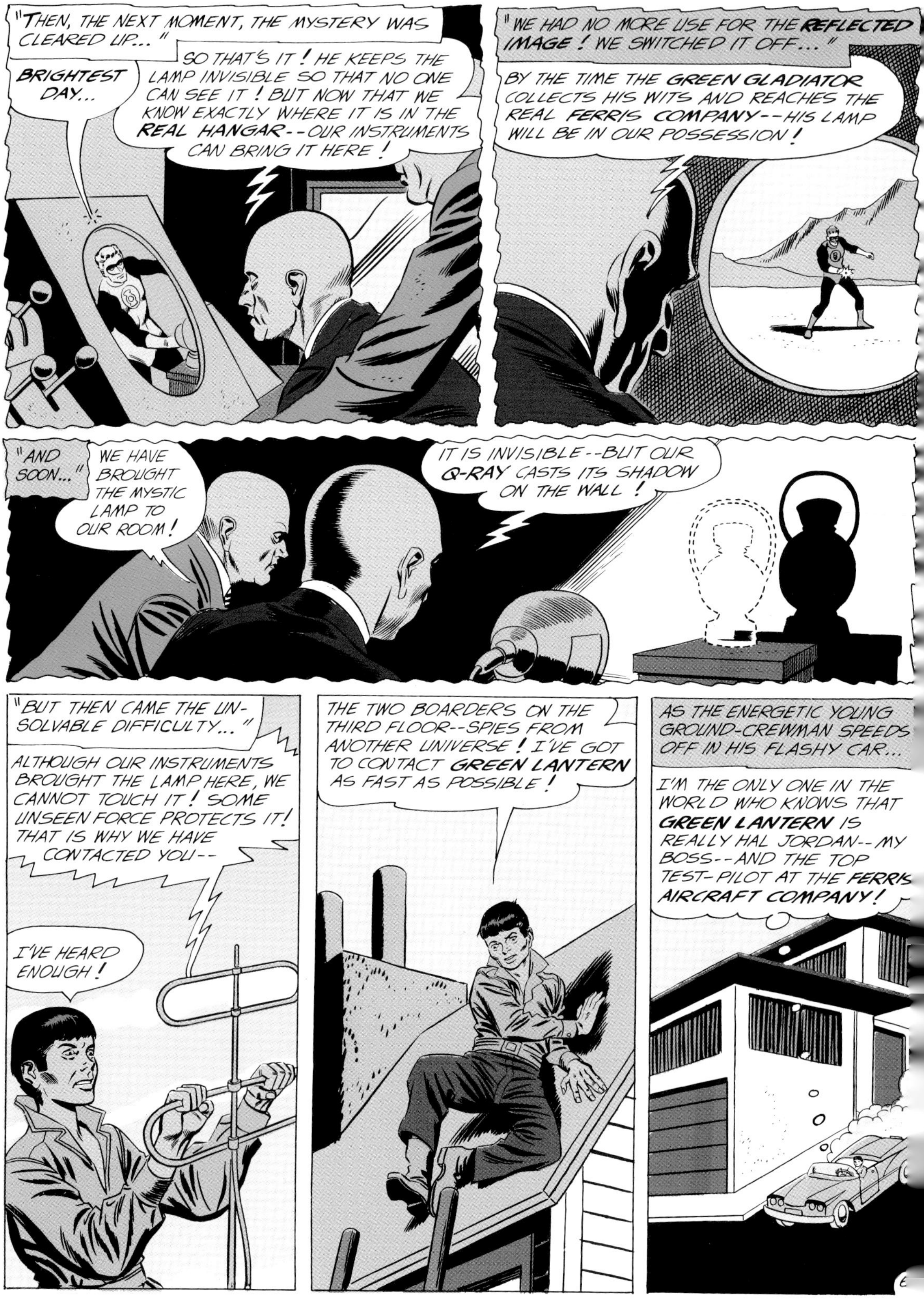
"THEN, THE NEXT MOMENT, THE MYSTERY WAS CLEARED UP..."
BRIGHTEST DAY...
SO THAT'S IT! HE KEEPS THE LAMP INVISIBLE SO THAT NO ONE CAN SEE IT! BUT NOW THAT WE KNOW EXACTLY WHERE IT IS IN THE REAL HANGAR--OUR INSTRUMENTS CAN BRING IT HERE!
"WE HAD NO MORE USE FOR THE REFLECTED IMAGE! WE SWITCHED IT OFF..."
BY THE TIME THE GREEN GLADIATOR COLLECTS HIS WITS AND REACHES THE REAL FERRIS COMPANY--HIS LAMP WILL BE IN OUR POSSESSION!
"AND SOON..."
WE HAVE BROUGHT THE MYSTIC LAMP TO OUR ROOM!
IT IS INVISIBLE--BUT OUR Q-RAY CASTS ITS SHADOW ON THE WALL!
"BUT THEN CAME THE UNSOLVABLE DIFFICULTY..."
ALTHOUGH OUR INSTRUMENTS BROUGHT THE LAMP HERE, WE CANNOT TOUCH IT! SOME UNSEEN FORCE PROTECTS IT! THAT IS WHY WE HAVE CONTACTED YOU--
I'VE HEARD ENOUGH!
THE TWO BOARDERS ON THE THIRD FLOOR--SPIES FROM ANOTHER UNIVERSE! I'VE GOT TO CONTACT GREEN LANTERN AS FAST AS POSSIBLE!
AS THE ENERGETIC YOUNG GROUND-CREWMAN SPEEDS OFF IN HIS FLASHY CAR...
I'M THE ONLY ONE IN THE WORLD WHO KNOWS THAT GREEN LANTERN IS REALLY HAL JORDAN--MY BOSS--AND THE TOP TEST-PILOT AT THE FERRIS AIRCRAFT COMPANY!

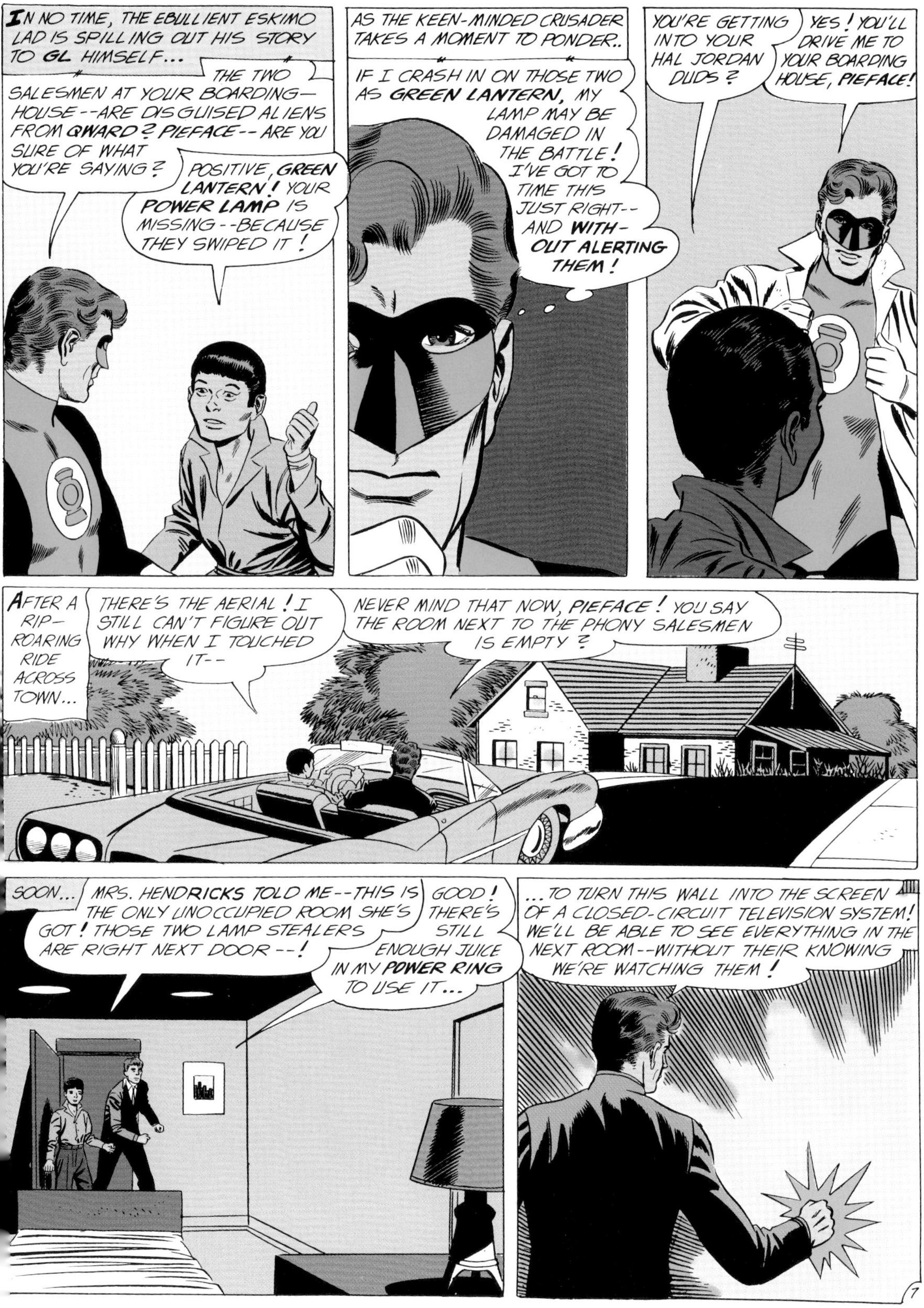
IN NO TIME, THE EBULLIENT ESKIMO LAD IS SPILLING OUT HIS STORY TO GL HIMSELF...
THE TWO SALESMEN AT YOUR BOARDING-HOUSE--ARE DISGUISED ALIENS FROM QWARD? PIEFACE--ARE YOU SURE OF WHAT YOU'RE SAYING?
POSITIVE, GREEN LANTERN! YOUR POWER LAMP IS MISSING--BECAUSE THEY SWIPED IT!
AS THE KEEN-MINDED CRUSADER TAKES A MOMENT TO PONDER..
IF I CRASH IN ON THOSE TWO AS GREEN LANTERN, MY LAMP MAY BE DAMAGED IN THE BATTLE! I'VE GOT TO TIME THIS JUST RIGHT--AND WITH-OUT ALERTING THEM!
YOU'RE GETTING INTO YOUR HAL JORDAN DUDS?
YES! YOU'LL DRIVE ME TO YOUR BOARDING HOUSE, PIEFACE!
AFTER A RIP-ROARING RIDE ACROSS TOWN...
THERE'S THE AERIAL! I STILL CAN'T FIGURE OUT WHY WHEN I TOUCHED IT--
NEVER MIND THAT NOW, PIEFACE! YOU SAY THE ROOM NEXT TO THE PHONY SALESMEN IS EMPTY?
SOON...
MRS. HENDRICKS TOLD ME--THIS IS THE ONLY UNOCCUPIED ROOM SHE'S GOT! THOSE TWO LAMP STEALERS ARE RIGHT NEXT DOOR--!
GOOD! THERE'S STILL ENOUGH JUICE IN MY POWER RING TO USE IT...
...TO TURN THIS WALL INTO THE SCREEN OF A CLOSED-CIRCUIT TELEVISION SYSTEM! WE'LL BE ABLE TO SEE EVERYTHING IN THE NEXT ROOM--WITHOUT THEIR KNOWING WE'RE WATCHING THEM!
7

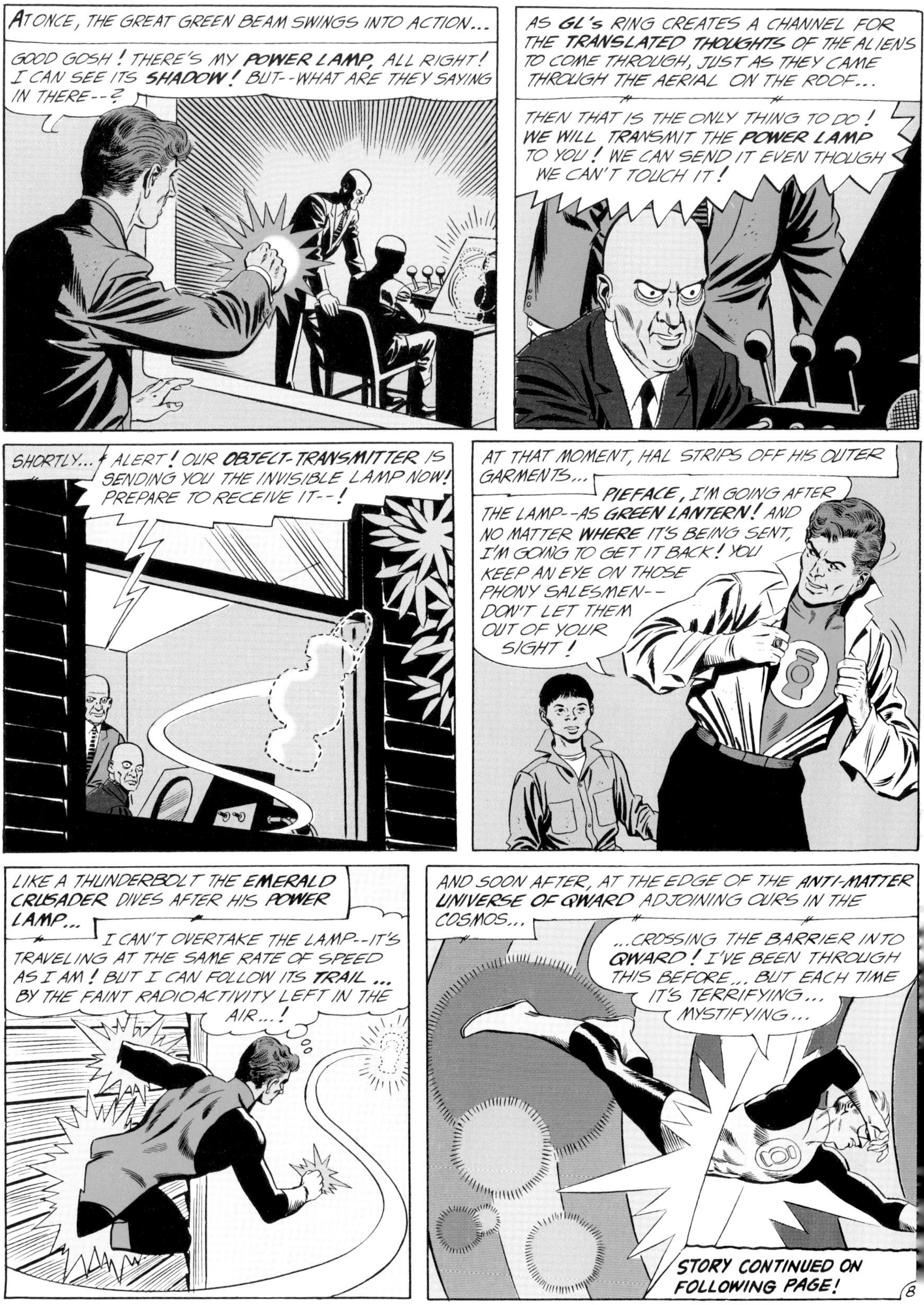
AT ONCE, THE GREAT GREEN BEAM SWINGS INTO ACTION...
GOOD GOSH! THERE'S MY POWER LAMP, ALL RIGHT! I CAN SEE ITS SHADOW! BUT--WHAT ARE THEY SAYING IN THERE--?
AS GL's RING CREATES A CHANNEL FOR THE TRANSLATED THOUGHTS OF THE ALIENS TO COME THROUGH, JUST AS THEY CAME THROUGH THE AERIAL ON THE ROOF...
THEN THAT IS THE ONLY THING TO DO! WE WILL TRANSMIT THE POWER LAMP TO YOU! WE CAN SEND IT EVEN THOUGH WE CAN'T TOUCH IT!
SHORTLY...
ALERT! OUR OBJECT-TRANSMITTER IS SENDING YOU THE INVISIBLE LAMP NOW! PREPARE TO RECEIVE IT--!
AT THAT MOMENT, HAL STRIPS OFF HIS OUTER GARMENTS...
PIEFACE, I'M GOING AFTER THE LAMP--AS GREEN LANTERN! AND NO MATTER WHERE IT'S BEING SENT, I'M GOING TO GET IT BACK! YOU KEEP AN EYE ON THOSE PHONY SALESMEN--DON'T LET THEM OUT OF YOUR SIGHT!
LIKE A THUNDERBOLT THE EMERALD CRUSADER DIVES AFTER HIS POWER LAMP...
I CAN'T OVERTAKE THE LAMP--IT'S TRAVELING AT THE SAME RATE OF SPEED AS I AM! BUT I CAN FOLLOW ITS TRAIL... BY THE FAINT RADIOACTIVITY LEFT IN THE AIR...!
AND SOON AFTER, AT THE EDGE OF THE ANTI-MATTER UNIVERSE OF QWARD ADJOINING OURS IN THE COSMOS...
...CROSSING THE BARRIER INTO QWARD! I'VE BEEN THROUGH THIS BEFORE... BUT EACH TIME IT'S TERRIFYING... MYSTIFYING...
STORY CONTINUED ON FOLLOWING PAGE!
8

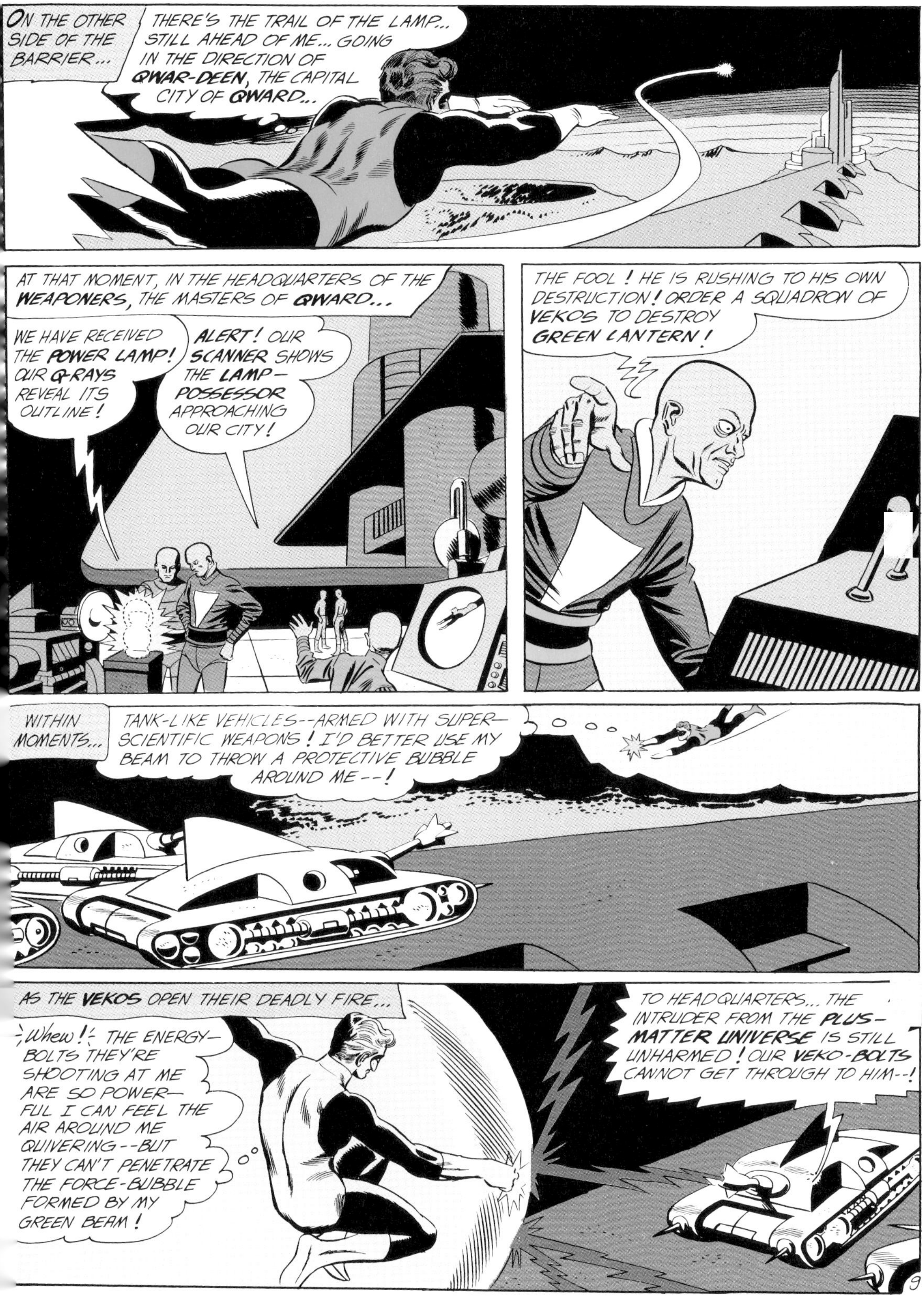
ON THE OTHER SIDE OF THE BARRIER...
THERE'S THE TRAIL OF THE LAMP... STILL AHEAD OF ME... GOING IN THE DIRECTION OF QWAR-DEEN, THE CAPITAL CITY OF QWARD...
AT THAT MOMENT, IN THE HEADQUARTERS OF THE WEAPONERS, THE MASTERS OF QWARD...
WE HAVE RECEIVED THE POWER LAMP! OUR Q-RAYS REVEAL ITS OUTLINE!
ALERT! OUR SCANNER SHOWS THE LAMP-POSSESSOR APPROACHING OUR CITY!
THE FOOL! HE IS RUSHING TO HIS OWN DESTRUCTION! ORDER A SQUADRON OF VEKOS TO DESTROY GREEN LANTERN!
WITHIN MOMENTS...
TANK-LIKE VEHICLES--ARMED WITH SUPER-SCIENTIFIC WEAPONS! I'D BETTER USE MY BEAM TO THROW A PROTECTIVE BUBBLE AROUND ME--!
AS THE VEKOS OPEN THEIR DEADLY FIRE...
Whew! THE ENERGY-BOLTS THEY'RE SHOOTING AT ME ARE SO POWERFUL I CAN FEEL THE AIR AROUND ME QUIVERING--BUT THEY CAN'T PENETRATE THE FORCE-BUBBLE FORMED BY MY GREEN BEAM!
TO HEADQUARTERS... THE INTRUDER FROM THE PLUS-MATTER UNIVERSE IS STILL UNHARMED! OUR VEKO-BOLTS CANNOT GET THROUGH TO HIM--!
9

THERE IS ONE CERTAIN WAY WE CAN DEFEAT *GREEN LANTERN!* WE MUST *DELAY HIM* UNTIL THE POWER IN HIS RING GIVES OUT! HERE IS WHAT WE WILL DO...

AS THE *WEAPONERS* ENCASE THE *POWER LAMP* IN A *YELLOW DOME...*

THIS WILL PREVENT THE EARTHMAN FROM REACHING HIS LAMP! OUR AGENTS HAVE REPORTED THAT ALL LAMP-POSSESSORS HAVE *NO POWER* OVER ANYTHING *YELLOW!* *

* *Editor's Note:* DUE TO A NECESSARY IMPURITY IN ITS VERY NATURE, *GREEN LANTERN'S* MYSTIC LAMP IS POWERLESS OVER ANYTHING *YELLOW!*

THUS HE WILL BE UNABLE TO PENETRATE THE DOME, AND WHEN HIS RING GIVES OUT--

ALERT! HERE HE COMES NOW! EVERYONE AWAY FROM HERE!

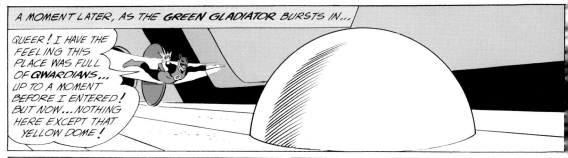

A MOMENT LATER, AS THE *GREEN GLADIATOR* BURSTS IN...

QUEER! I HAVE THE FEELING THIS PLACE WAS FULL OF *QWARDIANS...* UP TO A MOMENT BEFORE I ENTERED! BUT NOW...NOTHING HERE EXCEPT THAT YELLOW DOME!

AND GREAT SCOTT! THE TRAIL OF THE LAMP... IT LEADS TO THIS YELLOW DOME! I CAN'T GET AT IT--UNLESS THERE HAPPENS TO BE AN *OPENING* INTO IT--!

IN VAIN, *GREEN LANTERN* PROBES THE SURFACE OF THE STRUCTURE, SEEKING A CREVICE OR CRACK IN IT...

I'VE *GOT* TO FIND A WAY IN THERE! MY TIME--THE TWENTY-FOUR HOURS OF POWER I GET WHEN I CHARGE MY RING AT THE LAMP-- IS ALMOST UP!

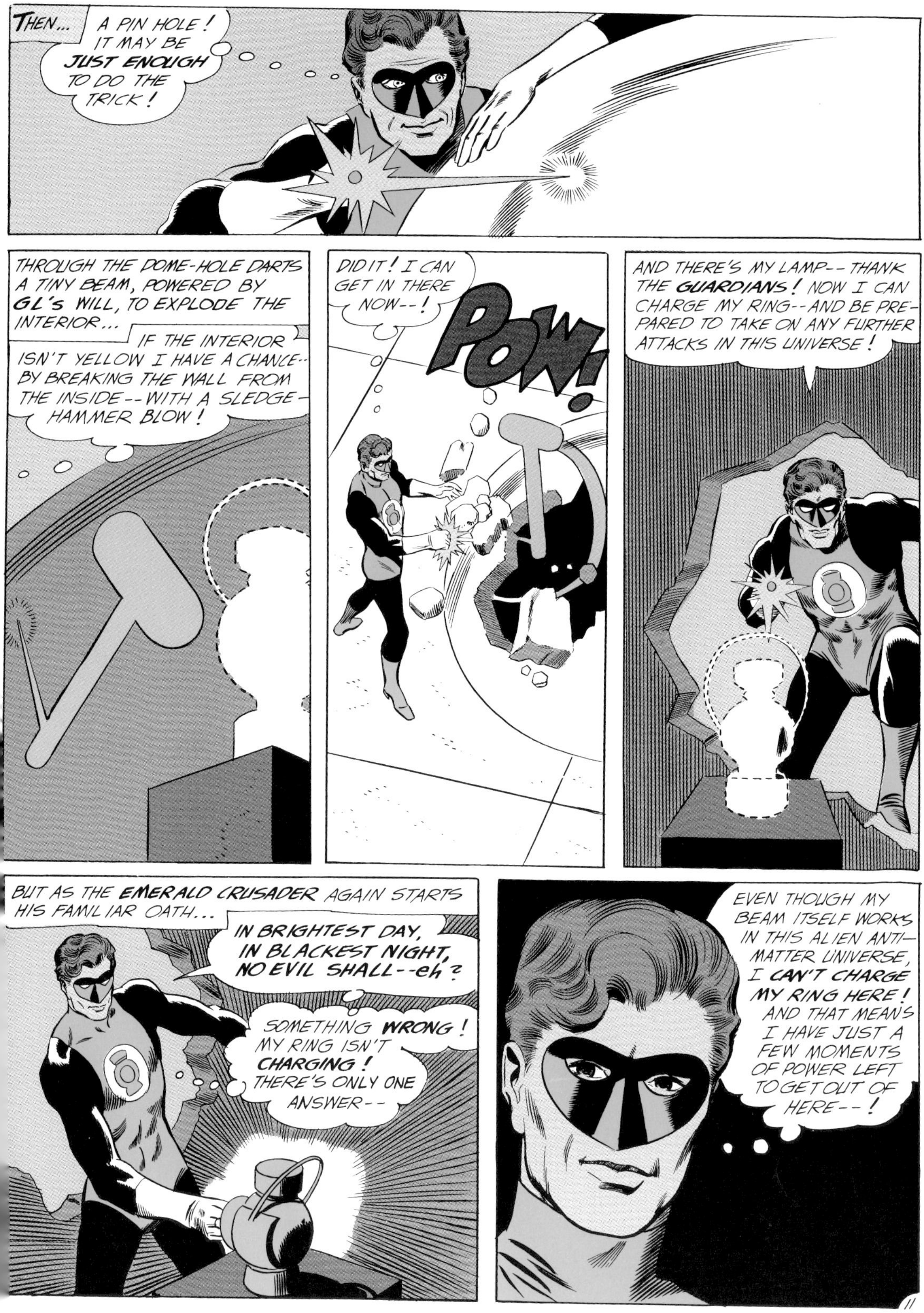
THEN...
A PIN HOLE! IT MAY BE JUST ENOUGH TO DO THE TRICK!
THROUGH THE DOME-HOLE DARTS A TINY BEAM, POWERED BY GL'S WILL, TO EXPLODE THE INTERIOR...
IF THE INTERIOR ISN'T YELLOW I HAVE A CHANCE-- BY BREAKING THE WALL FROM THE INSIDE--WITH A SLEDGE-HAMMER BLOW!
DID IT! I CAN GET IN THERE NOW--!
POW!
AND THERE'S MY LAMP--THANK THE GUARDIANS! NOW I CAN CHARGE MY RING--AND BE PREPARED TO TAKE ON ANY FURTHER ATTACKS IN THIS UNIVERSE!
BUT AS THE EMERALD CRUSADER AGAIN STARTS HIS FAMILIAR OATH...
IN BRIGHTEST DAY, IN BLACKEST NIGHT, NO EVIL SHALL--eh?
SOMETHING WRONG! MY RING ISN'T CHARGING! THERE'S ONLY ONE ANSWER--
EVEN THOUGH MY BEAM ITSELF WORKS IN THIS ALIEN ANTI-MATTER UNIVERSE, I CAN'T CHARGE MY RING HERE! AND THAT MEANS I HAVE JUST A FEW MOMENTS OF POWER LEFT TO GET OUT OF HERE--!
11

AT THAT INSTANT, IN THE THOUGHT—MONITORING CONTROL ROOM WHERE THE **GWARDIAN** CHIEFTAINS ARE CONCEALED...

...CAN'T CHARGE MY RING...! ONLY A FEW MOMENTS OF POWER LEFT...

WE MUST PREVENT THE LAMP-POSSESSOR FROM GETTING AWAY! ALL OUR FUTURE PLANS--FOR THE INVASION OF HIS PLUS—MATTER UNIVERSE--DEPEND ON IT!

SURROUND THE DOME! ON ALL SIDES-- AND BE READY TO FIRE--WITH YELLOW-FIRING RAY-GUNS!

HERE HE COMES! OPEN FIRE--! HE WILL NOT BE ABLE TO WITHSTAND US ALL--!

ZZZZZZT!

AFTER THE OPENING VOLLEY...

WE DID IT! WE HAVE SLAIN THE LAMP—POSSESSOR!!

BUT UNKNOWN TO THE **QWARDIAN** LEADERS AT THAT MOMENT...

WITH THE LAST OUNCES OF POWER LEFT IN MY RING I MADE MYSELF **INVISIBLE** AND CREATED A **FALSE IMAGE** OF MYSELF TO LEAD THE **QWARDIANS** ASTRAY! THEY BLASTED THE **IMAGE**--

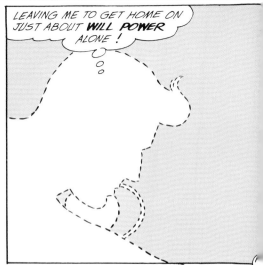

LEAVING ME TO GET HOME ON JUST ABOUT **WILL POWER** ALONE!

SHORTLY, AS *GREEN LANTERN* PASSES THE BARRIER INTO OUR UNIVERSE, A LONG OVERDUE ACT TAKES PLACE...

IN BRIGHTEST DAY, IN BLACKEST NIGHT, NO EVIL SHALL ESCAPE MY SIGHT! LET THOSE WHO WORSHIP EVIL'S MIGHT BEWARE MY POWER--*GREEN LANTERN'S LIGHT!*

AND IN *COAST CITY* NOT LONG AFTERWARD, WITH THE *POWER LAMP* SECURELY HIDDEN AWAY...

WE'LL TURN THESE TWO *QWARDIANS* OVER TO THE AUTHORITIES, *PIEFACE!* THANKS FOR KEEPING AN EYE ON THEM!

A PLEASURE, GL!

AFTER THE SPIES FROM *QWARD* HAVE BEEN PLACED IN CUSTODY AND AN *INVESTIGATION* OF THEIR PRESENCE HERE HAS BEGUN...

IT'S TIME WE GOT BACK TO WORK, *PIEFACE!* HANG ON--I'LL USE MY RING TO GET US TO THE *FERRIS PLANT!*

LET'S GO!

POLICE

LATER, AS HAL JORDAN AND HIS MECHANIC LABOR OVER A JET MOTOR...

WELL! DID YOU TWO TAKE THE *MORNING OFF?* I DIDN'T SEE YOU ANY--WHERE!

ER--WE HAD THINGS TO DO, CAROL!

The End

13

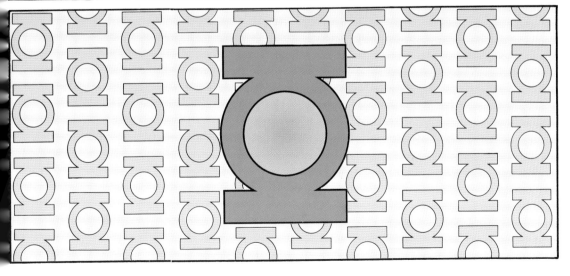

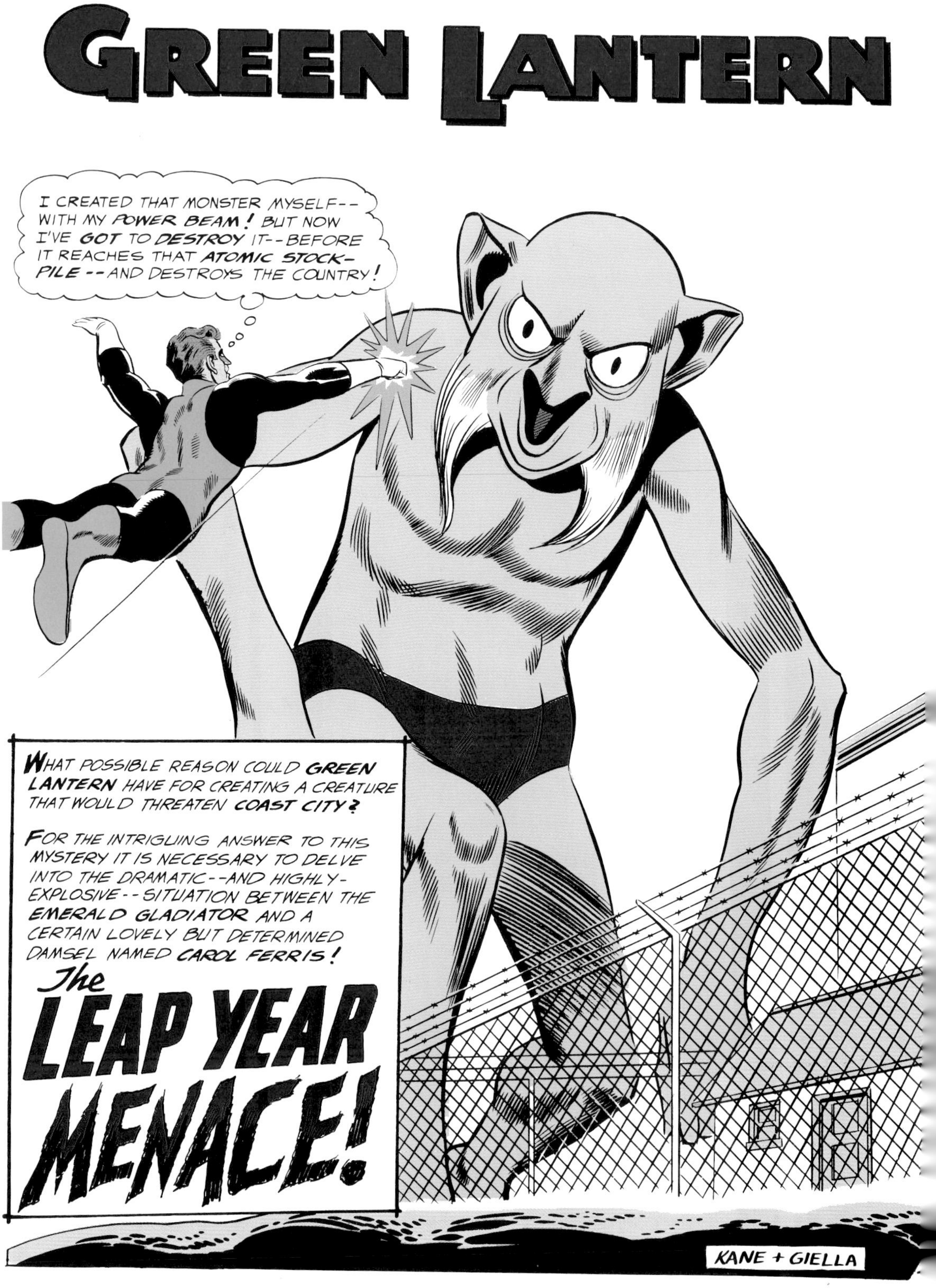
GREEN LANTERN
I CREATED THAT MONSTER MYSELF-- WITH MY POWER BEAM! BUT NOW I'VE GOT TO DESTROY IT--BEFORE IT REACHES THAT ATOMIC STOCK-PILE--AND DESTROYS THE COUNTRY!
WHAT POSSIBLE REASON COULD GREEN LANTERN HAVE FOR CREATING A CREATURE THAT WOULD THREATEN COAST CITY?
FOR THE INTRIGUING ANSWER TO THIS MYSTERY IT IS NECESSARY TO DELVE INTO THE DRAMATIC--AND HIGHLY-EXPLOSIVE--SITUATION BETWEEN THE EMERALD GLADIATOR AND A CERTAIN LOVELY BUT DETERMINED DAMSEL NAMED CAROL FERRIS!
The LEAP YEAR MENACE!
KANE + GIELLA

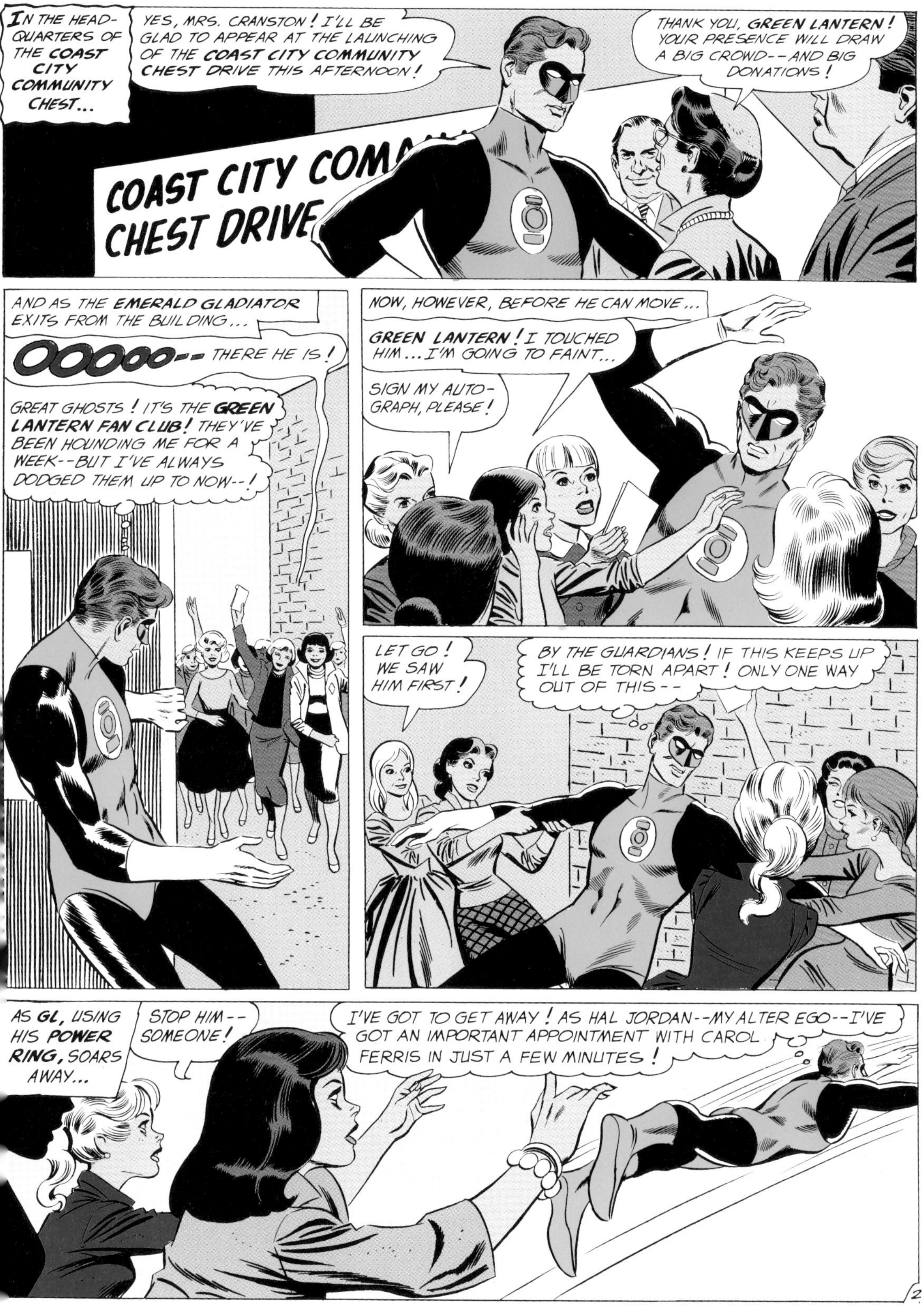
IN THE HEAD-QUARTERS OF THE COAST CITY COMMUNITY CHEST...
YES, MRS. CRANSTON! I'LL BE GLAD TO APPEAR AT THE LAUNCHING OF THE COAST CITY COMMUNITY CHEST DRIVE THIS AFTERNOON!
THANK YOU, GREEN LANTERN! YOUR PRESENCE WILL DRAW A BIG CROWD--AND BIG DONATIONS!
COAST CITY COMM
CHEST DRIVE
AND AS THE EMERALD GLADIATOR EXITS FROM THE BUILDING...
OOOOO-- THERE HE IS!
GREAT GHOSTS! IT'S THE GREEN LANTERN FAN CLUB! THEY'VE BEEN HOUNDING ME FOR A WEEK--BUT I'VE ALWAYS DODGED THEM UP TO NOW--!
NOW, HOWEVER, BEFORE HE CAN MOVE...
GREEN LANTERN! I TOUCHED HIM... I'M GOING TO FAINT...
SIGN MY AUTO-GRAPH, PLEASE!
LET GO! WE SAW HIM FIRST!
BY THE GUARDIANS! IF THIS KEEPS UP I'LL BE TORN APART! ONLY ONE WAY OUT OF THIS--
AS GL, USING HIS POWER RING, SOARS AWAY...
STOP HIM--SOMEONE!
I'VE GOT TO GET AWAY! AS HAL JORDAN--MY ALTER EGO--I'VE GOT AN IMPORTANT APPOINTMENT WITH CAROL FERRIS IN JUST A FEW MINUTES!
2

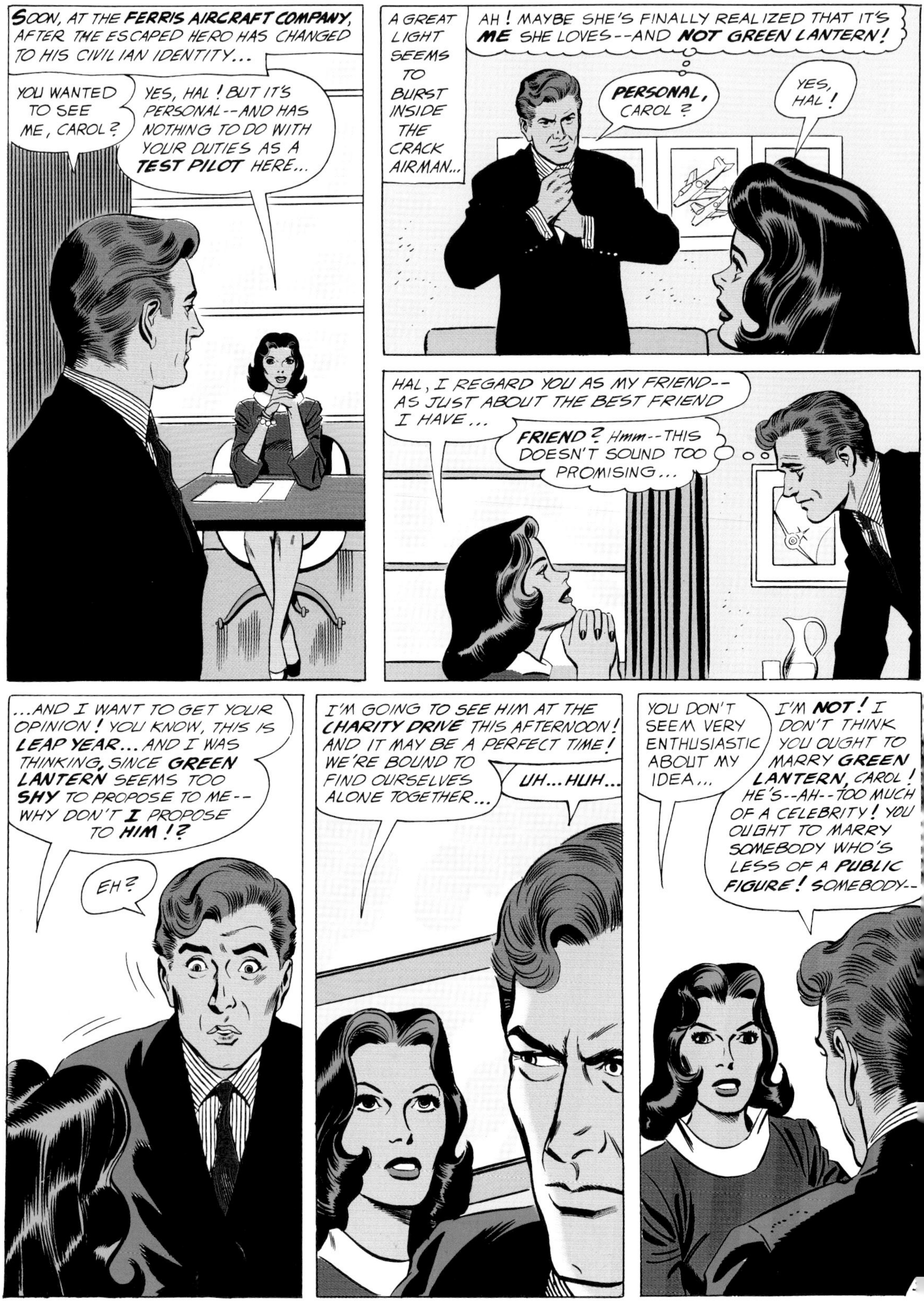
SOON, AT THE FERRIS AIRCRAFT COMPANY, AFTER THE ESCAPED HERO HAS CHANGED TO HIS CIVILIAN IDENTITY...
YOU WANTED TO SEE ME, CAROL?
YES, HAL! BUT IT'S PERSONAL--AND HAS NOTHING TO DO WITH YOUR DUTIES AS A TEST PILOT HERE...
A GREAT LIGHT SEEMS TO BURST INSIDE THE CRACK AIRMAN...
AH! MAYBE SHE'S FINALLY REALIZED THAT IT'S ME SHE LOVES--AND NOT GREEN LANTERN!
PERSONAL, CAROL?
YES, HAL!
HAL, I REGARD YOU AS MY FRIEND--AS JUST ABOUT THE BEST FRIEND I HAVE...
FRIEND? Hmm--THIS DOESN'T SOUND TOO PROMISING...
...AND I WANT TO GET YOUR OPINION! YOU KNOW, THIS IS LEAP YEAR... AND I WAS THINKING, SINCE GREEN LANTERN SEEMS TOO SHY TO PROPOSE TO ME--WHY DON'T I PROPOSE TO HIM!?
EH?
I'M GOING TO SEE HIM AT THE CHARITY DRIVE THIS AFTERNOON! AND IT MAY BE A PERFECT TIME! WE'RE BOUND TO FIND OURSELVES ALONE TOGETHER...
UH...HUH...
YOU DON'T SEEM VERY ENTHUSIASTIC ABOUT MY IDEA...
I'M NOT! I DON'T THINK YOU OUGHT TO MARRY GREEN LANTERN, CAROL! HE'S--AH--TOO MUCH OF A CELEBRITY! YOU OUGHT TO MARRY SOMEBODY WHO'S LESS OF A PUBLIC FIGURE! SOMEBODY--

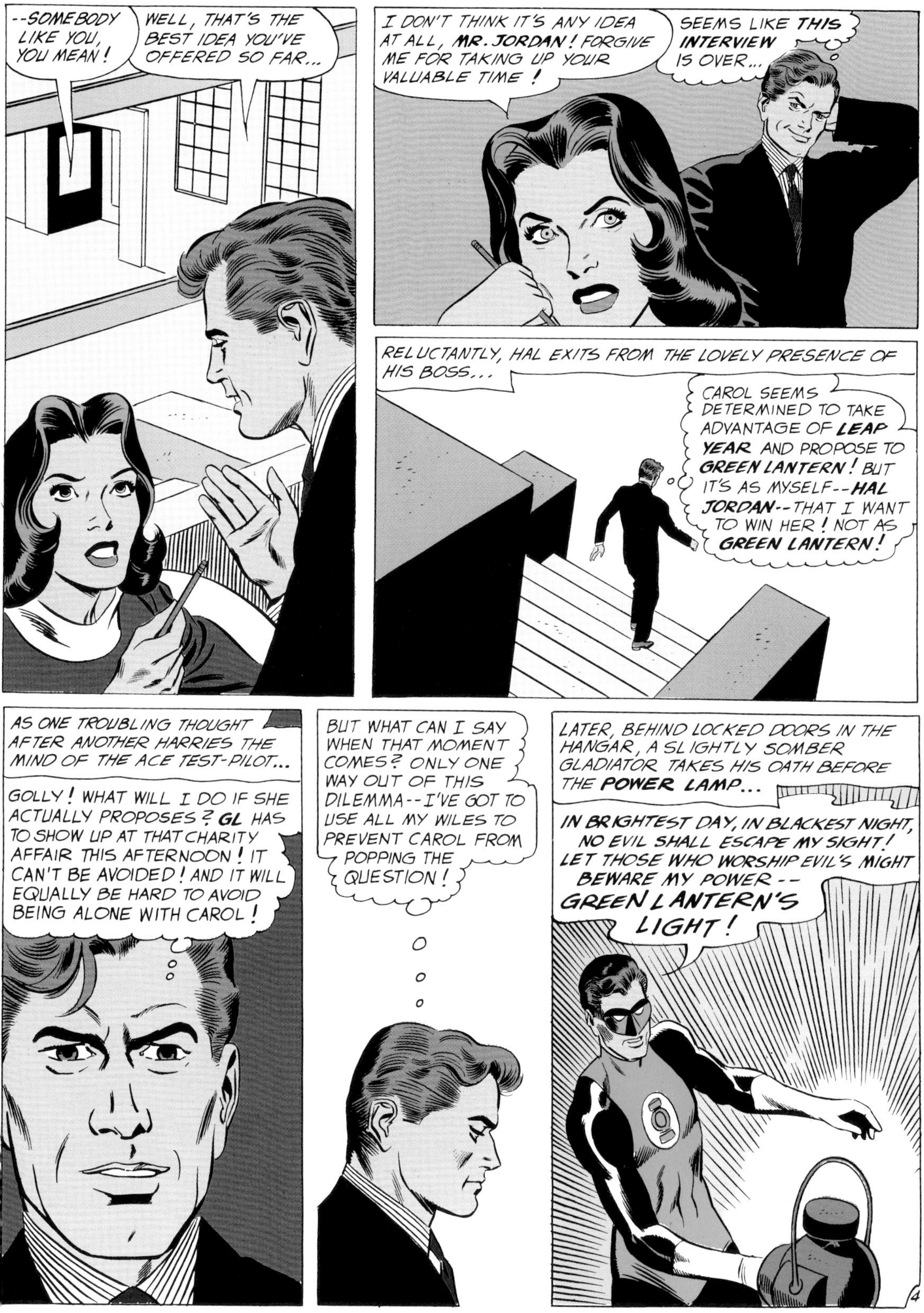
--SOMEBODY LIKE YOU, YOU MEAN!
WELL, THAT'S THE BEST IDEA YOU'VE OFFERED SO FAR...
I DON'T THINK IT'S ANY IDEA AT ALL, MR. JORDAN! FORGIVE ME FOR TAKING UP YOUR VALUABLE TIME!
SEEMS LIKE THIS INTERVIEW IS OVER...
RELUCTANTLY, HAL EXITS FROM THE LOVELY PRESENCE OF HIS BOSS...
CAROL SEEMS DETERMINED TO TAKE ADVANTAGE OF LEAP YEAR AND PROPOSE TO GREEN LANTERN! BUT IT'S AS MYSELF--HAL JORDAN--THAT I WANT TO WIN HER! NOT AS GREEN LANTERN!
AS ONE TROUBLING THOUGHT AFTER ANOTHER HARRIES THE MIND OF THE ACE TEST-PILOT...
GOLLY! WHAT WILL I DO IF SHE ACTUALLY PROPOSES? GL HAS TO SHOW UP AT THAT CHARITY AFFAIR THIS AFTERNOON! IT CAN'T BE AVOIDED! AND IT WILL EQUALLY BE HARD TO AVOID BEING ALONE WITH CAROL!
BUT WHAT CAN I SAY WHEN THAT MOMENT COMES? ONLY ONE WAY OUT OF THIS DILEMMA--I'VE GOT TO USE ALL MY WILES TO PREVENT CAROL FROM POPPING THE QUESTION!
LATER, BEHIND LOCKED DOORS IN THE HANGAR, A SLIGHTLY SOMBER GLADIATOR TAKES HIS OATH BEFORE THE POWER LAMP...
IN BRIGHTEST DAY, IN BLACKEST NIGHT, NO EVIL SHALL ESCAPE MY SIGHT! LET THOSE WHO WORSHIP EVIL'S MIGHT BEWARE MY POWER -- GREEN LANTERN'S LIGHT!
4

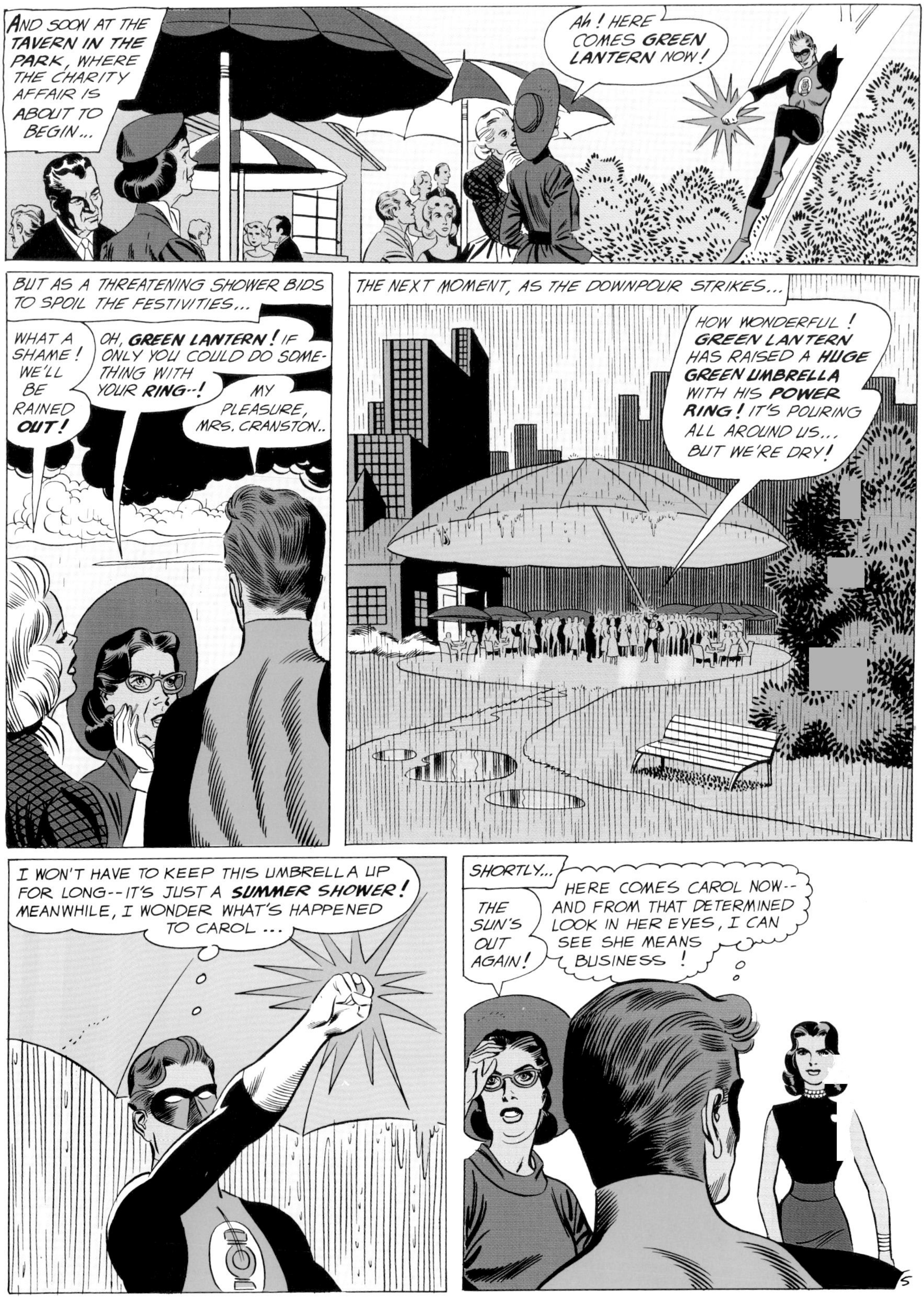
AND SOON AT THE TAVERN IN THE PARK, WHERE THE CHARITY AFFAIR IS ABOUT TO BEGIN...
AH! HERE COMES GREEN LANTERN NOW!
BUT AS A THREATENING SHOWER BIDS TO SPOIL THE FESTIVITIES...
WHAT A SHAME! WE'LL BE RAINED OUT!
OH, GREEN LANTERN! IF ONLY YOU COULD DO SOMETHING WITH YOUR RING--!
MY PLEASURE, MRS. CRANSTON..
THE NEXT MOMENT, AS THE DOWNPOUR STRIKES...
HOW WONDERFUL! GREEN LANTERN HAS RAISED A HUGE GREEN UMBRELLA WITH HIS POWER RING! IT'S POURING ALL AROUND US... BUT WE'RE DRY!
I WON'T HAVE TO KEEP THIS UMBRELLA UP FOR LONG--IT'S JUST A SUMMER SHOWER! MEANWHILE, I WONDER WHAT'S HAPPENED TO CAROL ...
SHORTLY...
THE SUN'S OUT AGAIN!
HERE COMES CAROL NOW--AND FROM THAT DETERMINED LOOK IN HER EYES, I CAN SEE SHE MEANS BUSINESS!
5

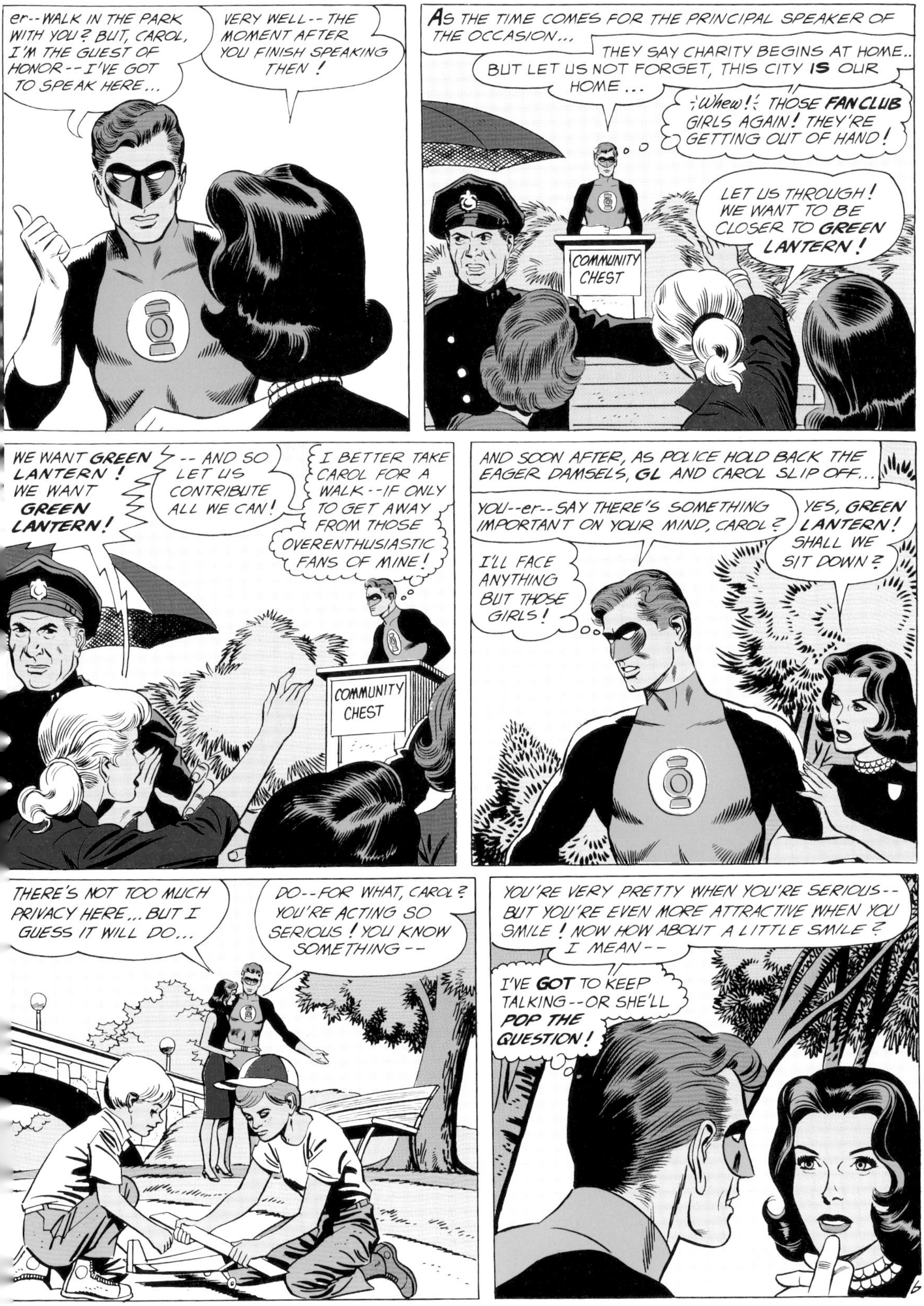
er--WALK IN THE PARK WITH YOU? BUT, CAROL, I'M THE GUEST OF HONOR--I'VE GOT TO SPEAK HERE...
VERY WELL--THE MOMENT AFTER YOU FINISH SPEAKING THEN!
AS THE TIME COMES FOR THE PRINCIPAL SPEAKER OF THE OCCASION...
THEY SAY CHARITY BEGINS AT HOME.. BUT LET US NOT FORGET, THIS CITY IS OUR HOME...
Whew! THOSE FAN CLUB GIRLS AGAIN! THEY'RE GETTING OUT OF HAND!
LET US THROUGH! WE WANT TO BE CLOSER TO GREEN LANTERN!
COMMUNITY CHEST
WE WANT GREEN LANTERN! WE WANT GREEN LANTERN!
--AND SO LET US CONTRIBUTE ALL WE CAN!
I BETTER TAKE CAROL FOR A WALK--IF ONLY TO GET AWAY FROM THOSE OVERENTHUSIASTIC FANS OF MINE!
COMMUNITY CHEST
AND SOON AFTER, AS POLICE HOLD BACK THE EAGER DAMSELS, GL AND CAROL SLIP OFF...
YOU--er--SAY THERE'S SOMETHING IMPORTANT ON YOUR MIND, CAROL?
YES, GREEN LANTERN! SHALL WE SIT DOWN?
I'LL FACE ANYTHING BUT THOSE GIRLS!
THERE'S NOT TOO MUCH PRIVACY HERE... BUT I GUESS IT WILL DO...
DO--FOR WHAT, CAROL? YOU'RE ACTING SO SERIOUS! YOU KNOW SOMETHING--
YOU'RE VERY PRETTY WHEN YOU'RE SERIOUS--BUT YOU'RE EVEN MORE ATTRACTIVE WHEN YOU SMILE! NOW HOW ABOUT A LITTLE SMILE? I MEAN--
I'VE GOT TO KEEP TALKING--OR SHE'LL POP THE QUESTION!
6

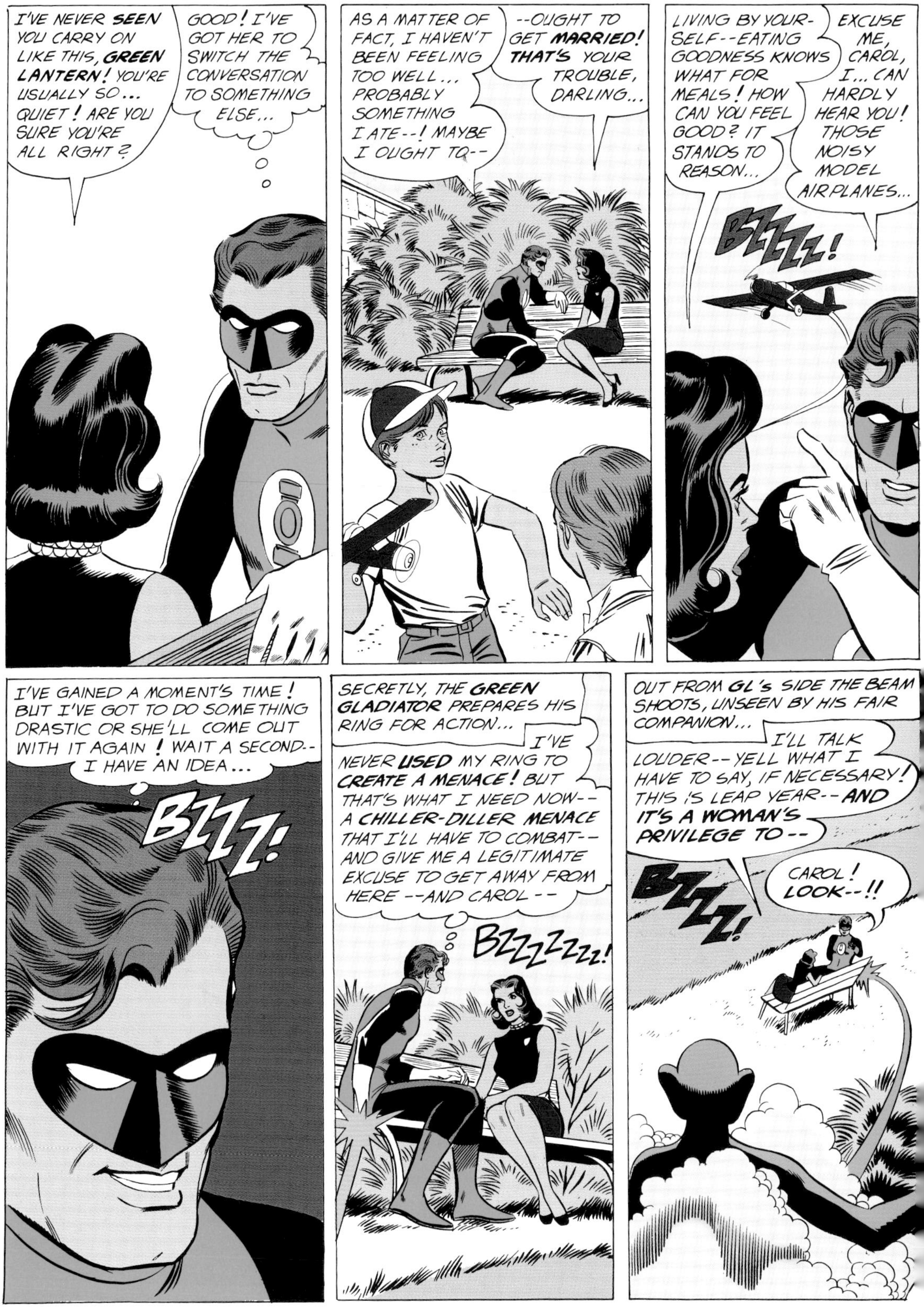
I'VE NEVER SEEN YOU CARRY ON LIKE THIS, GREEN LANTERN! YOU'RE USUALLY SO... QUIET! ARE YOU SURE YOU'RE ALL RIGHT?
GOOD! I'VE GOT HER TO SWITCH THE CONVERSATION TO SOMETHING ELSE...
AS A MATTER OF FACT, I HAVEN'T BEEN FEELING TOO WELL... PROBABLY SOMETHING I ATE--! MAYBE I OUGHT TO--
--OUGHT TO GET MARRIED! THAT'S YOUR TROUBLE, DARLING...
LIVING BY YOURSELF--EATING GOODNESS KNOWS WHAT FOR MEALS! HOW CAN YOU FEEL GOOD? IT STANDS TO REASON...
EXCUSE ME, CAROL, I... CAN HARDLY HEAR YOU! THOSE NOISY MODEL AIRPLANES...
BZZZZ!
I'VE GAINED A MOMENT'S TIME! BUT I'VE GOT TO DO SOMETHING DRASTIC OR SHE'LL COME OUT WITH IT AGAIN! WAIT A SECOND-- I HAVE AN IDEA...
BZZZ!
SECRETLY, THE GREEN GLADIATOR PREPARES HIS RING FOR ACTION...
I'VE NEVER USED MY RING TO CREATE A MENACE! BUT THAT'S WHAT I NEED NOW-- A CHILLER-DILLER MENACE THAT I'LL HAVE TO COMBAT-- AND GIVE ME A LEGITIMATE EXCUSE TO GET AWAY FROM HERE --AND CAROL--
BZZZZZZZ!
OUT FROM GL'S SIDE THE BEAM SHOOTS, UNSEEN BY HIS FAIR COMPANION...
I'LL TALK LOUDER--YELL WHAT I HAVE TO SAY, IF NECESSARY! THIS IS LEAP YEAR--AND IT'S A WOMAN'S PRIVILEGE TO--
BZZZ!
CAROL! LOOK--!!

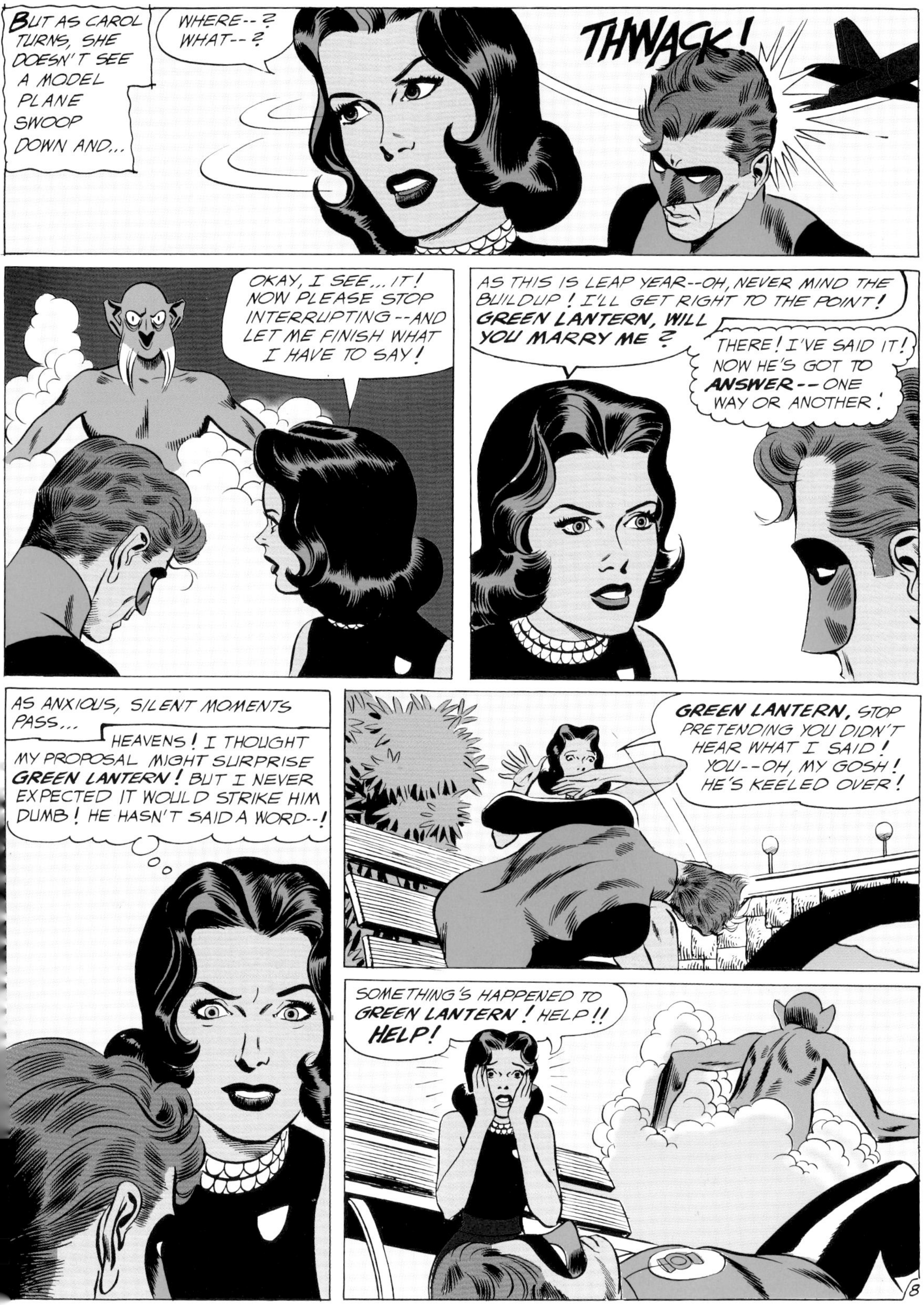
BUT AS CAROL TURNS, SHE DOESN'T SEE A MODEL PLANE SWOOP DOWN AND...
WHERE--? WHAT--?
THWACK!
OKAY, I SEE...IT! NOW PLEASE STOP INTERRUPTING--AND LET ME FINISH WHAT I HAVE TO SAY!
AS THIS IS LEAP YEAR--OH, NEVER MIND THE BUILDUP! I'LL GET RIGHT TO THE POINT! GREEN LANTERN, WILL YOU MARRY ME?
THERE! I'VE SAID IT! NOW HE'S GOT TO ANSWER--ONE WAY OR ANOTHER!
AS ANXIOUS, SILENT MOMENTS PASS...
HEAVENS! I THOUGHT MY PROPOSAL MIGHT SURPRISE GREEN LANTERN! BUT I NEVER EXPECTED IT WOULD STRIKE HIM DUMB! HE HASN'T SAID A WORD--!
GREEN LANTERN, STOP PRETENDING YOU DIDN'T HEAR WHAT I SAID! YOU--OH, MY GOSH! HE'S KEELED OVER!
SOMETHING'S HAPPENED TO GREEN LANTERN! HELP!! HELP!
8

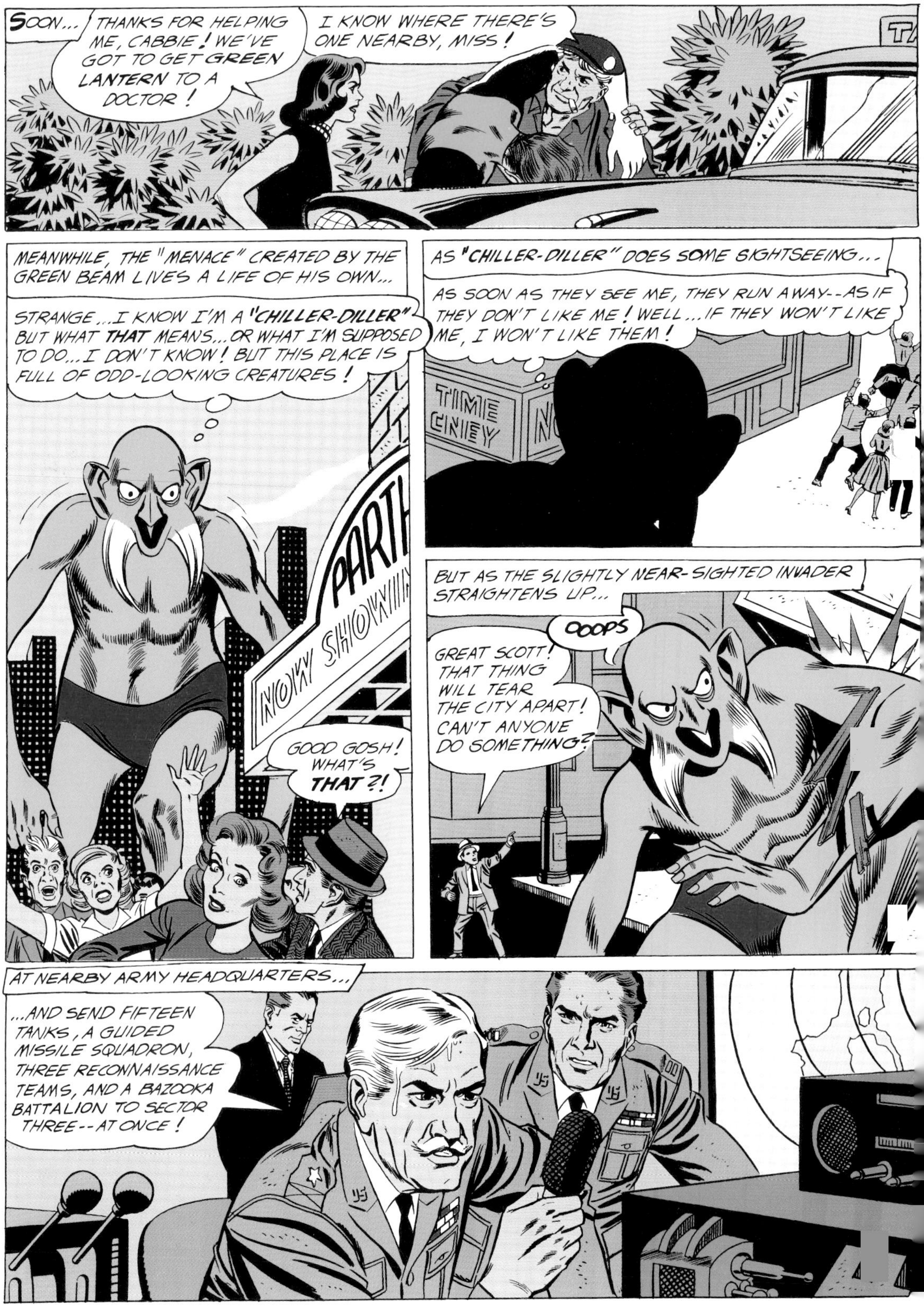
SOON...
THANKS FOR HELPING ME, CABBIE! WE'VE GOT TO GET GREEN LANTERN TO A DOCTOR!
I KNOW WHERE THERE'S ONE NEARBY, MISS!
MEANWHILE, THE "MENACE" CREATED BY THE GREEN BEAM LIVES A LIFE OF HIS OWN...
STRANGE... I KNOW I'M A "CHILLER-DILLER" BUT WHAT THAT MEANS... OR WHAT I'M SUPPOSED TO DO... I DON'T KNOW! BUT THIS PLACE IS FULL OF ODD-LOOKING CREATURES!
PARTH
NOW SHOWI
GOOD GOSH! WHAT'S THAT?!
AS "CHILLER-DILLER" DOES SOME SIGHTSEEING...
AS SOON AS THEY SEE ME, THEY RUN AWAY--AS IF THEY DON'T LIKE ME! WELL... IF THEY WON'T LIKE ME, I WON'T LIKE THEM!
TIME
CNEY
BUT AS THE SLIGHTLY NEAR-SIGHTED INVADER STRAIGHTENS UP...
OOOPS
GREAT SCOTT! THAT THING WILL TEAR THE CITY APART! CAN'T ANYONE DO SOMETHING?
AT NEARBY ARMY HEADQUARTERS...
...AND SEND FIFTEEN TANKS, A GUIDED MISSILE SQUADRON, THREE RECONNAISSANCE TEAMS, AND A BAZOOKA BATTALION TO SECTOR THREE--AT ONCE!

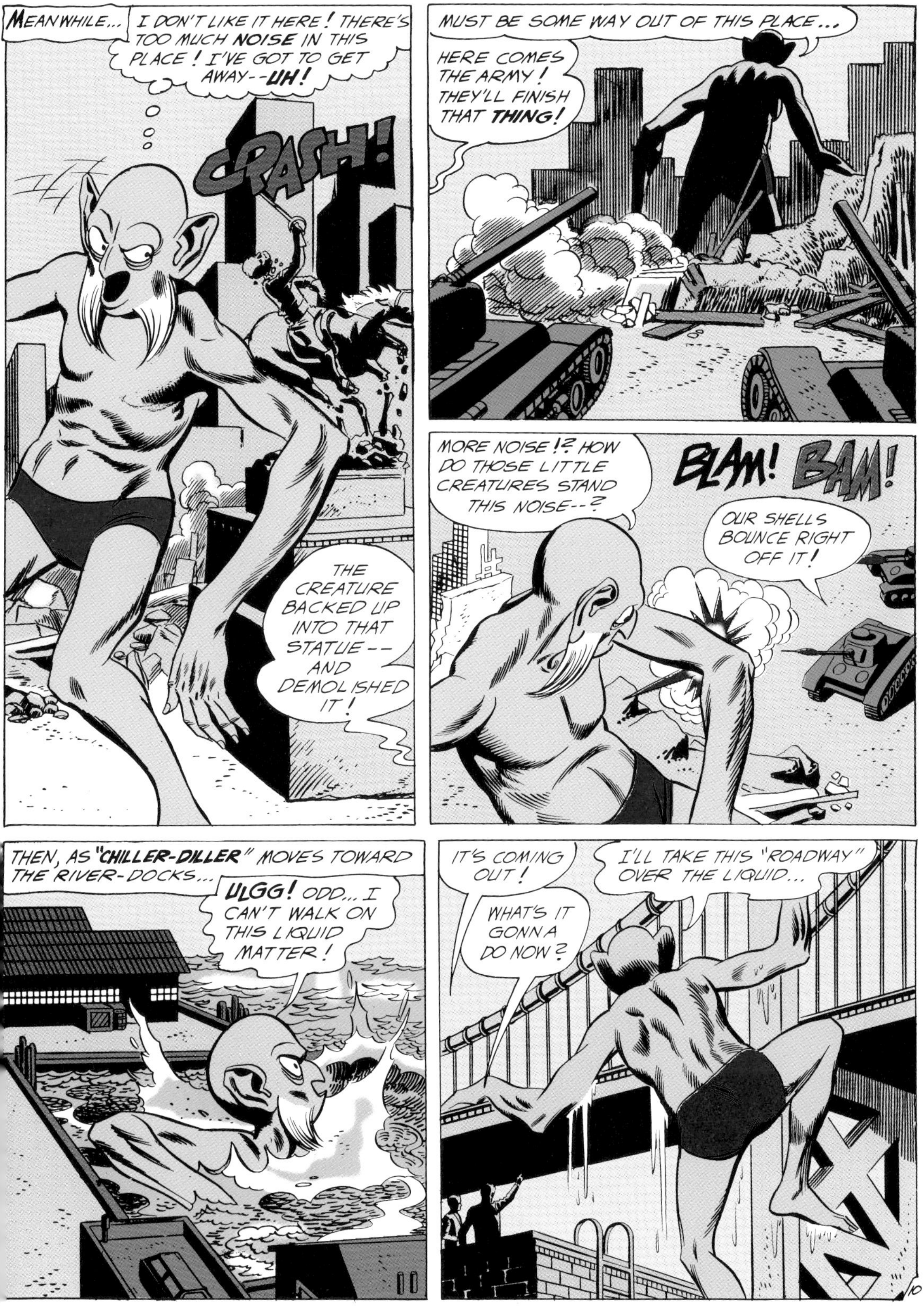
MEANWHILE...
I DON'T LIKE IT HERE! THERE'S TOO MUCH NOISE IN THIS PLACE! I'VE GOT TO GET AWAY--UH!
CRASH!
THE CREATURE BACKED UP INTO THAT STATUE--AND DEMOLISHED IT!
MUST BE SOME WAY OUT OF THIS PLACE...
HERE COMES THE ARMY! THEY'LL FINISH THAT THING!
MORE NOISE!? HOW DO THOSE LITTLE CREATURES STAND THIS NOISE--?
BLAM! BAM!
OUR SHELLS BOUNCE RIGHT OFF IT!
THEN, AS "CHILLER-DILLER" MOVES TOWARD THE RIVER-DOCKS...
ULGG! ODD... I CAN'T WALK ON THIS LIQUID MATTER!
IT'S COMING OUT!
WHAT'S IT GONNA DO NOW?
I'LL TAKE THIS "ROADWAY" OVER THE LIQUID...
10

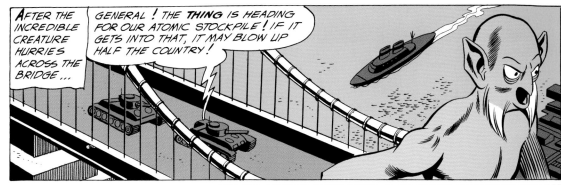

AFTER THE INCREDIBLE CREATURE HURRIES ACROSS THE BRIDGE...

GENERAL! THE **THING** IS HEADING FOR OUR ATOMIC STOCKPILE! IF IT GETS INTO THAT, IT MAY BLOW UP HALF THE COUNTRY!

MR. PRESIDENT, THIS IS GENERAL WILLIS! WE NEED REINFORCEMENTS, SIR! **COAST CITY** IS ABOUT TO BE BLOWN OFF THE MAP!

AT THAT MOMENT, IN THE DOCTOR'S OFFICE WHERE **GREEN LANTERN** *HAS BEEN TAKEN...*

...AND THE INVULNERABLE CREATURE IS **STILL GOING!** THE NEXT FEW MINUTES WILL TELL! IT IS TOO LATE TO EVACUATE THE CITY!

HOLY SMOKE! ACCORDING TO THE DESCRIPTION OVER THE RADIO...

...IT'S THE "MENACE" I MADE WITH MY **POWER BEAM** -- TO DISTRACT CAROL -- THAT'S CAUSING ALL THE TROUBLE! I'VE GOT TO GET GOING -- FAST!

GREEN LANTERN! ARE YOU ALL RIGHT?

HE DIDN'T ANSWER--!

HE MUST BE ALL RIGHT-- LOOK AT HIM GO!

AND IN THE VERY NICK OF TIME...

GREEN LANTERN SAVED US -- HE DISSOLVED THE **MONSTER!**

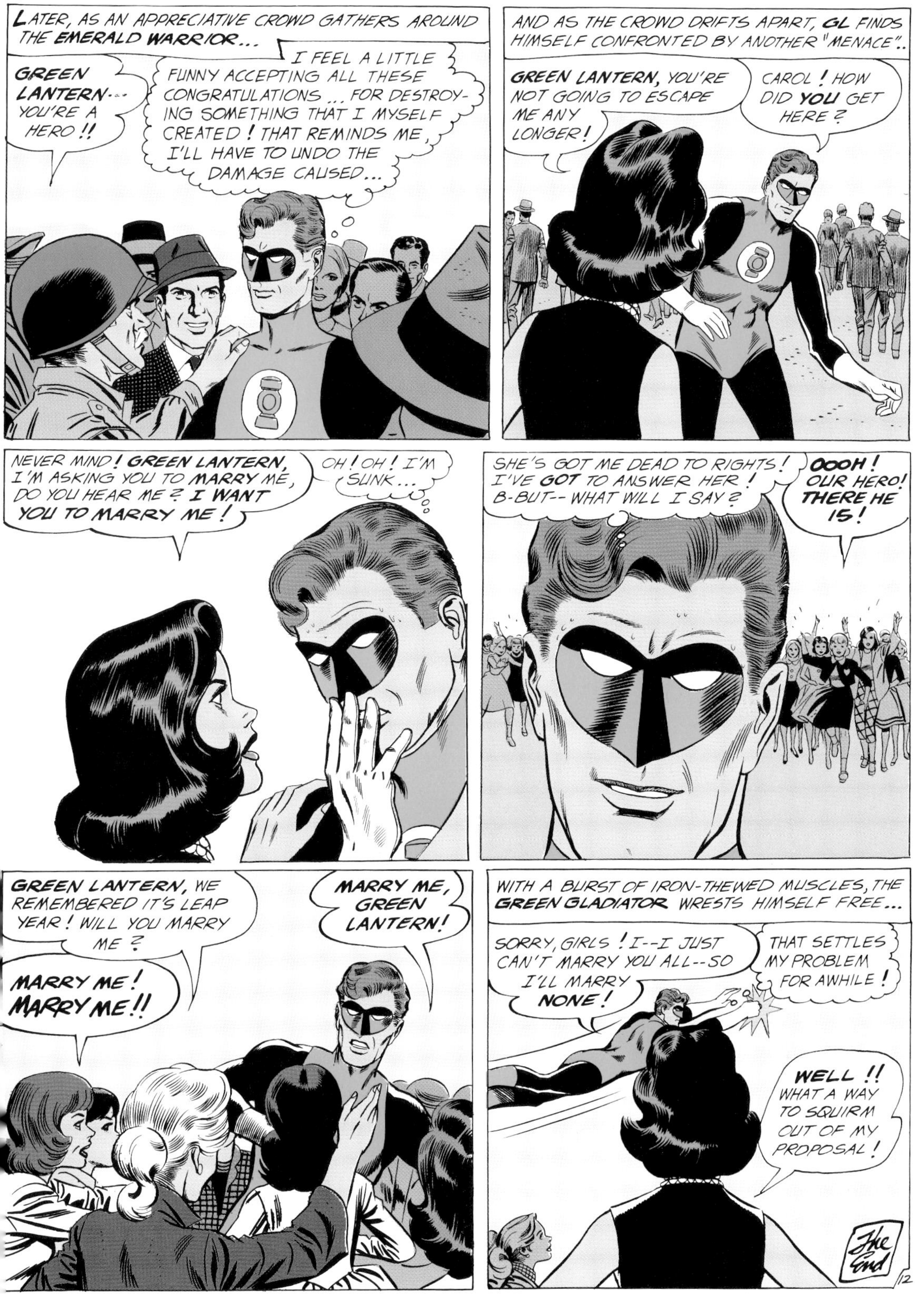
LATER, AS AN APPRECIATIVE CROWD GATHERS AROUND THE EMERALD WARRIOR...
GREEN LANTERN... YOU'RE A HERO !!
I FEEL A LITTLE FUNNY ACCEPTING ALL THESE CONGRATULATIONS ... FOR DESTROYING SOMETHING THAT I MYSELF CREATED ! THAT REMINDS ME, I'LL HAVE TO UNDO THE DAMAGE CAUSED...
AND AS THE CROWD DRIFTS APART, GL FINDS HIMSELF CONFRONTED BY ANOTHER "MENACE"..
GREEN LANTERN, YOU'RE NOT GOING TO ESCAPE ME ANY LONGER!
CAROL ! HOW DID YOU GET HERE ?
NEVER MIND ! GREEN LANTERN, I'M ASKING YOU TO MARRY ME, DO YOU HEAR ME ? I WANT YOU TO MARRY ME !
OH ! OH ! I'M SUNK...
SHE'S GOT ME DEAD TO RIGHTS ! I'VE GOT TO ANSWER HER ! B-BUT-- WHAT WILL I SAY ?
OOOH ! OUR HERO! THERE HE IS !
GREEN LANTERN, WE REMEMBERED IT'S LEAP YEAR ! WILL YOU MARRY ME ?
MARRY ME, GREEN LANTERN!
MARRY ME ! MARRY ME !!
WITH A BURST OF IRON-THEWED MUSCLES, THE GREEN GLADIATOR WRESTS HIMSELF FREE...
SORRY, GIRLS ! I--I JUST CAN'T MARRY YOU ALL--SO I'LL MARRY NONE !
THAT SETTLES MY PROBLEM FOR AWHILE !
WELL !! WHAT A WAY TO SQUIRM OUT OF MY PROPOSAL !
The End
12

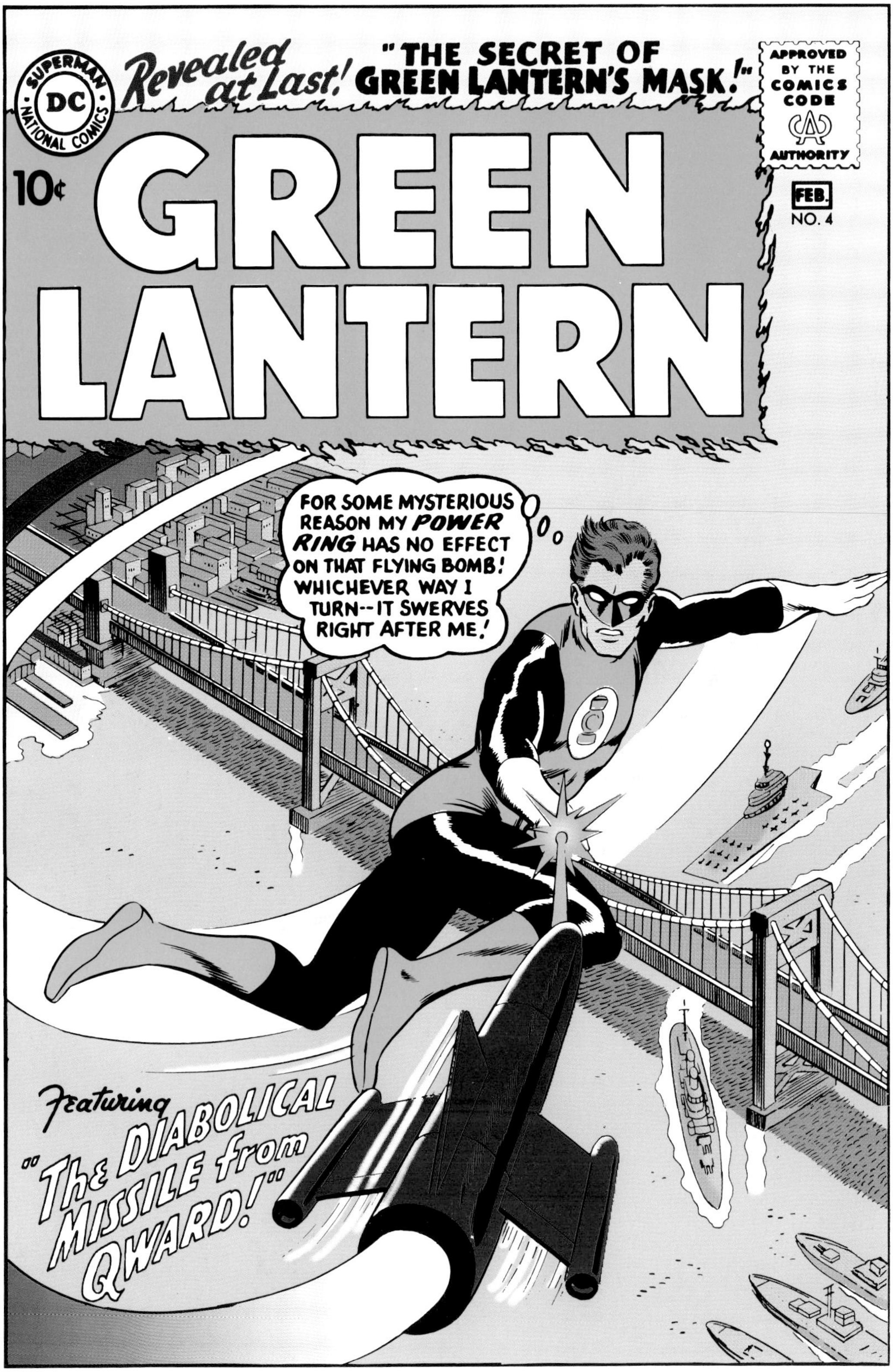
SUPERMAN DC NATIONAL COMICS
10¢
Revealed at Last! "THE SECRET OF GREEN LANTERN'S MASK!"
APPROVED BY THE COMICS CODE AUTHORITY
FEB. NO. 4
GREEN LANTERN
FOR SOME MYSTERIOUS REASON MY POWER RING HAS NO EFFECT ON THAT FLYING BOMB! WHICHEVER WAY I TURN--IT SWERVES RIGHT AFTER ME!
Featuring "The DIABOLICAL MISSILE from QWARD!"

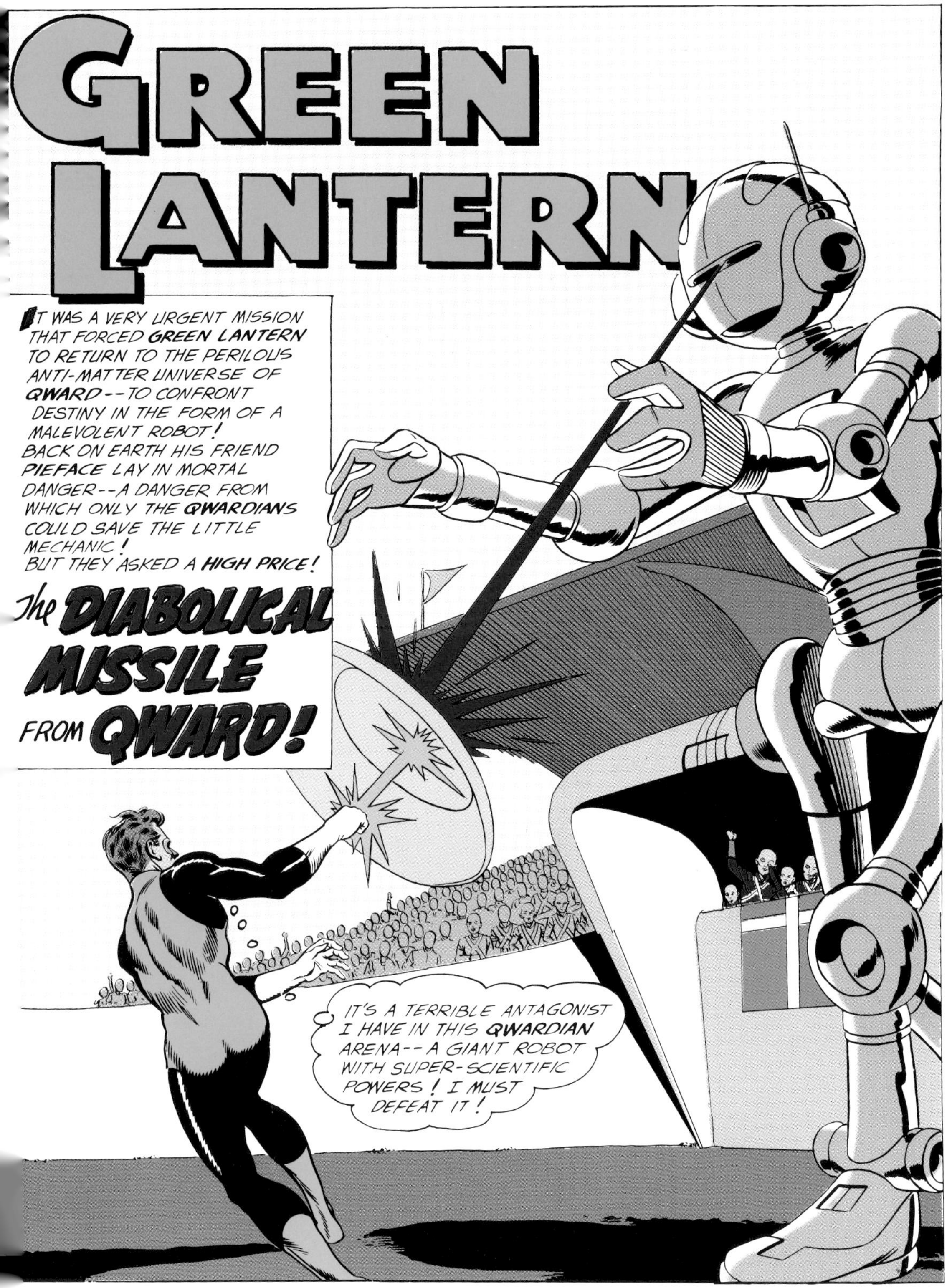
GREEN LANTERN
IT WAS A VERY URGENT MISSION THAT FORCED GREEN LANTERN TO RETURN TO THE PERILOUS ANTI-MATTER UNIVERSE OF QWARD--TO CONFRONT DESTINY IN THE FORM OF A MALEVOLENT ROBOT! BACK ON EARTH HIS FRIEND PIEFACE LAY IN MORTAL DANGER--A DANGER FROM WHICH ONLY THE QWARDIANS COULD SAVE THE LITTLE MECHANIC! BUT THEY ASKED A HIGH PRICE!
The DIABOLICAL MISSILE FROM QWARD!
IT'S A TERRIBLE ANTAGONIST I HAVE IN THIS QWARDIAN ARENA--A GIANT ROBOT WITH SUPER-SCIENTIFIC POWERS! I MUST DEFEAT IT!

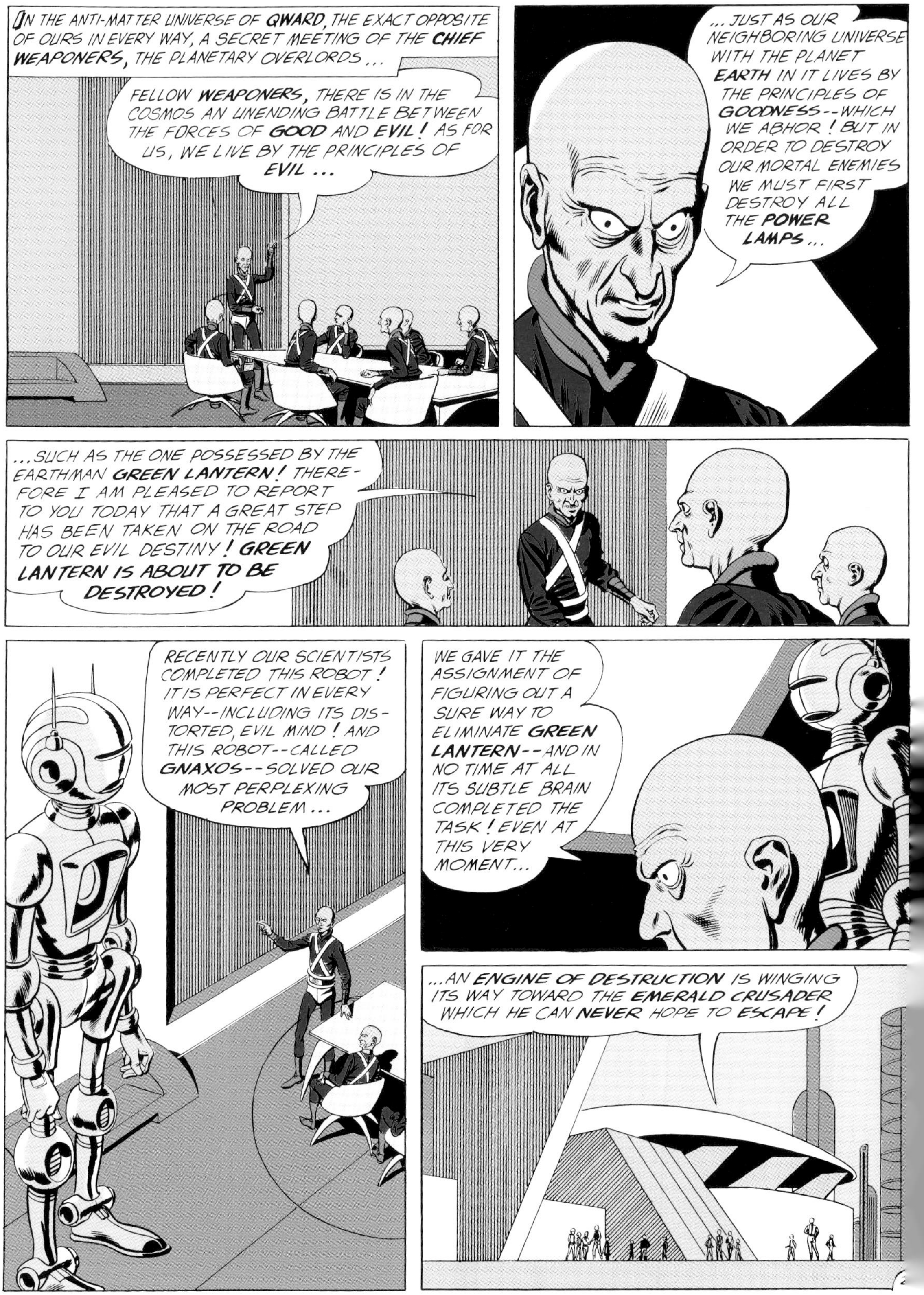

ON THE ANTI-MATTER UNIVERSE OF QWARD, THE EXACT OPPOSITE OF OURS IN EVERY WAY, A SECRET MEETING OF THE CHIEF WEAPONERS, THE PLANETARY OVERLORDS ...
FELLOW WEAPONERS, THERE IS IN THE COSMOS AN UNENDING BATTLE BETWEEN THE FORCES OF GOOD AND EVIL! AS FOR US, WE LIVE BY THE PRINCIPLES OF EVIL ...
... JUST AS OUR NEIGHBORING UNIVERSE WITH THE PLANET EARTH IN IT LIVES BY THE PRINCIPLES OF GOODNESS--WHICH WE ABHOR! BUT IN ORDER TO DESTROY OUR MORTAL ENEMIES WE MUST FIRST DESTROY ALL THE POWER LAMPS ...
... SUCH AS THE ONE POSSESSED BY THE EARTHMAN GREEN LANTERN! THEREFORE I AM PLEASED TO REPORT TO YOU TODAY THAT A GREAT STEP HAS BEEN TAKEN ON THE ROAD TO OUR EVIL DESTINY! GREEN LANTERN IS ABOUT TO BE DESTROYED!
RECENTLY OUR SCIENTISTS COMPLETED THIS ROBOT! IT IS PERFECT IN EVERY WAY--INCLUDING ITS DISTORTED, EVIL MIND! AND THIS ROBOT--CALLED GNAXOS--SOLVED OUR MOST PERPLEXING PROBLEM ...
WE GAVE IT THE ASSIGNMENT OF FIGURING OUT A SURE WAY TO ELIMINATE GREEN LANTERN--AND IN NO TIME AT ALL ITS SUBTLE BRAIN COMPLETED THE TASK! EVEN AT THIS VERY MOMENT...
...AN ENGINE OF DESTRUCTION IS WINGING ITS WAY TOWARD THE EMERALD CRUSADER WHICH HE CAN NEVER HOPE TO ESCAPE!

AND AT THE **FERRIS AIRCRAFT COMPANY** WHERE HAL JORDAN, ACE TEST PILOT, IS EMPLOYED...

HAL, YOU SEEM A BIT WORRIED TODAY! IS ANYTHING WRONG?

I'M NOT SURE, **PIEFACE** ! YOU SEE...

...MY **POWER RING**--WHICH I KEEP HERE IN THIS POCKET WHEN I'M NOT WEARING IT--HAS BEEN EMITTING A PECULIAR TYPE OF ENERGY FOR THE PAST HOUR! IT'S AS IF...AS IF IT'S TRYING TO WARN ME OF SOME **DANGER** !

GREAT FISH-- HOOKS !

AND THAT REMINDS ME, I'D BETTER RECHARGE MY RING--JUST IN CASE ! YOU KEEP AN EYE OUT, WILL YOU, **PIEFACE**?

SURE THING, HAL ! DON'T WORRY--NO ONE WILL GET PAST **ME** !

Editor's Note :

PIEFACE--OR THOMAS KALMAKU, HAL'S CRACK ESKIMO AIRPLANE MECHANIC, TO GIVE HIM HIS REAL NAME -- IS THE ONLY PERSON ON EARTH WHO KNOWS THAT HAL JORDAN IS IN REALITY **GREEN LANTERN** ! WHICH EXPLAINS THE TEST PILOT'S FREE-DOM IN DISCUSSING SUCH **TOP SECRET** MATTERS AS HIS RING AND ITS POWERS !

BEHIND CLOSED DOORS IN HAL'S DRESSING ROOM AT THE HANGAR, A SOLEMN OATH IS REPEATED...

IN BRIGHTEST DAY, IN BLACKEST NIGHT, NO EVIL SHALL ESCAPE MY SIGHT ! LET THOSE WHO WORSHIP EVIL'S MIGHT BEWARE MY POWER--**GREEN LANTERN'S LIGHT** !

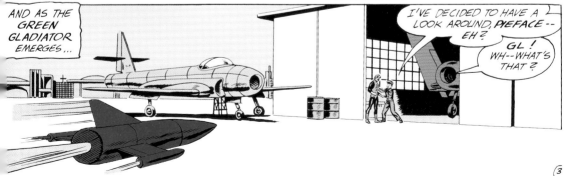

AND AS THE **GREEN GLADIATOR** EMERGES...

I'VE DECIDED TO HAVE A LOOK AROUND, **PIEFACE**--EH?

GL ! WH--WHAT'S THAT ?

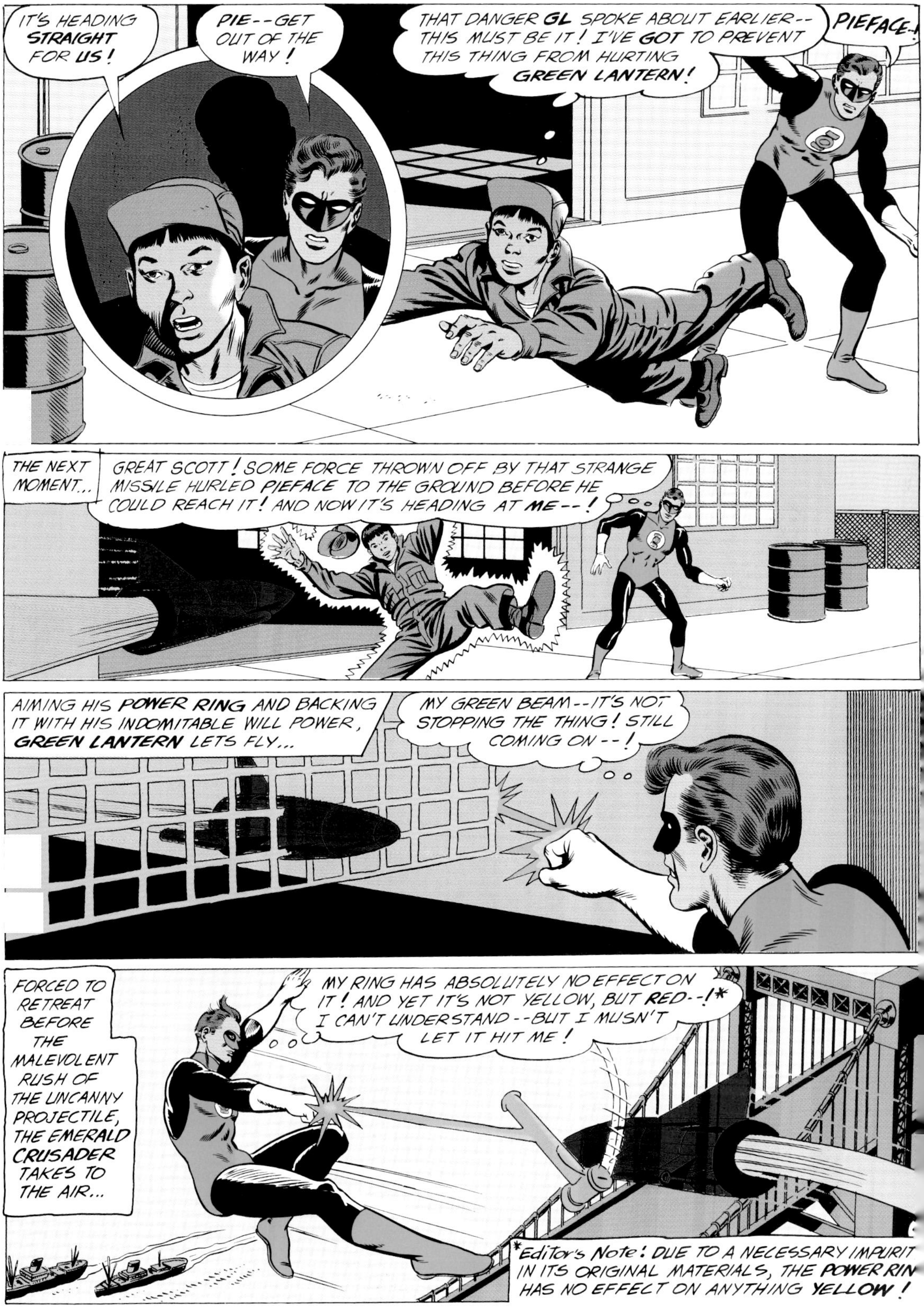
IT'S HEADING STRAIGHT FOR US!
PIE--GET OUT OF THE WAY!
THAT DANGER GL SPOKE ABOUT EARLIER--THIS MUST BE IT! I'VE GOT TO PREVENT THIS THING FROM HURTING GREEN LANTERN!
PIEFACE-!
THE NEXT MOMENT...
GREAT SCOTT! SOME FORCE THROWN OFF BY THAT STRANGE MISSILE HURLED PIEFACE TO THE GROUND BEFORE HE COULD REACH IT! AND NOW IT'S HEADING AT ME--!
AIMING HIS POWER RING AND BACKING IT WITH HIS INDOMITABLE WILL POWER, GREEN LANTERN LETS FLY...
MY GREEN BEAM--IT'S NOT STOPPING THE THING! STILL COMING ON--!
FORCED TO RETREAT BEFORE THE MALEVOLENT RUSH OF THE UNCANNY PROJECTILE, THE EMERALD CRUSADER TAKES TO THE AIR...
MY RING HAS ABSOLUTELY NO EFFECT ON IT! AND YET IT'S NOT YELLOW, BUT RED--!* I CAN'T UNDERSTAND--BUT I MUSN'T LET IT HIT ME!
*Editor's Note: DUE TO A NECESSARY IMPURIT IN ITS ORIGINAL MATERIALS, THE POWER RIN HAS NO EFFECT ON ANYTHING YELLOW!

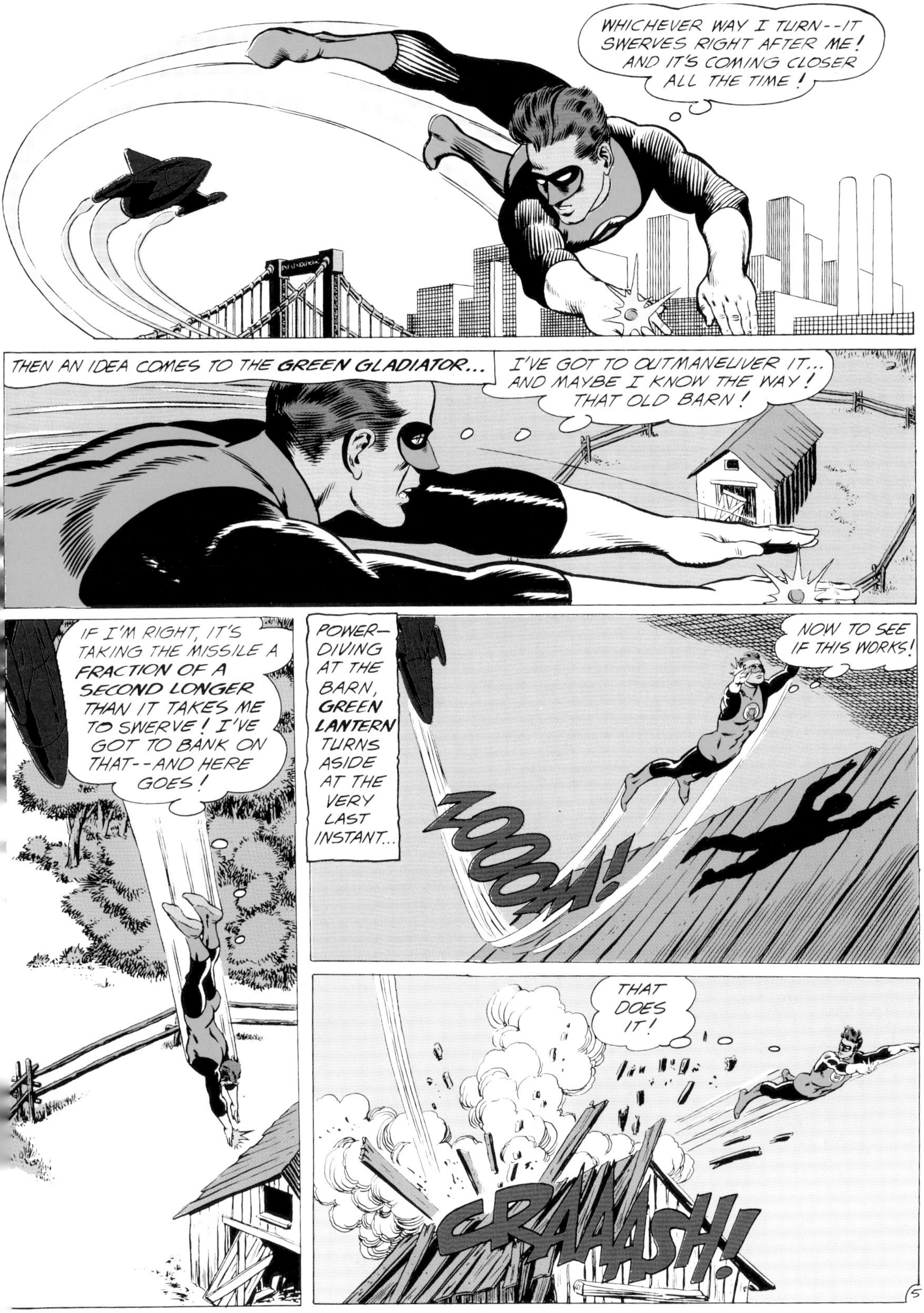
WHICHEVER WAY I TURN--IT SWERVES RIGHT AFTER ME! AND IT'S COMING CLOSER ALL THE TIME!
THEN AN IDEA COMES TO THE GREEN GLADIATOR...
I'VE GOT TO OUTMANEUVER IT... AND MAYBE I KNOW THE WAY! THAT OLD BARN!
IF I'M RIGHT, IT'S TAKING THE MISSILE A FRACTION OF A SECOND LONGER THAN IT TAKES ME TO SWERVE! I'VE GOT TO BANK ON THAT--AND HERE GOES!
POWER-DIVING AT THE BARN, GREEN LANTERN TURNS ASIDE AT THE VERY LAST INSTANT...
NOW TO SEE IF THIS WORKS!
ZOOOOM!
THAT DOES IT!
CRAAAASH!
5

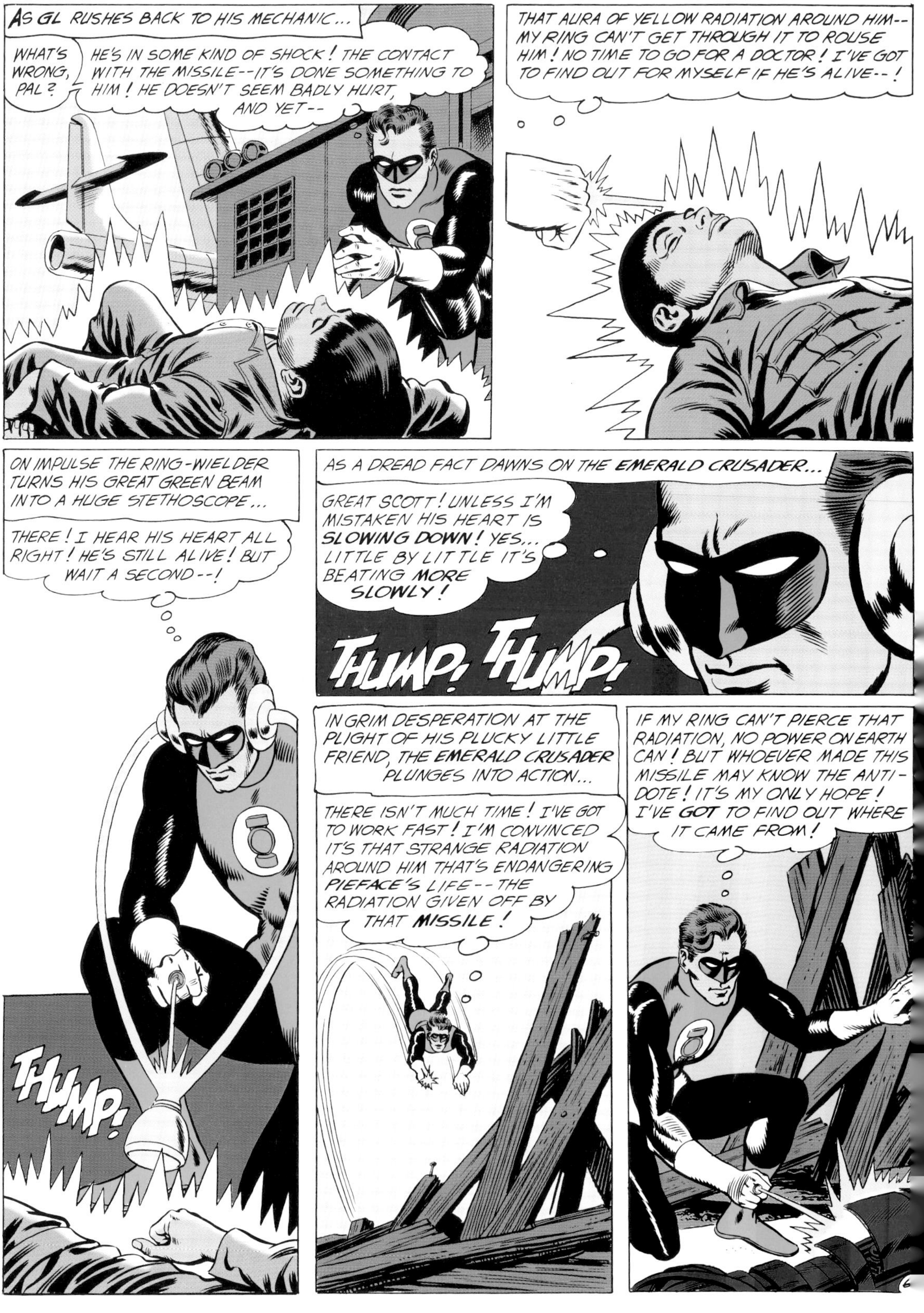
AS GL RUSHES BACK TO HIS MECHANIC...
WHAT'S WRONG, PAL?
HE'S IN SOME KIND OF SHOCK! THE CONTACT WITH THE MISSILE--IT'S DONE SOMETHING TO HIM! HE DOESN'T SEEM BADLY HURT, AND YET--
THAT AURA OF YELLOW RADIATION AROUND HIM--MY RING CAN'T GET THROUGH IT TO ROUSE HIM! NO TIME TO GO FOR A DOCTOR! I'VE GOT TO FIND OUT FOR MYSELF IF HE'S ALIVE--!
ON IMPULSE THE RING-WIELDER TURNS HIS GREAT GREEN BEAM INTO A HUGE STETHOSCOPE...
THERE! I HEAR HIS HEART ALL RIGHT! HE'S STILL ALIVE! BUT WAIT A SECOND--!
THUMP!
AS A DREAD FACT DAWNS ON THE EMERALD CRUSADER...
GREAT SCOTT! UNLESS I'M MISTAKEN HIS HEART IS SLOWING DOWN! YES... LITTLE BY LITTLE IT'S BEATING MORE SLOWLY!
THUMP! THUMP!
IN GRIM DESPERATION AT THE PLIGHT OF HIS PLUCKY LITTLE FRIEND, THE EMERALD CRUSADER PLUNGES INTO ACTION...
THERE ISN'T MUCH TIME! I'VE GOT TO WORK FAST! I'M CONVINCED IT'S THAT STRANGE RADIATION AROUND HIM THAT'S ENDANGERING PIEFACE'S LIFE--THE RADIATION GIVEN OFF BY THAT MISSILE!
IF MY RING CAN'T PIERCE THAT RADIATION, NO POWER ON EARTH CAN! BUT WHOEVER MADE THIS MISSILE MAY KNOW THE ANTI-DOTE! IT'S MY ONLY HOPE! I'VE GOT TO FIND OUT WHERE IT CAME FROM!
6

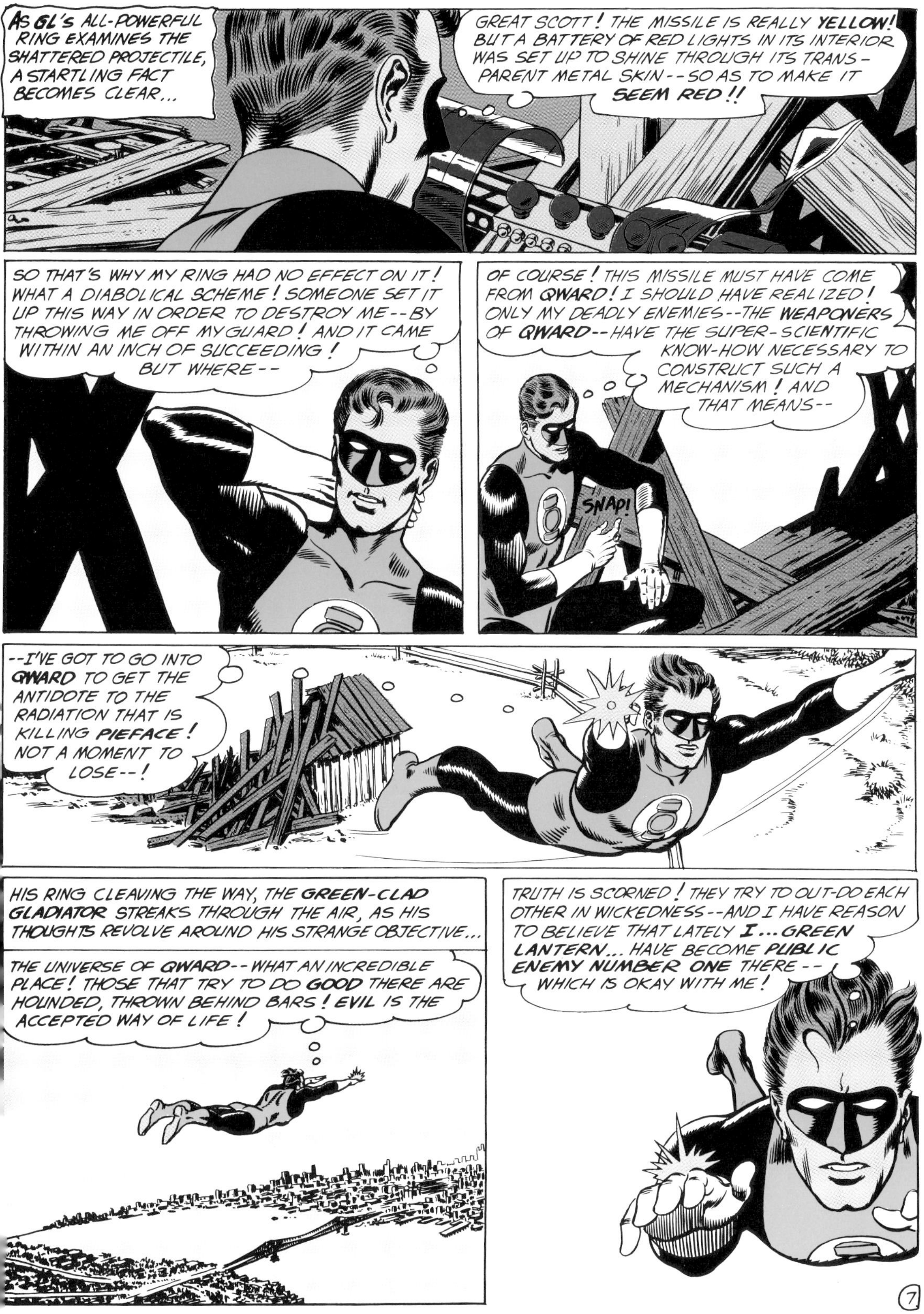
AS GL'S ALL-POWERFUL RING EXAMINES THE SHATTERED PROJECTILE, A STARTLING FACT BECOMES CLEAR...
GREAT SCOTT! THE MISSILE IS REALLY YELLOW! BUT A BATTERY OF RED LIGHTS IN ITS INTERIOR WAS SET UP TO SHINE THROUGH ITS TRANS-PARENT METAL SKIN--SO AS TO MAKE IT SEEM RED!!
SO THAT'S WHY MY RING HAD NO EFFECT ON IT! WHAT A DIABOLICAL SCHEME! SOMEONE SET IT UP THIS WAY IN ORDER TO DESTROY ME--BY THROWING ME OFF MY GUARD! AND IT CAME WITHIN AN INCH OF SUCCEEDING! BUT WHERE--
OF COURSE! THIS MISSILE MUST HAVE COME FROM QWARD! I SHOULD HAVE REALIZED! ONLY MY DEADLY ENEMIES--THE WEAPONERS OF QWARD--HAVE THE SUPER-SCIENTIFIC KNOW-HOW NECESSARY TO CONSTRUCT SUCH A MECHANISM! AND THAT MEANS--
SNAP!
--I'VE GOT TO GO INTO QWARD TO GET THE ANTIDOTE TO THE RADIATION THAT IS KILLING PIEFACE! NOT A MOMENT TO LOSE--!
HIS RING CLEAVING THE WAY, THE GREEN-CLAD GLADIATOR STREAKS THROUGH THE AIR, AS HIS THOUGHTS REVOLVE AROUND HIS STRANGE OBJECTIVE...
THE UNIVERSE OF QWARD--WHAT AN INCREDIBLE PLACE! THOSE THAT TRY TO DO GOOD THERE ARE HOUNDED, THROWN BEHIND BARS! EVIL IS THE ACCEPTED WAY OF LIFE!
TRUTH IS SCORNED! THEY TRY TO OUT-DO EACH OTHER IN WICKEDNESS--AND I HAVE REASON TO BELIEVE THAT LATELY I...GREEN LANTERN...HAVE BECOME PUBLIC ENEMY NUMBER ONE THERE--WHICH IS OKAY WITH ME!
7

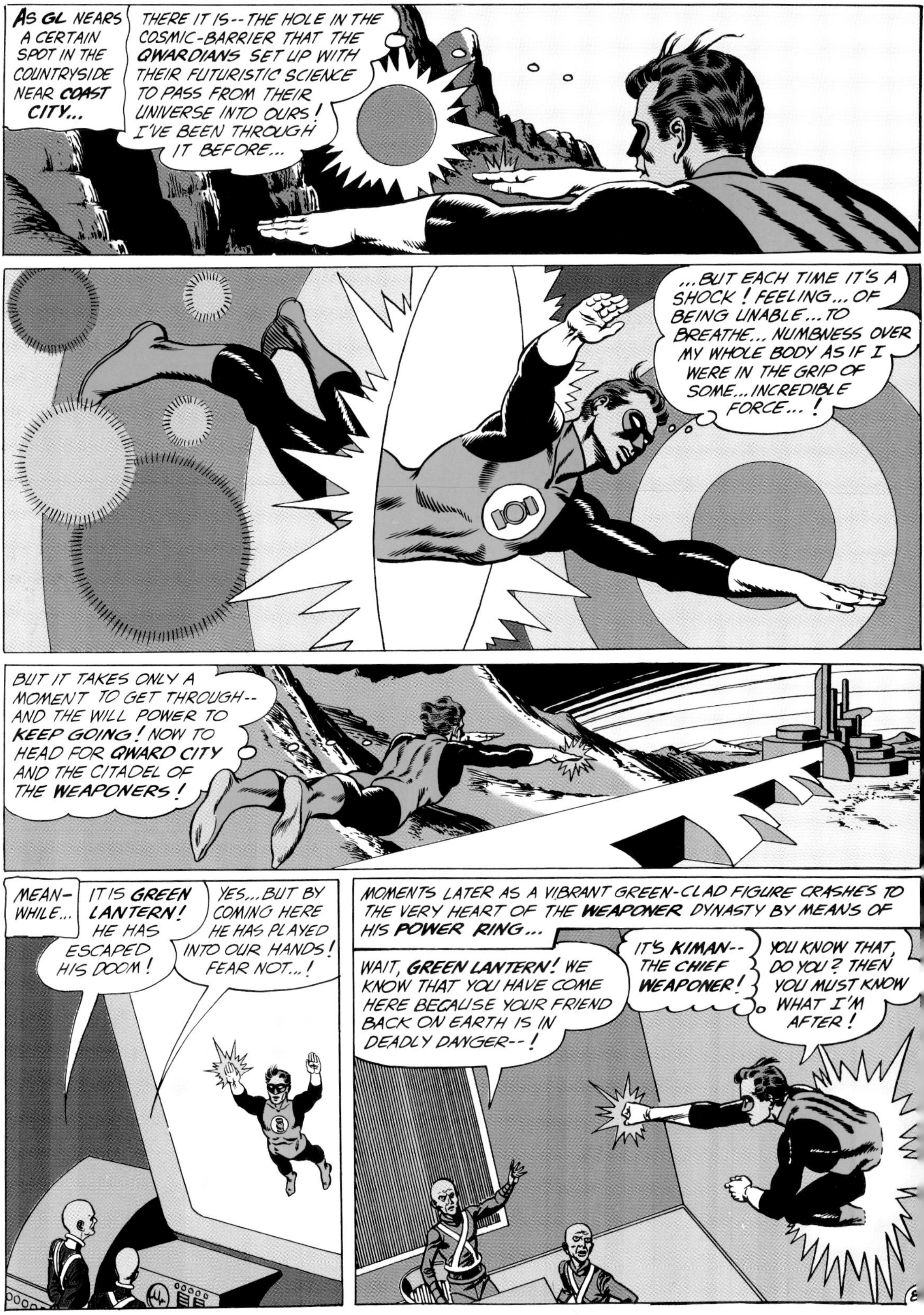
AS GL NEARS A CERTAIN SPOT IN THE COUNTRYSIDE NEAR COAST CITY...
THERE IT IS--THE HOLE IN THE COSMIC-BARRIER THAT THE QWARDIANS SET UP WITH THEIR FUTURISTIC SCIENCE TO PASS FROM THEIR UNIVERSE INTO OURS! I'VE BEEN THROUGH IT BEFORE...
...BUT EACH TIME IT'S A SHOCK! FEELING...OF BEING UNABLE...TO BREATHE...NUMBNESS OVER MY WHOLE BODY AS IF I WERE IN THE GRIP OF SOME...INCREDIBLE FORCE...!
BUT IT TAKES ONLY A MOMENT TO GET THROUGH--AND THE WILL POWER TO KEEP GOING! NOW TO HEAD FOR QWARD CITY AND THE CITADEL OF THE WEAPONERS!
MEAN-WHILE...
IT IS GREEN LANTERN! HE HAS ESCAPED HIS DOOM!
YES...BUT BY COMING HERE HE HAS PLAYED INTO OUR HANDS! FEAR NOT...!
MOMENTS LATER AS A VIBRANT GREEN-CLAD FIGURE CRASHES TO THE VERY HEART OF THE WEAPONER DYNASTY BY MEANS OF HIS POWER RING...
WAIT, GREEN LANTERN! WE KNOW THAT YOU HAVE COME HERE BECAUSE YOUR FRIEND BACK ON EARTH IS IN DEADLY DANGER--!
IT'S KIMAN--THE CHIEF WEAPONER!
YOU KNOW THAT, DO YOU? THEN YOU MUST KNOW WHAT I'M AFTER!
8

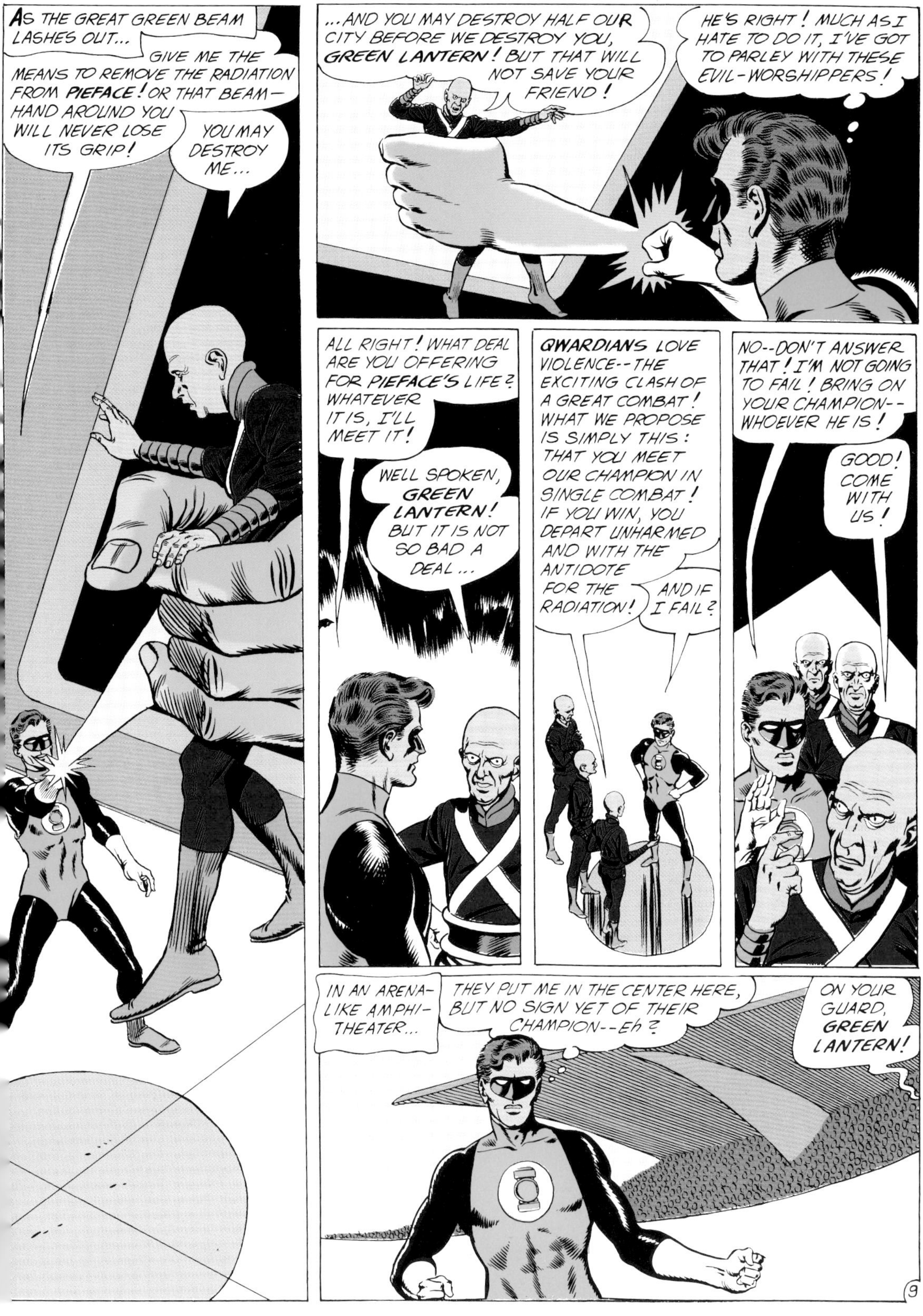
AS THE GREAT GREEN BEAM LASHES OUT...
GIVE ME THE MEANS TO REMOVE THE RADIATION FROM PIEFACE! OR THAT BEAM-HAND AROUND YOU WILL NEVER LOSE ITS GRIP!
YOU MAY DESTROY ME...
...AND YOU MAY DESTROY HALF OUR CITY BEFORE WE DESTROY YOU, GREEN LANTERN! BUT THAT WILL NOT SAVE YOUR FRIEND!
HE'S RIGHT! MUCH AS I HATE TO DO IT, I'VE GOT TO PARLEY WITH THESE EVIL-WORSHIPPERS!
ALL RIGHT! WHAT DEAL ARE YOU OFFERING FOR PIEFACE'S LIFE? WHATEVER IT IS, I'LL MEET IT!
WELL SPOKEN, GREEN LANTERN! BUT IT IS NOT SO BAD A DEAL...
QWARDIANS LOVE VIOLENCE--THE EXCITING CLASH OF A GREAT COMBAT! WHAT WE PROPOSE IS SIMPLY THIS: THAT YOU MEET OUR CHAMPION IN SINGLE COMBAT! IF YOU WIN, YOU DEPART UNHARMED AND WITH THE ANTIDOTE FOR THE RADIATION!
AND IF I FAIL?
NO--DON'T ANSWER THAT! I'M NOT GOING TO FAIL! BRING ON YOUR CHAMPION--WHOEVER HE IS!
GOOD! COME WITH US!
IN AN ARENA-LIKE AMPHI-THEATER...
THEY PUT ME IN THE CENTER HERE, BUT NO SIGN YET OF THEIR CHAMPION--Eh?
ON YOUR GUARD, GREEN LANTERN!
9

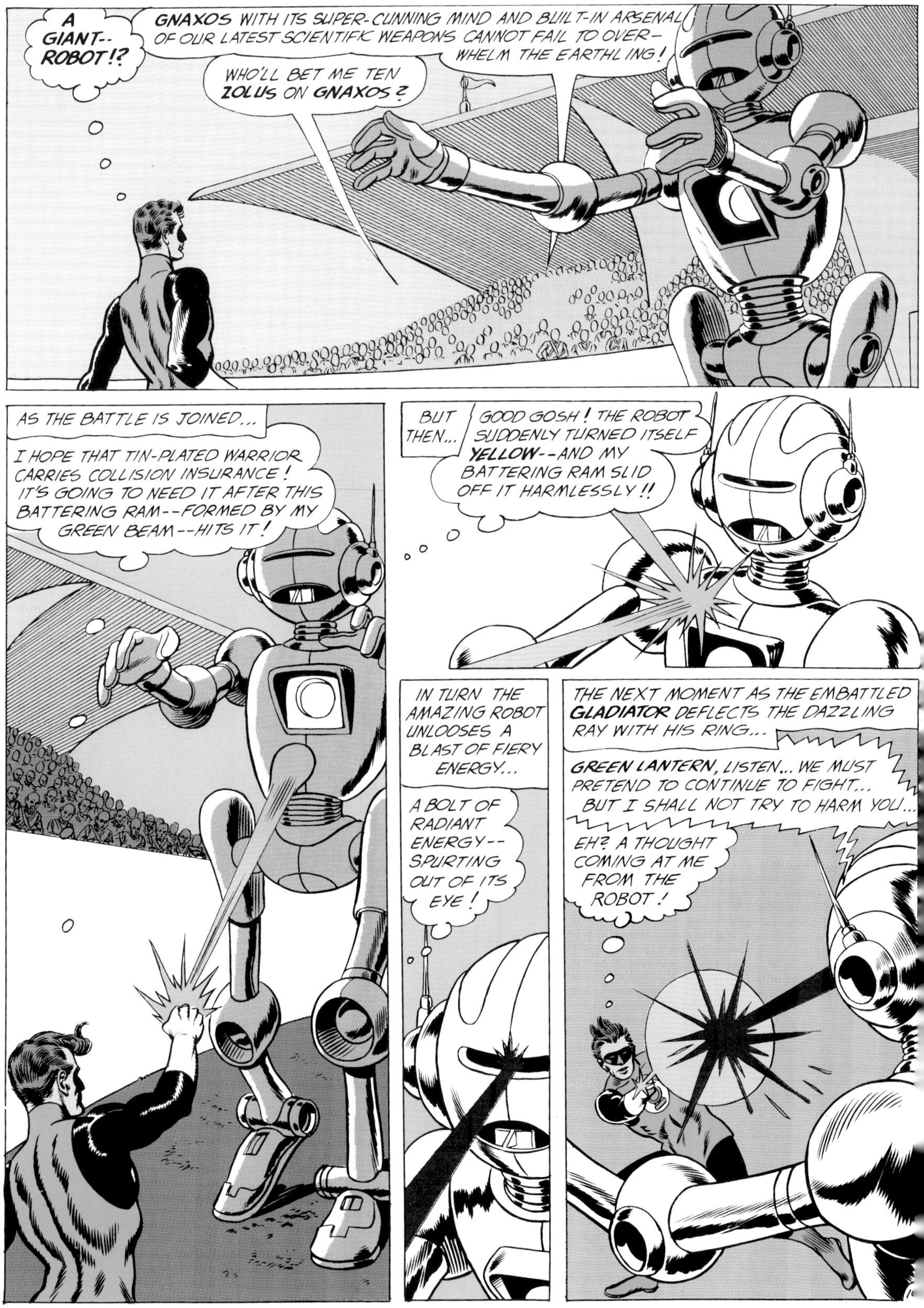
A GIANT--ROBOT!?
GNAXOS WITH ITS SUPER-CUNNING MIND AND BUILT-IN ARSENAL OF OUR LATEST SCIENTIFIC WEAPONS CANNOT FAIL TO OVERWHELM THE EARTHLING!
WHO'LL BET ME TEN ZOLUS ON GNAXOS?
AS THE BATTLE IS JOINED...
I HOPE THAT TIN-PLATED WARRIOR CARRIES COLLISION INSURANCE! IT'S GOING TO NEED IT AFTER THIS BATTERING RAM--FORMED BY MY GREEN BEAM--HITS IT!
BUT THEN...
GOOD GOSH! THE ROBOT SUDDENLY TURNED ITSELF YELLOW--AND MY BATTERING RAM SLID OFF IT HARMLESSLY!!
IN TURN THE AMAZING ROBOT UNLOOSES A BLAST OF FIERY ENERGY...
A BOLT OF RADIANT ENERGY--SPURTING OUT OF ITS EYE!
THE NEXT MOMENT AS THE EMBATTLED GLADIATOR DEFLECTS THE DAZZLING RAY WITH HIS RING...
GREEN LANTERN, LISTEN... WE MUST PRETEND TO CONTINUE TO FIGHT... BUT I SHALL NOT TRY TO HARM YOU...
EH? A THOUGHT COMING AT ME FROM THE ROBOT!

THEN, ANOTHER BOLT--AND ANOTHER THOUGHT MESSAGE FLASHES AT THE *EMERALD CRUSADER*...

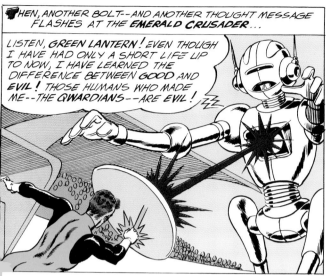

LISTEN, *GREEN LANTERN*! EVEN THOUGH I HAVE HAD ONLY A SHORT LIFE UP TO NOW, I HAVE LEARNED THE DIFFERENCE BETWEEN *GOOD* AND *EVIL*! THOSE HUMANS WHO MADE ME--THE *QWARDIANS*--ARE *EVIL*!

I, *GNAXOS*, WAS MADE TO BE EVIL BUT SOMETHING HAPPENED TO MY BRAIN AND I HAVE BECOME *GOOD*--AND I WANT TO HELP YOU BECAUSE I HAVE LEARNED FROM PROBING YOUR MIND THAT YOU TOO ARE GOOD!

JUMPIN' JUPITER! I--I'VE FOUND AN ALLY!

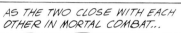

AS THE TWO CLOSE WITH EACH OTHER IN MORTAL COMBAT...

TAKE THIS, *GREEN LANTERN*! IT WILL COUNTERACT THE DEADLY RADIATION THAT IS AFFECTING YOUR FRIEND! TAKE IT-- AND FLEE!

BUT WHAT ABOUT YOU, *GNAXOS*? THE *QWARDIANS* ARE ALREADY BECOMING SUSPICIOUS! THEY'LL DISCOVER WHAT YOU'VE DONE-- THEY'LL DESTROY YOU!

PERHAPS-- IF THEY CAN!

BUT IF THEY DO, I SHALL PERISH THE WAY I WANT TO PERISH--FIGHTING FOR GOOD AND AGAINST EVIL! GO, *GREEN LANTERN*! I WILL HOLD THEM BACK--PREVENT THEM FROM ATTACKING YOU!

THE *QWARDIANS* KNOW SOMETHING IS UP NOW! THEY'RE RISING-- PULLING OUT WEAPONS--!

NO, *GNAXOS*! I'M NOT LEAVING YOU TO DEAL WITH THIS MOB ALONE! WE'LL BOTH FIGHT THEM--AND WE'LL BOTH GET OUT OF HERE TOGETHER! COME ON--!

"WE"!?

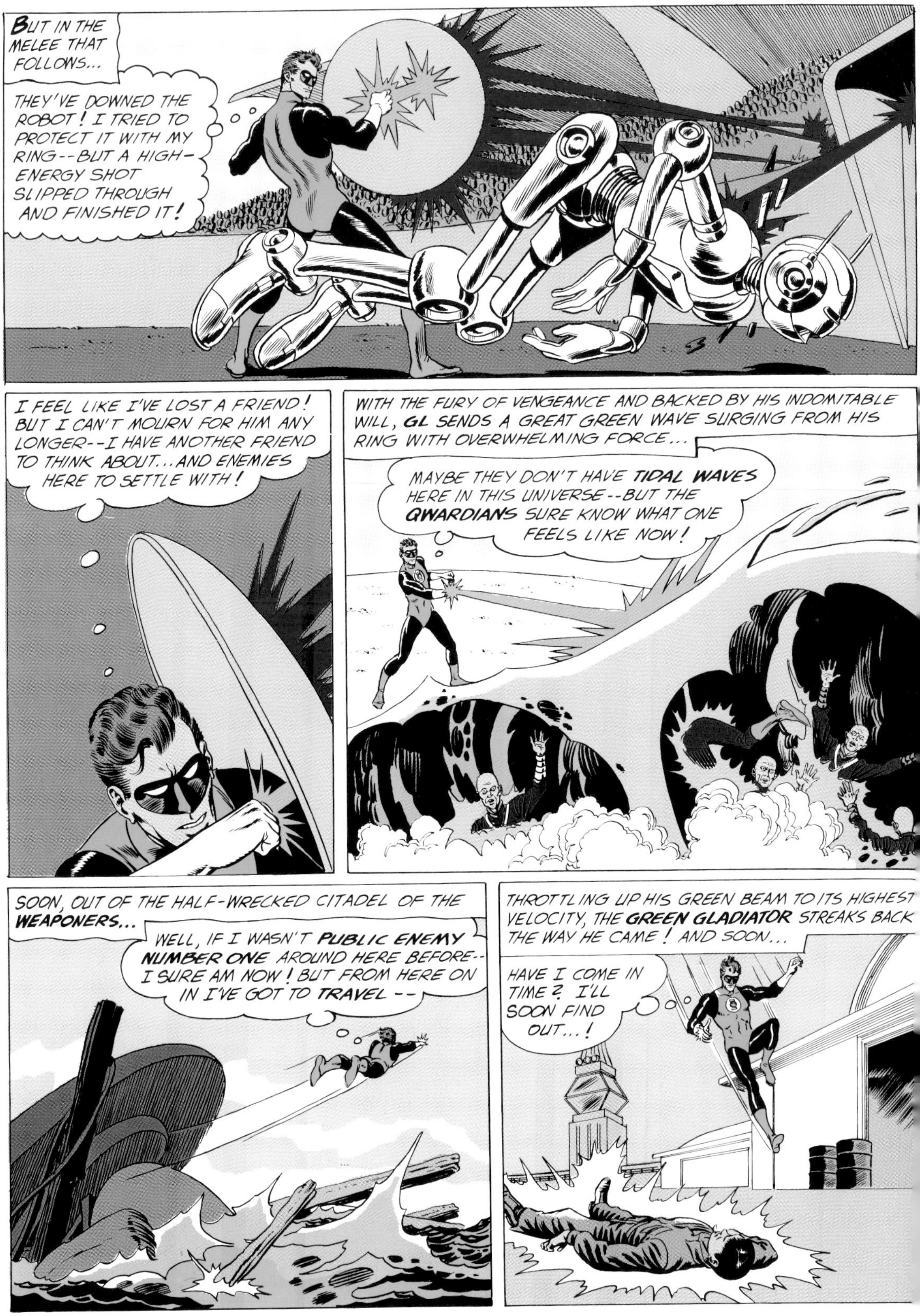
BUT IN THE MELEE THAT FOLLOWS...
THEY'VE DOWNED THE ROBOT! I TRIED TO PROTECT IT WITH MY RING--BUT A HIGH-ENERGY SHOT SLIPPED THROUGH AND FINISHED IT!
I FEEL LIKE I'VE LOST A FRIEND! BUT I CAN'T MOURN FOR HIM ANY LONGER--I HAVE ANOTHER FRIEND TO THINK ABOUT...AND ENEMIES HERE TO SETTLE WITH!
WITH THE FURY OF VENGEANCE AND BACKED BY HIS INDOMITABLE WILL, **GL** SENDS A GREAT GREEN WAVE SURGING FROM HIS RING WITH OVERWHELMING FORCE...
MAYBE THEY DON'T HAVE **TIDAL WAVES** HERE IN THIS UNIVERSE--BUT THE **QWARDIANS** SURE KNOW WHAT ONE FEELS LIKE NOW!
SOON, OUT OF THE HALF-WRECKED CITADEL OF THE **WEAPONERS...**
WELL, IF I WASN'T **PUBLIC ENEMY NUMBER ONE** AROUND HERE BEFORE--I SURE AM NOW! BUT FROM HERE ON IN I'VE GOT TO **TRAVEL**--
THROTTLING UP HIS GREEN BEAM TO ITS HIGHEST VELOCITY, THE **GREEN GLADIATOR** STREAKS BACK THE WAY HE CAME! AND SOON...
HAVE I COME IN TIME? I'LL SOON FIND OUT...!

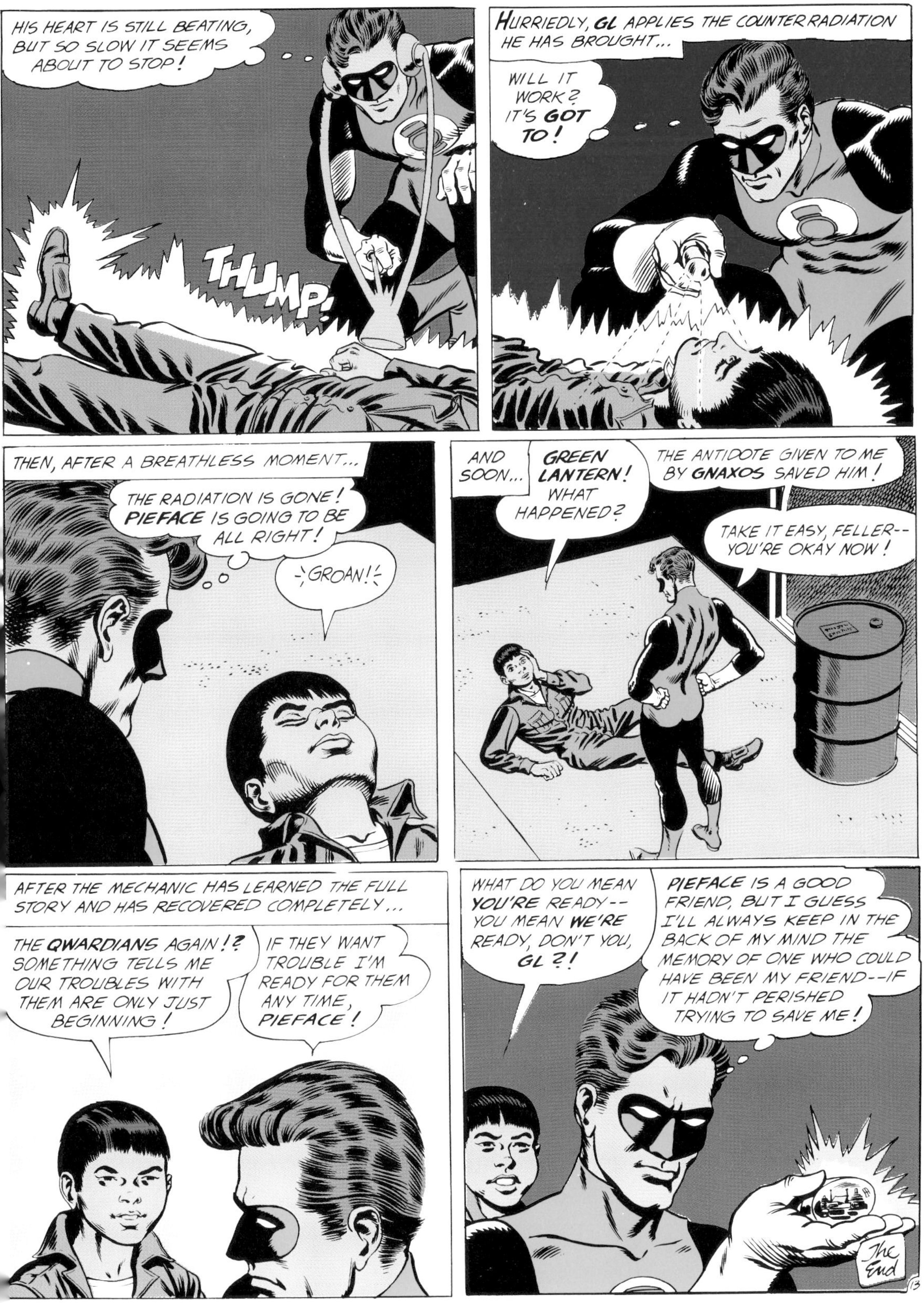
HIS HEART IS STILL BEATING, BUT SO SLOW IT SEEMS ABOUT TO STOP!
THUMP!
HURRIEDLY, GL APPLIES THE COUNTER RADIATION HE HAS BROUGHT...
WILL IT WORK? IT'S GOT TO!
THEN, AFTER A BREATHLESS MOMENT...
THE RADIATION IS GONE! PIEFACE IS GOING TO BE ALL RIGHT!
GROAN!
AND SOON...
GREEN LANTERN! WHAT HAPPENED?
THE ANTIDOTE GIVEN TO ME BY GNAXOS SAVED HIM!
TAKE IT EASY, FELLER-- YOU'RE OKAY NOW!
AFTER THE MECHANIC HAS LEARNED THE FULL STORY AND HAS RECOVERED COMPLETELY...
THE QWARDIANS AGAIN!? SOMETHING TELLS ME OUR TROUBLES WITH THEM ARE ONLY JUST BEGINNING!
IF THEY WANT TROUBLE I'M READY FOR THEM ANY TIME, PIEFACE!
WHAT DO YOU MEAN YOU'RE READY-- YOU MEAN WE'RE READY, DON'T YOU, GL?!
PIEFACE IS A GOOD FRIEND, BUT I GUESS I'LL ALWAYS KEEP IN THE BACK OF MY MIND THE MEMORY OF ONE WHO COULD HAVE BEEN MY FRIEND--IF IT HADN'T PERISHED TRYING TO SAVE ME!
The End
13

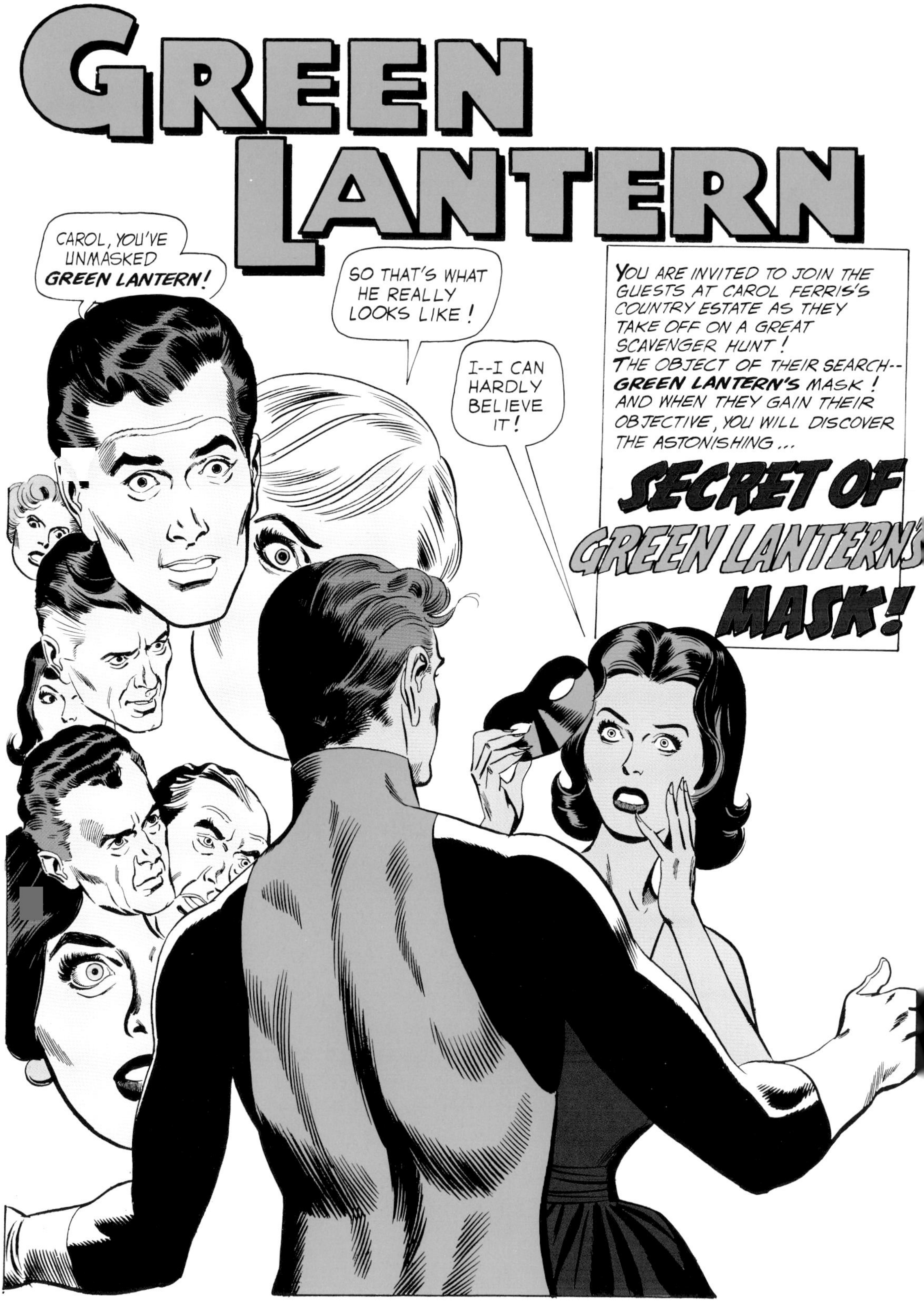
GREEN LANTERN
CAROL, YOU'VE UNMASKED GREEN LANTERN!
SO THAT'S WHAT HE REALLY LOOKS LIKE!
I--I CAN HARDLY BELIEVE IT!
YOU ARE INVITED TO JOIN THE GUESTS AT CAROL FERRIS'S COUNTRY ESTATE AS THEY TAKE OFF ON A GREAT SCAVENGER HUNT! THE OBJECT OF THEIR SEARCH-- GREEN LANTERN'S MASK! AND WHEN THEY GAIN THEIR OBJECTIVE, YOU WILL DISCOVER THE ASTONISHING...
SECRET OF GREEN LANTERN'S MASK!

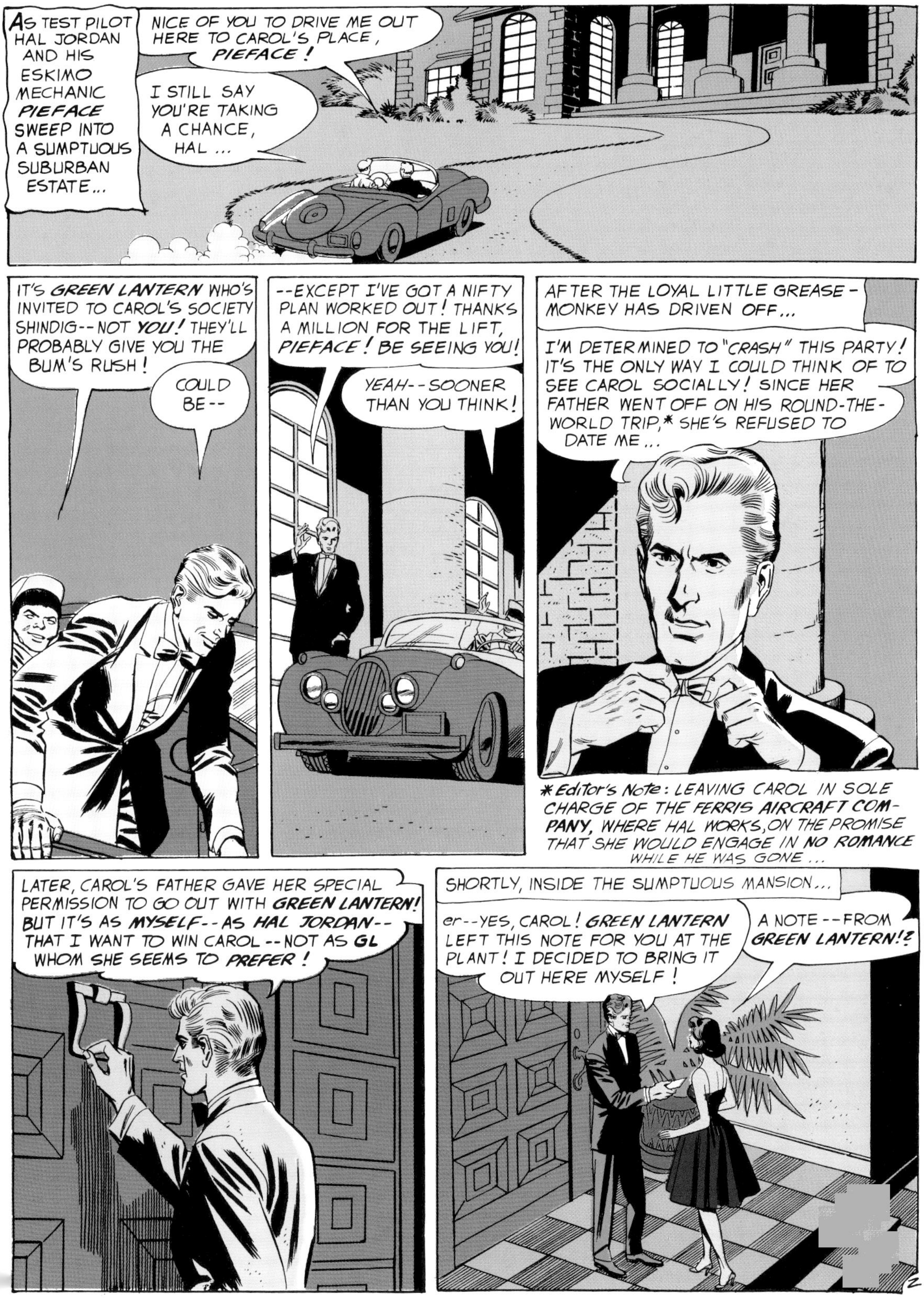
AS TEST PILOT HAL JORDAN AND HIS ESKIMO MECHANIC PIEFACE SWEEP INTO A SUMPTUOUS SUBURBAN ESTATE...
NICE OF YOU TO DRIVE ME OUT HERE TO CAROL'S PLACE, PIEFACE!
I STILL SAY YOU'RE TAKING A CHANCE, HAL ...
IT'S GREEN LANTERN WHO'S INVITED TO CAROL'S SOCIETY SHINDIG--NOT YOU! THEY'LL PROBABLY GIVE YOU THE BUM'S RUSH!
COULD BE--
--EXCEPT I'VE GOT A NIFTY PLAN WORKED OUT! THANKS A MILLION FOR THE LIFT, PIEFACE! BE SEEING YOU!
YEAH--SOONER THAN YOU THINK!
AFTER THE LOYAL LITTLE GREASE-MONKEY HAS DRIVEN OFF...
I'M DETERMINED TO "CRASH" THIS PARTY! IT'S THE ONLY WAY I COULD THINK OF TO SEE CAROL SOCIALLY! SINCE HER FATHER WENT OFF ON HIS ROUND-THE-WORLD TRIP,* SHE'S REFUSED TO DATE ME...
*Editor's Note: LEAVING CAROL IN SOLE CHARGE OF THE FERRIS AIRCRAFT COMPANY, WHERE HAL WORKS, ON THE PROMISE THAT SHE WOULD ENGAGE IN NO ROMANCE WHILE HE WAS GONE...
LATER, CAROL'S FATHER GAVE HER SPECIAL PERMISSION TO GO OUT WITH GREEN LANTERN! BUT IT'S AS MYSELF--AS HAL JORDAN--THAT I WANT TO WIN CAROL--NOT AS GL WHOM SHE SEEMS TO PREFER!
SHORTLY, INSIDE THE SUMPTUOUS MANSION...
er--YES, CAROL! GREEN LANTERN LEFT THIS NOTE FOR YOU AT THE PLANT! I DECIDED TO BRING IT OUT HERE MYSELF!
A NOTE--FROM GREEN LANTERN!?
2

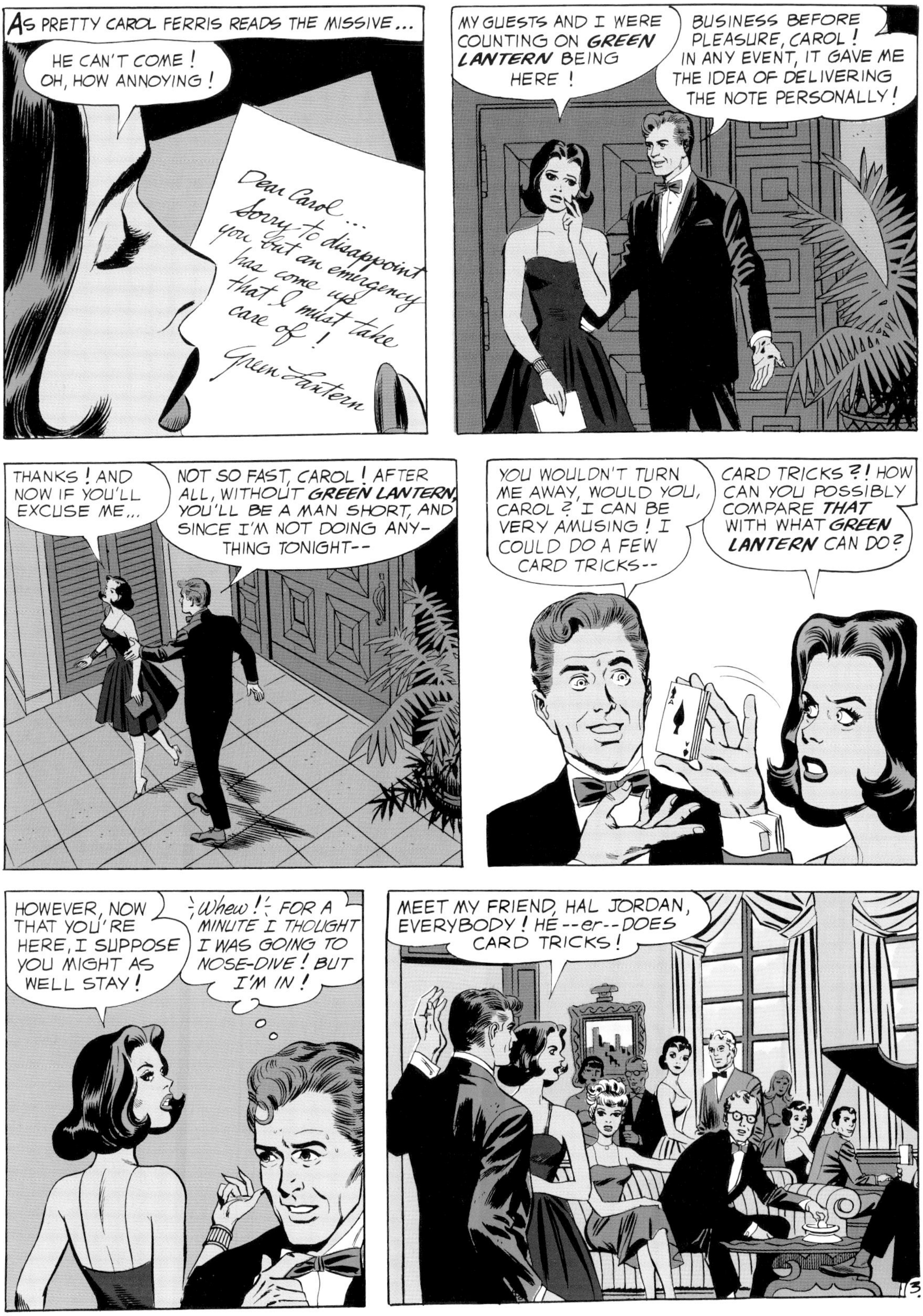
AS PRETTY CAROL FERRIS READS THE MISSIVE...
HE CAN'T COME! OH, HOW ANNOYING!
Dear Carol...
Sorry to disappoint
you but an emergency
has come up
that I must take
care of!
Green Lantern
MY GUESTS AND I WERE COUNTING ON GREEN LANTERN BEING HERE!
BUSINESS BEFORE PLEASURE, CAROL! IN ANY EVENT, IT GAVE ME THE IDEA OF DELIVERING THE NOTE PERSONALLY!
THANKS! AND NOW IF YOU'LL EXCUSE ME...
NOT SO FAST, CAROL! AFTER ALL, WITHOUT GREEN LANTERN, YOU'LL BE A MAN SHORT, AND SINCE I'M NOT DOING ANYTHING TONIGHT--
YOU WOULDN'T TURN ME AWAY, WOULD YOU, CAROL? I CAN BE VERY AMUSING! I COULD DO A FEW CARD TRICKS--
CARD TRICKS?! HOW CAN YOU POSSIBLY COMPARE THAT WITH WHAT GREEN LANTERN CAN DO?
HOWEVER, NOW THAT YOU'RE HERE, I SUPPOSE YOU MIGHT AS WELL STAY!
Whew! FOR A MINUTE I THOUGHT I WAS GOING TO NOSE-DIVE! BUT I'M IN!
MEET MY FRIEND, HAL JORDAN, EVERYBODY! HE --er-- DOES CARD TRICKS!
3

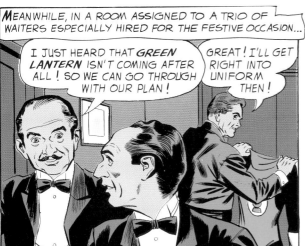

MEANWHILE, IN A ROOM ASSIGNED TO A TRIO OF WAITERS ESPECIALLY HIRED FOR THE FESTIVE OCCASION...

I JUST HEARD THAT *GREEN LANTERN* ISN'T COMING AFTER ALL! SO WE CAN GO THROUGH WITH OUR PLAN!

GREAT! I'LL GET RIGHT INTO UNIFORM THEN!

AND SOON...

HOW DO I LOOK?

PERFECT, *WOOZY!* *GREEN LANTERN'S* OWN MOTHER WOULD BE FOOLED! NOW PUT ON YOUR MASK AND LET'S GET STARTED!

OUT IN THE DRAWING ROOM WHERE THE NEW ARRIVAL IS ENTERTAINING THE COMPANY...

HAL JORDAN TELLS THE MOST AMUSING STORIES, CAROL! HE'S REALLY FUN!

HAL *IS* OUTDOING HIMSELF TODAY! I'VE NEVER SEEN HIM LIKE THIS!

I GUESS IT'S BECAUSE HE'S TRYING TO TAKE *GREEN LANTERN'S* PLACE! BUT THAT'S IMPOSSIBLE! HE COULD NEVER IN A MILLION YEARS MATCH--eh?

LOOK-- IT'S *GREEN LANTERN!*

THIS TINY GREEN FLASHLIGHT I HAD MADE IN THE FORM OF A RING IS WORKING LIKE A CHARM!

HI, EVERY-BODY!

GREEN LANTERN, YOU'RE HERE! HOW WONDERFUL!

I FOUND I COULD MAKE IT, CAROL--SO I JUST OPENED THE THROTTLE ON MY GREEN BEAM-- AND HERE I AM! BUT DON'T LET ME INTERRUPT THINGS!

WHAT'S GOING ON HERE?

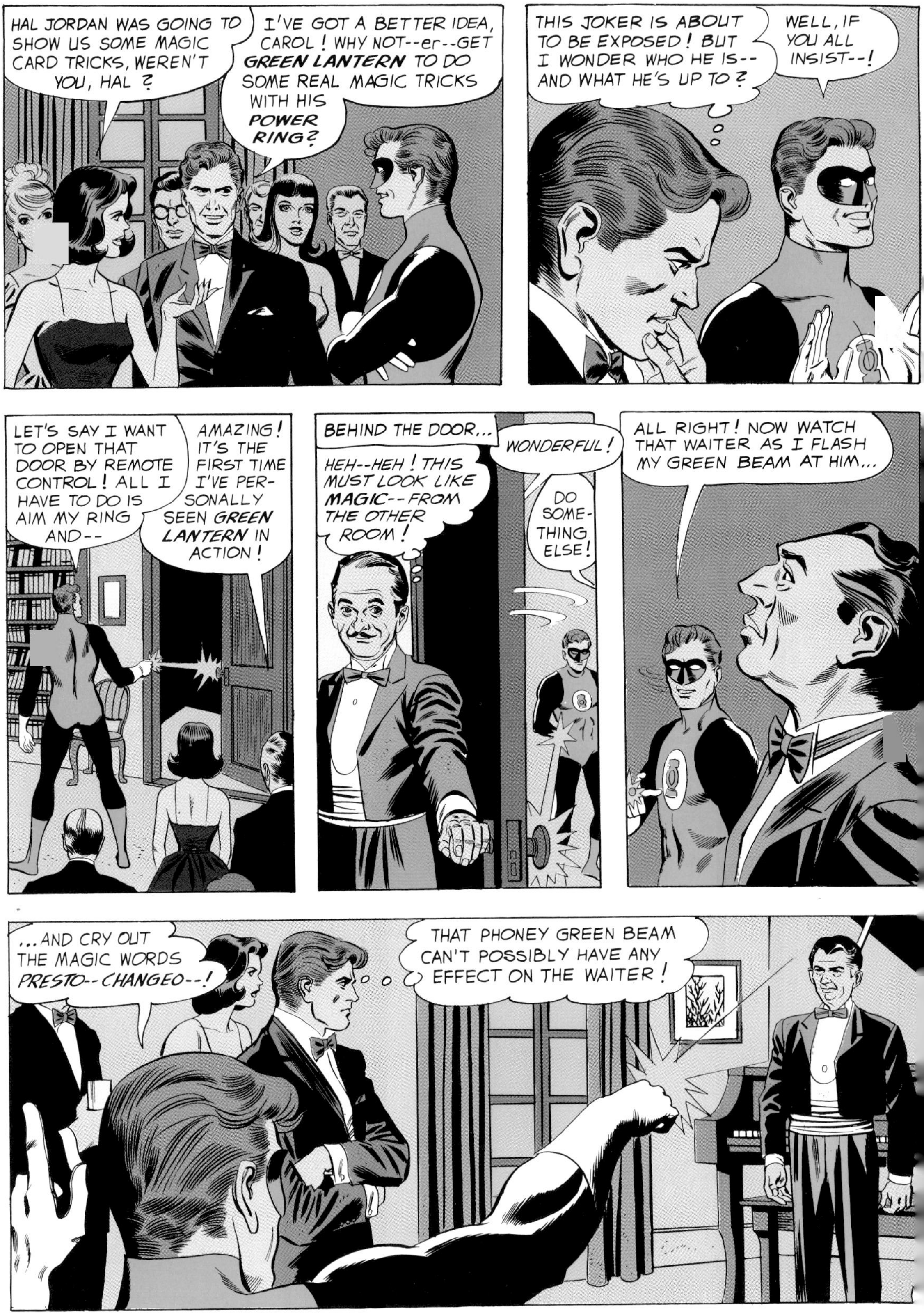
HAL JORDAN WAS GOING TO SHOW US SOME MAGIC CARD TRICKS, WEREN'T YOU, HAL ?
I'VE GOT A BETTER IDEA, CAROL ! WHY NOT--er--GET GREEN LANTERN TO DO SOME REAL MAGIC TRICKS WITH HIS POWER RING?
THIS JOKER IS ABOUT TO BE EXPOSED ! BUT I WONDER WHO HE IS-- AND WHAT HE'S UP TO ?
WELL, IF YOU ALL INSIST--!
LET'S SAY I WANT TO OPEN THAT DOOR BY REMOTE CONTROL ! ALL I HAVE TO DO IS AIM MY RING AND--
AMAZING ! IT'S THE FIRST TIME I'VE PERSONALLY SEEN GREEN LANTERN IN ACTION !
BEHIND THE DOOR...
HEH--HEH ! THIS MUST LOOK LIKE MAGIC--FROM THE OTHER ROOM !
WONDERFUL !
DO SOMETHING ELSE !
ALL RIGHT ! NOW WATCH THAT WAITER AS I FLASH MY GREEN BEAM AT HIM...
...AND CRY OUT THE MAGIC WORDS PRESTO--CHANGEO--!
THAT PHONEY GREEN BEAM CAN'T POSSIBLY HAVE ANY EFFECT ON THE WAITER !

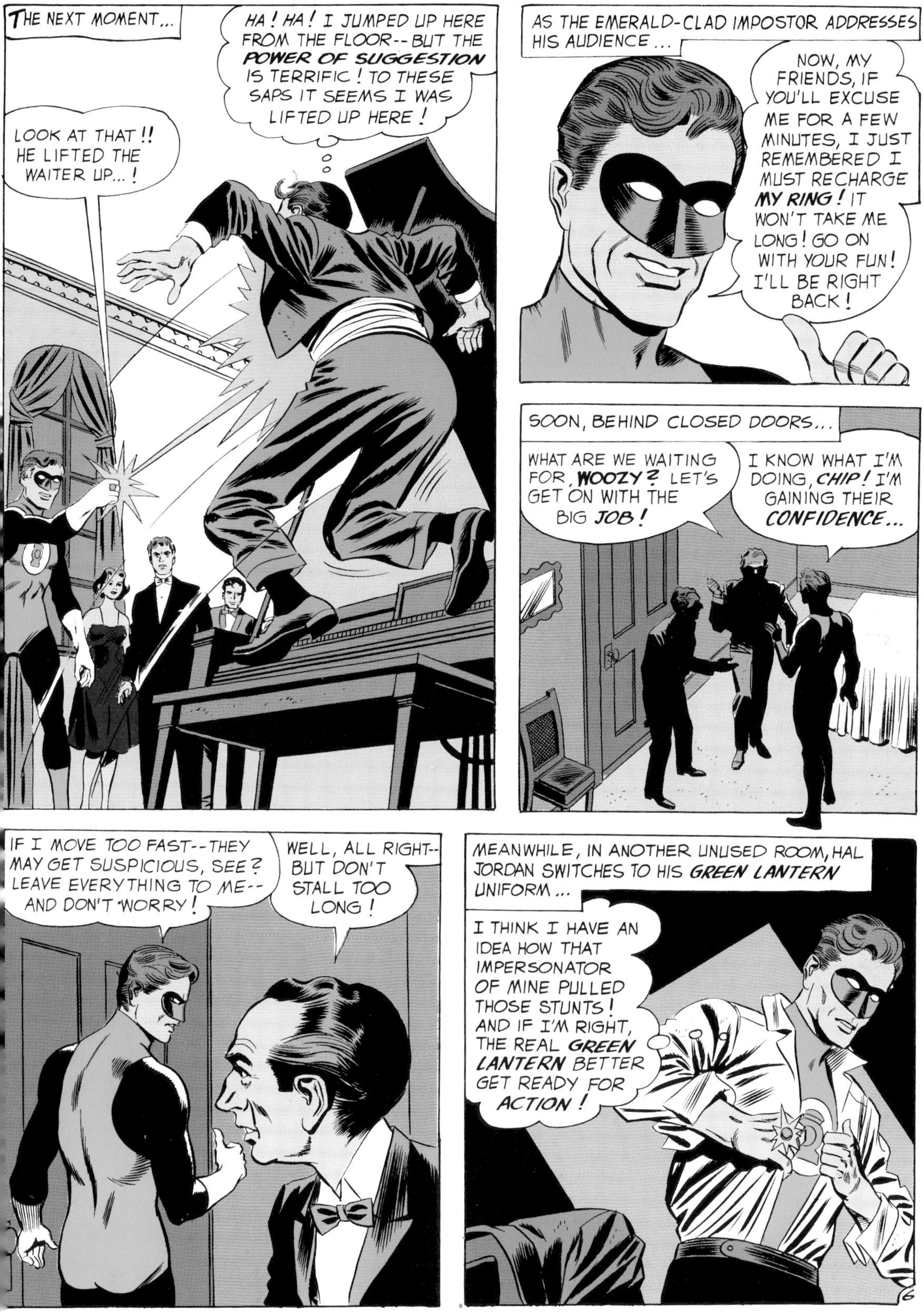

THE NEXT MOMENT...
HA! HA! I JUMPED UP HERE FROM THE FLOOR--BUT THE POWER OF SUGGESTION IS TERRIFIC! TO THESE SAPS IT SEEMS I WAS LIFTED UP HERE!
LOOK AT THAT!! HE LIFTED THE WAITER UP...!
AS THE EMERALD-CLAD IMPOSTOR ADDRESSES HIS AUDIENCE...
NOW, MY FRIENDS, IF YOU'LL EXCUSE ME FOR A FEW MINUTES, I JUST REMEMBERED I MUST RECHARGE MY RING! IT WON'T TAKE ME LONG! GO ON WITH YOUR FUN! I'LL BE RIGHT BACK!
SOON, BEHIND CLOSED DOORS...
WHAT ARE WE WAITING FOR, WOOZY? LET'S GET ON WITH THE BIG JOB!
I KNOW WHAT I'M DOING, CHIP! I'M GAINING THEIR CONFIDENCE...
IF I MOVE TOO FAST--THEY MAY GET SUSPICIOUS, SEE? LEAVE EVERYTHING TO ME--AND DON'T WORRY!
WELL, ALL RIGHT--BUT DON'T STALL TOO LONG!
MEANWHILE, IN ANOTHER UNUSED ROOM, HAL JORDAN SWITCHES TO HIS GREEN LANTERN UNIFORM...
I THINK I HAVE AN IDEA HOW THAT IMPERSONATOR OF MINE PULLED THOSE STUNTS! AND IF I'M RIGHT, THE REAL GREEN LANTERN BETTER GET READY FOR ACTION!
6

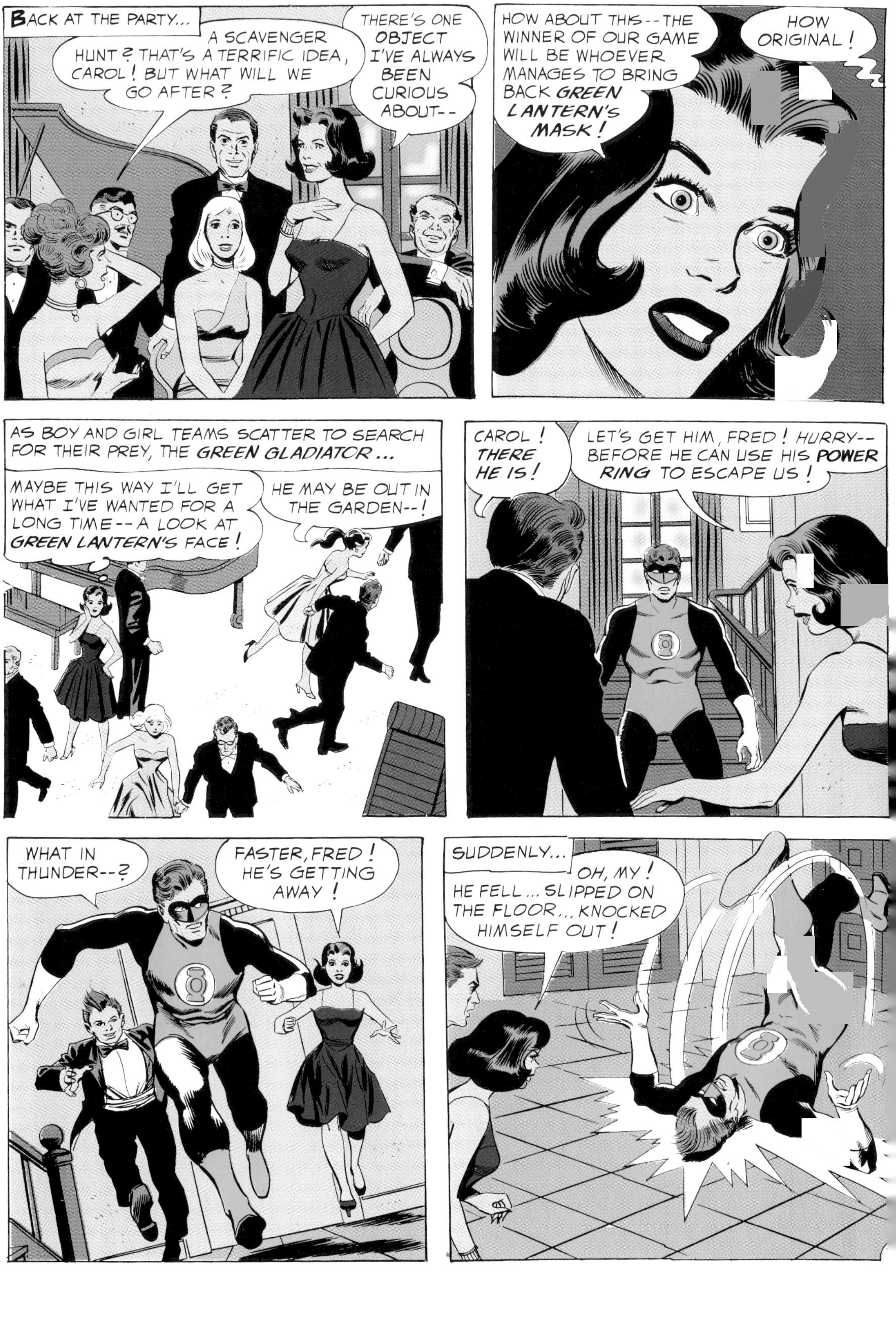
BACK AT THE PARTY...
A SCAVENGER HUNT? THAT'S A TERRIFIC IDEA, CAROL! BUT WHAT WILL WE GO AFTER?
THERE'S ONE OBJECT I'VE ALWAYS BEEN CURIOUS ABOUT--
HOW ABOUT THIS--THE WINNER OF OUR GAME WILL BE WHOEVER MANAGES TO BRING BACK GREEN LANTERN'S MASK!
HOW ORIGINAL!
AS BOY AND GIRL TEAMS SCATTER TO SEARCH FOR THEIR PREY, THE GREEN GLADIATOR...
MAYBE THIS WAY I'LL GET WHAT I'VE WANTED FOR A LONG TIME--A LOOK AT GREEN LANTERN'S FACE!
HE MAY BE OUT IN THE GARDEN--!
CAROL! THERE HE IS!
LET'S GET HIM, FRED! HURRY--BEFORE HE CAN USE HIS POWER RING TO ESCAPE US!
WHAT IN THUNDER--?
FASTER, FRED! HE'S GETTING AWAY!
SUDDENLY...
OH, MY! HE FELL... SLIPPED ON THE FLOOR... KNOCKED HIMSELF OUT!

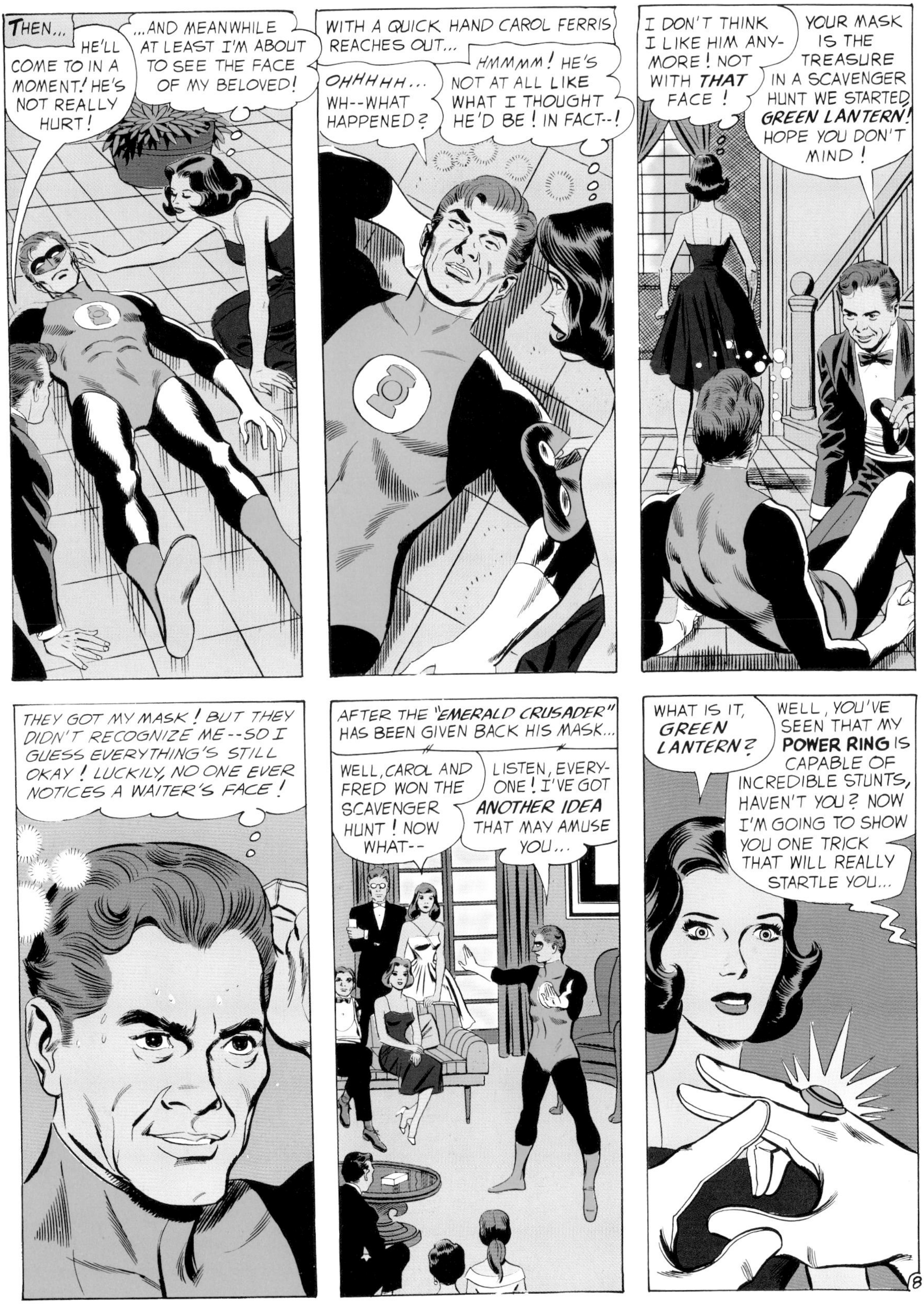
THEN...
HE'LL COME TO IN A MOMENT! HE'S NOT REALLY HURT!
...AND MEANWHILE AT LEAST I'M ABOUT TO SEE THE FACE OF MY BELOVED!
WITH A QUICK HAND CAROL FERRIS REACHES OUT...
OHHHHH... WH--WHAT HAPPENED?
HMMMM! HE'S NOT AT ALL LIKE WHAT I THOUGHT HE'D BE! IN FACT--!
I DON'T THINK I LIKE HIM ANY-MORE! NOT WITH THAT FACE!
YOUR MASK IS THE TREASURE IN A SCAVENGER HUNT WE STARTED, GREEN LANTERN! HOPE YOU DON'T MIND!
THEY GOT MY MASK! BUT THEY DIDN'T RECOGNIZE ME--SO I GUESS EVERYTHING'S STILL OKAY! LUCKILY, NO ONE EVER NOTICES A WAITER'S FACE!
AFTER THE "EMERALD CRUSADER" HAS BEEN GIVEN BACK HIS MASK...
WELL, CAROL AND FRED WON THE SCAVENGER HUNT! NOW WHAT--
LISTEN, EVERY-ONE! I'VE GOT ANOTHER IDEA THAT MAY AMUSE YOU...
WHAT IS IT, GREEN LANTERN?
WELL, YOU'VE SEEN THAT MY POWER RING IS CAPABLE OF INCREDIBLE STUNTS, HAVEN'T YOU? NOW I'M GOING TO SHOW YOU ONE TRICK THAT WILL REALLY STARTLE YOU...
8

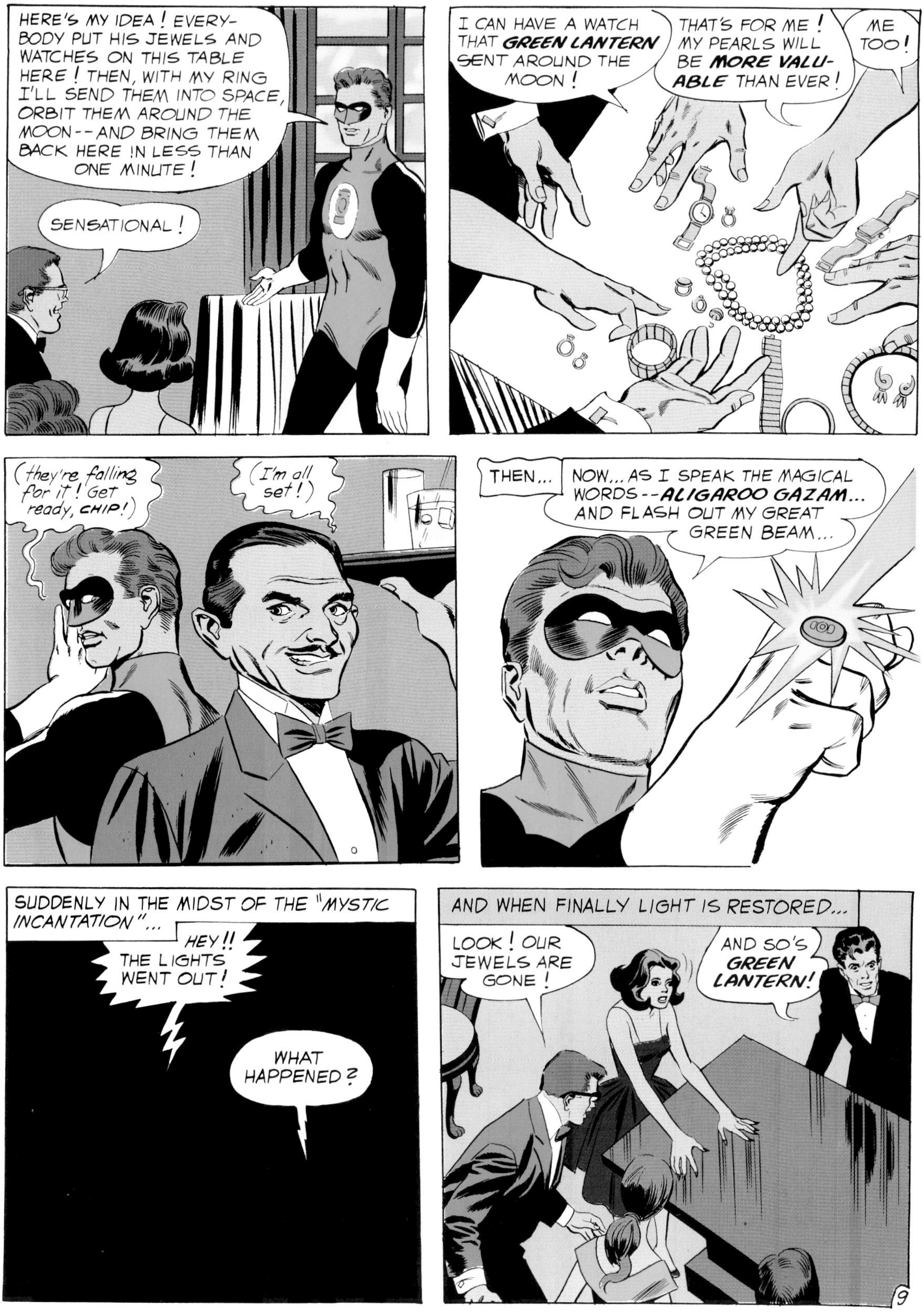
HERE'S MY IDEA! EVERYBODY PUT HIS JEWELS AND WATCHES ON THIS TABLE HERE! THEN, WITH MY RING I'LL SEND THEM INTO SPACE, ORBIT THEM AROUND THE MOON--AND BRING THEM BACK HERE IN LESS THAN ONE MINUTE!
SENSATIONAL!
I CAN HAVE A WATCH THAT GREEN LANTERN SENT AROUND THE MOON!
THAT'S FOR ME! MY PEARLS WILL BE MORE VALUABLE THAN EVER!
ME TOO!
(they're falling for it! Get ready, CHIP!)
(I'm all set!)
THEN...
NOW... AS I SPEAK THE MAGICAL WORDS--ALIGAROO GAZAM... AND FLASH OUT MY GREAT GREEN BEAM...
SUDDENLY IN THE MIDST OF THE "MYSTIC INCANTATION"...
HEY!! THE LIGHTS WENT OUT!
WHAT HAPPENED?
AND WHEN FINALLY LIGHT IS RESTORED...
LOOK! OUR JEWELS ARE GONE!
AND SO'S GREEN LANTERN!
9

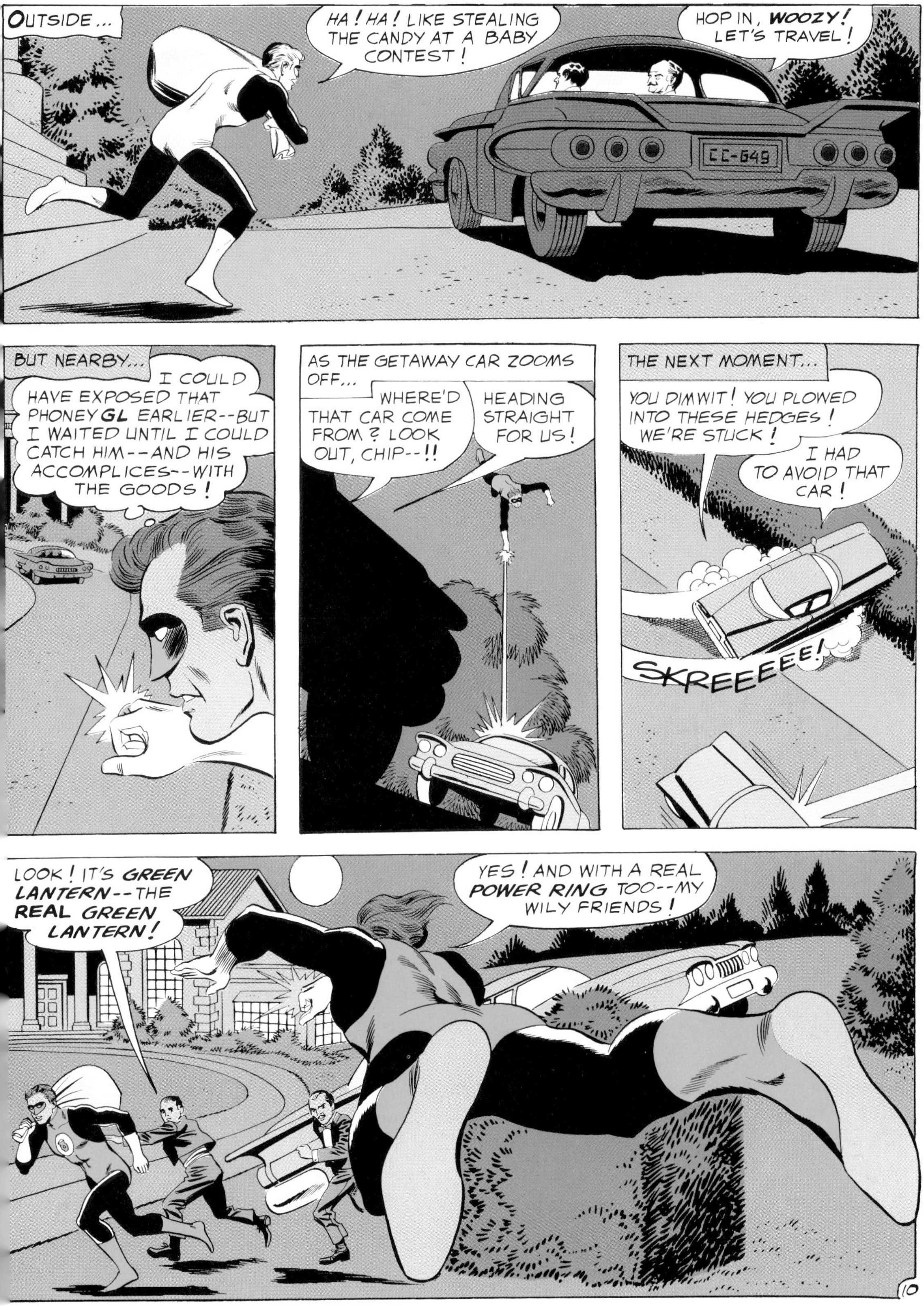
OUTSIDE...
HA! HA! LIKE STEALING THE CANDY AT A BABY CONTEST!
HOP IN, WOOZY! LET'S TRAVEL!
CC-649
BUT NEARBY...
I COULD HAVE EXPOSED THAT PHONEY GL EARLIER--BUT I WAITED UNTIL I COULD CATCH HIM--AND HIS ACCOMPLICES--WITH THE GOODS!
AS THE GETAWAY CAR ZOOMS OFF...
WHERE'D THAT CAR COME FROM? LOOK OUT, CHIP--!!
HEADING STRAIGHT FOR US!
THE NEXT MOMENT...
YOU DIMWIT! YOU PLOWED INTO THESE HEDGES! WE'RE STUCK!
I HAD TO AVOID THAT CAR!
SKREEEEEE!
LOOK! IT'S GREEN LANTERN--THE REAL GREEN LANTERN!
YES! AND WITH A REAL POWER RING TOO--MY WILY FRIENDS!
10

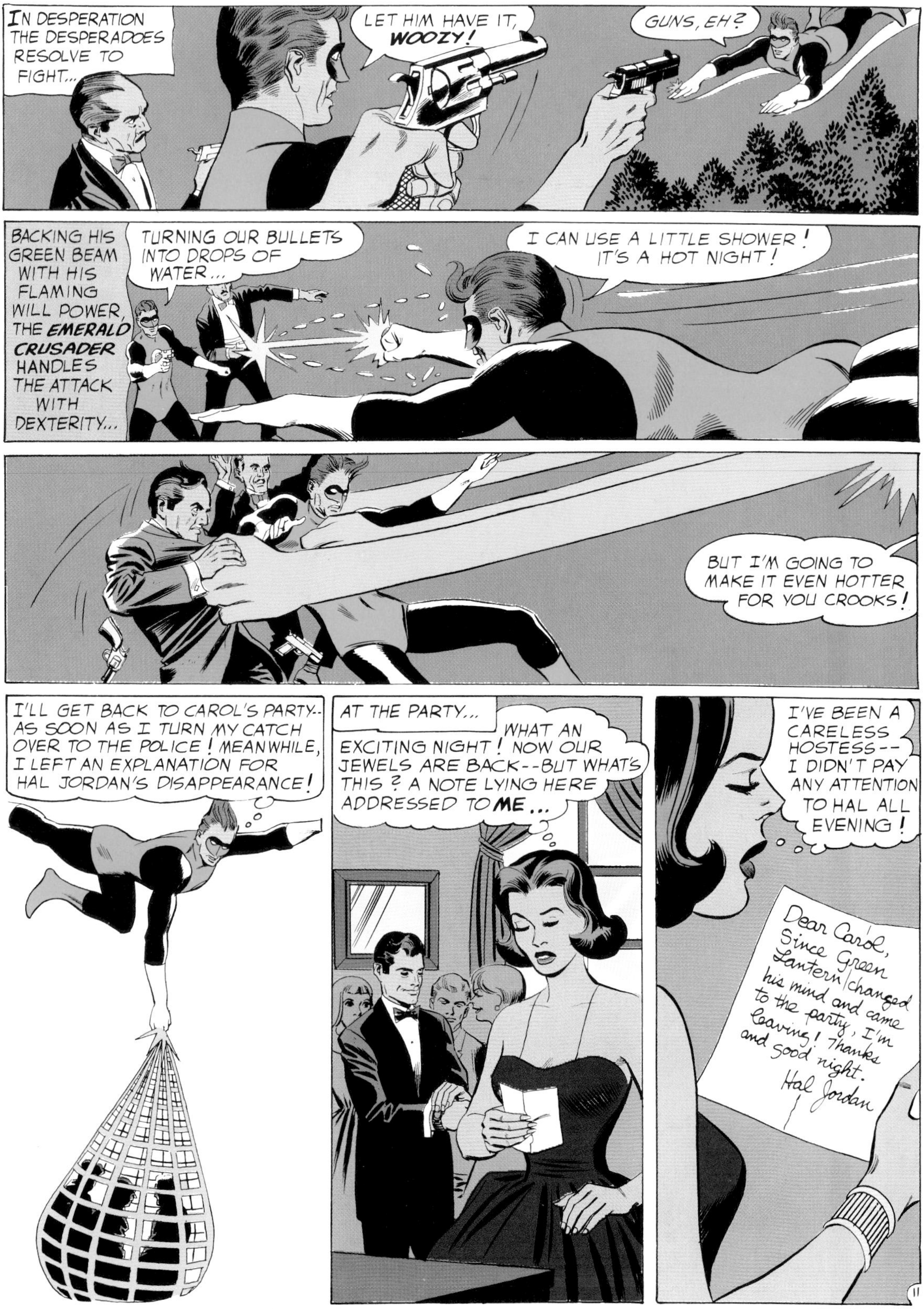
IN DESPERATION THE DESPERADOES RESOLVE TO FIGHT...
LET HIM HAVE IT, WOOZY!
GUNS, EH?
BACKING HIS GREEN BEAM WITH HIS FLAMING WILL POWER, THE EMERALD CRUSADER HANDLES THE ATTACK WITH DEXTERITY...
TURNING OUR BULLETS INTO DROPS OF WATER...
I CAN USE A LITTLE SHOWER! IT'S A HOT NIGHT!
BUT I'M GOING TO MAKE IT EVEN HOTTER FOR YOU CROOKS!
I'LL GET BACK TO CAROL'S PARTY-- AS SOON AS I TURN MY CATCH OVER TO THE POLICE! MEANWHILE, I LEFT AN EXPLANATION FOR HAL JORDAN'S DISAPPEARANCE!
AT THE PARTY...
WHAT AN EXCITING NIGHT! NOW OUR JEWELS ARE BACK--BUT WHAT'S THIS? A NOTE LYING HERE ADDRESSED TO ME...
I'VE BEEN A CARELESS HOSTESS-- I DIDN'T PAY ANY ATTENTION TO HAL ALL EVENING!
Dear Carol, Since Green Lantern changed his mind and came to the party, I'm leaving! Thanks and good night. Hal Jordan
11

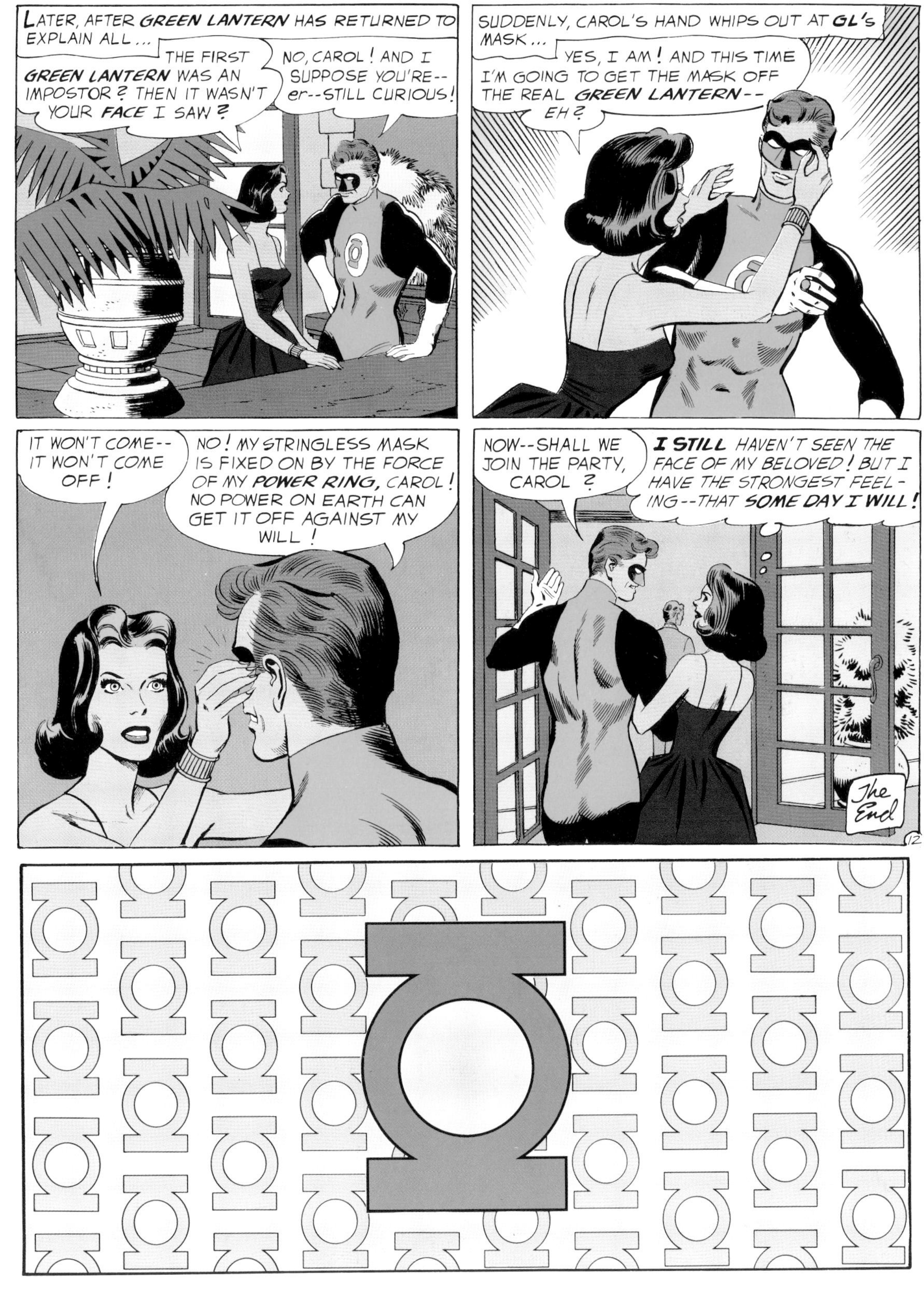
LATER, AFTER GREEN LANTERN HAS RETURNED TO EXPLAIN ALL ...
THE FIRST GREEN LANTERN WAS AN IMPOSTOR? THEN IT WASN'T YOUR FACE I SAW?
NO, CAROL! AND I SUPPOSE YOU'RE-- er--STILL CURIOUS!
SUDDENLY, CAROL'S HAND WHIPS OUT AT GL's MASK ...
YES, I AM! AND THIS TIME I'M GOING TO GET THE MASK OFF THE REAL GREEN LANTERN--
EH?
IT WON'T COME-- IT WON'T COME OFF!
NO! MY STRINGLESS MASK IS FIXED ON BY THE FORCE OF MY POWER RING, CAROL! NO POWER ON EARTH CAN GET IT OFF AGAINST MY WILL!
NOW--SHALL WE JOIN THE PARTY, CAROL?
I STILL HAVEN'T SEEN THE FACE OF MY BELOVED! BUT I HAVE THE STRONGEST FEEL-ING--THAT SOME DAY I WILL!
The End
12

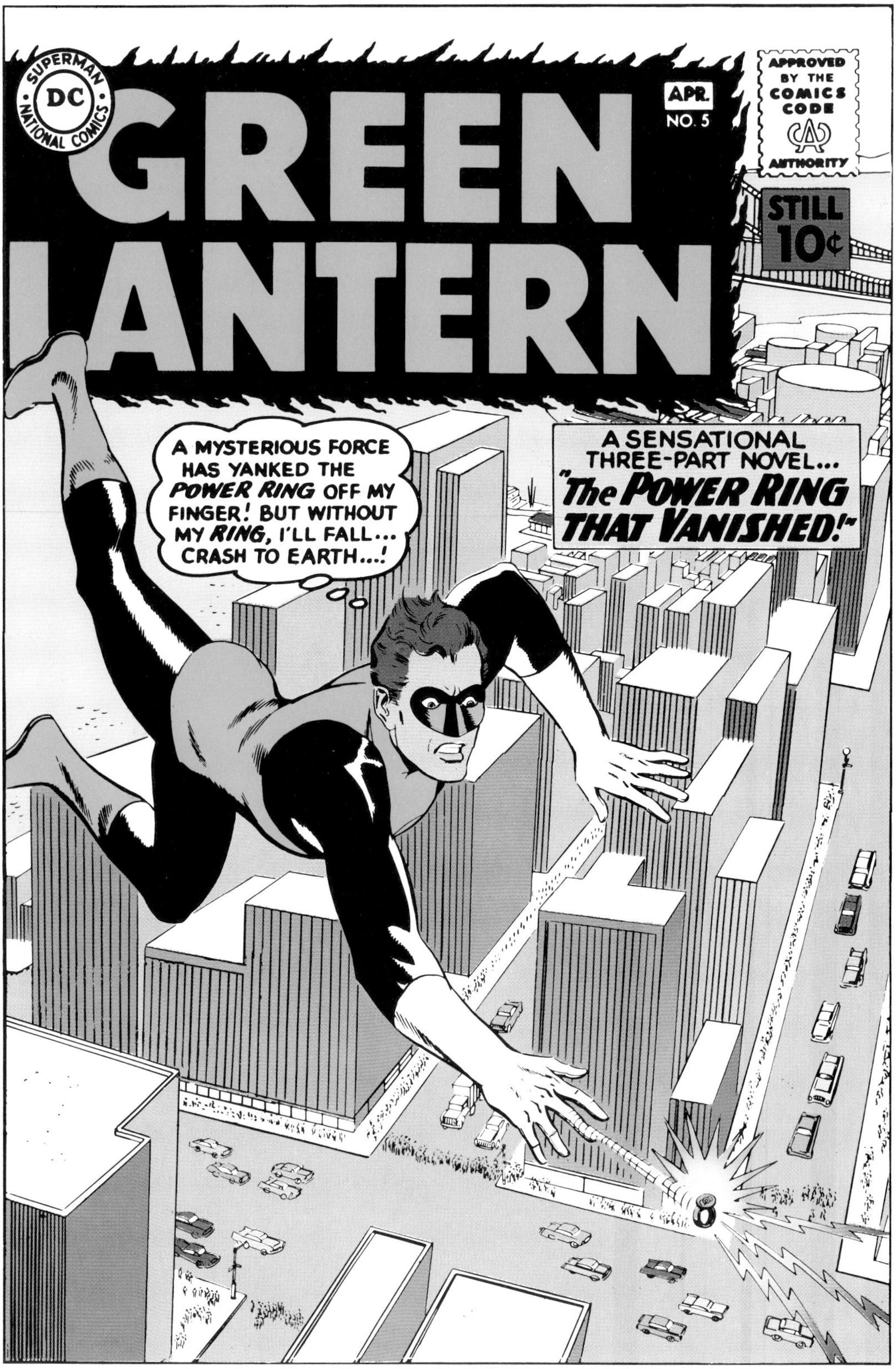
SUPERMAN DC NATIONAL COMICS
GREEN LANTERN
APR. NO. 5
APPROVED BY THE COMICS CODE AUTHORITY
STILL 10¢
A MYSTERIOUS FORCE HAS YANKED THE POWER RING OFF MY FINGER! BUT WITHOUT MY RING, I'LL FALL... CRASH TO EARTH...!
A SENSATIONAL THREE-PART NOVEL... "The POWER RING THAT VANISHED!"

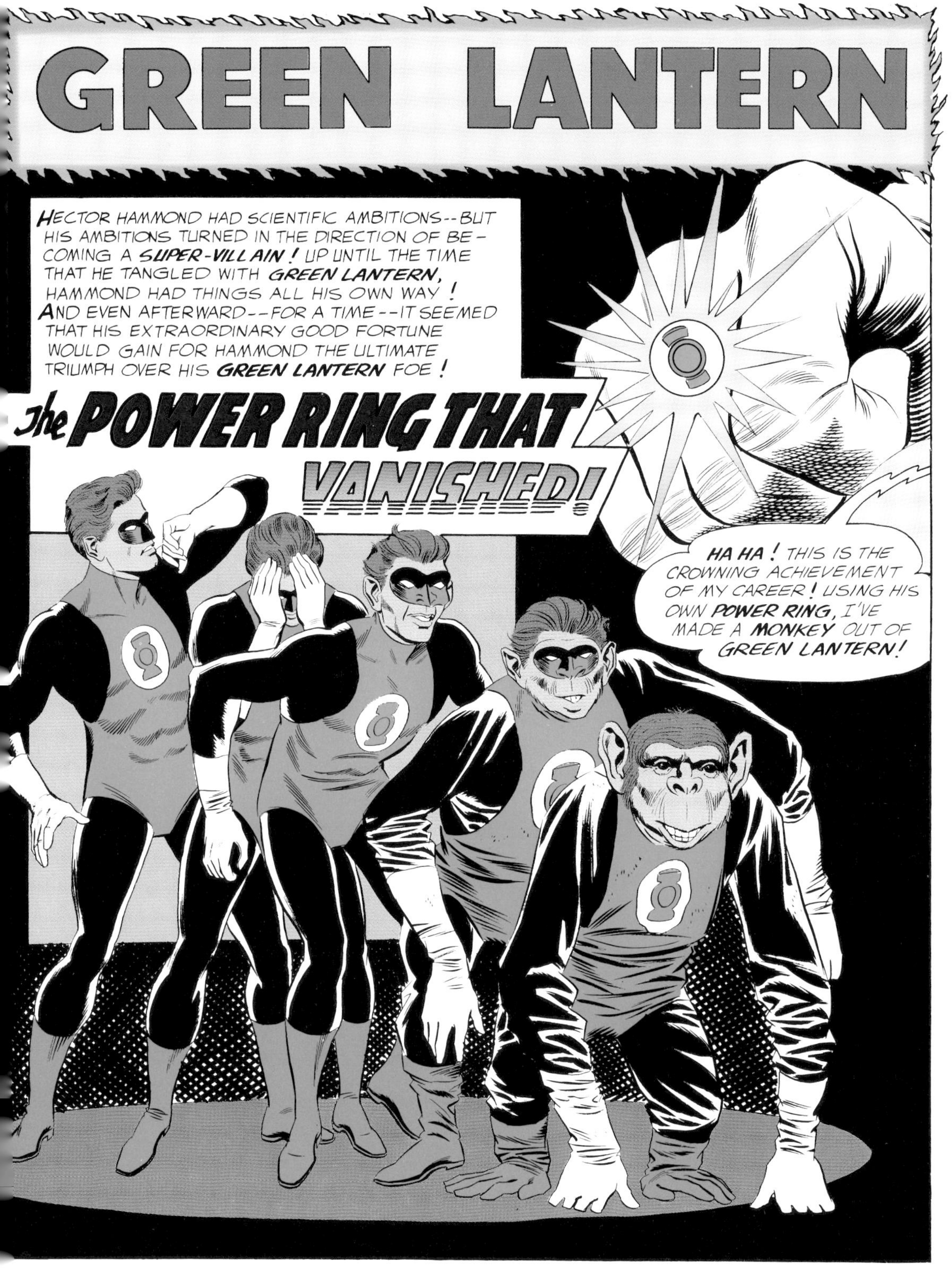
GREEN LANTERN
HECTOR HAMMOND HAD SCIENTIFIC AMBITIONS--BUT HIS AMBITIONS TURNED IN THE DIRECTION OF BE-COMING A SUPER-VILLAIN! UP UNTIL THE TIME THAT HE TANGLED WITH GREEN LANTERN, HAMMOND HAD THINGS ALL HIS OWN WAY! AND EVEN AFTERWARD--FOR A TIME--IT SEEMED THAT HIS EXTRAORDINARY GOOD FORTUNE WOULD GAIN FOR HAMMOND THE ULTIMATE TRIUMPH OVER HIS GREEN LANTERN FOE!
The POWER RING THAT VANISHED!
HA HA! THIS IS THE CROWNING ACHIEVEMENT OF MY CAREER! USING HIS OWN POWER RING, I'VE MADE A MONKEY OUT OF GREEN LANTERN!

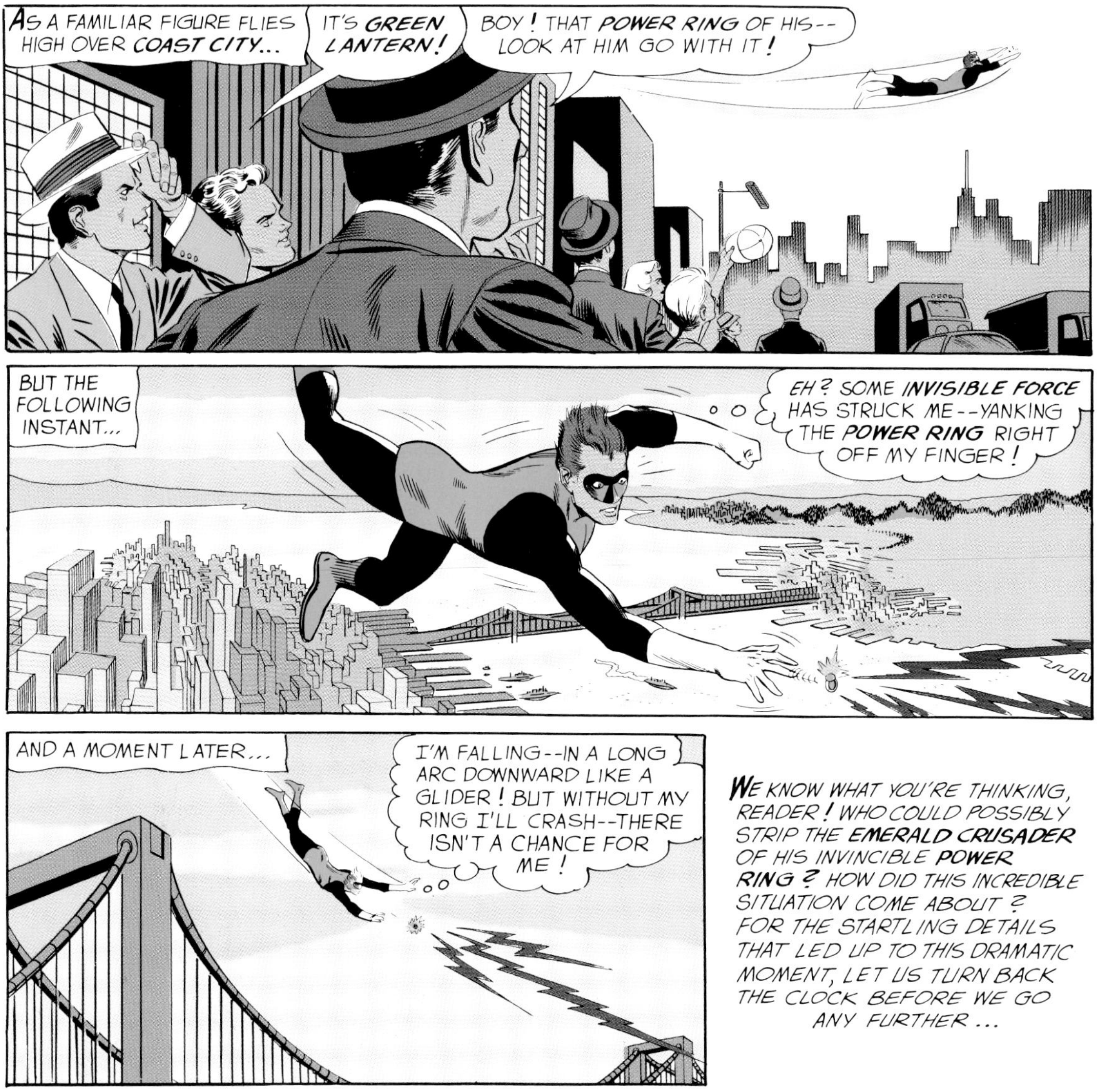
AS A FAMILIAR FIGURE FLIES HIGH OVER COAST CITY...
IT'S GREEN LANTERN!
BOY! THAT POWER RING OF HIS-- LOOK AT HIM GO WITH IT!
BUT THE FOLLOWING INSTANT...
EH? SOME INVISIBLE FORCE HAS STRUCK ME--YANKING THE POWER RING RIGHT OFF MY FINGER!
AND A MOMENT LATER...
I'M FALLING--IN A LONG ARC DOWNWARD LIKE A GLIDER! BUT WITHOUT MY RING I'LL CRASH--THERE ISN'T A CHANCE FOR ME!

WE KNOW WHAT YOU'RE THINKING, READER! WHO COULD POSSIBLY STRIP THE **EMERALD CRUSADER** OF HIS INVINCIBLE **POWER RING**? HOW DID THIS INCREDIBLE SITUATION COME ABOUT? FOR THE STARTLING DETAILS THAT LED UP TO THIS DRAMATIC MOMENT, LET US TURN BACK THE CLOCK BEFORE WE GO ANY FURTHER...

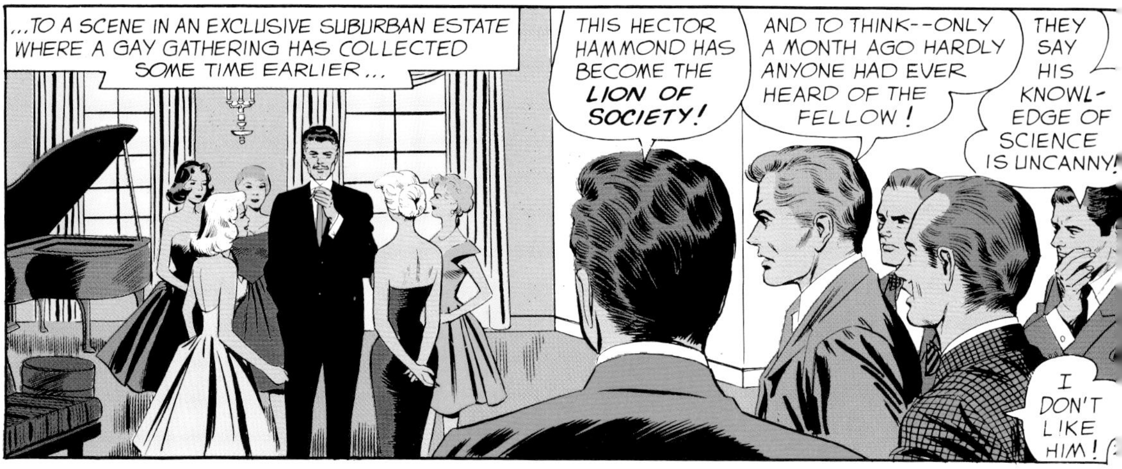
...TO A SCENE IN AN EXCLUSIVE SUBURBAN ESTATE WHERE A GAY GATHERING HAS COLLECTED SOME TIME EARLIER...
THIS HECTOR HAMMOND HAS BECOME THE LION OF SOCIETY!
AND TO THINK--ONLY A MONTH AGO HARDLY ANYONE HAD EVER HEARD OF THE FELLOW!
THEY SAY HIS KNOWLEDGE OF SCIENCE IS UNCANNY!
I DON'T LIKE HIM!

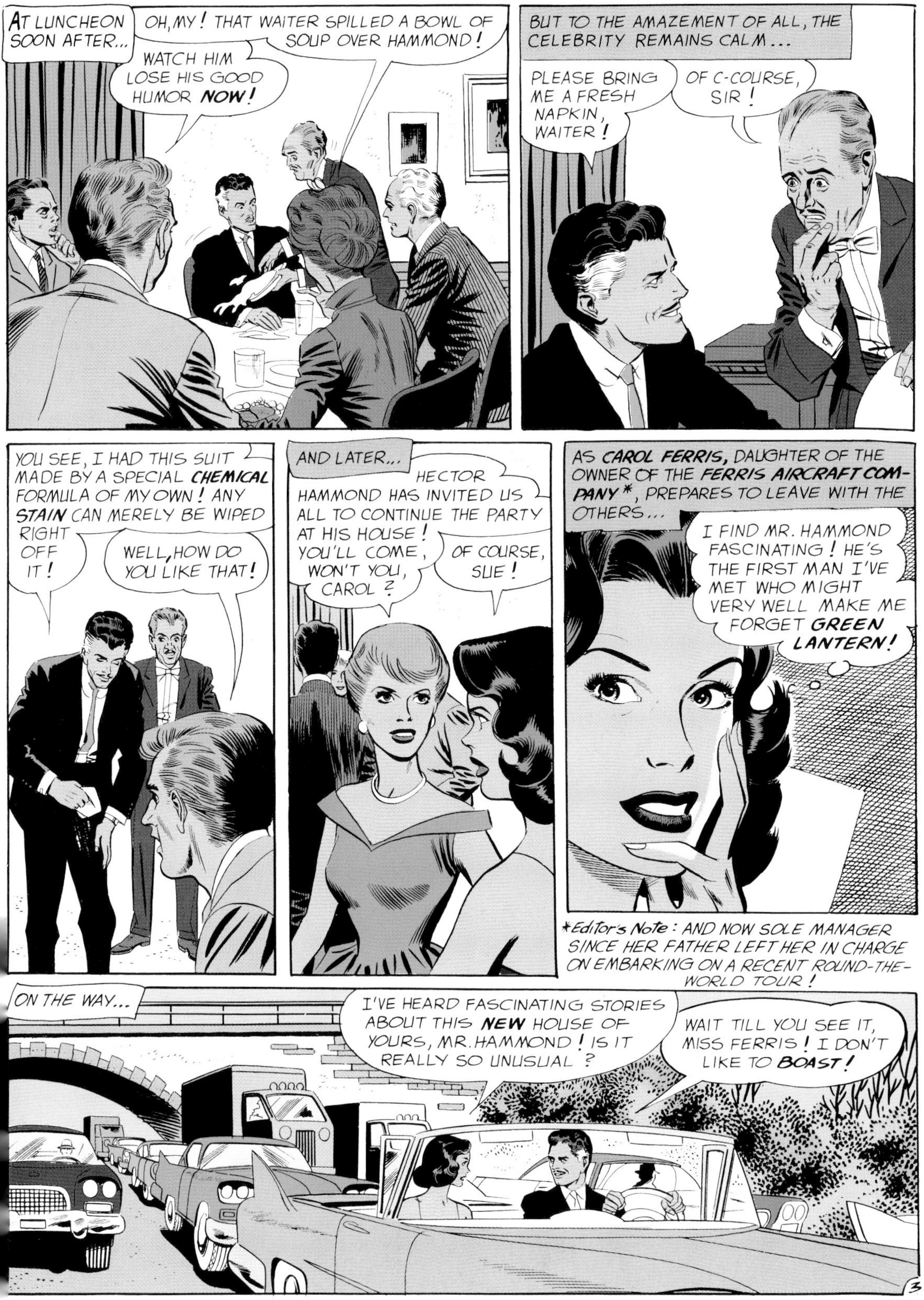
AT LUNCHEON SOON AFTER...
OH, MY! THAT WAITER SPILLED A BOWL OF SOUP OVER HAMMOND!
WATCH HIM LOSE HIS GOOD HUMOR NOW!
BUT TO THE AMAZEMENT OF ALL, THE CELEBRITY REMAINS CALM...
PLEASE BRING ME A FRESH NAPKIN, WAITER!
OF C-COURSE, SIR!
YOU SEE, I HAD THIS SUIT MADE BY A SPECIAL CHEMICAL FORMULA OF MY OWN! ANY STAIN CAN MERELY BE WIPED RIGHT OFF IT!
WELL, HOW DO YOU LIKE THAT!
AND LATER...
HECTOR HAMMOND HAS INVITED US ALL TO CONTINUE THE PARTY AT HIS HOUSE! YOU'LL COME, WON'T YOU, CAROL?
OF COURSE, SUE!
AS CAROL FERRIS, DAUGHTER OF THE OWNER OF THE FERRIS AIRCRAFT COMPANY*, PREPARES TO LEAVE WITH THE OTHERS...
I FIND MR. HAMMOND FASCINATING! HE'S THE FIRST MAN I'VE MET WHO MIGHT VERY WELL MAKE ME FORGET GREEN LANTERN!
*Editor's Note: AND NOW SOLE MANAGER SINCE HER FATHER LEFT HER IN CHARGE ON EMBARKING ON A RECENT ROUND-THE-WORLD TOUR!
ON THE WAY...
I'VE HEARD FASCINATING STORIES ABOUT THIS NEW HOUSE OF YOURS, MR. HAMMOND! IS IT REALLY SO UNUSUAL?
WAIT TILL YOU SEE IT, MISS FERRIS! I DON'T LIKE TO BOAST!
3

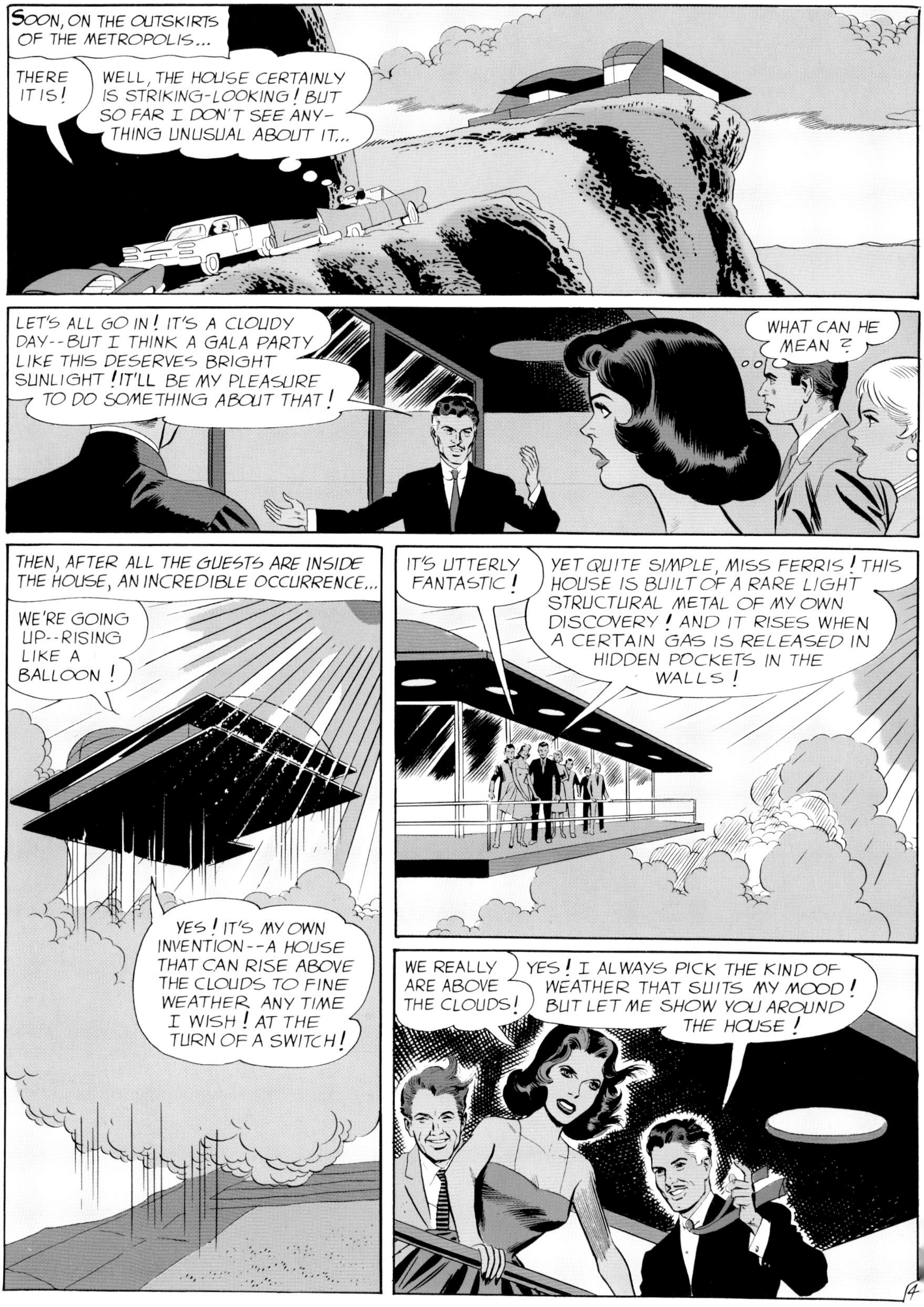
SOON, ON THE OUTSKIRTS OF THE METROPOLIS...
THERE IT IS!
WELL, THE HOUSE CERTAINLY IS STRIKING-LOOKING! BUT SO FAR I DON'T SEE ANYTHING UNUSUAL ABOUT IT...
LET'S ALL GO IN! IT'S A CLOUDY DAY--BUT I THINK A GALA PARTY LIKE THIS DESERVES BRIGHT SUNLIGHT! IT'LL BE MY PLEASURE TO DO SOMETHING ABOUT THAT!
WHAT CAN HE MEAN?
THEN, AFTER ALL THE GUESTS ARE INSIDE THE HOUSE, AN INCREDIBLE OCCURRENCE...
WE'RE GOING UP--RISING LIKE A BALLOON!
YES! IT'S MY OWN INVENTION--A HOUSE THAT CAN RISE ABOVE THE CLOUDS TO FINE WEATHER ANY TIME I WISH! AT THE TURN OF A SWITCH!
IT'S UTTERLY FANTASTIC!
YET QUITE SIMPLE, MISS FERRIS! THIS HOUSE IS BUILT OF A RARE LIGHT STRUCTURAL METAL OF MY OWN DISCOVERY! AND IT RISES WHEN A CERTAIN GAS IS RELEASED IN HIDDEN POCKETS IN THE WALLS!
WE REALLY ARE ABOVE THE CLOUDS!
YES! I ALWAYS PICK THE KIND OF WEATHER THAT SUITS MY MOOD! BUT LET ME SHOW YOU AROUND THE HOUSE!
4

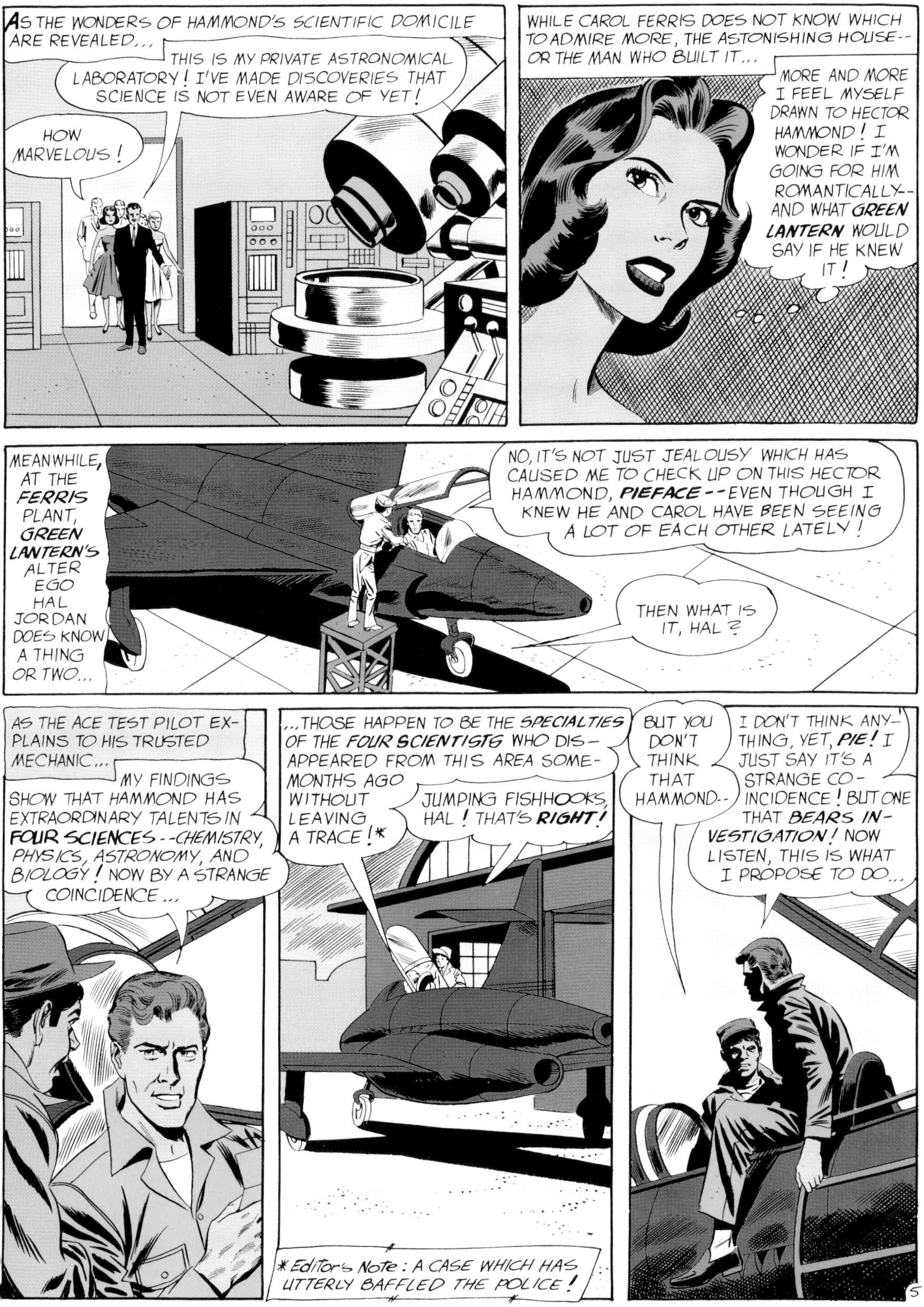

AS THE WONDERS OF HAMMOND'S SCIENTIFIC DOMICILE ARE REVEALED...
THIS IS MY PRIVATE ASTRONOMICAL LABORATORY! I'VE MADE DISCOVERIES THAT SCIENCE IS NOT EVEN AWARE OF YET!
HOW MARVELOUS!
WHILE CAROL FERRIS DOES NOT KNOW WHICH TO ADMIRE MORE, THE ASTONISHING HOUSE-- OR THE MAN WHO BUILT IT...
MORE AND MORE I FEEL MYSELF DRAWN TO HECTOR HAMMOND! I WONDER IF I'M GOING FOR HIM ROMANTICALLY-- AND WHAT GREEN LANTERN WOULD SAY IF HE KNEW IT!
MEANWHILE, AT THE FERRIS PLANT, GREEN LANTERN'S ALTER EGO HAL JORDAN DOES KNOW A THING OR TWO...
NO, IT'S NOT JUST JEALOUSY WHICH HAS CAUSED ME TO CHECK UP ON THIS HECTOR HAMMOND, PIEFACE--EVEN THOUGH I KNEW HE AND CAROL HAVE BEEN SEEING A LOT OF EACH OTHER LATELY!
THEN WHAT IS IT, HAL?
AS THE ACE TEST PILOT EXPLAINS TO HIS TRUSTED MECHANIC...
MY FINDINGS SHOW THAT HAMMOND HAS EXTRAORDINARY TALENTS IN FOUR SCIENCES--CHEMISTRY, PHYSICS, ASTRONOMY, AND BIOLOGY! NOW BY A STRANGE COINCIDENCE...
...THOSE HAPPEN TO BE THE SPECIALTIES OF THE FOUR SCIENTISTS WHO DISAPPEARED FROM THIS AREA SOME MONTHS AGO WITHOUT LEAVING A TRACE!*
JUMPING FISHHOOKS, HAL! THAT'S RIGHT!
*Editor's Note: A CASE WHICH HAS UTTERLY BAFFLED THE POLICE!
BUT YOU DON'T THINK THAT HAMMOND--
I DON'T THINK ANYTHING, YET, PIE! I JUST SAY IT'S A STRANGE COINCIDENCE! BUT ONE THAT BEARS INVESTIGATION! NOW LISTEN, THIS IS WHAT I PROPOSE TO DO...
5

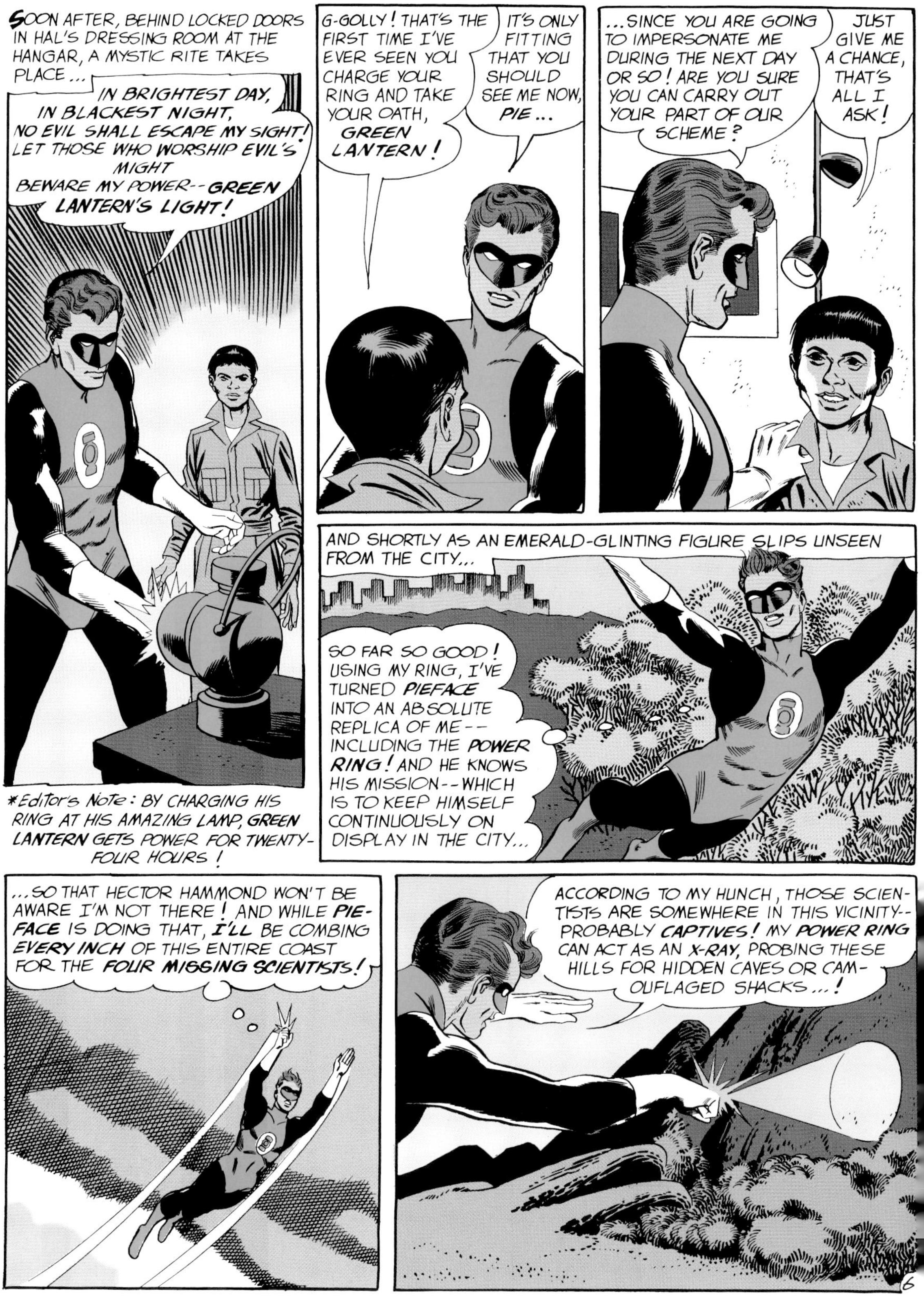
SOON AFTER, BEHIND LOCKED DOORS IN HAL'S DRESSING ROOM AT THE HANGAR, A MYSTIC RITE TAKES PLACE...
IN BRIGHTEST DAY, IN BLACKEST NIGHT, NO EVIL SHALL ESCAPE MY SIGHT! LET THOSE WHO WORSHIP EVIL'S MIGHT BEWARE MY POWER--GREEN LANTERN'S LIGHT!
*Editor's Note: BY CHARGING HIS RING AT HIS AMAZING LAMP, GREEN LANTERN GETS POWER FOR TWENTY-FOUR HOURS!
G-GOLLY! THAT'S THE FIRST TIME I'VE EVER SEEN YOU CHARGE YOUR RING AND TAKE YOUR OATH, GREEN LANTERN!
IT'S ONLY FITTING THAT YOU SHOULD SEE ME NOW, PIE...
...SINCE YOU ARE GOING TO IMPERSONATE ME DURING THE NEXT DAY OR SO! ARE YOU SURE YOU CAN CARRY OUT YOUR PART OF OUR SCHEME?
JUST GIVE ME A CHANCE, THAT'S ALL I ASK!
AND SHORTLY AS AN EMERALD-GLINTING FIGURE SLIPS UNSEEN FROM THE CITY...
SO FAR SO GOOD! USING MY RING, I'VE TURNED PIEFACE INTO AN ABSOLUTE REPLICA OF ME--INCLUDING THE POWER RING! AND HE KNOWS HIS MISSION--WHICH IS TO KEEP HIMSELF CONTINUOUSLY ON DISPLAY IN THE CITY...
...SO THAT HECTOR HAMMOND WON'T BE AWARE I'M NOT THERE! AND WHILE PIEFACE IS DOING THAT, I'LL BE COMBING EVERY INCH OF THIS ENTIRE COAST FOR THE FOUR MISSING SCIENTISTS!
ACCORDING TO MY HUNCH, THOSE SCIENTISTS ARE SOMEWHERE IN THIS VICINITY--PROBABLY CAPTIVES! MY POWER RING CAN ACT AS AN X-RAY, PROBING THESE HILLS FOR HIDDEN CAVES OR CAMOUFLAGED SHACKS...!
6

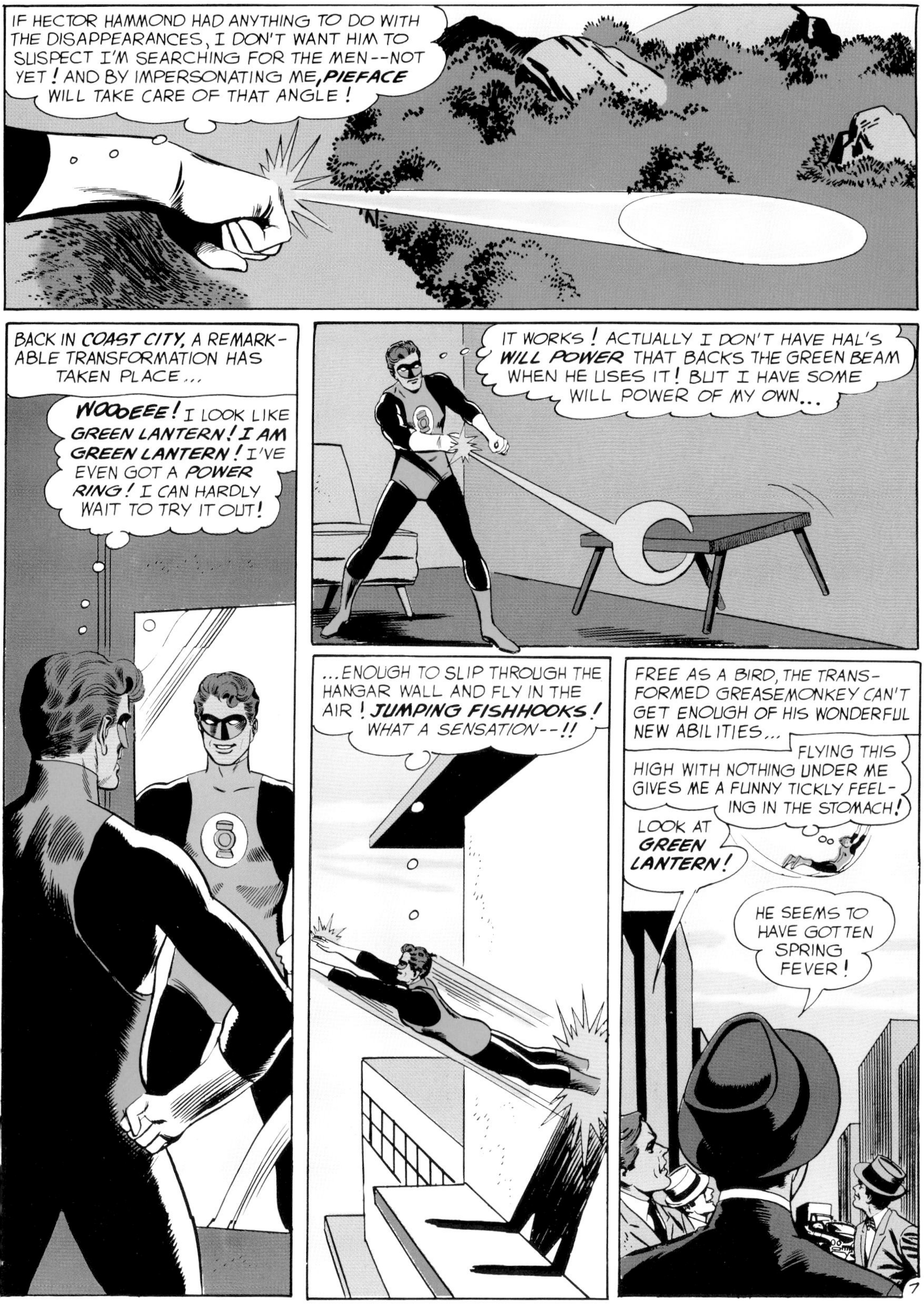
IF HECTOR HAMMOND HAD ANYTHING TO DO WITH THE DISAPPEARANCES, I DON'T WANT HIM TO SUSPECT I'M SEARCHING FOR THE MEN--NOT YET! AND BY IMPERSONATING ME, PIEFACE WILL TAKE CARE OF THAT ANGLE!
BACK IN COAST CITY, A REMARKABLE TRANSFORMATION HAS TAKEN PLACE...
WOOOEEE! I LOOK LIKE GREEN LANTERN! I AM GREEN LANTERN! I'VE EVEN GOT A POWER RING! I CAN HARDLY WAIT TO TRY IT OUT!
IT WORKS! ACTUALLY I DON'T HAVE HAL'S WILL POWER THAT BACKS THE GREEN BEAM WHEN HE USES IT! BUT I HAVE SOME WILL POWER OF MY OWN...
...ENOUGH TO SLIP THROUGH THE HANGAR WALL AND FLY IN THE AIR! JUMPING FISHHOOKS! WHAT A SENSATION--!!
FREE AS A BIRD, THE TRANSFORMED GREASEMONKEY CAN'T GET ENOUGH OF HIS WONDERFUL NEW ABILITIES...
FLYING THIS HIGH WITH NOTHING UNDER ME GIVES ME A FUNNY TICKLY FEELING IN THE STOMACH!
LOOK AT GREEN LANTERN!
HE SEEMS TO HAVE GOTTEN SPRING FEVER!
7

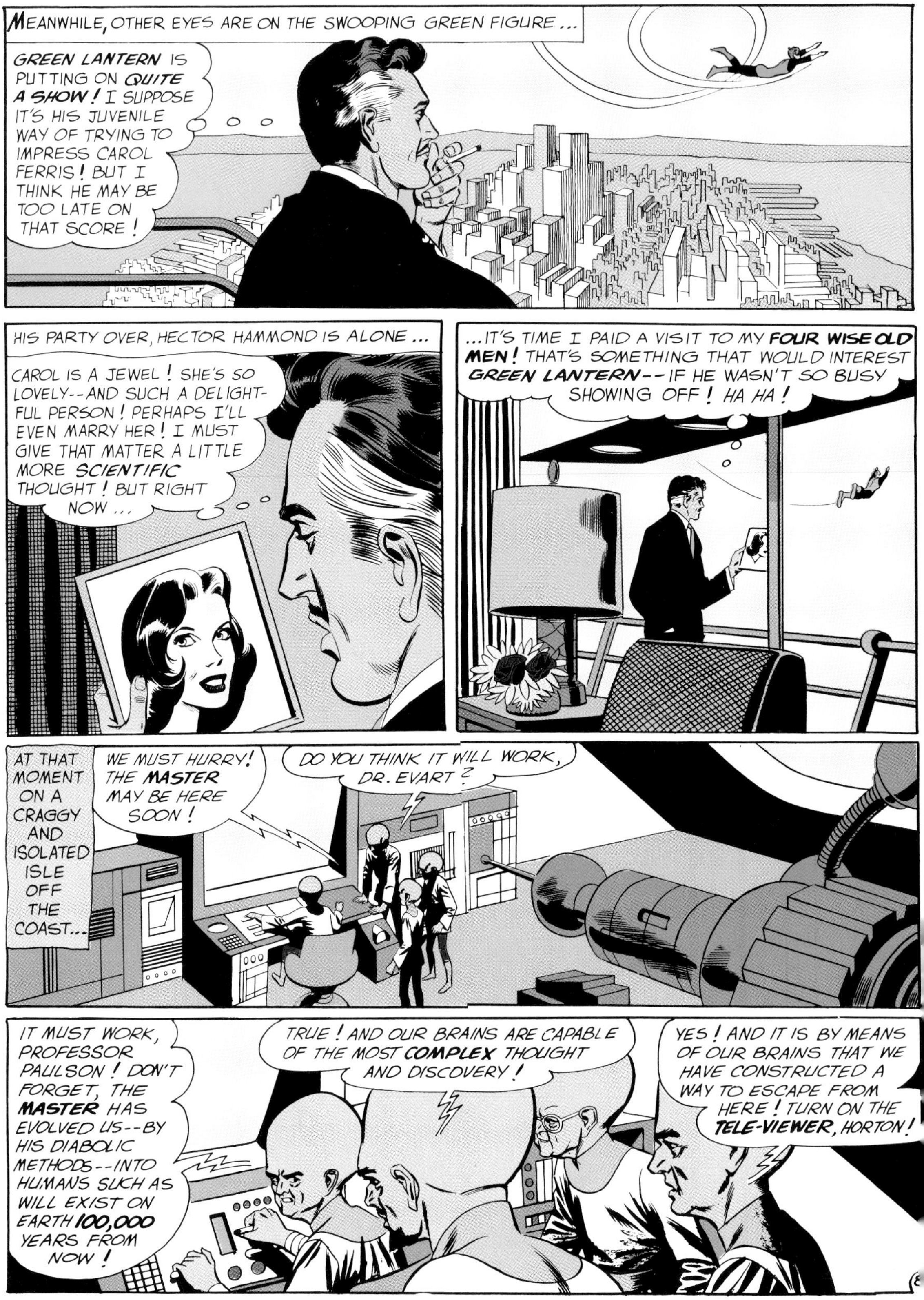
MEANWHILE, OTHER EYES ARE ON THE SWOOPING GREEN FIGURE...
GREEN LANTERN IS PUTTING ON QUITE A SHOW! I SUPPOSE IT'S HIS JUVENILE WAY OF TRYING TO IMPRESS CAROL FERRIS! BUT I THINK HE MAY BE TOO LATE ON THAT SCORE!
HIS PARTY OVER, HECTOR HAMMOND IS ALONE...
CAROL IS A JEWEL! SHE'S SO LOVELY--AND SUCH A DELIGHTFUL PERSON! PERHAPS I'LL EVEN MARRY HER! I MUST GIVE THAT MATTER A LITTLE MORE SCIENTIFIC THOUGHT! BUT RIGHT NOW...
...IT'S TIME I PAID A VISIT TO MY FOUR WISE OLD MEN! THAT'S SOMETHING THAT WOULD INTEREST GREEN LANTERN--IF HE WASN'T SO BUSY SHOWING OFF! HA HA!
AT THAT MOMENT ON A CRAGGY AND ISOLATED ISLE OFF THE COAST...
WE MUST HURRY! THE MASTER MAY BE HERE SOON!
DO YOU THINK IT WILL WORK, DR. EVART?
IT MUST WORK, PROFESSOR PAULSON! DON'T FORGET, THE MASTER HAS EVOLVED US--BY HIS DIABOLIC METHODS--INTO HUMANS SUCH AS WILL EXIST ON EARTH 100,000 YEARS FROM NOW!
TRUE! AND OUR BRAINS ARE CAPABLE OF THE MOST COMPLEX THOUGHT AND DISCOVERY!
YES! AND IT IS BY MEANS OF OUR BRAINS THAT WE HAVE CONSTRUCTED A WAY TO ESCAPE FROM HERE! TURN ON THE TELE-VIEWER, HORTON!

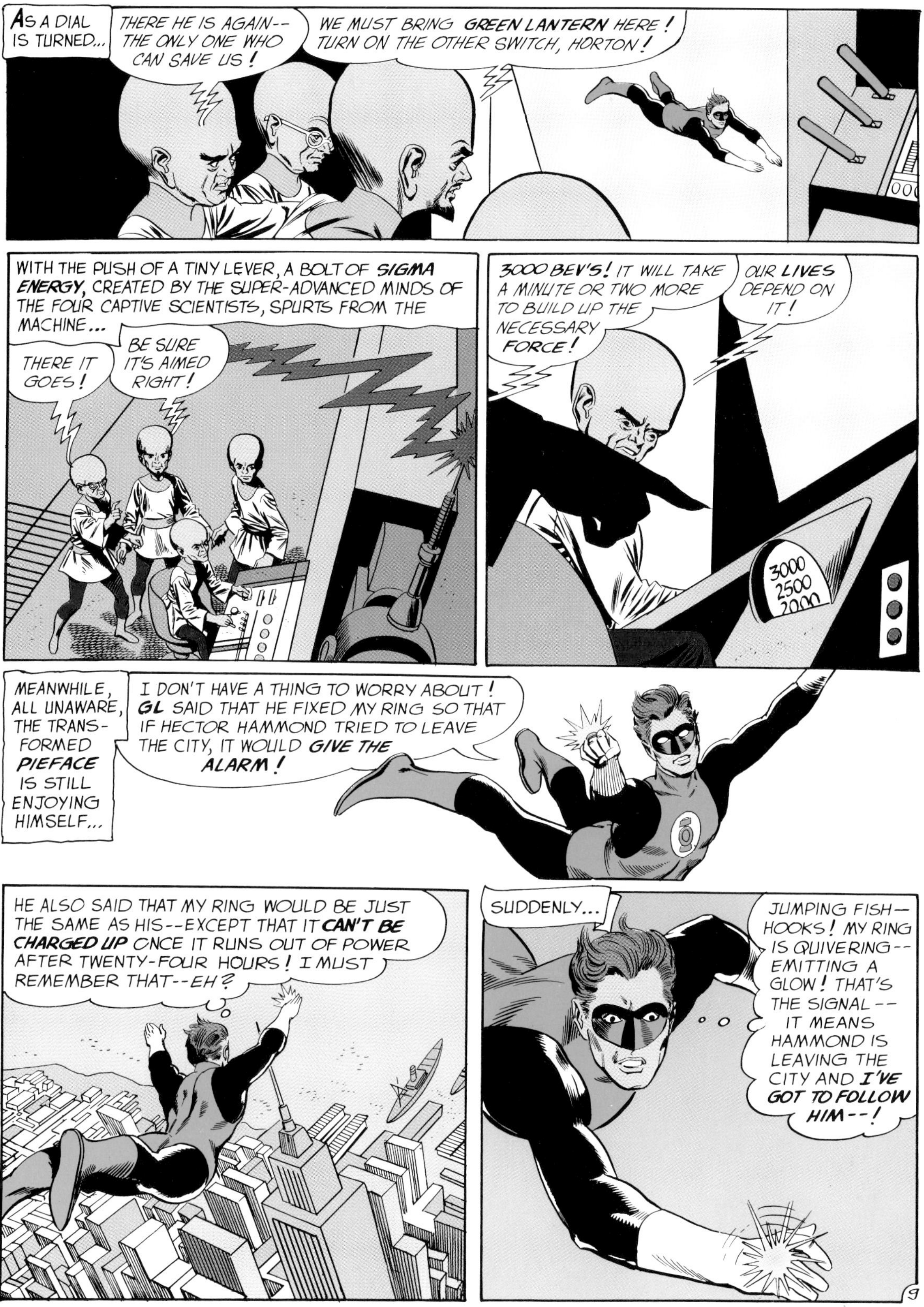
AS A DIAL IS TURNED...
THERE HE IS AGAIN-- THE ONLY ONE WHO CAN SAVE US!
WE MUST BRING GREEN LANTERN HERE! TURN ON THE OTHER SWITCH, HORTON!
WITH THE PUSH OF A TINY LEVER, A BOLT OF SIGMA ENERGY, CREATED BY THE SUPER-ADVANCED MINDS OF THE FOUR CAPTIVE SCIENTISTS, SPURTS FROM THE MACHINE...
THERE IT GOES!
BE SURE IT'S AIMED RIGHT!
3000 BEV'S! IT WILL TAKE A MINUTE OR TWO MORE TO BUILD UP THE NECESSARY FORCE!
OUR LIVES DEPEND ON IT!
3000
2500
2000
MEANWHILE, ALL UNAWARE, THE TRANS-FORMED PIEFACE IS STILL ENJOYING HIMSELF...
I DON'T HAVE A THING TO WORRY ABOUT! GL SAID THAT HE FIXED MY RING SO THAT IF HECTOR HAMMOND TRIED TO LEAVE THE CITY, IT WOULD GIVE THE ALARM!
HE ALSO SAID THAT MY RING WOULD BE JUST THE SAME AS HIS--EXCEPT THAT IT CAN'T BE CHARGED UP ONCE IT RUNS OUT OF POWER AFTER TWENTY-FOUR HOURS! I MUST REMEMBER THAT--EH?
SUDDENLY...
JUMPING FISH-HOOKS! MY RING IS QUIVERING--EMITTING A GLOW! THAT'S THE SIGNAL--IT MEANS HAMMOND IS LEAVING THE CITY AND I'VE GOT TO FOLLOW HIM--!
9

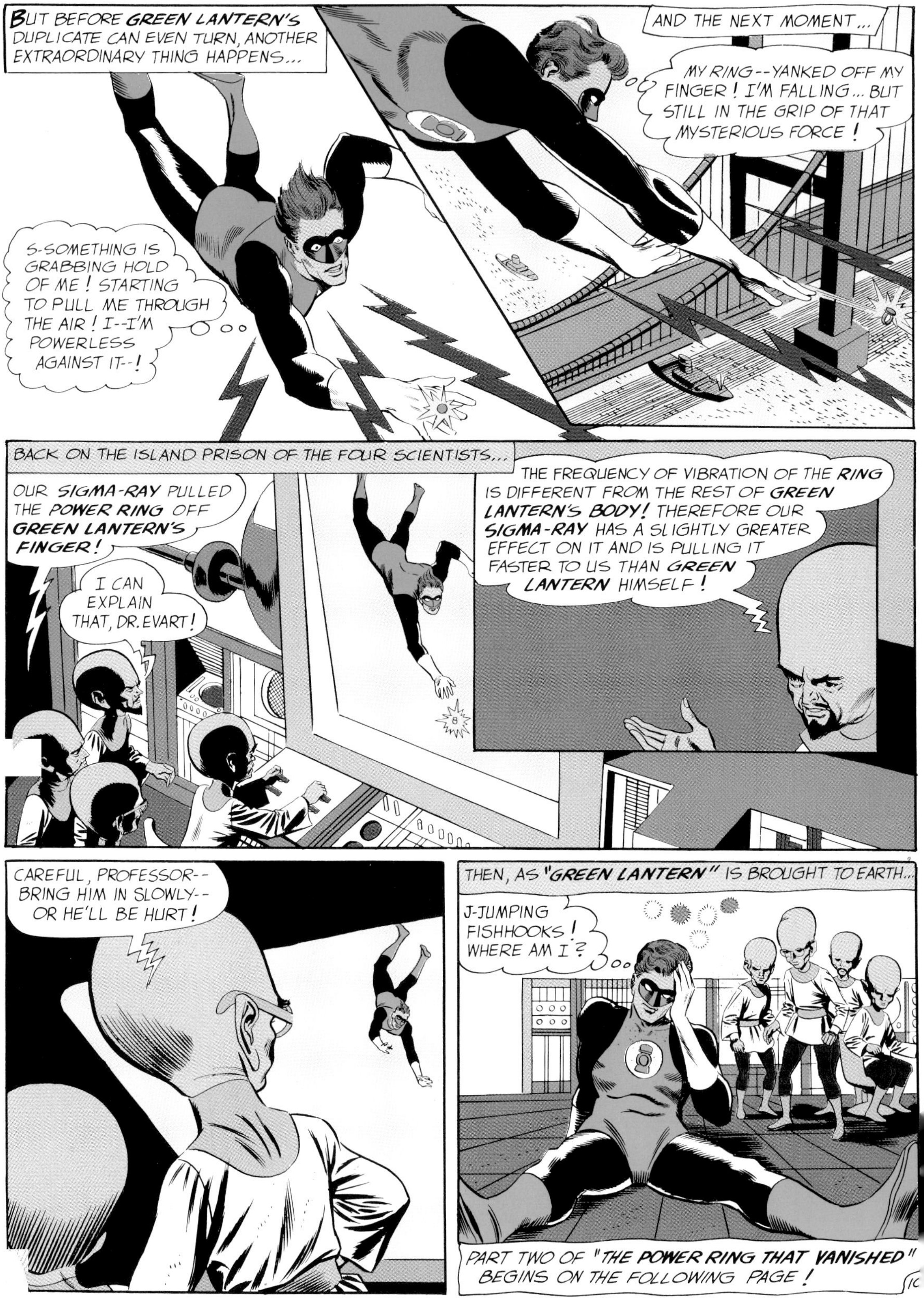
BUT BEFORE GREEN LANTERN'S DUPLICATE CAN EVEN TURN, ANOTHER EXTRAORDINARY THING HAPPENS...
S-SOMETHING IS GRABBING HOLD OF ME! STARTING TO PULL ME THROUGH THE AIR! I--I'M POWERLESS AGAINST IT--!
AND THE NEXT MOMENT...
MY RING--YANKED OFF MY FINGER! I'M FALLING... BUT STILL IN THE GRIP OF THAT MYSTERIOUS FORCE!
BACK ON THE ISLAND PRISON OF THE FOUR SCIENTISTS...
OUR SIGMA-RAY PULLED THE POWER RING OFF GREEN LANTERN'S FINGER!
I CAN EXPLAIN THAT, DR. EVART!
THE FREQUENCY OF VIBRATION OF THE RING IS DIFFERENT FROM THE REST OF GREEN LANTERN'S BODY! THEREFORE OUR SIGMA-RAY HAS A SLIGHTLY GREATER EFFECT ON IT AND IS PULLING IT FASTER TO US THAN GREEN LANTERN HIMSELF!
CAREFUL, PROFESSOR--BRING HIM IN SLOWLY--OR HE'LL BE HURT!
THEN, AS "GREEN LANTERN" IS BROUGHT TO EARTH...
J-JUMPING FISHHOOKS! WHERE AM I?
PART TWO OF "THE POWER RING THAT VANISHED" BEGINS ON THE FOLLOWING PAGE!
10

The POWER RING THAT VANISHED! PART TWO

THESE CREATURES MUST BE THE MISSING SCIENTISTS! THEY WERE *CHANGED* SOMEHOW BY *HECTOR HAMMOND* -- HE'S KEEPING THEM PRISONER HERE! AND THEY EXPECT *ME* TO HELP THEM *ESCAPE* --!

YOU *MUST* HELP US ESCAPE, *GREEN LANTERN!*

I HATE TO TELL THEM I'M *NOT* GREEN LANTERN! BUT THE TROUBLE IS, EVEN IF I WAS -- I COULDN'T HELP THEM ...

I HAVEN'T GOT MY RING!

YOUR RING --!?

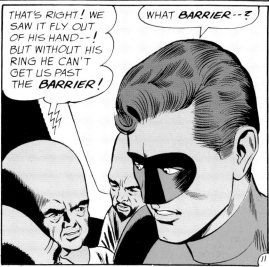

THAT'S RIGHT! WE SAW IT FLY OUT OF HIS HAND --! BUT WITHOUT HIS RING HE CAN'T GET US PAST THE *BARRIER!*

WHAT *BARRIER* --?

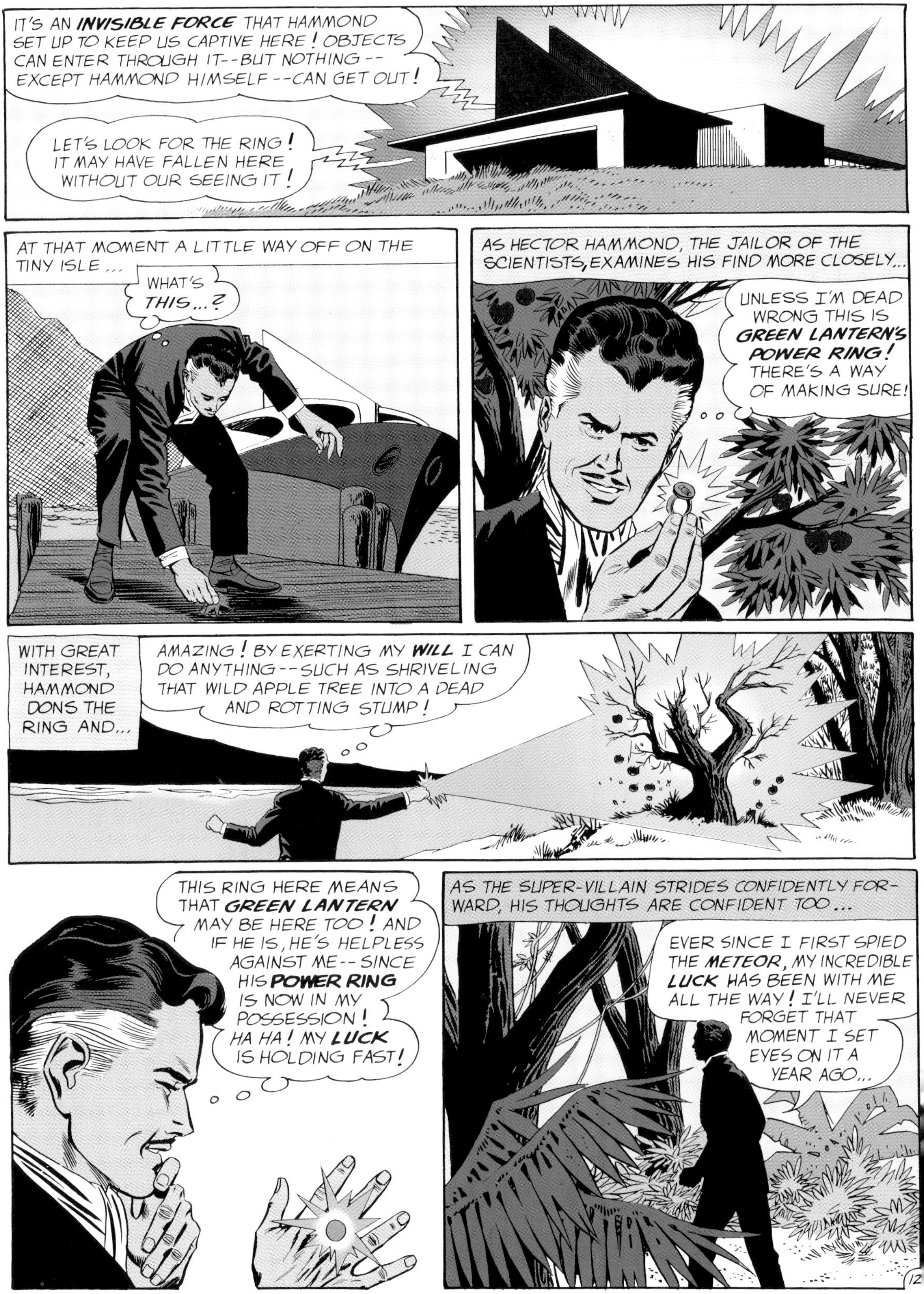
IT'S AN INVISIBLE FORCE THAT HAMMOND SET UP TO KEEP US CAPTIVE HERE! OBJECTS CAN ENTER THROUGH IT--BUT NOTHING--EXCEPT HAMMOND HIMSELF--CAN GET OUT!
LET'S LOOK FOR THE RING! IT MAY HAVE FALLEN HERE WITHOUT OUR SEEING IT!
AT THAT MOMENT A LITTLE WAY OFF ON THE TINY ISLE...
WHAT'S THIS...?
AS HECTOR HAMMOND, THE JAILOR OF THE SCIENTISTS, EXAMINES HIS FIND MORE CLOSELY...
UNLESS I'M DEAD WRONG THIS IS GREEN LANTERN'S POWER RING! THERE'S A WAY OF MAKING SURE!
WITH GREAT INTEREST, HAMMOND DONS THE RING AND...
AMAZING! BY EXERTING MY WILL I CAN DO ANYTHING--SUCH AS SHRIVELING THAT WILD APPLE TREE INTO A DEAD AND ROTTING STUMP!
THIS RING HERE MEANS THAT GREEN LANTERN MAY BE HERE TOO! AND IF HE IS, HE'S HELPLESS AGAINST ME--SINCE HIS POWER RING IS NOW IN MY POSSESSION! HA HA! MY LUCK IS HOLDING FAST!
AS THE SUPER-VILLAIN STRIDES CONFIDENTLY FORWARD, HIS THOUGHTS ARE CONFIDENT TOO...
EVER SINCE I FIRST SPIED THE METEOR, MY INCREDIBLE LUCK HAS BEEN WITH ME ALL THE WAY! I'LL NEVER FORGET THAT MOMENT I SET EYES ON IT A YEAR AGO...
12

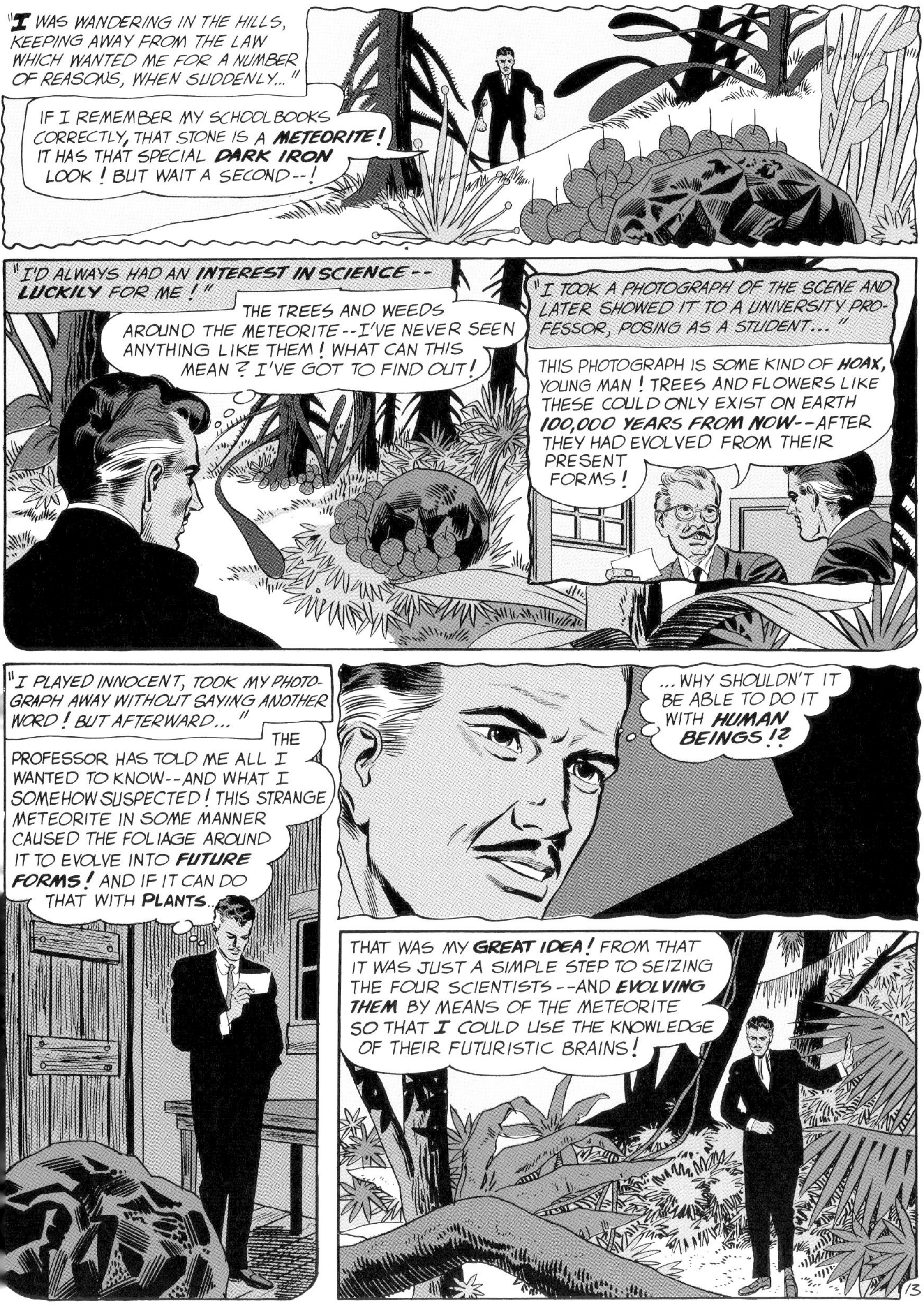
"I WAS WANDERING IN THE HILLS, KEEPING AWAY FROM THE LAW WHICH WANTED ME FOR A NUMBER OF REASONS, WHEN SUDDENLY..."
IF I REMEMBER MY SCHOOLBOOKS CORRECTLY, THAT STONE IS A METEORITE! IT HAS THAT SPECIAL DARK IRON LOOK! BUT WAIT A SECOND--!
"I'D ALWAYS HAD AN INTEREST IN SCIENCE--LUCKILY FOR ME!"
THE TREES AND WEEDS AROUND THE METEORITE--I'VE NEVER SEEN ANYTHING LIKE THEM! WHAT CAN THIS MEAN? I'VE GOT TO FIND OUT!
"I TOOK A PHOTOGRAPH OF THE SCENE AND LATER SHOWED IT TO A UNIVERSITY PROFESSOR, POSING AS A STUDENT..."
THIS PHOTOGRAPH IS SOME KIND OF HOAX, YOUNG MAN! TREES AND FLOWERS LIKE THESE COULD ONLY EXIST ON EARTH 100,000 YEARS FROM NOW--AFTER THEY HAD EVOLVED FROM THEIR PRESENT FORMS!
"I PLAYED INNOCENT, TOOK MY PHOTOGRAPH AWAY WITHOUT SAYING ANOTHER WORD! BUT AFTERWARD..."
THE PROFESSOR HAS TOLD ME ALL I WANTED TO KNOW--AND WHAT I SOMEHOW SUSPECTED! THIS STRANGE METEORITE IN SOME MANNER CAUSED THE FOLIAGE AROUND IT TO EVOLVE INTO FUTURE FORMS! AND IF IT CAN DO THAT WITH PLANTS...
...WHY SHOULDN'T IT BE ABLE TO DO IT WITH HUMAN BEINGS!?
THAT WAS MY GREAT IDEA! FROM THAT IT WAS JUST A SIMPLE STEP TO SEIZING THE FOUR SCIENTISTS--AND EVOLVING THEM BY MEANS OF THE METEORITE SO THAT I COULD USE THE KNOWLEDGE OF THEIR FUTURISTIC BRAINS!
13

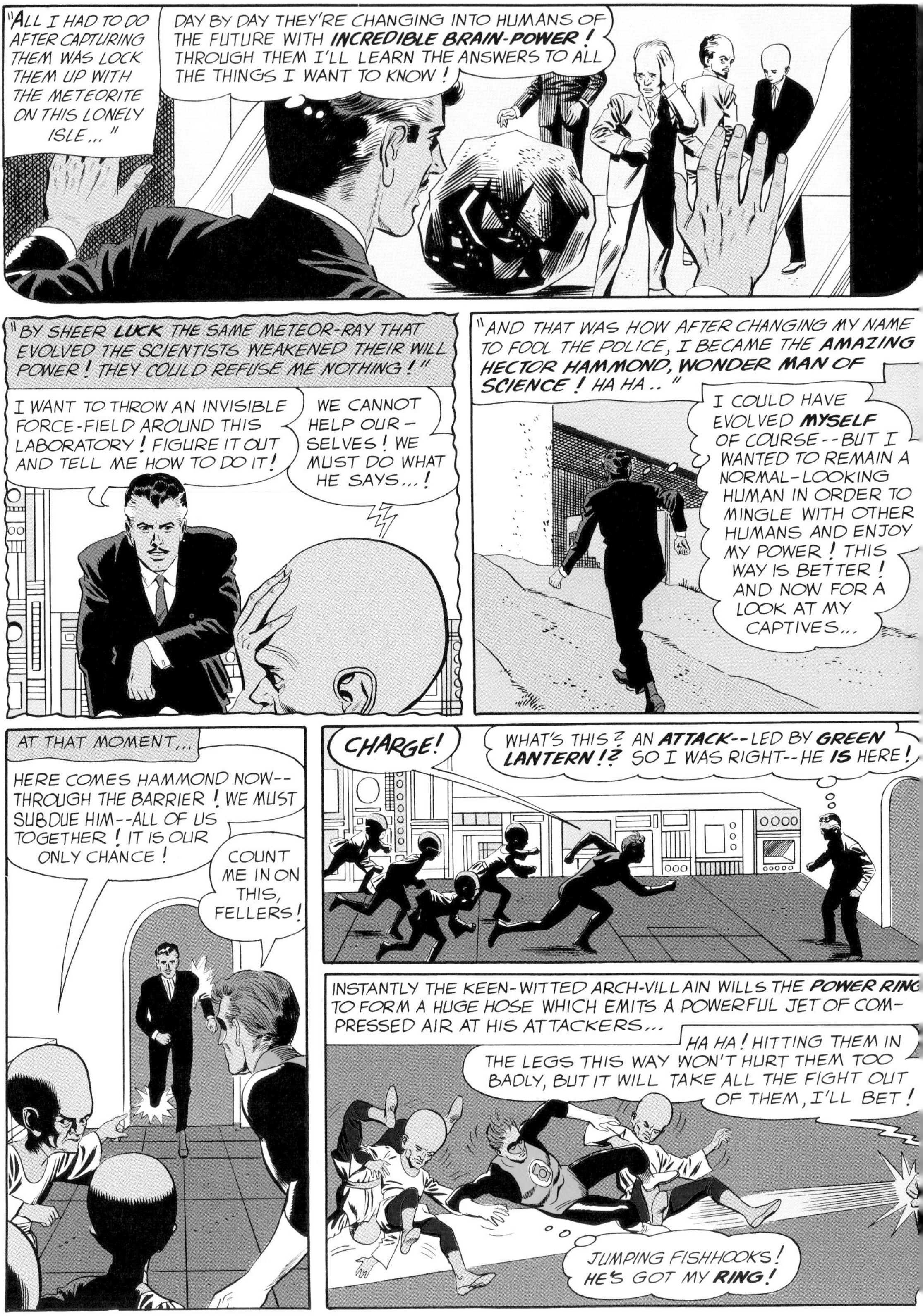
"ALL I HAD TO DO AFTER CAPTURING THEM WAS LOCK THEM UP WITH THE METEORITE ON THIS LONELY ISLE..."
DAY BY DAY THEY'RE CHANGING INTO HUMANS OF THE FUTURE WITH INCREDIBLE BRAIN-POWER! THROUGH THEM I'LL LEARN THE ANSWERS TO ALL THE THINGS I WANT TO KNOW!
"BY SHEER LUCK THE SAME METEOR-RAY THAT EVOLVED THE SCIENTISTS WEAKENED THEIR WILL POWER! THEY COULD REFUSE ME NOTHING!"
I WANT TO THROW AN INVISIBLE FORCE-FIELD AROUND THIS LABORATORY! FIGURE IT OUT AND TELL ME HOW TO DO IT!
WE CANNOT HELP OUR-SELVES! WE MUST DO WHAT HE SAYS...!
"AND THAT WAS HOW AFTER CHANGING MY NAME TO FOOL THE POLICE, I BECAME THE AMAZING HECTOR HAMMOND, WONDER MAN OF SCIENCE! HA HA.."
I COULD HAVE EVOLVED MYSELF OF COURSE--BUT I WANTED TO REMAIN A NORMAL-LOOKING HUMAN IN ORDER TO MINGLE WITH OTHER HUMANS AND ENJOY MY POWER! THIS WAY IS BETTER! AND NOW FOR A LOOK AT MY CAPTIVES...
AT THAT MOMENT...
HERE COMES HAMMOND NOW--THROUGH THE BARRIER! WE MUST SUBDUE HIM--ALL OF US TOGETHER! IT IS OUR ONLY CHANCE!
COUNT ME IN ON THIS, FELLERS!
CHARGE!
WHAT'S THIS? AN ATTACK--LED BY GREEN LANTERN!? SO I WAS RIGHT--HE IS HERE!
INSTANTLY THE KEEN-WITTED ARCH-VILLAIN WILLS THE POWER RING TO FORM A HUGE HOSE WHICH EMITS A POWERFUL JET OF COM-PRESSED AIR AT HIS ATTACKERS...
HA HA! HITTING THEM IN THE LEGS THIS WAY WON'T HURT THEM TOO BADLY, BUT IT WILL TAKE ALL THE FIGHT OUT OF THEM, I'LL BET!
JUMPING FISHHOOKS! HE'S GOT MY RING!

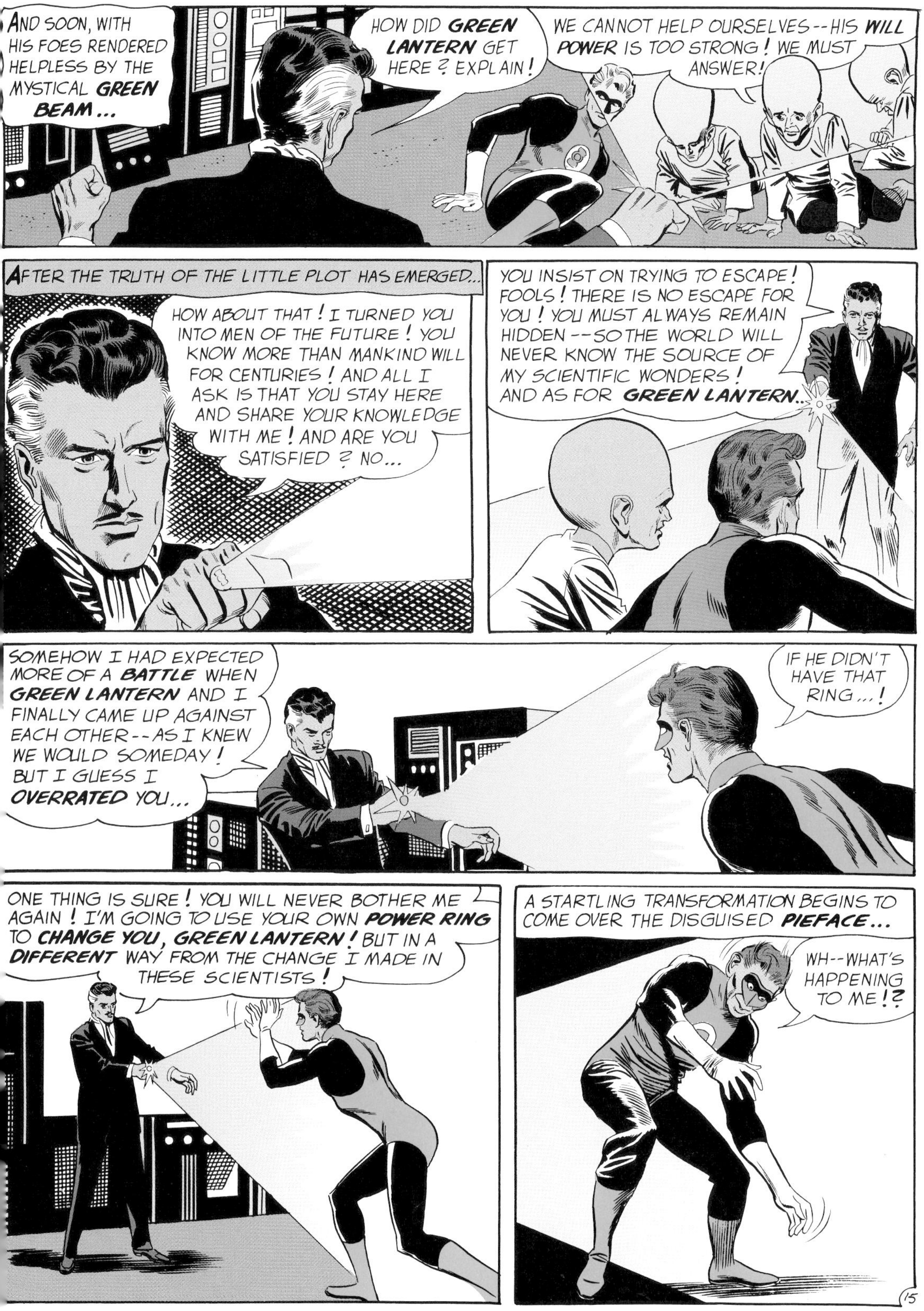
AND SOON, WITH HIS FOES RENDERED HELPLESS BY THE MYSTICAL GREEN BEAM...
HOW DID GREEN LANTERN GET HERE? EXPLAIN!
WE CANNOT HELP OURSELVES--HIS WILL POWER IS TOO STRONG! WE MUST ANSWER!
AFTER THE TRUTH OF THE LITTLE PLOT HAS EMERGED...
HOW ABOUT THAT! I TURNED YOU INTO MEN OF THE FUTURE! YOU KNOW MORE THAN MANKIND WILL FOR CENTURIES! AND ALL I ASK IS THAT YOU STAY HERE AND SHARE YOUR KNOWLEDGE WITH ME! AND ARE YOU SATISFIED? NO...
YOU INSIST ON TRYING TO ESCAPE! FOOLS! THERE IS NO ESCAPE FOR YOU! YOU MUST ALWAYS REMAIN HIDDEN--SO THE WORLD WILL NEVER KNOW THE SOURCE OF MY SCIENTIFIC WONDERS! AND AS FOR GREEN LANTERN...
SOMEHOW I HAD EXPECTED MORE OF A BATTLE WHEN GREEN LANTERN AND I FINALLY CAME UP AGAINST EACH OTHER--AS I KNEW WE WOULD SOMEDAY! BUT I GUESS I OVERRATED YOU...
IF HE DIDN'T HAVE THAT RING...!
ONE THING IS SURE! YOU WILL NEVER BOTHER ME AGAIN! I'M GOING TO USE YOUR OWN POWER RING TO CHANGE YOU, GREEN LANTERN! BUT IN A DIFFERENT WAY FROM THE CHANGE I MADE IN THESE SCIENTISTS!
A STARTLING TRANSFORMATION BEGINS TO COME OVER THE DISGUISED PIEFACE...
WH--WHAT'S HAPPENING TO ME!?
15

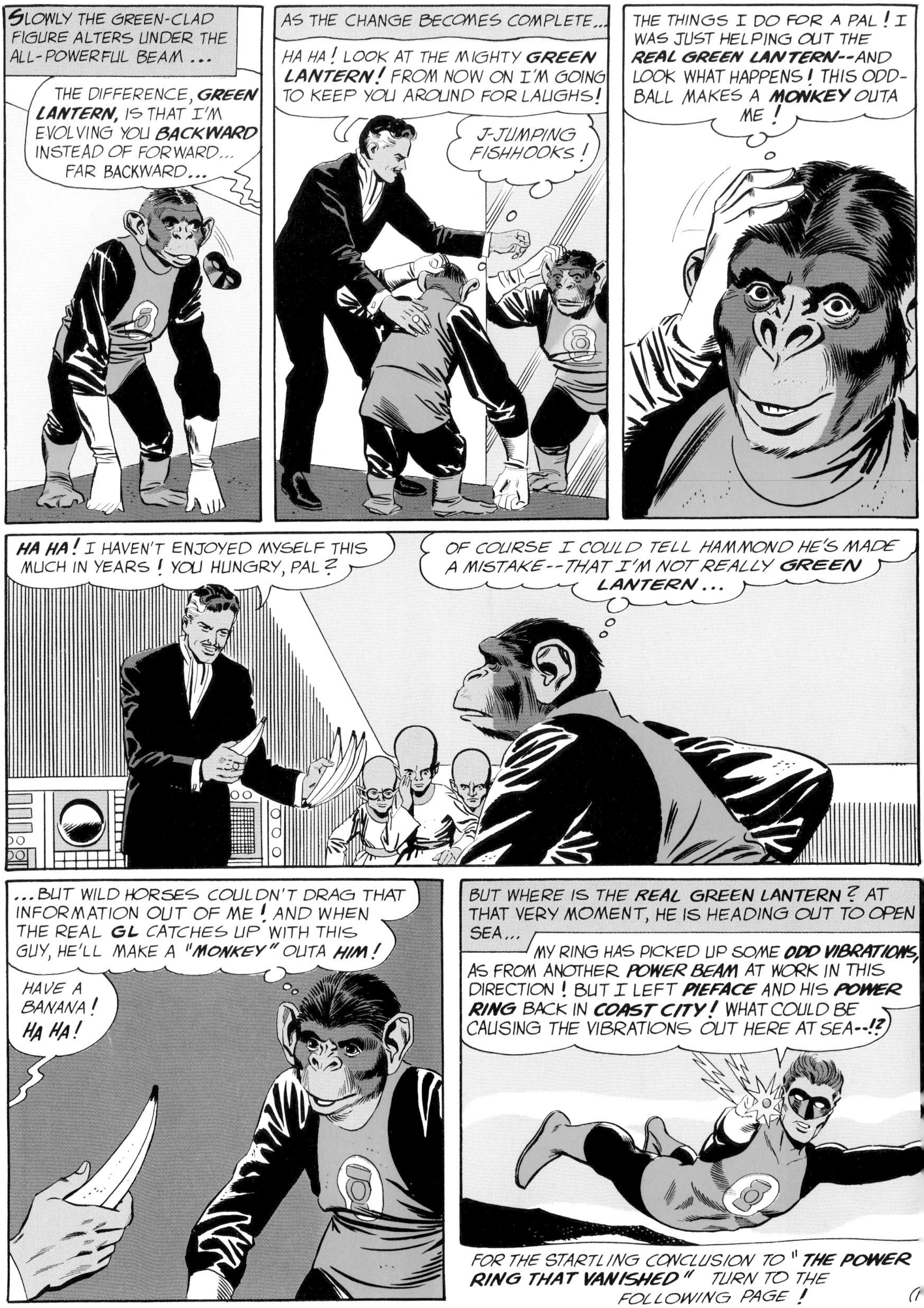
SLOWLY THE GREEN-CLAD FIGURE ALTERS UNDER THE ALL-POWERFUL BEAM ...
THE DIFFERENCE, GREEN LANTERN, IS THAT I'M EVOLVING YOU BACKWARD INSTEAD OF FORWARD... FAR BACKWARD...
AS THE CHANGE BECOMES COMPLETE...
HA HA! LOOK AT THE MIGHTY GREEN LANTERN! FROM NOW ON I'M GOING TO KEEP YOU AROUND FOR LAUGHS!
J-JUMPING FISHHOOKS!
THE THINGS I DO FOR A PAL! I WAS JUST HELPING OUT THE REAL GREEN LANTERN--AND LOOK WHAT HAPPENS! THIS ODD-BALL MAKES A MONKEY OUTA ME!
HA HA! I HAVEN'T ENJOYED MYSELF THIS MUCH IN YEARS! YOU HUNGRY, PAL?
OF COURSE I COULD TELL HAMMOND HE'S MADE A MISTAKE--THAT I'M NOT REALLY GREEN LANTERN...
...BUT WILD HORSES COULDN'T DRAG THAT INFORMATION OUT OF ME! AND WHEN THE REAL GL CATCHES UP WITH THIS GUY, HE'LL MAKE A "MONKEY" OUTA HIM!
HAVE A BANANA! HA HA!
BUT WHERE IS THE REAL GREEN LANTERN? AT THAT VERY MOMENT, HE IS HEADING OUT TO OPEN SEA...
MY RING HAS PICKED UP SOME ODD VIBRATIONS, AS FROM ANOTHER POWER BEAM AT WORK IN THIS DIRECTION! BUT I LEFT PIEFACE AND HIS POWER RING BACK IN COAST CITY! WHAT COULD BE CAUSING THE VIBRATIONS OUT HERE AT SEA--!?
FOR THE STARTLING CONCLUSION TO "THE POWER RING THAT VANISHED" TURN TO THE FOLLOWING PAGE!

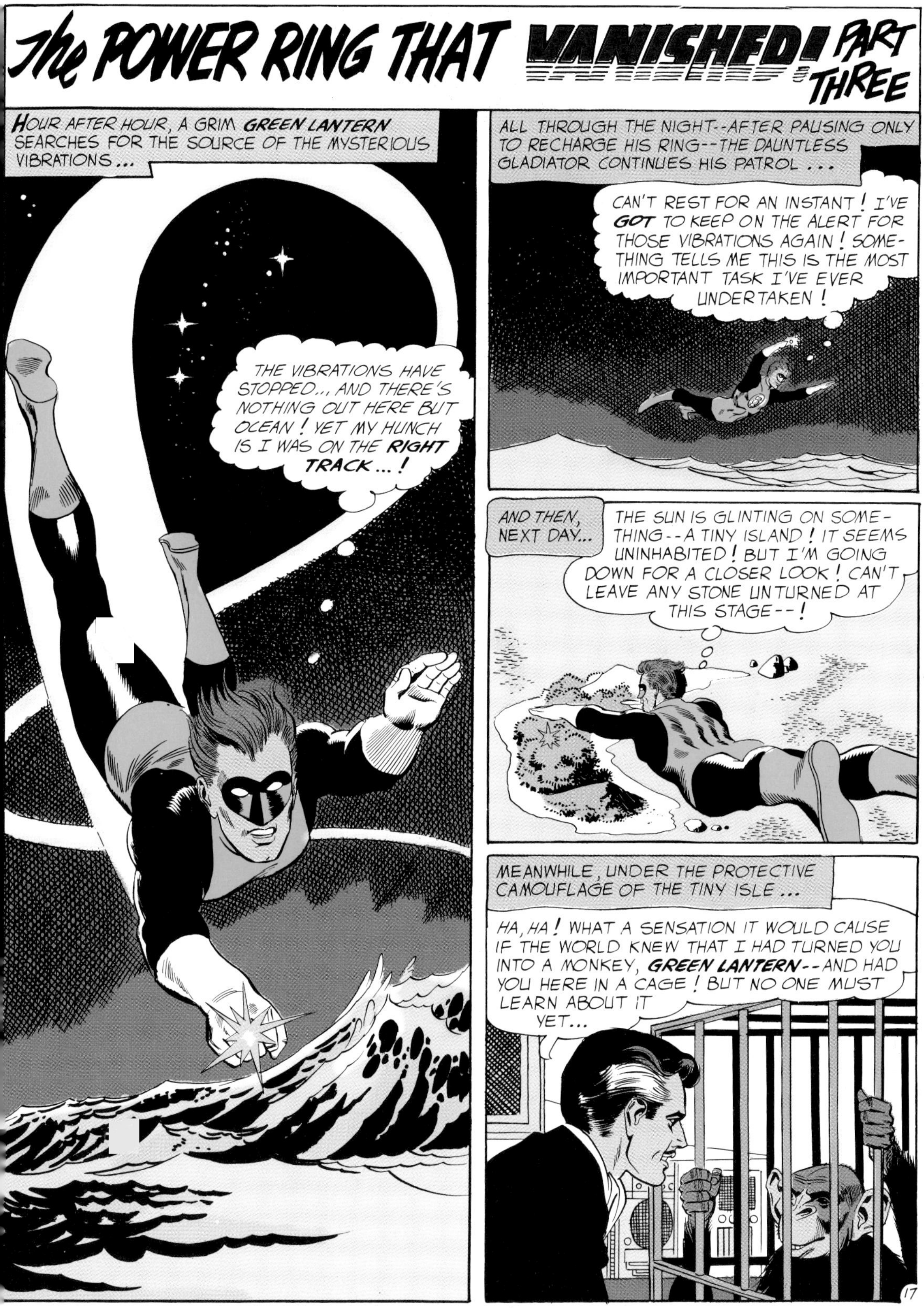
The POWER RING THAT VANISHED! PART THREE
HOUR AFTER HOUR, A GRIM GREEN LANTERN SEARCHES FOR THE SOURCE OF THE MYSTERIOUS VIBRATIONS...
THE VIBRATIONS HAVE STOPPED.., AND THERE'S NOTHING OUT HERE BUT OCEAN! YET MY HUNCH IS I WAS ON THE RIGHT TRACK...!
ALL THROUGH THE NIGHT--AFTER PAUSING ONLY TO RECHARGE HIS RING--THE DAUNTLESS GLADIATOR CONTINUES HIS PATROL...
CAN'T REST FOR AN INSTANT! I'VE GOT TO KEEP ON THE ALERT FOR THOSE VIBRATIONS AGAIN! SOMETHING TELLS ME THIS IS THE MOST IMPORTANT TASK I'VE EVER UNDERTAKEN!
AND THEN, NEXT DAY...
THE SUN IS GLINTING ON SOMETHING--A TINY ISLAND! IT SEEMS UNINHABITED! BUT I'M GOING DOWN FOR A CLOSER LOOK! CAN'T LEAVE ANY STONE UNTURNED AT THIS STAGE--!
MEANWHILE, UNDER THE PROTECTIVE CAMOUFLAGE OF THE TINY ISLE...
HA, HA! WHAT A SENSATION IT WOULD CAUSE IF THE WORLD KNEW THAT I HAD TURNED YOU INTO A MONKEY, GREEN LANTERN--AND HAD YOU HERE IN A CAGE! BUT NO ONE MUST LEARN ABOUT IT YET...
17

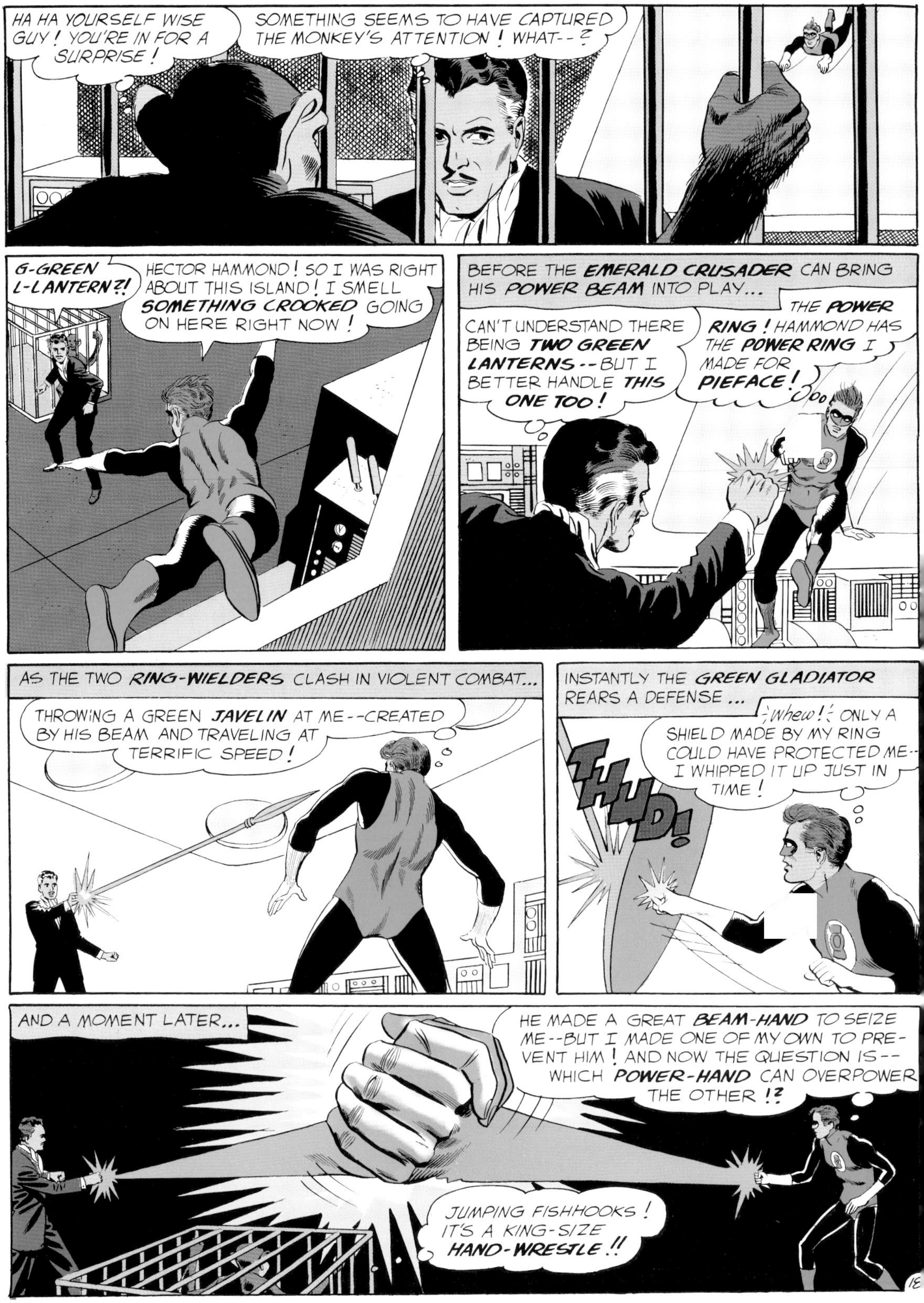
HA HA YOURSELF WISE GUY! YOU'RE IN FOR A SURPRISE!
SOMETHING SEEMS TO HAVE CAPTURED THE MONKEY'S ATTENTION! WHAT--?
G-GREEN L-LANTERN?!
HECTOR HAMMOND! SO I WAS RIGHT ABOUT THIS ISLAND! I SMELL SOMETHING CROOKED GOING ON HERE RIGHT NOW!
BEFORE THE EMERALD CRUSADER CAN BRING HIS POWER BEAM INTO PLAY...
CAN'T UNDERSTAND THERE BEING TWO GREEN LANTERNS--BUT I BETTER HANDLE THIS ONE TOO!
THE POWER RING! HAMMOND HAS THE POWER RING I MADE FOR PIEFACE!
AS THE TWO RING-WIELDERS CLASH IN VIOLENT COMBAT...
THROWING A GREEN JAVELIN AT ME--CREATED BY HIS BEAM AND TRAVELING AT TERRIFIC SPEED!
INSTANTLY THE GREEN GLADIATOR REARS A DEFENSE...
THUD!
Whew! ONLY A SHIELD MADE BY MY RING COULD HAVE PROTECTED ME--I WHIPPED IT UP JUST IN TIME!
AND A MOMENT LATER...
HE MADE A GREAT BEAM-HAND TO SEIZE ME--BUT I MADE ONE OF MY OWN TO PREVENT HIM! AND NOW THE QUESTION IS--WHICH POWER-HAND CAN OVERPOWER THE OTHER!?
JUMPING FISHHOOKS! IT'S A KING-SIZE HAND-WRESTLE!!
18

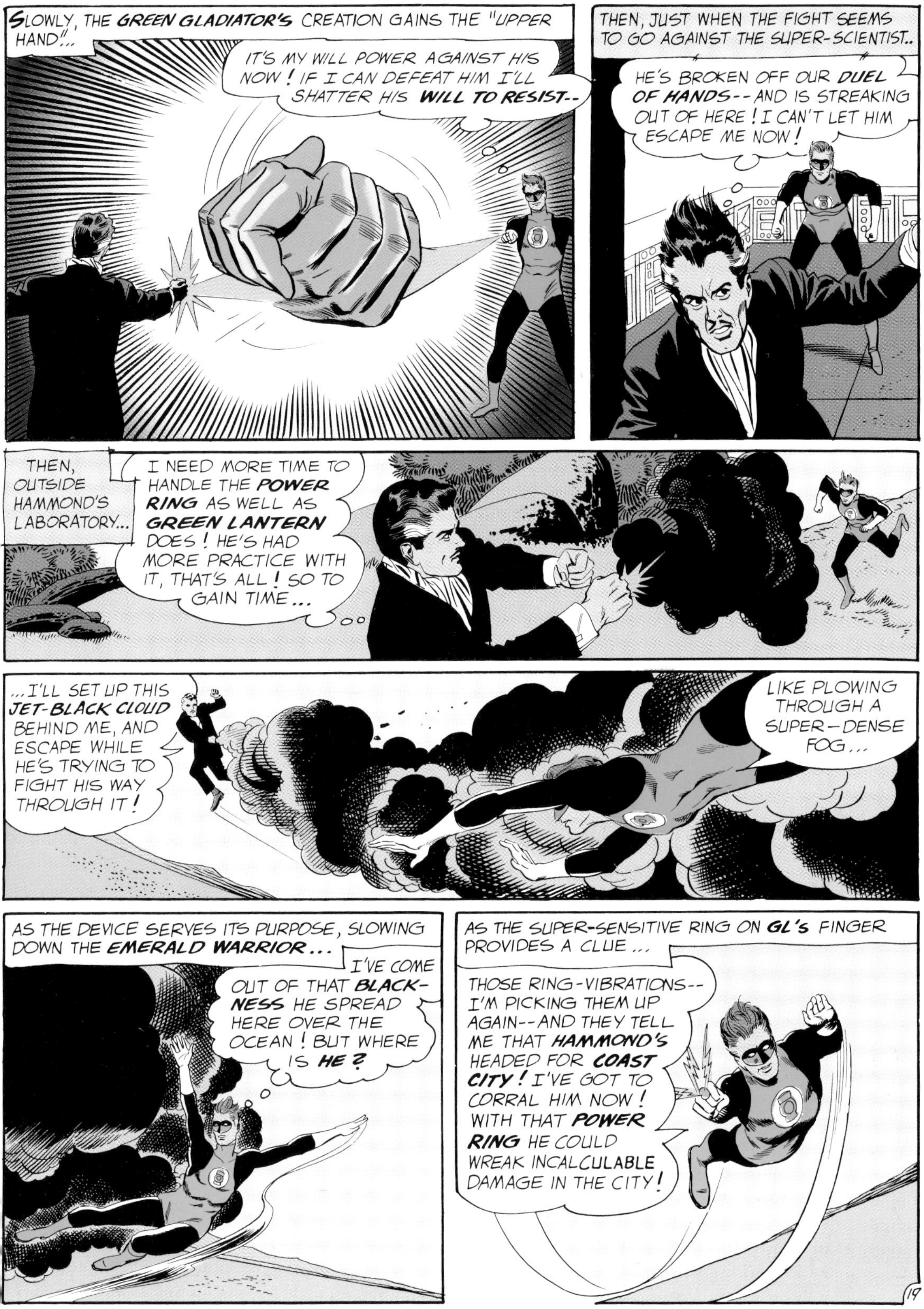
SLOWLY, THE GREEN GLADIATOR'S CREATION GAINS THE "UPPER HAND"...
IT'S MY WILL POWER AGAINST HIS NOW! IF I CAN DEFEAT HIM I'LL SHATTER HIS WILL TO RESIST--
THEN, JUST WHEN THE FIGHT SEEMS TO GO AGAINST THE SUPER-SCIENTIST..
HE'S BROKEN OFF OUR DUEL OF HANDS--AND IS STREAKING OUT OF HERE! I CAN'T LET HIM ESCAPE ME NOW!
THEN, OUTSIDE HAMMOND'S LABORATORY...
I NEED MORE TIME TO HANDLE THE POWER RING AS WELL AS GREEN LANTERN DOES! HE'S HAD MORE PRACTICE WITH IT, THAT'S ALL! SO TO GAIN TIME...
...I'LL SET UP THIS JET-BLACK CLOUD BEHIND ME, AND ESCAPE WHILE HE'S TRYING TO FIGHT HIS WAY THROUGH IT!
LIKE PLOWING THROUGH A SUPER-DENSE FOG...
AS THE DEVICE SERVES ITS PURPOSE, SLOWING DOWN THE EMERALD WARRIOR...
I'VE COME OUT OF THAT BLACKNESS HE SPREAD HERE OVER THE OCEAN! BUT WHERE IS HE?
AS THE SUPER-SENSITIVE RING ON GL'S FINGER PROVIDES A CLUE...
THOSE RING-VIBRATIONS--I'M PICKING THEM UP AGAIN--AND THEY TELL ME THAT HAMMOND'S HEADED FOR COAST CITY! I'VE GOT TO CORRAL HIM NOW! WITH THAT POWER RING HE COULD WREAK INCALCULABLE DAMAGE IN THE CITY!
19

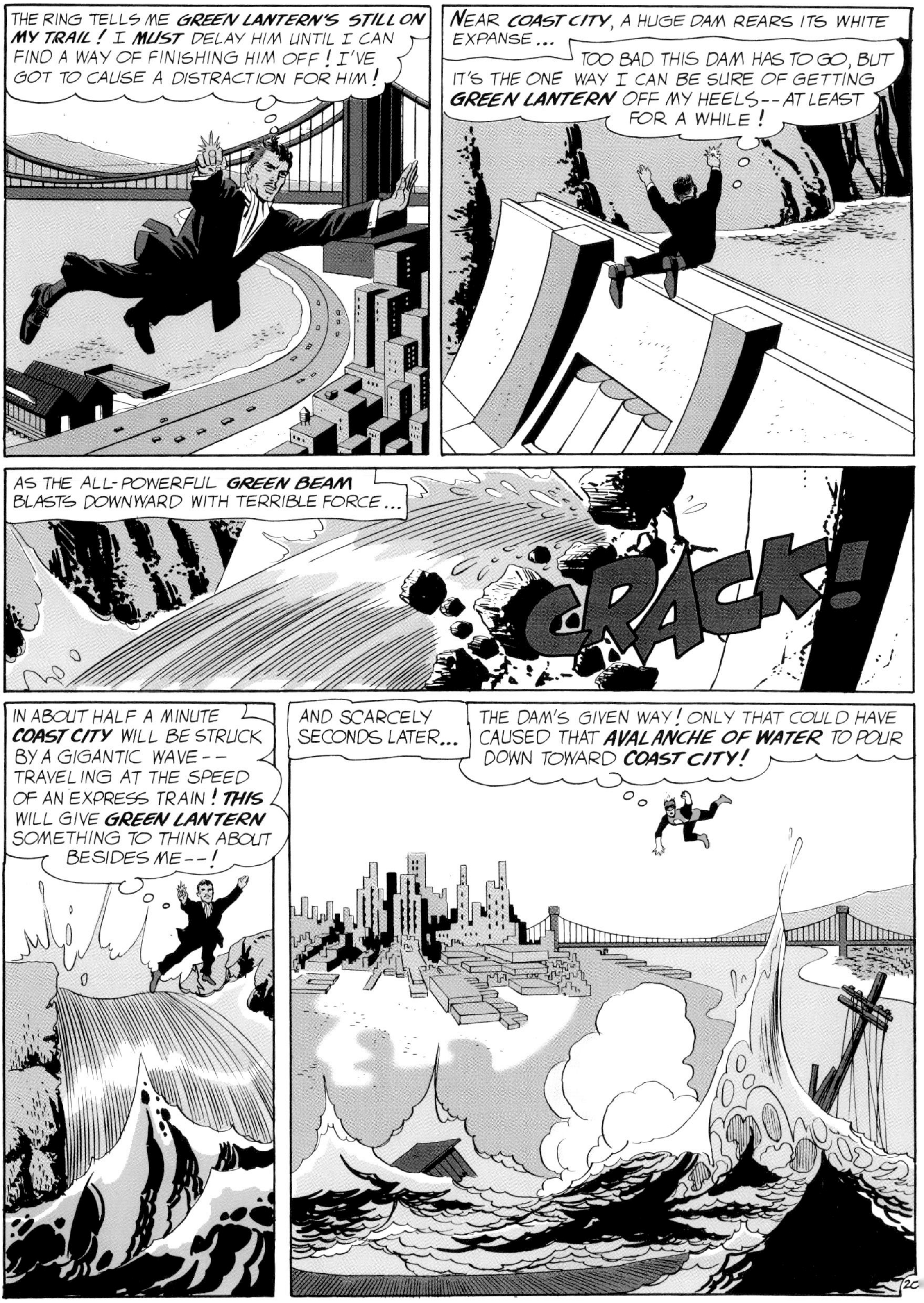
THE RING TELLS ME GREEN LANTERN'S STILL ON MY TRAIL! I MUST DELAY HIM UNTIL I CAN FIND A WAY OF FINISHING HIM OFF! I'VE GOT TO CAUSE A DISTRACTION FOR HIM!
NEAR COAST CITY, A HUGE DAM REARS ITS WHITE EXPANSE...
TOO BAD THIS DAM HAS TO GO, BUT IT'S THE ONE WAY I CAN BE SURE OF GETTING GREEN LANTERN OFF MY HEELS--AT LEAST FOR A WHILE!
AS THE ALL-POWERFUL GREEN BEAM BLASTS DOWNWARD WITH TERRIBLE FORCE...
CRACK!
IN ABOUT HALF A MINUTE COAST CITY WILL BE STRUCK BY A GIGANTIC WAVE--TRAVELING AT THE SPEED OF AN EXPRESS TRAIN! THIS WILL GIVE GREEN LANTERN SOMETHING TO THINK ABOUT BESIDES ME--!
AND SCARCELY SECONDS LATER...
THE DAM'S GIVEN WAY! ONLY THAT COULD HAVE CAUSED THAT AVALANCHE OF WATER TO POUR DOWN TOWARD COAST CITY!
20

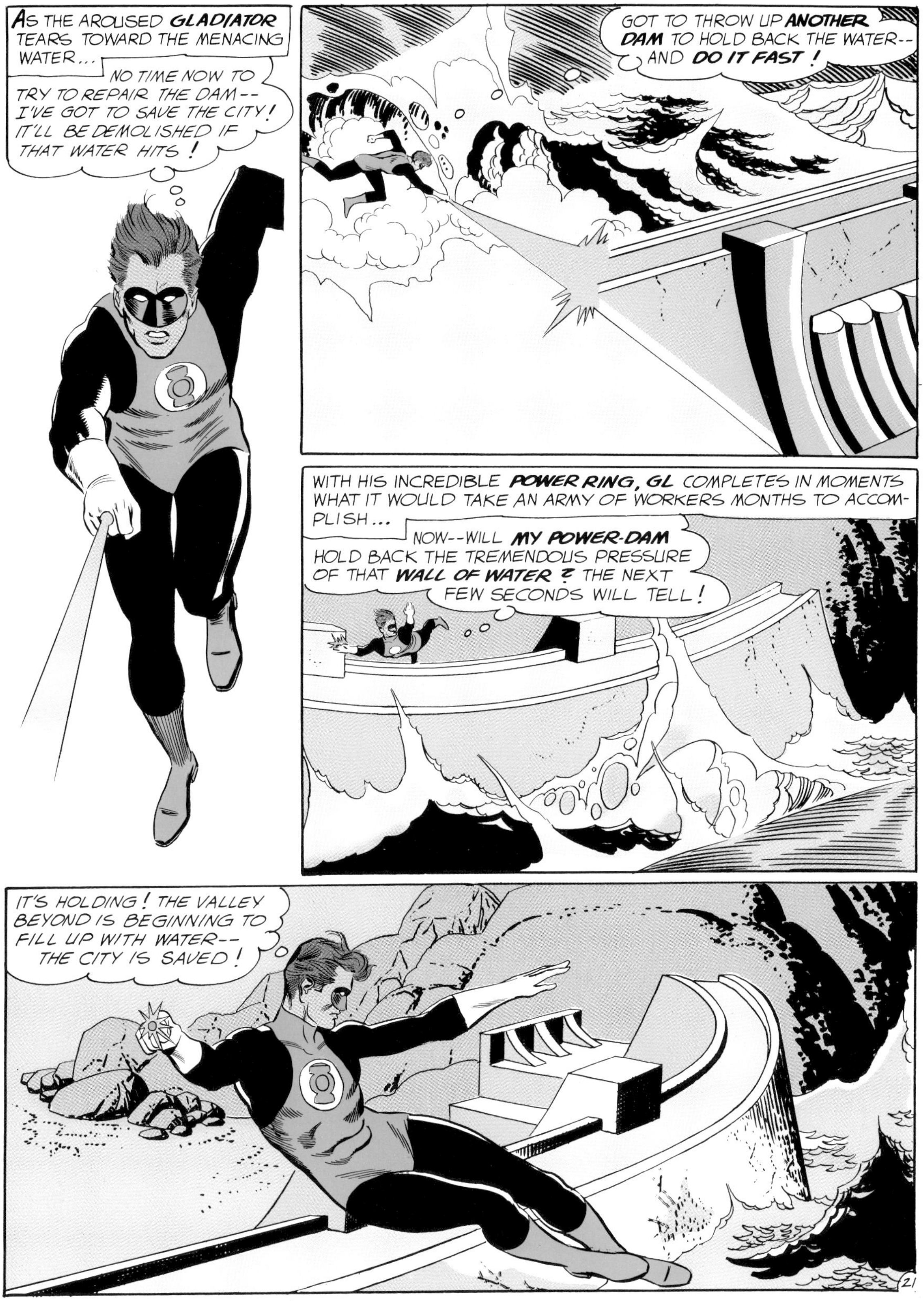
AS THE AROUSED GLADIATOR TEARS TOWARD THE MENACING WATER...
NO TIME NOW TO TRY TO REPAIR THE DAM-- I'VE GOT TO SAVE THE CITY! IT'LL BE DEMOLISHED IF THAT WATER HITS!
GOT TO THROW UP ANOTHER DAM TO HOLD BACK THE WATER-- AND DO IT FAST!
WITH HIS INCREDIBLE POWER RING, GL COMPLETES IN MOMENTS WHAT IT WOULD TAKE AN ARMY OF WORKERS MONTHS TO ACCOMPLISH...
NOW--WILL MY POWER-DAM HOLD BACK THE TREMENDOUS PRESSURE OF THAT WALL OF WATER? THE NEXT FEW SECONDS WILL TELL!
IT'S HOLDING! THE VALLEY BEYOND IS BEGINNING TO FILL UP WITH WATER-- THE CITY IS SAVED!
21

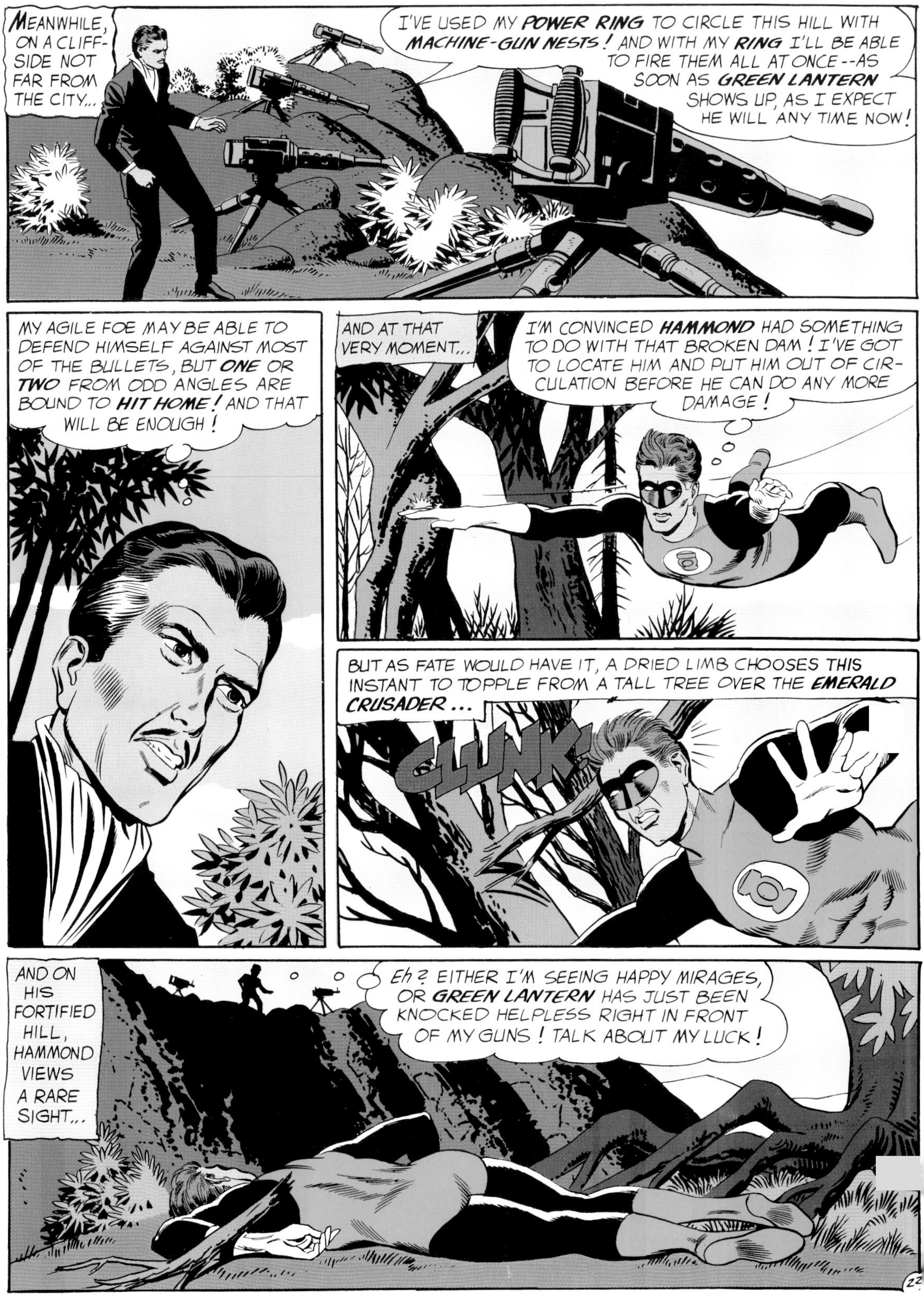
MEANWHILE, ON A CLIFF-SIDE NOT FAR FROM THE CITY...
I'VE USED MY POWER RING TO CIRCLE THIS HILL WITH MACHINE-GUN NESTS! AND WITH MY RING I'LL BE ABLE TO FIRE THEM ALL AT ONCE--AS SOON AS GREEN LANTERN SHOWS UP, AS I EXPECT HE WILL ANY TIME NOW!
MY AGILE FOE MAY BE ABLE TO DEFEND HIMSELF AGAINST MOST OF THE BULLETS, BUT ONE OR TWO FROM ODD ANGLES ARE BOUND TO HIT HOME! AND THAT WILL BE ENOUGH!
AND AT THAT VERY MOMENT...
I'M CONVINCED HAMMOND HAD SOMETHING TO DO WITH THAT BROKEN DAM! I'VE GOT TO LOCATE HIM AND PUT HIM OUT OF CIR-CULATION BEFORE HE CAN DO ANY MORE DAMAGE!
BUT AS FATE WOULD HAVE IT, A DRIED LIMB CHOOSES THIS INSTANT TO TOPPLE FROM A TALL TREE OVER THE EMERALD CRUSADER...
CLUNK!
AND ON HIS FORTIFIED HILL, HAMMOND VIEWS A RARE SIGHT...
Eh? EITHER I'M SEEING HAPPY MIRAGES, OR GREEN LANTERN HAS JUST BEEN KNOCKED HELPLESS RIGHT IN FRONT OF MY GUNS! TALK ABOUT MY LUCK!
22

As the super-villain starts to take swift advantage...

I'LL FIRE ALL THE GUNS AT ONCE! FOR *GL* TO COME OUT OF THIS ALIVE, HE'LL HAVE TO BE A REAL *WONDER— WORKER!*

BUT THEN, AS WAS BOUND TO HAPPEN, HAMMOND'S LUCK FINALLY RUNS OUT...

THE *RING*-- SUDDENLY IT'S LOST ITS *POWER!* I CAN'T SEEM TO MAKE IT WORK-- NO MATTER HOW MUCH WILL POWER I SUMMON UP!

AND WHEN HAMMOND, IN DESPERATION, ABANDONS USE OF THE RING AND SCRAMBLES TOWARD ONE OF HIS GUNS...

I'LL BLAST HIM BY HAND! I--EH?

TOO LATE, MY FRIEND! THAT LITTLE DELAY WAS ALL I NEEDED TO COME TO MY SENSES --AND DISCOVER WHAT YOU WERE UP TO!

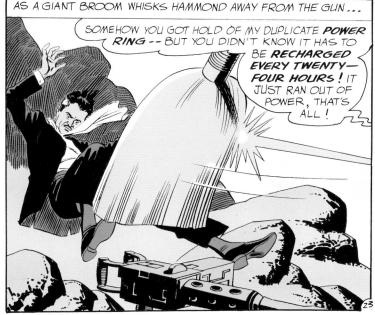

AS A GIANT BROOM WHISKS HAMMOND AWAY FROM THE GUN...

SOMEHOW YOU GOT HOLD OF MY DUPLICATE *POWER RING* -- BUT YOU DIDN'T KNOW IT HAS TO BE *RECHARGED EVERY TWENTY— FOUR HOURS!* IT JUST RAN OUT OF POWER, THAT'S ALL!

23

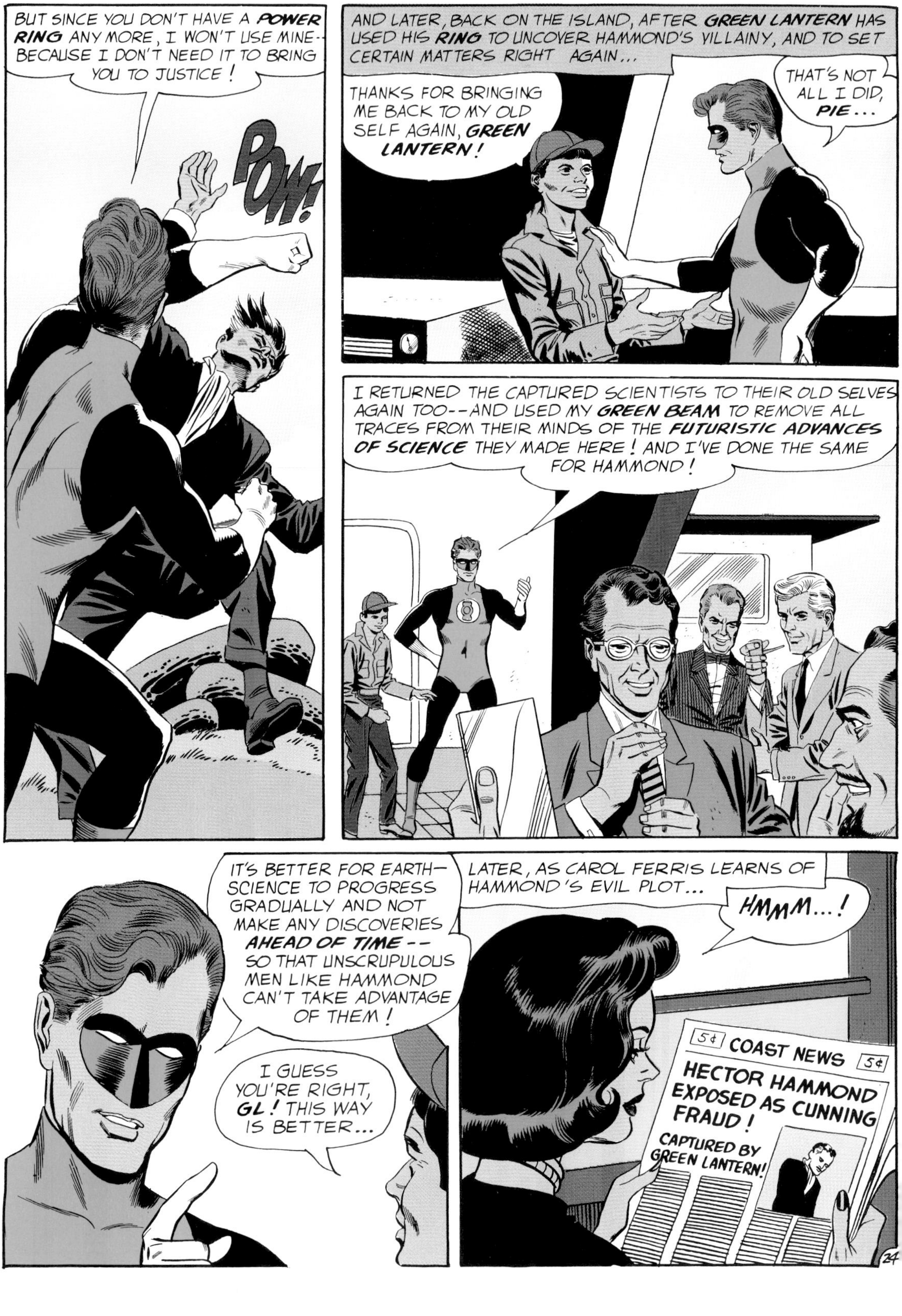
BUT SINCE YOU DON'T HAVE A POWER RING ANY MORE, I WON'T USE MINE--BECAUSE I DON'T NEED IT TO BRING YOU TO JUSTICE!
POW!
AND LATER, BACK ON THE ISLAND, AFTER GREEN LANTERN HAS USED HIS RING TO UNCOVER HAMMOND'S VILLAINY, AND TO SET CERTAIN MATTERS RIGHT AGAIN...
THANKS FOR BRINGING ME BACK TO MY OLD SELF AGAIN, GREEN LANTERN!
THAT'S NOT ALL I DID, PIE...
I RETURNED THE CAPTURED SCIENTISTS TO THEIR OLD SELVES AGAIN TOO--AND USED MY GREEN BEAM TO REMOVE ALL TRACES FROM THEIR MINDS OF THE FUTURISTIC ADVANCES OF SCIENCE THEY MADE HERE! AND I'VE DONE THE SAME FOR HAMMOND!
IT'S BETTER FOR EARTH-SCIENCE TO PROGRESS GRADUALLY AND NOT MAKE ANY DISCOVERIES AHEAD OF TIME--SO THAT UNSCRUPULOUS MEN LIKE HAMMOND CAN'T TAKE ADVANTAGE OF THEM!
I GUESS YOU'RE RIGHT, GL! THIS WAY IS BETTER...
LATER, AS CAROL FERRIS LEARNS OF HAMMOND'S EVIL PLOT...
HMMM...!
5¢ COAST NEWS 5¢
HECTOR HAMMOND EXPOSED AS CUNNING FRAUD!
CAPTURED BY GREEN LANTERN!
24

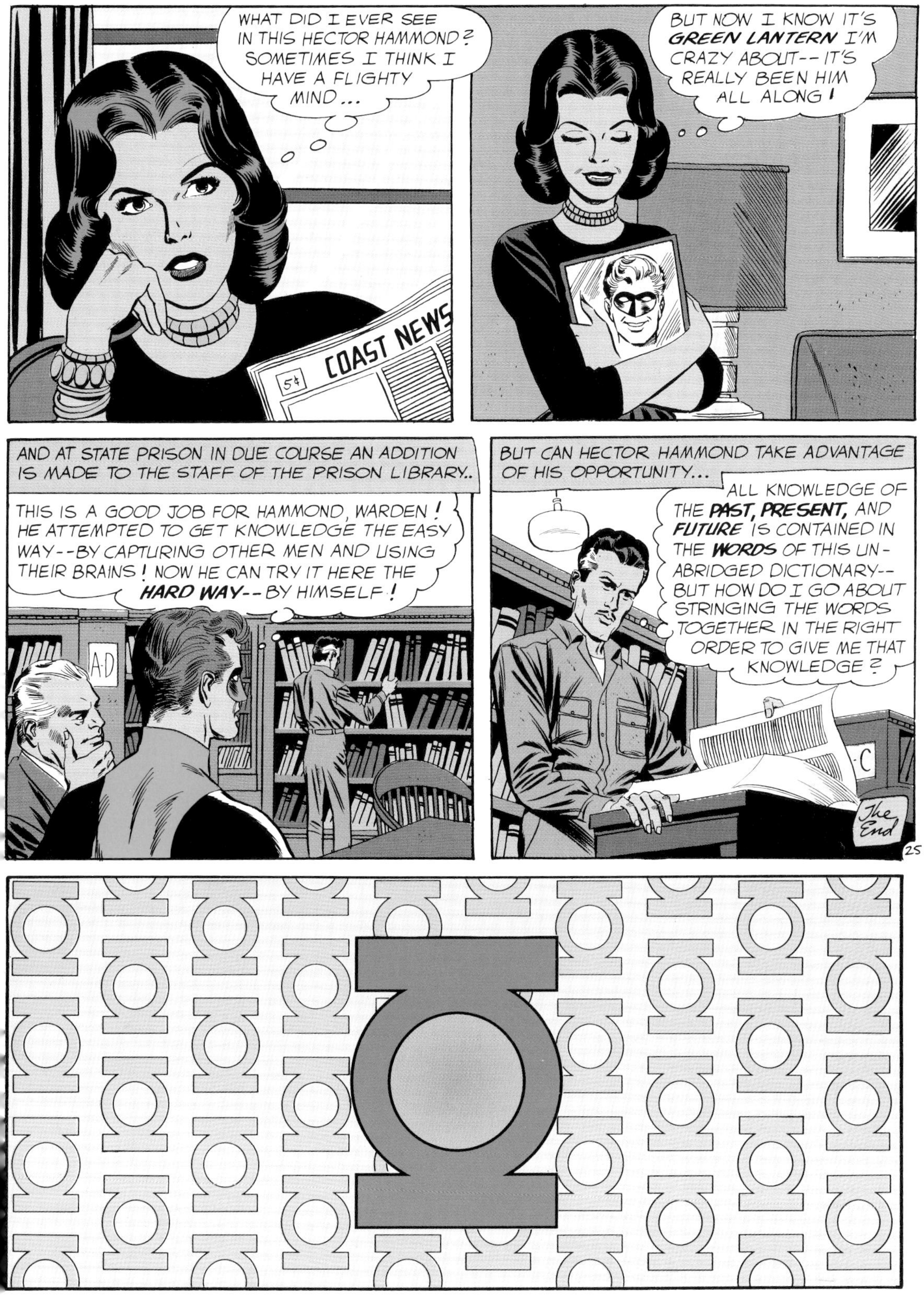
WHAT DID I EVER SEE IN THIS HECTOR HAMMOND? SOMETIMES I THINK I HAVE A FLIGHTY MIND...
COAST NEWS
5¢
BUT NOW I KNOW IT'S GREEN LANTERN I'M CRAZY ABOUT-- IT'S REALLY BEEN HIM ALL ALONG!
AND AT STATE PRISON IN DUE COURSE AN ADDITION IS MADE TO THE STAFF OF THE PRISON LIBRARY..
THIS IS A GOOD JOB FOR HAMMOND, WARDEN! HE ATTEMPTED TO GET KNOWLEDGE THE EASY WAY--BY CAPTURING OTHER MEN AND USING THEIR BRAINS! NOW HE CAN TRY IT HERE THE HARD WAY--BY HIMSELF!
A-D
BUT CAN HECTOR HAMMOND TAKE ADVANTAGE OF HIS OPPORTUNITY...
ALL KNOWLEDGE OF THE PAST, PRESENT, AND FUTURE IS CONTAINED IN THE WORDS OF THIS UN-ABRIDGED DICTIONARY-- BUT HOW DO I GO ABOUT STRINGING THE WORDS TOGETHER IN THE RIGHT ORDER TO GIVE ME THAT KNOWLEDGE?
The End
25

JOHN BROOME

Though he was well-versed in all genres, writer John Broome was best known for the science-fiction-oriented work he produced during his long career in comics, both under his own name and under the oft-used pen names "John Osgood" and "Edgar Ray Merritt." Recruited from the SF pulps in the early 1940s by DC editor Julius Schwartz, Broome adapted his skills effortlessly from prose to illustrated fiction.

Throughout the '40s, '50s and '60s, Broome penned a myriad of features for Schwartz, including the Justice Society of America, Captain Comet, Detective Chimp, and the Atomic Knights. Today, however, comics historians are most familiar with his work on the Silver Age FLASH and GREEN LANTERN, the two series that best allowed him to exercise his greatest strength: imbuing even the most straight-laced super-heroes with a whimsical sense of humor and strong, solid characterization.

John Broome retired from comic books in 1970 to travel the world; he passed away on March 14, 1999 of a heart attack while traveling in Thailand.

GIL KANE

Born in 1926, Kane and his family moved from their native Latvia to New York City when Kane was three. An artistic prodigy by the time he reached his late teens, Kane had left his mark on every major comics publisher of the day, including MLJ, Prize, Quality, Marvel—and DC, for whom he produced Wildcat, Johnny Thunder, and a plethora of Western, science-fiction and true crime tales. In 1959, he joined with John Broome to revive the Golden Age hero Green Lantern, in the process totally revamping the look of the strip and giving the Emerald Gladiator the trademark sleek, stream-lined costume he wears to this day.

Over the years, Gil Kane's work has come to stand as the textbook definition of dynamic drawing. A master of style, Kane imbued each of his drawings with an unequaled sense of power and motion. Though Kane continued to illustrate GREEN LANTERN throughout the 1960s, he lent pencil and pen to many other series as well, such as Marvel Comics' Spider-Man and Captain America and Tower's Thunder Agents. Gil Kane, an artist whose work defined comics, passed away January 31, 2000.

JOE GIELLA

Joe Giella began his long career as a comic-book artist in the 1940s, working for Hillman Publications and for Timely, the company that was later to become Marvel Comics. Giella came to DC in 1951 and over the next three decades worked predominantly as an inker, lending his clean, tight line to thousands of pencilled pages and to every major character the company published. During the 1960s, at the height of the TV-fueled "Batmania," Giella pencilled and inked the daily Batman newspaper strip. He continues his syndicated comic-strip work to this day, illustrating the venerable Mary Worth feature.

MURPHY ANDERSON

Heavily influenced by artists Lou Fine and Will Eisner, Murphy Anderson entered the comics arena in 1944 as an artist for Fiction House. Following a tour of naval duty during World War II, he returned to comics, lending his talents both to comic books and to newspaper strips such as Buck Rogers. In 1950, he began his lifelong associa-tion with DC Comics, pulling double duty as both a full illustrator and as an inker over artists as diverse in style as Carmine Infantino and Gil Kane. In particular, Anderson's occasional work with Kane on GREEN LANTERN gave him an opportunity to draw the kind of

Biographical material researched and written by Mark Waid

swashbuckling science fiction and space opera that has always been his first love. Presently Murphy enjoys a well-earned retirement.

JULIUS SCHWARTZ

More than any other editor, Julie Schwartz helped shape the face of the comic-book medium. Born in New York in 1915, Schwartz was one of the earliest and most vocal fans of the literary genre that became known as "science fiction," in time establishing himself as an agent for Ray Bradbury, Henry Kuttner, Robert Bloch, and other giants of the SF and fantasy field. Hired as a DC editor in 1944, Schwartz's inventive mind and dedication to the craft of storytelling soon made him a legend in his own right, a man known for employing only the finest and most talented writers and artists in the field. His true legacy, however, came to flower in the 1950s and early 1960s, at a time when the future of comics was at best dubious. Schwartz—together with John Broome, Robert Kanigher, Gardner Fox, and others—revived and revitalized the all-but-abandoned super-hero genre, transforming such nearly forgotten heroes as the Flash and Green Lantern into super-stars. Without their infusion of energy, comic books might well have gone the way of the penny postcard, the automat and the drive-in movie—faded icons of a bygone era.